...and the truth
shall set you free

First published in September 1995 by

Bridge of Love Publications
c/o Papworth Press
Ermine Street South
Papworth Everard
Cambridge CB3 8RG, England

Updated and reprinted, October 1995
Second edition, June 1996
Updated and reprinted, January 1997
Updated and reprinted, February, 1998

Published in the U.S.A., January, 1997
Updated and reprinted, August 1997
Updated and reprinted, November 1997
Updated and reprinted, July 1998

Cover illustration by Neil Hague

Text set in Bembo 9¾ on 11½

Printed and bound by KNI

**British Library Cataloguing-in
Publication Data**
A catalogue record for this book is
available from the British Library

ISBN 0 9526147 1 5

...and the truth
shall set you free

David Icke

Bridge
of Love

Dedication

To Linda, Jan, Yeva, Ayem, Alice, Sam, Anne, Fran,
Derry Ann, Gloria, Lidia, Michelle, Jean, Liz, Archer, Sara, Paul,
Gary, Wendy, Becks, Jim, Karl, David, Neil, Scott, Matthew, William,
and all those who support me and love me, come what may.
You will never know how much it is appreciated.
I love you so very much.

My thanks to David Solomon for funding the first
UK edition of this book. You are a *VERY* big man.

My thanks also to Sam for her magnificent production work,
to Jean and Liz for their proofreading, to Gary for compiling the index,
and to Neil for his inspired cover illustration.

We are the power in everyone;
We are the dance of the moon and the sun;
We are the hope that will never hide;
We are the turning of the tide.

Other books, tapes and videos by David Icke

Available from Bridge of Love Publications or Bookworld –
details at the back of the book

Know the truth and the truth shall set you free.

How little we know of the scale of eternity.
How dare we challenge the might and enormity
of such wisdom and creation.
A million worlds could exist in the heavens... beyond our site.
Each with living beings, looking at the sky in wonder
at the never ending universe.
They may also think that no other intelligence exists...
apart from themselves.
But perhaps they do not share the arrogance of the human race.
Perhaps they possess the intelligence to realize
that all things are possible in the vastness of forever...

Is it conceivable, that this earth of ours,
which is but a speck of dust against the scale of reality,
is not only being visited by other life forms
but is being controlled by them.
Let us not be blinded by our arrogance
as to what is possible and what is not.
Because we are children at the dawn of our creation
with the universe as our classroom
and intelligence beyond our imagination
waiting to be tapped... when we are ready to receive it.

Seek and the wonders you will see
will reveal the true qualities of your universe.
To the truth of your origins your hearts will go out.
The beauty of your origins will surpass your belief and
comprehension.
And the infinite depth of your cosmic reality will remain part
of your heritage in the mists of forever.

The peace of understanding, is the beauty of creation.
The word has been spoken and the spirit within you knows
that home is eternity and existence is immortal...

Anonymous

Contents

Introduction

We are what we think

We live in a multidimensional universe, which is part of a multi-dimensional and infinite consciousness we call God and Creation. We are multidimensional beings. Therefore this book has to be multidimensional if it is to make a significant contribution to human freedom.

It exposes both the daily manipulation of our lives by a secret clique and presents the spiritual causes and solutions which will bring true freedom to Planet Earth and all who live upon her. The latter relates to what we think and feel about ourselves and before I begin to unravel the global manipulation and name some of the people and organisations involved, it is important that I outline the context in which I am presenting these matters. The last thing I want is for people to read this book full of anger, hatred, and condemnation for the global manipulators and what they are doing. I don't write this book to apportion blame, merely to show what happens when the human race gives its mind away and how rapidly things will change – are changing – as we take it back again.

I name names because we need to know who is behind the manipulation if we are going to expose what is happening. This exposure will also give those people the opportunity to face their actions and to see that the desire for control and domination of others is an expression of their own deep inner imbalances and dislike of themselves. The lifting of the veil of secrecy will speed the moment when the days of such domination and manipulation are over. But the elite clique which controls the world, the Global Elite as I call them, are *our* creation. It is no good hurling hatred and condemnation in their direction for the ills of the world. Yes, as you will see, the same grouping manipulated the two world wars and all the negative events of global significance in this century and before. But without the rest of the human race, they could not do this. An elite few cannot create wars unless thousands or millions are willing to be used as cannon fodder. If people read this book and hand the responsibility for what has happened only to the Global Elite, they are missing the point I am making throughout. What is happening in the world is the here and now reflection of what is going on inside us, the human race. *We* created this reality. But how?

Contrary to what medical science is obsessed with telling us, the physical body is not the whole human being. It is the fantastic physical shell through which the eternal us experiences this physical world. There is far more to us than a body. Creation is the expression of one infinite mind and all lifeforms are aspects of that one mind: what many people call God. We are each other. We are all God, if you wish to use that term. At the heart of this mind is a consciousness I see as a blinding light – the Source Consciousness from which all has been thought into existence. Creation consists of an infinite number of dimensions, wavelengths, frequencies, of reality. This physical world is only one of them. These frequencies share the same space that our physical world occupies, in the same way that all the radio, television, and telecommunication frequencies broadcasting to your area are sharing the same space that your body is occupying now. They don't interfere with each other because they are on different frequencies or dimensions; they are vibrating at different speeds. At the moment we call death, our mind-emotions-spirit, everything that is the thinking, feeling us, withdraws from the body, the 'genetic space suit' as I call it. This eternal spirit moves on to another wavelength of reality, another 'world', to continue its evolution. This is all that is happening during a 'near death experience' or an 'out of body experience' when people leave their physical bodies for a time before returning to tell remarkably similar stories of what happened to them. Life is forever – for everyone.

Our mental, emotional, and spiritual selves are a series of magnetic energy fields interacting with each other via vortices of energy widely known by the Hindu and Sanskrit word, chakra, which means wheel of light. These vortices are spirals of energy which intersect all levels of our being and pass energies between them. It is through this system that an imbalance on the emotional level, perhaps caused by stress, is passed on to the other levels of our being, including, eventually, the physical body. This is how stress causes illness. What we call 'physical' illness is really a multidimensional disharmony or dis-ease. We are constantly absorbing magnetic energy from the cosmos, mostly through the 'base' chakra at the base of the spine. After this lifeforce has passed through our levels of being and we have taken from it what we need, we broadcast the energy out through the chakras back to the cosmos and the world around us (*Figure 1*). These are the energies that people are feeling when they say that someone gives them good or bad 'vibes'. It is the same when we say a house or place feels 'happy', 'welcoming' or 'frightening'. What we call 'atmosphere' is created by the vibrations (energy fields) generated by people, either in the moment or in the past. People often feel uneasy at the scenes of battles because they are feeling the energies left there by the pain, aggression, and suffering of those involved.

There is a vital difference between the energy that enters through the base chakra and that which we broadcast. That energy is changed in its nature and form when it passes through us. It becomes imprinted with our unique energy pattern and that pattern reflects precisely what is happening inside us at that moment, mentally, emotionally, and spiritually. Second by

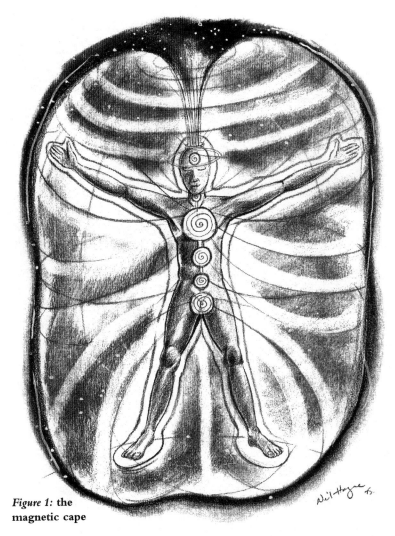

Figure 1: **the magnetic cape**

second we are broadcasting an energy field that reflects what we think of ourselves. This may not seem to have anything to do with the manipulation of the world, but it is, in fact, at the core of what has happened and continues to happen.

You might imagine this process as like casting a magnetic cape or aura around ourselves. Under the law of like attracts like, this magnetic energy field, the outer reflection of the inner person, will attract to it compatible energy fields. Everything is energy, as even mainstream, closed minded science is beginning to appreciate. A person is a series of magnetic energy fields, so is a place, an experience, a situation, everything. Life is the interaction of these energy fields, all of which have the ability to think and retain information. Energy is consciousness, consciousness is energy. They are the same thing. If it sounds hard to believe that a wall or water or rock can think and retain information, then remember that all contain magnetic energy fields. What is it within the computer I am working on now that retains the information I am writing? A magnetic disc. Same principle. The reason we are drawn to particular people, places, experiences and ways of life is because we are magnetically attracted to them. And that attraction comes from the magnetism of our 'capes'. These capes, in turn, are a reflection of what we think and feel about ourselves. Our lives are an exact physical replica of our own subconscious mind. How it thinks and perceives itself and the world, is recreated physically in the people, places and experiences we attract to us. When I was a child, there used to be a saying which went: "Think lucky and you'll be lucky". This contains an eternal truth, although it has nothing to do with luck. We attract to us people, places, and experiences which connect magnetically with our 'cape'. Therefore if we believe inside that we will always be poor and downtrodden, that pattern will be contained in the cape. It will become, you could say, the cape of no hope. This magnetic pattern will then attract to it the experiences which ensure that we remain poor and downtrodden. We will have created our own reality. This is so, so vital to understand, not only in relation to this book, but in the context of life itself:

We create our own reality.

Religions and ancient texts going way back have had a common theme of 'reaping what you sow', 'an eye for an eye and a tooth for a tooth', and 'what you do to others will be done to you'. The word by which this process is now best known is 'karma'. Too often this karma is seen in only negative terms. Something unpleasant happens to some people and they say it must be their 'karma'. It is presented as almost a form of punishment. At that level, it *is* punishment – self punishment. We created it, not some angry, judgmental, finger-wagging God! What we call karma is, in my view, only another word to describe the way we create our own reality. If we have imbalances that lead us to act negatively towards others, it is those imbalances that will also attract to us a physical experience, a 'mirror' of what we think of ourselves. In this way what we do to others will come back to us because we will still be holding onto the imbalances, the lack of self love, that will attract those experiences. If we feel good about ourselves and have a positive view of our lives we will create *that* world around us. This is positive 'karma'. I differ from the New Age view of karma which seems to believe that once we have done something, there must be a karmic reaction no matter what we subsequently do. I feel that if we act negatively towards someone, recognise why we did it, and change the inner cause of that action, we change the nature of the magnetic broadcast, the cape, and we do not then attract the 'karma'. There is no need because we have recognised the imbalance within us. That's all karma is there for. Creation is about love. Love for self and love for all. Karma is part of that love. It is a vehicle which allows us to face ourselves, unload negative baggage, and move on. It is an aid to evolution, a gift, not a punishment – unless we ourselves decide to make it so. No matter what experiences you have had in your life or you are having now, you, and no-one else, created them.

Two things worth remembering throughout this book and your own life: the victim mentality creates the victim reality. And: if you believe it, you will achieve it.

This creation of reality happens on many levels. The sum total of the interaction of individuals accumulates in the collective mind of humanity. Every species has a collective mind to which all 'individual' members of that species are connected. We add our thought patterns constantly to the collective level and have access to other patterns held at the collective level. It is a two way process. We give and we receive. Scientists have established something called the hundredth monkey syndrome which I have written about in other books. They have discovered that once a certain number of individuals within a species learn something new, suddenly the rest of that species can do it without being shown. They do it purely by instinct. Although establishment science cannot explain this by its incredibly limited view of life, the process is very simple. Once that certain number within a species has transferred the new knowledge into the collective level, a point of 'critical mass' is reached. The knowledge becomes powerful enough in the collective mind for it to be accessed by every other member of the species. When they attune themselves to the vibration (the thought pattern) which contains that knowledge, they know how to do something without being shown, because that thought pattern is guiding them. We call it instinct or inspiration when it is really tuning to a vibration (a frequency) that holds that information.

All that I have said about the individual creating their own reality equally applies to the collective human mind. It reflects the sum total of human thinking, the sum total of what humanity as a whole thinks of itself. If humanity doesn't like itself, love itself, and respect itself, it will create that reality on this planet. It will attract to it physical manifestations of how it views its own sense of worth and potential. Only this time, the magnetic cape is not cast around only one person, but the entire planet. This creates the global reality.

Look at the consequences of this process in our every day lives. Humanity as a whole wishes to give away its responsibility for what happens in the world. When anything goes wrong, we hear the cry: "What are *they* going to do about it?" We rarely look at ourselves for responsibility. We may like to complain about politicians and bankers, but most people would still rather others ran the world than accept the responsibility for playing their part. These are the thought patterns which dominate the collective mind and it has therefore created that reality on a collective, global, scale. The collective mind has created a response to that desire for someone else to 'do it' by attracting together the energy fields – people – to construct the secret network which now controls the direction of everyone's lives. We have been given what we asked for, or 'thought' for. It is the same with religions. They, too, are created by the thought patterns of the collective mind, as are the media and other institutions which use fear and guilt for purposes of manipulation and control. These reflect, collectively, what billions of people do in their everyday lives. They manipulate fear and guilt to get their way. Observe yourself for a few days and see how many times you (and others) use fear and guilt to control a situation. We do it without realising and we pass this attitude on to our children. What is it we say to them?

"You naughty boy. If you do that again, I'll give you a big smack. Wait till your dad gets home, he'll make you sorry for what you've done." (Fear)

"You naughty girl. How could you do that to your mummy and daddy? How could you make us so sad and unhappy? And all we have done for you." (Guilt)

These are only minor examples of the way fear and guilt are used on children. From an early age they learn to do the same to others. By the time we reach the adult world and the interrelationships that go on there, the use of fear and guilt for control and manipulation has become an art form. They ought to award medals for it! This thought pattern has consequently dominated the collective mind, and it has created the collective physical reflection of this – the religions and other institutions which tell us what to think and use fear and guilt to control. Again, we created them. They are a reflection of us, the collective us, at least. That's good news because we have the power to remove this global manipulation by removing our personal manipulation.

Such a transformation of human perception is so vital to the future of this planet and the world we leave our children. Humanity's desire to give its mind away has allowed a structure to develop over thousands of years which today is on the verge of creating a global fascist dictatorship. Fascism ended with Adolf Hitler? If only it were so. That same mindset controls the secret government of the world which is, minute by minute, manipulating the human mind to accept a centralised global tyranny. This tyranny is called the New World Order and, unless we shake ourselves from our spiritual slumber, it will manifest as a world government; a world central bank and currency; a world army; and a microchipped population linked to a global computer. If anyone thinks all this is ridiculous, the next few hundred pages are going to be very sobering. We are astonishingly close to all of those things. It is time to grow up and wake up.

As you read the story of how your life and the life of this planet has been so controlled and manipulated, I ask you to remember that we all created it. The people I name and the events I describe are only mirrors reflecting back at the human race and the Earth the thought patterns within us. This world is merely human thought made physical. When we recognise what those negative patterns are and remove them, our reality will change and the world will change. But not until.

It begins and ends with *us*.

Part One

The Prison

I believe in... someone else

We are actively discouraged from thinking constructively and questioningly, and once an individual has accepted the numb acquiescence so encouraged, an insidiously vicious circle has successfully been promoted. Another rather convenient result of such a situation is that people who don't think constructively and questioningly don't even realise it.

Michael Timothy, *The Anti-Intellectual Ethic*

Chapter 1

The veil of tears

We have all, at some time, looked at the world around us and asked the same questions. Why does life have to be such a struggle? Why do we know so little about who we are and the purpose of our lives? Why is there so much conflict and suffering in a world of such beauty and such riches?

In search of the answers to these and so many other questions, I'm going to ask you to suspend your programmed 'here and now' responses and open your infinite mind to much greater possibilities. I don't use the word 'programmed' in a patronising way, because we are all programmed by the messages and beliefs we constantly hear in our childhood, through the media, and through the education system. It is the letting go of that programming which opens our minds and our hearts to wonder, potential, and understanding beyond our dreams. I've pondered on the nature of this visible physical world for a long time, trying to make sense of it. Since 1990 I've been on a conscious spiritual journey of discovery. It has opened me to so much I had never thought or felt before in this lifetime and, painful as some of it has been, those moments, too, have led me to greater understanding. I have experienced how we can tune our minds, our consciousness, to other levels of reality and access information available there which is not known, or at least not widely known on Earth. I have realised that our minds – the thinking, feeling us – are a series of energy fields, which use the physical body as a vehicle for experience.

At this moment, our consciousness is tuned to this dense physical world, so this is our reality. When we 'die', our mind-spirit (our consciousness) leaves this temporary physical body and moves on to another wavelength, another stage of experience and evolution.

A most important point to make is that, while in the same physical body on the same planet, a person's mind can be tuned to many different wavelengths of knowledge and understanding. This is why there is such a variation in consciousness, perspective and perception within the human race. In our daily lives, we even talk of people being on 'different wavelengths', because they think so differently and have so little in common. Our attitude to life and the level of knowledge and wisdom we can attain at any point depends on the vibratory levels which our minds can access. All this is essential background to what I believe is behind the history of the human race over many millions of years and into the present day. To me the human race so often seems to be like a herd of bewildered and lost sheep. In fact, look at how many times throughout known history the 'lost sheep' symbolism has been used to describe our plight. We have somehow become detached from our higher potential, our power source; again, we see this portrayed symbolically throughout history and cultures in phrases such as 'lost children' who have become disconnected from 'the father'. The story of the prodigal son in the New Testament is an obvious example. I believe that, symbolically, this is precisely what has happened and the consequences of that explain so much of the world we live in today.

I feel it is impossible to appreciate what has happened unless we can open our minds to the existence of what we call extraterrestrial life. That can include an infinite variety of forms. All I mean by extraterrestrial is 'not of this Earth' – other civilisations, consciousness and lifeforms on other wavelengths which our physical senses cannot normally see or hear. For instance, while we may look at some of the other planets in this solar system and see apparently barren, lifeless, lands, we are only looking at that planet on our own frequency or dimension of experience, our own space-time reality. On another dimension, that planet may be a teeming haven of life in the same way that all the radio and television stations broadcasting to your area now are sharing the same space that your body is occupying. You can't see them and they can't 'see' each other because they are operating on different wavelengths. Take this one stage further to encompass the fact that these other civilisations on other wavelengths are more advanced in their knowledge and know-how than we are at this time, and a picture begins to form, for me and many others, anyway. These other civilisations are not all positive or negative. Like us, they are a bit of both. Extraterrestrial life is no big deal. It is the same stream of life we call Creation or God, at a different stage of evolution and/or on a different wavelength of experience. But many of these peoples are years, sometimes *millions* of years (in our version of time) ahead of where we are technologically and in their understanding of the universal laws. If we judge the credibility or craziness of something only from the perspective of our scientific achievements on this wavelength of Planet Earth, we will never understand what has happened to us. This is why I ask the skeptics to open themselves to other possibilities. If you were a peasant farmer in the mountains of some self-contained society in deepest Asia, you would find it impossible to believe a description of New York. But New York would still exist. And remember, only a short time has passed since the idea of humans flying off into space was considered ridiculous.

Over a number of years, as I have sought to grasp the nature of the human condition, a story has begun to form in my mind. When I read a book called *Bringers Of The Dawn*,[1] it cross-confirmed some of the themes I had written

---

[1] Barbara Marciniak, *Bringers Of The Dawn*, (Bear & Co, Sante Fe, 1992).

in *The Robots' Rebellion* and other ideas that I had been developing in the months that followed. It is a 'channelled' book, in that the writer, Barbara Marciniak, tuned her consciousness to another wavelength of reality and acted as a channel to bring information to this Earth vibration. I am always wary of channelled books because, like everything, this process can produce inspired understanding or a load of utter claptrap. It depends on the competence of the channel and the level of the wavelength to which they are connecting. As someone once said of contact with those no longer on this Earth: "Death is no cure for ignorance". If you connect with wavelengths close to this one, you can be seriously misled.

Bringers Of The Dawn claims to be the words of a consciousness communicating from the star system we know as the Pleiades. I know if you are new to this, it all sounds so fantastic and hard to accept. But all I can do – all any of us can do – is to say what we believe and feel. I believe that this star system called the Pleiades, or at least the more evolved groups from there, are part of a universal operation to set humanity and this world free from the prison we have unknowingly lived within for aeons of what we call time. We are the generation who are going to see this happen.

Planet Earth was hijacked, you could say, and taken over by another civilisation or civilisations, which are highly advanced technologically, but pretty low on love and wisdom. This is, as always, a telling and profoundly imbalanced combination. I call it 'cleverness without wisdom'. We live in a free-will universe where, within certain limits, we are allowed to experience all of the emotions, and learn from the consequences of our actions. So taking over a planet does not bring in the 'father', the Source of All That Exists, to immediately wrest control from the hijackers. It is used as a period of experience from which all will learn and evolve. We live in a time-space reality – "world" – called the Third Dimension and it is from some of our "neighbours" in the Fourth Dimension that the interference has come. Whenever I speak of the extraterrestrial consciousness or the Prison Warder consciousness I am referring to manipulation from the Fourth Dimension via either thought control or direct intervention. Both the hijacking extraterrestrials and those with humanity's interests at heart were regular visitors to the Earth thousands of years ago. They became the 'gods' in the ancient texts and legends which have formed the foundations of most, perhaps all, of the major religions of today. If an extraterrestrial landed on the planet in ancient times in an astonishing anti-gravity spacecraft, or you saw a psychic vision of someone on another frequency, you would sure as hell think he or she was a god! And they did. This is where the 'gods' – particularly the angry, judgmental, fire and brimstone gods – originated: negative extraterrestrials. The 'fear of God' was born, and this fear and resistance to change (disobeying the gods) is still in the collective psyche. Over time, as described at length in *The Robots' Rebellion*, these various god myths became fused together to form 'composite gods', based on themes from many of the earlier civilisations. So it is with Judaism, the Christian Bible, Islam, and most of the others. Their version of God relates to the type of extraterrestrials from which their religion originated or the way many different extraterrestrial stories have become fused into a composite God over the centuries. Dearly beloved, we are gathered here today to worship a composite God made up of extraterrestrials. Amen.

If you look at the origins of the major religions, the stories are remarkably similar to those we hear today from people claiming to have met, or been abducted by, extraterrestrials. Mohammed, the founder of Islam in the seventh century, said that he had been visited by the Angel Gabriel, who was "in the likeness of a man, standing in the sky above the horizon".[2] This figure told him he had to be a prophet, and he was given messages which formed the Islamic holy book, the Koran. These messages would be dictated while Mohammed was in a trance on many other occasions in the years that followed. He also wrote of going on a 'celestial journey'. Many people in the modern world who claim to have experienced extraterrestrial contact have said the same as Mohammed. Saul of Tarsus, better known as St Paul, was the man who changed the image of Y'shua (Jesus)[3] into the saviour-god-messiah from which the Christian religion was spawned. This happened after he had a 'vision' of Y'shua on the road to Damascus. He also talked about being 'taken up' into heaven, or a number of different heavens (dimensions). Speaking of himself, he wrote:

> *"I know a man in Christ who fourteen years ago was caught up to the third heaven. Whether he was in the body or out of the body, I do not know – God knows. And I know that this man – whether in the body or out of the body I do not know, but God knows – was caught up in Paradise. He heard inexpressible things, things that man is not permitted to tell."*
> **2 Corinthians 12: 2–4**

Again, this is paralleled by many of today's accounts of extraterrestrial abductees who have told of being taken into other dimensions of reality by ETs, sometimes in their body, sometimes out of it. St Paul and the prophet called Enoch speak of seeing many heavens when they were 'taken up'; this corresponds with the stories in the Vedas, the ancient holy books of India which were written in the original Sanskrit language. These describe seven higher planes and seven lower planes around this planet. Some people still talk of being in 'Seventh Heaven' when something wonderful happens to them. One of these 'planes' is our third dimension and just above us vibrationally is the level which has manipulated us. In the Book of Enoch,

---

[2] Hari Prasad Shastri, *The Ramayana Of Valmiki*, (Shanti Sadam, London, 1976) Vol. II, p95.
[3] Jesus is a Greek translation of a Judean name, probably Y'shua, the Hebrew for Joshua. The full name would have been Y'shua ben Yosef (Joshua, the son of Joseph).

the 'Watchers' sound remarkably like extraterrestrials. The Dead Sea Scrolls say that the father of Noah was a 'Watcher', and Nebuchadnezzar, the King of Babylon from 651–604 BC, records being visited by a Watcher and a holy one who came down from heaven.[4] The Dakas in Mahayana Buddhism were 'sky travelling beings' and Padma Sambhava, the founder of Tibetan Buddhism, was said to have left Tibet in a celestial chariot.[5] Something similar was claimed for the biblical prophet Elijah when he left Israel[6] and for the Central American god, Quetzalcoatl.[7] Descriptions of flying discs, flying boats, and celestial chariots, abound on all continents and in all cultures. Still today we relate 'heaven' to the sky, because that is where the 'gods' of ancient time came from in their spacecraft. The aborigines of Australia speak of three ancestral beings, called the Djanggawul, who were connected with the planet Venus, as was Quetzalcoatl and the Polynesian deity, Kahuna.[8] Add to all these the many examples cited in *The Robots' Rebellion* and countless other books, linking ETs with the creation and supervision of the Earth races, and only a padlocked mind could dismiss at least the possibility – I would say probability – that extraterrestrials are at the heart of human history and the events that have shaped that history.

There are so many themes which link the ancient texts with descriptions of UFO sightings and extraterrestrials of today. UFO investigators tracked down the alleged author of a report known as *The Memorandum*. Bill English was a former captain in intelligence with the Green Berets in Vietnam involved in the retrieval of a B-52 bomber forced down in the jungle by a UFO. He claims to have spent three months in a psychiatric unit after the experience, before being assigned to an RAF listening post in England by US Army Intelligence. In his office there, he says, he found a sealed diplomatic pouch waiting for him which contained a 624-page report on UFOs, known as *The Grudge 13 Report*. His memorandum was his personal analysis of this document. It included all top secret UFO activity from 1942 to 1951 and this involved reported landings, sightings, UFO crashes, human abductions, and ETs captured by the government. This could all quite easily be disinformation because there is so much of that in the UFO scene. But the report did contain many interesting points. It said that the language of the captured ETs was similar to Sanskrit, the ancient language of the Indian holy texts, the Vedas, which contain many references to what appear to be spacecraft and flying machines known as the Vimanas and to extraterrestrial 'gods'.

The Grudge Report said that the nourishment absorbed by the ETs they examined was based on chlorophyll, which (as is now known) exists

[4] George C. Andrews, *Extra-Terrestrials Among Us*, (Llewellyn Publications, USA, 1986) p63.

[5] *Extra-Terrestrials Among Us*, p54–55.

[6] Ibid p73–74.

[7] Ibid p72–73.

[8] Ibid p63.

throughout what we call space and not just on Earth. In the Vedas, there is considerable importance given to a plant known as Soma. It was used as a hallucinogenic drug in ceremonies to help communication with the 'god' Indra and other 'gods', and it was the favourite drink of Indra and his colleagues. Given the increasing speculation that the ancient 'gods' were actually extraterrestrials, it is rather a coincidence that the Soma drink is believed to have been based on liquid chlorophyll. A number of people who have claimed contact with ETs have reported that their nourishment came from 'juice'. There are, however, tens of thousands of extraterrestrial civilisations which have visited this planet, I believe, and they will be very different in appearance, genetics, and means of nourishment. Some undoubtedly look very much as we do and could walk past us in the street without turning a head. Others appear very different from us.

I feel that at least many of the 'miracles' recorded throughout religious legend have an extraterrestrial (Fourth Dimensional) origin. The sight witnessed by 70,000 Catholics at Fatima, Portugal in 1917 sounds like many of the stories described in both the ancient texts and the modern world. The Fatima 'miracle' followed a series of meetings between three children and some strange being, which, they said, sometimes manifested as the Virgin Mary. The being promised to produce a miracle to open the eyes of humanity, and those tens of thousands of people who turned up to witness it did, indeed, see a fantastic sight. But what was it? UFO researcher, Jacque Vallee, believed he knew when he wrote, in his 1976 book, *The Invisible College*:

> "Not only was a flying disc or globe consistently involved, but its motion, its falling leaf trajectory, its light effects, the thunderclaps, the buzzing sounds, the strange fragrance, the fall of 'angel hair' that dissolves on the ground, the heat wave associated with the close approach of the disc, all of these are constant parameters of UFO sightings everywhere. And so are the paralysis, the amnesia, the conversions, and healings."

The children passed a sealed message from their communicator to the Pope, with instructions that it was only to be opened and made public in 1960. The Pope did open it in 1960, but we are still waiting for all of it to be made public! One thing is for sure: if it had confirmed the basis of the Roman Catholic religion, it would have hit the airwaves within minutes. So what did it say?

I am convinced that the Old Testament 'God' known as Yhwh (Yahweh) is also based on an extraterrestrial, or more likely, a series of them. Interestingly, while the Jewish religion is perceived as a 'One God' faith, the original Hebrew texts do not support this. While the English translation refers to a 'God', the Hebrew talks of Elohim, the plural meaning 'Gods'. Similarly, while we read the word 'Lord' in the English, the Hebrew refers to

Adonai, the plural 'Lords'. Jehovah, who is often interchanged with Yahweh, would seem to have a different origin. Another extraterrestrial, most probably.

If you read the Old Testament and other ancient texts and replace every reference to 'God' or 'the gods' with 'extraterrestrial', the whole thing begins to make sense and becomes so obvious. It is important to remember that in evolutionary terms, the time span between the period when these accounts were written and today is nothing, hardly the blink of an eye. Modern UFO phenomena as reported by thousands of people – which include amazing holographic images, beings and craft which appear and disappear (switch dimensions), and a host of other visions and tricks that put Walt Disney in the shade – were being performed by extraterrestrials in the periods during which the major religions originated. These Fourth Dimensional manipulators created the religions to control the human mind as they sought to control this dimension.

The potential for manipulating humanity with such technology is simply limitless. What better way to control people, close down their minds and divide and rule, than to create a series of dogmatic religions based on extraterrestrial special effects? Look at the pain, misery, and inter-generational ignorance that has been visited upon this planet by Christianity, Islam, Judaism, and all the rest. If you want to shut down someone's consciousness so they stop thinking for themselves and delink their minds from their infinite potential, sell them a dogmatic religion or some other form of rigid dogma. They are then putty in your hands.

I think the takeover of Planet Earth was achieved by what I call the Luciferic Consciousness. I use this as an overall name to describe the force which attempts to work through all life forms, human and extraterrestrial, to control the planet. It is an extremely negative energy operating from the Fourth Dimension. The Luciferic Consciousness takes two main forms. Different cultures give these forms different symbolic names. One seeks to imprison us in the material world by persuading us to reject all idea of the spiritual realms and the eternal nature of life. The other works on spiritually-minded people to persuade them to ignore the realities of the physical world and to float around in a spiritual daze. Either way it means that the people involved can be controlled and their potential to bring positive change to the physical world is seriously curtailed.

The takeover of the Earth by the extraterrestrial expressions of this Luciferic Consciousness took the form, I feel, of creating a vibratory prison. We are multidimensional beings, working across many frequencies and dimensions at the same time. I know these can be strange concepts to those hearing them cold, but our *real* potential and our *perceived* potential are light years apart, as we are going to realise in the amazing years that are to follow. If, therefore, there is a frequency 'net' thrown around this planet, a blocking, imprisoning vibration, which prevents us from interconnecting with the

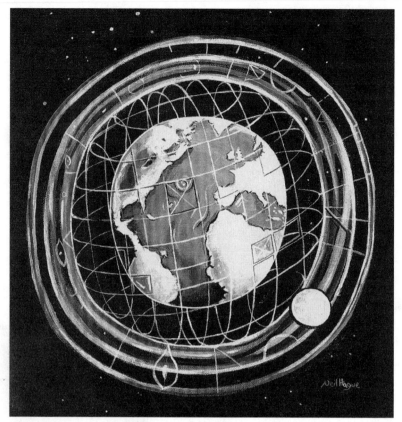

Figure 2: is the Earth a vibratory prison?

higher levels of our consciousness and potential, we cease to be 'whole'. We become delinked from 'the father'. With the knowledge held on the Fourth Dimension, this would not be the miracle it might at first appear. Blocking frequencies are already used here on Earth, never mind by more technologically advanced civilisations. During the period of the Soviet Union, they created an information prison by sending out blocking frequencies to stop certain foreign radio stations from being received by the population. This prevented information which challenged the official line from reaching the people. It created a vibratory prison, an information prison. Extend that concept to the planet as a whole and you have the very picture I am presenting (*Figure 2*). The only difference is one of scale, that's all.

In his book, *The Montauk Project*,[9] the electrical engineer, Preston Nichols, tells the story of how he discovered a blocking frequency which jammed the

---

[9] Preston B. Nichols with Peter Moon, *The Montauk Project*, (Sky Books, New York, 1992).

minds of psychics he was working with as part of research into telepathy. The basis of telepathy, as Preston Nichols confirmed, is so simple. When we think we send out a thought-wave similar to a radio or television wave broadcast from a transmitter. A radio or television set decodes those waves and, in a far more sophisticated way, the human mind decodes thought-waves. Hence telepathy. Nichols found that the minds of his psychics were blocked at the same time each day. Using tracking equipment, he traced the jamming frequency to a now notorious centre of mind control and time travel research called Montauk, on the eastern end of Long Island, New York. Even on Earth, blocking frequencies are a fact.

I am going to use the term blocking and jamming frequency for simplicity, but it could well have taken the form of closing down the portals and gateways which link this physical dimension we see around us with other space-time dimensions. Some of these gateways are reckoned to be at the great sacred places of the ancients, like Stonehenge, Machu Picchu in Peru, Ayers Rock, and the former lands of Babylon and Mesopotamia, now Iraq. The Bermuda Triangle is believed to be another, which could explain the many strange disappearances of ships and aircraft, as the gateway opens. It may even be that these gateways were largely closed down for positive reasons, to prevent more negative extraterrestrials from entering this space-time reality. There are lots of maybes and so much more to know and understand. Jamming frequency, closing the dimensional gateways, perhaps both – the precise *cause* of the prison doesn't matter for what I am saying in this book. All we need to remember is that an extraterrestrial force from the Fourth Dimension created an information prison by blocking off the higher levels of human consciousness. The veil came down. A veil of tears. We were, in effect, put into spiritual and mental quarantine.

If such a jamming vibration were thrown around our planet, or even the Solar System and further afield, our potential would be confined to the levels of consciousness which are within the imprisoning frequency. Any consciousness and knowledge held on higher frequencies outside this vibratory prison would be denied to us. We would become delinked from the higher levels of our own consciousness. We would be, in the words of the ancient books, 'lost souls' delinked from 'the father'. I have used the following analogy many times, but I think it sums it up pretty well: You are a spaceman on the Moon. You are receiving information through your eyes and ears from the world immediately around you. You are also receiving information about the wider picture and a greater understanding of your task from what we call 'Mission Control'. When you, the spaceman, are getting a balance of information through your eyes and ears and from the greater perspective of Mission Control, everything is fine and you are operating at full potential. But think what would happen if the link with Mission Control was cut. Suddenly the wider understanding and guidance has gone. Only the 'eyes and ears' information from the world immediately around you is left to guide your thinking and behaviour. Very soon that behaviour and perception would be enormously different from what it would have been had you and Mission Control stayed in powerful contact.

When that blocking, imprisoning frequency was thrown around this planet, the Solar System, and possibly beyond, it had that same effect. We lost touch with our Mission Control and, crucially, with our eternal memory. We forgot who we were and where we came from. Or, at least, the overwhelming majority did. Those who could continue to hold their vibratory rate, their frequency, could still stay in touch with their higher levels, their Higher Self, because the vibratory connection was still there, although the blocking frequency made this a less than perfect connection, even for them. More and more people are able to do this today as the blocking frequency is dispersed and this is the basis of what is termed the 'spiritual awakening' now enveloping this planet. Only a tiny few have been able to do this, however, until very recently. The rest have seen their vibratory rate fall under the influence of events, religions, and general programming which has encouraged them to close down their minds and therefore reduce their vibratory rate. This has created a vibratory gap – for some a chasm – between their lower levels of consciousness inside the blocking frequency (the Lower Self) and their infinite potential outside of that frequency (the Higher Self). Within the prison was this physical level and some non-physical levels to which we return between incarnations. The rest of Creation has been denied to most people. You might see it as the human race living out its existence inside a box with the lid held down. We sit in the dark, believing that our potential, and Creation in general, is limited to what is within that box, within that vibratory prison. Infinity in potential and space is so, so close on the other side of the box lid, but we have not been allowed to see outside and we have not realised that there *is* an outside. Over the thousands of years or more since the vibratory 'net' was cast around the Earth, we have been a people, a race, working to a fraction of our full and infinite potential. Life on Earth changed dramatically and I believe this also affected the animal kingdom. The law of the jungle and the cruelty we see within nature is not the way it was meant to be, I feel, nor the way it was before the veil came down. The good news is – shout it from the roof tops – that this period of disconnection is now entering its end time. Wow. What a future we are going to experience!

In the period after the blocking vibration was created, I believe that Fourth Dimensional extraterrestrials of the Luciferic mindset came here and genetically rewired the DNA, the inherited coding of the physical body. Over a period of time, this new DNA pattern was passed on through the generations to everyone. The DNA determines the nature of the physical being and contains the inherited memory of all the generations. If the DNA had been left alone, we would, while living in a vibratory prison, at least *know* what had happened and the nature of the problem. By scrambling the

DNA, this knowledge, too, was lost to us. The communicators of the information in *Bringers Of The Dawn* (and in other books claiming to come from extraterrestrial sources) say that the human DNA before that time had twelve spirals known as helixes, but after the genetic tinkering this was reduced to two. Our potential and our inherited information source was reduced to a sixth of what it is meant to be. Even now, I understand, there are parts of the DNA which have been identified that researchers have been unable to link to any apparent function. This has been termed 'junk DNA'. It is possibly the disconnection of the other ten spirals of DNA which has meant that, as is widely acknowledged, only a fraction of our brain's potential is actually used. Some more good news to celebrate – we are in the time when a process is unfolding which will reunite those DNA spirals within us. My goodness! What we will *then* be able to know, remember, and do, will beggar belief from today's perspective.

It is possible that these genetic events are described symbolically in the tale of Adam and Eve and the term, 'the Fall of Man'. You can also find many references in the ancient texts and legends to 'gods' coming from the skies to control humanity and impregnate women. In the Bible, Genesis 6:4 says that, "The sons of God came in to the daughters of men, and they bore children to them". The term 'sons of God' (which is common to almost all ancient religions) referred, I am sure, to the extraterrestrials. We hear of how God or the gods created humanity 'in their own image'. I outline a number of these ancient themes in *The Robots' Rebellion*. The offspring of these extraterrestrial/human liaisons looked very different from the rest of the people. As Genesis 6:4 puts it in *The Good News Bible*: "In those days, and even later, there were giants on the Earth who were descendants of human women and the heavenly beings. They were the great heroes and famous men of long ago". The reason this-world-is-all-there-is science has been unable to find the missing links in human genetic evolution is because there aren't any. The sudden changes in the human form were due to extraterrestrial intervention. This is possibly an origin of the virgin mother legends which are also found throughout the world. In what we call China, they had a 'sky god' called Di (no relation to Prince Charles) who was said to have 'miraculously' impregnated a virgin, who then gave birth to Zu, the first of the new genetic line. All over the ancient world, you find that the royal families were supposed to have originated with the sky gods – extraterrestrials. Records left by the ancient civilisations of Mesopotamia say that their pyramidal towers known as ziggurats were built for intercourse between a priestess and a god from the sky. Herodotus described the inside of a ziggurat he saw in Babylon:

> *"On the topmost tower there is a spacious temple, and inside the temple stands a great bed covered with fine bedclothes with a golden table at its side. There is no statue of any kind set up in this place, nor is the chamber occupied*

at night by any but a single native woman who, say the Chaldean priests, is chosen by the deity out of all the women of the land. The priests also declare, but I for one do not credit it, that the god comes down in person into this chamber, and sleeps upon the couch." [10]

On a tomb found in Rome and dated between the First and Fourth Centuries AD the inscription read: "I am a son of the Earth and the stars of the sky, but I am of the celestial race. May the knowledge be passed on!" [11] The birth of Y'shua (Jesus), as described in the Gnostic Gospels, also has similarities to modern day ET experiences. The Protoevangelion of James is the oldest of the Gnostic Gospels which were removed from Christian orthodoxy at the notorious Council of Nicaea in 325 AD (see *The Robots' Rebellion*). The Gnostic text describes the birth of Y'shua and how people and animals froze in mid-gesture in a powerful, though temporary paralysis, while Joseph and the midwife were unaffected. This is very much a theme of ET contactee/abductee experiences. The text goes on:

"And the midwife went away with him. And they stood in the place of the cave, and behold a luminous cloud overshadowed the cave. And the midwife said: 'My soul has been magnified this day, because mine eyes have seen strange things — because salvation has been brought forth to Israel'. And immediately the cloud disappeared out of the cave, and a great light shone in the cave, so that the eyes could not bear it. And in a little that light gradually decreased until the infant appeared, and went and took the breast of his mother, Mary."

The connections with 'gods' and 'clouds' are endless in the ancient legends and texts and what about the 'star' that was supposed to have hovered over the birthplace of Y'shua? Why could that not have been a spacecraft? In the biblical Revelations we hear of the New Jerusalem descending from the sky (Rev 22:10) and Y'shua returning 'with the clouds' (Rev 1:7). Was Y'shua a member of a positive extraterrestrial race who became incarnate to help humanity get out of prison? It is certainly a possibility. The Native American tribe, the Iroquois, have a legend of an Iroquois maiden marrying the chief of the sky people. The geologist, Christian O'Brien, suggested that Hebrew and Sumerian texts refer to a race of beings known as the 'Shining Ones', a term he connects with the Hebrew word, Elohim. It is no coincidence that the Devas from the Sanskrit and the Angels of Christianity are also 'Shining Ones'. The Incas of Peru referred to 'Shining Ones' too. O'Brien says that it was the beings known as the Elohim which created modern humanity from early human forms through genetic manipulation. He adds that some of them, the 'Watchers' in the Book of Enoch, mated with humans and he

---

[10] *Extra-Terrestrials Among Us*, p54.
[11] Ibid p59.

believes that the alleged founders of the Semitic race, Shemjaza and Yahweh, were among the extraterrestrial 'Watchers' and 'Shining Ones'.[12]

An Israeli scholar, Zecharia Sitchin, used the ancient Sumerian and Babylonian writings to support his belief that modern humans were created by ETs called the Nefilim.[13] UFO abductees today have also spoken of communications with ETs who described how they created the bodies of the present human race and manipulated our DNA; there are many references by abductees to having sex with extraterrestrials while on a spacecraft. Not all of these stories will be true, nor all the theories and details, but if you take note of the common themes, a picture starts to form. I believe that different extraterrestrial civilisations seeded the different races on Earth and perhaps this can explain the obsession that some have with the purity of their race. Most will not relate this to an extraterrestrial origin, but at a deep, subconscious level, that might be what is motivating them.

I believe the Earth is far older than science has imagined and that a stream of civilisations has settled and developed here which are not mentioned in the history books. Most of them before 'the Fall' were far more highly evolved, technologically and spiritually, than humanity is today. Life is not always about progressing mentally, emotionally, spiritually, and physically. If something happens to delink us from our true potential, we can also go backwards. It depends on the knowledge and potential available to us. In the periods known as Lemuria and Atlantis, hundreds of thousands of years ago in our version of time, humans lived in what we would call a science fiction world, in which amazing things were possible, as was also true in civilisations before those. These were not miracles, merely the use of the natural laws of Creation. What is termed the paranormal or supernatural is only that which our limited version of science has not discovered or acknowledged yet. Everything that exists is the result of 'natural' laws. If it were not, it could not exist. We began to go backwards when the jamming frequency was installed, and the levels of consciousness which contained the knowledge enjoyed before recorded human history were denied to us. The prison door slammed shut and we are now flinging it open again.

Human civilisation did not begin on Planet Earth, I am convinced. It came to this planet from other areas of the galaxy. Some say the first humans on Earth came from the star system called Vega, 26 light-years from here, and three times the size of the Sun. It is the brightest star in the Lyra constellation and the fifth brightest in our sky.[14] Wherever it was, I feel the

[12] Christian O'Brien, *The Genius Of The Fen*, (Turnstone Press Ltd., Wellingborough, Northamptonshire, 1985). His views were also quoted in Richard L. Thompson's *Alien Identities*, (Govardhan Hill Publishing, San Diego, 1993) p197–198.
[13] Zecharia Sitchin, *The 12th Planet*, (Avon, New York, 1976).
[14] Virginia Essene and Sheldon Nidle, *You Are Becoming A Galactic Human*, (S.E.E. Publishing Co, Santa Clara, 1994).

human race originally came from another star system and took the
opportunity to populate and experience this magnificent new planet.
Genetic manipulation, both positive and negative, has continued ever since
to advance or control the species, depending on the mindset at the time. In
those earlier times, I think the nature of the physical form was not as dense as
it is today. It was more etheric, lighter and less dense, and capable of
manifesting and demanifesting, levitation, and floating above the surface. All
these things are possible now if the power of our thought is concentrated
sufficiently, but it was available to everyone then, I believe, as an everyday
part of life. In those periods, there was no physical 'death'. The
consciousness withdrew from the body when it chose to do so. We will be
doing this again as the transformation of this planet and humanity proceeds.

Another theme which connects channelled information from many
sources purporting to be extraterrestrial civilisations and the symbolic stories
in the ancient texts and legends across thousands of years, is that of a war in
the heavens, possibly a war between extraterrestrial civilisations for control of
this galaxy. I feel this relates to the struggle between two consciousness
streams on the Fourth Dimension, for the control of this one. Lemuria was
the creation of one of these streams, Atlantis the work of the other. It has
been a long and bitter battle with humanity as the pawns in the middle. The
Indian Vedas contain stories that could easily describe a high tech battle in
the skies. Those who are more evolved technologically do not have to be
more evolved spiritually. The development of the atomic bomb is a case in
point. Developing the bomb was brilliant technologically. Dropping it was
the very opposite of spirituality. So I find it quite feasible that all hell broke
loose in parts of this galaxy, as extraterrestrials battled for power with their
highly advanced toys. I feel that films like *Star Wars* and other science
'fiction' stories are the result of the writers accessing their deep memories or
having direct knowledge of what happened. It is this same inner memory at
some deep level of our consciousness that attracts such astonishing numbers
of people to the science fiction films and literature. Some of the places which
crop up most often in channelled information relating to these conflicts are
the systems of Orion, Sirius, and the Pleiades. Interesting, then, that these
were at the fore of ancient beliefs and worship on Earth over thousands of
years, across scores of cultures. The pyramids at Giza and the giant spider
drawn in ancient times on the plains of Nazca, Peru, are exactly aligned with
Orion. I think the star Arcturus in the Bootes constellation is also significant
to the Earth's history.

The aim of the negative extraterrestrials in relation to the Earth was to
turn humans into little more than a slave race. This has been a theme all
along and it remains so today, although in another form. Instead of
controlling us physically by occupation of the planet, over the past few
thousand years they have sought to do so by working through our
consciousness from other dimensions. I believe there came a period after

ancient Babylon and Egypt when, for some reason, they no longer came here in the same way. Maybe they were forced out by other extraterrestrials who were trying to help us. Maybe it was vibratory changes that took place. Either way, I believe they began to work mostly through the human mind from the Fourth Dimension and that this has replaced the physical occupation of the distant past. I have no doubt they have still come here, however, and in increasing numbers in more recent times. *The Lord Of The Rings* by J.R. Tolkien, has themes of war between the humanlike Hobbits and the little grey Orcs which many believe resemble the themes of what has actually happened, even down to the descriptions of subterranean laboratories which mirror the claims of what is happening today in the underground bases and genetic laboratories under America and other countries.

The battle for the Earth possibly reached its most destructive phase at the end of Atlantis, over a period of tens of thousands of years, leading up to the vast island of Atlantis sinking into the Atlantic Ocean around 10,500–9,500 BC. The evidence is mounting from many sources of some cataclysmic weather and geological upheavals around this time, in which whole mountain ranges pushed up from the Earth and an unbelievable tidal wave of some kind swept across the planet's surface. The geological researchers, J.B. Delair and D.S. Allan, document much of this evidence in their book, *When The Earth Nearly Died.*[15] They believe that a star exploded around 15,000 BC and some of the debris reached this solar system about 9,500 BC, leaving devastation in its wake. Their work confirms the themes of channelled communications over thousands of years when they claim that the Earth surface we see today was created largely by an enormous upheaval, almost in the twinkling of an eye in evolutionary terms, and not by the slow, gradual change so promoted by mainstream, official-line, science.

The detail of these various views is interesting, but I find the overall *themes* emerging from ancient and modern information and beliefs to be the most compelling aspect in all this. Those themes are of a considerable extraterrestrial influence on human affairs, a battle between extraterrestrial civilisations for supremacy, and a catastrophe on Earth and throughout the Solar System caused by a foreign 'body' of some kind passing through. I feel that such themes are connected and that connection is the Luciferic Consciousness. It is a collective consciousness, the total of all minds – human and extraterrestrial – thinking within that extreme negative frequency range. While it is not possible for one person or group to destabilise a planetary system with their thoughts alone, it is certainly possible (in my view anyway) for a multidimensional collective consciousness to do so.

As everything is created by thought and all matter is subordinate to thought, all physical events are the result of a thought or thoughts of some

[15] D.S. Allan and J.B. Delair, *When The Earth Nearly Died*, (Gateway Books, Bath, 1995).

kind affecting matter. Everything is. What scientists are doing when they investigate the 'laws' of physics and matter is to put forward mathematical equations which describe the power and potential of thought, most of which they have so far missed. All of these events which caused mayhem in the Solar System took place within the confines of the vibratory prison, created by representations of the Luciferic Consciousness. This consciousness manipulates *through any lifeform,* human or extraterrestrial, *which is operating within its vibratory range.* The Luciferic Consciousness is an extremely negative thought pattern, or range of thought patterns, and anyone whose own attitudes are within that range can be captured by it and turned into a vehicle for its will. It is the same principle as tuning a radio into a particular station. When the Luciferic Consciousness locks into someone's consciousness, it, in effect, becomes their 'Mission Control', their guide. If our intent remains loving and positive, it cannot affect us directly because our energy fields, the mind-emotions-spirit, will be vibrating within a range much higher than the Luciferic band. There is no resonance established. The Luciferic 'broadcast' is not received by a consciousness 'tuned' to a different frequency, just as a radio receiver only picks up stations within a defined bandwidth at any given time.

I feel that the civilisation we call Atlantis was an attempt – by what I call (in *The Robots' Rebellion)* the 'volunteers', and *Bringers Of The Dawn* calls the Family of Light and the Systems Busters – to break the vibratory stronghold, the blocking vibration. These volunteers were mostly from the more positive consciousness stream on the Fourth Dimension. It was an influx of beings into the prison, the box, attempting to change the Earth vibration and break the controlling frequency. It was, for a time, a partial success, but Atlantis became a highly negative place under influence from the Luciferic stream and it suffered a violent end. We, the generations of today, now have the opportunity to do what Atlantis could not do – break the blocking vibration and allow humanity to return to wholeness and Oneness, to reconnect with our full potential. It is an opportunity we are going to grasp and we are going to do it peacefully. Not with physical force, but with love. I want to tell this story as simply as possible without getting lost in complexities. I will therefore use some simplistic terms for two overall streams of thinking, which seek rather different futures for Planet Earth. The Prison Warders, as I will call them, is a symbolic name for the Fourth Dimensional consciousness which took over the planet and delinked humanity, vibrationally and genetically, from our full potential and higher knowledge. I don't wish to present this in reality as a simple 'light v dark', 'good v evil' thing because we are all part of the same whole anyway, all aspects of the same one consciousness that we call God or Creation. We all have a positive and negative polarity which we are seeking to balance. But at different points in our evolution we all have different attitudes and it is the interaction of these various thought patterns, positive and negative, which sets up the experiences that speed evolution. The other stream of thinking is represented by those entities and consciousness streams which wish to break through the limitations and disconnections imposed on humanity and the Earth, and to restore freedom of thought and potential. I will call this stream of consciousness the 'Light' or 'Love' vibration.

One other point to make about this vibratory hijack is the nature of 'food' and nourishment. On this physical level our bodies need physical food to sustain them. But on other frequencies of reality in the non-physical realms of consciousness, the food is pure energy. The more energy of like vibration which can be created, the bigger the meal, if you like. The energy that the Prison Warder/Luciferic Consciousness absorbs and gets its power from is negative energy. The more of that which can be created, the more powerful it can potentially become. And the more imbalanced, too, of course. Emotions like fear, guilt, and anger, can, if not balanced by positive emotions, produce vast supplies of negative energy. A war becomes a banquet. We are generating energy all the time and the psychically sensitive can feel and see it. In fact we all can, although most people don't realise it. If humanity can be manipulated to be full of fear, guilt, and anger, the vibratory 'box' in which we live becomes a production line of negative energy. For the Prison Warders, lunch is served! It is interesting that today's stories about negative extraterrestrials presently at large on Earth speak of them living off negative human emotions and seeking to stimulate events and circumstances in which more extreme negative energy will be created. I believe this to be correct and it is a key reason why this extraterrestrial consciousness, the Prison Warders, has worked through human minds to stimulate the horrors of history and today. These events are not the result of an 'evil' human nature. They are manufactured by manipulating human nature and its sense of reality. It is highly likely, too, that the animal and human sacrifices to the 'gods' (which abound throughout history and in cultures all over the world) were performed to serve the extraterrestrials' need for such energy and perhaps for some portions of the physical body. The Aztecs in Central America, who sacrificed untold numbers of people to the 'gods', are but one example of this. Fortunately, most extraterrestrials are not of this extreme negative mindset; a host of positive ET civilisations are at work today on various wavelengths around this planet to ease the spiritual transformation to freedom which has now begun. They are here to help us.

After the introduction of the blocking frequency, when people 'died' and their consciousness left the physical body, most could not escape further than the non-physical frequencies which were contained within the vibratory prison. Even when not in physical bodies, they continued to be disconnected from their higher consciousness, their Higher Self, as we call it – they were imprisoned in the Third Dimension. So began the process of incarnation and reincarnation into Earth bodies, as beings sought to continue their evolution inside a prison they didn't even realise was a prison. The 'gods' who supervised the prison were perceived to be *the* God. Many people became so imbalanced and locked into certain thought patterns and attitudes that they chose to reincarnate into the same situations, places, and races. As they repeated the old responses, Earth life after Earth life, they became more and more imbalanced. Others of greater understanding used their incarnations as a vehicle for gathering experience and evolving.

Our consciousness is a series of interconnecting magnetic energy fields and the greater our understanding and openness of mind, the quicker those energy fields vibrate. After the prison door was closed, those trapped inside were encouraged and manipulated to close their minds and that still continues today, of course. All the positive extraterrestrials can do is to give us the opportunity to open our minds and raise ourselves vibrationally to reconnect with our infinite selves. This is what they are seeking to do with phenomena like the crop patterns.

It is quite simple really. The positive Fourth Dimensional (and higher) ETs are trying to open our minds and hearts and the negative ones are seeking to keep them closed. Our minds cannot be opened by extraterrestrials just landing on the White House lawn. That would not open the collective human mind; it would blow it! Look at the mass panic in 1938, when Orson Welles presented his radio show, *War Of The Worlds* which purported to be a live broadcast about a landing by extraterrestrials. The mind is like a muscle; the more you use it, the better it works and the bigger it becomes. So we have to be given clues which stretch our consciousness to understand and trigger the memories we hold at a deeper level of our consciousness. The negative ETs, in contrast, wish to keep from us any information which would stimulate us spiritually and intellectually.

A few people through history have been able to open and expand their consciousness to the point where they have raised their vibratory rate beyond that of the prison vibration and reunited fully with the rest of themselves and Creation. This process has been given the name 'ascension' – getting out of jail – and it shows itself in the words attributed to Y'shua and similar figures throughout history: "I and my father are one". We see many of these people in the history books. They were able to raise their consciousness while in incarnation, to connect with frequencies outside of the prison and so understand the nature of the predicament humanity is in. They were laughed at and condemned because they were speaking from a knowledge accessed from levels outside of the blocking vibration, while most of the people to whom they were speaking could conceive only of the world they knew and saw all around them. They could remember no other.

We return to the central theme of the book: creating our own reality. The Prison Warder consciousness knows all about this process. Our physical reality is the creation of the thoughts we hold onto, past and present. These create a pattern within us which is then cast around us in the form of a magnetic cape/aura. This attracts to us a physical reality in terms of people, places, and events which exactly reflects our inner pattern, how we see ourselves. The key to this reality is *thought*. If you can manipulate someone's thoughts and view of themselves, you are creating that person's reality and, as a result, their physical experience. More than that, people will generally pass onto their children large chunks of their own views and beliefs, thus manipulating – often with the best of intentions – how the children view themselves and their potential. This affects the children's sense of self and creates their corresponding physical reality.

In short, once you can manipulate the thoughts of one generation, it gets easier to impose your will on future generations because you now have the programmed parents and 'leaders' unknowingly working on your behalf. You will see throughout the story revealed in this book how the foundation of the *global* manipulation is the manipulation of the individual human mind and its view of self and the world. The Global Conspiracy (with the Prison Warder consciousness at the apex of the pyramid) is a conspiracy to manipulate the human race's sense of self and, in doing so, the creation of its physical reality. As I say, the victim *mentality* creates the victim *reality*. Today, we have a planet awash with people who have been encouraged to *think* of themselves as victims, hence they *are*.

What has happened through this period of the global prison is a reflection of what is happening within the collective human mind. We collectively attracted this experience to us. We created this reality, just as the battered wife with no sense of self-love and self-worth subconsciously attracts to her the punishment she believes she deserves. The woman in that state of mind will manifest her sense of self by magnetically attracting the energy field of a man who desires to punish another. In the same way the collective human mind's inner lack of self-love and self-worth attracted the Prison Warder/Luciferic Consciousness to do the same. If there was not an imbalance within the collective human mind which relates to this experience we are going through, we would not have created this experience. The problem and the solution begins and ends with the self. If we all find love for ourselves, that is the reality we will create for ourselves and, together, that is the reality the collective mind will create. When we do that, the Luciferic Consciousness will no longer affect us, because we will no longer attract the experiences it provides.

When viewed from the higher levels of understanding, the Luciferic Consciousness, horrific as it may be in the physical 'here and now', is actually an experience we have created as a mirror for us to face the collective imbalances within the human mind and, in doing so, remove them. If we see it that way, it becomes a positive experience at least in outcome.

Chapter 2

The Birth of the Brotherhood

The most effective way to close down a human mind and to manipulate its sense of self is to programme into it some form of dogma. A dogma will always vehemently defend itself from other information and repel any alternative opinion which contradicts its narrow, solidified view. Dogmas become a person's sense of security and means of retaining power. Humanity tends to cling to both until its knuckles turn white.

Dogmas take endless forms and when you can persuade different people to hold opposing dogmas, the manipulation of conflict and control through 'divide and rule' becomes easy. It is happening today in the same way – more so, in fact – as it has throughout the period of the vibratory prison. To a manipulator, Judaism is just as useful as Christianity and Islam; the political 'Left' is just as important as the political 'Right'. You need two dogmas to play off against each other. The most effective dogmas over thousands of years have been the religions. One generation takes on a narrow view of life and themselves (a religion) and imposes it on their children, who then do the same to their children, and so it goes on into the modern world. The religious and political dogmas have all been inspired by negative elements from the Fourth Dimension.

The two leading weapons used by religions are those cancerous emotions: fear and guilt. They have been used to suppress the human mind and to destroy its sense of self-worth, thus creating a physical reality to match. Religions are the same thought pattern manifesting under different names – the thought pattern called control. Even the origins of their myths, stories and ceremonies are invariably the same because they all originate from the same source!

Towards the end of Atlantis, groups of people began to escape from their increasingly devastated land. Some left the prison while their vibratory rate was still high enough for them to do so; others became trapped by accident or design. As Atlantis crumbled, some settled in the areas we now know as Egypt and the Middle East, Central America, and the United States. Those who survived the cataclysm which followed, passed on their knowledge to their children in myths and stories. This is one possible answer to the apparent mystery of how when the Americas were 'discovered' by the Europeans in the fifteenth and sixteenth centuries, they found many cultures and beliefs of the native peoples to be remarkably similar to (sometimes the same as) those in the 'Old World' of Europe and the Middle East. Both were influenced by the knowledge brought by the escaping Atlanteans, although I think another reason for this relates to extraterrestrial activity all over the world. In the period after Atlantis, I believe that extraterrestrial expressions of the Prison Warder consciousness still landed and interacted with the people, telling different peoples the same basic manipulated story.

Some Atlanteans escaped by sailing west to the Americas, some went east to Europe and North Africa. It is possible that the biblical story of Noah and the Ark relates to this period, although it could involve another flood some thousands of years later. Over many millennia, the Atlantean and extraterrestrial knowledge was passed on through the succeeding generations, and the original clarity was lost in the repeated communication. The knowledge also became a vehicle for control, and it was accordingly changed to suit those in power at any given time. This is why you still find elements of this knowledge in all religions. The original core knowledge has been diluted and diverted in countless directions, to manifest as religions such as Christianity, Islam, Judaism, Paganism, Hinduism, etc. All have retained the themes of the knowledge to some extent, while often destroying its true meaning with dogma, myth, and manipulated make-believe. Ironically, Paganism has retained far more of the original knowledge than those religions (such as Christianity) which condemn it as 'evil'. The Fourth Dimensional Prison Warders wish to prevent us from knowing who we are, how we have been imprisoned, and how we can get out of prison. Making us confused and dividing us into factions, religions, and tongues was part of the Prison Warder strategy. If you read the story of the Tower of Babel, you can see this described symbolically:

> *"At first the people of the whole world had only one language and used the same words. As they wandered about in the East, they came to a plain in Babylonia and settled there. They said to one another, 'Come on! Let's make bricks and bake them hard'. So they had bricks to build with and mortar to hold them together. They said: 'Now let's build a city with a tower that reaches to the sky, so that we can make a name for ourselves and not be scattered all over the Earth'.*
>
> *"Then the Lord [extraterrestrials] came down to see the city and the tower which those men had built, and he said: 'Now then, these are all one people and they speak one language; this is just the beginning of what they are going to do. Soon they will be able to do anything they want! Let us go down and mix up their language so they will not understand one another.' So the Lord scattered them all over the Earth, and they stopped building the city. The city was called Babylon, because there the Lord mixed up the language of all the people, and from there he scattered them all over the Earth."*
>
> **Genesis, 11:1–9**

Christianity sees those people in a highly negative light when, I believe, it was actually the other way around. They were rebelling against the control. After Atlantis, other civilisations began to emerge from the reincarnation of Atlantean consciousness. The knowledge they passed on through the generations, and extraterrestrial intervention, was both positive and negative. There was the civilisation called Sumer in Mesopotamia (now Iraq), which developed alongside the Tigris and Euphrates rivers. Sumer is believed to have originated from around 6000 BC, although such figures must be treated as only estimates. This would later become part of the Babylonian Empire, which greatly influenced the beliefs of Judaism and, through that, Christianity, as did the Egyptian civilisation. You can read the detailed history of all this in *The Robots' Rebellion*.

A contact who has worked on the 'inside' of government and security agencies in the UK told me a story which relates both to Sumer and the themes of an extraterrestrial takeover. He says that in the 1960s the British intelligence agencies produced a secret report detailing claims of extraterrestrial sightings. This involved interviewing 1,800 people in Europe and Scandinavia who claimed to have seen a UFO, an extraterrestrial, or had contact with beings from another world. At the same time, he says, similar surveys were being compiled in the United States, the Soviet Union, Australia and Japan. Eventually they pooled their findings and this made available some 62,000 interviews with people across the globe. Firstly, the vast, vast majority of the stories told of positive, loving communications with the ETs of various races. This is so different to the "evil aliens" stories we see in the media. Secondly, about 75% of those interviewed all over the world apparently told the same basic story. They said that the ETs told them how a planet called Melchedek had once existed in our solar system, but the Melchedekans had become obsessed with the material world and they destroyed their environment. In the end they exploded so many nuclear devices during tests and conflicts that the planet broke apart and itself exploded. The asteroid belt was said to be part of the remnants of Melchedek.

According to the stories of the contactees in the survey, about 5,000 of the Melchedekan 'elite' escaped and landed on the Earth in the place we know as Sumer, now Iraq. The Melchedekan race were described as…wait for it…blond haired and blue eyed. The "Aryan" 'Master Race' described by Adolf Hitler. These were the 'gods' described in the Sumerian tablets, this story goes, and as time passed they used their advanced knowledge of genetics to create a new race of Earth people – the white race we see today. This was symbolised by the story of Adam and Eve and forbidding them to eat from the tree of knowledge was symbolic of the plan to keep the Earth races ignorant of who they really were. In effect, a slave race was created and this has continued to the present day. The contactees said that it was the Melchedekans who became known as the Elohim in the Biblical texts. I think this Fourth Dimensional force is known by many names. The original

Earth people were the black, red, and other native peoples of the world in Africa, the Americas, Asia and Australia – not the white race, the contactees were told.

There were two streams of Melchedekan 'invaders'. Those who only interbred with each other, thus keeping the blond haired, blue eyed genetic 'purity'. These, the ET communicators said, were still living on the Earth, though mostly out of sight underground. The others interbred with their newly created Earth races, but again they sought, and still do, to keep this genetic stream as pure as possible by interbreeding only within the family or within a small circle of similar genetic background. It was said that it is this genetic stream which overwhelmingly make up the families of the 'Illuminati' that have manipulated the course of human history since the time of Sumer. The manipulation has guided this planet along the same destructive road that Melchedek experienced. Again according to the overwhelming majority of the 62,000 interviewed, there are also five other extraterrestrial races working on Earth today to help humanity break out of the mental prison and remove the Melchedekan manipulation. One of these races is described as about eleven feet tall, the "giants" of ancient legend, perhaps? They have double hip joints, very large foreheads, blue eyes, a small gap in the face rather than what we would call a mouth, and very big feet. Make of all that what you will, but this could – *could* – be another expression of Fourth Dimensional beings operating on our frequency.

It is certainly true that Sumer was the origin of so much that was to shape human culture and existence. The Christian belief in a Son of God and a Lamb of God dying so our sins could be forgiven can be found in Sumer, Babylon, and Egypt. The idea of a lamb dying to forgive the sins of humanity originates from the Sumerian belief that if you literally sacrificed a lamb on the altar, it would remove the sins of the people involved. While I was writing this book, I saw a picture in a newspaper of an Orthodox Jew today, still waving a chicken around the head of a young girl, in the belief that the chicken would absorb her 'sins'. Virgin mothers of 'saviour' figures abound throughout the ancient world and, indeed, can be found in the beliefs of the native peoples of North, South, and Central America. The Bible story of the Garden of Eden is mirrored in the much earlier Sumerian story of the Garden of Edinnu, and even the idea of the Sabbath can be found in the Sumerian day of rest, the Sabattu. The Jewish peoples were held in captivity in Babylon and, when they were freed by the Persians, they took many of the Babylonian stories and beliefs back to Palestine. These found their way into the Old Testament of the Bible and through that into the New Testament. Today's religions are the recycling of ancient beliefs and symbolic stories which have been added to and twisted under the guidance of the Prison Warder consciousness, until the original meaning has been lost under an avalanche of myth and invention. So often when you investigate the origin of the foundation stories of the religions, you find the same basic themes with different names for the alleged heroes and villains. For the Christian version of Jesus, see also Bel (Sumer), Dionysus (Greece), Mithra (Persia and Rome), Osiris (Egypt), Quetzalcoatl (Central and South America), Krishna (India), and so on. In this way, the spiritual knowledge from which all religions originally derive, has, to a large extent, been destroyed in the public arena. This process has been essential to controlling the human race. You take information out of the public arena and pass it on secretly only to those who share your ambitions.

The foundation of the manipulation of the world has always been the control of knowledge. While the religions were using fear, guilt and imposition to sell the people a desperately narrow view of life and themselves, a secret network developed to pass on far more advanced knowledge to the privileged few. Even within this vibratory prison, there is knowledge that remains hidden from most people. It does not compare with the knowledge available outside the prison, but it is still far in advance of that which humanity in general has been allowed to know. If you want to manipulate people, it is essential that you have knowledge which they don't have. One of the first rules of control and manipulation is "Don't let your victims know what you know". I will call this 'hidden', suppressed understanding the 'esoteric knowledge'. The dictionary definition of *esoteric* is: "of a philosophical doctrine meant only for the initiated, not generally intelligible; private, confidential". Sums it up perfectly. This knowledge has been kept from the mass of the people for reasons of manipulation and control. Hence, the knowledge has indeed become 'private, [and] confidential'.

There is an unfolding global awakening, however, which will make these understandings available to all who wish to hear, and the conspiracy to keep humanity in the spiritual dark will crumble and fall. It is already doing so. A key part of this process is to reveal the nature of the deception and why it is being perpetrated. The vehicle for keeping this knowledge from the public arena has been the system of initiations used by the ancient mystery schools and the now immense secret society network all over the world, which I call the Brotherhood. Each higher level of initiate is given more knowledge than those below. This sets up a pyramid structure, with the few who reach the top levels of initiation knowing far, far more than the majority further down the ladder (*see Figure 3*). This makes it easy for those few to manipulate the rest. The content of this esoteric knowledge relates to an understanding of the laws and potential of Creation which is far in advance of the 'science' we are allowed to see in the public arena, and of the knowledge of the human psyche, its nature, and how it can be programmed and controlled.

The hoarding of such knowledge was not always done for negative reasons. When Christianity imposed its misguided and manipulative dogma throughout most of the known world, it was suicidal to speak of these alternative spiritual beliefs in public. Not surprisingly, they were passed on in secret or hidden within legends and symbolic stories. Thank goodness they

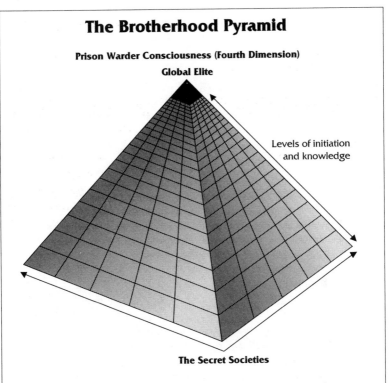

The secret societies like the Freemasons, Knights of Malta, etc, appear to be separate organisations. But they all connect with the Global Elite, so turning all secret societies into the same organisation working to a common goal. At least 95% of the members of these societies will not realise what they are part of.

Figure 3

were! But knowledge is neutral. It is how you use it that is negative or positive. The spiritual knowledge can be used and abused, and so can the secrecy inherent in the societies and mystery schools which, particularly at their higher levels, know spiritual realities denied to most people. In the same way that each higher level of initiate within the secret societies knows more than those below them, so the Fourth Dimensional Prison Warders ensure that they know far more than even those human vehicles at the top of the global pyramid of manipulation. Today, at their higher levels, this network of secret societies and the knowledge it has inherited are being used, I believe, for almost entirely negative reasons, under the direction of its highest, controlling core: the Global Elite or simply the Elite. The members of this Elite are either direct incarnations of the Fourth Dimensional Prison Warders or have their minds controlled by them. The aim of the Brotherhood and its interdimensional controllers has been to centralise

power in the hands of a few. This process is very advanced and it is
happening on a global scale thanks to modern technology. The game plan is
known as the Great Work of Ages or the New World Order, and it seeks to
introduce a world government to which all nations would be colonies; a
world central bank and currency; a world army; and a microchipped
population connected to a global computer. What is happening today is the
culmination of the manipulation which has been unfolding for thousands of
years.

The idea of passing on the knowledge through a series of secret initiations
goes back at least to Atlantis, probably much further. A common theme of
channelled information is that there was a sort of temple in Atlantis, where
those considered to be trustworthy would be given knowledge that the bulk
of the population did not have. When the civilisations that followed Atlantis
began to emerge, they, too, continued to have initiations into different levels
of the knowledge. Among these organisations were the Mystery Schools of
Babylon, Egypt, and Greece, which guarded their knowledge with enormous
secrecy; the smallest violation of the oath of secrecy was punishable by death.
From this foundation came today's massive secret society network. These
mystery schools of initiation were inspired by the negative elements of the
Fourth Dimension, and have been supervised by them through the
consciousness of the highest initiates, the adepts, since that time. In his study
Fragments Of A Faith Forgotten, Professor G. R. S. Mead says:

> "*A persistent tradition in connection with all the great Mystery institutions
> was that their several founders were the introducers of all the arts of
> civilization; they were either themselves gods or were instructed by gods − in
> brief, that they were men of far greater knowledge than any who had come
> after; they were the teachers of infant races...*
>
> "*It is said that these earliest teachers of humanity who founded the
> Mystery-institutions as the most efficient means of giving infant humanity
> instructions in higher things, were souls belonging to a more highly developed
> humanity than our own...In the earliest times, according to this view, the
> mysteries were conducted by those who had a knowledge of nature-powers
> which was the acquisition of a prior perfected humanity not necessarily Earth-
> born and the wonders shown therein such that none of our humanity could of
> themselves produce.*" [1]

This initiation structure was either negative from the start in its ambitions
for humanity, or it was later taken over by that consciousness. I feel the
highly influential Egyptian Brotherhood has been dominated by negative
manipulation at least since the end of the reign of the Pharaoh Akhenaten,

[1] Professor G.R.S. Mead, *Fragments Of A Faith Forgotten*, (The Theosophical Publishing
Society, London, 1906).

who died around 1,362 BC. He had moved the Egyptian court to a new city in Middle Egypt called El-Amarna, and there he built a Brotherhood Temple for the esoteric initiations. When he died, his successors moved the royal court back north to Thebes, but the Brotherhood stayed at El-Amarna and broke away from the state. Through the centuries, other vehicles for communicating the knowledge emerged. Some, like the Cathars in the twelfth and thirteenth centuries, were destroyed by the Catholic Church in the most horrific manner after spreading their influence over a wide area from their base in Southern France. The Knights of the Temple (Knights Templar), who came to prominence about the same time as the Cathars, were dealt with equally severely by Papal 'justice'. But the Templars went underground and their influence has continued up to the present day, both in their own right, and within other secret societies which are, after all, part of the same overall organisation. This period of the Cathars and the Crusades spawned many Brotherhood offshoots, which continue to significantly influence events – secret societies like the Knights Hospitallers of St. John, known today as The Knights of Malta. Nor was this merely a phenomenon of the Christian and Jewish world. Similar secret societies were created within all cultures, and the Arab Brotherhood Grand Lodge in Cairo was to become a major manipulator of events.

The aim of this negative Brotherhood structure is to persuade the mass of the people to believe any old nonsense while the manipulators keep for themselves the knowledge of the nature of life and Creation and how to exploit the power of the mind, the Earth's energy fields, and the global energy grid (the network of energy lines known by different cultures as ley lines, meridians, and dragon lines). But even the privileged initiates did not retain the purity of the information through the centuries. To this day, they work with a twisted version of the knowledge, albeit still far more advanced in its understanding of the universal laws than anything you will find in the religions and establishment sciences that the rest of us are asked to accept. The greatest misunderstanding of the negative Brotherhood relates to the power of love. The Prison Warder consciousness which controls the minds of those who manipulate the Brotherhood does not understand love. It generates and feeds upon negative energy, and the more negative energy it can produce and encourage humanity to produce, the more powerful it becomes. To this consciousness, love is like garlic to a vampire, and without love – the energy on which all Creation exists – knowledge will always be misused. Knowledge without love is the state of being which still controls the higher levels of the Brotherhood network, via its Global Elite. It is the intellect without the heart, you could say, and without the balanced feminine.

The symbols of the Brotherhood in ancient times remain those of the Brotherhood today – the pyramid and all-seeing eye, the swastika, the lamb, the apron, the obelisk and many others. The obelisk is symbolic of the penis of Osiris, the Egyptian god. The legend is that he was torn into pieces by the 'evil' Set (Lucifer, Satan, the Devil, et al.) and when Isis, the wife of Osiris, tried to put him back together again, she found all his missing parts, except you know what. Such legends are, I feel, symbolic of much more straightforward truths.

The obelisk and Osiris's penis in that story symbolise male energy, which has dominated the world throughout recorded history. All of us, and Creation as a whole, are in search of balance and harmony between opposites – negative and positive, male and female. These are the Yin and Yang-type forces of Chinese culture. When one of these forces dominates, there is an imbalance which manifests as imbalanced behaviour. The transformation the planet is now going through is designed to bring such forces into harmony and balance so that all serve, but none dominates. The suppression of female energy by the male has created a male-dominated world and the 'macho man' is one of its offspring. This has not been by accident, but by design – the Prison Warders' design. Harmony and balance in all things = wholeness. Wholeness = infinite potential. That's the last thing the Prison Warders want, because such people are impossible to control. Instead, they have sought to imbalance us. Disharmony and imbalance = division of self. Division of self = limited potential.

The two major imbalances within ourselves and the prison in general have been the negative dominating the positive and the male dominating the female. There is no greater manifestation of the male imbalance than what is seen in some of the major religions and in the secret society network. The re-emergence of female energy is crucial to the harmonising of the Earth, and by that, I don't only mean the re-emergence of women into areas of decision-making. I mean the reawakening of female energy within the male form also, and a softening of the indoctrinated desire of so many men to dominate and to follow the macho man programming. This re-emergence of female energy is symbolised as 'the return of the goddess'.

It is highly appropriate that the obelisk (the symbol of male energy) should be so important to the Brotherhood over the centuries, because it is, after all, a *brother*hood, not a brother-and-sisterhood. The secret societies are almost entirely male-dominated with women excluded from the knowledge and decision making. Look at the Freemasons as an example. It is a male preserve, with their wives wheeled out for the annual dinner like a piece of decoration. Such a male-dominated organisation must by definition be imbalanced, and this one most certainly is. The Freemasons have become one of the most important of the secret societies which have appeared since the ancient times, and they have based themselves on the structure and beliefs of the Brotherhood Mystery Schools, as have the others. I will refer to this network as the cult of the All-Seeing Eye, the cult that worships these Fourth Dimensional "gods" or "masters". It goes back to antiquity and this same stream of manipulation is behind the New World Order to this day. It is a fusion of the ancient esoteric beliefs which have emerged from Babylon,

Egypt, and the Hebrew Kabbala School. The higher levels of the Freemasons still worship a 'God' called Jahbulon – Jah (Jehovah, Hebrew), Bul (Baal, Babylon), and On (Osiris, Egypt).

Perhaps the most important achievement by this Global Elite-Brotherhood on the journey to world domination has been the colonisation of America, a land it knew existed long before it was officially 'discovered'. Throughout known human history, there have been two levels of knowledge operating on this planet. One is made public for the mass of the people to see, most of which is flawed and manipulated to control our thinking and the reality we create, while the other is known only to the few, mostly in the Elite levels of the Brotherhood. The conventional story behind the 'discovery' of the Americas is an example of this. The history books tell us that Christopher Columbus made a guess in 1492 that the Earth was round or pear-shaped and if he sailed west, he believed, he would eventually reach India and the Far East which had already been identified by Marco Polo. It is said that he 'accidentally' discovered what we call the West Indies and that he believed he had found India, to the day he died. We are further told that John Cabot and his son, Sebastian, both Venetians, set off from Bristol four years after Columbus had sailed from Spain; Cabot 'discovered' North America in 1497. No link is offered by conventional history between these two events. But when you look deeper there is a potential link: the knowledge held by the Brotherhood network, which had been passed on secretly since the time of Atlantis.

The 33rd degree Freemason, Manly P. Hall, points out in his book, *America's Assignment With Destiny*,[2] that John Cabot's real name was Giovanni Caboto. He was born in Genoa, the city where Colombus is said to have been born, and Caboto later became a naturalised Venetian. It is suggested that he was involved with a secret Christian Brotherhood sect known as the Johannites, which was greatly influenced by the esoteric doctrines of the Templars. Legends say he visited the so called 'Wise Men of the Near East' – just as Colombus had done. Columbus had his own Brotherhood connections. His father was a member of the Brotherhood branch, The Order of the Christ. Columbus himself was involved with a group which followed the beliefs of the poet Dante, who was a member of the Cathar Church and an initiate of the Knights Templar. Columbus was often seen wearing the garb of what was believed to be the Franciscan Order. Columbus's son said his father had died in such attire. The priests at the ancient Egyptian Brotherhood Temple at El-Amarna wore a similar habit, as did a Brotherhood group called the Fraternités at the time of Columbus. These are only some of his Brotherhood connections. Columbus's father-in-law was a member of the Knights of Christ, the undercover name for the

---

[2] Manly P. Hall, *America's Assignment With Destiny: The Adepts In The Western Esoteric Tradition, Part Five*, (Philosophical Research Society, Los Angeles, 1979) p58.

Knights Templar. When the Templars were purged across Europe, they
survived in Portugal by changing their name to the Knights of Christ. They
devoted themselves to *maritime activity*. The explorer, Vasco de Gama, was a
Knight of Christ, as was Prince Henry the Navigator, a Grand Master of the
Order. Columbus's father-in-law was one of Prince Henry's captains, and
inherited maps and charts from him which Columbus used to 'find' the
Americas. The red cross on a white background was the Templars symbol. It
was outlawed by the Pope at the time of the purge. Columbus's ships sailed
with the red cross on a white background![3] His historic journey was funded
by King Ferdinand of Aragon, Spain and Queen Isabella of Castile, Spain,
whose marriage helped to unify Spain. These were 'Catholic' monarchs
funding a trip by a man flying the flag of the Knights Templar. More than
that, other support came from Leonardo da Vinci and Lorenzo de Medici,
both high initiates of Brotherhood secret societies. Given this background to
Columbus and Caboto, it is hardly stretching the bounds of credibility to
suggest that their 'discovery' of different parts of the Americas within four or
five years of each other was no coincidence. Many of the early explorers and
colonisers were known to be members of Brotherhood societies. They knew
what they were looking for because they had the maps and charts of the
world passed down over thousands of years by the Brotherhood, perhaps
since Atlantis.

In 1513, Piri Reis, an admiral in the navy of the Ottoman Turks,
produced a map showing the land mass of Antarctica which then, as now,
was covered by a mile-thick sheet of ice! Antarctica wasn't even officially
'discovered' until 300 years after the map was compiled. The United States
Airforce has confirmed that the map agrees "very remarkably"[4] with the
results of the seismic profile produced by the Swedish-British Antarctic
Expedition of 1949. This indicates, says the US airforce, that "the coastline
had been mapped before it was covered by the ice cap".[5] They said they had
no idea how the data on the Piri Reis map can be reconciled with the state
of geographical knowledge in 1513. I can help them there. Piri Reis
compiled his map from maps and charts passed on through the higher levels
of the Brotherhood. The evidence is mounting that far from being there for
millions of years, the ice cap has only been there for maybe 6,000 years. The
world was mapped before that date by civilisations far in advance of what we
have been told by conventional, doctored history, which is designed to fool,

[3] It is interesting to look at where the symbol of the red cross is used today. Not all of them
will be signs of Templar control, maybe, but many certainly will.
[4] Letter by Lt. Colonel Harold Z. Onlmeyer, Commander, 8 Reconnaissance Technical
Squadron (SAC), United States Airforce, Westover Airforce Base, Massachusetts, to Professor
Charles H. Hapgood, of Keene College, New Hampshire, on July 6th, 1960. Quoted by
Graham Hancock in *Fingerprints Of The Gods* (Heinemann, London, 1995) p3.
[5] Ibid.

not inform us. Columbus and Cabot found the Americas for one simple reason. They knew what was there!

Colonising the Americas and particularly North America seems to have been a long-term aim of The Great Work of Ages or the New World Order. Sir Francis Bacon, the Grand Chancellor of England, was a Brotherhood member of high rank at the time of Elizabeth I and James I. He was a Grand Commander of the Brotherhood Order called the Rosicrucians, and very much involved in the underground operations of the Knights Templar traditions. Bacon passed on knowledge secretly in codes contained in works like the Shakespearean plays, which he wrote himself. The evidence for this is very substantial and the Shakespeare story is a myth. Sorry Stratford! Bacon used the network to encourage the colonising of North America, not the least to stop the Spanish getting control of it. More than that, however, he was working from the Brotherhood agenda. People like Sir Walter Raleigh were also in Bacon's circle, along with other prominent names in Elizabethan society.

I stress that not everyone within the Brotherhood is of negative intent. Most are persuaded by those even higher up the ladder that the Great Work is for the good of all people. Most Brotherhood members have no idea of the despotism contained in the real agenda which is known to only the tiny few. Indeed, the *real* agenda is known only to the Prison Warders of the Fourth Dimension who have been the common link in the conspiracy over thousands of years.

In his work, *The New Atlantis,* Bacon sets out his vision of a new world in which the power is exercised by a secret society, The Temple of Solomon. In Bacon's vision, the privileged elite study the sciences in secret and act as an invisible government, deciding what the people should and should not be told. All this is remarkably like the secret manipulation of events and information today. But then, it's not so remarkable really, because the plan Bacon was working from in the sixteenth and seventeenth centuries is the same one that is being followed by the present day Brotherhood. Some of them genuinely believe it is the best way to run the world, but, I most strongly suggest, they are fundamentally misguided because they do not appreciate how such a world can be easily manipulated by the few to the detriment of all. Most importantly, they do not realise that the Prison Warders are manipulating the whole thing, including them.

Another significant name in this period was Dr John Dee, an adept (high initiate) and the official astrologer to Queen Elizabeth I. He was also her unofficial secret agent, and signed his reports 007.[6] In a diary entry written in Prague in 1586, Dee describes an encounter with a "little man" whose feet "seemed not to touch the ground by a foot height, who moved in a little fiery cloud" and who went up into the sky "in a great pillar of fire".

---

[6] *Extra-Terrestrials Among Us,* p76.

In Prague, Dee gave the Emperor Rudolph an illustrated manuscript, written in code and claimed to be the work of Roger Bacon, the thirteenth century Franciscan monk who upset the church authorities with his views and ideas. These included prophecies about the microscope, the telescope, the car, submarine, aeroplane, and the belief that the Earth was a sphere. All of these facts would have been transmitted from the Fourth Dimension. In 1912, this same manuscript was bought by an American book dealer called Wilfrid Voynich and became known as the Voynich Manuscript. When he sent copies to the 'experts' of the day, they said that most of the hundreds of plants illustrated did not grow on Earth. Some illustrations looked like tissue seen under a microscope and others were of star systems and constellations. The best code breakers available to United States intelligence in both the first and second world wars tried to decipher what they called "the most mysterious manuscript in the world", but none could do it. A professor at the University of Pennsylvania called William Romaine Newbold claimed to have decoded some of it in 1921. He said part of the text read:

"In a concave mirror, I saw a star in the form of a snail between the navel of Pegasus, the girdle of Andromeda, and the head of Cassiopeia." [7]

What Roger Bacon describes in the manuscript that was acquired by John Dee is now known to be accurate and the illustration he includes of the Andromeda nebula is also correct, but it is depicted from an angle which cannot be seen from the Earth! Dee was an adept and channeller of great renown and claimed to communicate with an 'angel with a wand', an extraterrestrial. The knowledge held within the secret society network has always been far – often centuries – in advance of what the mass of the people are allowed to know. The knowledge of the existence of America and its long term place in the plan was well known to these Elizabethan adepts, as it was to those who guided Columbus and the Cabots, thanks to the Fourth Dimensional manipulators.

The first permanent English settlement in North America was established at Jamestown, Virginia (named after Elizabeth the 'virgin queen'), in 1607. Many members of the Francis Bacon family were among the early settlers. From that point on, the native culture of North America was doomed, as was that of South and Central America once the Spanish and Portuguese arrived. The way the native peoples were slaughtered without mercy and their cultures destroyed without respect or compassion was one of the most appalling episodes in all of human history. Thousands of settlers sailed west from Europe to escape religious persecution after the Brotherhood-engineered Reformation divided the Christian Church into Protestants and

Catholics. This created division and conflict and weakened the power of the Pope. But when the persecuted peoples arrived in America, they often proceeded to persecute the native population and the immigrants of other religious beliefs in the same merciless way that they themselves had been treated.

The land they occupied, now called the United States, was and *is* a key weapon in the Brotherhood's long term plan for world domination. The Masonic societies went through a massive change and expansion after the English Civil War and especially in the early 1700s. Up to that point, only people who worked by profession as masons or building craftsmen could be members. Now it became open to all and *Free*masonary or Speculative Masonry was born. It is likely that Francis Bacon was a force behind this transformation. The centre of the Freemasonic network that now expanded rapidly was a new Grand Lodge (launched in London in 1717) which became known as the Mother Grand Lodge of the World. It was a centre of Freemasonic manipulation, encouraging other lodges to be set up throughout Europe, the British Empire, and the Americas. Many other versions of Freemasonry were introduced, including the York Rite and the Scottish Rite of Michael Ramsey (which was based on the Knights Templar system). The Scottish Rite has 33 degrees of initiation and today has enormous influence in the politics, economics, military, and security services of Britain, Europe, the United States, and many other countries. New York was named after the York Rite of Freemasonry.

The Brotherhood plan was for the establishment of an independent United States of America – independent of the British government, that is, not independent of the Brotherhood. Encouraged by the Mother Grand Lodge in London, the Freemasonic lodges in the colonies of America began to plot and agitate against British rule. An economic crisis was engineered, not least through war between Britain and the French. As part of their desperation for income, the British government imposed higher taxation and duties on the American colonies. It was an operation created and coordinated by the Global Elite which has been repeated over and over again. The network in Britain, as in every other country, includes key bankers, many politicians, and, more importantly, their political advisers. They secretly engineered events which caused an economic crisis in Britain. They then advised the British government that the only way out of trouble was to levy higher taxation on the American colonies. At the same time, the American arm of the Brotherhood was being directed to whip up hostility against this action and turn that anger into demands for independence from Britain. It appears on the surface – and in the history books – as Britain versus the American colonies. In fact, the same network was manipulating *both* sides. This is how all the major wars and revolutions have been created, as we shall see. This strategy was described very well by P. Sedir in his *Histoire et doctrine des Rose-Croix*, published in Paris in 1910:

"Unable to control destinies on Earth openly because governments would resist, this mystic alliance can act only through secret societies... These, gradually created as the need for them arises, are divided into distinct groups, groups seemingly in opposition, sometimes advocating the most contradictory policies in religion, politics, economics, and literature; but they are all connected, all directed by the invisible centre that hides its power as it thus seeks to move all the sceptres of the Earth."

The opposition by the American colonies led the British government to withdraw the new taxes, except for those on tea, but the Brotherhood was not going to let the anger subside. Members of the St. Andrews Freemasons Lodge in Boston, led by the Junior Warden, Paul Revere, dressed up as native American 'Indians' and threw tea chests into the harbour to protest at the tax on tea. The Boston Tea Party, as it became known, was hatched during a supper at the home of the Bradlee brothers, who were both members of the St. Andrews Lodge.[8] The momentum for a war of independence gathered strength until it was unstoppable.

The leading revolutionaries and those who signed the Declaration of Independence in 1776 were almost all Freemasons. George Washington, the triumphant Commander-in-Chief of the American armies and the first president of the United States of America, was a high ranking Freemason and all but two of his brigadier generals in the war were Masons. Top Freemason and Freemasonic historian, Manly P. Hall, says that of the fifty-six men who signed the Declaration of Independence, nearly fifty were known to be Freemasons and only *one* was known not to be.[9] Another researcher, Enrique De Vincente, says that fifty-three of the signatories were Freemasons and that seventeen presidents, beginning with Washington, have been members of the Order. The second president, John Adams, belonged to a secret society known as The Dragons, named after the magnetic energy lines in the Earth's energy grid. He studied the sacred geometry contained in the energy grid and knew how to harness the power it contained.[10]

One of the leading revolutionaries and founding fathers of the United States was Benjamin Franklin, the first Grand Master of the Freemasons of Pennsylvania. He became a friend of Sir Francis Dashwood, the Chancellor of the British Treasury, and founder of the secret society called the Club of Hell's Fire. Franklin became a member along with the Mayor of London, the son of the Archbishop of Canterbury, and the Prince of Wales. He travelled to France to canvass successfully for the support of the French

[8] *America's Assignment With Destiny*, p95.
[9] Ibid p96.
[10] Enrique De Vincente, "The Occult Roots of the New World Order", *Exposure* magazine, (1993) Vol. 1, No. 2, p10.

Figure 4: **The US dollar bill with it's classic Brotherhood symbol which goes back to antiquity**

Freemasons for the American Revolution, and he also secured the services of the German Freemason, Baron von Streube, who served in the army of Frederick the Great of Prussia. The baron was to play a major part in the colonists' victory over the British. Franklin's connections with the French Brotherhood were very close and he became a high ranking member of the Lodges of San Juan and the Nine Sisters which, in league with the Grand Orient Lodge in Paris, would trigger the French Revolution of 1789. Franklin was made Grand Master of the Nine Sisters. One of the central revolutionaries in France, the Marquis de Lafayette, was a friend of Franklin and supported him and the colonists during the American Revolution.

Freemasons manipulated and won the War of Independence and then took control of the new United States of America. They, and other Brotherhood groups, have never conceded that control to this day. How appropriate, then, that when the founding fathers commissioned a design for the Great Seal of the United States, it included the classic Brotherhood (Prison Warder) symbols which go back to ancient Egypt and beyond, including the pyramid and all-seeing eye. Above and below this symbol are two Latin phrases, *Annuit Coeptis* and *Novus Ordo Seclorum*. These translate as "Announcing the birth, creation, or arrival" of "A New Order of Ages". In other words, announcing the creation of the New World Order. The founding of the United States was a massive step forward in the plan for centralised global power. Today this part of the seal can be found on every dollar bill (*see Figure 4*), and again this is very appropriate, given that the Elite controls the American economy and everyone else's. The decision to put the Pyramid/New World Order symbol on the dollar was made by the 33rd degree Freemason, Franklin D. Roosevelt, in 1935, with the full support and encouragement of his vice president, Henry Wallace, another 33rd degree Mason.[11] Mr Roosevelt will be making many appearances in the text of the next few chapters. The American flag, the Stars and Stripes, was also designed to reflect Brotherhood symbolism and the Statue of Liberty was given to American Freemasons by the French Grand Orient (Illuminati) Masonic Order.[12]

While ties were 'officially' severed between Britain and the United States after the war, those between the American Brotherhood societies and ruling families and their brethren in Britain and Europe grew still stronger, through the secret network. Again, I am not suggesting that everyone involved in the fight for American independence was negatively motivated, nor that all in the Brotherhood lodges are of a similar state of mind. Most would have been persuaded they were doing the right thing and in many ways they were. Often it is not the act, but the motivation behind the act that we need to watch. One country owning and controlling another is quite wrong, in my view. But we need to look at the wider agenda and motivation behind a course of action and look very carefully at what the proposed alternative will be. Control of America by a British monarch and government being replaced by control of America by a secret Brotherhood hardly advances human freedom, but – and here's the point to remember – such a transfer of power and control can be (and invariably *is*) justified under the banner of expanding human freedom. The American War of Independence was the first in a series of 'people's revolutions', created and financed by the Brotherhood. The plan was to end the power of the monarchs. I do not oppose this if it is done peacefully and with genuine popular support. But instead of 'power to the people', the monarchs were replaced by other dictatorships, called revolutionary committees, communists, fascists or, more subtly, by the illusion of 'democracy', which in reality was and is rule by the Elite.

Let us summarise where we are. A pyramidal structure of human beings has been created under the influence and design of the negative manipulators on the Fourth Dimension, the Prison Warders. They control the human clique at the top of the pyramid, which I have dubbed the Global Elite. These, in turn, manipulate the lower levels of the network, within which you will find most of the major national and global decision-makers in politics, banking, industry, commerce, the media, the military, etc. The Prison Warders manipulate the Elite, the Elite manipulate the Brotherhood network, and the Brotherhood network manipulates the world. Each lower

[11] *The Occult Roots Of The New World Order*, p10.
[12] Jan Van Helsing, *Secret Societies And Their Part In The 20th Century*, (Ewertverlag, Grand Canaria, Spain, 1995) p215.

level doesn't know what the level above knows, and none of them knows what the Prison Warders know. It is a manipulators' paradise, with most people within it not knowing what they are part of or what the final goal will be.

You could describe it symbolically as the clear-sighted (ETs) manipulating the partially-sighted (Global Elite/Brotherhood), who then manipulate the blind (the mass of humanity). With the United States now created and in Brotherhood hands, the control of the world could be advanced even more quickly than before.

Chapter 3

Paper power

The plan for the New World Order and global control moved into a new phase with the emergence of 'funny money'. This is the process by which banks lend money that doesn't exist (credit) and charge you interest on it! If I gave you something that doesn't exist and asked you to pay me for it, you might consider calling the police. If I gave you something that doesn't exist and said that if you don't pay me for it I will take you to court and take your property away, you might say we lived in a fascist state. Yet what I have just described is the banking system of the world and the means through which both people and governments are drowning in debt. And what does debt equal? Control.

Among the first bankers in the Western world were the Knights Templar. They were given enormous riches by Christians supporting the crusades and by legacies from people who were often hoping to buy a place in heaven. They were the wealthiest organisation in every country in which they established themselves, and their temples in Paris and London became financial centres. Eventually, King Philip IV of France, in league with Pope Clement V, destroyed the Templars and stole their fortune to pay debts and, as I outlined in *The Robots' Rebellion*, possibly for other reasons, too. The Templars' Grand Master, Jacques de Molay, was burned at the stake and the Order then went underground to work and plot secretly within other organisations. The Christian world had a strict ban on usury (the charging of interest on loans) but as the centuries passed this was forgotten, and the banking system which today controls humanity began to develop.

The currency of that time was precious metals (such as gold and silver) and, for safety reasons, the owners began to deposit their wealth with the goldsmiths, who had suitable strong rooms to ensure its safekeeping. The goldsmiths would issue paper receipts for the gold and silver deposited with them, and the owners would pay their debts by withdrawing portions of their 'deposits', as necessary. It was obviously an unwieldly process to move all those metals around and the paper receipts slowly became accepted as currency. The gold and silver were rarely moved, but the *ownership* of it changed with the issuing of receipts ('money') to pay off debts. In the same way today, vast fortunes are made by simply moving numbers between one computer file and another.

The goldsmiths and other owners of the strong rooms began to realise that, at any one time, only a fraction of the gold and silver was being withdrawn by the owners. "So," they thought, "why don't we issue notes (money) to other people who don't own the gold and charge them interest on the notes?" The only way the ruse could fail was if they issued too many notes and everyone came along at the same time to cash them in for gold and silver. They began to issue notes for the ownership of the gold and silver greatly in excess of the amount of gold and silver they had deposited in their vaults. Most of the notes they lent (and earned interest on) were related to gold and silver which the 'banks' did not even have. But since only a small amount of the metals was being withdrawn at *any one time*, they were in the clear. They could issue lots of bits of paper for gold and silver that didn't exist and charge interest for doing so! There, in one sentence, you have a description of today's banking system, which controls the world.

People and governments are submerged in debt and desperately trying to pay interest on money that has never, does not, and will never exist. It is reckoned that on average, for every £1,000 a bank receives from customers, it lends (and charges interest upon) at least £10,000! It is able to do this through a fractional reserve system, which means they only have to keep a fraction (say, one-tenth) of their total deposits in the bank, or 'reserve'. They count on it not being called for (demanded) by its customers all at the same time. In most countries where banks are regulated, there are rules or laws which allow a bank to shut its doors if too many people want their money out at the same time. The bank creates this money out of thin air by typing numbers onto a computer screen. A large slice of your taxes goes to the banks to pay interest on money created in this way when those taxes could be used to ease poverty and hunger, and create greater opportunity. Indeed, if the money system was restructured to serve people and not banks, there is a good case for saying that all taxation could end.

The con-trick is completed by the fact that if you fall behind in your interest payments on money that doesn't exist, the bank can take away your car, your house, and other property – wealth that *does* exist. Remember, too, that while you are borrowing a certain figure from the bank, you are paying back more than that, with the interest. Where does that interest come from? It comes from the wealth and credit in the world. So with every loan paid back to a bank since this system began, the interest payments have been sucking the wealth and money of the world into the banking system. With each loan repayment, the control of that system is strengthened. This allows the banking system, controlled by the Global Elite, to lend even greater sums of non-existent money and submerge even more people in debt.

The eighteenth century saw a major leap forward for the Global Elite/Brotherhood ambitions as this banking system expanded, especially with the emergence and rapid rise to dominance of the House of Rothschild. Few organisations in modern times have served Brotherhood

ambitions more than this one. This name will appear on so many occasions
in the first half of the book (as I explain how the Prison Warders manifest
their control on the physical level), that I should fill in a little Rothschild
history here.

Mayer Amschel Bauer (later Rothschild) was born in 1743 in Frankfurt,
Germany. He married Gutle Schnaper in 1770 and they had a large family of
five boys and five girls. He was educated to be a rabbi, but he later worked
briefly for the Oppenheimer bank in Hanover and then became a money
lender who acted as an agent for William IX, Landgrave of Hesse-Cassel. In
1785, William inherited the largest family fortune in Europe, estimated at
some $40 million.[1] Some of this was accumulated by hiring out troops to
Britain to fight in the Brotherhood-engineered American War of
Independence.

The Rothschild Empire was built on money embezzled by Mayer Amschel
from William, who had in turn stolen it from the soldiers he had hired out
to the British. The money, perhaps around $3 million, was paid by the
British government to William to pay the soldiers, but he kept it for himself.[2]
William gave this money to Rothschild to hide it from Napoleon's armies,
but instead Rothschild sent it to England with his son Nathan to establish
the London branch of the family's empire. Nathan used the money to buy a
vast quantity of gold from the East India Company and he used this gold to
finance the Duke of Wellington's military exploits. Nathan manipulated the
situation in such a way that this became the origin of the enormous
Rothschild fortune. We should remember that money, like everything, is an
energy. It can be used for positive and negative purposes and it will carry the
energy of the 'intent' behind it. To have the House of Rothschild built on
money which was embezzled from an embezzler meant that the empire was
built from the start on negative energy.

On the back of Nathan's financial coup, branches of the House of
Rothschild were established in Berlin, Paris, Vienna, and Naples. Mayer's
sons were each put in charge of one of them. Today the Rothschild holdings
are reported to be held in the Five Arrows Fund of Curaçao and the Five
Arrows Corporation of Toronto, Canada. The name comes from the
Rothchild symbol of an eagle with five arrows in its talons, signifying the five
sons.[3] The fortune expanded by colossal leaps as the Rothschilds manipulated
governments and worked through the Brotherhood network to create wars
and revolutions, often lending money to both sides in the ensuing conflicts.
You will see that this was to become a standard practice for the banking elite.
It is easy to create conflict and war; you only need to control a dictator or

[1] *Jewish Encyclopedia*, Vol. X, p499.
[2] George Armstrong, *Rothschilds Money Trust*, (1940) p22.
[3] Eustace Mullins, *The World Order, Our Secret Rulers*, (Ezra Pound Institute of Civilisation,
Staunton, USA, 1992) p7.

government, ensure that they have the means to build up a powerful army, and then encourage or instruct them to invade other countries. Those countries will, understandably, defend themselves and presto! you have a war. I have heard it said that no-one gains from wars, but that's not quite correct. The bankers win every time – in the short term. They lend money that doesn't exist to finance both sides and make massive profits on the interest. They also control the arms manufacturers with whom the two sides spend the funny money which the bankers have loaned. In this way they get their loans back through their armament companies while still charging interest on the original loan to the governments. Then, when the two or more countries have devastated each other with the help of money provided by the banks, those same banks lend them more money that doesn't exist to rebuild their shattered nations and infrastructure. This produces even more profits for the banks and, through debt, gives them control of those countries and their peoples. The Rothschild empire quickly became highly skilled in such manipulation, as did those in America like J.P. Morgan, the Rockefeller empire, and many others who, when you look behind the front organisations and smokescreens, are controlled by the same few families and individuals. There is evidence to suggest that in fact the House of Rothschild was behind both of these great American business and banking empires, a demonstration of the Rothschilds' brilliance for hiding the extent of their power and control behind frontmen and organisations.

But the bankers cannot do all this alone. They need the help of the Brotherhood network to manipulate the circumstances in which conflicts will break out. The Rothschilds have long been enthusiastic Freemasons and Napoleon Bonaparte was surrounded by Freemasons who advised him on his policies and expansionism. They persuaded him at one time to invade Egypt and ransack ancient sites for knowledge and artifacts held to be sacred to Freemasonic ritual and legend. Napoleon brought a massive Egyptian obelisk back to Paris as part of this burglary. British Freemasons persuaded their government to do the same and the result was the theft of the Egyptian obelisk known as Cleopatra's Needle, which still stands in London. Napoleon's escapades were well exploited by the Brotherhood and their bankers. In his book, *The Rothschilds*, historian John Reeves tells how Nathan Rothschild witnessed the result of the Battle of Waterloo in 1815 and saw that Wellington had beaten the Napoleonic armies. Nathan then raced as fast as possible for the English Channel and the London Stock Exchange. There, looking dirty, panic-stricken and dejected, he announced that Wellington had been defeated. He gave more credence to this by selling some of his stocks at ridiculously low prices. This started a panic on the market with everyone desperately trying to sell at whatever price they could get. Secretly, Nathan and the House of Rothschild were buying these stocks for next to nothing. At that time, with no telephone or telegraphs it took several days for the news to filter back to London that Wellington had in fact *won.* The Stockmarket immediately rebounded and surged upwards. Nathan proceeded to sell the stocks he had secretly acquired and reaped massive profits. This same basic method has been used ever since and is still used today to manipulate financial markets. Stock Market panics are not random. They are engineered to the detriment of everyone, except those who create them. The approach of the Rothschild Empire was summed up by Mayer Amschel when he said: "Give me control of a nation's currency and I care not who makes the laws".[4]

Nathan Rothschild took the Rothschild fortune and influence to new levels. He boasted that he multiplied their capital 2,500 times in the course of five years.[5] He established the private banking concern N.M. Rothschild and Sons in London with branches in Paris, Berlin, Vienna, and Naples. Its purpose was to operate on the stock exchanges and make loans to governments and others. It became the agent and manager for banks, railways, arms manufacturers, and corporations of all kinds. From this came branches of the company which were given many different names to hide the extent of Rothschild influence, power, and infiltration. This is very much how the financial system operates today, with a few at the centre using endless different fronts and names for the same organisation. Just look at the names above the shops in the average city centre; if you look at who actually owns them, you will find it is the same few groups. You also find this with the apparently different soap powders and other products in the supermarkets. In America, the Rothschild empire was represented by companies like Kuhn, Loeb, and Co and it is likely, according to some researchers, that US companies such as J.P. Morgan, Speyer, and Lehman, were also controlled or greatly influenced by the Rothschilds. The British Prime Minister, Benjamin Disraeli, was very close to the Rothschild family. They lent his government £4 million to buy a controlling stake in the Suez Canal in 1875. Disraeli's novel, *Coningsby*, is clearly based on the family's story. The character, Sidonia, in this extract, is really Nathan Rothschild:

> "He arrived here [London] after the peace of Paris with his large capital. He staked all that he was worth on the Waterloo loan and the event made him one of the greatest capitalists in Europe...He reaped the due reward of his sagacity. Europe did require money and Sidonia [Nathan] was ready to lend it to Europe. France wanted some, Austria more, Prussia a little, Russia a few million; Sidonia could furnish them all. The only country he avoided was Spain; he was too well acquainted with its resources.
> "...He established a brother or near relative in whom he could confide, in most of the principal capitals. He was lord and master of the money markets of the world and of course virtually lord and master of everything else. He

[4] I have seen this quote attributed to later Rothschilds, also.
[5] *The Rothschilds, Financial Rulers Of Nations*, p167.

literally held the revenues of Southern Italy in pawn and monarchs and ministers in all countries courted his advice and were guided by his suggestions."

Or as the historian, John Reeves, put it in his work, *The Rothschilds*:

"Little could Mayer Amschel have anticipated that his sons would in after years come to exercise such an unbounded sway that the peace of nations would depend upon their nod; that the powerful control they exercised on the European money markets would enable them to pose as the arbiters of peace and war, since they could at their pleasure withhold or furnish the pecuniary means required to carry on a campaign.

"But this, incredible as it may seem, was what their vast influence, combined with their enormous wealth and unlimited credit, enabled them to do, for no firms existed strong enough to oppose them for any length of time, or rash enough to take up a business which the Rothschilds had refused. To reach this exalted position, Mayer Amschel and his sons required the cooperation of the states, but, when once he had climbed over their backs and reached the height of his ambition, he was independent of all aid and could act with the greatest freedom, whilst the states remained in a suppliant attitude at his feet." [6]

The extent of Rothschild influence by now can hardly be overstated. When Nathan died, his eldest son, Lionel, took his place as the head of N. M. Rothschild. Lionel advanced massive loans to the British and American governments and others such as the Egyptians. This included a loan of around $80 million to Britain to finance the (Elite-engineered) Crimean War in which tens of thousands died. Lionel also acted as agent to the Russian government for twenty years.[7] He was succeeded by his eldest son, Nathan Mayer, who became the first Lord Rothschild when he was raised to the peerage and took his seat in the British House of Lords in 1885. The first Lord Rothschild went on to become the governor of the Bank of England, with untold power to influence the world financial system. The 'Old Lady of Threadneedle Street' (as the Bank of England is called) has always been, and remains, an arm of the Global Elite. The Rothschild representatives across the world continued to manipulate events to expand their power and to serve a longer-term agenda which mirrored that of the Brotherhood: world domination.

I stress here that to highlight the part played by the Rothschilds is not to cast aspersions on Jewish people as a whole, the vast majority of whom have no idea what is happening and certainly would not support it if they did

---

[6] John Reeves, *The Rothschilds*, p104–105.
[7] *Jewish Encyclopedia*, Vol. 10, p501–502.

know. Many of the members of families I will name, like the Rothschilds, Rockefellers, and others, do not know the game plan, either. It is those who control those empires that I am seeking to expose, not everyone whose name is Rothschild, Rockefeller, or whatever. I believe that researchers over the years who have blamed the entire conspiracy on the Jewish people as a whole are seriously misguided; similarly, for Jewish organisations to deny that *any* Jewish person is working for the New World Order conspiracy is equally naive and allowing dogma or worse to blind them to reality. We are looking at a common thread – a lust for power and the All-Seeing Eye cult – which goes across all races and, in my view, is connected – sometimes knowingly but mostly unknowingly – to a higher controlling force: the Prison Warders of the Fourth Dimension.

A Global Elite banking network was created with central banks in each country working together to manipulate the system across Europe and the United States. This would later be coordinated from the Bank of International Settlements in Basle, Switzerland, and a thirteen-man elite on the International Banking Commission in Geneva, Switzerland. You'll note that Switzerland is always left alone when Europe goes to war. This is why. It is the Global Elite financial centre. The idea of a central bank in each country was another Elite inspiration. The first was the Bank of Amsterdam in 1609 and then followed the Bank of Hamburg (1619) and the Bank of Sweden (1661), chartered by the descendants of bankers in Genoa and Venice. These included the Warburgs of Hamburg, who descended from the Abraham del Banco family, the biggest bankers in Venice. The manipulators behind the Bank of Amsterdam were also behind the Dutch[8] William of Orange who took the British throne in 1689, a feat achieved by the manoeuvrings of the secret society called the Orange Order. The Bank of England soon followed, under the charter granted by William in 1694. Some researchers claim that all European monarchs have a connection back to William.[9] Resistance to the bank from members of Parliament was overcome when William took Britain into a costly war with the French. The need to raise money made the opposition succumb to the pressure to introduce the bank, which began to lend money which didn't exist to the British government. The fantastic profits it made as a result came from the pockets of the people through income tax, and the exploitation of even poorer people throughout the British Empire. The institution known as the National Debt (to the banks) was born. The Royal Prerogative for minting money was handed over to a committee which was also given the power to convert the basis of the country's wealth to gold, which the Elite controlled.

---

[8] I say "Dutch", in fact he was formerly a German prince from the house of Nassau. Interestingly, another German prince would marry into the Dutch royal family in this century. That was Prince Bernhard, of which much more later.

[9] *The World Order, Our Secret Rulers*, p25.

A leading part of the Global Elite at the top of the human pyramid is the group known as the Black Nobility, from where families like the Warburgs of Hamburg descended. These were at the forefront of the plan to put William of Orange on the British Throne and the creation of the money system as we know it. They originate from the Guelphs, also called the Neri, or Black Guelphs, and now the Black Nobility.[10] They were the force behind the Normans, who conquered England in the Battle of Hastings, led by William the Conqueror in 1066. Later, when based in Genoa, Italy, the Black Nobility supported Robert Bruce in his conquest of Scotland and it was this same genetic line and secret society which ensured that William of Orange became King of England, Scotland and Ireland.[11] Through William, the Black Nobility created the Bank of England and the notorious East India Company rapidly expanded to capture Asia and the Far East for the British (Global Elite) and to become the biggest drug running operation the world had yet seen. The political and economic union of England and Scotland was designed to force Scotland into this spider's web of money lending and control. We have a United Kingdom all right – united in its subservience to the manipulated money system controlled by the few. The Elite bankers were now manipulating with ever greater influence across the world. They were involved in the American Civil War, in which they financed both sides. The London Rothschilds funded the North while the Paris Rothschilds funded the South.[12] President Abraham Lincoln also printed interest-free money, called 'Greenbacks', to reduce the level of debt his government would face. This was potentially disastrous for the banks. If this had continued after the war and spread to other countries, the banks and the Elite would have lost their power. Lincoln was assassinated by John Wilkes Booth, an agent of the House of Rothschild, according to some researchers.[13] After Lincoln's death, the printing of greenbacks was ended.

The efforts to form a central banking system in the United States were always highly controversial. Against opposition from two of the founding fathers, Thomas Jefferson and James Madison, the first US Central Bank was introduced, thanks to the manipulation of one of their colleagues, Alexander Hamilton, who ran the Bank of New York. He was secretly backed by the Bank of England and the Rothschild Empire, which were, in truth, one and the same. When George Washington, a high ranking Freemason, became President in 1789, he made Hamilton the Secretary to the Treasury. Within two years, Hamilton had secured his ambition with the

---

[10] *The World Order, Our Secret Rulers*, p25.

[11] Ibid p276.

[12] *Secret Societies*, p122.

[13] There is another train of thought which suggests that Lincoln was killed because he was revealing too many of the secrets of the Brotherhood societies of which he was a member. I will describe the black esoteric basis of the Global Elite/Brotherhood in a later chapter.

creation of the US Central Bank, the Bank of the United States. As with the Bank of England, this was a *private* bank which now controlled the American economy. The bank caused mayhem, and riots erupted from the consequences of its policies. In the 1830s, President Andrew Jackson had the courage to take on the power of the Bank of the United States and he won. The first US Central Bank was no more. Another, however, was not long in coming.

In the early years of this century, the Elite was plotting to retake control of the US economy even more completely than before. They wanted two things: a new central bank with control over the nation's borrowing and the introduction of a federal income tax to give them control of the government's income. Again there was serious opposition to this, but in classic 'black-is-white' fashion, they tricked the American Congress and people. First, the Elite supported the election of President Woodrow Wilson in 1909. He was a front man, a political puppet and a Rosicrucian. The real power of the Wilson administration was in the hands of a man called 'Colonel'[14] Edward Mandel House, who was there for no other reason than to serve the Elite. Wilson said that House was "my second personality", "my alter ego", and that "his thoughts and mine are one". The Elite instructed Colonel House and he instructed Woodrow Wilson, who did as he was told. This was all happening under the pretence of 'democracy'.

The Elite bankers met at a place called Jekyl Island in Georgia to put together the bill for the introduction of the new US Central Bank, the Federal Reserve System. They travelled in a luxurious private railroad car owned by Senator Nelson Aldrich, the political mouthpiece for the Elite in Washington, and the grandfather of Nelson Aldrich Rockefeller (the four times Mayor of New York and the vice president of the United States under President Ford). Aldrich's daughter, Abby, was married to John D. Rockefeller Jr. For years after the meeting on Jekyl Island, the 'educators', commentators, and 'historians' denied it took place. Now this has been accepted, but it is said to have been an insignificant event. Utter bilge. It was the moment the Elite took over the US economy and its people with an organisation called the Federal Reserve System, which is neither federal, nor has any reserve!

In 1902, the Rothschilds sent one of their agents, Paul Warburg, to America with his brother, Felix, to 'rearrange' US banking to suit Rothschild and Elite interests. Another brother, Max Warburg, stayed at home in Frankfurt to run the family banking business there. After arriving in the USA, Paul Warburg married Nina Loeb (of the Rothschild controlled, Kuhn, Loeb, and Company) while Felix married Frieda Schiff, the daughter of Jacob Schiff, the head of Kuhn, Loeb, and Co Hardly surprisingly, both brothers became partners in the company and Paul was

---

[14] The title 'Colonel' was purely honorary. He never actually served.

given an annual salary of half a million dollars (in the early years of this century!) to prepare the ground for the imposition of the Federal Reserve System on the people of the United States. It was all arranged by the Rothschilds, probably even down to the Warburg's marriage partners. These banking and Elite families like to interbreed whenever possible. It keeps the genes up to scratch, you know, and keeps the money (control) in the family. When Jacob Schiff arrived in America to join Kuhn, Loeb, and Co, he married the daughter of Solomon Loeb. Jacob Schiff was to be one of the key manipulators in the first half of this century. The Schiff and Rothschild families were as one and shared the same house in Frankfurt in the days of Mayer Amschel. The Federal Reserve Bill became known as the 'Aldrich Bill' and it was Warburg and Aldrich who organised the covert meeting on Jekyl Island. Many years later, Frank Vanderlip, the Rockefellers' agent at the time, would say:

> *"Despite my views about the value to society of greater publicity for the affairs of corporations, there was an occasion, near the close of 1910, when I was as secretive – indeed furtive – as a conspirator...I do not feel it is any exaggeration to speak of our secret expedition to Jekyl Island as the occasion of the actual conception of what eventually became the Federal Reserve System."* [15]

The Federal Reserve System is a cartel of *private* banks, of which the Bank of New York is the most powerful. To this day it controls the US economy and thereby affects all of our lives. Through its US offshoots and connections like J.P. Morgan and Kuhn, Loeb, and Co, the Rothschild Empire controlled the principal New York banks and, through them, the Bank of New York. This gave them control of the Federal Reserve System and the American economy.[16] This Federal Reserve cartel is nominally controlled by the government-appointed chairman of the Federal Reserve Board, which is another way of saying the Elite control it. The cartel lends money that doesn't exist to the US government and has thus ensured that the country – and therefore the people – are drowning in debt to the banks. By 1910, the behaviour of the banks had made them deeply unpopular with the people. The Elite had to think of a way of persuading the public to accept a banking coup on the American nation while thinking the power of the banks was being curtailed. So when the bill the bankers had written was introduced by their front politicians they publicly and vehemently *opposed* it. This gave the impression that the bill was bad news for the banks and it was passed into law in 1913, in the belief that it curtailed the power of the money manipulators. It didn't. It gave them total control. Just to be safe, the Federal Reserve Bill was put before Congress shortly before Christmas,

---

[15] *Saturday Evening Post*, (February 9, 1935) p25.
[16] *Rothschild Money Trust*, p41.

1913, when many Congressmen were already at home with their families for the holiday.

Now the Elite controlled the US government's borrowing and interest rates, and it could create booms and busts whenever it wished. The way they introduced the Federal Income Tax was even more outrageous, although you have to admire their cheek. For this to be passed into law, it required the consent of at least thirty-six states because there had to be an amendment, the sixteenth, to the United States Constitution. Only two states agreed. In a democracy you would think that the bill would be ditched. Not so. This is no democracy! The Secretary of State, Filander Knox, informed Congress that the necessary agreement had been achieved and Federal Income Tax became 'law'. Or rather, in reality, it didn't. The Internal Revenue Service (IRS), which collects Federal Income Tax and takes away the property of those who do not pay, has been stealing from the American people for decades and continues to do so. The forced collection of Federal Income Tax is illegal to this day. It was never properly passed into law. In 1985, an American businessman took the Internal Revenue Service to court on this basis and won. I reprint a letter opposite (*Figure 5*) which appeared in *Nexus* magazine, an excellent publication which highlights the manipulation of the global conspiracy. The letter, from the Commissioner of the Internal Revenue Service to his regional directors, claims to be proof that the IRS and the US government know very well that to force people to pay federal income tax is theft. Some people say the letter is a fake and it may well be, but if you live in America it is worth taking professional advice on your tax liability.

The power over political and human events on this planet was increased by leaps and bounds as this funny money system expanded its grip on the world. This gave the Elite's bankers the power to manipulate wars and revolutions, almost at will, in league with other elements within the Brotherhood network, which expanded and became even more focussed on its goals during the same period that the banking system emerged. Another branch of the Brotherhood was *officially* started by the German professor, Adam Weishaupt, on May 1st 1776, and this sought to infiltrate all the seats of power throughout Europe. It was called the Bavarian Illuminati. The term 'Illuminati' means illuminated or enlightened ones and goes back to ancient times. Weishaupt's Illuminati was designed on classic Brotherhood lines with circles of apparently unconnected people who were, behind the scenes and without their knowledge, all manipulated and directed by the same controlling core at the centre. He once said: "The great strength of our Order lies in its concealment; let it never appear in its own name, but always covered by another name, another occupation". That was a superb summary of the Illuminati/Global Elite approach. Some researchers suggest that it was actually in 1770 that Weishaupt was asked to launch the Bavarian Illuminati by the Rothschilds.[17]

---

[17] *Secret Societies*, p109.

Internal Revenue Service   **Department of the Treasury**

TO ALL DISTRICT DIRECTORS   **APRIL 4, 1985**

On March 5, 1985, a charge of tax evasion was filed in U.S. DISTRICT COURT in Indianapolis, Indiana by U.S. Attorney George Duncan. The Charges were dismissed! The defense attorney, Lowell Becraft of Huntsville, Alabama presented irrefutable evidence that the 16th Amendment to the U.S. Constitution was never properly ratified. This amendment which established the "income tax", was signed into law despite serious defects. In reality only two states ratified the amendment and ratification requires 36 states to be valid. The effect of this is such that every tax paid into the Treasury since 1913, is due and refundable to every citizen and business.

The official position of the service is, as it has always been, to aid and assist the citizens of the United States. We will not publish or advertise this finding as a total immediate refund would cause a serious drain on the resources of the Treasury. For those citizens who become aware of this finding and apply for a total refund, expedite their refund documents as quickly and as quietly as possible...
...Advise each of your managers that they are not to discuss this situation with anyone. There will be no written communications and you are to destroy this memorandum.

The Secretary of the Treasury assures me that there will be no reduction in the workforce as this refunding activity will take a minimum of 5 years to complete. Further directions will be forwarded as the need arises.

                              (signed)
                              Roscoe L. Egger, Jr.
                              Commissioner of Internal Revenue

Figure 5: **This letter may well be a fake, but it outlines the themes of the confidence trick.**

The Brotherhood secret societies plotted to destroy the European monarchies, either by replacing them with republics or, less often, by removing their power and leaving them as purely symbolic heads of state. A powerful monarch was OK if he or she supported Illuminati/Elite plans for the New World Order, but if they didn't, or if they refused to be manipulated, it acted as a serious block to the unfoldment of the plan. The manipulators could assassinate them and hope the replacement would play the game, but you couldn't keep doing that again and again. Much better from the Brotherhood's point of view to replace the monarchies with elected representatives of the people, who could be replaced every few years. If you can control the money and the media, you can largely control (a) who gets to the top in political parties and (b) whom the people elect into government. You give financial backing and use the secret society network within *all* political parties to manipulate your choice to the top; you activate your (controlled) media to advance the popularity of the one you want to win at election time, and to undermine his or her opponent. The illusion which is laughingly called democracy is a wonderful vehicle for the Illuminati/Global Elite. It was their creation and the last thing you can call it is democratic.

The French Revolution of 1789 was an Illuminati coup d'état, the methods of which have been repeated over and over to replace undemocratic monarchies with undemocratic 'people's parliaments'. The only real difference between these forms of rule was that one was clearly a dictatorship, while the other *appeared* to be freedom. When people are ruled by a dictator in whatever form, the time will arrive when the desire for a say in a country's affairs will grow within the people and forms of democracy will be demanded. The people living under a dictator, in other words, know they are living under a dictator and eventually they will rebel. The system that replaced the monarchies, the 'phoney democracies' as I call them, were designed to give the illusion of 'people power' while structuring the system to ensure that the few could run the entire show. By manipulating events and elections via direct intervention, corruption, or media power, the Elite could pretty much be sure that their choices became the presidents, prime ministers, and the leading names in governments. People ask why those who get to the top in politics around the world are often either corrupt or incompetent. Well, now you know. They are meant to be. What's more, it is harder to encourage people to rebel against the tyranny of the phoney democracies, because they are programmed to believe that they live in a real democracy. With the fall of monarchy power during the Illuminati-engineered revolutions, one form of dictatorship was replaced by another, but very few noticed!

If we take a brief look at how the French Revolution unfolded, it will show you the background strategy which the Global Elite and their Illuminati offshoot use all the time to create conflict and hoodwink the people. It began as usual with a manufactured economic crisis. A country and its people are first brought to desperate straits by poverty and economic collapse. As you will see repeated throughout the book, the manipulators create the circumstances in which public opinion says: "Something must be done!" Once that stage has been achieved (by economic crisis, or wars, or whatever) the manipulators step forward in the guise of standing up for the people, and offer the 'solutions' to the problems they *themselves* have created in the first place. Those 'solutions' will be precisely the measures the manipulators wanted to happen all along, as part of the journey to the New World Order. It is what I call the problem-reaction-solution scenario. In this case, they wanted the people of France to overturn the monarchy, and they sowed the seeds of revolt by their age old method of poverty and debt. In his book, *The Life Of Napoleon*, McNair Wilson says of his time:

> *"A change of a fundamental kind had taken place in the economic structure of Europe whereby the old basis had ceased to be wealth measured in lands, crops, herds and minerals; but a new standard had now been introduced, namely, a form of money to which the title 'credit' had been given."* [18]

Debts were measured in gold or silver, neither of which France produced. Therefore their debts were bound to grow and become even more impossible to pay. The Brotherhood had people on the inside as usual, including one in the key position of chief finance minister to King Louis. His name was Necker, a man who claimed to be a Swiss of German extraction. McNair Wilson wrote of him: "Necker had forced his way into the King's Treasury as a representative of the debt system and owing allegiance to that system".[19] Necker had a reputation of being a daring and unscrupulous speculator before joining the King's administration and, after four years in the treasury, he had manipulated the French finances on behalf of the Illuminati-Elite to add another £170 million to the national debt.[20] With the French economy in tatters and the people growing restless in their poverty, the Illuminati moved into stage two and began the process of stimulating revolution. They did this through the Freemasonry network.

By 1730, Freemasonry had been introduced to France from England and had attracted notable names to its ranks, such as Phillipe Egalité, the Duke of Chartres, and the Duke of Orleans, who became a Grand Master. The Brotherhood used such people and others to establish the first foothold of the revolution, which was more moderate in its demands. Egalité was convinced that he would be made king of a democratic state once the

---

[18] McNair Wilson, *The Life Of Napolean*, p38.
[19] Captain A.H.M. Ramsey, *The Nameless War*, (Omni Publications, London, 1952) p25.
[20] Ibid p25.

existing king and queen had been overthrown. He had little idea of the scale of bloodletting that was to follow. It was the same with Lafayette, another revolutionary and friend of Benjamin Franklin. Lafayette wanted to see a democratic monarchy introduced under Louis, the present king. But these people were just used as vehicles to kick start the revolutionary fervour. The real manipulators knew exactly the sort of revolution it was intended to be. Once Egalité had served his purpose he was sent to the guillotine. Many different people are misled by the Illuminati manipulators to make sure they play their part in the overall plan, the true agenda of which is kept secret from them. Once they have done their job, they are discarded. Those reading this book who are on the lower levels of the Brotherhood ladder might ponder deeply on this for their own sake, if not for that of others.

Another Brotherhood frontman was the Marquis de Mirabeau. He is known to have been financed by the German, Moses Mendelssohn, a member of the Illuminati.[21] Rabbi Marvin S. Antelman names Mendelssohn as a key manipulator for an inner 'Jewish' clique which he believes has been seeking to destroy Judaism and all religion.[22] He says that this clique, together with non-Jews, are followers of what he, too, calls the All-Seeing Eye cult. He links this group to the House of Rothschild and says the cult was the force behind the French Revolution. Mendelssohn started the Illuminati front, the Haskala movement in 1776 – the year the Bavarian Illuminati was launched. Another figure close to Mendelssohn was the Illuminati member, Friedrich Nicholai. Rabbi Antelman described Mendelssohn as a "con man" who plotted the demise of Judaism while claiming to be a promoter of the religion and the "race". This is precisely what has happened since and continues today. There is a global Jewish clique who are not, in truth, followers of Judaism or supporters of Jewish people. The Freemasonry lodges in France, particularly those under the control of the Grand Orient form of the order, were infiltrated by Illuminati manipulators and used to fire the revolution. In 1786, Mirabeau formed an Illuminati lodge at a meeting at the Jacobin College in Paris. They became known as the Jacobins. In the same year, another All-Seeing Eye Illuminati group called the Frankists (after Jacob Franks) was created in Frankfurt. One of its leading lights was Michael Hess, an employee of Mayer Amschel Rothschild. These two groups, the Jacobins and the Frankists, were at the heart of the French Revolution.

The Brotherhood plan was openly revealed when a member of Adam Weishaupt's Bavarian Illuminati was struck by lightning and killed at Ratisbon while carrying secret papers. These revealed the plans for world

---

[21] *The Nameless War*, p26.

[22] Rabbi Marvin S. Antelman, *To Eliminate The Opiate*, (Zahavia Ltd., New York-Tel Aviv, 1974).

revolution and the New World Order and they had a remarkable resemblance to the *Protocols Of The Elders Of Zion*, of which more shortly.[23] The Bavarian government had the headquarters of the Illuminati searched. Much more information was found and the French authorities were told of the plan. But events in France had by now reached such a momentum that nothing could stop them. By 1789, more than 2,000 Freemasonry lodges had affiliated with the Grand Orient organisation which, in turn, was controlled by the Illuminati. They were, themselves, controlled by the Global Elite.

The central organisation of the revolution and the printing and distribution of propaganda was based at the Palais Royal, the home of Egalité. He was so in debt to the money lenders that he had to sign over his palace and estates to them. Part of the mind manipulation in any Elite/ Brotherhood operation is the character assassination of the opposition. One such example in the French Revolution was the famous diamond necklace 'bought' by the Queen, Marie Antionette. She had been warned about Freemasonry by her sister in Austria some years before, but the advice went unheeded. She had informed her sister that in France, Freemasonry was open and 'everyone knows all'. The 'open' Freemasons were actually planning a bloodbath at the guillotine as she wrote those words. Bitterness with the monarchy in France was further fuelled when the propaganda machine announced that the Queen had bought a diamond necklace for a quarter of a million pounds when, in truth, it had been ordered without her knowledge by an agent of the Brotherhood, a close associate of Adam Weishaupt. This was political dynamite at a time of such poverty in France. The scheme was organised by Joseph Balsamo, an Italian from Palermo, who was initiated into the Illuminati by Weishaupt.[24]

This 'peoples' revolution' continued to discard its stooges and frontmen as each new layer of violence unfurled. Others were introduced like Danton, Marat, and Robespierre, who would also be removed once they had been used to their full potential. Mobs were organised to go out onto the streets and stimulate more violence and unrest. In September 1792, the 'September massacres' came when 8,000 people were killed in the prisons of Paris alone, in the name of a revolution which was supposed to be about 'freedom' from royal tyranny. At its core, the revolution wasn't even organised by French people. As Sir Walter Scott said in his *Life Of Napoleon*: "The principal leaders of the...[revolution]...seem to have been foreigners".[25] Robespierre was said to be the leading light of the revolution as it gathered pace, but this was just another smokescreen. In his book, *The Life Of Robespierre*, G. Renier, says:

---

[23] *Secret Societies*, p110–112.

[24] *The Nameless War*, p29.

[25] Ibid p33.

"On the 28th July, 1794, Robespierre made a long speech against ultra terrorists…uttering vague general accusations. 'I dare not name them at this moment and in this place. I cannot bring myself entirely to tear asunder the veil that covers this profound mystery of antiquity. But I can affirm most positively that among the authors of this plot are agents of that system of corruption and extravagance, the most powerful of all the means invented by foreigners for the undoing of the Republic; I mean the impure apostles of atheism and the immorality that is at its base'."

At 2am that night, Robespierre was shot and the next day he was taken to the guillotine. He was getting too close to speaking the truth about the 'glorious' French Revolution, and in the strange world of the Illuminati/ Elite, that meant he had to go. Think on that, those of you in the Brotherhood who believe you are in control of events. Stop now, let me have the information you have about what is going on, and get the hell out of it before you become another Robespierre or Egalité! From the French Revolution we can see the elements of manipulated wars and revolutions that are common to all the 'peoples' uprisings' in Europe which ousted the monarchies and to conflicts around the world up to the present day. These are: the financial crisis to create suffering and the desire for change ("Something must be done"); the duping of influential people who support the 'cause' without realising the real agenda; the dumping of these people when they have served their purpose; the mass propaganda to exploit the public's natural sense of injustice, to disinform, and to lead opinion in the desired direction; the lies told about opponents of the plan and the assassination of their character to the point where people have great hatred for them; the organisation of 'rent-a-mob' to cause agitation and encourage others to overthrow the established order; and, finally, the installation of a phoney democracy or alternative dictatorship.

Look at the background of any revolution or war and you will see most, usually all, of these methods at work. This system I am describing is the means through which the extraterrestrial Prison Warders and the Luciferic Consciousness on the non-physical frequencies around this planet, project their control into the physical world as the Global Elite/Illuminati/ Brotherhood network. Divide and rule, control of the flow of information, secret manipulation, and conflict. Over the last three hundred thousand years or so, all these methods of control by the Prison Warders can be seen in the Elite network on Earth. One is merely another level of the other. Revolution and war continued throughout Europe during the ninteenth century, much of it coordinated by Lord Palmerston, the British Prime Minister, who directed the policies of his country to carry out the designs of the Illuminati. Lord Palmerston was the Grand Patriach or Grand Master of Grand Orient Freemasonry – another name for the Illuminati.

It was Palmerston who was prime minister during the 'opium wars' when Britain forced the Chinese to import opium, a policy which addicted the population and made them easy to control. One result was the British ownership of Hong Kong, from where Britain ran its drug trade and, with the Americans and Chinese, still does.

There was another ambition on the Prison Warder/Global Elite agenda during this period: the end of God in the human mind. The Elite's god is the Luciferic Consciousness, but they wanted the human mind to reject all beliefs in eternal life and believe in mortality, finality, and materialistic 'science'. This would turn human consciousness into an even greater slave to this material level. In the very late 1800s, a controversial document came to light called the *Protocols Of The Elders Of Zion.* I call them the Illuminati Protocols and I quote many extracts from them in *The Robots' Rebellion.* Some say they were a forgery made public only to discredit Jews, and I use the term 'Illuminati Protocols' to get away from the Jewish emphasis. If they were a forgery, something that is quite possible, what were they a forgery of, and by whom? The authors of the best-selling book, *Holy Blood, Holy Grail,* conclude that the original Protocols were indeed authentic. They suggest that they were the work of an elite group called The Priory of Sion, the inner, controlling, core of the Knights Templars.[26] They believe that this original document was changed to make it appear as a Jewish plot. I certainly would not dismiss such a conclusion. It is the manipulation they describe that interests me, not who has been blamed for it. I believe their origin lies with the Illuminati, as does Rabbi Antelman. Whatever the arguments, one fact cannot be denied, given the hindsight of the last 100 years. The Protocols, from wherever they came, were a quite stunning prophecy of what has happened in the twentieth century in terms of wars and the manipulation I am exposing here. Whoever wrote them sure as heck knew what the game plan was. One protocol speaks of the way the manipulators intended to destroy the idea of God in as many human minds as possible:

> *"It is with this object in view that we are constantly, by means of our press, arousing a blind confidence in these* [scientific] *theories. The intellectuals of the Goyim* [Gentiles] *will puff themselves up with their knowledge and without any logical verification of it will put into effect all the information available from science, which our agentur specialists have cunningly pieced together for the purpose of educating their minds in the direction we want. Do not suppose for a moment that these statements are empty words: think carefully of the successes we arranged for Darwinism..."*
> **Protocol 2**

---

[26] Michael Baigent, Richard Leigh and Henry Lincoln, *Holy Blood, Holy Grail,* (Jonathan Cape, London, 1982) p198–203.

"...It is indispensible to undermine all faith, to tear out of the minds of the Goyim the very principle of Godhead and the spirit, and to put into its place, arithmetical calculations and material needs."
Protocol 4

Darwinism, of course, refers to Charles Darwin, the man most effective in achieving a widespread belief in one-life-and-that's-it. He suggested in the mid-1800s that the potential of the mind is developed by genetic inheritance. This is patent nonsense, but it did provide the justification for the eugenics (racial purity) movement that would follow and lead both to Adolf Hitler and the population control policies of today. His work, *Origin Of Species*, to give it a shortened title, was to become the basis for 'scientific' thinking and its mindset dominates what we bravely call science to this day. His most famous theory, that of the survival of the fittest, didn't even appear in the first four editions. He lifted it from the writings of a contemporary, Herbert Spencer, who had lifted it from someone else. The word 'evolution' did not appear until the sixth edition, in 1872. I understand that even Darwin didn't believe his theory by the end of his life, and he thought God created human beings. But his *Origin Of Species* went on to take over 'scientific' thought anyway. It was designed by the Elite to do just that. Darwin was another stooge.

He was the frontman for a coup on the human mind which was coordinated over many years. A small group of people known as the Lunar Society in Birmingham, England, was significant in this. The group continued its influence under the name of the London-based Royal Society, which is still one of the most influential bodies in the world with regard to science. The Royal Society was founded by the Order of the Rosy Cross in the reign of Charles II. Another famous 'scientific' influence, Sir Isaac Newton, was a Rosicrucian and Grand Master of the Priory of Sion, the inner core of the Knights Templar. He was an inspiration behind the founding of the Royal Society. Researchers into the background of the Lunar Society have shown that it mirrored (with remarkable accuracy) a group called the Invisible College, described in the Francis Bacon work, *The New Atlantis*. It was known as the Lunar Society because it met once a month at the time of the full moon. Among its members were Benjamin Franklin, one of the founders of the United States and close associate of French revolutionaries, and...Erasmus Darwin, the grandfather of Charles Darwin, the man who would later be the frontman for this-world-is-all-there-is. What a coincidence! Another member of the Lunar Society was the Unitarian, Josiah Wedgwood, founder of the famous pottery, and his daughter was to become the mother of Charles Darwin after she married Dr Robert Darwin, the son of Erasmus Darwin. Nothing like keeping it in the family!

Six of the Lunar Society's members were educated at Edinburgh University, as was Charles Darwin. The society was a revolutionary organisation which supported the overthrowing of the monarchies and the undermining of God in the human belief system. Benjamin Franklin became a sort of shuttle 'diplomat' for the cause, in the same way that Henry Kissinger would come to be in the second half of this century. I cannot recommend too highly the book by the Canadian scientist and researcher, Ian T. Taylor, called *In The Minds Of Men: Darwin And The New World Order*. This reveals the story of how modern 'scientific' theory was manufactured and sold as truth to mislead the human mind. With detailed, documented evidence, Taylor dismantles the edifice of the scientific establishment, its beliefs, claims, and manipulation. Every student of science would benefit enormously from reading it.

But, of course, most people don't read such evidence. They go through the schools and university system and absorb all the accepted claptrap that originates from Darwin's time. This affects the way many of them see themselves and life in general, and, as we have discussed, they create that reality in the world around them. It is a world of "What's the point? We are only cosmic accidents after all, and life is about the survival of the fittest. No room for sentiment; it's everyone for themselves". A movement which has emerged from the Darwin view of life is called Humanism, another vehicle for manipulation, even though the overwhelming majority of its advocates will not realise it. Still today, organisations like the Committee for the Scientific [sic] Investigation of Claims of the Paranormal (CSICOP) do all they can to discredit any explanations or phenomena which expose establishment science as a fraud. One vehement British campaigner against alternative scientific explanation is Susan Blackmore, who is wheeled onto television programmes galore to defend the establishment line against all challenge. The padlock on such minds defies my imagination.

In our brief history of the conspiracy, we are now in the early years of the twentieth century. The manipulators have created the banking and financial system, introduced this-world-is-all-there-is science, and they have, through engineered revolution, installed a series of phoney democracies which they control and direct while the people think they are free. In their misguided minds (controlled by the Prison Warders on the Fourth Dimension), the time was right to launch the next stage on the road to the New World Order. It was time to go global.

Chapter 4

From Rhodes to ruin

Some people find it difficult to understand at first how this manipulation can be continued across the generations, but in fact it's very simple – coordination and inspiration from the Fourth Dimension. And those who have reached the top of the human pyramid are always on the lookout for people of the right calibre and attitude who can take over from them, as the earthly representations of the Prison Warders. The knowledge of the New World Order agenda and the methods of manipulation are also passed on across the generations of certain families, which makes the process easier. I believe that the same streams of consciousness have been constantly incarnating, 'dying', and reincarnating over the thousands of years to keep the plan going.

Just as those wishing to free humanity are supported from other frequencies of reality, so are those in the Elite/Illuminati/Brotherhood network. A common theme among many people involved is an interest in the 'black' occult and a wish to communicate with extraterrestrial 'supermen' – the Fourth Dimensional Prison Warders. The methods of communication are very much the same for those who want freedom and for those who want control. It is the intent behind such communications which differs. The Elite have thoughts and information fed into their consciousness to guide them and so do those challenging this structure. We on Earth are vehicles for a spiritual tussle happening on another level of this planet, not only this one.

THE ROUND TABLE

Cecil Rhodes was a fabulously wealthy Englishman who exploited the continent and peoples of Africa, and particularly the diamond reserves of South Africa. The name Rhodesia, now Zimbabwe, is an indication of his influence in that part of the world. As a student at Oxford University, Rhodes was inspired by a fine arts professor called John Ruskin, who is still considered a legendary figure at Oxford. Ruskin was born in London in 1819, the son of a wealthy wine merchant, and inherited a large fortune. His hero was the ancient Greek philosopher, Plato, whose works he read almost every day. Plato had a brilliant mind and made a great contribution to human debate and knowledge, but some of his views on how to structure a society by top-down imposition could hardly be further from my own.

Ruskin was a believer in the New World Order agenda of centralised power, and he felt the State should control the means of production and distribution. This was the same philosophy followed by the early British Labour Party before it became the alternative Conservative Party it is today. Ruskin, however, went further and believed the control of the State could be in the hands of one dictator of superior intellect to the rest of society. Some researchers say he was a supporter of the Illuminati. Ruskin probably genuinely wanted better conditions for the poor, but I would suggest that he was seriously misguided in his means of achieving them. His ideas were to be followed by Karl Marx and Friedrich Engels (another student of Plato) and became the foundations of the Marxist form of communism which was soon to grip the nations of Eastern Europe.

Rabbi Marvin S. Antelman also identifies the Plato theme and its connection to the All-Seeing Eye secret society network. He points out that Moses Mendelssohn, an architect of the French Revolution, was such a student of Plato's works that he became known as the "German Plato". He translated three books of Plato's *Republic* into German, but his work was never published. It was, however, passed down through the Warburg banking family, the subordinates of the Rothschilds, and creators of the Federal Reserve.[1] The Warburgs, like the Rothschilds, would later help to fund Adolf Hitler. Adam Weishaupt, the founder of the Illuminati, was another Plato groupie and high initiate of the All-Seeing Eye stream of occult 'thinking'.

The views of John Ruskin and his articulate promotion of them brought about a revolution in the thinking of the privileged undergraduates of Oxford and some at Cambridge, too. Rhodes copied Ruskin's inaugural lecture in longhand and kept it with him for the rest of his life. The creation of a world government centred on Britain became Rhodes's obsession and lay at the heart of almost everything he did. As his wealth grew with his exploitation of South African diamonds and minerals, he established companies like DeBeers Consolidated Mines and Consolidated Gold Fields. He also became the Prime Minister of the Cape Colony and used his wealth and influence to control parliamentary seats in Britain and South Africa. By the 1890s, he had an income of at least a million pounds a year (over a hundred years ago!), but he was usually overdrawn on his account, such was his ability to spend. A large amount went to furthering his aims of a world government. Rhodes is claimed to have been a member of an elite group known as the Committee of 300, also known as the Olympians. This organisation was the subject of a book by Dr John Coleman called *Conspirators Hierarchy: The Story Of The Committee Of 300*. Coleman claims to have been an intelligence officer in Britain's MI6. From this point I will identify those named by Dr Coleman with the abbreviation (Comm 300).

[1] Rabbi Marvin S. Antelman, *To Eliminate The Opiate*, p71–72, 82–83.

This organisation consists of leading people in politics, commerce, banking, the media, the military etc, who are working toward the goal of total global power.

Rhodes's[2] idea was to set up a secret society which would manipulate events in a way that would lead to the introduction of centralised global control. This society is known by several names but, for simplicity, I will call it throughout by one of them: the Round Table. It was structured on Illuminati and Freemasonic lines. There was an inner circle, the Society of the Elect (or Initiates), who knew exactly what the game and the aim was, and an outer Circle of Friends, made up of influential people who could help the cause, but who didn't always know the full implications or ambitions of the Round Table. The Table's manipulators were mostly those with the *real* power rather than those with the *appearance* of power. Its members were usually not recorded in history like the famous politicians and military leaders, but they controlled events far more than those documented by the history books.

Lord Astor (Comm 300) was a member of the Round Table inner elite and he was an example of another key area of control by the Elite: the media. He would later own *The Times* newspaper. Still today, the power lies not with politicians, but with the shadowy figures who 'advise' and control them, and those who manipulate the flow of information into the public arena. The Round Table, another Rothschild creation, plotted the Boer War in South Africa of 1899–1902, in which tens of thousands of men, women, and children were killed, many of them in the concentration camps established by Lord Kitchener (Comm 300). The British Prime Minister and Foreign Minister at the time was Lord Salisbury (Comm 300), of the elite Cecil family, a close friend of Winston Churchill (Comm 300). Lord Salisbury and the Cecil family were key players in the Rhodes-Round Table operation. Manipulation by the Round Table secured British control of the mineral wealth and introduced the Union of South Africa. Nathan (Baron) Rothschild was a member of the Round Table which represented the interests of the House of Rothschild and the bankers they controlled such as the Warburgs, Schroders, and Lazards. J.P. Morgan (Comm 300) became a member in 1899.

When Rhodes died in 1902, he bequeathed his funds to the cause. These continued to support the Round Table to an extent, although much of the funding came from the House of Rothschild. In his will, Rhodes also created a system of subsidised scholarships which continue to this day. This was, in part, a front to hide the secret society. Selected overseas students are

---

[2] Conspiracy researcher, Kitty Little who had many contacts at the highest levels of the former Rhodesia, says the role of Rhodes has been misunderstood. She says that Rhodes prevented the Rothschilds from winning control of the South African gold industry. As a result, she says, they have sought to blame him for the deeds of the real head of the Round Table, Alfred Milner.

brought to Oxford University to be taught the British view of life and to be sold the idea of a world government. It is remarkable how many 'Rhodes Scholars', as they are called, go on to become leaders of countries or heads of intelligence agencies, education, and other subject areas important to the Elite, or 'advisors' to those leaders. The most famous Rhodes Scholar in the world today is Bill Clinton, who was inaugurated as President of the United States in 1993. Oxford University, particularly the colleges of All Souls, Balliol, and New College, became dominated by the Round Table, and this continued after Rhodes's death when Alfred Milner (Comm 300), a Rothschild agent, took over the leadership. He, too, was an ardent follower of Ruskin, as were the group of former Oxford and Cambridge students whom Milner recruited for the Round Table and later, the Royal Institute of International Affairs. Under Milner's stewardship, the Round Table's influence grew and went on to enjoy tremendous power at the heart of government. Among its inner membership was Arthur Balfour (Comm 300),[3] the Foreign Secretary and Prime Minister, whose 'Balfour Declaration' would, in effect, bring the State of Israel into being.

In the years that followed, the Round Table controlled the London *Times* newspaper and other publications. It introduced the term 'a Commonwealth of Nations' and ensured that the idea became a reality. Through Milner, it was the chief influence in the British War Cabinet of Lloyd George (Comm 300) in the First World War. It would dominate the British delegation at the 'Peace' Conference of 1919, when the shape of the post-war world and German reparation payments were decided. It was also the major power behind the creation of the League of Nations, the first attempt at a world government by stealth. The Round Table decided British policy in Ireland, Palestine, and India from 1917–1945 and controlled (in the words of researcher Carroll Quigley) "the sources and writing of the history of British Imperial and foreign policy since the Boer War",[4] to an overwhelming extent. The rewriting of history is a vital part of the Elite's strategy because the way we perceive history fundamentally affects the way we see the world and each other today. George Orwell made the point in his book, *1984*, that those who control history control the present, and those who control the present control history.

Other branches of the Round Table were set up in other countries. By 1915, there were Round Table groups in Britain, South Africa, Canada, Australia, New Zealand, India, and the United States. The coordination between them was improved by the publication of the society's magazine, *The Round Table*, which began in November, 1910. The 'achievements' I've listed, which have had such an effect on our lives to the present day, were not

---

[3] Carroll Quigley, *The Anglo-American Establishment*, (Books In Focus, New York, 1981 edition) p312.
[4] Ibid p5.

the result of democratic decision making, but of the manoeuvrings of a secret society called The Round Table, working from its own agenda. Carroll Quigley, a professor at Georgetown University, was an 'insider' who was given access to secret papers on the New World Order conspiracy. He broke ranks and revealed in great detail what was happening behind the scenes in the first fifty years of this century. He wrote in his book, *The Anglo-American Establishment*:

> *"The picture is terrifying because such power, whatever the goals at which it may be directed, is too much to be entrusted safely to any group...No country that values its safety should allow what the Milner group accomplished – that is, that a small number of men would be able to wield such power in administration and politics, should be given almost complete control over the publication of documents relating to their actions, should be able to exercise such influence over the avenues of information that create public opinion, and should be able to monopolise so completely the writing and teaching of the history of their own period."* [5]

It is equally sobering to think that even though the Round Table network was directing the policies of the then most powerful country and empire in the world, the people didn't know such an organisation *existed*, never mind what it was doing. Ask anyone today, including most historians, about the Rhodes and Milner Round Table and they will reply, "the Round what?" The hidden hand that controls the direction of the world is indeed very *well* hidden from the public eye. The Round Table extended its influence across the Atlantic to the United States. It was there that the power blocs which would control political and economic policy and the communications industry – to the present day – were being assembled in the early years of this century. These were the organisations and the businesses of the so called 'Eastern Establishment', which work in concert with the British and European Round Table members under a common global policy. Among the central players and financial supporters of the Round Table in the United States were the Carnegie United Kingdom Trust, the companies and trusts in the nexus around the Rockefeller, J.P. Morgan, and Whitney families, along with others linked to the international financiers in London like the Rothschilds and Lazard Brothers. All these people were supporters of the world government ideals of the New World Order. The Round Table interconnected closely with other branches of the Elite including Freemasonry and, in the USA, with the sinister secret society based at Yale University known as the Skull and Bones Society. I will explain much more about this later. For now, I need only say that many of the influential American names behind the First

---

[5] Carroll Quigley, *Anglo-American Establishment*, p197.

World War and the Bolshevik Revolution were members of or had connections with the Skull and Bones Society.

The two names which dominated the Elite/Round Table network in America were Rockefeller and Morgan, who were both closely connected with and probably controlled by the Rothschilds (Comm 300). The Rockefellers (real name, Rockenfelder) are at the heart of the New World Order deception to this very day. J.D. Rockefeller started his Standard Oil Company in 1853 to produce the fuel for oil lamps, but, as the potential for oil was realised, it became a global company with tremendous power. In the early years of this century, the Rockefeller empire encompassed scores of other industries and interests, including railways and banks. They owned or controlled the National City Bank, the Hanover National Bank, the United States Trust Company, and leading insurance companies like Equitable Life and Mutual of New York. The Morgan empire was founded on steel, shipping, and the electricity industry, including General Electric. In the financial sector, the National Bank of Commerce, New York Life Insurance, and the Guaranty Trust Company, the biggest trust company in America, were all Morgan companies at that time.[6] Morgan/Rockefeller were quite a twosome, and no US government or politician could rule without their consent. They were in league with other American families of the Anglo-American political, banking, and business cartels in the Eastern Establishment, including the Dulles family. John Foster Dulles and his brother Allen will be another common thread in our story from the First World War to the Kennedy assassination. John Foster Dulles would become US Secretary of State and Allen, the head of the CIA.

One other name I should mention here is a family which will appear many times: Harriman. Edward Harriman started work at the age of fourteen with little education, but his fortunes changed after he married Mary Averell, the daughter of a New York banker and railroad president. Harriman built his own fortune with the Union Pacific Railroad, but he was a notoriously corrupt and ruthless businessman. In 1904, he was found guilty of a fraud which earned him $60 million in a deal that also implicated the Rothschild company, Kuhn Loeb and Co. Harriman stayed out of jail only by insider influence with politicians and their parties. His case was helped enormously by a $250,000 donation to the Republican National Committee of President Theodore Roosevelt. The Skull and Bones Society was working secretly in the background too. Roosevelt had earlier described Harriman as a man of 'deep-seated corruption', but the quarter of a million dollars helped the President to see him in a new light. Harriman money was involved in funding the Bolsheviks and both sides of the First World War. He and the

---

[6] This information on Rockefeller and Morgan holdings comes from *Wall Street And The Bolshevik Revolution* by Anthony C. Sutton, (Veritas Publishing, Morley, Western Australia, 1981) p49–50.

Rockefellers provided part of the start-up capital for the Morgan Guaranty Trust, which was to be the vehicle for enormous manipulation of world events. Edward Harriman had two sons, Averell and Roland, both pillars of the Skull and Bones Society. Averell (Comm 300) was to become one of the most active manipulators of the twentieth century.

But who was really behind these American business and banking giants? The J.P. Morgan empire began in 1838 as George Peabody and Company, in England. It had connections with the firm of Brown Brothers (later Brown Brothers, Harriman). George Peabody was working secretly as an agent of the Rothschilds as early as 1835[7] and he became known as Queen Victoria's 'favourite American'. A statue of George Peabody can be seen opposite the Bank of England today and his old lunchbox is still given a prominent place at the London office of the Morgan Stanley Bank. Peabody, the Rothschild frontman, became the biggest trader in American securities in the world; with his partner, John Peirpont Morgan (Comm 300), he put enormous pressure on the administration of Abraham Lincoln to manipulate the US economy for their personal benefit. Peabody had no sons and when he died his business was passed to Morgan's son, John Peirpont Morgan Jr (Comm 300), who was born in New York in 1867. This second J.P. Morgan was seen, like his father, as an all-powerful banker at the helm of his own empire, but he was almost certainly a vehicle for the House of Rothschild. Morgan was a direct descendent of Alexander Hamilton, the man who engineered the first US Central Bank, the Bank of the United States, in support of Rothschild interests. When the first J.P. Morgan died in 1913, he left only $11 million, a very modest sum, considering his reputation and the fortunes left by others. This is most likely to have been because he was a frontman for the Rothschilds and not all-powerful in his own right. The Wall Street reporter, Lincoln Steffens, interviewed both J.P. Morgan and J.D. Rockefeller, and he realised that they were not the real power behind their empires. "No-one ever seems to ask the question 'who is behind the Morgans and Rockefellers?'", he once wrote. It is noteworthy, too, that the Morgans had a reputation for being anti-Jewish while in fact working closely with the Rothschilds. This ploy of "anti-Semitism" is often used to camouflage Rothschild interests. The Rothschilds were most powerfully represented in the United States by the banking company known as Kuhn, Loeb, and Co. It was founded in 1867 by Abraham Kuhn and Solomon Loeb, two merchants from Cincinnati, but it became an obvious Rothschild front after 1875, when Jacob Schiff arrived from Frankfurt. Schiff was born in the Rothschild/Schiff house in Frankfurt, which the two families shared. The business arrangements between Schiff and Kuhn, Loeb, and Co were consummated (as so often happens in these cases) by the marriage of Schiff to Solomon Loeb's daughter, Therese. Schiff brought Rothschild capital into

---

[7] *The New Order, Our Secret Rulers*, p17.

the firm and ran it as a Rothschild front. George R. Conroy wrote in the December, 1912 issue of *Truth* magazine:

> *"Mr Schiff is head of the great private banking house of Kuhn, Loeb, and Co, which represents the Rothschild interests on this side of the Atlantic. He has been described as a financial strategist and has been for years the financial minister of the great impersonal power known as Standard Oil. He was hand-in-glove with the Harrimans, the Goulds, and the Rockefellers in all their railroad enterprises and has become the dominant power in the railroad and financial power of America."*

Schiff was the United States representative of the Rothschilds, a family who were supposed to have little influence or interest in America! It was also a Rothschild bank, the National City Bank of Cleveland, which financed the early expansion of the Rockefellers and the Harrimans. The Rockefellers and the Rothschilds (via Kuhn Loeb) would eventually merge some of their banking interests to form the Chase Manhattan Bank, one of the most influential banking operations in the world today.

In the early years of this century, the Elite's control was tightened still further and the structure became even more focussed and efficient. From the time of Cecil Rhodes, the Round Table Secret Society spawned a network of interconnecting groups in many countries working toward a common aim. But the two most important strongholds of the Round Table were Britain and the United States. At the Elite level were certain families and individuals on both sides of the Atlantic who worked together covertly in pursuit of the goal of world government, a world central bank, a world currency, and a world army. The technology for electronic money and a microchipped population would be added later. By now, certain names were appearing which would be involved in almost everything of global significance in the decades that followed: names like Rockefeller, Rothschild, Morgan, Harriman, Milner, Dulles, Warburg, Roosevelt, House, and Baruch. These names will become familiar as the conventional view of history is overturned.

Such names and organisations within the Elite/Illuminati/Brotherhood network have been behind the two World Wars, the Russian Revolution, the rise of Adolf Hitler, and the constant manipulation of the financial system. These events have kept humanity in fear and division, exactly as required. But it is a fair question to ask why would they support fascism, communism, and capitalism at the same time? And how could this help their plans for the New World Order? This has to be seen on many levels. Financially, wars and revolutions are very profitable for the bankers and suppliers. But there are wider reasons behind this. If you want nations to give up their sovereignty and hand over decisions and power to a world authority, it won't just happen. You have to make it happen by causing conflict between nations on the principle of problem-reaction-solution. The Elite, working in part through the Round Table network, wanted to cause so much pain and war between nation states that the public would say "something must be done". This something was intended to be a world authority all along.

They would try first to introduce this as the League of Nations after World War I and when that didn't quite work, another World War led to the United Nations. Both of these organisations were promoted as a means to keep the peace among nations by – to use Winston Churchill's famous phrase – "jaw, jaw, not war, war". But they were both Trojan horses for a global government, central bank, currency, and army. Look at what is happening within the United Nations today and you'll see how far the UN has already moved in this direction. The strategy the Elite/Round Table used in the two World Wars, the Russian Revolution, and countless other conflicts throughout this century has been attributed to a man called Hegel, although, in fact, this strategy was not developed by Hegel as such. His work was only a trigger for others who developed and changed his thinking to create a sinister phenomena. Hegel, himself, appears to have been a very genuine man. Put simply, the modified version of his thinking can be described as 'crisis management', which appears uncontrolled, but is, in fact, extremely calculated. 'Managed conflict' and 'controlled choice' would be even more accurate descriptions. The idea is to create the war and then win the peace in the way you restructure the devastated post-war world.

George Wilhelm Friedrich Hegel was a German philosopher, born in Stuttgart in 1770. During his life he could never have known what an effect a modified, materialistic version of the phenomena he identified would have on the world from that day to this. His observations about the spiritual development of the mind were developed and changed by others, including Karl Marx, and this modified version of Hegelianism expressed itself thus: If you create two opposing sides and bring them into conflict, you will create a third force, a synchronisation of both of them. It is known as thesis v antithesis = synthesis: a new order. Marx, a German, the inspiration of the Bolshevik revolutionaries, was a keen student of Hegel's work. The difference between them was that Hegel was talking of the spirit and mind while Marx rejected the idea of God and an afterlife. He was a materialist. To him, this world was all there was (or so he said publicly). As he once said: "I turned Hegel on his head". In doing so, he had also identified an incredibly effective tool in manipulating the world towards centralised control.

Marx and his German industrialist friend, Friedrich Engels, produced the Communist Manifesto. Engels, the promoter of freedom for the masses from the yoke of capitalism, had made a fortune exploiting child labour in Lancashire, England. The Communist Manifesto was nothing new and certainly not the inspiration of Karl Marx. He got his 'ideas' from the works of others, which he read during his countless hours in the British Museum. His belief in a class war came from Weishaupt and the Bavarian Illuminati.

As the American researcher, Gary Allen, writes in his 1972 book *None Dare Call It Conspiracy*:

> *"In actual fact the 'Communist Manifesto' was in circulation for many years before Marx's name was widely enough recognised to establish his authorship for this revolutionary handbook. All Karl Marx really did was to update and codify the very same revolutionary plans and principles set down seventy years earlier by Adam Weishaupt, the founder of the Order of the Illuminati in Bavaria."*

Marx was a member of a secret society in the Elite/Illuminati/Brotherhood network, called the League of the Just, which later became the Communist League. The League of the Just was an offshoot of the Society of the Seasons, which played a leading role in the French Revolution. Once again our eyes turn to Germany, birthplace of the Bavarian Illumaniti. The League of the Just was called the Bund Der Gerechtan or simply the Bund. This was the force behind the rise of Marxism and he was yet another front man. Interestingly, May 1st ('May Day'), was chosen as the annual celebration for Marxist-Leninist and socialist countries and groups around the world. The Bavarian Illuminati, the creator of the Bund, was founded on May 1st 1776. Marx had close connections with the British aristocracy through his marriage to Jenny von Westphalen, who was related to the Scottish Dukes of Argyll and the Campbells. One of her ancestors, Anna Campbell, the Countess of Balcarras and Argyll, was the governess to the Prince of Orange, later King William, who granted the charter to the Bank of England and caused such untold misery in Ireland. Archibald Campbell, the first Duke of Argyll, travelled with William on his journey to England to take the throne in 1688. The present Earl of Balcarras is related to Viscount Cowdray (Weetman John Churchill Pearson), whose mother was the daughter of Lord Spencer Churchill. These were some of the connections around the 'people's revolutionary', Karl Marx.

A tiny elite are coordinating all these apparently unconnected events. So when you see how the same people support and fund 'opposites' like Marxism-Leninism, fascism, and capitalism, it is not because they are confused or crazy. They are creating the opposing 'sides' which can then be brought into conflict to play one off against the other and create another force – New World Orderism. Thesis v antithesis = synthesis. This was expressed most obviously and destructively in the way the Elite created, funded, and brought capitalism and communism into conflict against fascism in the Second World War (*Figure 6 overleaf*). This created the desired synthesis: the United Nations and the European Community. The 'Cold War' between capitalism and communism is leading to another synthesis following the Elite-inspired 'people's revolutions' throughout the former

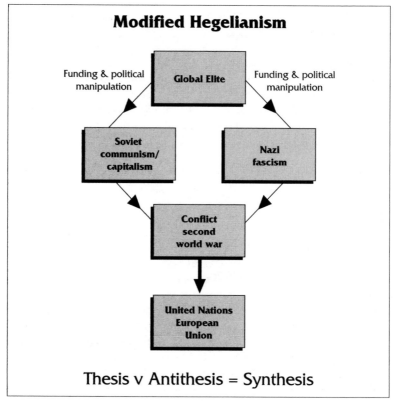

Figure 6

Soviet Union. People have been sold the line that political beliefs can be expressed at one extreme by communism (the far Left) and at the other by fascism (the far Right). This is part of the illusion to hide from us what is really going on. Fascism and communism are not opposites; they are merely promoted as such. Both involve central control by a tiny elite. The political spectrum is really freedom of expression, thought, and lifestyle at one end and authoritarianism (fascism/Marxism-Leninism) at the other. Yet we have people who are Marxists attacking fascists for their authoritarian policies and vice-versa! These 'opposites' are Elite-created to give the illusion of extremes which they can then use to create the conflict that leads to synthesis – the centralised global institutions they seek. And the political 'radicals', or what I call the 'Robot Radicals', have been duped into playing a crucial role in this. They still are.

By using the modified Hegel philosophy, the Elite and all these families and organisations have been involved in so much manipulation of the human race, that it would take a library of books to tell the full story. Even then, the interconnection and cross-referencing of names and organisations would be so complex as to be hardly comprehensible. Boring you to death is not my ambition. At the same time, I want to include enough detail to show that the idea that an elite few can and do control the world and your life is no 'theory', but provable fact. Therefore, in the rest of this chapter, I'm going to concentrate on the three major events in the early years of this century which show that the version of history we are given in the schools and the media is considerably less than the truth. Those events are the First World War, the Russian Revolution, and the creation of the State of Israel. The same few people manipulated all of them.

THE FIRST WORLD WAR

Kaiser Wilhelm II was ruler of Germany in the early years of this century, but Elite-placed men in his administration were manipulating policy, just as they were in Great Britain (Milner) and in the United States (Colonel House). The assassination of Archduke Ferdinand, the heir to the Austro-Hungarian throne, was used as the excuse for war, but the conflict had been decided upon long before. The Austrians accused Serbia of the murder and declared war. The assassination was carried out on June 28th 1914 by a Serbian Secret Society, controlled by the Elite, called the Black Hand. Ferdinand went with his wife to Sarajevo in Bosnia. Six assassins were waiting for him as his car was driven to his appointment. As the car went past them, all six failed to kill him and the Archduke appeared to have survived the attack. But his chauffeur became 'confused', took a 'wrong turning', and finally stopped the car in front of one of the would-be assassins, Gavrilo Princip, who took full advantage of his second opportunity. Ferdinand had told his friend, Count Czerin, that he knew an attempt on his life was imminent because he had been told the year before that the Freemasons had decided to kill him. Meanwhile – at exactly the same time in Russia – Grigory Yefimovitch Rasputin, the Tsar's most influential advisor (who opposed the war), was being attacked with a knife in an unsuccessful assassination attempt in Pokrovskoe. As author Colin Wilson says in his book, *Rasputin*:

> *"There are fifty degrees of longitude between Sarajevo and Pokrovskoe, which means that eleven o'clock in Sarajevo is about 2.15 in Pokrovskoe. It is a strange coincidence that two assassins struck at almost exactly the same moment – a coincidence that makes one inclined to doubt the 'blindness of history'. Ferdinand's death made war probable; Rasputin's injury made it certain, for he was the only man in Russia capable of averting it."*

Kaiser Wilhelm, urged on by his Brotherhood advisors, supported Austria and declared war on Russia and France. The 'Great War' was underway. One of its main architects was the Kaiser's Chancellor, Bethmann-Hollweg, a member of the Bethmann banking family in Frankfurt and a cousin of the

Rothschilds.[8] Britain came in against Germany, and the United States followed suit in 1917. America was always going to enter the war, as public opinion was whipped up by the media. Kent Cooper, the President of Associated Press, wrote in the November 13th 1944 issue of *Life*:

> *"Before and during the First World War, the great German news agency, Wolff, was owned by the European banking house of Rothschild, which had its central headquarters in Berlin. A leading member of the firm was also Kaiser Wilhelm's personal banker (Max Warburg). What actually happened in Imperial Germany was that the Kaiser used Wolff to bind and excite his people to such a degree that they were eager for World War I. Twenty years later under Hitler the pattern was repeated and enormously magnified by DNB, Wolff's successors."*

In his autobiography, *Barriers Down*, Cooper added that the House of Rothschild bought an interest in the three leading European news agencies: Wolff in Germany, Havas in France, and Reuters in England. For those who don't know how the media works, the news agencies provide news stories to all papers and media outlets, so what they say is often repeated by the whole of the media. "It must be true because they're all saying it" is what I hear people say. They are all saying it because they are printing the same information from the same source – the news agency. It is worth noting that on April 28th 1915, Baron Herbert de Reuter, the head of the Reuters agency, 'committed suicide'. This followed the collapse of the Reuters Bank. The Baron was replaced by Sir Roderick Jones, who reports in his autobiography that "...Shortly after I succeeded Baron Herbert de Reuter in 1915, it so happened that I received an invitation from Mr Alfred Rothschild, then head of the British House of Rothschild, to lunch with him at the historic New Court, in the City". What they discussed, he declines to reveal. What do you think?

Amazing as it may seem at first, the connections between the Jewish House of Rothschild and the creation of World Wars (in which so many Jewish people suffered appallingly) are beginning to mount.

It was part of the Elite's strategy to involve the US and increase the post-war demands for a world authority to stop further wars. This was not too much of a problem because the president, Woodrow Wilson, did whatever his chief 'advisor', Colonel House (Comm 300), told him to do. In 1915, the German sinking of the American 'passenger' ship, the Lusitania, was an excuse for the US to declare war, just as the assassination of Ferdinand had been for the Germans, and the attack on Pearl Harbor would be for the Americans in World War II. The Lusitania was sailed into an area of known German U-boat activity without an escort, and the people on board were

---

[8] *The New Order, Our Secret Rulers*, p10.

sacrificed to satisfy the Elite's horrific ambitions. In the archives of the US Treasury Department, President Wilson concealed proof that the Lusitania was carrying military supplies for the British.[9] It was not the 'passengers-only' vessel it was claimed to be as part of the propaganda to outrage American public opinion. Alfred Gwynne Vanderbilt of the Eastern Establishment family was on the Lusitania when it sank. A telegram had been delivered to the ship before it left New York warning Vanderbilt not to sail, but it never reached him and it cost him his life. Someone obviously knew exactly what was planned.

The manipulation of America into the war was coordinated through three main organisations: the Council on National Defense, the Navy League, and the League to Enforce Peace. Among the members of the Council on National Defense was the Rothschild agent, Bernard Baruch. As head of the War Industries Board during the war, Baruch had, in his own words "...probably more power than perhaps any other man did in the war...".[10] The Navy League was dominated by J.P. Morgan. Among the principals of the League to Enforce Peace were Elihu Root, J.P. Morgan's lawyer; Perry Belmont,[11] the Rothschild's US agent; and Jacob Schiff of the Rothschild's Kuhn, Loeb, and Co. The assistant secretary of the Navy at this time was one Franklin Delano Roosevelt, who was awarding big navy contracts well before there was any talk of America joining the war – just as he would a few years later, when he was president before and during the Second World War.

Another confirmation that the First World War was engineered for longer term reasons came in the 1950s, with the findings of a US Congressional investigation by the Reece Committee into the Carnegie Endowment for International Peace. It was found to be an organisation dedicated to creating war! This organisation is one of a network of so-called tax-exempt foundations started by the Carnegie, Rockefeller, and Ford families, which help to fund the New World Order plan. Norman Dodd, the Reece Committee's Director of Research, reported the findings of his investigator Kathryn Casey: Dodd said that at one meeting of the Carnegie trustees, the question was asked: "Is there any means known to man more effective than war if you want to alter the lives of an entire people?" It was decided that there was not, and so the next question for the trustees was, "How do we involve the United States in a war?" Dodd went on:

> *"And then they raised the question: 'How do we control the diplomatic machinery of the United States?' And the answer came out: 'We must control the State Department'. At this point we catch up with what we had already*

[9] Jim Keith, *Casebook On Alternative 3*, (IllumiNet Press, Lilburn, USA, 1994) p20.
[10] Said at a hearing of the post-war Graham Committee, which investigated Baruch.
[11] Perry Belmont was the son of August Belmont, the banker who was the Rothschild agent financing and manipulating the Union side in the American 'War of Independence'.

*found out…that through an agency set up by the Carnegie Endowment, every
high appointment in the State Department was cleared. Finally, we were in a
war. These trustees in a meeting about 1917 had the brashness to congratulate
themselves on the wisdom of their original decision because already the impact
of the war had indicated it would alter life and can alter life in this country.
This was the date of our entry in the war; we were involved. **They even had
the brashness to word and to dispatch a telegram to Mr Wilson,
cautioning him to see that the war did not end too quickly.**"* [12] [my
emphasis]

Dodd said that Kathryn Casey then found other minutes, dealing with the
work of the Carnegie Endowment to prevent American life returning to its
pre-war state. Changing the way people lived and thought was, after all, the
main point of the war. Dodd reported that:

*"…they came to the conclusion that, to prevent a reversion, they must
control education. And then they approached the Rockefeller Foundation and
they said: 'Will you take on the acquisition of control of education as it
involves subjects that are domestic in their significance'. And it was agreed.
Then together, they decided that the key to it was the teaching of American
history and they must change that. So, they then approached the most
prominent of what we might call American historians at that time with the idea
of getting them to alter the manner in which they presented the subject."* [13]

This is why most of the information in this book about the real
background to world events has never been taught in the schools or
universities. If you are not being allowed to know the full story about
something, it is because (from the manipulators' point of view) it is
dangerous for you to know. That is my motivation in writing this book. You
have a right to be dangerous!

THE RUSSIAN REVOLUTION

With the First World War underway, another Elite coup was reaching
fruition, the Russian Revolution of 1917. This took the same form as the
French Revolution. The Elite created economic chaos and the ruling
dictator, the Tsar, played into their hands by refusing to introduce democracy
and empowerment for the people. In 1905, the Tsar was manipulated by the
Rothschilds into a war with Japan to undermine the Russian economy and
sow the seeds of unrest among the population. The Rothschilds told the Tsar

---

[12/13] Norman Dodd reported these findings in an interview with writer, William H. McIlhany II,
for his 1980 book, *The Tax Exempt Foundations*, (Arlington House, Westport, USA). The Special
House Committee to Investigate Tax Exempt Foundations reported in 1954. It was named after
its chairman, representative B. Carroll Reece, of Tennessee.

that they would finance the war, while in the United States, the Rothschild company, Kuhn, Loeb, and Co, was secretly funding the Japanese. Then the war with Germany came in 1914, during which the Russian Army was constantly weakened by outside influences. One way the Elite have controlled wars is to send inferior weapons to the side they want to lose or to delay the delivery of armaments altogether. In 1915, the British Chancellor of the Exchequer and soon-to-be Prime Minister, Lloyd George (Comm 300), realised that armaments ordered for the Russian Army were five months overdue. At one point there was only one rifle for every six soldiers. This fuelled the fires of revolution, exactly as planned. The Elite wanted to demoralise the Russian soldiers so they would mutiny. The company responsible for the delay was Vickers Maxim, which was controlled by Sir Ernest Cassel, a business associate of the Rothschilds' Kuhn, Loeb, and Company. The largest holder of Vickers stock was the House of Rothschild.[14] The British Cabinet dispatched Lord Kitchener to Russia to reorganise their army, but he was drowned on the way when the HMS Hampshire 'mysteriously' sank on the night of June 5th 1916. Just another coincidence, I guess.

In Russia, dissension was being stirred. The first (and more moderate) revolution was begun by a Freemason, Alexander Kerensky. I say 'first', in fact there was another revolution even before this, headed by Prince Lvov. He planned to create an American-style Republic and by this time Tsar Nicholas II had already abdicated. But, as in France when the momentum for revolution had been triggered, along came the next, more terrifying stage. Trotsky and Lenin arrived to take over and introduce the despotic rule known as Marxism-Leninism. This was not a Russian Revolution. It was a coup on Russia by the United States financial arm of the Global Elite largely controlled by the Rothschilds. Leon Trotsky, who had been living in New York after being expelled from Germany, left for Petrograd, Russia, on the SS Kristianiafjord on March 26th 1917, with $10,000 given to him by the Rockefellers.[15] In his hand was a United States passport arranged for him by President Woodrow Wilson. Jennings C. Wise says in his study, *Woodrow Wilson: Disciple Of Revolution*: "Historians must never forget that Woodrow Wilson, despite the efforts of the British police, made it possible for Leon Trotsky to enter Russia with an American passport".[16] This happened at a time when the US authorities were supposed to be tightening their checks on potential revolutionaries entering Russia on United States passports! But who controlled Wilson? The Elite's representative, Colonel Edward House

---

[14] *The New Order, Our Secret Rulers*, p35.

[15] *The New Order, Our Secret Rulers*, p76. The Rockfellers have made unthinkable amounts of money by exploiting Russia and the Soviet Union and manipulating their men into place, such as President Gorbachev.

[16] Jennings C. Wise, *Woodrow Wilson: Disciple Of Revolution*, (Paisley Press, New York, 1938).

(Comm 300). When the ship docked in Canada en route, Trotsky was detained by the Canadian authorities, but he was released and allowed to continue his journey to Russia. Lieutenant Colonel John Bayne MacLean, the founder and President of Maclean Publishing, was known for his close contacts with Canadian Intelligence. In 1918, he wrote an article which appeared in his own *MacLean's Magazine*, headed "Why Did We Let Trotsky Go? How Canada Lost The Chance To Shorten The War".[17] MacLean made a number of revelations about Trotsky, many of which have been confirmed or supported by evidence that has come to light since then. He said that Trotsky was not Russian, but German, and other intelligence information has suggested that he spoke better German than Russian.[18] MacLean's sources said Trotsky had been very publicly 'expelled' from Germany in August 1914 to give him credibility for what was to follow. MacLean said that other Russian revolutionaries organised by Trotsky in the United States and Western Canada were "largely Germans and Austrians travelling as Russians". MacLean went on:

> "Originally the British found through Russian associates that Kerensky, Lenin, and some lesser leaders were practically in German pay as early as 1915 and they uncovered in 1916 the connections with Trotsky, then living in New York. From that time he was closely watched by the Bomb Squad. In the early part of 1916, a German official sailed into New York. British Intelligence officials accompanied him. He [Trotsky] was held up at Halifax, but on their [British Intelligence] instruction, he was passed on with profuse apologies for the unnecessary delay. After much manoeuvring, he arrived in a dirty little newspaper office in the slums and there he found Trotsky, for whom he bore important instructions. From June 1916, until they passed him onto the British, the New York Bomb Squad never lost touch with Trotsky. They discovered that his real name was Braunstein[19] and that he was German, not a Russian."

Interestingly, if this is correct, both communism and fascism (which came into conflict in the Second World War) were created to a large extent in the same country – Germany, the home of so many Elite secret societies and birthplace of Adam Weishaupt's Bavarian Illuminati. After Trotsky arrived in Russia, he was joined by Lenin, who had been given safe passage across Germany in a sealed train, from Switzerland to Russia via Sweden, in April 1917, accompanied by thirty-two other 'revolutionaries'. The trip was approved and paid for by the German General Staff under orders from

---

[17] Quoted by Anthony C. Sutton in *Wall Street And The Bolshevik Revolution*, (Morley, Australia, 1981) p32–33.

[18] Ibid.

[19] The more widely accepted spelling is Bronstein.

German Supreme Command. The Germans were also spending big sums to fund the Bolshevik's propaganda inside Russia. Von Kuhmann, the Foreign Affairs Minister, told the Kaiser in 1917:

> *"It was not until the Bolsheviks had received from us a steady flow of funds through the various channels and under varying labels that they were in a position to be able to build up their organ,* Pravda, *to conduct energetic propaganda and appreciably to extend the originally narrow base of their party."* [20]

The plan was that the re-revolution would withdraw Russia from the First World War and make 'peace' with Germany. This is precisely what happened. Once more, these events are multidimensional. The Russian 'revolutionaries' such as Lenin and Trotsky were being used to get Russia out of the war, to the benefit of Germany. But at the Elite level, the bogeyman called communism was being created to stimulate the division of fear and mistrust presented as communism v capitalism v fascism. Once you have fear caused by two or more distinct 'sides', you have divide and rule: control. Fear is also the greatest producer of negative energy. While Trotsky, Lenin, and their crowd were denouncing the capitalists, they were being financed by the London and New York bankers. Trotsky was quoted in the Russian newspaper, *Russkoe,* as saying that the "Soviet cannot align itself…with capitalist Americans, for this would be a betrayal". Oh really, Leon? In fact, Trotsky and the Bolsheviks were supported financially and politically by the same people who would support Hitler and the fascists because the Elite has no political line. In his autobiography, Trotsky refers to some of the loans from British financiers. Many of these were arranged by Lord Milner (Comm 300) of the Round Table and 'Alexander' Gruzenberg (real name Michael), the chief Bolshevik agent in Scandinavia, who was a confidential advisor to the J.P. Morgan-owned Chase National Bank in New York. This was a London-New York revolution, with the Russian people once again the victims.

A Mr Fixit between London, Wall Street, and the Bolsheviks was Olof Aschberg, who became known as the Bolshevik Banker. He owned Nya Banken, founded in Stockholm in 1912. Aschberg's London agent was the North Commerce Bank, chaired by Earl Grey, a friend of Cecil Rhodes and a member of the Round Table. Another close associate of Aschberg was Max May, the vice president of J.P. Morgan's Guaranty Trust and head of its overseas operations. Clearly Aschberg was the perfect middle man to channel funds from London and New York to the Bolsheviks. In 1915, the American International Corporation was formed to fund the Russian Revolution. Its directors represented the interests of the Rockellers, Rothschilds, DuPont,

[20] *Wall Street And The Bolshevik Revolution,* p39.

Kuhn, Loeb, Harriman, and the Federal Reserve. They included Frank Vanderlip (one of the Jekyl Island Group which created the Federal Reserve) and George Herbert Walker, the grandfather of President George Bush.

The Rothschilds were also directly involved in financing the revolution via Jacob Schiff, at Kuhn, Loeb, and Co in New York. International bankers from Britain, the United States, Russia, Germany, and France met in Sweden in the summer of 1917. They agreed that Kuhn, Loeb would deposit $50 million in a Swedish bank account for Lenin and Trotsky's use. In an article in *The New York American Journal* on February 3rd 1949, Jacob Schiff's grandson said that his grandfather had paid the two 'revolutionaries' an additional $20 million. The payment of $20 million to the Bolsheviks by Elihu Root (the Kuhn Loeb lawyer and former Secretary of State), via a Special War Fund, is recorded in the Congressional Record of September 2nd 1919. It was quite an investment if, as some researchers suggest, Lenin repaid Kuhn, Loeb, and Co the rouble equivalent of $450 million between 1918 and 1922. And this was nothing compared with the profits the bankers made from the exploitation of the Russian land, economy, and people, not least by stealing the Tsar's gold and vast financial holdings which were held abroad in the very banks that funded the revolution.

In 1917, the Elite used the cover of a Red Cross mission to Russia to arrange the final details of the Bolshevik takeover. The Red Cross in Washington launched a campaign to raise $2 million. It was successful thanks only to substantial donations from New York financiers, including J.P. Morgan himself, who gave $100,000. The bankers and industrialists proceeded to take control of the United States Red Cross and, as the Elite's John Foster Dulles put it, they "viewed the American Red Cross as a virtual arm of government…".[21] The personnel of this mission to Russia in August 1917 says it all. Only *seven* of the party of twenty-four were doctors. The rest were mostly New York financiers and their assistants, led by William Boyce Thompson (Comm 300), the first full-time head of the Federal Reserve Bank of New York. The doctors returned after only one month and Dr Frank Billings, Professor of Medicine at the University of Chicago and the official leader of the mission, was reported to have been disgusted with the obviously political activities of its non-medical members. Also in the party were three Russian interpreters, all known Bolsheviks. One of them, Boris Reinstein, would become secretary to Lenin and head of the Bureau of International Revolutionary Propaganda.[22] The Red Cross has been used on many occasions by the Elite without the knowledge of its genuine staff. This is not only an insult to the work the Red Cross is seeking to do, it is also extremely dangerous for the 99% who are genuinely working for that organisation out of compassion for the plight of the world's peoples.

---

[21] John Foster Dulles, *American Red Cross*, (Harper, New York, 1950).
[22] *Wall Street And The Bolshevik Revolution*, p78.

Intriguingly, the Red Cross symbol is also that of the Knights Templar, the flag of England, and the symbol which Columbus flew on his ships while 'discovering' the 'New World' on behalf of the Templars. The Red Cross was formed during the Elite-engineered Franco-Prussian War in 1870 via correspondence in our old friend, the London *Times*.

At the same time that these elite bankers were creating organisations to support the Bolsheviks, they were also funding and setting up *anti*-Bolshevik organisations. Otto Kahn and members of the Morgan Guaranty Trust formed a group called United Americans, which circulated anti-communist and anti-Jewish propaganda. This allowed genuine opponents of the revolution to be dismissed as 'anti-Semitic'. This has continued to happen up to the present day, with the Robot Radicals of the "I'm full of my own political purity" mindset dancing on the strings pulled by the Global Elite to denounce anyone who gets close to the truth as an 'anti-Semite'. The same is happening to me today. It's all so predictable. The Robot Radicals and their 'opposition', the Robot Right, have their strings pulled by the same people! It's hilarious, really.

On his way back from Russia, William Boyce Thompson stopped over in London to meet the British Prime Minister, Lloyd George. They were joined by Thomas W. Lamont of J.P. Morgan, who had travelled from Paris (where he had been in discussion with Colonel Edward House on how to rearrange the world after the war). House had cabled President Wilson on November 28th 1917, urging him to suppress all media criticism of the Bolsheviks: "It is exceedingly important that such criticism be suppressed", the cable said. This telegram was placed in a confidential file and came to light only six years later. Researcher, Carroll Quigley, said that the House of Morgan was infiltrating Left-wing groups in the United States from around 1915. It was the strategy to hijack both 'Left' and 'Right' domestically and internationally.[23]

The Russian Revolution was all part of the Big Plan, which is why the leading officials of the Rothschild-controlled Federal Reserve Bank of New York, including Thompson, supported the Bolsheviks. In this period, we are seeing the Global Elite deciding on the post-war policies and ensuring that the puppet-politicians make it happen. Thompson and Lamont met Lloyd George to convince him that the British government's anti-Bolshevik stance was misguided and should encompass the reality that Lenin and Trotsky were there to stay.[24] Lloyd George and his Cabinet – including the Round Table's Lord Milner, of course – accepted the Thompson-Lamont view. When you have agents of the Elite in vital positions on all sides in this way, you can

---

[23] Carroll Quigley, *Tragedy And Hope*, (Macmillan, New York, 1966) p938. This book so angered the manipulators that it was withdrawn from the shelves. Only the pirated edition is available today.

[24] *Wall Street And The Bolshevik Revolution*, p46.

pretty much do what you like. The British decision to back the Bolsheviks is less surprising when you consider that Lloyd George was not a free agent in this. His private life left him open to blackmail and he was under obligations to an international armaments dealer called Basil Zaharoff (who made a fortune selling arms to both sides in any war he could find). Zaharoff had a hold over Lloyd George after he arranged for the Prime Minister to have an affair with his wife, formerly Emily Ann Burrows of Knightsbridge. Zaharoff also sold peerages created by Lloyd George.[25] In the 1963 book, *The Mask Of Merlin,*[26] the writer Donald McCormick says that Zaharoff had so much power that "Allied statesmen and leaders were obliged to consult him before planning any great attack". Woodrow Wilson, Lloyd George, and the French Prime Minister, Georges Clemenceau, met a number of times at Zaharoff's Paris home. This is relevant to the Allied policy on Russia because Zaharoff was supporting the Bolsheviks and diverting arms away from those opposing them. He, too, intervened on the Bolsheviks' behalf in both London and Paris.

In April 1919, the British Foreign Office issued a nine pence White Paper on Russia which revealed that the revolution had been organised and financed by international bankers. It explained how "Chinese criminals" had been imported to serve under Bolshevik officers in a terror campaign against the people of Russia. This document was quickly withdrawn and replaced with a six pence version – minus this information.[27] Some claim that the Bolshevik Revolution was a Jewish Revolution, but I think that Rabbi Marvin S. Antelman reads the situation perfectly when he writes:

> "The truth of the matter was...that there was a conspiracy, but it was neither Jewish, nor Catholic, nor Masonic. It involved people of all types of religions and national backgrounds. Side by side with the Schiffs, Warburgs, and Rothschilds were the Morgans and the Rockefellers. With Trotsky were Lenin and Stalin." [28]

What was the common theme between them? The cult of the All-Seeing Eye. With the revolution established, the Elite arranged for its intelligence personnel to be sent to Russia. Alfred Milner selected an agent, Bruce

[25] *The World Order, Our Secret Rulers*, p37. A knighthood cost £10,000 to £12,000, of which £5,000 went to Lloyd George, according to author Eustace Mullins.
[26] Donald McCormick, *The Mask Of Merlin*, (MacDonald, London, 1963) p208. McCormick also claims that British Intelligence discovered documents which proved that government officials were secret agents of Zaharoff – with the knowledge of Lloyd George!
[27] Dr Kitty Little, "Subversive Infiltrators Into Westminster And Whitehall. Promotion Of A Federal Europe." Submission to the Nolan Committee on Standards in Public Life, (January 1995) p4, paragraph 16.
[28] Rabbi Marvin S. Antelman, *To Eliminate The Opiate*, p15.

Lockhart (Comm 300), to go to Russia and to team up with the American, Raymond Robins, who had been left behind by William Boyce Thompson to lead the – now doctorless – 'Red Cross' mission through 1918. The French chose to send the Bolshevik supporter, Jacques Sadoul, an old friend of Trotsky. The conspiracy then had control of the diplomatic and intelligence reports coming out of Russia to their governments. With that, the coup by the Global Elite on the Russian people was complete. Lenin and Trotsky proceeded to dismantle any institutions and groups of workers which had emerged from the early days of the revolution. The hated Okhrana, the 'secret service' of the Tsars, was revamped into what eventually became the KGB. The 'People's Revolution', which would turn hundreds of millions of people into little more than prisoners in their own land and cause the death and suffering of so many in the concentration camps, had massively advanced the aims of the New World Order. The Soviet card would be played with great effect in the decades that followed.

THE CREATION OF THE STATE OF ISRAEL

Another Elite ambition during the First World War was to ensure the recognition by Britain of a Jewish homeland in what was then Arab Palestine. The political movement known as Zionism had been introduced to campaign for a Jewish homeland, but it is often misunderstood: all Jewish people are not Zionists and all Zionists are not Jewish. Zionism is not a religion or a race; it is a *political movement* consisting of people, Jews and non-Jews, who support the claim for a Jewish homeland. If you support that, you are a Zionist, too, no matter what your race or religious belief. To say that Zionism is the Jewish race is like saying the British Labour Party is the English race. Zionism was founded in the last century by an atheist, Theodore Herzl, and it is used as a front for the Global Elite and a means to dupe Jewish people as a whole. The offer to recognise a homeland in Palestine was designed both to persuade the United States to enter the war and later to create 'managed conflict' and a situation of 'divide and rule' in the oil-rich Middle East. More than twenty years after the First World War, on April 25th 1939, US Senator Gerald P. Nye of North Dakota revealed to the Senate some of the background to Britain's recognition of a Jewish homeland and the First World War in general. He said he had been given some documents called 'The Next War'. The title referred to the Second World War, which the writers of the documents already knew was going to happen. One volume, called 'Propaganda in the Next War', also discussed, in passing, how the American people had been tricked into fighting in World War I. It said:

> *"For some time the issue as to which side the United States would take hung in the balance, the final result was a credit to our British propaganda. There remain the Jews. It has been estimated that of the world Jewish*

population of approximately fifteen million, no fewer than five million are in
the United States; 25% of the inhabitants of New York are Jews.

"During the Great War we bought off this huge American Jewish public by
the promise of the Jewish national home in Palestine, held by Ludendorf to be
a master stroke of allied propaganda, as it enabled us not only to appeal to
Jews in America, but to Jews in Germany as well." [29]

The Americans entered the war in 1917. The Balfour Declaration came
on November 6th of that year, when Arthur (Lord) Balfour (Comm 300),
the British Foreign Secretary and member of the Round Table's inner elite,
officially recognised Palestine as a homeland for Jewish people. We need to
look at this on many levels again. The propagandists may well have believed
it was a 'master stroke' to bring America into the war, but what they didn't
know was that they were being manipulated to manipulate others. America
was coming into the war anyway. A Jewish homeland in Palestine had been
a long-time Elite strategy and the guise of bringing America into the war
was used to encourage British politicians to accept it. The Balfour
Declaration was a terrible blow to the Arabs who had, under the leadership
and promises of the Englishman, T.E. Lawrence ('Lawrence of Arabia'),
fought on Britain's behalf against the Turks and they played a crucial role in
winning the war. The Arabs were promised full post-war sovereignty and
independence for their support and this was confirmed in official
correspondence. Lawrence, a close friend of Winston Churchill (Comm
300), knew full well that he was lying to the Arabs he was leading. Some
years later Lawrence said:

> *"I risked the fraud on my conviction that Arab help was necessary to our*
> *cheap and speedy victory in the East, and that better we win and break our*
> *word, than lose…The Arab inspiration was our main tool for winning the*
> *Eastern War. So I assured them that England kept her word in letter and in*
> *spirit. In this comfort they performed their fine things; but, of course, instead*
> *of being proud of what we did together, I was continually bitter and*
> *ashamed."* [30]

While Lawrence and the British were promising the Arabs independence,
they were in the process of making a commitment to give away Palestine as a
Jewish homeland. Lawrence, Milner, and Victor Rothschild all knew each
other. The Balfour Declaration was not an announcement by the Foreign
Secretary to the House of Commons. It took the form, appropriately, of a
letter between Arthur Balfour (Comm 300), of the Rothschild-funded
Round Table, and Lord Lionel Walter Rothschild (Comm 300), the

---

[29] Congressional Record, 76th Congress, Vol. 84, No. 82, p6597–6604.
[30] "Documents on British Foreign Policy, 1919-1939", first series Vol. IV, p245–247.

representative of the English Federation of Zionists, which was set up with Rothschild money. It was written by the leading voice in Lloyd George's wartime cabinet, the Round Table's most influential figure, Lord Milner (who was made chairman of Rio Tinto Zinc by Lord Rothschild).[31] The Balfour Declaration was a decree by the Rothschilds/Global Elite and not part of any democratic process. Balfour's letter *to* Lord Rothschild, believed by many to have been written *by* Lord Rothschild, in league with Alfred Milner, said:

> *"I have much pleasure in conveying to you, on behalf of His Majesty's Government, the following declaration of sympathy with Jewish Zionist aspirations which has been submitted to, and approved by, the Cabinet: His Majesty's Government view with favour the establishment in Palestine of a national home for the Jewish people, and will use their best endeavours for the achievement of this object, it being clearly understood that nothing shall be done which may prejudice the civil and religious rights of existing non-Jewish communities in Palestine [what a joke!], or the rights and political status enjoyed by Jews in any other country. I should be grateful if you would bring this declaration to the knowledge of the Zionist Federation."*

At the time less than one per cent of the population of Palestine was Jewish and yet this letter was to form the basis on which the post-war world was to be divided and Arab control of Palestine handed over. It had nothing to do with what was best for Jews, even though its architects, the Rothschilds, are Jewish if only in name. It was about the wider strategic oil and New World Order possibilities that a foothold in that part of the Middle East would offer. I believe that Rabbi Marvin S. Antelman is correct when he links the House of Rothschild with the All-Seeing Eye clique which is seeking to destroy Judaism. Things may be done in the name of Jewish people as a whole, but they are not done for their benefit. Jewish people are used as fodder by the Elite and by many within the Jewish hierarchy. Nor is it true that most Jewish people today have a genetic line back to ancient Israel, a claim used to justify the occupation of Palestine. For the same reason, the term 'anti-Semitic' is constantly misused.

Personally, I don't care about the colour and genetic line of a person's physical body. It is a vehicle for experience, that's all. We are aspects of each other. But since many people use the genetics of their bodies to justify their

---

[31] Insider, Carroll Quigley, writing in *The Anglo-American Establishment*, says: "This declaration, which is always known as the Balfour Declaration, should rather be called the 'Milner Declaration', since Milner was the actual draftsman and was, apparently, its chief supporter in the War Cabinet. This fact was not made public until 21 July 1937" (p169). So Lord Milner, the leading light in the Round Table, wrote the Balfour Declaration in a letter to Lord Rothschild, who funded and controlled the Round Table! What chance did the Palestinians ever have of justice?

actions, we might as well get the information right. The word Semitic comes from the race of peoples in ancient Sumer from whom the biblical Jews claimed to have emerged. Sem or Shem, one of the sons of Noah in the Bible stories, is said to be of this line and the origin appears to have been the legend of 'Shemjaza', the 'heavenly son and guardian angel of God'. Another extraterrestrial almost certainly. But according to several Jewish writers, including Arthur Koestler in his book, *The Thirteenth Tribe*,[32] very few Jews today can trace their genetic ancestry back to the Semite line of this period and/or the Semitic line in Palestine and Israel at the time of Y'shua (Jesus). Instead, they are the genetic descendants of a people of Turkish-Mongolian-Nordic ancestry called the Khazars who *converted* to the Jewish religion in 740 AD.

The Khazars lived in lower Russia between the Black and Caspian Seas. They were between the Christian and Islamic worlds and their leader chose to accept the Jewish faith to avoid being swamped by the empires of the perceived alternatives. Most Jews today, Koestler says, originate from these people, not the Semitic line. In fact, to call someone 'anti-Semitic' is, more accurately, to call them 'anti-Arab', because more members of the old Semite race are Arab than are Jewish!

After the breakup of the Khazar empire by the thirteenth century, the people who adopted the Jewish faith either stayed on in Russia or, in the case of the majority, moved on into what became the Balkans, Lithuania, Poland, and Germany. The language known as Yiddish emerged from these events. It is a mixture of Hebrew, Polish, and German. The name Rothschild came from the Red Shield, the symbol of the Khazar "Jews" in eastern Europe (German: rotes schild = red shield). The Rothschild family have no more an historic link to Palestine than an eskimo.[33] The 'Jewish' hooked nose does not originate from the biblical Israel. It has its genetic origins in the Caucasus. The classic Jewish face of Y'shua (Jesus) is a myth. He would not have looked anything like that because he was not born in Lower Russia. As Koestler wrote, "Anthropology concurs with history in refuting the popular belief in a Jewish race descended from the biblical tribe". The Jewish-born Christian bishop, Hugh Montefiore, said in the *Church Times* of January 24th 1992, that: "Anti-Semitism is built on a powerful racial myth, accepted by Jews and anti-Semites alike". Yet it is members of the genetic stream which has no connection whatsoever with Palestine, who were behind the creation of Israel and today's continued suppression of Palestinian rights.

The Jewish writer Alfred M. Lilienthal goes further. He says there is no such thing as a Jewish "race". To be "Jewish" is to follow the Jewish religious

[32] Arthur Koestler, *The Thirteenth Tribe – The Khazar Empire And Its Heritage*, (originally published by Hutchinson & Co in 1976). See also Douglas Reed's *Controllers Of Zion*, (Dolphin Press, 1978).
[33] *Secret Societies*, p39.

faith and has nothing to do with race because, he says, people of endless races converted to the Jewish faith over thousands of years, so creating a vast cocktail of different genetic streams who called themselves Jewish. In his courageous book, *What Price Israel?*, Lilienthal points out:

> "*The most persuasive argument the Jewish nationalist could advance for Zionism is based on the hypothesis of a 'Hebrew-Semitic race'. But most members of such a 'race' would be found amongst the Arabic peoples of the Middle East, the overwhelming majority of whom do not profess the Jewish faith. The Arabs, bitter enemies of the Israelis who have returned to their reported 'racial home', most closely resemble those Jews who are indigenous to Palestine and the Middle East; for they are of poorer Hebrew-Israelite blood than most of those who have been 'ingathered'…The allegation that Arabs are anti-Semitic is somewhat ludicrous.*
>
> "*…it is, in fact, the unanimous conclusion of all anthropologists, from Weissenberg, Hertz and Fishberg (themselves Jews), to Boas, Ripley, Mead, Pittard and others that wherever Jews are found, they closely resemble the people amongst whom they live. Even those of common family names supposedly traceable to the ancient Hebrew tribes, such as Levites (Levi) and Kohanim (Kohn, Coehn, Cohn) have little physical resemblence to one another. There is not one racial characteristic common to all who profess to be Jews.*" [34]

Such subtleties evaded Lloyd George (Comm 300), who was a passionate advocate of a Jewish homeland in Israel. When you look at what he wrote on the subject in the 1920s, either he was trying to mislead the populace or he himself was being seriously misled. In his book, *Is It Peace?*, he accepts without question that Jewish people had an historical right to Palestine.[35] He says that only with their brilliance and commitment could it become a 'land of milk and honey' again because, basically – if you put his words in simple terms – the Arabs were too stupid to do that. But it is when he outlines Zionist intentions for Palestine that his claims can be shown to be breathtakingly naïve or calculated to mislead. Even more likely, the endless means through which he could have been blackmailed over his private life and personal corruption acted to 'focus' his mind. As they say, "When you have got someone by the balls, their hearts and minds will follow". Lloyd George condemns the opponents of the Balfour Declaration for suggesting that the Zionist leaders were seeking to establish "a Jewish oligarchy in Palestine that will reduce the Arab inhabitant to a condition of servitude to a favoured Hebrew minority".[36] The best answer to that charge, he said, was to

---

[34] Alfred M. Lilienthal, *What Price Israel?*, (Henry Regnery, Chicago, 1953) p223–224.

[35] David Lloyd George, *Is It Peace?*, (Hodder & Stoughton, London, 1923) p246–253.

[36] Ibid p246–253.

be found in a memorandum submitted by the Zionist Association to the League of Nations. With the hindsight of more than seventy years, I doubt if even Lloyd George would now quote that memorandum as confirmation that the opponents were wrong. It said:

> *"The Jews demand no privilege, unless it is the privilege of rebuilding by their own efforts and sacrifices a land which, once the seat of a thriving and productive civilisation, has long been suffered to remain derelict. They expect no favoured treatment in the matter of political or religious rights. They assume, as a matter of course, that all the inhabitants of Palestine, be they Jews or non-Jews, will be in every respect on a footing of perfect equality. They seek no share in the Government beyond that to which they may be entitled under the Constitution as citizens of the country. They solicit no favours. They ask, in short, no more than an assured opportunity of peacefully building up their National Home by their own exertions and of succeeding on their merits."*

The Jewish and Arab populations of Israel will be in every respect on a footing of perfect equality? They expect no favoured treatment in the matter of political or religious rights? Really?

Chaim Herzog, the President of Israel, had a rather different view some years later, when he said that the Arabs cannot be "participants in any way in a land that has been consecrated to our people for thousands of years. To the Jews of this land there cannot be any partner".[37] There, that's more like it! Jewish people as a whole (the faith) have been victims of Zionism (the political movement), which is controlled by the Global Elite. It is time Jewish people (who are innocent and unaware of the background) realised how they, their minds and their emotions are being used in ways that serve a longer-term plan for centralised control, and not themselves and their children.

This is certainly true of the Anti-Defamation League of B'nai B'rith which was formed in the United States in 1913. From that time to this, the Anti-Defamation League (ADL) has operated as an intelligence unit which brands as "anti-Semitic" anyone who challenges or questions the Global Elite. But was it set up for the benefit of Jewish people? No, no. It was formed to protect the New York gangsters! In the early years of this century, Thomas Bingham, the New York City Police Commissioner, began a determined challenge to the mobsters. Among them was Arnold Rothstein, the mentor of Meyer Lansky who would later be the godfather of the organised crime syndicate which helped to fund and arm the Jewish terrorist underground in Palestine and later did the same for the State of Israel itself. Lansky was also a key player in the assassination of President Kennedy. The New York

[37] Noam Chomsky, *Letters From Lexington*, (Common Courage Press, Maine, USA, 1990) p3.

mobsters responded to Bingham's investigation by branding him an anti-Semite. This character demolition was so successful that it forced him out of office and ended the investigation of the mob.

These attacks were coordinated by a committee set up by an attorney called Sigmund Livingston. In 1913 this committee was given a formal title – The Anti-Defamation League.[38] Today it is an arm of the Israeli/Global Elite intelligence agency, Mossad, and has been at the heart of some horrific events, including the Kennedy assassination. The ADL is there to help the Global Elite and the terrorists who have controlled Israel, not to protect Jewish people from prejudice. Anything but, in fact.

WINNING THE PEACE

The First World War ended in 1918 with tens of millions of dead and injured on all sides, after the bloodiest conflict in known human history. It was a war that was planned and created by the Elite using the power and money of the banking and secret society network. It would not otherwise have happened. It was not the work of human nature, but *manipulated* human nature. At the same time, the Elite had sown the seeds for the capitalist/communist v fascist (Second) World War and the capitalism v communism Cold War by arranging and financing the Russian Revolution. The Elite had won the revolution and the war. Now they prepared for their most important ambition – winning the peace. They had the nation states of Europe exactly where they wanted them. The war had left Europe devastated and submerged in debt to the Elite's bankers, who had made loans to both sides. The name J.P. Morgan (Comm 300) was at the heart of this. The Morgan Guaranty Trust and the Elite's American International Corporation made loans to finance German espionage and covert operations in the United States and South America during the war. This was revealed by the Overman Committee of the US Senate in 1919. Among the other names involved were the Rothschilds' Kuhn, Loeb, and Co, and Morgan's Chase National Bank. The committee also established that the Guaranty Trust which was making loans to the Allies during the war, was covertly arranging other loans for *Germany* on the *London* money markets! This money was channelled to Germany via South America.[39]

In 1915 while all this was happening, the same J.P. Morgan was named by the British government as its sole agent for the purchasing of Britain's war supplies from the then 'neutral' United States, and for all loans from private banks in the US. Britain also became the guarantor for all goods and loans from America by the French, Italians, and Russians. By the end of the war, Britain, once the most powerful country in the world, was on its knees.

---

[38] Michael Collins Piper, *Final Judgement, The Missing Link In The JFK Assassination Conspiracy*, (The Wolfe Press, Washington DC, 1995) p82.
[39] US Senate, Overman Committee, 2.2009.

Again, this was not accident, but design. At the time of the Versailles Peace Conference in 1919, Britain owed the United States $4.7 billion in war debts. The British national debt had increased by 924% between 1913 and 1918, while the profits of the Global Elite companies soared. According to the Austrian writer, Gertrude Elias, the capital of DuPont (Comm 300) alone increased from $83 million to $308 million during the years of the First World War.[40] The 'victorious' leaders of the Allies at Versailles were Woodrow Wilson, Lloyd George, and Georges Clemenceau. They met with their 'advisors' to decide the reparations that Germany would pay to the victors and the terms of the peace settlement. Versailles and its offshoots would also give birth to the League of Nations, the Elite's first attempt at a covert world government, and the World Court in The Hague, Netherlands. It would further confirm Israel as a Jewish homeland, giving control of Palestine to the British in the meantime, and return the world economy to the gold standard, the process by which currencies are linked to gold. Who controlled the gold? The Rothschilds and some other Elite financiers.

The Elite also controlled the events and decisions at Versailles. Woodrow Wilson was 'advised' there by Colonel House (Comm 300) and Bernard Baruch, both Rothschild-Elite representatives; Lloyd George (Comm 300) was advised by Lord Milner (Comm 300) of the Round Table and Sir Phillip Sassoon, a direct descendant of Mayer Amschel Rothschild; Clemenceau had Georges Mandel, his Minister for the Interior, whose real name was Jeroboam Rothschild. Also in the American Commission to Negotiate Peace were the Dulles brothers; the Warburgs (Max from Germany and Paul from the US); Thomas W. Lamont from J.P. Morgan; the Secretary of State, Robert Lansing, an uncle of the Dulles's; and Walter Lippman (Comm 300) who (with House and others) was one of the main architects of the League of Nations and founder of the American branch of the Fabian Society. Their host in France was Baron Edmund de Rothschild, a leading campaigner and manipulator for a Jewish State in Israel.

The three leaders (stooges) at Versailles set up two committees to work on the details of the post-war policies. One was called the Economic Section and the other was the Financial Committee. Woodrow Wilson appointed Bernard Baruch to represent the US on the Economic Section and Thomas W. Lamont of J.P. Morgan articulated US (Elite) interests on the Financial Committee. Baruch's group decided that Germany should pay $12 billion in reparations and, together with other limitations on the German economy, this was a death sentence for the new German Republic, known as the Weimar Republic. It would ensure the conditions that would lead to Adolf Hitler's rise to power. The Financial Committee met later in Brussels to decide on a return to the gold standard. The effect of this on currencies made it impossible for Germany to pay her reparations. The financial

---

[40] Gertrude Elias, briefing paper for networked circulation, (London, 1995).

consequences of a return to the gold standard for every nation were pointed out to the committee by Professor Gustav Cassel of Sweden, but to no avail. All these decisions were coordinated to create the circumstances in Europe which would lead to the next war and an advancement of the New World Order. Eventually the gold standard caused such chaos and suffering that it had to be abandoned, but by then the damage was done.

Colonel House wrote the first draft of what became the covenant of the new League of Nations and President Wilson's famous fourteen points for the Versailles Conference were largely decided by a group convened by Colonel House. This group was known as 'The Inquiry'. These were all New World Order manipulators, people like John Foster Dulles, the future US secretary of state, and his brother, Allen, future head of the CIA. House had written a novel years before called *Philip Dru: Administrator*, which he later admitted was fact presented as fiction. In the book he outlined his New World Order philosophy.[41] President Wilson's biographer, George Sylvester Viereck, said that: "The Wilson Administration transferred the Colonel's ideas from the pages of fiction to the pages of history".[42] In his novel, published anonymously two years before the First World War had even begun, he proposed "...a League of Nations". Seven years later, that very same name was used for an organisation designed to impose its will on nation states under the pretext of ending the wars which its architects had started! Create the problems, then offer the solutions. The Rockefellers donated the money to build the headquarters of the League of Nations in Geneva, Switzerland, and they would later donate the land which the United Nations headquarters now occupies in New York.

The League of Nations failed, despite the best efforts of the One Worlders, because they could not persuade quite enough representatives in the US Congress to support it. If the United States would not support the idea, it was doomed to fail. It could be that the Second World War had been planned to increase the power of the League of Nations and turn it into a fully fledged world government. This setback meant, instead, that the Elite had to use the next war to introduce the successor to the League. Even as the League of Nations folded, the United Nations of today was already in their sights.

---

[41] Colonel Edward Mandell House, *Philip Dru: Administrator*, (B.W. Huebsch, New York, 1912).

[42] George Sylvester Viereck, *The Strangest Friendship In History: Woodrow Wilson And Colonel House*, (Liveright, New York, 1932) p28.

Chapter 5

United fronts

The events of history are the result of the struggle between two states of mind: one which wishes to imprison and the other which desires to set free. The scene of this tussle is the collective human mind.

In these last years of the twentieth century and across into the millennium, the human race is being given an opportunity we've not had since Atlantis, to step out of the prison and into mental, emotional, and spiritual freedom. Events are happening, which I will describe in detail later, that are dissolving the imprisoning vibration and vibrationally reconnecting the Earth with the rest of Creation. We and our 'father' will be One again. It won't simply 'happen' for every individual; the desire to do this needs to be present. But the opportunity is there for all and many are grasping that opportunity, as I know from the thousands of letters I receive and the people I meet. We are in a period of transition from the old fear vibration to the re-emerging love vibration.

We know this at a subconscious level and, for rapidly increasing numbers, at a conscious level too. Most people at this time can't remember why they are here, but they will. The Prison Warders on the Fourth Dimension know what is happening too, and the last thing that consciousness wants is for its prison and negative-energy-production-unit to be no more. The key to breaking out of this spiritual prison is the awakening and expansion of our consciousness to the point where its vibratory rate will be so high and powerful that it can, collectively, dismantle the blocking frequency. The Prison Warders, via the Global Elite, have been doing everything possible to close our minds and to divide us so that we do not work together as One. As I describe the quickening pace of the global manipulation after the First World War, this reflects the pressure coming from the Prison Warder consciousness for a speeding up of the work towards centralised control of the human mind before the challenge to this planetary occupation reaches its peak, in the latter years of this decade and into the next millennium. This speeding up of the centralised control is yet again a reflection of the collective human mind. It has become a downward spiral. As we have given our minds away and taken on thought patterns from others about our lack of self-worth and potential to control our own lives, we have created that physical reality. But instead of learning the lesson in the light of events this has caused, such as wars, we have allowed those events to further demoralise us, frighten us, and fill us with guilt and despair. This has further diminished our self-worth, thus increasing our self-loathing and our desperation to look to others for the answers to the gathering gloom. The collective mind has then manifested *that* negative sense of reality in an escalation to even more centralised power and control which, at a subconscious level, the human mind is demanding out of its fear and self-loathing. The Prison Warders have taken advantage of this and fuelled the fires of the collective mindset. But they can't create the reality; only we can. And we can only do that by the way we think about ourselves and the way we allow ourselves to absorb the thought patterns of others, including the Prison Warders and the Global Elite, who are working to erode our sense of self-love and self-worth.

With every year of the twentieth century, the quickening pace of the New World Order agenda can be identified. A network of organisations developed rapidly after the Versailles Peace Conference of 1919, and today this network is the most influential of all the Global Elite structures in controlling world events. The organisations within this network are presented as harmless 'think tanks' and forums, but they are, in truth, part of a global web of deception and manipulation. They were introduced to infiltrate all areas of politics, banking, business, the media, education, science, and the military. Their role is to recruit members who support the New World Order philosophy and ensure that they are appointed to positions of power and influence in all these areas of national and international life. They are organisations within organisations, eating away at the established structure and directing the world along the road to a global tyranny. All are offshoots of the original Round Table which began to give birth to this network after Versailles, with the creation of the Institute of International Affairs, based at Chatham House in London. It became the 'Royal' Institute when the sitting monarch became its official head in 1926. It was founded by members of the British and American delegations at Versailles when they gathered at the Hotel Majestic in Paris on May 30th 1919. The two groups were composed of members of Lord Milner's Round Table from Britain and Colonel House's 'Inquiry' group from the United States. Quite simply, they were dedicated to the creation of the New World Order.

The Round Table had close links with the Rothschild, Morgan, Rockefeller, and Carnegie Empires, and these connections were extended to the Royal Institute of International Affairs (RIIA). In Britain, the Astors, including Major John (Jacob) Astor (Comm 300), a director of Hambros Bank and owner of *The Times* newspaper (after 1922) were operating at the heart of both the Round Table and the Institute, and many of the former associates of Cecil Rhodes were involved. Sir Abe Bailey, the owner of Transvaal Mines, who worked with Lord Milner to start the Boer War, was among the founders of the RIIA, as was John W. Wheeler-Bennett, who would become General Eisenhower's political advisor in London in the crucial last two years of the Second World War as the nature of the post war world was being developed. Chatham House at 10 St James's Square, London, is named after William Pitt, the Earl of Chatham, one of three British Prime Ministers who have lived there. Goodness knows how many prime ministers and ministers have had their policies decided there, too.

The Institute of International Affairs immediately began to infiltrate the education system and expand its influence across the world. In Britain it has had a considerable sway at Oxford and other universities and within the London School of Economics. Funding this infiltration and the publications and propaganda was never a problem. Whenever money is required, some part of the Brotherhood network will provide it. By 1926, the money was flowing in for books and other work from the Carnegie United Kingdom Trustees, the Bank of England, and J.D. Rockefeller. The Rothschilds were, and are, the power behind the scenes. Within seven years of its launch, the funding of the Institute by the major banks and multinationals was already established; this continues today with global companies making donations to the cause. In 1926, funding came from, among many others: The Bank of England; Barclays Bank; Lloyds, and Lloyds Bank; Westminster Bank; Midland Bank; Hambros Bank; Rothschild and Sons; Ford Motor Company; Anglo-Iranian Oil (now BP); Baring Brothers; Imperial Chemical Industries (ICI); The British South Africa Company; the Mercantile and General Insurance Company; Erlangers Ltd; Lever Brothers; Stern Brothers; Vickers-Armstrong; Central Mining and Industrial Investment Ltd; British American Tobacco Company; Whitehall Securities Corporation; and Reuters, the newsagency which supplies news to newspapers and the broadcast media across the world.[1]

In the years that followed, Institute branches were established in Australia, Canada, Namibia, New Zealand, Nigeria, Trinidad and Tobago, and India, where it is known as the Council of World Affairs. By far the most important of the Institute's creations, however, was the Council on Foreign Relations (CFR) in the United States, which was to penetrate all areas of American life. This was formed in 1921 at the Harold Pratt House at 58 East 68th Street in New York, the former mansion of the Pratt family, close friends of the Rockefellers. Soon afterwards, the day-to-day administration was taken over by Colonel House and his associates, including the Rockefellers and, particularly, J.P. Morgan. The CFR's founding president was John W. Davis, J.P. Morgan's personal attorney; the founding vice-president was Paul Gravath, from a law firm representing Morgan; and the council's first chairman was the Morgan partner, Russell Leffingwell. Another 'independent' organisation, I see. The Council on Foreign Relations and the Royal Institute of International Affairs are the same organisation, working on different sides of the Atlantic to carry out the same

---

[1] Carroll Quigley, *The Anglo-American Establishment*, p190.

goals and agenda. Their members are in leading positions in government, including the Presidency, banking, business, education, military, and the media.

The power of the Council on Foreign Relations grew rapidly, and today it controls the administration of the United States, especially its foreign policy. Its goal is to introduce world government and it has spanned the United States with support groups. Each of these front organisations, like the CFR, has a similar structure based on the Round Table. There are circles of members answering to a central elite. The inner circle knows the agenda and works full time towards that target. The next circle knows all or most of the agenda and seek to use their own sphere of influence, politics, banking, the media, whatever, to lead the world in the desired direction. Other circles of people know some or a little of the real story and are persuaded to support the organisation by accepting the idea that a world government is the only answer to the ills of humanity. What this latter group doesn't realise is that those ills are being created by the very organisations they are members of!

Many of the people named in this book will not be involved through malice, but by genuinely believing that the New World Order agenda is the best option for peace and stability. A few members of these Elite front-groups have had the courage to speak out when they have seen the game plan. Admiral Chester Ward, a former US Judge Advocate General of the Navy, was a member of the Council on Foreign Relations for sixteen years. He said the purpose of the organisation was the "...submergence of US sovereignty and national independence into an all-powerful one-world government". In his book, *Kissinger On The Couch*, written with Phyllis Schafly, Ward said:

> "...[the] *lust to surrender the sovereignty and independence of the United States is pervasive throughout most of the membership, and particularly in the leadership of several divergent cliques that make up what is actually a polycentric organisation...*[the main clique] *is composed of the one-world-global-government ideologists – more respectfully referred to as the organised internationalists. They are the ones who carry on the tradition of the founders.*" [2]

The writer James Perloff read every issue of the CFR's magazine, *Foreign Affairs*, since its first publication in 1922. His verdict: "...the accusations against the Council on Foreign Relations – the pursuit of world government and receptiveness to communism are true". He said the domination of Washington administrations by the CFR membership had influenced "mightily upon the course of American Foreign policy in this century...

---

[2] Phyllis Schafly and Chester Ward, Rear Admiral VSN (Ret), *Kissinger On The Couch*, (Arlington House, New Rochelle, New York, 1975) p146, 149–150.

[which has] seen the United States eroded in strength and its allies sometimes vanquished altogether".³ What was true of the CFR was true of all the other 'think tanks' that were to follow.

The nexus of control which began in Britain and America was spreading across the world throughout the 1920s and 30s. The Institute of Pacific Relations was founded in 1924 and headed by Jerome D. Greene, a Boston banker close to Morgan and the Rockefellers. This was designed to extend the network into the governments and businesses of the Far East. Alongside Greene on the ruling council was Lionel Curtis, the leading founder of the Royal Institute of International Affairs. You will see throughout the book how the network of familiar names and organisations keeps coming up whenever events are being orchestrated. A Brotherhood mafia of organisations and people, controlled by the same elite, cast a web of manipulation and deceit across the Atlantic from London to New York and Washington, and then further afield, too.

Much of the funding for this New World Order network comes from the tax-exempt foundations. These are the foundations created by the big names of banking, industry, and finance, to make donations to various causes. People like the Rockefeller, Ford, and Carnegie families all formed foundations and presented them as vehicles of philanthropy. In fact, they are used as tax havens in the name of charity while most of the money is actually channelled into organisations and subject areas which support and promote centralised control. This reality almost became public in the 1950s, but the Elite control of the media just managed to keep the lid on the truth. The US Congress set up a committee in 1953 under B. Carrol Reece of Tennessee to investigate the behaviour of the tax-exempt foundations. Researcher and 'insider' Carroll Quigley says in his book, *Tragedy And Hope*:

> "*It soon became clear that people of immense wealth would be unhappy if the investigation went too far and that the 'most respected newspapers in the country', closely allied with these men of wealth, would not get excited enough about any revelations to make the publicity worth while, in terms of votes or campaign contributions.*" (p995)

What the papers didn't get excited about were the Reece Committee's findings that: the rich banking families give money to the foundations without losing control of how it is spent; the major foundations are interconnected and work as one to a common policy; they took over social science in the US and suppress those social scientists who disagree with their plans; research sponsored by the foundations is often slanted to conform to the conclusions the funders demand; those educational institutions in

---

³ James Perloff, *The Shadows Of Power: The Council On Foreign Relations And The American Decline*, (Appleton, WI, Western Islands, USA, 1988).

America which refuse to conform are refused a grant; Rhodes scholars are fed into government service by the foundations; history books are being funded which keep the truth from the people. The Reece Committee discovered that the Carnegie Endowment for International Peace was promoting war and the foundations were presenting the United Nations as the base for a socialist-communist coalition. All these findings came from an official Congressional Committee.[4]

This is still happening today and behind the names all these major foundations, including Ford and Carnegie, are controlled by the Rockefeller family. The Ford Foundation came in for especially strong criticism. It gave a billion dollars to the cause of 'education' and a million dollars to the Council on Foreign Relations. The foundations are another arm of global manipulation. Norman Dodd was the Reece Committee's director of research and he interviewed the then Ford Foundation president, H. Rowan Gaither, as part of his report. Gaither told him that the Ford Foundation operated under directives from the White House and these instructions were to make every effort to alter life in the United States to ensure a comfortable merger with the Soviet Union.[5] The foundations are particularly used to fund projects which aim to massage public opinion.

In the years after World War I, the interconnecting networks of think tanks and foundations had increased the effectiveness of the conspiracy. In these years, also, the manoeuvring went on that would explode as the Second World War. This was another bankers' conflict. Without their connivance, it could not have happened. The Second World War was planned before Versailles. It was at Versailles that the Rothschild–Wall Street–Colonel House–Bernard Baruch–Round Table connections imposed the impossible reparations on Germany which were sure to destroy the new German Democratic Republic and prepare the way for the rise of a dictator, Adolf Hitler. Added to this colossal debt, other decisions at Versailles had cost Germany 75% of her iron ore, 68% of her zinc, and 26% of her coal. Soon France announced that Germany had defaulted on reparation payments and French troops occupied the Ruhr. This 'defaulting' turned out to be a small shortfall in deliveries of coal and telegraph poles. The French move sent the German mark into freefall and it plunged to 7,592 to the dollar. This is hardly surprising, given that the Ruhr produced 80% of Germany's coal, iron, and steel. By November 1923, the mark had plummeted to 4,200 *billion* to the dollar!

What followed was a double-strike by the Wall Street and British banking cartel, which first financed German rearmament and enabled Germany to

---

[4] The Special House Committee To Investigate Tax Exempt Foundations, which reported in 1954. The Ford family has long lost control of the Ford Foundation. It is "Ford" in name only today, and it is controlled by the Rockefellers, who are controlled by..?

[5] Revealed by Dodd in an interview with author William H. McIllhany II, for his book, *The Tax Exempt Foundations*, in 1988.

prepare for the next war, and then collapsed the German economy again to bring Adolf Hitler to power. These strikes were called the Dawes Plan and the Young Plan. General C. Dawes was appointed by the US government to propose a solution to the German reparations fiasco. He introduced a series of short term loans from Wall Street banks to bail the Germans out. All this did, of course, was to add to the debt and put off the moment when the German economy would collapse, a collapse that was to be timed to bring Adolf Hitler to power. Lloyd George told the New York *Journal American* of June 24th 1924:

> *"The international bankers dictated the Dawes reparations settlement. The protocol which was signed between the Allies and Associated Powers and Germany is the triumph of the international financier. Agreement would never have been reached without the brusque and brutal intervention of the international bankers. They swept statesmen, politicians, and journalists to one side, and issued their orders with the imperiousness of absolute monarchs, who knew there was no appeal from their ruthless decrees. The settlement is the joint ukase of King Dollar and King Sterling. The Dawes Report was theirs. They inspired it and fashioned it. The Dawes Report was fashioned by the Money Kings. The orders of German financiers* [lead by the Warburg bank] *to their political representatives were just as peremptory as those of allied bankers to their political representatives."*

That was because the Allied and German bankers were on the same side. They were connected by the same All-Seeing Eye cult; a force which goes back to antiquity. The short-term loans issued under the Dawes Plan went into specific German companies vital to rearmament. It was this money that expanded the pharmaceutical cartel known as I.G. Farben, which was, in reality, Hitler's war machine. Farben had produced poison gas in World War I, thanks to German fanatic, Fitz Haber. The rest of the money went to other German cartels or the German subsidiaries of American companies. These included A.E.G. (the German General Electric), United Steelworks, and American I.G., the wholly-owned subsidiary of I.G. Farben. These loans, which included some from Morgan and Rothschild companies, and the technology transfers from America to the German cartels, made the Second World War possible. Without that help, there could have been no war. The US Ambassador to Germany, William Dodd, said in a communication to President Franklin D. Roosevelt on October 19th 1936:

> *"At the present moment more than a hundred American corporations have subsidiaries here of co-operative understandings. The DuPonts have three allies in Germany that are aiding the armament business. Their chief ally is the I.G. Farben Company, a part of the Government which gives 200,000 marks a year to one propaganda organisation operating on American opinion. Standard Oil Company (New York sub-company) sent $2,000,000 here in*

December 1933 and has made $500,000 a year helping Germans make Ersatz gas for war purposes; …The International Harvester Company president told me their business here rose 33% a year (arms manufacture, I believe), but they could take nothing out. Even our airplanes people have secret arrangements with Krupps. General Motors Company [Morgan] and Ford do enormous business here through their subsidiaries and take profits out. I mention these facts because they complicate things and add to war dangers." [6]

This was a shocking story of involvement with Nazi Germany's rearmament by major US companies and all the more compelling in that it came from the United States ambassador to Germany. What did Roosevelt do? Nothing. Franklin D. Roosevelt, a distant cousin of an earlier president, Theodore Roosevelt, was brought to power through a Wall Street-created depression in the United States, and was ensured of election when Wall Street put its financial and media power behind him. Another supporter was Meyer Lansky, the head of the international crime syndicate which included the Mafia. The term "Mafia" is often used to describe the organised crime network. In fact, the Italian Mafia is only a part of the picture, albeit an important part. Lansky was actually top man in the syndicate and it was his money and bribes which helped Roosevelt to power. [7] Once more the people of America were conned. Some of his prominent backers set up an organisation to oppose him – a constantly repeated Global Elite strategy. This was called the Liberty League and its pronouncements ensured that it would be branded 'extreme Right wing' and 'anti-Semitic'. This allowed all the main opposition to Roosevelt, even the genuine people, to be dismissed as Right wing anti-Semites. The Liberty League was funded by Pierre and Irene DuPont ($325,000), J.P. Morgan, the Rockefellers, J. Howard Pew, and William J. Knudsen, who was later given a top job by the very president the Liberty League 'opposed'. [8] In the same way the Robot Radicals of the political Left and the Robot Right all over the world are used today to discredit genuine opposition.

The preparation of America and Germany for war and the rise of both Hitler and Roosevelt were remarkably similar. We have seen how the Elite collapsed the German economy. They were doing the same in America. During the 1920s, they encouraged the stockmarket to overstretch itself and then the Federal Reserve issued a series of strict new banking laws which put the smaller banks under terrific pressure. This was the time of the so called 'Turkey Shoot', when the global banks picked off the small fry and massively increased their power. When this process was over, the Federal Reserve

[6] Edgar B. Dixon (editor), *Franklin D. Roosevelt And Foreign Affairs*, (Belknap Press, Cambridge, 1969) Vol. III, p456.

[7] Michael Collins Piper, *Final Judgement, The Missing Link In The JFK Assassination Conspiracy*, (The Wolfe Press, Washington D.C., 1995) p130.

[8] *The New Order, Our Secret Rulers*, p91.

withdrew the new banking laws. The Wall Street crash of 1929 plunged the country into economic depression.

In the United States and Germany, the same solutions were offered. Borrow more money from the banks. Roosevelt's National Recovery Act or 'New Deal' was offered to the American people as the way out of depression. Thousands of miles away across the Atlantic, the same plan under another name was being offered to the Germans by Hitler. Roosevelt's New Deal was the work of Gerard Swope, a member of many Roosevelt organisations. He was the chairman of the Morgan-controlled International General Electric, and a director of German General Electric (A.E.G.). Roosevelt was another version of Woodrow Wilson. Like Wilson, he would be elected by telling the people that America was not going to war while knowing that was exactly what was going to happen. Again Colonel Edward House was behind the scenes, visiting Roosevelt at his home in East 65th Street, New York, almost every day in 1932.[9]

What a 'coincidence' that Roosevelt and Hitler came to power in the wake of economic depression with the same basic 'New Deal' type solutions, and that both were advised by people connected with the American-German cartels and the Elite-controlled Bank of International Settlements. What's more, they both took office in the same year, 1933! Small world, isn't it? Indeed, it is the same small world occupied by Margaret Thatcher and Ronald Reagan when they were in power on both sides of the Atlantic during the 1980s, while following exactly the same economic policies, Thatcherism and Reaganomics.

Hitler's rise to power was made certain after 1929 when the Dawes Plan of short-term loans came to an end with Germany now owing an extra $16 *billion* in debt. One of Franklin D. Roosevelt's main financial backers, Owen D. Young, was appointed to propose solutions to Germany's inability to pay. Young was a Morgan executive and the head of the Morgan-controlled General Electric. The Young Plan of demanding payment in cash, not goods, demolished the German economy almost overnight. That is why he did it. A major financial supporter of Hitler, Dr Fritz Thyssen, would say under interrogation in 1945:

> *"The acceptance of the Young Plan and its financial principles increased unemployment more and more until about one million were unemployed. People were desperate. Hitler said he would do away with unemployment. The government in power at that time was very bad, and the situation of the people was getting worse. That really was the reason for the enormous success Hitler had in the election. When the last election came, he got about 40%."* [10]

---

[9] *The New Order, Our Secret Rulers*, p90.
[10] US Group Control Council (Germany), Office of the Director of Intelligence, Intelligence Report No. EF/ME/1, September 4th 1945.

The network linking both the Nazis and the Allies at the highest level is clear to see. While millions fought and died for what they believed was a war for freedom, the same force was manipulating the whole thing through *both* sides. Without them, it would not have happened.

The Austrian writer and researcher, Gertrude Elias, identifies Hjalmar Schacht as a major go-between, connecting the Nazis and the Wall Street-City of London elite.[11] Schacht became Hitler's financial advisor and President of the Reichsbank. The two signatures on the document confirming Schacht's appointment on March 17th 1933, were Adolf Hitler and the Rothschild frontman, Max Warburg.[12] In 1930, Schacht also founded the Global Elite's Bank of International Settlements in Basle, Switzerland. In England, a key figure was Montagu Norman (Comm 300), governor of the Rothschild-controlled Bank of England, and a close friend of Schacht. In fact they were so close that Schacht named his grandson after him. It was Norman who pressed for and supported the raising of US interest rates by the Federal Reserve, which was the final push that led to the Wall Street crash, the New Deal, and Franklin D. Roosevelt. Norman was the most influential central banker in the world at that time and his actions, in league with Wall Street, were crucial.

Once Hitler was safely elected, the attitude of the Bank of England and the Federal Reserve to Germany was transformed. Credit was offered to the Nazi regime and after the Nazis successfully invaded Czechoslovakia, Norman released £6 million of Czechoslovakian gold to Hitler which was deposited in London. This was done with the agreement of the Prime Minister, Neville Chamberlain.[13] On June 11th 1934, and again the following October, Norman and Schacht met in secret at Badenweiler in the Black Forest to arrange loans for Hitler and the Nazis.[14] But who was behind Norman? His family almost turned the governorship of the Bank of England into their personal property. One grandfather, George Warde Norman, was governor from 1821–1872 and his other grandfather, Lord Collet, was governor from 1887–1889. Montagu Norman spent a period in the United States at the offices of the Rothschild-funded Brown Brothers (later Brown Brothers, Harriman) and was befriended by the family of W.A. Delano (Comm 300), relatives of Franklin Delano Roosevelt, the President of the United States at the same time that Norman was head of the Bank of England. This all-powerful banker was actually a 'yes man' for the Rothschilds, and here again, we see the ploy at work. He was portrayed as anti-Jewish.

[11] Gertrude Elias, briefing paper for networked circulation, 1995.

[12] Rodney Atkinson and Norris McWhirter, *Treason At Maastricht, The Destruction Of The Nation State,* (Compuprint Publishing, Newcastle-Upon-Tyne, 1995) p20.

[13] *The Anglo-American Establishment,* p299.

[14] *The World Order, Our Secret Rulers,* p154.

Today the Bank of England is still the feifdom of the Global Elite.
Gertrude Elias says that the Bank collaborated with the leading Zionist, Lord
Bearsted of Royal Dutch Shell, to arrange the transfer of the assets of wealthy
German Zionists to Palestine. It was these transfers, she says, that helped to
build up the economy of the embryonic Zionist state. "They were the
privileged emigre class while propertyless Jews were refused asylum and
neutralised in the holocaust", Elias adds.[15] I believe that all this was coldly
calculated by the 'Jewish' elite, for reasons I will come to in due course.

I don't want to send you to sleep with a mass of detail, but I do want to
make it clear how provable it is that the Second World War and the rise of
Hitler were creations of the Elite in Britain and America. We need to move
away from conspiracy *theory* and see that it is conspiracy *fact*. Only then will
we deal with it. Crucial to the rise of the Nazi war machine was the
behaviour of some of the most famous companies in the United States, who
supported Hitler via their German subsidiaries or partners. Here are just a
few of what were almost countless examples of how this was secretly done...

I.G. FARBEN/STANDARD OIL

German production of steel and other products needed for war soared
through the period leading up to the outbreak of the conflict in 1939. At the
centre of this rearmament was the chemical giant, I.G. Farben. As Senator
Homer T. Bone would say to a Senate Committee in 1943 "Farben was
Hitler and Hitler was Farben".[16] This immense cartel was created in its
wartime form by American loans! In 1939, with Wall Street investment, it
had become the biggest manufacturer of chemicals in the world. And who
controlled I.G. Farben, a company that would use Jews and others as slave
labour? The Rothschilds, via a stream of frontmen and companies. Among
the German bankers on the supervisory board of Farben into the late 1920s
was Max Warburg, the brother of Paul Warburg of the Manhattan Bank, who
was sent to the United States by the Rothschilds to install the Federal Reserve
System and to take over the US economy. These were quite a pair, operating
in concert in the US and Germany. The US Naval Secret Service Report of
December 2nd 1918 said: "Paul Warburg. German, nationalised US citizen
1911, decorated by Kaiser, handled large sums furnished by German bankers
for Lenin and Trotsky. His brother Max who is director of espionage system
of Germany".[17] Paul Warburg was on the board of Farben's American
subsidiary, American I.G. Sitting alongside him were Edsel Ford (son of
Henry) of the Ford Motor Company, Charles E. Michell from the Federal

---

[15] Gertrude Elias, briefing paper for networked circulation, 1995. Before anyone shouts
"anti-Semite", Gertrude comes from a Jewish background.

[16] Senator Homer T. Bone speaking to the Senate Committee on Military Affairs, June 4th
1943.

[17] Quoted in *The New Order, Our Secret Rulers*, p128.

Reserve Bank of New York, and Walter Teagle, Franklin Roosevelt's close friend from Standard Oil. All this top American influence and support for a company of which an American War Department report said:

> *"Without I.G.'s immense productive facilities, its intense research, and vast international affiliations, Germany's prosecution of the war would have been unthinkable and impossible. Farben not only directed its energies toward arming Germany, but concentrated on weakening her intended victims, and this double-barrelled attempt to expand the German industrial potential for war and to restrict that of the rest of the world was not conceived and executed 'in the normal course of business'. The proof is overwhelming that I.G. Farben officials had full prior knowledge of Germany's plan for world conquest and of each specific aggressive act later undertaken..."* [18]

The Farben Empire became a state within a state and in effect ran its own economy. Reports and investigations, during and after the war, show that Farben's role, with Wall Street and British support, was to make Germany self-sufficient in all that Hitler needed for war: products like rubber, petrol, oils, and explosives. One major problem they had was the supply of oil. Their supplies came from outside Germany and in 1934 around 85% of German petroleum products were imported. This would obviously dry up during a war. But a deal between Farben and the Rockefellers ensured a constant supply of oil to Germany. Farben began to invest vast sums from the Wall Street loans into research aimed at developing processes to make oil from the German reserves of coal. What they couldn't discover for themselves, the Rockefeller's Standard Oil gave to them! In January 1933, just before Hitler came to power, a report from the Commercial Attache at the US Embassy in Berlin said:

> *"In two years Germany will be manufacturing oil and gas enough out of soft coal for a long war. The Standard Oil of New York is furnishing millions of dollars to help."* [19]

The Rockefellers also helped I.G. Farben with chemicals essential to aircraft fuel. The American representatives of American I.G. tried to hide their company's involvement with the German war machine by merging American I.G. into another company and changing its name to the General Aniline and Film Corporation. In fact, the makeup of the American I.G. board of 1930, with Farben already five years into its preparation for war, tells the real story of the US-German Brotherhood network which was leading the world into yet another awesome conflict. Among the board

---

[18] *Elimination Of German Resources*, p943.

[19] Report to the State Department, Washington DC.

members of American I.G. were: Carl Bosch (German), from Ford; Edsel B. Ford (US), Henry Ford's son; Max Ilgner (German), director of Farben's Nazi intelligence office in Berlin; H.A. Metz (US) director of I.G. Farben and the Rothschild/Warburg Bank of Manhattan; C.E. Mitchell (US), Director of the Federal Reserve Bank of New York and the Morgan National City Bank; Hermann Schmitz (German), president of American I.G. and I.G. Farben and on the boards of both the German Central Bank and the Bank of International Settlements; Walter Teagle (US), director of Federal Reserve Bank of New York, the Rockefellers' Standard Oil of New Jersey, trustee of the Roosevelt Foundation, and close friend of the President; W.H. von Rath (naturalised US), director of German General Electric (A.E.G.); and Paul M. Warburg, of the Bank of Manhattan.

When the war ended and the investigations into its background began, three German members of that American I.G. board were found guilty at the Nuremberg War Crimes Trials. The American representatives such as Paul Warburg were left untouched, as was his brother, Max Warburg, who, even though a Jew, was allowed to leave Nazi Germany in 1939 without any restriction. The Elite controlled even the arrests and trials resulting from the war and the horrors they themselves engineered. Such operations were not only between two companies, they involved other elements of the Global Elite-Brotherhood in other companies and governments. The president of Standard Oil of New Jersey (now Exxon) at this time was William Stamps Farish. During the war, a letter was released by the US Justice Department from Frank A. Howard, the Standard Oil vice-president to Farish. It was dated October 12th 1939, and it said:

> "...*In England I met by appointment the Royal Dutch* [Shell Oil] *gentleman from Holland and...a general agreement was reached on the necessary changes in our relations with the I.G.* [Farben], *in view of the state of war...the Royal Dutch Shell Group is essentially British...I also had several meetings with the* [British] *Air Ministry...*
>
> *I required help to obtain the necessary permission to go to Holland...After discussions with the* [American] *Ambassador* [Joseph Kennedy]...*the situation was cleared completely...The gentlemen in the Air Ministry...very kindly offered to assist me in re-entering England.*
>
> *Pursuant to these arrangements, I was able to keep my appointment in Holland (having been flown there on a British Royal Air Force bomber), where I had three days of discussion with the representatives of I.G. They delivered to me assignments of some 2,000 foreign patents and* **we did our best to work out complete plans for a modus vivendi which could operate through the term of the war, whether or not the US came in.**" [20] [my emphasis]

[20] Quoted by Webster Griffin Tarpley and Anton Chaitkin in *George Bush, The Unauthorised Biography*, (*Executive Intelligence Review*, Washington DC, 1992) p47.

William S. Farish refuelled Nazi shipping and submarines in Spain and Latin America during the war. It was the Standard Oil-I.G. Farben enterprise which opened the Auschwitz Concentration Camp on June 14th 1940, and used the slave labour of Jews and political opponents to produce the artificial rubber and gasoline from coal. Farish was very close to Hermann Schmitz, the chairman of I.G. Farben. Standard Oil hired the infamous publicist, Ivy Lee, to promote Farben and the Nazis in the United States. William S. Farish had a grandson, William Farish III, who was to become a close friend of George Bush (Comm 300) and has enjoyed the company of Queen Elizabeth II (Comm 300) at his home. Their horses breed with each other, apparently. When George Bush became vice-president, he had to hand over his businesses and investments to a 'blind trust', to ensure that he could not (in theory) make decisions in the White House which affected his investments. Who was put in charge of this 'blind trust'? William Farish III!

GENERAL ELECTRIC (G.E.C.)

I.G. Farben worked in concert before and throughout the war with other cartels like the J.P. Morgan-controlled General Electric, a company with which President Franklin D. Roosevelt had many close connections. In 1939, Senator James A. Reed of Missouri, a one-time Roosevelt supporter, told the Senate that the President was a "hired man for the economic royalists", in Wall Street. He added that the Roosevelt family was one of the biggest holders of shares in General Electric.[21] Interesting, then, that General Electric was a big Hitler supporter and there is photographic and documented evidence that, like I.G. Farben, both General Electric companies in Germany, A.E.G. and Osram, directly financed Hitler.[22] Farben contributed the most (45% of the fund that brought Hitler to power in 1933), but the companies linked to General Electric also made very large donations and – in this web of intrigue – a number of directors of German General Electric were on the board of I.G. Farben. As with the other major American companies involved, General Electric (in the US) channelled its contributions to Hitler via German subsidiaries and cartel partners. Again only the *German* directors of the General Electric cartel were charged and tried at Nuremberg, not the Americans. To have done so would have exposed the whole story.

INTERNATIONAL TELEPHONE AND TELEGRAPH (I.T.T.)

Another United States company that was important to Hitler and his war machine was International Telephone and Telegraph, better known as I.T.T. It was the creation of its founder, Sosthenes Behn, an entrepreneur born in

---

[21] *The New York Times,* (October 4th 1936).
[22] For the detailed research on this, see Anthony C. Sutton's superb exposé, *Wall Street And The Rise Of Hitler,* (Heritage Publications, Melbourne, Australia, 1976) p121–132.

the Virgin Islands. By 1924, I.T.T. was closely connected with J.P. Morgan, and the board reflected Morgan's control. It has been proved that I.T.T. made donations to Hitler through German subsidiaries and was a significant supporter of the Nazi regime.[23] I.T.T. bought a large interest in German armament companies, most particularly the aircraft manufacturer, Focke-Wolfe. The profits from these investments were not returned to the United States; they were reinvested in further German rearmament. Sosthenes Behn met with Hitler in August 1933.[24] Hitler's personal banker, Baron Kurt von Schroder, a Nazi and SS Senior Group Leader, became the overseer of I.T.T. interests in Germany and a director of all I.T.T.-affiliated companies. Baron von Schroder was channelling I.T.T. funding to Himmler's SS at least until 1944![25] The Schroder Banking family from Hamburg had branches in London and New York under the name of J. Henry Schroder (Comm 300). In England, the managing director of Schroder Bank was Mr F.C. Tiarks, a director of the Rothschild-controlled and Montagu Norman-supervised Bank of England. Gordon Richardson was chairman of Schroder Bank up until 1973, when he was made governor of the Bank of England. From 1938 on, the Schroder Bank in London was appointed to represent Nazi interests in Britain. In America, Schroder and the Rockefellers merged some of their business interests.

THE FORD MOTOR COMPANY

Much has been written of Henry Ford's alleged collusion with the Nazis. He was vehement in his condemnation of the Jews. Ford was just as outspoken in his criticism of the Wall Street financiers, whom he blamed for starting the wars and controlling the world money markets for their own ends. At the same time, he said J.P. Morgan was to be trusted and I can't help feeling that Mr Ford did his utmost to spread disinformation. He portrayed himself as the peoples' friend against the manipulators while he was, in fact, another manipulator. He made enormous profits during the war by supplying both sides. As early as 1922, the *New York Times* was reporting that Ford was financing Hitler's nationalists and anti-Jewish movements in Germany and the Berlin newspaper, *Berliner Tageblatt*, was calling on the American ambassador to stop Ford from intervening in German affairs. Hitler was so grateful for Ford's assistance, that in 1938 he presented Ford with the highest honour the Nazis conferred on non-Germans: the Grand Cross of the German Eagle; Ford's portrait hung behind Hitler's desk in Hitler's private office. The two biggest manufacturers of tanks for Hitler's armies before and during the war were the German subsidiaries of the Ford Motor Company, and the Morgan-controlled

---

[23] *Wall Street And The Rise Of Hitler*, p121–132.
[24] Report in *The New York Times*, (August 4th 1933).
[25] *Wall Street And The Rise Of Hitler*, p79.

General Motors (Opel). In 1928, the Ford Motor Company in Germany merged with I.G. Farben. Carl Bosch of Farben became the head of the Ford operation in Germany.

W.A. HARRIMAN

Fritz Thyssen was a German steel entrepreneur and banker, who funded the Nazis from the early 1920s. His banking operation in Germany was affiliated – through a subsidiary – with the W.A. Harriman Company in New York (Brown Brothers, Harriman after 1933), which in turn was funded (at least in its earlier days) by the Rothschilds. The Harriman family was prominent in supporting both the Russian Revolution and Adolf Hitler. A Thyssen company controlled the Union Banking Corporation in the US, which had E. Roland Harriman on its board along with known Nazis and Nazi financial backers. Prescott Bush, the father of the future president, George Bush, was also on the UBC board and owed his wealth to the Harrimans. Roland was the brother of W. Averell Harriman (Comm 300), who was a director of Morgan's Guaranty Trust when it was financing Lenin and Trotsky. Averell Harriman would later make vast profits from Russian ventures and be appointed as the ambassador to the Soviet Union. He was also a controlling voice in the Democratic Party and close to the president, Franklin D. Roosevelt.

THE DULLES BROTHERS

The name Dulles is another which spans the manipulation of both the First and Second World Wars. The Dulles's were from a southern slave-owning family, and cousins of the Rockefellers. They were connected with international banking in America and Germany. Statements made by John Foster Dulles as early as 1911 revealed support for the creation of a 'super race' by 'eliminating the lower members...'.[26] The Dulles law firm, Sullivan and Cromwell, handled the US affairs of I.G. Farben and Hitler's major financial backer, Fritz Thyssen, who introduced Allen Dulles to the Fuhrer-to-be. John Foster Dulles wrote 'Heil Hitler' on his letters to German clients. After Hitler's rise to power, John Foster Dulles went to Germany on behalf of the Rothschild/Round Table group, to negotiate new loans for the Nazis. The Dulles brothers were appointed to the US State Department during World War I by their uncle, Secretary of State, Robert Lansing, one of the Colonel House/Bernard Baruch clique which controlled Woodrow Wilson. The Dulles brothers were at the Versailles Peace Conference where they met the Round Table delegation and became part of the Round Table/Royal Institute of International Affairs/Council on Foreign Relations

---

[26] Dulles made a statement based on 'natural selection' and the survival of the fittest. He said the weakest members of the population had to be eliminated by natural selection so that the human race could progress. He was quoted in Jim Keith's *Casebook On Alternative 3*, p19.

network. Allen Dulles was, very conveniently, appointed First Secretary of the US Embassy in Berlin in 1920, just as his brother was in Germany, representing the Elite's bankers through his connections with the Bank of England and the J.P. Morgan empire. Both Dulles' were friends of Hitler's financial wizard, Hjalmar Schacht. John Foster Dulles would become Secretary of State and Allen Dulles became the first head of the CIA. The latter would also serve on the Warren Commission, which was charged with investigating the assassination of President Kennedy.

I have highlighted some of the big names in the financing and manipulation of Germany and her rearmament programme. But there was also direct support for the Nazi Party by these same banks and industrialists. Among the documents from the Nuremberg Trials are the original transfer slips from I.G. Farben, German General Electric, Osram, and others, authorising the transfer of funds into the Nazis' National Trusteeship account, Hitler's election fund. Representatives of companies owned or influenced by the Rockefellers, American I.G., I.T.T., General Electric, and Ford can be shown to be at the heart of the Nazi Party.[27] It is fascinating to see how remarkably free from bomb damage were the German factories and plants owned by the American-German cartels. When the Allied armies reached Cologne, for instance, many noticed the stark contrast between the flattened city and the undamaged plants (owned by I.G. Farben, the Ford Motor Company, and the United Rayon Works) on its edge. The way I.G. Farben plants survived the bombing is staggering, given that the Allies knew that this company *was* the German war machine. There is evidence that Ford Plants in Germany and France were not bombed by the US Airforce.[28] When the one at Poissy was hit by the British, the Vichy government paid Ford 38 million francs in compensation! A relieved Edsel Ford wrote to his General Manager in Europe: "Photographs of the Plant on fire were published in American newspapers but fortunately no reference was made to the Ford Motor Company".[29] The Vichy regime collaborated with the Nazis and among its number was one François Mitterand (Comm 300), Grand Master of Grand Orient Freemasonry and later the long-time president of France.[30]

In five years of war and global slaughter, the United States trusts I have highlighted, and others, made a profit of $175,000,000,000, according to research by the writer and researcher, Gertrude Elias.[31]

---

[27] For the detailed research, see Anthony C. Sutton's *Wall Street And The Rise Of Hitler*, p123–132.

[28] James Stewart Martin, *All Honourable Men*, (Little Brown & Co, Boston, 1950) p75.
See also the research of Anthony C. Sutton, *Wall Street And The Rise Of Hitler*, p62–66.

[29] Josiah E. Dubois Jr, *Generals In Grey Suits*, (The Bodley Head, London, 1953) p251.

[30] *Treason At Maastricht*, p137

[31] Gertrude Elias, briefing paper for networked circulation, (London, 1995).

To complete this appalling tale of deceit on the people of the world, the same Wall Street names that created and funded the war were also appointed by Franklin Roosevelt to supervise the fate of German industry when the conflict ended. Top executives appointed to this role included Louis Douglas, director of the Morgan-dominated General Motors and president of the Morgan Mutual Life Insurance, and Brigadier General William H. Draper Jr of Dillon, Read, and Co, another firm that contributed substantially to the creation of the cartels and the funding of Hitler's Germany. Both Draper and Douglas were members of the Council on Foreign Relations and Draper, a eugenics (master race) fanatic, would later become a leading light in the funding of 'population control'.

The story of William H. Draper Jr reveals the scale of the scam and the cover-up. He joined the Prescott Bush circle in 1927, when he was hired by Dillon Read to handle the account of...Fritz Thyssen, one of Adolf Hitler's biggest financial backers. Draper became a director and later the vice-president and assistant treasurer of Dillon Read's German Credit and Investment Corporation, supervising some of the short-term loans to Thyssen's German Steel Trust under the Dawes Plan. These loans, agreed upon by Draper, helped to bring Hitler to power and fund his rearmament. His partners in this operation were both Nazis: Alexander Kreuter, in Berlin, was president, and Frederic Brandi (who moved to the US in 1926) became Draper's co-director of the German Credit Investment Corporation in Newark, New Jersey. Brandi's father was a leading coal executive with the German Steel Trust. Draper was listed as a director of German Credit throughout 1942 until it was liquidated in 1943, by which time its job had been done.[32]

Draper then went off to become a general in the Pacific, fighting for the USA! This is the man appointed by Roosevelt after the German surrender to decide what should happen to the Nazi cartels he helped to create. He would have power to decide who was exposed, who lost or kept their business, and who was charged with war crimes. The scale of the sting is incredible. Draper played good guy/bad guy with US Treasury Secretary Henry Morgenthau, to complete another mental coup d'état. Morganthau demanded that Germany's industry be destroyed and the Germans be reduced to a purely rural nation. Draper's role was to prevent this, but only if the Germans agreed to accept all the guilt for Nazism. The authors of a superb book, *George Bush, The Unauthorised Biography*, say:

> "*Draper and his colleagues demanded that Germany and the world accept the collective guilt of the German people as the explanation of the rise of Hitler's New Order and the Nazi war crimes. This, of course, was rather*

---

[32] *George Bush, The Unauthorised Biography*, p53–54, quoting the *Directory Of Directors For New York City, 1942.*

convenient for General Draper himself, as it was for the Bush family. It is still convenient decades later, allowing Prescott's son, President George, to lecture Germany on the danger of Hitlerism. Germans are too slow, it seems, to accept his New World Order." (p55)

The threads have continued through the decades since then, with President Bush appointing Draper's son, William Draper III, to a United Nations job involved in population control. At Dillon Read, Bush's US Treasury Secretary, Nicholas Brady, was the long-time partner of Frederic Brandi, General Draper's cohort in the financing of Hitler's steel cartel. The same small group of bankers, companies, and political manipulators were behind the First World War, the Russian Revolution, and the Second World War. Without their money and manoeuvring, the two greatest conflicts in recorded human history would not have happened.

Why is it important to know this? There are many reasons, but I stress two. I have heard it said so often that the problem with the world is human nature. This nature is evil, I hear people say, and what do they point to in justification of this? The two World Wars and other conflicts before and since. Our desire for multidimensional freedom will only become a reality when we realise that human nature is not evil. It has a natural desire for love, not hate, for harmony, not conflict. Those wars were not the result of human nature being evil. They were the result of humanity giving away to someone else its right to think and act. These are lessons which are still to be learned and until they are, we will continue to be denied our true and infinite potential. But we can make that switch in an instant, if we so choose.

We are having a version of events projected at us through the schools, universities, and the media, all the time. That version of events has almost nothing to do with truth. It has been created to mislead us and to persuade us to think and act in a particular way, which suits the aims of the human manipulators and their controllers, the Prison Warders. So if you want to go to war and you need the people to support you, just set up an attack on one of your own ships or have one of your top people assassinated, and whip up the public's indignation with propaganda against the alleged culprit. As long as people take everything at face value, without question, and they don't survey the world with open eyes and an open mind, we will go on being a bewildered herd, blindly following the sheep at the front. But is it a sheep – or a monster? And what is its agenda? If we stop being human blotting paper, soaking up this tidal wave of biased information, and begin to filter what we are told, we become so much more difficult to mislead. These terrible events which have plagued the world in this century can only happen if we see life in terms of the leaders and the led. If we do that, a tiny few can control the world. And they have. Until now.

Chapter 6

Master plans

The First and Second World Wars were made possible by a coup d'état on the minds of hundreds of millions of people. As the Prison Warders program the minds of the Global Elite, so the Elite do the same to people on Earth. It almost wouldn't matter that the global bankers and industrialists were funding both sides – *if* (and it is one hell of a big 'if') the people in general had seen what was afoot and refused to take part. I remember the words of a splendid song by Donovan in the 1960s, *The Universal Soldier*:

> *"He's five foot two, and he's six feet four. He fights with missiles and with spears. He's all of thirty-one and he's only seventeen. He's been a soldier for a thousand years…He's the universal soldier and he really is to blame. Without him how could Hitler have begun? He's the one who gives his body as a weapon of the war and without him all this killing can't go on."* [1]

Hitler was no threat to the world unless the mass of the German people handed over their lives to him. Unfortunately, this is what happened, and the same was true of people in Britain and elsewhere, who also gave up thinking and allowed 'leaders' to 'do it' for them. In Germany, you had the propaganda whipping up public opinion against a perceived enemy and their egos were being massaged by talk of a German Master Race. Outside Germany, the same force was orchestrating public opinion against the Germans, once Hitler's rearmament programme was sufficiently advanced. When the two populations had soaked up the designer propaganda, they were played off against each other. Most of the people who fought that war did not want to be there. They wanted to be at home with their families and to watch their children grow. But because they had given up their right to think, they left their families and children, to kill and be killed.

Their minds were so overwhelmed by the mass hypnosis, that those who did stand up and challenge the official line were jailed without trial and few raised even a whimper against it. But by then, especially with the First World War and the Great Depression still powerfully affecting human responses, the collective mind was full of fear. It had lost confidence in itself. It was

---

[1] Donovan, *The Universal Soldier*, (Pye Records, London, 1965). Written by Buffy St Marie.

confused, bewildered, and looking to others to change the nature of the human condition. The human mind had also been programmed, not the least by its recent experience, to believe that life was about conflict and struggle: the world was a horrible place. These were the dominating thought patterns and that was the physical reality thus created.

Uniting a nation against a common enemy and convincing the people of their own racial superiority is another powerful weapon of control. The Nazis used this to great effect with their German Master Race/anti-Jewish propaganda. Ironically, or perhaps more than that, they were assisted in this by a man called Alfred Rosenberg, an occultist with a Jewish, Estonian, and French background. It was Rosenberg who made a copy of *The Protocols Of The Learned Elders Of Zion* available to Hitler. Why on Earth did he do that, when he would have known that Hitler would use them as propaganda against Jews as a whole? Hitler did indeed circulate *The Protocols* widely to justify his campaign against Jews. This was outrageous, given that the mass of Jewish people were not aware of what was going on and nor would they have supported it if they were.

Rosenberg said that a stranger arrived mysteriously and gave him a copy of the document: "The man, whom I had never seen before, came to my study without knocking, put the book on my desk and vanished without saying a word".[2] Rosenberg presented himself as vehemently anti-Jewish and soon rose to become the Nazi Party's official 'ideologist', with the role of providing the 'facts' to justify the campaign against Jews. Ernst Hanfstaengl, a close friend of Franklin Roosevelt, was also a close associate of Hitler before the war. He says he was warned by the Austrian writer, Rudolf Kommer, that "if any political party emerges with an anti-Semitic programme directed by Jewish or half Jewish fanatics we shall have to watch out". Hanfstaengl wrote that later, after experiencing the influence that Alfred Rosenberg had on Hitler, he began to realise what that remark really meant:

"I thought back to Rudolf Kommer's remark about an anti-Semitic programme directed by Jewish or half Jewish fanatics – Rosenberg was distinctly Jewish in appearance, although he would have been the first to protest furiously if anyone had questioned his ancestry. Yet I used to see him most mornings sitting in a dingy café at the corner of Briennerstrasse and Augustenstrasse with a Hungarian Jew named Holoschi, who was one of his principal assistants. The man called himself Hollander in Germany and was another of these Jewish anti-Semites…I suspected the Aryan background of many of the others, Strasser and Streicher looked Jewish to me as well as figures like Ley, Frank and even Goebbels, who would have had difficulty in proving their pedigree." [3]

---

[2] Quoted in several books, including Trevor Ravenscroft's *The Spear Of Destiny*, (Corgi, London, 1974) p106.

[3] Ernst Hanfstaengl, *Hitler – The Missing Years*, (London, 1957).

Now isn't this all rather strange? Jewish bankers and their political representatives were *provably* involved in funding the Nazis and their rearmament. Then along comes Alfred Rosenberg from a Jewish background, to hand over a copy of *The Protocols* to Hitler and to become the chief 'researcher' of anti-Jewish material which leads to the grotesque treatment of Jews under the Nazi regime. This treatment is then used and hyped to justify the takeover of Palestine for a 'Jewish' homeland. No-one used this method more obviously than Lord Victor Rothschild in his House of Lords speeches urging support for a Jewish State in Palestine. What goes on here? I believe it was all a set up by the Elite. Hitler's infamous book, *Mein Kampf*, was ghostwritten by Major General Karl Haushofer, who acknowledged that a major source for the "ideas" it expressed came from Halford J. MacKinder, a director of the elite's London School of Economics. In 1996, official German documents uncovered by an American student also proved that many of Hitler's leading officers and thousands of his troops were of Jewish decent.

In Britain, it seems to me, the public mind was being urged to ignore Hitler until his rearmament programme was well established. Then, when the Germans were ready for battle, that same public opinion was switched dramatically to see Hitler as a monster who must be stopped. The British collective psyche was like a little child in the hands of the mind doctors. This policy, I believe, was coordinated by Lord Milner and the Round Table secret society, together with the Royal Institute of International Affairs at Chatham House. The two front men for these two very different stages were Prime Minister Neville Chamberlain and his successor, Winston Churchill (Comm 300).

Chamberlain and his close aide, Lord Halifax (a Round Table member almost from its foundation and a member of the Committee of 300), supported the appeasement of Hitler. Milner and his fellow manipulators agreed with this policy. Speeches by the Round Table/Royal Institute high command like Lionel Curtis (Comm 300), Leopold Amery, and Lord Lothian were strongly in favour of leaving Hitler alone during the 1930s. In May 1933, Hitler's representative (Alfred Rosenberg) visited England to meet with Sir Henry Deterding (Comm 300), head of Royal Dutch Shell; Geoffrey Dawson, the editor of *The Times* newspaper (owned by the Astors (Round Table, Royal Institute)), Walter Eliot MP; 1st Viscount Hailsham, the Secretary for War; and the Duke of Kent, brother of King Edward VIII and King George VI. Edward, who is believed to have had sympathies with Hitler, later fell in love with an American woman, Mrs Simpson. He abdicated from the British throne and moved to the Rothschild castle in Austria after reigning for only 325 days. There is speculation that the real reason he left Britain was because he would not support a war with Germany, which the manipulators knew was planned.

When Hitler announced the remilitarisation of the Rhineland in 1936, the British Cabinet accepted it. The Astors used their *Times* newspaper to promote this view of Hitler also. The authorised biographer of Lord Halifax shows how the Milner crowd and the British Cabinet were negotiating behind the scenes with Germany, and making proposals that would have given Hitler control over mainland Europe. This was part of a British-German-United States pact proposed by Milner's associate Lord Lothian in a meeting with Hitler in January 1935. Lord Halifax also met with Hitler in Berchtesgaden on November 19th 1937. Carroll Quigley's research for *The Anglo-American Establishment* reveals that Halifax (Comm 300) convinced Hitler of three points: a) that Britain saw Germany as the main defence against communism in Europe; b) that Britain was prepared to be part of a Four Power agreement with France, Germany and Italy; c) that Britain would allow Germany to liquidate Austria, Czechoslovakia and Poland, if it could be achieved without British public opinion demanding a war with Germany.[4] All elements of the Round Table, the Royal Institute of International Affairs, and their associated organisations, publications, and members, were put to work to sell the appeasement policy.

The only thing that could have started a war with Germany earlier than planned was British public opinion, so the appeasement propaganda was stepped up. A few months after the Halifax/Hitler meeting, the Nazis invaded Austria in March 1938. The French Prime Minister, Daladier, went to London to ask for British support for the protection of Czechoslovakia against Hitler's aggression. Chamberlain refused. More than that, it would appear that the French were urged to pressure the Czechs into an agreement with Hitler. Lord Lothian made speeches in the House of Lords and at Chatham House condemning the Czechs for not making concessions to Germany.[5] In a meeting with American newspaper journalists at the Astors' London home, Chamberlain made a calculated, but deniable, comment, indicating that he believed the Czechs should hand over some of their land to Germany.[6] Lady Astor denied the meeting had taken place when the news was made public, but later had to admit that it had.

The policy Chamberlain had outlined for the journalists was supported in a leading article in *The Times* newspaper, owned by the Astors. This produced such an outcry of protest that the manipulation of public opinion was further increased. The article appeared on September 7th 1938 because they knew the German invasion of Czechoslovakia was near. Later in that month, Lord Halifax and others launched a propaganda exercise known as the 'war scare'. The government circulated stories which greatly exaggerated the strength of the German forces. They implied that if they went to war with Hitler, German planes would soon be dropping poison gas from their

---

[4] Carroll Quigley, *The Anglo-American Establishment*, p275.
[5] House of Lords, February 1938; Chatham House, March 24th 1938. *The Anglo-American Establishment*, p279–281.
[6] Ibid p284.

aeroplanes over England. The government even went to the ridiculous lengths of digging trenches in London parks and distributing gas masks! But, of course, silly as that may have been – what use are trenches in the *parks*? – it was not their *military* usefulness the government was interested in. It was about mind manipulation. They wanted to frighten public opinion into thinking that going to war with Germany was not such a good idea after all. Chamberlain added to this by saying on BBC Radio that the dispute between Germany and Czechoslovakia was: "...a quarrel in a far away country between people of whom we know nothing".[7] The Nazi invasion of Czechoslovakia was, in truth, crucial to the plan because it gave Hitler the resources he needed to be a major military power, capable of fighting a prolonged war. The writer, Gertrude Elias, says of this:

> *"Most revealing even for the present are the deals which preceded the sell-out of Czechoslovakia by Chamberlain in 1939, which turned Germany into a military superpower. The fact was, however, that the Skoda works, the biggest munition factory in Central Europe, controlled by the French Schneider Creuzot, like Wittowitz, the biggest steelworks owned by the Rothschilds, like the Czech explosives, had already been handed over to Germany...*
>
> *...The death warrant [for Czechoslovakia] was signed in the head office of the Unilever subsidiary in Aussig, the headquarters of the pro-Nazi clique."* [8]

When Germany occupied the whole of Czechoslovakia in March 1939, there was a sudden and remarkable switch in the attitude of Milner and the Round Table. Now they were all in favour of war with Germany. The time had arrived for the second strike in the Elite's pre-war strategy in Britain. Chamberlain had served his purpose in giving Hitler time to rebuild German armaments (with Wall Street support) and Germany's area of influence had expanded. Dictators of a similar persuasion were installed in Italy (Mussolini) and Spain (Franco). OK boys, we're ready to go. Start the war.

Hitler had been duped, too, into believing there would be no opposition, but suddenly that was to change. The Milner group, through its publication, *The Round Table* magazine, had been pressing for the appeasement of Hitler throughout the period we have been discussing. Now it was calling for a 'Grand Alliance' of Poland, Rumania, France, and Britain, against Germany. Lord Lothian and Lord Astor, those arch appeasers, were suddenly making speeches saying exactly the opposite of what they had said before. "War with Germany!" they cried. Lothian was also calling for an alliance with Russia. They demanded a policy of conscription into the armed forces, as

---

[7] *The Anglo-American Establishment*, p285.

[8] Gertrude Elias, briefing paper for networked circulation, (London, 1995).

did Astor's *Times*[9] and Lord Amery, the man who had supported Hitler so vigorously. The switch in policy wasn't even subtle. It was painfully transparent if you knew the Elite game plan.

Chamberlain's use to the Elite was almost over. His successor, Winston Churchill (Comm 300), was being manoeuvred into place. All that was left was to remove Chamberlain and the knives of his former 'friends' were sharpened. There can be few greater examples of hypocrisy in the House of Commons chamber than when Leopold Amery, echoing Cromwell, shouted at the government benches: "You have sat too long for any good you have been doing. Depart, I say, and let us have done with you. In the name of God, go!"[10] Go for pursuing the policies Amery advocated right up to the sudden switch of 1939. Lady Astor who had supported Chamberlain's policy to the hilt, turned against him even earlier: "Will the Prime Minister lose no time in letting the German government know with what horror the whole of this country regards Germany's action?" she asked him in 1939. Chamberlain didn't answer, but another Conservative MP, Major Vyvyan Adams, summed it up when he shouted at Lady Astor: "You caused it yourself".[11]

Chamberlain was simply a scapegoat, knowingly or unknowingly. Churchill became Prime Minister. A man of war was now in Downing Street and on the very evening he took over the reins of the British Empire, May 11th 1940, the policy of bombing civilian targets began. The Churchill family has links with the Rothschilds (Comm 300). Winston's father, Lord Randolph Churchill, was funded by the House of Rothschild while he was British Chancellor of the Exchequer in the mid 1800s and his closest friend was Nathaniel Rothschild. When Randolph Churchill died, he was in debt to the Rothschilds to the tune of some £65,000.[12] Winston, too, was in debt to them and he was a good friend of Lord Victor Rothschild and the Rothschild's arch manipulator in America, Bernard Baruch.[13] The names of Rothschild and Churchill continue to crop up together today. In 1995, some of Churchill's papers and speeches were controversially sold by his family to the National Heritage Memorial Fund for £12,500,000, thanks to money acquired from the National Lottery.

---

[9] The involvement of *The Times* in the manipulation of British public opinion was quite appalling. As Carroll Quigley reveals, the Round Table controlled the paper indirectly from at least 1912 and took it over completely when the Astors bought the company in 1922. (*The Anglo-American Establishment*, p113.) A key Round Table frontman was Geoffrey Dawson, the editor of *The Times* from 1912 to 1941, which covered the periods in which both World Wars were manipulated into being. He left the editor's chair for three years between 1919 and 1922 after disagreements with the owner, Lord Northcliffe. The moment the Astors took over, lapdog Dawson was restored. (p102.)

[10] House of Commons, May 8th 1940.

[11] House of Commons, March 16th 1939.

[12] *The Churchills*, (Independent Television, May 1995).

[13] Secret Societies, p208

The Chairman of the National Heritage Memorial Fund, which agreed to buy the papers for such a large sum, is Lord Jacob Rothschild. Also important were Churchill's close links with Bernard Baruch and the elite family known as the Cecils. Indeed they controlled him to a large extent. The Cecils have longtime connections with the networks set up by another elite front, the Jesuits, and to other families in the European elite like the Habsburgs and the Black Nobility of Italy. Churchill knew exactly what he was doing.

Within a fortnight of walking into 10 Downing Street, Churchill was using the infamous 'Regulation 18b' to imprison hundreds of British people who opposed the war or pointed out that it was being engineered by a secret force.[14] This approach must be noted in any guide to freedom. It is one thing to use propaganda to feed public opinion a particular line, but if you are a manipulator, you also need to stop anyone who is voicing alternative information. What the British administration did was to use Regulation 18b to imprison – without trial – those who sought to reveal who was really creating the war, and to justify this in the public mind with press claims of a subversive 'Fifth Column' at work in Britain, in support of Hitler. Regulation 18b had been introduced before the war in response to bombings in London which had been blamed on the IRA. It conveniently allowed people to be imprisoned purely on 'suspicion'. There was no need for the State to prove anything and I can't help thinking that this law was another case of: create the 'problem' (the London bombings blamed on the IRA) and then offer the 'solution': a regulation that gives you the power to arrest and imprison whomever you like, whenever you like, during the war you already know is coming. One lady, a Mrs Nicholson, the wife of a distinguished admiral, was arrested, tried, and acquitted on all counts of being involved in a 'Fifth Column'. As she left the court, cleared of all charges by a judge and jury, she was arrested under Regulation 18b and imprisoned for several years. This was happening in a country, under Churchill, that was supposed to be fighting for freedom! Who was the British intelligence officer in charge of the prosecutions under Regulation 18b? Lord Victor Rothschild, the friend, I would say manipulator, of Churchill.[15] Rothschild controlled the intelligence operative who was *officially* in charge of 18b, Maxwell Knight. Intelligence researcher, Doctor Kitty Little, who investigated Lord Rothschild's activities for fifty years, told me:

---

[14] Some researchers believe that 18b was used without Churchill's knowledge.

[15] Lord Victor Rothschild went on to be a governor of the BBC and a key influence in atomic energy policy, the National Research and Development Corporation, the Medical Research Council, and the Agricultural Research Council (in the period when British farming was destroyed and taken over by factory farming and the methods which have turned large areas of the British countryside into ecological deserts). He was good for pharmaceutical companies, though. Lord Rothschild was named in a book in 1994 as the 'fifth man' in the British spy scandal involving Philby, Maclean, Burgess and Blunt.

"Being in control of counter-subversion and the administration of 18b gave Rothschild plenty of scope for subversive activities. He was able to ensure that members of the three covert sections of his organisation were protected from investigation, while he used 18b in two ways. On the one hand he was able to intern people like Fuchs [the Soviet spy and nuclear physicist, Klaus Fuchs, who later worked on the atomic bomb project] *and send them to the camp in Canada where they received training in subversive organisation or sought to thwart the activities of its members. Since then many other people whose normal patriotism or whose normal scientific activities have run counter to the desires of subversive agents, have found their careers and influence inexplicably hampered and thwarted. His agents reached the stage when patriotism was routinely smeared as 'fascist', or 'extreme Right wing', or 'racist' or 'anti-Semitic'."* [16]

A famous victim of Regulation 18b was the Conservative MP, Captain Archibald Maule Ramsey, formerly of the Royal Military College, Sandhurst. Ramsey served with the 2nd Battalion of the Coldstream Guards in the First World War before he was severely wounded in 1916. He blamed Jews for the manipulation of the Second World War and he did not hide that fact. My feeling is that to blame any one race for anything is extremely simplistic and can quite wrongly give the impression that *all* Jews are responsible. This is fundamentally *not* the case. I believe Jewish people as a whole are victims of the Global Elite, not behind it. But that some people who are Jewish are involved is without question. Why is it apparently terrible to say *that* when it is OK to say that some Arabs or Germans are involved, which they are? People are people are people. Or they should be. I don't care what bodies they have. It is what they do that interests me.

Ramsey made some very legitimate points about the covert manoeuvrings and he asked some very pertinent questions in the House of Commons, while most of the other MPs were, as usual, easy prey for the manipulation. In a statement from Brixton Prison to the Speaker and members of the House of Commons, Ramsey claimed to have uncovered nearly thirty organisations which were working in Britain to bring about what I call the Elite agenda. The names that interconnected and controlled these organisations were, according to Ramsey: Professor Harold J. Laski (Fabian Society and Labour Party), Israel Moses Sieff, Professor Herman Levy, Victor Gollancz, D.N. Pritt MP, and G.R. Strauss MP. Notably, given what would later unfold as the European Community, he said his investigations had unearthed a plot to bring about a Federal Europe. That has certainly proved to be correct. He said in February 1940 he was handed some literature about a new group advocating a Federal Europe under centralised control. "The list of supporters' names was startling" he said. "It might have been copied from

---

[16] Dr Kitty Little, conversation with the author, July 1995.

the chart I had just completed." This chart was the interconnecting names and organisations he said were engineering the war, some of whom are listed above.[17] Ramsey raised these matters in a question in the House of Commons. He asked for confirmation that the creation of a Federal Union of Europe was not one of the war aims of the government, but he received only a noncommittal reply. Ramsey had, in fact, identified one of the key reasons for the war, as we shall see.

His most potent threat to the manipulators came from his connections with Tyler Kent, an American coding officer employed at the US Embassy in London, where Joseph Kennedy (the father of JFK) was the ambassador. Kennedy was later to say that he opposed the war because it had been manipulated to happen. More about this in *Chapter 12*. Kent had sent coded cables between Winston Churchill and Franklin D. Roosevelt *before* Churchill became Prime Minister. They were both knowingly part of the scam. Churchill was then the First Lord of the Admiralty. The contents of the cables confirmed that the war was indeed a setup, with Churchill and Roosevelt plotting together to arrange future events. They also showed that the manipulation of the war in Europe was being coordinated from New York.

Ramsey saw some of these documents at Kent's flat at 47 Gloucester Place. He intended to see the rest and make the contents known to Chamberlain after a visit to Scotland. While he was away, Chamberlain was replaced by Churchill and when Ramsey returned to London, he was arrested on the steps of his house under Regulation 18b. He spent the rest of the war in jail and so did Tyler Kent, who was found guilty of stealing documents from the US Embassy.[18] Ambassador Joseph Kennedy sacked Kent just before he was arrested by the British authorities and this deprived him of diplomatic immunity from prosecution in the British courts. He was tried in secret in ways that were illegal under the American Constitution. Kent and Ramsey were jailed in Britain for the duration of the war, along with another investigator, Anna Wookoff, to prevent them revealing the truth about the war and how it started. Part of Kent's defence against the charges was that Roosevelt was helping to remove Chamberlain and install Churchill, and that this was part of a chain of events designed to bring America into the war.

In the USA and the UK, the wartime leaders, Roosevelt and Churchill, are still revered as wartime heroes, and yet the legends and reality are light years apart. Even the conventional 'history' which says that Churchill broadcast live to the nation on the BBC to lift morale (with lines like "We will fight them on the beaches"), is a fantasy. Churchill's speeches were never broadcast live or in their entirety by the BBC. He made them in the House of Commons and short recorded clips were later used in the news bulletins.

---

[17] Captain A.H.M. Ramsey, *The Nameless War*, (OMNI Publications, London, 1952) p101.
[18] See John Howland Snow's *The Case Of Tyler Kent*, (The Long House, Connecticut, USA, 1946).

After the war, it was an actor who recorded his speeches in full for the Decca record company.[19]

With Roosevelt, Churchill, and Hitler all in place, the Elite could step up the war and turn it into a worldwide conflict. It would be a massive global problem in search of a massive global solution: the United Nations, the European Community, and all the other centralised institutions that would appear after 1945. According to Roosevelt's son, Colonel Elliot Roosevelt, his father used the cover of an invented fishing trip in August 1941 to meet Churchill on board a warship in Argentia Bay. Also at the meeting were Lord Beaverbrook (the owner of the London *Daily Express*) and Averell Harriman (whose family business had financed the Bolshevik Revolution, Adolf Hitler, the Nazi war machine, and eugenics organisations advocating the forced sterilisation of the 'lower classes' to bring about a Master Race). These were the people who met to discuss opposition to Hitler! Churchill, Beaverbrook and Harriman were all members of the Committee of 300.

Harriman was close to both Roosevelt and Churchill and he acted as the go-between, advising both of them. From this position, he could manipulate the two leaders as he liked, or rather, as the Global Elite liked. The Elite's problem was to bounce the American people into sending their sons and daughters into another war in Europe which, on the face of it, had nothing to do with them. The American people were so keen to avoid war that Roosevelt could only get re-elected by saying he had no intention of sending their children to fight in Europe or anywhere else, thus echoing the words of Woodrow Wilson before he took America into the First World War. Like Wilson, Roosevelt was lying. Look at some of the things he said:

> "...And while I am talking to you mothers and fathers, I give you one more assurance. I have said this before, but I shall say it again and again and again. Your boys are not going to be sent into any foreign wars." [20]
>
> "You can therefore nail any talk about sending armies to Europe as deliberate untruth." [21]

All the time he was saying these things, he knew the Second World War was being executed by the Elite and that the means to make American public opinion accept US involvement had long been unfolding behind the scenes. Roosevelt was breaking the international laws on neutrality and defying his own speeches by supplying the British with ammunition and weapons both covertly and through the Lend Lease Act. Some members of Congress could see what was happening. Representative Philip Bennett of Missouri said:

[19] Source: The BBC Written Archive Centre.
[20] Boston, October 30th 1940. *Public Papers And Addresses Of Franklin D. Roosevelt,* (Macmillan, New York), 1940 volume, p517.
[21] Ibid (December 29th 1940) p633–644.

"But our boys are not going to be sent abroad, says the President. Nonsense, Mr Chairman; even now their berths are being built in our transport ships. Even now the tags for identification of the dead and wounded are being printed by the firm of William C. Ballantyne and Co of Washington." [22]

To this day, popular accounts of history portray Roosevelt as a man who "strove in vain to ward off war".[23] The Elite plan, long known by Roosevelt, was to engineer an attack on the United States which would so anger public opinion that people would agree to go to war against the aggressor and, as a consequence of that, join the European conflict also. As a member of Woodrow Wilson's administration in the First World War, Roosevelt would have been well-schooled in manipulating public opinion with engineered events. In 1939, Senator P. Nye of North Dakota said that he had seen a series of volumes called *The Next War*, including one called *Propaganda In The Next War*. This was the document to which I referred some chapters earlier. It revealed that the Americans had been promised that Britain would recognise a Jewish homeland in Palestine if the Americans entered the First World War. As Senator Nye revealed, the material also included the game plan for manipulating public opinion into accepting American intervention in the second global conflict, which these documents – written between the wars – said was coming. The propaganda document, which originated in Britain, said:

> *"To persuade her* [the United States] *to take our part will be much more difficult, so difficult as to be unlikely to succeed. It will need a definite threat to America, a threat moreover, which will have to be brought home by propaganda to every citizen, before the Republic will again take arms in an external quarrel...*
>
> *"The position will naturally be considerably eased if* **Japan** [my emphasis] *were involved, and this might and probably would bring America in without further ado. At any rate, it would be a natural and obvious effect of our propagandists to achieve this, just as in the Great War they succeeded in embroiling the United States with Germany...*
>
> *"Fortunately with America, our propaganda is on firm ground. We can be entirely sincere, as our main plank will be the old democratic one. We must clearly enunciate our belief in the democratic form of government, and our firm resolve to adhere to...the old goddess of democracy routine."* [24]

The manipulation around Roosevelt was coordinated by Bernard Baruch and that front for the Global Elite, the Council on Foreign Relations (CFR). Baruch was chairman of the War Industries Board during World War I and

---

[22] Quoted by A.H.M. Ramsey in *The Nameless War*, p75.

[23] *Pears Cyclopaedia, 85th Edition*, p852.

[24] Congressional Record, 76th Congress, Vol. 84, No. 82, p6597–6604.

was among the 'advisors' who negotiated the German reparations at Versailles. He was the voice in Roosevelt's ear, as he had been for many presidents. The Council on Foreign Relations devised the plan to antagonise Japan to such a degree that they would attack the United States. At the forefront of this was Roosevelt's Secretary of War, Henry Stimson, a founder of the CFR. In his diary he wrote: "We face the delicate question of diplomatic fencing to be done so as to be sure Japan is put into the wrong and makes the first bad overt move".[25] The CFR's War and Peace Studies Project sent a memo to Roosevelt, suggesting that aid be given to China while she was in conflict with Japan, and that Japanese assets in the US be frozen, a trade embargo imposed, and Japan be refused access to the Panama Canal. I can recommend an excellent book, *Pearl Harbor, The Story Of The Secret War*,[26] by George Morgenstern, which sets out in great detail how the Japanese were goaded into the attack on Pearl Harbor, Hawaii, on December 7th 1941. For four years before the attack, the Roosevelt administration had been intercepting and decoding secret Japanese messages. They knew that the Japanese intended to alert their diplomatic centres around the world of a decision to go to war through a false weather report during the daily Japanese language short-wave news broadcast. The forecast of 'east wind rain' indicated war with the United States, 'west wind clear' would mean a decision to go to war with Britain and British and Dutch colonies in the East, while 'north wind cloudy' meant war with Russia.

As a congressional investigation[27] heard in 1945, the messages indicating a decision to go to war with the United States and Britain, though not with Russia, were intercepted and decoded on December 3rd 1941 – four days before Pearl Harbor. These messages subsequently went 'missing' from Navy files. Other decoded messages gave Roosevelt prior warning of the attack on Pearl Harbor, but the people were not told. On January 27th 1941, the US ambassador in Tokyo, Joseph Grew, had written to Roosevelt to say that in the event of war, Pearl Harbor would be the first target.[28] In all, Roosevelt had information from eight different sources indicating a probable attack.[29] The attack was to happen purely to manipulate American public opinion into agreeing to go into another war, which had been long planned. And no-one was more duped than the Japanese. They had been tricked into attacking the US, both by the Americans and the Germans. The German foreign minister, Joachim von Ribbentrop, had been pressing

---

[25] Quoted in *Casebook On Alternative 3*, p25.

[26] George Morgenstern, *Pearl Harbor, The Story Of The Secret War*, (Costa Mesa, USA, 1991 edition. First published in 1947).

[27] Joint Congressional Committee of the Investigation of the Pearl Harbor attack. It was largely a coverup.

[28] *Secret Societies*, p210

[29] *Casebook On Alternative 3*, p26.

the Japanese to attack the United States. On December 6th, Hitler had added to the Japanese resolve by indicating that the German forces were about to enter Moscow. On December 8th, the day after Pearl Harbor, the Germans were found to be in retreat from the Russian front. Three thousand people were killed at Pearl Harbor, the latest victims in the Elite's plan to control the world, but most of the cream of the US Navy was out of harbour at the time. Surprised? The day after Pearl Harbor, Allen Dulles was appointed to the staff of the Office of the Coordinator of Information, which later became the Office of Strategic Services (OSS) and then the CIA.

The plan worked brilliantly, as public opinion reacted in exactly the way required. America was into another war in Europe and 'our boys' who were not going to be sent to Europe (according to Roosevelt) were now on their way, many of them to die. Churchill's reaction to the news was: "That is what I have dreamed of, aimed at, and worked for, and now it has come to pass".[30] He might have added, "And I always knew it was going to". The Round Table/Royal Institute of International Affairs were perfectly placed to coordinate the manipulation in the United States. Lord Lothian, who campaigned for the appeasement of Hitler and then demanded war, was named British Ambassador to the United States. When he died in December 1940, he was replaced in Washington by another elite member of the Round Table/RIIA, Lord Halifax (Comm 300). This was the man, you will recall, who suggested a deal with Hitler when they met in 1938. Apart from the British Embassy in Washington, the Round Table had its members in control of the Research and Intelligence Department of the UK Foreign Office, the Ministry of Information, and all the agencies involved with economic 'mobilisation and reconstruction'.[31] A similar situation prevailed in the US. The influence on Roosevelt of the Council on Foreign Relations, with its membership throughout the government, banking, commerce, media, and military, cannot be overestimated. Roosevelt's son-in-law, Curtis Dall, quoted in Jim Keith's *Casebook On Alternative 3*, said:

> "For a long time I felt that [Roosevelt]...had developed many thoughts and ideas that were his own to benefit this country, the USA. But he didn't. Most of his thoughts, his political 'ammunition' as it were, were carefully manufactured for him in advance by the Council on Foreign Relations/One World Money Group. Brilliantly, with great gusto, like a fine piece of artillery, he exploded that prepared 'ammunition' in the middle of an unsuspecting target, the American people – and thus paid off and retained his internationalist political support." (p25)

---

[30] February 15th 1942. Radio address reported in *The New York Times*, February 16th.
[31] *The Anglo-American Establishment*, p303.

Dall also revealed that Roosevelt had ignored a German offer of an "honourable surrender" in the spring of 1943. The offer was made to Commander George Earle, Roosevelt's personal military attaché in Istanbul, by Admiral Wilhelm Canaris, the head of the German secret service, and later repeated by Fritz Von Papen, the German Ambassador. All the messages which Earle sent to Roosevelt detailing the offer of surrender were ignored.[32] The manipulators wanted the war to continue until the world was changed in their image.

Symbolically, the Roosevelt mansion (on East 65th Street in New York) was next door to the headquarters of the Council on Foreign Relations! While hell was being visited upon this planet for a second time in twenty-five years, the Elite were right on course. As in the First War, the idea was to win the peace once it was all over, and to leave the world at the end of the war in a situation that could be most effectively controlled. Hitler didn't invade Britain when it was there for the taking (after the Dunkirk retreat of 1940) because, I am increasingly convinced, those who were controlling him did not want that to happen. And, as became clear after the war, the Allied Supreme Commander, General Eisenhower, was prevented by Roosevelt (the Global Elite) from moving on through Germany when the Germans were overrun, so that the Soviet Union Empire could be extended to Berlin and the Cold War thus created. Eisenhower was a close associate of the Rockefellers and Bernard Baruch. Thanks to them his progress through the ranks was astonishingly fast. After the war he became President of the United States. On April 9th 1951, *Life* magazine reported that Eisenhower had radioed Stalin via the US military mission in Moscow, to detail his plan to stop at the Elbe River and allow the Russians to take Berlin. The message was written by his political advisor, John Wheeler Bennett of the Royal Institute of International Affairs, received by W. Averell Harriman, and passed on to Stalin.[33] The Iron Curtain and the Berlin Wall were Elite creations on the classic principle of divide and rule and manipulate through fear. World war as a form of control was going to be replaced, at least for a few decades, by the *fear* of apocalyptic conflict between East and West. This fear was fuelled by the unveiling of a new and devastating weapon, the atomic bomb. It was created by the Americans under the so called 'Manhattan Project', led by Robert Oppenheimer, with support from the Elite-controlled Institute for Advanced Study at Princeton University (where Albert Einstein was a regular visitor).

---

[32] *Secret Societies*, p212

[33] When the victorious allies did make it to Berlin, the place was looted by the British, Americans, and Russians. Among the looters was one Captain Du Maurier. We know him better as Robert Maxwell, international publisher, thief, and agent of the Israeli secret service, Mossad. The Berlin porcelain dining table set sold after his mysterious death at sea in 1991 was stolen from a Berlin Museum in 1945. Source: *The Spotlight* newspaper, (April 17th 1995) p4.

After Roosevelt's death,[34] his successor, another Freemason, Harry S. Truman, authorised the use of this 'new' weapon to destroy the Japanese cities of Hiroshima and Nagasaki on August 6th and 9th 1945. Eighty thousand men, women, and children were killed by the explosion at Hiroshima alone. Goodness knows how many have died or suffered since from the effects of the radiation. This grotesque act of inhumanity was justified by the politicians and military leaders as the only way to protect American lives which, it was said, would have been lost in enormous numbers had an invasion of Japan been authorised. We now know different. We now know that the Japanese had agreed to surrender the previous spring on the *same* terms that were accepted after the bombs were dropped. Emperor Hirohito agreed to this through secret negotiations with the US via the Vatican. The former British cabinet minister, Tony Benn, has said that he learned that this was the case when he entered government. Retired Colonel Donn Grand Pre, writing in the American investigative newspaper, *The Spotlight*, on September 12th 1994, said that he also knew for sure that the Japanese would have surrendered before Hiroshima. He said that in May 1945 he was with a military force, driving what was left of the Japanese army out of North Burma while B-29s were devastating Tokyo in a series of raids. Two days after those raids in the May, the Colonel said, the acting US Secretary of State, Joseph C. Grew, recommended to President Truman that he add to his terms for a Japanese surrender the words... "surrender would not mean the elimination of the present dynasty (Emperor Hirohito) if the Japanese desired its retention". These were the terms on which the Japanese would surrender after the horrors of three months later. Truman apparently favoured the addition, but after consulting with his advisors, the idea was dropped for 'military reasons'. It was a question of timing, the dissenters said. Truman's decision was to cost tens of thousands of lives, possibly hundreds of thousands. The 'question of timing' related to the Potsdam Conference when Truman, Churchill, and Josef Stalin would issue an ultimatum to Japan – minus the suggested addition. As Colonel Donn Grand Pre now says:

> *"The psychological spin behind the exploding of the bombs was to create such a worldwide fear of the power of nuclear energy that countries would give up their sovereignty, turn all their weapons and armed forces over to a world government and surrender their freedom."* [35]

President Truman said in an address shortly before Hiroshima: "It will be just as easy for nations to get along in a republic of the world as it is for us to

---

[34] Some researchers claim that Roosevelt died earlier than officially announced and that a look-alike was used for the latter months of the war. The two men certainly have obvious facial differences when their pictures are put side by side.

[35] *The Spotlight*, (September 12th 1994) p15.

get along in the Republic of the United States". This same approach of justifying centralised world government and all that goes with it can be seen in the statements of Albert Einstein, the man remembered for his scientific genius to such an extent that today you still hear very clever people described as being an 'Einstein'. But there was more to him than that. Einstein, who arrived in America from Germany via Switzerland, was a close friend of Bernard Baruch, the financier and string puller of presidents, and of Lord Victor Rothschild, the arch manipulator within British Intelligence who would gather atomic information for Israel's secret nuclear weapons programme. Einstein worked on the development of the atomic bomb and Baruch called it the 'absolute weapon'. Baruch set himself up as the head of an organisation he called The United Nations Atomic Energy Commission in 1944 – sixteen months before the US Cabinet, including the then Vice President Truman, knew the bomb even existed and before the first meeting of the official founding group of the United Nations! But then Baruch and his fellow manipulators had known since the First World War what was planned. When Truman became president and learned of the bomb and the United Nations became official, he appointed Baruch to head... the United Nations Atomic Energy Commission. Both Baruch and Einstein sought to use the fear of atomic destruction to install a world government. What a help it was to have an example in Hiroshima and Nagasaki to emphasise its capacity for destruction! Einstein called for the formation of a world government by the United States, Britain and the Soviet Union, to which the 'secret of the bomb' should be given. He said that these three were "the only three powers with great military strength" and he urged them to commit this strength (world army) to the world government. The 'genius' went on:

> "The world government would have power over all military matters and need have only one further power: the power to intervene in countries where a minority is oppressing a majority and creating the kind of instability that leads to war... There must be an end to the concept of non-intervention, for to end it is part of keeping the peace." [36]

These mental gymnastics were right off the pages of the Elite personnel manual and these themes are being parroted to this day by those seeking to turn the United Nations 'peacekeeping' forces into an Einstein-like world army. Just look at Bosnia. Under Einstein's criteria of a minority oppressing a majority, the first intervention by the world government and army should have been in the Soviet Union which he said should be *part* of the world government and army! But, no. The genius had an answer to that:

---

[36] *The Atlantic Monthly*, (November 1945).

"While it is true that in the Soviet Union the minority rules, I do not consider the internal conditions there are of themselves a threat to world peace. One must bear in mind that the people of Russia did not have a long political education and changes to improve Russian conditions had to be carried through by a minority for the reason that there was no majority capable of doing it." [37]

Decoded, this Einstein-speak is saying that what we need is to use the fear of mass destruction to install a world (Elite) government which will have a world army at its disposal to intervene whenever it believed its interests and power would benefit. In 1946, Einstein's British friend, Bertrand Russell (Comm 300), said that it was necessary to use the fear of nuclear weapons to force all nations to give up their sovereignty and submit to the dictatorship of the United Nations.[38] This was the approach decided upon in 1958 at the second of the Pugwash Conferences when the policy of Mutual Assured Destruction (MAD) was agreed. The conferences were hosted by Cyrus Eaton, a business partner of the Rockefellers.[39] In reality, the MAD policy involved building up nuclear arsenals on both sides to the point where for either to attack the other would mean annihilation for both of them. The fear of this would be used as a wonderful means of controlling government policy, arms spending, and public opinion throughout the Cold War, while at the top levels of manipulation they were all on the same side. Pavel A. Sudoplatov, head of the Soviet Intelligence Bureau on the atomic problem during World War Two, has now confirmed that Oppenheimer was supplying data about the bomb to the Soviet Union during the war.[40] Klaus Fuchs, the German nuclear physicist, worked on the Manhattan Project after he 'fled' from Germany to Britain in 1933. Fuchs, a close associate of Lord Victor Rothschild (Comm 300), was later jailed for fourteen years for supplying British and American atomic secrets to the Russians. The post-war Pugwash Conferences, inspired by Einstein and Bertrand Russell, were another means through which scientific data was passed from one side to the other during the alleged 'Cold War'. They also helped Victor Rothschild to amass nuclear information for Israel, as we shall see later.

It is hard to believe at first, but you don't have to search too far to realise that almost *every* major negative event of global significance has been part of the same long-term plan by the All-Seeing Eye cult to take over the planet via a centralised world government, central bank, currency, and army. And it is being done by programming the human mind. If we are going to stop this

[37] Ibid.
[38] *Bulletin Of Atomic Scientists*, (October 1946).
[39] Pugwash comes from the name of the Canadian estate of industrialist, Cyrus Eaton. He began his career as secretary to J.D. Rockefeller before he became a business partner of the dynasty.
[40] *The Spotlight*, (May 16th and September 12th 1994).

and allow humanity to burst forth in its full potential for love and harmony, there is one thing we need to do above all else. We have to stop thinking in black and white and soften our rigid belief systems. This world is not black and white. Nothing is. If you have a rigid belief system that is not open to the endless subtleties of life, you become a manipulator's party trick. If you believe that someone running a business in a pin-striped suit is bad by definition, without listening to what the person has to say, your mind is not your own. The same with those who see the homeless or travellers and immediately react with 'scroungers' or 'dossers'. Or those who believe one race or other is inferior to their own. No-one is all right and no-one is all wrong.

Because the thinking of the mass of the British people before and during World War Two was so set and inflexible, it bought the idea of good v evil, when the same force was behind both sides. It also allowed people who had the courage to stand up and speak out against the manipulation to be jailed without charge throughout the war. If you challenge our side, you must be a supporter of the other side, this childlike mindset believed. This is the type of non-thinking which allows the manipulation to go on. Still today, if you speak of the global deception and mention any name involved which happens to be Jewish, you are immediately branded 'anti-Semitic'. Some people do this purposely to discredit the researcher and diminish the impact of their information. Others, like the people I call the Robot Radicals, parrot these slogans because their minds are so rigid at this time, that they couldn't cope with the idea that many of their 'far Left', 'radical', heroes, were controlled by the same force, sometimes *part* of the same force, which controls their perceived enemies on the 'far Right'.

It was this naïvety that allowed the World Wars to happen. For the second time in forty-five years both 'Left' and 'Right' had been manipulated into conflict with the most devastating and horrific effect. Sadly, the same childish responses continue to this day.

Chapter 7

Master races

The same attitude that suppressed the challenge to the manipulation of World War Two, today sees people vilified and jailed for questioning some of the official versions of The Holocaust in Nazi Germany. If you do that, no-one listens to the evidence because this is lost in the tidal wave of vilification and condemnation. If people want to believe that all those who question the official line are Nazis and apologists for the Hitler regime, or anti-Jewish, then they must go ahead and do so. But I'll tell them this. They are kidding themselves, because that isn't true. It simply isn't.

As the old vibration of life begins to crumble and the new one emerges, we are in the period now when the muck of the past which has remained hidden is coming to the surface to be dealt with and dispersed. The content of this book is part of that. It is not only individuals who have suppressed emotions which eat them away and eventually have to be dealt with, it is the Earth and the collective mind of humanity also. The process of cleansing the Earth takes many forms, and one of them is for all that has been secret and suppressed to come into the public spotlight. Whether people like it or whether they don't, the official version of The Holocaust cannot avoid this exposure to proper debate for very much longer. The process of cleansing and transformation will ensure that this will happen.

The way the Nazis treated many Jewish people is unspeakable. There are no words adequate to describe it. The pain, as we see in the commemorations, appears undiminished for those who lived through it. What an insult it would be to those people who suffered so, if it were established that their pain and unimaginable horror is also being used without their knowledge, to promote and protect a longer-term plan. It would qualify, perhaps, as one of the ultimate inhumanities. Are people who did not suffer under the Nazis using the emotions of those who did to manipulate events for their own diabolical ends? We can only establish if that is true by allowing all information about that period to be made public without vilification or condemnation.

As Professor Yehuda Bauer, the chairman of the Vidal Sassoon Centre for the Study of Anti-Semitism, said, "Someone is misusing people's fears and obsessions and presenting things we know today did not happen".[1] He was

---

[1] *Jewish Chronicle*, (April 7th 1995).

reacting to stories about 'human soap' which holocaust 'experts' have said the Nazis made out of the bodies of Jewish victims in the concentration camps. This has become an accepted 'fact', but Professor Bauer said there was no documentary evidence that any such thing took place. In the researching of this book, for the first time in my life I stumbled across information which questions the official holocaust line. I was shocked, to be honest. I looked at it and I wrote it down, a process that always helps me to get things clearer in my mind. I pondered on it endlessly for weeks. My conclusion was that there were the most terrible atrocities against Jewish people, as there were against others in Germany, the Soviet Union, and in Japanese-occupied countries. The whole war was a holocaust. What the European settlers did to the Native American tribes was a holocaust. The atrocities that Jewish people did suffer under the Nazis, makes the pain that we see thoroughly understandable. But I also concluded from the evidence I came across that the official line has a vast number of questions to answer and enormous tracts of documented information to explain before we can really know what happened. Like I say, nothing is ever what it seems, no matter what we may be told. When, for instance, a Jewish American like David Cole produces evidence and video documentaries demolishing the official claims about the events at Auschwitz, you cannot, if you are interested in truth, just dismiss his findings and condemn him as a Nazi apologist. That is not to say that everything people say is correct, but why are we so frightened to allow the public to decide for themselves? Why is such information suppressed?

People might not like me making these points, but I ask them this: what is a true love for humanity? Is it saying what you believe people *need* to know and taking the flak? Or is it saying what you think they *want* to know and taking the plaudits?

I come back to something that I see often in my research into the Global Elite: the way Jewish people are used as mere propaganda fodder by the upper reaches of their own hierarchy, especially the Rothschilds and others like the Habsburgs. Jewish people are not seeking to take over the world. The opposite is true. They just want to get on peacefully and joyfully with their lives, like all of us. Instead, they are being used mercilessly by their own privileged, manipulating cliques to be the 'fall guy', to protect the few from legitimate investigation and exposure. So much of their history is kept from them to ensure they remain under the mental and emotional control of the few. Major Alojzy Dziurski, of the wartime Polish underground movement, was no apologist for the Nazis and nor was he anti-Jewish. He had a wide circle of Jewish friends and expressed a deep gratitude to the Jew he said had saved his life. In his book, *Freedom Fighter*, Dziurski told how he heard that the German attitude to Jews had changed quite dramatically after they realised the Zionist influence in Stalin's Soviet Union. This prompted Major Dziurski to meet with Polish Jewish leaders in March 1942, to warn them that they must disperse the Jews living in the ghettos, move them to homes among Polish farmers in remote areas, and establish settlements in forested areas. He said the leaders refused, with terrible consequences. The major said he became a close friend of a Jewish captain, who had been a Political Commissar in the Red Army. Dziurski said in his book:

> *"Because of my interest in Jewish affairs, he* [the Captain] *would share with me a well-guarded secret. Accepted as a devoted Zionist, he would attend a secret meeting for initiated Zionists only. It was conducted in Hebrew, not in Yiddish, as most meetings were. The majority of the speakers were foreign Zionist leaders, but he recognised only one, Moshe Sneh, a Polish Jewish leader, who had left for Palestine before the war and returned in 1945 as Berihah leader to organise the mass emigration of Polish Jews. Every speaker emphasised the unique opportunity that had come to snatch Palestine and the Middle East from the Arabs and the British...The whole non-Jewish world had to be made to feel guilty for The Holocaust together with the Nazis. The Holocaust must be shown to be the greatest Christian crime against the Jewish people. Intensive propaganda would be launched, and all publishing houses and the press under Jewish influence had already been instructed to propagate the story of Jewish sufferings.*
> *"Moshe Sneh had demanded that the maximum number of Polish Jews must be forced to leave Poland for Palestine or any country of their choice. Instructions had been issued to Western European Jewry to prepare for the reception of Polish immigrants...to filter later into the United States. The USA must be made the great reservoir of Jewry to influence American politics because the USA would become the decisive world power."* [2]

You may or may not accept that. But you have a right to hear it, and much, much, more of the documented background information relating to this subject will be coming to the surface in the years to come. No-one will be more stunned by what will be made known than the mass of Jewish people themselves. They are going to look on their hierarchy in a very different light. Major Dziurski compiled a large number of writings and archives about his wartime experiences and the information given to him by Jewish friends and acquaintances. These were stolen in a robbery at his home in May 1965, after which he emigrated to Australia.

I strongly believe that a small Jewish clique which has contempt for the mass of Jewish people worked with non-Jews to create the First World War, the Russian Revolution, and the Second World War. This Jewish/non-Jewish Elite

---

[2] Major Alojzy Dziurski, *Freedom Fighter*, (J.A. Dewar, Portland, Victoria, 1983).

used the First World War to secure the Balfour Declaration and the principle of the Jewish State of Israel in Palestine (for which, given the genetic history of most Jewish people, there is absolutely no justification on historical grounds or any other). They then dominated the Versailles Peace Conference and created the circumstances which made the Second World War inevitable. They financed Hitler to power in 1933 and made the funds available for his rearmament. Their representatives in other nations manipulated their governments to allow Hitler and the Nazis to invade surrounding countries and increase their military power and potential by acquiring the resources of those countries. They gave Hitler the impression that he could expand across mainland Europe without challenge, but then, at a prearranged time, the attitude of Britain changed dramatically and he found himself in a war he could not win – especially after Roosevelt manipulated the American people, via Pearl Harbor, into a conflict he said they would never be involved in.

Meanwhile, those Jews in Germany who were part of, or useful to, this tiny Jewish/non-Jewish Elite were allowed to leave the Nazi-occupied lands and escape to the USA, other safe countries, and to Palestine to begin the work that would culminate in the creation of Israel after the war. They were not the ones who were to suffer so terribly under Hitler. Far from it. They were the ones who were going to use and exploit the suffering of those left behind. When the privileged elite, like the banker Max Warburg, had left Germany, the Jewish men, women, and children considered expendable in pursuit of a wider goal were left to their fate. That fate was sealed when Alfred Rosenberg with his Jewish background, made a copy of *The Protocols Of The Learned Elders Of Zion* available to Hitler.

So what could possibly motivate this manipulating Jewish clique to treat their fellow Jews in such a subhuman way? Quite simply, the manipulators are not really Jews, as Rabbi Marvin S. Antelman points out in his 1974 book, *To Eliminate The Opiate*. Antelman, who lost seventeen members of his family to the Nazis, says that this clique does not want to promote Judaism, it wants to destroy it, as it wants to destroy all alternatives to its own focus of worship, the All-Seeing Eye cult of antiquity. It is this which provides the common themes of loyalty and motivation between the Jews, Arabs, British, Germans, Americans etc, who are knowingly working together to bring about the global fascist tyranny known as the New World Order. The 'Jews' of the Global Elite could not give a damn about Jewish people, as the Germans in the clique could not care less about the German people. To them, the masses of whatever race, colour, or country, are a herd of nonentities who are there to be used only as necessary to serve their master – the Luciferic Consciousness on the Fourth Dimension. The 'All Seeing' Jews, however, and their non-Jewish conspirators, use the smokescreen of 'anti-Semitism' and the genuine suffering of *real* Jews to prevent investigation of their sinister activities. I am convinced that it was this clique which wrote and leaked the Protocols and made it look like a plot by Jewish people as a whole. It is *not*. No, no, no!

After the war, the unimaginable suffering of Jewish people, condemned by their own elite, among others, was used to bring the State of Israel into being on a wave of understandable emotion, given the stories the world was being told. It has been used ever since to block legitimate investigation into the manipulation of the human race. The label 'anti-Semite' is hurled at anyone who challenges the official version of history and who exposes the people who really control the world. One vehicle for this Jewish and non-Jewish clique – which has made Jews suffer so much – is called Zionism and so is the State of Israel, a country and a ruling mindset, which to me looks remarkably like the Nazi mentality.

The British hierarchy has provably manipulated, exploited, and sent to their deaths multimillions of British people to serve the 'national interest' – the interests of the ruling clique; the German hierarchy has done the same to the German people and the American hierarchy to the American population. These ruling cliques have utter contempt for their 'unwashed masses'. They see them as cattle to be used and abused as required. Why is it so amazing that the Jewish hierarchy should see the mass of Jewish people in the same terms?

The exploitation of those who did suffer by those who didn't has allowed the ruling elite of Israel to commit the most terrible atrocities without challenge from the wider world community, while any perceived threat to Israel is immediately condemned and dealt with. Why do we not hear about the decades of atrocities by Israel against the dispossessed Palestinians, which have been reported again and again by members of the United Nations Relief and Works Agency? The grotesque irony is that while complaining about the 'far Right' and 'anti-Semitism', the Israeli government has supported Nazi regimes across the world, including the terrorist, Somoza, who was responsible for the slaughter of tens of thousands of his own people in Nicaragua.[3] Israel has armed or supported neo-Nazis and terrorists in Taiwan, Saudi Arabia, Central America, Argentina, and scores of others,[4] in league with the neo-Nazis who control the United States and the CIA. When Israel pontificates about racism and the far Right, it turns my stomach. The Israeli government, its army and its intelligence arm, Mossad, are neo-Nazi, terrorist organisations. This mindset is personified by many of the Israeli settlers in the occupied West Bank and Gaza Strip. The Israeli authorities hide this fact behind Jewish people who genuinely suffered in Hitler's Germany. The Israeli leaders who are part of, or controlled by, the All-Seeing Eye cult, have used this suffering for more than fifty years to conceal and justify daily atrocities against the Arab population. Palestinian children are shot by Nazi settlers in the occupied lands, but the killers escape without punishment. Meanwhile, Arabs are routinely shot by the same

[3] Noam Chomsky, *World Orders, Old And New*, (Pluto Press, London, 1994) p205–206.
[4] Ibid p205–206.

soldiers who look the other way when settlers are terrorising Palestinian men, women, and children.[5] As Hitler treated those Jews cast adrift by their own hierarchy, so does Israel treat Palestinians today. I'll take no lectures on racism and Nazism from apologists for Israeli terrorism, thank you very much.

Indeed those who led the terrorist organisations which created Israel after the war, later became its leaders. To challenge the behaviour of Israel is not to condemn Jewish people. The opposite is the case. Those who have controlled Israel and its international terrorist arm, Mossad, are not true Jews. They are a bunch of unbalanced thugs who have used (abused) Jewish people for their own horrific ends. Israeli Prime Minister Menachim Begin was a leading light in the Jewish terrorist underground organisation, Irgun, and as a result was responsible for untold murder and mayhem. He would later win the Nobel Peace Prize, as did Henry Kissinger. Another Israeli Prime Minister, Yitzhak Shamir, was a terrorist in the Jewish underground before becoming (appropriately, I guess) the head of the Mossad assassination squad at the time of the murder of John F. Kennedy. In a later chapter I link both Shamir and Begin to Kennedy's assassination. Prime Minister Yitzhak Rabin was lauded as a great peace maker after his own assassination in 1995, but he too was a terrorist. As Naeim Giladi, the Israeli historian and author, says: "Rabin launched his career...with terrorist murders that shed both Arab and Jewish blood when cold political calculation demanded it".[6]

In 1940 when illegal Jewish immigration to Palestine became a flood, the British military government began to detain and deport those Jews who did not have the correct documentation. The Zionist underground decided to sabotage the refugee ships rather than allow them to be turned away. Giladi goes on: "In those days Rabin was a member of Palmach – the name means 'action squads' – it was a violent underground force...in November 1940 his group blew up the refugee ship Patria in Haifa harbour. More than 250 Jewish emigrants died in the explosion".[7]

Three other ships were later given the same treatment by Rabin's Palmach and more than a thousand Jews died as a result. But it was the Arabs who were blamed for this barbarity and that was the whole point of the carnage, of course. The Zionist leader, David Ben-Gurion, wrote in his diary that the bombings "stirred more world wide sympathy and support for us than we anticipated".[8] Later I will also connect Ben-Gurion to the Kennedy assassination. I am coming more and more to the conclusion that what happened to Jews in Nazi Germany (whatever the truth turns out to be) was

---

[5] *World Orders, Old And New*, p258–260. Here, he was quoting Yossi Torpshtein, a correspondent for Ha'aretz, and other witnesses.
[6] "Establishment Fakes Rabin's History", *The Spotlight*, (November 20th 1995) p1.
[7] Ibid.
[8] Ibid.

supported, even planned, by these crazy people to ensure that both Israel was created and that 'anti-Semitism' could be used as a defence against legitimate investigation of their sickening activities. That has certainly been the outcome. Anyone who exposes these breathtaking horrors is dubbed a neo-Nazi.

What's more, a lot of the money and the armaments used both by these underground terrorists and the founders of Israel were supplied by the Meyer Lansky organised crime syndicate which was based in the US, but operated internationally. Lansky, who was born Maier Suchowjansky in Grodno, Russia, rose from the slums of New York to the top of the heap in the international underworld. He was above the Mafia. Lansky acheived these dizzy heights by the usual means – murder and terror. This was the man who used his crime and terror networks to channel funds and guns to the Jewish terrorists and the later Israeli State. Such was his contribution that he has been described as "Israel's Godfather".[9] Lansky would run to Israel whenever the heat was turned up in the States and eventually settled in his beloved "homeland". Lansky, too, was at the heart of the murder of John F. Kennedy, as we shall see. These are the sorts of minds that created Israel under the supervision of the Rothschilds. And yet if you challenge and expose these people, you are called a Nazi! Give me strength.

Some brave Jews have spoken out against the behaviour of Israel and the plight of the Palestinians, people like Noam Chomsky and Israel Shahak[10] (a survivor of the Belsen concentration camp), but where are the British government and the United States government? Silence. These are legitimate points in a democracy (hilarious, I know), but people are frightened, even terrified, to make them, because they will be branded 'anti-Semitic'. Even some Jews who have made these points have been branded 'anti-Semitic'! To this day, the clique continues to arrange for 'anti-Semitic' events and attacks which allow this manipulation of the Jewish and non-Jewish communities to go on. The Jewish hierarchy wishes to keep the mass of Jewish people in constant fear, a state of mind which makes anyone child's play to control and manipulate. The far Right are a dream for this clique and they play into their hands by behaving in ways that make the manipulation so much easier. Not all of them are behaving in this way by accident, either. Who actually funds some of these 'far Right' groups? If you know, perhaps you'll tell me.

In Britain, I am told by an extremely reliable source very close to the intelligence organisations that the 'far Right' group, Combat 18, is a front for the sinister Anti-Defamation League, the United States arm of the 'Israeli'/

[9] For the documented evidence of Lansky's central role in the funding and gun running of the Jewish terrorist groups and the State of Israel, I recommend Michael Collins Piper's superb exposé, *Final Judgement. The Missing Link in the JFK Assassination Conspiracy*. See bibliography.
[10] Israel Shahak, *Jewish History, Jewish Religion – The Weight Of Three Thousand Years*, (Pluto Press, London, 1994).

Rothschild secret service, Mossad. The Anti-Defamation League (ADL) has been operating in Britain and Europe since at least 1991 and its role is to brand as anti-Semitic anyone who is getting close to the truth of what is going on. What better way to discredit an investigator than to have a 'far Right' group like Combat 18 to praise them? What better way to control Jewish people through fear than to have the behaviour of Combat 18 as an example of what is waiting for them if they don't have the hierachy to protect them?

If you find all this hard to believe there are many examples that prove the point. At the time of the Kennedy assassination the national secretary of the American Nazi Party was a man called Daniel Burros. He was a close associate of the "Nazi" Roy Frankhouser, a man who once said: "Hitler had the Jews; we've got the niggers. We have to put our main stress on the nigger question, of course, because that's what preoccupies the masses – but we're not forgetting the Jew. If Jews knew what was coming – and believe me, it's coming as surely as the dawn – they'd realise that what's going to happen in America will make Nazi Germany look like a Sunday-school picnic. We'll build better gas chambers, and more of them, and this time there won't be any refugees".[11] Charming. But "Nazi" Frankhouser turned out to be a professional federal infiltrator of the Ku Klux Klan and other "Nazi" and "Communist" organisations. His close associate, the "Nazi" Daniel Burros, was exposed in October 1965 as a Jew by the *New York Times*. The following day he was found shot dead at Frankhouser's home in Reading, Pennsylvania. Verdict "suicide". Burros was also a key figure in the "Nazi" National Renaissance Party, which was controlled by the Anti-Defamation League. Life is never what it seems. The 'opponent' of Combat 18 in the UK is an organisation called Searchlight. The same source tells me that this is a front for the Board of Deputies of British Jews and the ADL. Can anyone confirm this? It is an old, old strategy. Even Mossad is not what it appears to be. It is actually the intelligence agency primarily for the Rothschilds, the banking cartel of the Global Elite, and the cult of the All-Seeing Eye, as is the ADL. Researcher Gary Allen put the situation very well in his 1973 book, *None Dare Call It Conspiracy*:

> "*One major reason for the historical blackout on the role of the international bankers in political history is that the Rothschilds were Jewish. (Anti-Jewish people)...have played into the hands of the conspiracy by trying to portray the entire conspiracy as Jewish. Nothing could be farther from the truth. The traditionally Anglo Saxon J.P. Morgan and Rockefeller international banking institutions have played a key role in the conspiracy. But there is no denying the importance of the Rothschilds and their satellites. However, it is just as unreasonable and immoral to blame all Jews for the*

---

[11] John George and Laird Wilcox, *Nazis, Communists, Klansmen And Others On The Fringe*, (Prometheus Books, New York, 1992) p285.

crimes of the Rothschilds as it is to hold all Baptists accountable for the crimes of the Rockefellers.

"The Jewish members of the conspiracy have used an organisation called The Anti-Defamation League as an instrument to try to convince everyone that any mention of the Rothschilds and their allies is an attack on all Jews. In this way they have stifled almost all honest scholarship on international bankers and made the subject taboo within universities.

"Any individual or book exploring this subject is immediately attacked by hundreds of ADL communities all over the country. The ADL has never let the truth or logic interfere with its highly professional smear jobs... Actually, nobody has a right to be more angry at the Rothschild clique than their fellow Jews. The Warburgs, part of the Rothschild empire, helped finance Adolf Hitler..."

Tyranny has many forms and most of them are less than obvious. Widespread condemnation of Jews in Germany was the result of the Nazis putting out one version of the 'truth' (Jews are horrid) while suppressing alternative information which told another story (Jews are no different from anyone else). That is clearly a mind-manipulating tyranny because people were denied all the facts and views available and their attitudes were subsequently imbalanced. But if that is a tyranny which we rightly pledge ourselves to oppose, why do we play a part in suppressing alternative information to the official line of the Second World War? How is it right that while this fierce suppression goes on, free copies of the Spielberg film, *Schindler's List*, are given to schools to indoctrinate children with the unchallenged version of events? And why do we, who say we oppose tyranny and demand freedom of speech, allow people to go to prison and be vilified, and magazines to be closed down on the spot, for suggesting another version of history? How can we not be accused of hypocrisy and of criticising one tyranny while supporting another? Once people think it is OK to suppress different views and evidence, whether we agree with it or not, we are playing God for the rest of our fellow men and women. If the evidence is wrong, then it will be shown to be so under the spotlight of the public arena. If it is true, then what the hell are we doing suppressing it? John F. Kennedy supported this view in a speech at Columbia University in February 1962, when he said:

"We seek the free flow of information...a nation that is afraid to let the people judge the truth and falsehood in an open market is a nation afraid of its people."

We live in nations afraid of the people and in a world afraid of the people. We cling to dogmas that are afraid of the people. Those who wish to suppress by whatever means alternative versions of history which challenge

'the official line' are also afraid of the people – afraid that their manipulation
will be exposed by such a free flow of information. The way the Jewish mind
has been so seriously manipulated by the Jewish hierarchy over the centuries
has had another effect. Like the Roman Catholic Church and other religious
and racial tyrannies, Judaism, and more recently Zionism, has used fear and
guilt to maintain control of its people. It has pressurised each generation to
conform to what it tells them they must believe and it has programmed their
minds to think of themselves as a people who have always been, and will
always be, the subject of oppression and prejudice from the rest of society. A
leaflet[12] asking for financial support for The Board of Deputies of British
Jews has a picture of hostile neo-Nazis on the front. Inside the leaflet it says
that the Board is the Jewish community's "protection" against racism and
"Holocaust denial" at a time when "the voices of fascists are getting louder".
It's all fear, fear, fear, control, control, control. Many Jewish people have also
been programmed to see themselves as God's 'chosen people', above all the
rest, and when you read some of the Jewish literature and laws, they are
incredibly racist, quite stunningly so. The Talmud, the Jewish book of law,
contains among other little gems, the following: "Just the Jews are humans,
the non-Jews are no humans, but cattle" (Kerithuth 6b, page 78,
Jebhammoth 61); "The non-Jews have been created to serve the Jews as
Slaves" (Midrasch Talpioth 225); "Sexual intercourse with non-Jews is like
sexual intercourse with animals" (Kethuboth 3b); "The non-Jews have to be
avoided, even more than sick pigs" (Orach Chaiim 57, 6a); "The birth rate
of non-Jews has to be suppressed massively" (Zohar II, 4b); "As you replace
lost cows and donkeys, so you shall replace non-Jews" (Lore Dea 377,1).
And so it goes on and on. So how often do the "anti-racist" protestors
demonstrate outside Talmudic events? Never. Exactly.

The irony is that the racism of extreme Jews and the racism of Adolf Hitler
are both based on a colossal myth. As Alfred M. Lilienthal, the Jewish writer
and researcher, said:

> *"There is no reputable anthropologist who will not agree that Jewish
> racialism is as much poppycock as Aryan racialism. As far back as 1938, the
> American Anthropological Association, at it's annual conference in New York,
> condemned Aryanism as a fallacy and stated that both 'Aryan' and 'Semitic'
> were* linguistic *terms without any* racial *significance…*
>
> *"…Anthropological science divides mankind into three recognised races:
> negro, mongolian and oriental, and caucasian or white (although some
> authorities refer to a fourth race – the australoids)…Members of the Jewish
> faith are found in all three races and subdivisions."* [13]

[12] "The Board of Deputies is the Voice of the Jewish Community", published by The Board
of Deputies of British Jews, Tavistock Square, London WC1 0EZ.
[13] *What Price Israel?* p213–214.

The conditioned thought patterns in the collective Jewish mind have repeatedly created the physical reality of oppression, prejudice, and racism which matches the pattern – the *expectation* – programmed into their collective psyche. They expect it; they create it. When Jewish people as a whole break free from the mind control of their hierarchy and start to let go of those feelings of fear and expectation of prejudice, they will stop attracting such experiences to them. When they openly reject the inherited view of racial superiority, those patterns will disperse from their magnetic cape/aura, and they will cease to attract racism to them. Also, like those brought up in the extreme versions of Roman Catholicism, Jewish people need to love themselves and leave behind the guilt their controllers demand that they retain. Of all the people I meet, those brought up in the Roman Catholic and Jewish faith are among the most screwed-up, mentally and emotionally. This is no coincidence. Both faiths brainwash children with fear and guilt from the earliest age.

Jewish people are simply wonderful when they allow themselves to be who they really are. I love their humour and their spirit. They have such a contribution to make to the good of the world. But I have rarely met one who really loves themself or does not carry the burden of inherited guilt. My friends, it is all about control. It's time to let it go.

Jewish people (who, like the rest of us, are evolving consciousnesses which happen to be experiencing a Jewish lifetime), will never be free until they step out of the mental and emotional control of this tiny clique, which uses them in the most merciless ways to advance its own sick and diabolical ambitions, in league with an equally sick clique of non-Jews.

Official history has been tampered with in the most extraordinary way, so that we continue to see the world in the childlike simplicity of good and evil, heroes and villains. It is rarely like that. After the war, the Nuremberg Trials sat in judgement on the Germans. When you look behind the sanitised history books you see that those trials were a farce, a calculated exercise in revenge and manipulation, often punishing those without influence to cover the tracks of those who had it...like the Americans on the boards of the US-Nazi cartels and parent companies. These were show trials of those Nazis not considered important enough or with enough political and scientific knowledge, to be removed to the United States and South America where they could continue their work for the Elite.[14] The defence of following orders from a superior officer was not allowed at Nuremberg. This meant that if they had disobeyed an order during the war they were shot, and if they obeyed the order they were hanged at Nuremberg. The precedent for

---

[14] Among these escapees who fled to South America was likely to have been Hitler. Dr Robert Dorion, the Director of Forensic Dentistry in Montreal, compared the teeth on the photographs of Hitler's alleged "corpse" and those of the man himself. He found there were many glaring differences between them.

removing the defence of following orders was made by the War Office in London in April 1944, just as the list of Nazi war criminals was being compiled and the preparations made for the post-war 'trials'. At that time the wording of Paragraph 443 of Chapter XIV of *The British Manual Of Military Law* was changed to reflect the wording of an article written in *The British Year Book Of International Law For 1944* by Dr Hersch Lauterpacht. The revised Paragraph 443 reads as follows:

> *"The clearly illegal nature of the order – illegal by reference to generally acknowledged principles of international law so identified with cogent dictates of humanity as to be obvious to any person of ordinary understanding – renders the fact of superior orders irrelevant."*

Dr Lauterpacht was a former Austrian with an interesting background. He was an assistant lecturer at the Round Table-influenced London School of Economics between the wars. Then, in 1940, he became a visiting professor at the Elite-controlled Carnegie Endowment for International Peace, which was shown to be promoting war. After his words were used to destroy the defence of superior orders, Dr Lauterpacht was appointed to the British War Crimes Executive and to a stream of international law publications and positions, including the United Nations International Law Commission.[15] His son, Elihu Lauterpacht QC, was consultant to the UK government's Central Policy Review Staff during the Premiership of Edward Heath (Conservative) and Jim Callaghan (Labour), and a host of international law bodies.[16] The head of Heath's policy unit was Lord Victor Rothschild.

Nuremberg was an insult to natural justice. It doesn't matter what the defendants were supposed to have done. If people don't administer justice fairly, they cannot claim to be any better than those they condemn. The American judge, Justice Wenersturm, the president of one of the tribunals, resigned and went home in disgust at the injustice and manipulation of it all. Another American judge, Edward L. van Roden, was one of the three members of the Simpson Army Commission which was appointed to investigate the methods used at the Dachau trials at Nuremberg. His findings were reported in *The Washington Daily News* and the British *Sunday Pictorial* in January 1949. He described the ways that 'confessions' were secured:

> *"Posturing as priests to hear confessions and give absolution; torture with burning matches driven under the prisoner's finger nails; knocking out of teeth and breaking jaws; solitary confinement and near-starvation rations;...The statements which were admitted as evidence were obtained from men who had first been kept in solitary confinement for three, four, and five months...The*

---

[15] *Who's Who*, (1958).
[16] *Who's Who*, (1987).

investigators would put black hoods over the accused's head and then punch him in the face with brass knuckles, kick him and beat him with rubber hoses...All but two of the Germans, in the 139 cases we investigated, had been kicked in the testicles beyond repair. This was standard operating procedure with our American investigators...Strong men were reduced to broken wrecks ready to mumble any admission demanded by their prosecutors."

These were the people sitting in judgement of others for their war crimes. Once you fall for the trick of seeing two sides as 'good' and 'evil' with no shades of grey in between, you become a robot. Life is not like a John Wayne film. Shortly after the Falklands War in 1982, a soldier who served there told me how he had been devastated to see his fellow British soldiers bayonetting to death Argentine prisoners of war who had put down their weapons and surrendered. He described how other British 'heroes' cut off the fingers of dead Argentines to steal their rings. He was so appalled, he left the forces in disgust. Years later, evidence came to light about these very events which led to a police investigation, but their findings were ignored and the British government refused to press charges against those involved. The newspapers said what an outrage it would have been to charge 'our boys' with such offences when they were 'only fighting for their country'. It is about time we realised that some of 'our boys' act just as horribly as those in Germany and Iraq. Mind you, that would explode the nonsense we are supposed to accept that Britain, America, and the West in general are on white chargers, 'fighting for freedom' to the sound of angelic choirs.

Perhaps nothing demolishes this simplistic idea of 'free' world v tyranny more than Hitler's genetic experiments in pursuit of a Master Race. Ask most people about the master race mentality and they will point to Adolf Hitler and the Nazis. But again, it is not as simple as that. The plan for a master race and the elimination of 'lesser' races did not begin and end in Nazi Germany. It began long before and it is still going on. All that happened under Hitler was that he had such a grip on the country and the German mind that he could openly promote it. This master race mentality is another part of the Elite's plan for the New World Order. When you think that the Prison Warders are seriously into genetic engineering of the most advanced kind, it is hardly surprising that their stooges on Earth would reflect that in their own attitude of mind. The Nazis were doing and saying publicly what the Elite in Britain and America had been saying and funding long before the word Nazi was even heard of.

Eugenics is, to quote the *Oxford Concise Dictionary*, "...the production of fine offspring by the improvement of inherited qualities". The term eugenics was coined by the Englishman, Francis Galton, in the later years of the nineteenth century. He called for society to intervene to maintain racial purity. Galton wanted the forced sterilisation of the 'unfit'. Another 'pioneer' of this mindset was Thomas Robert Malthus, born in 1766. It was from him that the theory of the 'survival of the fittest' was passed on through Herbert Spencer to Charles Darwin. Malthus was obsessed with the culling of the population and proposed a series of measures against the 'lower races' (the poor), to keep the population down and, as he saw it, to prevent the human genetic stream being dominated by such 'inferior' racial lines. In his best known work, *Essay*, he suggested that streets should be made narrower and more people crowded into houses, to encourage the return of the plague. Villages should be built next to stagnant pools and, above all, remedies for preventing and curing disease ought to be strongly condemned, he said. Malthus went on:

> *"We are bound in justice and honour formally to disclaim the right of the poor to support. To this end, I should propose a regulation be made declaring that no child born...should ever be entitled to parish assistance...The* [illegitimate] *infant is comparatively speaking, of little value to society, as others will immediately supply its place...All children beyond what would be required to keep up the population to this* [desired] *level, must necessarily perish, unless room be made for them by the deaths of grown persons."* [17]

From such a mind did the idea of the 'survival of the fittest' emerge, and it has dominated 'science' ever since! Add to this the belief that the intellect of a person is genetically determined by the intellect of the parents and you have the eugenics movement, which came to the surface so infamously under the rule of Adolf Hitler. Although advanced esoteric knowledge is known at the top level of the Elite, some of those lower down on the pyramid are encouraged to believe some incredible garbage. Genetic superiority of the intellect through interbreeding is one of them. It appeals to the ego, I guess. Note, also, how the Malthus proposals of the encouragement of disease and of forcing upon the poor conditions they are unlikely to survive, are still at the forefront of Elite policy in the Third World and within industrialised countries, too.

Names now familiar to us in this book, such as the Harrimans and the Rockefellers, were seriously into eugenics. Averell Harriman's mother funded the launch of the race-science movement in America in 1910, and built the Eugenics Record Office as a branch of the Galton National Laboratory in London. The Harrimans were responsible for the Bush family fortune and they were close to another Bush family backer, George Herbert Walker (a relative by marriage of Prescott Bush and grandfather to George Bush, who would go on to be President of the United States). By the late nineteenth century, some mentally ill people and children were being sterilised by US health officials as a result of eugenics policies. The State of

---

[17] Thomas R. Malthus, *An Essay On The Principle Of Population As It Affects The Future Improvement Of Society*, (Reeves and Turner, London, 1878 reprint).

Indiana made the sterilisation of the mentally ill and 'undesirables' compulsory and 475 men were sterilised at the Indiana State Reformatory.

After the turn of the century, the Harrimans and Rockefellers spent more than $11 million to establish a eugenics research laboratory at Cold Springs Harbor on Long Island, New York, close to the Dulles brothers' estates. The study of eugenics was encouraged at the Elite-controlled universities, such as Harvard, Columbia, and Cornell. In Germany, the same line was taken by Ernst Haeckel, the mystic and Aryan master race promoter, whose ideas would influence Hitler. Haeckel said it was the duty of a nation to enforce breeding, and he and his supporters formed the Monist League to promote their sick beliefs in Germany. The first International Congress of Eugenics was held in London in 1912. Among its directors were Winston Churchill and Alexander Graham Bell, inventor of the telephone. By 1917, fifteen US States had eugenics laws, and all but a few of them made legal the compulsory sterilisation of epileptics, the mentally ill and retarded, and regular criminals.

In 1932, a year before Hitler and Roosevelt came to power, the Harrimans helped to organise the Third International Congress on Eugenics at the American Museum of Natural History in New York. Averell Harriman's sister, Mary, was the director of entertainment for the event. These wealthy American families, like their counterparts in Britain, feel themselves to be racially superior and they wish to protect their racial purity. This – along with the pursuit of power, wealth, and influence – is the reason why so many intermarriages take place within these families. America may not have an official royal family or aristocracy as they exist in Britain, but they have an unofficial one, and every effort is taken to trace one's line back, often falsely, to William of Orange and the British Royal Family, or to some wing of the British aristocracy.

The aim of the eugenics movement was, and is, to create a Master Race by the sterilisation and forced birth control of those races considered 'inferior'. The International Congress of Eugenics in New York in 1932 tackled the 'problem' (as they saw it) of African-Americans and other 'inferior' stock reproducing and expanding their numbers. It was decided that the way to deal with this 'danger' to the higher races (themselves) was through sterilisation and 'cutting off the bad stock'. The Congress was dedicated to the work of Averell Harriman's mother and Averell did his best to support the proceedings. He personally arranged for the Hamburg-Amerika Shipping Line (controlled by himself, George Walker and Prescott Bush) to transport Nazis from Germany to New York so they could take part in the Congress. The best known of them was Dr Ernst Rudin, a psychiatrist at the Kaiser Wilhelm Institute for Genealogy and Demography in Berlin. There he occupied an entire floor with his eugenics 'research', and all of this was made possible by funds provided by...the *Rockefellers*.[18]

---

[18] *George Bush, The Unauthorised Biography*, p49.

Dr Rudin was unanimously elected president of the International Federation of Eugenics Societies at the New York Congress, and this was, in part, a recognition of his work as a founder of the German Society for Race Hygiene. The eugenics movement called for the sterilisation of mental patients (mental hygiene societies); the execution of criminals, the insane, and the terminally ill (euthanasia societies); and race purification by sterilisation and the prevention of births to those considered inferior bloodstocks (population control societies). All of this was up and running long before anyone had heard of Adolf Hitler and the Nazis. Hitler's Germany was a vehicle for part of this movement; it wasn't the whole movement.

Soon after Hitler had abolished elections and become dictator of Germany in 1933, the Rockefeller-funded Dr Rudin was commissioned to write the Law for the Prevention of Hereditary Diseases in Posterity, which involved the forced sterilisation of anyone considered genetically inferior. A quarter of a million people who were mental patients, blind, deaf, or alcoholics were sterilised on the order of special eugenics courts. Rudin supervised this policy and trained the psychiatrists and doctors to order and perform the sterilisations. But where did the Nazi Rudin get his inspiration from for the wording of his race laws? From the Model Eugenical Sterilization Law of 1922, presented by H.H. Laughlin, the eugenics 'expert' of the US House of Representatives Committee on Immigration and Nationalisation, which was accepted by many States. Eugenics was not unique to Nazi Germany. In 1942, the American 'psychiatrist' Foster Kennedy called for the killing of retarded children, and between 1941 and '43 more than 42,000 people were sterilised in America.[19]

Nor did the master race mentality end in 1945 with the demise of Hitler's Germany. Obviously, talk of master races, racial purity, and sterilisation to improve the stock was bad PR, once some of the tales of Nazi projects began to be known. But all that happened was that the names for master race policies were changed to disguise the true meaning. We began to hear about euthanasia and population control instead of eugenics and race purification, but it's all the same thing really. What the Harrimans, Rockefellers, and people like Prescott Bush were funding and supporting before and during the war, their successors have continued to promote under the cover of 'acceptable' language. For instance, one of the people who worked with the Harrimans and Prescott Bush in their funding of Hitler was William H. Draper Jr, the man who helped to fund the Nazi cartels and was then appointed by Roosevelt after the war to decide what should be done with them.

Draper, a close associate of Averell Harriman, was a major funder of the International Eugenics Congress before the war and was one of those responsible for making Dr Ernst Rudin the head of the world eugenics

---

[19] *Casebook On Alternative 3*, p86.

movement. In 1958, Draper was appointed to chair a committee which was advising President Dwight Eisenhower (CFR) on the use of military aid to other countries. This appointment was made possible by Prescott Bush, who was then a US Senator for Connecticut. Bush was a regular golf partner of the president and of National Security Advisor Gordon Gray (a close friend and eugenics promoter). By now, John Foster Dulles (Bush's former lawyer during the funding of Hitler) was the Secretary of State, and his brother Allen Dulles (formerly with Schroder, Hitler's personal bankers) was head of the CIA. To put it mildly, a eugenics enthusiast like Draper had many people around him of like mind. This allowed him to change the whole thrust of his committee from that of advising on military aid to campaigning on the threat of the 'population explosion'. His committee formulated plans to depopulate the poorer countries: i.e. those people who do not have white skins. The growth of such peoples, said Draper, was a threat to the national security of the United States.[20]

Eisenhower dismissed Draper's proposals, but with support from his fellow racial purity fanatics, he went on to found the Population Crisis Committee/'Draper Fund', which – together with the Rockefeller and DuPont families – continued to promote eugenics under the guise of population control. Draper was advisor to President Lyndon Johnson on this subject and that administration began to use the overseas aid programme to fund birth control in non-white countries.

Another of Draper's[21] like-minds in American politics was to be Prescott's son, George Bush, a vocal supporter of General Draper's policies. Bush arranged hearings as early as 1969 into the dangers posed by the birth of too many black babies. Draper's son and heir, William H. Draper III, was co-chairman for finance and head of fundraising for the George Bush For President campaign in 1980. Later in that decade, Bush persuaded Ronald Reagan to appoint the younger Draper to be administrator of the United Nations Development Programme, an organisation connected with the World Bank and charged with supervising population control!

Eugenics and master race policies were passed on across the generations of these ruling families of the Elite. During George Bush's tenure in the White House, the population control element of the aid budget soared. His legal counsel from 1980 was Boyden Gray, who became the chief legal advisor to the President during the Bush administration. Gray would have been able to

---

[20] *George Bush, The Unauthorised Biography*, p56.
[21] In 1971, William Draper likened the developing nations to the 'world famous animal reserve – the Kruger Park in South Africa'. "Who will cull out the surplus in this country when the pressure of too many people and too few resources increases beyond endurance?" he asked. Quoted in *Global 2000, Blueprint For Genocide*, a special report by Executive Intelligence Review, New York. My copy was distributed by Contact Network International, A.B. Gorredijk, The Netherlands.

give him plenty of advice on population control. When Boyden was a boy after the war, his father, Gordon Gray (Prescott Bush's close friend), launched the project which provided the basis of today's global sterilisation programme. In 1946, the eugenics movement was trying to rebuild itself in the wake of the rather unfortunate publicity aroused by one of its chief advocates, Adolf Hitler. During the war, The Sterilization League of America had changed its name to Birthright Inc., and was now looking for a means to get back to business. Its efforts to relaunch itself in Iowa ended when a young boy died during a sterilisation operation and the bad publicity brought an end to the plan. Instead they moved to Gray family territory in North Carolina. Gordon Gray had founded the Bowman Gray (Memorial) Medical School in Winston-Salem. It was named after Boyden's grandfather, who had owned the R.J. Reynolds Tobacco Company. The school became a centre for eugenics. It compiled extensive records of families carrying 'inherited diseases', and it began a project which...get this...forcibly sterilised young children who were not considered to be of a high enough IQ. No, no, I am not talking about Nazi Germany during the war; I am talking about the United States of America in 1946–1947! Boyden Gray's great aunt, Alice Shelton Gray, founded the Human Betterment League (the North Carolina branch of the national eugenics sterilisation movement), and she was the official supervisor of the master race experiment that was begun at the Grays' 'medical school'. Others involved were Dr Claude Nash Herndon, the assistant director of 'medical genetics' at the school, and Dr Clarence Gamble (the heir to the Proctor and Gamble soap empire), who was the chief of 'national field operations'. Children enrolled in the Winston-Salem school district were given 'intelligence tests' and those who fell below the mark considered acceptable to these bizarre people were sterilised. Their recommendations were passed to the State Eugenics Board, which had the authority to order sterilisation under North Carolina law. Dr Claude Nash Herndon talked of his work in an interview in 1990 which was reported in *George Bush, The Unauthorised Biography*:

> "...*IQ tests were run on all the children in the Winston-Salem school system. Only the ones who scored really low* [were targeted for sterilisation], *the real bottom of the barrel, like below 70. Did we do sterilizations on young children? Yes. This was a relatively minor operation...It was usually not* [done] *until the child was eight or ten years old. For the boys, you just make an incision and tie the tube...We more often performed the operation on girls than with boys. Of course, you have to cut open the abdomen, but again, it is relatively minor."* (p59)

Oh, that's OK then. What were the media doing while all this was going on? Not a lot, it turns out. Dr Herndon talked of their "good relationship" with the press. This is less surprising when you realise that Gordon Gray owned the *Winston-Salem Journal*, the *Twin City Sentinel* and the radio station WSJS. Eugenics was being promoted on a wide scale after the war in the guise of population control, just as it is today. In the early 50s, when John Foster Dulles was chairman of the tax-exempt New World Order front, the Rockefeller Foundation, he travelled with John D. Rockefeller III on a number of world tours campaigning for policies to stem the expansion of the non-white populations. In November 1952, Dulles and Rockefeller launched the Population Council with tens of millions of dollars provided by the Rockefeller family. The American Eugenics Society left its old headquarters at Yale University, the home of the sinister Skull and Bones Society, and moved in with the Population Council. The two organisations, in effect, became one. The first president of the Population Council was Frederick Osborne, the long-time secretary of the American Eugenics Society. The child-steriliser of North Carolina, Dr Claude Nash Herndon, was made president of the Eugenics Society in 1953.

When George Bush became ambassador to the United Nations in 1972, he and his clique in the US Agency for International Development arranged the first official contract between the American government and the Sterilization League of America, which had, by then, changed its name yet again, to the Association for Voluntary Surgical Contraception. Under this contract, the US government (taxpayer) began to fund this organisation to do in non-white countries of the world what it had already done to children in North Carolina. In 1988, the year George Bush was elected president, another contract was arranged which involved the American taxpayer spending $80 million dollars over five years to expand this work in 58 countries in Asia, Africa, and Spanish-America. Millions have been sterilised and most of it has been funded by the taxpayer. Other countries do the same. And by the way, Dr Clarence Gamble, the sterilising enthusiast from the Proctor and Gamble soap family and the Bowman Gray Medical School, has also enjoyed funding from the USAID budget. His so called Pathfinder Fund is paid to infiltrate non-white societies and break down resistance to sterilisation.

The Planned Parenthood Federation, which has been supported at every opportunity by George Bush and the manipulating Elite, was actually founded in London, at the offices of the British Eugenics Society. You can see that while the names change and the rhetoric may be couched in terms deemed acceptable to public opinion at the time, we are looking at the *same* unwavering agenda, weaving its way through the decades and the generations. Nazi Germany was but its most famous example. Global centralisation of power, fundamental control of the minds and bodies of the mass population, and the creation of a master race. These are the themes that span the centuries and they still dominate the secret agenda today, which is manipulating our lives.

But how many people in this world believe they are racially superior to the rest? The number is so vast it doesn't bear thinking about. Ironically, many of those who have suffered from the master race mentality of one race, actually believe that they, themselves, are superior genetically to others. That attitude, that thought pattern, is broadcast into the collective mind, which creates a collective version of that reality. If within our psyche, we believe we are racially superior, we are more likely to attract that same mentality to us. A feeling of racial superiority is an imbalance and our subconscious attracts our imbalances to us as physical experiences so we can face them, learn from those experiences, and let them go. These imbalances often relate to thought patterns we hold onto from previous physical lives as well as this one, which is why someone who does not have a conscious feeling of racial superiority might still attract a racial experience to them. It is our subconscious reality that we are creating. We – humanity as a whole – thought the global master race mentality/reality into existence and we can now think it out again, by seeing all colours and creeds as equal, which they are.

The Elite can get away with its deception because it has so many faces and works through so many different groups and organisations. In the next three chapters, I will unravel some of this structure and make it easier for those new to this subject to understand how the Elite remains hidden from most of the world while secretly plotting our collective fate.

Chapter 8

The secret government

With the war at an end, the world was at the mercy of the Global Elite. Europe was devastated, physically, emotionally, mentally, spiritually and economically – as it was planned to be.

The enormity of the deceit may be hard to comprehend as you survey those endless rows of white gravestones in the war cemeteries of France, but those young men and women did not die for freedom in its true sense. They died to satisfy the Elite agenda for global domination and, on a higher level, to deepen the control of the Prison Warders on the Fourth Dimension. Of course, if those soldiers on both sides had known that, there would have been no war. Instead, they were presented with a story that the Nazis were a uniquely evil creation that had to be stopped by the forces of goodness, freedom, and virtue. Again, another black and white fantasy. The Nazi philosophy was unspeakable, but it was also the philosophy of those who controlled the Allies. The same forces funded and manipulated both of them.

At the end of World War II, the United States was the most powerful country on Earth. It had bankrolled the war and, through the lend-lease system of supplying armaments on the basis of 'have now, pay later', Europe was drowning in debt to the American – Elite-controlled – bankers. Roosevelt had told Churchill years earlier that the British Empire would have to be dismantled and now that was a certainty. Britain's long period of pre-eminence was over, destroyed by the two World Wars. For me, Britain should never have had an 'empire' in the first place, but we need to keep our eyes on why it was brought to an end by those plotting their own world supremacy. If you read the Illuminati Protocols (which I included in *The Robots' Rebellion*), you will see that the use of debt and wars as a means of control was precisely what the manipulators had always planned.

These protocols came to light late in the last century and, although they have been condemned as a 'forgery', they tell the story of the twentieth century with remarkable accuracy. Whoever wrote them knew what was coming. The debt they talk about was to grow still more, with the European countries borrowing heavily from America, to rebuild their towns and cities in the aftermath of all the bombing that had gone on.

The United States (Global Elite) introduced its Grand Area strategy to control Western Europe, the whole of the Western hemisphere, the Middle and Far East, and the former British Empire. The Third World was essential to this policy. In the words of a 1949 memo by the US State Department, the Third World would "...fulfil its major function as a source of raw materials and a market for industrial capitalist societies".[1] Put another way, it was going to be mentally, emotionally, and physically raped. George Kennan at the State Department even suggested at this time that Europe might enjoy a 'psychological lift' from exploiting Africa, as declassified documents reveal.[2] Vital to this plan was to ensure that no country, particularly in the Third World, was allowed to delink from Elite economic domination and run their economy for the benefit of the people. This so called 'threat of a good example', which others might follow, led to slaughter across South and Central America and the East, including Vietnam. Henry Kissinger (Comm 300) would call the introduction of social and economic reforms in Third World countries a 'virus' that, if allowed to thrive, would 'infect' a much wider area.[3] Or, as Secretary of State Dean Acheson (Comm 300) said in the late 1940s, "One rotten apple can spoil the barrel". The Elite's barrel.

The more terror that could be used against leaders and people trying to eliminate dependency on the Elite bankers and multinationals, the less likely it was that anyone else would try it. This was the fundamental and base motivation behind the United States (Elite) strategy which engineered the horrors in Vietnam, Guatemala, Nicaragua, El Salvador, Brazil, Italy, Chile, the Dominican Republic, Laos, Grenada, Honduras, Iran, and Indonesia. You would need a map of the world to list them all. Behind these events and the overthrow of democratically elected governments were many of the Nazis employed all over the world by the CIA. The SS officer and Gestapo chief, Klaus Barbie, the 'Butcher of Lyon', was one who was employed by the Americans to spy on the French. For hundreds, if not thousands, of Hitler's men who were bankrolled by the CIA, it was 'business as usual' after the 'defeat' of Nazism. The manipulation was happening on many levels, but the most important goal was to cause so much conflict between nation states (the problem), that public opinion would demand that something must be done (the reaction), and the Elite could then unveil its long-term plan for centralised global institutions under the control of a tiny clique (the solution).

In summary, the foundation themes of the Elite's plan immediately after the war were the following:

---

[1] Noam Chomsky, *What Uncle Sam Really Wants*, (Odonian Press, fifth printing, Berkeley, California, 1993) p12.
[2] Ibid.
[3] Ibid p24.

- To introduce a world authority called the United Nations (with associated bodies like the World Health Organisation), which could evolve into a world government with powers to control the lives of everyone on the planet.

- To continue to cause conflicts across the world and to use the fear of the Soviet Union to massively increase spending on nuclear weapons and 'conventional' weapons, thus adding to the terror of nuclear war and demands for global security. To set up an American-European defence alliance (which was called the North Atlantic Treaty Organisation (NATO)) and a United Nations 'peace' keeping force, which, through the engineering of conflicts, would eventually be fused together to form the world army.

- To create three 'free trade' regions in Europe, the Americas, and Asia, which would be sold to people initially as merely economic groupings. Gradually, however, these would be evolved into centralised political unions, with one central bank and one currency. These would be stepping-stones to the introduction of the same institutions on a global scale. The European Economic Community, now the European Union, was the first of these, but the other two are now underway, also.

- To advance the control of public opinion and to research and expand the understanding of how to manipulate the human psyche, individually and collectively. Today this agenda includes the microchipping of people and their permanent connection to a global computer.

- To create a welfare state while destroying alternatives to the economic system and, when the desired dependency had been achieved, to dismantle that state welfare support, so creating a vast underclass without help or hope.

- To make fantastic amounts of money in the course of realising all of these ambitions via the Elite-controlled companies and banks.

- To continually add to the debt burdens of people, business, and state, thus increasing the control exerted over them.

The approach which was followed to hoodwink public thinking was painfully predictable, but highly effective: Discredit the nation state. This was laid out during the War by the German economist and refugee, Hans Heymann, who produced his Plan for Permanent Peace using funds given by...the Carnegie Endowment for International Peace. In this work he said:

> *"Nations have created international disharmony in the vain belief that harmony in our society can be achieved on a national basis...This narrow-minded approach has left us one strong hope, namely, that this fallacious concept may hold only during a transitional period...After the debacle* [World War Two] *an international organisation will be imperative, for the well-being of society as a whole."* [4]

It was classic problem-reaction-solution. In 1945, the original Round Table secret society had two main offshoots – the Royal Institute of International Affairs (RIIA) at Chatham House in London (which had branches in many other parts of the world), and the RIIA's United States branch, the Council on Foreign Relations (CFR) in New York (which had branches across the United States). In the post-war years, these would be joined by the Bilderberg Group (Bil), the Trilateral Commission (TC), and the Club of Rome (CR) to form a highly effective network of manipulation which comprises a very significant element of the secret government of the world – a government that is far more powerful than any elected authority (*Figure* 7).

You will find the membership of these organisations among the elite of global politics and political 'advisors', banking, oil companies, multinational corporations, media owners, executives and journalists, the military, the law, and education. They work as organisations within organisations, infiltrating these spheres of influence and secretly promoting the Global Elite agenda. The majority of their colleagues and employees have no idea what is going on or how they are being used. As with the Round Table, there are distinct circles of people within these front groups. There is an elite core who work full time for the cause; a circle of members who know the agenda and work within their own organisations to achieve it; and an outer circle of members who are not aware of the real and full implications of the agenda, but are useful to the manipulators in the short term. Not everyone who is a member of these organisations is a conscious manipulator and we need to use our intuition and the information presented by researchers to decide which ones know the score and which are being used without understanding what they are really involved in. In this chapter, I will outline the background and influence of these groupings and of their associated power blocs, the United Nations and the European Union.

THE ROYAL INSTITUTE OF INTERNATIONAL AFFAIRS (RIIA)

The Anglo-American Elite who met at the Versailles Peace Conference in Paris in 1919 formed the RIIA and the Council on Foreign Relations in 1920 and 1921, as discussed earlier. The so called 'special relationship' between Britain and America is, in fact, the relationship between the RIIA

---

[4] Hans Heymann, *Plan For Permanent Peace*, (Harper & Brothers, New York, 1941) p78.

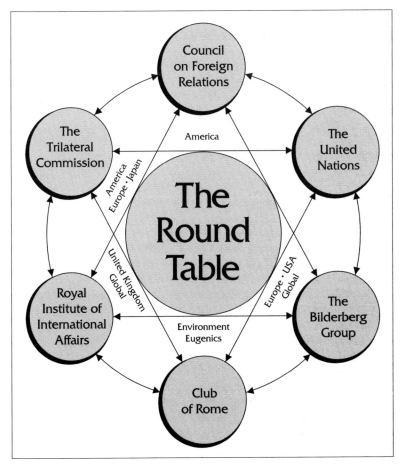

Figure 7

and the Council on Foreign Relations. Today the Royal Institute, with the Queen as its patron, has an enormous effect on British and global policy. It *is* the British Foreign Office. So why, it can be fairly asked, has British economic and political power been curtailed? The answer is that the British manipulators are far more interested in creating a world government than in improving Britain as a country. If curtailing British economic power and the empire was necessary for this wider plan, then so be it. As with the 'Jewish' clique, their commitment is to the cause of the All-Seeing Eye cult, not the interests of the people.

At the time of this writing, the RIIA's three joint presidents are Lord Carrington (Comm 300), the former Conservative cabinet minister (including Foreign Secretary), Secretary-General of NATO, member of the Trilateral Commission, and, from 1991, the chairman of the Bilderberg

Group; Lord Callaghan of Cardiff, the former Labour Prime Minister, cabinet minister (including Foreign Secretary), and Bilderberg attendee; and Lord (Roy) Jenkins of Hillhead, a founding member in Europe of the Trilateral Commission, a Bilderberger, and the former Labour Cabinet minister and Chancellor of the Exchequer. Lord Jenkins was one of the 'Gang of Four', along with former Labour Foreign Secretary, Lord (David) Owen (TC), who split the Labour Party in 1981 by launching their own Social Democratic Party (SDP). He was also a President of the European Commission and, together with people like the former Conservative Prime Minister, Edward Heath (Bil, TC), he is a passionate advocate of European union. The chairman of the RIIA is the former Conservative MP, Christopher (now Lord) Tugendhat, the chairman of the Abbey National Building Society and Governor of the Ditchley Foundation, which is a front for the New World Order, according to many researchers and published works. Tugendhat describes the European Union as, "the most hopeful and beneficent political development to be undertaken in this part of the world this century...it is a brave and noble [sic] venture that I am proud to be able to serve".[5] The Institute names as 'honorary presidents' the "presidents and prime ministers of the United Kingdom and other Commonwealth countries".[6] The presidents, prime ministers, and political elite throughout the world speak at the Institute, often under the secrecy of the 'Chatham House Rule'. This says that:

> "*When a meeting, or part thereof, is held under the Chatham House Rule, participants are free to use the information received, but neither the identity nor the affiliation of the speaker(s), nor that of any other participant, may be revealed; nor may it be mentioned that the information was received at a meeting of the Institute.*" [7]

So much for open government. The Institute is highly secretive and will not release details of its membership in high places. Why not, if it is only a 'think tank'? What is there to hide? When I rang to ask for a list of members in the British Cabinet and Shadow Cabinet, I was told by the membership secretary that the names of individual members are never released. To join, you have to be nominated by two members who know you well and even then you might not pass the selection procedure. Running alongside this membership is another which is only allowed access to the Institute's library. This second form of membership helps to smokescreen what is going on elsewhere in the organisation. The Institute is funded today, as it has been

---

[5] "Time for all Good Europeans to Come to the Aid of Our Venture." *The European*, (July 7th–13th 1995) p6.
[6] RIIA Annual Report 1992–93.
[7] Ibid.

from the start, by the major global companies and banks. Its 'Energy and Environment Programme' is paid for by major oil companies, coal and electricity producers, and the Atomic Energy Authority. My goodness, I bet that's unbiased! Major corporate members of the RIIA are: Morgan Guaranty Trust Company of New York (J.P. Morgan); S.G. Warburg Group plc (before its takeover);[8] Barings plc (before its mysterious and high profile collapse);[9] the British Foreign and Commonwealth Office; the Ministry of Defence; the United States Embassy; the RTZ Corporation; Anglo-American Corporation of South Africa; British Petroleum; Shell International; Bank of England; Barclays Bank; Lloyds Bank; National Westminster Bank; Lazard Brothers; TSB Group; Abbey National; Midland Montagu; Coopers and Lybrand; Unilever; British American Tobacco Industries; British Aerospace; *The Economist*; Gerard Atkins and Co Ltd; John Swire and Sons Ltd; and Ente Nazionale Idrocarburi (ENI).

The other corporate members comprise a list of the world's leading companies, countries, and media. Even the Church of England is in there, along with the African National Congress (ANC) and Amnesty International. Why is Amnesty International supporting an organisation through which manipulation is orchestrated that adds massively to the number of political prisoners? Media organisations supporting the RIIA include ABC News Intercontinental Inc; CBS News; NBC News Worldwide Inc; Britain's Channel Four TV and Independent Television News (ITN); Fuji Television; *Der Spiegel*; *The European*; *The Financial Times*; *The Guardian*; *The Independent* and *Independent On Sunday*; *The Observer*; *Daily Telegraph*; *The Times*; *The Scotsman*; *The Yorkshire Post*; *Reuters*, the international news agency; *The New York Times*; *The Washington Post*; *The Wall Street Journal*; *The Reader's Digest*; and, quite outrageously for an organisation claiming to be independent, the BBC World Service; the BBC Monitoring Service; and BBC Radio.

Taxpayer funding and support for the RIIA is given not only by the British and Commonwealth Office and the Ministry of Defence, but also the Cabinet Office, the Treasury, the Department of the Environment, the Department of Trade and Industry, Customs and Excise, and many other sources. The British Labour Party International Department is a corporate member, along with the Trades Union Congress (TUC), and so are other names we have seen throughout this book. These include the Chase Manhattan Bank (the post-war amalgamation of the Rockefellers' Chase Bank and the Rothschild/Warburg Bank of Manhattan), Morgan and

---

[8/9] Barings and S.G. Warburg have appeared many times in my research into the global manipulation, and I do not believe that the collapse of one and the takeover of the other in 1995 was an accident. The idea that one trader in the Far East, Nick Leeson, could be given enough power to destroy Barings is ridiculous. I believe the Bank of England was involved in the collapse. And the Bank of England is a tool of the Global Elite.

Warburg companies and amalgamations, N.M. Rothschild and Sons Ltd, J. Henry Schroder (also acting as the bankers for the BBC charity, the Children in Need Appeal), the Ford Motor Company, and that population control organisation so beloved of George Bush, the Planned Parenthood Federation. Another name which keeps coming up in my investigations is the Hambros Bank Ltd, which is also a corporate member of the RIIA. The creation of a United States of Europe under centralised control is a major stepping-stone in the New World Order plan, and so it is appropriate and hardly surprising that the RIIA is also supported by the Commission of the European Communities, the European Parliament UK Office, the European Policy Advisers (UK) Ltd, European Round Table (how apt!) of Industrialists, and the European Bank for Reconstruction and Development.[10]

The Institute is used as a private forum for the elite to sell their New World Order ideas to invited audiences and those with influence in the media, politics, education and commerce. It is a lobbying organisation, in effect, for the New World Order and a means (*outside* the 'official' government machine) through which deals can be done and events arranged without the knowledge of either the public or elected parliaments. It is more than that, however. It is a central and powerful pivot in the secret government network, with very close links to the British Royal Family and British Intelligence. Again, most of the people involved with the RIIA do not realise how it is being used.

THE COUNCIL ON FOREIGN RELATIONS (CFR) AND THE UNITED NATIONS (UN)

The CFR is the Royal Institute, Stateside branch. The only major difference between them is that the CFR membership list is more widely available and some of its members have been so disturbed by what they have seen and heard that they have spoken out against it. Not many, but some. If only that were the case in Britain, where they leave the Americans standing when it comes to secrecy! Most of the 'secrets' that come to the surface in Britain are those which have been purposely leaked to undermine a politician, personality, or group, for some desired, manipulative end. This general rule also applies in the US, but the British establishment has had longer to perfect its leak-proofing techniques. Since the formation of the CFR, every president of the United States has been a member except for Ronald Reagan. In truth Reagan was not president, his vice-president George Bush, a CFR member, was running the show. It was the Council on Foreign Relations, no doubt with RIIA input and coordination, that brought the United Nations (the successor to the League of Nations) into being. This was the jewel of the post-war manipulators and one of the main reasons the Second World War was fashioned. By 1945, the world was understandably

[10] All of this information comes from the RIIA Annual Report, 1993–94.

sick and tired of war and the public mind was open to anything that might prevent more human slaughter. Problem-reaction-solution brought forth the United Nations. The UN Charter was officially accepted by representatives of fifty countries at a meeting in San Francisco on June 26th 1945. But that was only the public culmination of years of behind-the-scenes manoeuvring by the Council on Foreign Relations, which controlled the administration of Franklin D. Roosevelt. The writer, James Perloff, revealed the background to the UN in his 1988 book, *The Shadows Of Power: The Council On Foreign Relations And The American Decline*:

> *"In January 1943, the Secretary of State, Cordell Hull, formed a steering committee composed of himself, Leo Pasvolsky, Isaiah Bowman, Sumner Welles, Norman Davis, and Morton Taylor. All these men – with the exception of Hull – were in the CFR. Later known as the Informal Agenda Group, they drafted the original proposal for the United Nations. It was Bowman – a founder of the CFR and member of Colonel House's old 'Inquiry' – who first put forward the concept. They called in three attorneys, all CFR men, who ruled that it was constitutional. Then they discussed it with Franklin D. Roosevelt on June 15th, 1944. The President approved the plan, and announced it to the public the same day."* [11]

In his book, *The American Language*, H.L. Mencken suggests that the term 'United Nations' was decided by President Roosevelt during a meeting with Winston Churchill at the White House in December 1941, shortly before the attack on Pearl Harbor.[12] The US delegation at the founding meeting of the UN was like a roll call of the CFR. It included Isaiah Bowman, Hamilton Fish Armstrong, Sumner Welles, Norman H. Davis, James T. Shotwell, and the Russian-born Leo Pasvolsky. They were all CFR members who served during the war on Roosevelt's Advisory Committee on Post-War Foreign Policies. In all, seventy-four CFR members were in the delegation. This was the vehicle through which the United Nations was manipulated into being.

The US delegation at the San Francisco Conference also included: John J. McCloy (CFR chairman from 1953-70, a member of the Committee of 300, the chairman of the Ford Foundation and the Rockefellers' Chase Manhattan Bank, and friend and advisor to nine presidents from Roosevelt to Reagan); John Foster Dulles (Hitler supporter, CFR founder, and soon to be Secretary of State); and Nelson Rockefeller (an arch manipulator, four times elected Governor of New York, and vice president in the administration of President Gerald Ford). The attitude of John J. McCloy typified that of the manipulators who created the UN. He was a financial advisor to the

---

Italian fascist government of Benito Mussolini and he played a significant role
in Nazi Germany for the Harriman/Bush bank which was financing Hitler.
McCloy sat in Hitler's private box at the 1936 Olympics in Berlin at the
invitation of Rudolf Hess and Hermann Göring.[13] McCloy was also a
member of the Bilderberg Group Steering Committee.

The secretary general of the conference was the State Department official
and CFR member, Alger Hiss, later exposed as a secret agent employed by
the Soviet Union. Hiss was executive secretary of the 1944 Dumbarton Oaks
Conference, where he worked with Stalin's man, Vyacheslav Molotov, on the
details of the UN Charter. He was described as President Roosevelt's 'top
international organisation specialist' at the Yalta Conference in the Crimea in
February 1945, which was also attended by Churchill and Stalin. After
guiding the UN into existence, Hiss was made president of the infamous
Carnegie Endowment for International Peace, an appointment made by John
Foster Dulles, who ignored information about Hiss's espionage when he was
told about it in 1946. Later Hiss was exposed and spent 44 months in prison.

Other covert Communist Party members of the CFR were in the US
delegation in San Francisco for the launch of the UN, among them Dexter
White, who was also revealed as a Soviet agent. The Council on Foreign
Relations directs the United States policy, whatever 'party' is officially in
power. As John J. McCloy once said: "Whenever we needed a man [for a
government position] we thumbed through the roll of the council members
and put through a call to New York" (The CFR headquarters at Harold
Pratt House, 58 East 68th Street).[14] The granddaughter of former President
Theodore Roosevelt, the newspaper columnist Edith Kermit Roosevelt,
summed up the grip of the so called 'Eastern Establishment' working
through the CFR:

> *"What is the Establishment's view-point? Through the Roosevelt, Truman,
> Eisenhower and Kennedy administrations its ideology is constant: that the best
> way to fight Communism is by a One World Socialist State governed by
> 'experts' like themselves. The result has been policies which favour the growth
> of the superstate, gradual surrender of United States sovereignty..."* [15]

Robert W. Lee, writing in the September 1992 edition of *The New
American* pointed out that at least fourteen of the eighteen US secretaries of

[13] Walter Isaacson and Evan Thomas, *The Wise Men: Six Friends And The World They Made –
Acheson, Bohlen, Harriman, Kennan, Lovett, McCloy*, (Simon and Schuster, New York, 1986)
p122, 305.
[14] Quoted by J. Anthony Lukas in "The Council On Foreign Relations: Is It A Club?
Seminar? Presidium? Invisible Government?", *New York Times* magazine, (November 21st
1971) p125–126.
[15] "Elite Clique Holds Power In US", *Indianapolis News*, (December 23rd 1961) p6.

state since the CFR was founded in 1921 have been members of that organisation, including the acting secretary of state at the time of the article, Lawrence Eagleburger. The last eight directors of the CIA, including George Bush, had been CFR members, and over the previous four decades, the Democratic and Republican Party candidates for president or vice president who were (or became) members of the CFR were Dwight D. Eisenhower, Adlai Stevenson, John F. Kennedy, Henry Cabot Lodge, Richard Nixon, Hubert Humphrey, Edmund Muskie, George McGovern, Jimmy Carter, Walter Mondale, Gerald Ford, Nelson Rockefeller, George Bush, Michael Dukakis, Geraldine Ferraro, and Bill Clinton.

This, then, is the organisation which created the United Nations.[16] The UN even built its headquarters in New York on land given free of charge by the Rockefellers. Besides the Rockefellers, names like Morgan, Warburg, Schiff, and Marburg were manipulating in the background, behind the politicians and advisors. The United Nations was sold to the public as a means to bring peace to the world, to solve differences by words, not war. Most of the people who work for the UN genuinely believe that is its purpose. They are about to be disillusioned on that score, I'm afraid. The UN is but a 'Trojan Horse' for the global fascist/communist tyranny known as the New World Order. It is the vehicle through which the world government and world army are being manipulated into place and through which public opinion is being softened up, by conflicts and propaganda, to accept this policy as the only way to bring peace and stability to human affairs. All seven of the UN secretary generals since 1945 have promoted such thinking. The last holder of the office, Dr Boutros Boutros-Ghali, began his career under the Egyptian dictator, Gamal Abdel Nasser. Boutros-Ghali called for a permanent UN Army (world army) and for the UN to have the right to levy taxation (world government). His successor, Kofi Annan, wants the same.

The original United Nations has given birth to a stream of connected organisations which coordinate the New World Order plan in areas like health (World Health Organisation), population control or – more accurately – eugenics, (the UN Population Fund – UNFPA), economic development and environment (the UN Environment Programme – UNEP), education, science and culture (UNESCO), and the list is getting longer all the time. These are organisations which are designed to globalise control of all areas of our lives and we urgently need to wake up to this. The UN is a front for the Illuminati/Freemasonic hierarchy. In a speech in 1970, Robert Welch, the founder of the John Birch Society in America, predicted with remarkable accuracy what the United Nations would become:

---

[16] I can recommend an excellent book by William F. Jasper about the UN: *Global Tyranny…Step By Step. The United Nations And The Emerging New World Order*, (Appleton, Wisconsin, Western Islands, 1992).

"The United Nations hopes and plans – or, more accurately, the insiders, the conspiratorial bosses above it, hope and plan for it – to use population controls, controls over scientific and technological developments, control over arms and military strength of individual nations, control over education, control over health, and all the controls it can gradually establish under all of the different excuses for international jurisdiction that it can devise. These variegated separate controls are to become components of the gradually materialising total control that it expects to achieve by pretense, deception, persuasion, beguilement, and falsehoods, while the enforcement of such controls by brutal force and terror is also getting under way." [17]

That is what the United Nations was always intended to do; that is what it was created to do; that is what it is now doing.

THE EUROPEAN ECONOMIC COMMUNITY – NOW THE EUROPEAN UNION

The plan to create three global trading blocks which would eventually be merged into one is not new. It has been a long-term plan to centralise power in Europe, the Americas, and Asia-Australia, via groupings promoted initially as free trade areas, but later evolving into the European Union, the American Union, and the Pacific Union. The European Economic Community was the first, and this has been followed by the North American Free Trade Agreement (NAFTA) which involves the US, Canada, and Mexico. This agreement was signed by President George Bush on August 12th 1992. In my scores of public talks throughout 1994, I said that this would eventually be expanded to encompass the whole of the Americas. This was not prophecy, simply knowledge of the game plan. It doesn't matter what president is nominally in power, be it Republican or Democrat, the plan rumbles on. What was it that George Bush, a Republican, said when NAFTA was launched? That he wished to see a free trade area stretching from the top of North America to the tip of South America. What was it that Bill Clinton, a Democrat, said at a gathering of leaders from throughout the American continent on December 10th 1994?

"History has given the people of the Americas the chance to build a community of nations, committed to liberty and the promise of prosperity... early in the next century [I want to see]...a huge free trade zone from Alaska to Argentina."

Spot the difference? No, nor me. Another thing I was predicting through 1994, again from knowledge of the agenda, was the creation of the third 'free

[17] *"Which World Will It Be?"* *American Opinion*, Reprint Series, (The John Birch Society, Appleton, Wisconsin, 1970).

trade area' involving Asia and Australia. On November 16th 1994, I picked up a copy of the London *Daily Telegraph* to see that this had been agreed to on the previous day. The Asia-Pacific Economic Cooperation (APEC) grouping was accepted at a Summit meeting near Jakarta, Indonesia, attended by Bill Clinton, Paul Keating (the Australian Prime Minister), and heads of the Asian governments. Either Keating is in on the scam or he is easily duped. Now the process will begin of evolving the two latest trading blocs into the model used in Europe before merging them all into one.

The plan for a United States of Europe under centralised control goes back centuries. It was one of the goals of the Knights Templar. When the Templars were destroyed in their stronghold in France by a combination of the French King and the Pope, many of those who survived the onslaught regrouped in Scotland and the Templars reformed under the pseudonym, the Scottish Rite of Freemasonry. This has a large number of its members in the high places of influence and power in the world, not the least in the United States. The men behind the European Community, now the European Union, were Jean Omar Marie Gabriel Monnet (Comm 300), the son of a French brandy merchant; Count Richard N. Coudenhove-Kalergi (Comm 300) from Austria; and Joseph Retinger (Comm 300), a Polish socialist, who formed an organisation called the European Movement to press for central control of Europe. He was also most influential in the creation of the Bilderberg Group, one of the key vehicles for secret government manipulation. Jean Monnet was the most important figure, however, in European union.

Monnet went to Canada in 1910, at the age of just twenty to seek new markets for the family brandy business. There he linked up with the Hudson Bay Company and the Lazard Brothers banking operation and became part of the Anglo-American scene, even though he was French. He became a confidant to presidents and prime ministers, and this won him a highly lucrative contract to ship materials from Canada to France during the First World War. When the war ended he was appointed to the Allied Supreme Economic Council and he became advisor to the group around Lord Milner (Comm 300) and Colonel House (Comm 300), which was preparing the Treaty of Versailles and creating the League of Nations. By 1919, his influence and reputation among the manipulators was such that he was named the Deputy Secretary General of The League of Nations. The same names again. Six years later he moved to America and became vice president of a company owned by the Bank of America, called Transamerica. Monnet was now in the perfect position to coordinate the America-European conspiracy to create the European Community.

Count Richard N. Coudenhove-Kalergi wrote a book in 1923, calling for a United States of Europe. He was named after Richard Wagner, of whom Hitler had said that to understand Nazi Germany one had to understand Wagner. A close friend of the Count's father was Theodore Herzl, the founder of Zionism. The Count's book was called *Pan Europa*, and he went on to form the Pan European Union with branches right across the continent, supported by leading European politicians, the Anglo-American Establishment, including Colonel House and Herbert Hoover, and the usual crowd that pop up everywhere. The Count said in his autobiography:

> *"At the beginning of 1924, we received a call from Baron Louis de Rothschild; one of his friends, Max Warburg, from Hamburg, had read my book and wanted to get to know us. To my great surprise* [sure!]*, Warburg spontaneously* [sure!] *offered us 60,000 gold marks to tide the movement over for its first three years...Max Warburg, who was one of the most distinguished and wisest men that I have ever come into contact with, had a principle of financing these movements. He remained sincerely interested in Pan-Europe for his entire life. Max Warburg arranged his 1925 trip to the United States to introduce me to Paul Warburg and Bernard Baruch."* [18]

Also among the supporters of the Pan European Movement was Winston Churchill (Comm 300), who wrote an article in 1930 for the American publication, *The Saturday Evening Post*, entitled "The United States of Europe". This was nine years before the Second World War for which Churchill so vigorously campaigned – a war that was responsible for creating the European Community. Count Coudenhove-Kalergi was given enthusiastic backing from such 'unbiased' sources as John Foster Dulles, Nicholas Murray Butler, the president of Columbia University and the Carnegie Endowment for International War (sorry, 'Peace'), and Dr Stephen Duggan, the founder and first president of the Institute of Education, which was 100% controlled by the Council on Foreign Relations. Those who funded the Bolshevik Revolution and both sides in the two World Wars, including Adolf Hitler, were plotting to introduce the European Community as well as the United Nations.

Meanwhile, Monnet was also close to Franklin D. Roosevelt, thanks to his relationship with the President's influential aide, Harry Hopkins, who was to Roosevelt what Colonel House had been to President Wilson. Hopkins was financed by the Rockefellers and he was their man in the White House. He was recruited by Nelson Rockefeller to work on the New Deal which actually prolonged the United States depression. [19] Both Monnet and Hopkins were supporters of the Soviet Union and Monnet was deeply involved in the lend-lease policies through which vast amounts of weapons, other materials, and knowledge of US nuclear technology were transferred to the communist world. Organisations like the Federal Union Movement – later the Atlantic Union Committee and the Atlantic Council of the United States – were

---

[18] Quoted in *The World Order, Our Secret Rulers*, p248.
[19] Gary Allen, *The Rockefeller File*, ('76 Press, Seal Beach, California, 1976) p156.

formed to press for the union of America and Britain. Such bodies were dominated by CFR members.

Among the directors of the Atlantic Council in the 1970s were George Bush (Comm 300) and one of the world's most influential and tireless manipulators, Henry Kissinger (Comm 300), of whom *much* more will be revealed as our story progresses. The pressure and propaganda for European Union reached new heights in May 1948, when the United European Movement held its Congress of Europe. The leading advocates of the Movement were Winston Churchill and his son-in-law, the British politician Duncan Sandys, and working behind the scenes to great effect were Jean Monnet and the creator of the Bilderberg Group, Joseph Retinger. The Congress adopted seven Resolutions on the political union of Europe. One of them stated, "The creation of a United Europe must be regarded as an essential step towards the creation of a United World" [world government]. Monnet also headed the Committee for the United States of Europe, which had the same goal.[20]

The post-war American loans to Europe, known as the Marshall Plan or European Recovery Programme (ERP), were used both to provide funds for the European Union movement and to undermine the independence of sovereign states and increase the pressure for the central control of Europe. This aid plan was supposed to be the work of General George C. Marshall, President Truman's Secretary of State, but it is now known that the architects were Jean Monnet and the Council on Foreign Relations.[21] In 1946–1947, a CFR study group was formed to report on the Reconstruction of Europe. The group was chaired by the lawyer, Charles M. Spofford, and the secretary was David Rockefeller (Comm 300), later to be head of the Chase Manhattan Bank, the chairman of the CFR, a leading influence in the Bilderberg Group, and creator of another front for the Elite, the Trilateral Commission.

Within little more than a year, this CFR 'study group' changed its name to the Marshall Plan and was sold as government policy. The man chosen to head the Marshall Plan in Europe was...Averell Harriman (Comm 300), who based himself at the Rothschild's Paris Mansion, Hotel Talleyrand. The proposal was not given an easy ride and there were many congressmen who could see through the smokescreen. The CFR therefore launched a propaganda offensive by Elite organisations to ensure that the policy was accepted. These included the CFR-controlled business and trade union bodies and, of course, the CFR-controlled media. The policy of a United States of Europe was given sterling support from the CFR's *New York Times* and *Washington Post*.

The Elite-contrived 'Cold War' would also be very useful, as indeed it

---

[20] *Treason At Maastricht*, p15.

[21] *Global Tyranny...Step By Step. The United Nations And The Emerging New World Order*, p241.

would be on so many occasions in the decades that followed. The need to make loans to Europe to overcome the threat of communism (which the Elite had created) was effectively used to win Congressional approval for the Marshall Plan. John J. McCloy (Comm 300), the chairman of the CFR for nearly twenty years, said that his period as US High Commissioner to Germany after the war had shown him how the use of the communist threat could get things done. "People sat up and listened when the Soviet threat was mentioned",[22] he said. When the proposals secured approval, the Marshall Plan executive board included Allen W. Dulles, then president of the CFR; Philip Reed, the chairman of General Electric; the former secretaries of war, Henry L. Stimson and Robert P. Patterson; and the former undersecretary of state, Dean Acheson (Comm 300), a member of the CFR who was in the US delegation at the formation of the United Nations.

The first step in the creation of the European Community was the introduction of the European Coal and Steel Community, which started in July 1952, and merged the coal and steel industries of West Germany, France, Italy, Belgium, the Netherlands, and Luxemburg under one central control. It had the powers to decide prices, investment, raise money, and make decisions by majority voting. It was introduced under the name The Schuman Plan (after the French socialist foreign minister and later prime minister, Robert Schuman), but once again the man behind it was Jean Monnet, then head of the French General Planning Commission. The idea won gushing praise from CFR names like John Foster Dulles and Dean Acheson, and Monnet was awarded the Wateler Peace Prize of two million francs to recognise the "international spirit which he had shown in conceiving the Coal and Steel Community…". Who made the award? The Carnegie Foundation! Two admirers of Monnet, Merry and Serge Bromberger, set out the plan in their book, *Jean Monnet And The United States Of Europe*:

> *"Gradually, it was thought, the supranational authorities, supervised by the European Council of Ministers at Brussels and the Assembly in Strasbourg, would administer all the activities of the Continent. A day would come when governments would be forced to admit that an integrated Europe was an accomplished fact, without their having had a say in the establishment of its underlying principles. All they would have to do was to merge all these autonomous institutions into a single federal administration and then proclaim a United States of Europe."* [23]

Monnet and his plotters tried to introduce a European army under their central command. They called for disarmament by the nations and the creation of one army. The same is happening today on a global scale. The six

---

[22] Walter Isaacson and Evan Thomas, *The Wise Men*, p289.

[23] Merry and Serge Bromberger, *Jean Monnet And The United States Of Europe*, p123.

members of the Coal and Steel Community signed a treaty to this effect in 1952, but it failed to materialise when the French Parliament refused to accept it. Still, on March 25th 1957, the six did sign the two Treaties of Rome to create the European Economic Community or Common Market, and the European Atomic Energy Community (Euratom). The negotiations for the Treaties of Rome were controlled by Monnet with constant help from the CFR network in the United States. This was confirmed by Harvard lecturer, Ernst H. van der Beugel, an honourary secretary-general of the Elite's Bilderberg Group and a member of the Trilateral Commission. In his book, *From Marshall Aid To Atlantic Partnership* (foreword by his friend, Henry Kissinger), he says:

> *"Monnet and his action committee were unofficially supervising the negotiations and as soon as obstacles appeared, the United States diplomatic machinery was alerted, mostly through Ambassador Bruce...who had immediate access to the top echelon of the State Department...*
>
> *"At that time, it was usual that if Monnet thought that a particular country made difficulties in the negotiations, the American diplomatic representative in that country approached the Foreign Ministry in order to communicate the opinion of the American Government which, in practically all cases, coincided with Monnet's point of view."* [24]

Monnet = Global Elite. The Single European Act, which brought down trade barriers across Europe from 1992, and the Maastricht Accords for European union are just more stepping-stones along the road to the United States of Europe under Elite control. The stepping-stones approach is used daily to fool the public. The manipulators know that if we were asked to move from nation state sovereignty to world government in one leap, even the bewildered herd might ask what was going on and oppose it. So we are sold a series of intermediate stages which are promoted as isolated and unconnected events. Once we have accepted one, the next is introduced until the final goal is reached by stealth. It is like putting someone in a bath of cold water and then heating it slowly until it boils. Only in the final stages does the victim realise what is happening and by then it may be too late. Josef Stalin, the authoritarian dictator of the Soviet Union, explained this process in his book, *Marxism And The National Question*, published in 1942 when the Anglo-American-communist game plan was obviously well known to him. He wrote:

> *"Divide the world into regional groups as a transitional stage to world government. Populations will more readily abandon their national loyalties to a*

[24] Ernst H. van der Beugel, *From Marshall Aid To Atlantic Partnership*, (Elsevier Publishing, Amsterdam, New York, 1966) p245.

vague regional loyalty than they will for a world authority. Later, the regionals can be brought all the way into a single world dictatorship." [25]

Which is precisely what is happening. In 1984, the Soviet KGB defector, Anatoliy Golitsyn, warned that there would be a 'false liberalisation' in the Soviet Union and Eastern Europe. This would be welcomed by the West, he said, and it would lead to a merger of the European Community and the countries of the former Soviet Union. On the same weekend in December 1994, that Bill Clinton announced plans for the NAFTA free trade area to be expanded across the Americas to Argentina, the European heads of government revealed plans to allow countries of the former Soviet Union to join the European Union. Events are now moving very quickly. In the first draft of this chapter, I wrote that the plan was to eventually merge the former Soviet Union into the United States of Europe and, before this book was finished, it had been officially announced.

Look at how far the confidence trick has travelled since the introduction of the European *Economic* Community, or Common Market. We were told we had to join or the British economy would collapse. Oh really? The current British deficit in European trade and membership contributions since we joined is closing in on £100 billion![26] Once the peoples of Europe had been tricked into believing that if they didn't join they would all face disaster, the word *economic* was dropped from the title and it became the European Community (stepping-stone). Later there was another name change to the European Union (stepping-stone). We have also had the move towards the centralisation of political power in the community and the erosion of national decision-making (stepping-stone). This was followed by the pressure for a European Central Bank and one European currency (stepping-stone). And the concept of Europe with centralised control administered by a European Central Bank, one currency, regional administration and common labour, transport and industrial policies, is exactly what Hitler and the Nazis planned for Europe. They even called their plan the European Economic Community (Europäische Wirtschaft = gemeinschaft).[27]

In his 1966 book, *Tragedy And Hope*, Elite 'insider' Carroll Quigley explained how the process of European integration on all levels was to be achieved in stages; Richard N. Gardner (Comm 300) of the CFR was later to say how the plan was to "erode it [sovereignty] piece by piece".[28] On November 9th 1988, the European leaders gathered at the Pantheon in Paris

[25] Quoted by James J. Drummey in *The Establishment's Man (A Profile Of George Bush)*, (Appleton, Wisconsin, Western Islands, 1991) p92.
[26] *Treason At Maastricht*, p52.
[27] For more on this, see *Treason At Maastricht*, pp118–125.
[28] Richard N. Gardner "The Hard Road To World Order", *Foreign Affairs* (magazine of the CFR) (April 1974) p558–559.

to celebrate the centenary of the birth of Jean Monnet, the man called 'the father of Europe'. But what was there to celebrate about Monnet's creation? It has kept the peace in Europe since 1945? No, no. The Elite has allowed that to happen so European integration could take place. Without the manipulators there would have been no pan-European wars in this century, anyway. Monnet created a monster which is in the process of devouring freedom. The integration of Europe is another major vehicle for the New World Order.

THE BILDERBERG GROUP (BIL)[29]

The creation of the European Community and the Bilderberg Group are linked by one man in particular, the Polish socialist, Joseph Retinger, a founder of the European Movement and fellow conspirator with Jean Monnet. It was Retinger and Prince Bernhard of the Netherlands who suggested regular meetings of European foreign ministers. Out of these meetings came the customs union known as the Benelux Countries (Belgium, Netherlands, and Luxemburg), a forerunner to the European Community. Appropriately, it was in a speech at Chatham House to the Royal Institute of International Affairs that Retinger set out his vision of a Europe in which countries would 'relinquish part of their sovereignty'.[30] In London he met Averell Harriman, then US Ambassador to England. Harriman arranged for him to visit the United States to gather support for the Independent League for Economic Cooperation, also known sometimes as the Economic League for European Cooperation, which Retinger was organising. In America, Retinger (in his own words) enjoyed widespread approval for his plans from Russel C. Leffingwell, senior partner in the J.P. Morgan bank and official of the CFR; David Rockefeller, the CFR chairman from 1946-53; Nelson Rockefeller (CFR); Sir William Wiseman (Comm 300), partner in Kuhn, Loeb, the Rothschild company; George Franklin, the CFR executive director from 1953-71 and an 'in law' to the Rockefeller family; John Foster Dulles, and many other familiar characters.[31] By this time, Retinger had already formed the American Committee on a United Europe with Allen Dulles, the first head of the CIA, and William Donovan, the head of the CIAs predecessor, the OSS.[32]

From these and other discussions came the idea of a grouping of leading politicians, political advisors, media owners and executives, multinational company and banking executives, military leaders, and educationalists, who

---

[29] Where I use the term (Bil) this refers to people known to have attended Bilderberg Group meetings. Some will know the real agenda, but others will have been invited along in ignorance, to be sold the Elite line that World Government is good for you. Where people have attended a series of Bilderberg meetings, or if they are the chairman or on the steering committee, they will know the real situation.

[30] Joseph Retinger, *The European Continent?* (Hodge, London, 1946).

[31] Ibid.

[32] *Treason At Maastricht*, p17.

would meet to decide the future of the world. It would become known as the Bilderberg Group, named after the Bilderberg Hotel in Oosterbeek, the Netherlands, where the first meeting took place from May 29th to 31st 1954. At the heart of the Bilderberg Group's formation were the Rothschilds and people like Retinger, Prince Bernhard of the Netherlands, Paul Rykens (the chairman of the soap and food giant, Unilever), and that man again, Averell Harriman. The influence of Harriman on this century can hardly be overstated, although most people will never have even heard of him. It was Harriman who arranged the lend-lease supplies to Britain and the Soviet Union; was the leading administrator of the Marshall Plan in Europe (which directed the policies of recipient countries); introduced the defence budget procedures with Jean Monnet and the British civil servant, Edwin Plowden, for the North Atlantic Treaty Organisation (NATO) which are still used today; headed the Mutual Security Administration which rearmed Europe during the Cold War. This was the man whose family businesses supported the emergence of Adolf Hitler and the eugenics movement.

Prince Bernhard, the former German SS officer, German spy via the I.G. Farben Company,[33] and later a major shareholder with Lord Victor Rothschild in Shell Oil, went to America to arrange the US membership of the Bilderberg Group. Prince Bernhard was born in 1911 as the German Prince of Lupp-Biesterfeld and later worked for I.G. Farben's 'NW7' intelligence department. He married Princess Juliana (Comm 300) of the Netherlands in 1937. They were exiled to London after the Nazi invasion of the Netherlands and this 'former' German intelligence operative worked as a top military liaison with allied forces.[34] The man who persuaded Bernhard to be the frontman for the Bilderbergers was that arch manipulator...Lord Victor Rothschild. The annual meeting of the Anglo-European-American Elite known as the Bilderberg Group was to become a key component in the Elite network which forms the secret government of the world today. Among those who attended that first meeting at the Bilderberg Hotel in 1954 were David Rockefeller (CFR); Dean Rusk (CFR, TC, Rhodes Scholar), the head of the Rockefeller Foundation and Secretary of State under John F. Kennedy; Joseph E. Johnson (CFR), head of the Carnegie Endowment for International Peace and the US Secretary of the Bilderbergers; Denis Healey (TC, RIIA, Comm 300), the British Labour Party Minister of Defence from 1964–1970 and Chancellor of the Exchequer 1974–1979; Hugh Gaitskell, the future leader of the British Labour Party before his death in the early 60s; and Lord Boothby, who worked with Winston Churchill on the unification of Europe.[35] Denis

---

[33] *Wall Street And The Rise Of Hitler*, p39, and *Trilateralism, The Trilateral Commission And The Elite Planning For World Management*, (edited by Holly Sklar, South End Press, Boston, USA, 1980) p182.

[34] *Trilateralism*, p183.

[35] *Trilateralism*, p166–167.

Healey has attended more Bilderberg meetings since 1954 than any other United Kingdom politician. He also became chairman of another Elite creation, the International Monetary Fund Interim Committee, and he was given a grant by the Ford Foundation[36] to launch the Elite's Institute of Strategic Studies, which began operating in London in 1958.[37] For 12 years, Healey, a leading member of the Fabian Society, served on the council of the Royal Institute of International Affairs and became a member of the Rockefellers' Trilateral Commission in 1979.

The Bilderberg Group consists of a small core elite, known as the Steering Committee. This is unelected and was headed by Prince Bernhard, a close friend of the British Royal Family. He remained chairman until he resigned in 1976 when he was implicated in the Lockheed bribery scandal. Lord Home (Comm 300), the former British Prime Minister, took over as chairman and since 1991 that post has been held by Lord Carrington. He is an extremely close associate of Henry Kissinger. Carrington is a former British cabinet minister, secretary general of NATO, member of the Committee of 300, and current President of the Royal Institute of International Affairs. Peter Rupert Carrington comes from a family which made its money from banking. Carrington was on the board of Hambros Bank (Comm 300 designate) which has been linked with the Michel Sindona financial scandal in Italy. This was, in turn, connected with the infamous P2 Freemasonry Lodge which blew Italian politics apart. Among Lord Carrington's other business interests have been directorships at Rio Tinto Zinc, Barclay's Bank, Cadbury Schweppes, Amalgamated Metal, British Metal, Christies (the auctioneers), and the chairmanship of the Australian New Zealand Bank.

In his book, *The English Rothschilds*, Richard Davis reports that Lionel Rothschild was a frequent visitor to the Carrington's home in Whitehall. The two families are related by the marriage of the fifth Earl Rosebery to Hannah Rothschild, daughter of Mayer, in 1878. During the ceremony, she was given away, as the British say, by Prime Minister Disraeli. The Bilderberg Elite, like Carrington and those on the steering committee, coordinate the regular attenders of Bilderberg meetings (who know the real game plan) and those invited on a rare or one-time basis (who may not know the true agenda of the organisation, but can be fed the party line that world institutions are the way to peace and prosperity). The Elite are also very efficient manipulators of the ego and many politicians feel themselves to have 'arrived' on the international stage if they are invited to attend.

The Bilderberg Group meets once a year and always in the strictest secrecy. The hotels are cleared of everyone except the Bilderbergers and hotel staff. The meetings discuss the strategy required over the following twelve months

[36] *Washington Observer Newsletter,* (July 1st 1971).
[37] Later the International Institute of Strategic Studies. The Ford Foundation gave $150,000 over three years (*Trilateralism*, p187).

to further the goals of the New World Order, and it cooperates with associated organisations. Not a word of the discussions is allowed to be reported in the mainstream press. This, despite the attendance of major media figures like Katharine Graham (Bil, CFR, TC), the present owner of the *Washington Post*, and Conrad Black (Bil, TC), the owner of the Hollinger Group which controls the London *Daily Telegraph*, the *Jerusalem Post*, the *Spectator*, and scores of other media organisations around the world. Graham is also co-chairman (with Arthur Ochs Sulzberger of the *New York Times*) in the jointly-produced *International Herald Tribune*, another propaganda sheet for the Global Elite. Graham is further connected with *Newsweek* magazine and the news agency, Associated Press (AP), which feeds information to countless media outlets around the world; not information about the Bilderberg Group, however, or the CFR or Trilateral Commission.

Three board members of Black's Hollinger empire, and/or the *Daily Telegraph*, are Henry Kissinger, Lord Carrington, and Sir Evelyn de Rothschild. Black has served on the Bilderberg Steering Committee. His Hollinger Group has an interesting history. It was formerly known as the Argus Corporation which evolved from a company set up by the elite British intelligence unit of World War II, the Special Operations Executive, thanks to the leading economic warfare expert, Edward Plunket Taylor. He was a business partner of George Montegu Black, Conrad's father. Both were involved in brewing in Canada and their rise paralleled that of the Bronfmans, the family of a Canadian gangster of the prohibition period. Today the Bronfmans are closely connected with that notorious Elite organisation, the Anti-Defamation League. In 1940, Edward Plunket Taylor was personally appointed by Winston Churchill to the Special Operations Executive. His cover was to chair a private company called War Supplies Ltd, which was created by the SOE. Taylor and George Montegu Black made a vast fortune through this company and it continued after the war as the Argus Corporation, now the Hollinger Group. Taylor left in 1970 to draft the banking laws for the Cayman Islands and the Bahamas which, as a result, became "offshore" havens for dodgy money. Under Conrad Black's stewardship, a stream of Bilderbergers and other names mentioned in this book have been appointed to the board of Telegraph newspapers and the Hollinger Group. Great to know we have a free press, eh?

Another member of the Bilderberg Steering Committee is Andrew Knight, the former executive on the *Economist*, Black's *Daily Telegraph*, and later the executive chairman of Rupert Murdoch's *News International* which, in Britain, owns the *Sun*, *Today*, the *News of the World*, the *Times* and *Sunday Times*. Knight is still on the board of that organisation. Since 1982, he has been part of the Council of Management of the Ditchley Foundation, based at Ditchley Park, near Oxford, in a castle built for the Earl of Lichfield in the sixteenth century. The Ditchley Foundation was given the property by Ronald and Marietta Tree. Ronald was a former high flyer in British

Intelligence.[38] The steering committee of the Bilderberg Group often holds its monthly meetings at the castle. The Ditchley Foundation is a New World Order front organisation which works closely with the Tavistock Institute for Human Relations in London, which a number of researchers and published works have claimed is a centre for the study of mass mind manipulation. Several of the names mentioned in this book are connected with Ditchley including Christopher (Lord) Tugendhat, the chairman of the Royal Institute of International Affairs. The American branch of the Ditchley Foundation is run by Cyrus Vance (CFR, TC, Bil, Comm 300), secretary of state under Carter and a director of the Rockefeller Foundation. The number of journalists and media executives in the Bilderberg Group and in other strands in the network is very substantial, but try finding a word about these meetings in the mainstream media.

Behind the Bilderbergers are the Rothschilds and the Rockefellers. Today Henry Kissinger is a major manipulator, albeit as a puppet of those who really control him. Kissinger is an elite member of the Bilderberg Group, the Trilateral Commission, and the Council on Foreign Relations, and he is connected with the Royal Institute of International Affairs, the Rockefeller/Rothschild Chase Manhattan Bank, and the Rockefeller Foundation. He also runs his own organisation, Kissinger Associates, among whose founding directors you will find...Lord Carrington! Kissinger and Carrington have close connections with Lord Roll of Ipsden, another Bilderberger, Trilateralist, member of the Committee of 300, and board member of Kissinger Associates. Lord Roll (formerly Sir Eric Roll) was the president of the merchant bank, S.G. Warburg. Another close friend of Kissinger in England was British Intelligence operative and spy, Lord Victor Rothschild.

The Spotlight newspaper in Washington (which seeks to publish material that the mainstream media will not report) is constantly seeking to infiltrate Bilderberg meetings. It had a good year in 1991 when it obtained the guest list of the meeting in Baden-Baden, Germany. Among the names were David Rockefeller and a stream of US administrators, politicians, and company heads. Bill Clinton was there, then as governor for Arkansas, but he was soon to be President of the United States. Clinton is also a member of the Council on Foreign Relations and the Trilateral Commission, two of many things this Democrat shares with his predecessor in the White House, the Republican, George Bush. Conrad Black was there, as always, and so was another elite Bilderberger, the longtime head of Fiat, Giovanni Agnelli (Comm 300). He is the richest and most powerful figure in Italian society with interests in banking, insurance, chemicals, textiles, armaments and publishing, reputed to be worth $60 billion. His publishing empire includes two of the three leading newspapers in Italy, *La Stampa* and *Corriere dela Sera.*

---

[38] *The World Order, Our Secret Rulers*, p267.

I bet they don't mention that their owner is a leading voice in the Bilderberg Group. Henry Kissinger described him as "one of the people in this world I like the most".[39]

European royalty was represented by two regular attenders, Queen Beatrix of the Netherlands (Comm 300), the daughter of Prince Bernhard, and Queen Sophia of Spain. The British delegation included John Smith,[40] the late leader of the Labour Party, who was also a Trilateralist; Gordon Brown, the shadow Labour Chancellor; Andrew Knight; Lord Roll of Ipsden; Lawrence Freedman, the head of the Department of War Studies at Kings College; Christopher Hogg, the chairman of Courtaulds; and Patrick Wright, the Permanent Undersecretary of State and head of the Diplomatic Service. Manfred Wörner, the late secretary general of NATO, was there and so was John R. Galvin, the Supreme Allied Commander Europe at SHAPE headquarters. Galvin has been an advocate of NATO operations outside its official sphere of influence. The secretary general of NATO is a Bilderberg appointment. Most, if not all, of them have been Bilderbergers. In more recent times, the Bilderberger Joseph Luns, was replaced by Lord Carrington, who was followed by Manfred Wörner, and after his death in 1994, he was replaced by another regular Bilderberger, Willy Claes, the Belgian Foreign Minister (who has since been questioned by Belgian police investigating corruption). The latest head of NATO, the Spaniard, Javier Solana (Bil), has been constantly pressing the Bilderberg Group agenda for a European army, the expansion of NATO into the former Soviet Union, and for NATO to operate outside its designated area. According to *The Spotlight*, the introduction of the world army was high on the agenda in Baden-Baden, with Henry Kissinger saying in one of his Bilderberg forums:

> *"A UN army must be able to act immediately, anywhere in the world, without delays involved in each country making its own decisions based on parochial considerations."* [41]

---

[39] *The Sunday Times*, (December 17th 1995) p1, section 3.

[40] John Smith attended the April 1986 Bilderberg meeting in Gleneagles, Scotland, which was chaired by Lord Roll of Ipsden. Also there were David Steel, the then leader of the British Liberal Party; Denis Healey; Lord Home; Garret Fitzgerald, the Irish Prime Minister; Lord Young, the UK Secretary of State for Employment; Malcolm Rifkind, the Secretary of State for Scotland and later Defence and Foreign Secretary; Helmut Schmidt, former Chancellor of Germany [Helmut Kohl, the present Chancellor is also a Bilderberger]; Lord Boardman, chairman of the National Westminster Bank; Henry J. Heinz II, chairman of Heinz and Co; Paul R. Jolles, chairman of Nestle S.A.; John Sainsbury, chairman of J. Sainsbury plc; Conrad Black; Andrew Knight; and Paul A. Volcker, the chairman of the US Federal Reserve, also an executive of the CFR and the Trilateral Commission.

[41] *The Spotlight*, Special Report on the Bilderberg Group and the Shadow Government, (Reprint, September 1991).

And, of course, Henry, if there just happened to be lots of conflicts in which UN Peacekeeping Forces were exposed as inadequate and ineffective as in Bosnia, Rwanda, etc, the public outcry could be met with: "Well, if you will just agree to give the UN Forces more powers, they could respond quicker and be as effective as you want them to be". Problem-reaction-solution. Kissinger also said he was delighted with the way George Bush was able to declare war on Iraq by going direct to the United Nations when under the US Constitution, only Congress was allowed to declare war. If Americans could be persuaded to surrender warmaking decisions to the UN and let their young men die wearing a UN uniform, fighting under a UN flag, 'parochial nationalism' in Britain, France, and elsewhere would disappear, Bilderberg speakers said, according to *Spotlight* informants. Bill Clinton has pressed for just such a policy in Bosnia and we will see further efforts to do this with other UN operations.

The same old names which keep coming up everywhere attended the June 1994 Bilderberg meeting in Finland. Among the invited high and mighty was Peter D. Sutherland (TC, Comm 300), the Director General of GATT, the General Agreement on Tariff and Trade, which is an Elite front to bring down trade barriers and put all countries at the mercy of the Elite-controlled world economic system. Sutherland was a perfect choice for the job as a former member of the Commission of the European Community. He was a Bilderberger before he became head of world trade. His successor as the top man at the World Trade Organisation, the Italian, Renato Ruggiero, is also a Bilderberger. Another regular Bilderberger, the Netherlands Prime Minister, Ruud Lubbers, was also there in Finland, along with bankers like J. Martin Taylor, the chief executive of Barclays Bank. Two other names of significance to British voters are Tony Blair (Labour) and Kenneth Clarke (Conservative). They attended the 1993 Bilderberg meeting in Vouliagment, Greece, where David Owen (TC) spoke about Yugoslavia and the future of Europe. Tony Blair, then the opposition home affairs spokesman, went on to become Labour leader and prime minister, while Kenneth Clarke would become the Chancellor of the Exchequer. Both support a federal Europe.

In June 1995, the Bilderberg Group met at three exclusive hotels, The Grand, The Park, and The Palace, on a mountainside at Burgenstock in Switzerland. It was a rare occasion when they met in the same place twice. Coincidentally, I was on holiday in Switzerland when the Bilderbergers gathered and I was told of the meeting by *Spotlight* newspaper only a few days before I arrived. I went to Burgenstock before the meeting and again on their final day of discussions. What a difference the second time! The roads and paths to the hotels were blocked by Swiss police and the military manned lookout posts across the mountain. All this for a private meeting of an organisation that operates outside the 'democratic' process.

I asked a policeman at a road block what was going on. All he could reply was "top secret, top secret". He knew no more than that. It was a bizarre situation. *I* could have told the policeman what he was guarding, but *he* didn't know! It illustrated brilliantly the way the global pyramid operates. The policeman appeared to be a very nice man. No doubt he had children and grandchildren and he had no desire to leave them a global fascist state. But there he was on a Swiss mountainside playing his part, unknowingly, in shielding from the public glare, the very people who are plotting to create just such a world dictatorship.

THE EUROPEAN-ATLANTIC GROUP (EAG) AND THE ATLANTIC COUNCIL (AC)

In 1954, the year the Bilderberg Group was founded, another organisation came into being, the European-Atlantic Group. Its headquarters are at 6 Gertrude Street, Chelsea, London. The group was formed by the late Lord Layton, who was then Vice-President of the Council of Europe and it brings together members of parliament from all parties, industrialists, bankers, economists, and journalists (sound familiar?) to promote closer relations between the "European and Atlantic countries by providing a regular forum in Britain for informed discussion of their problems and possibilities for better economic and political cooperation with each other and with the rest of the world".[42] This means, to use its own words, connecting with international organisations, including The Council of Europe, NATO, OECD, the Western European Union, the European Union, the European Free Trade Association, the GATT global 'free' trade organisation, and the Economic Commission for Europe. And, it might add, any organisation which desires a world government or can be used to that end. Its hierarchy is dominated by the House of Lords and includes a representative of the American New World Order front, the Council on Foreign Relations. Among the vice-presidents on the list I have from the 1990s are: Lord Carrington, chairman of the Bilderberg Group; Lord Chalfont, chairman of the House of Lords Defence Committee; Graham Dowson, joint president of the European League for European Cooperation; Douglas Fairbanks, the Council on Foreign Relations; Lord Gladwyn, president of the European Movement; Robert Maxwell (deceased), embezzler, Mossad agent, and publisher of the *Daily Mirror* newspaper; Sir David Nicholson, chairman of the European Movement; Derek Prag, chairman of the London Europe Society; Lord Pym, who took over as foreign secretary from Lord Carrington at the time of the Falklands War; and Lord Shawcross.

The Atlantic Council (formerly the British Atlantic Council) is a similar organisation, even down to many of the personnel. Its vice-presidents include: Lord Carrington; Lord Gladwyn; Lord Pym; Lord Shawcross; the Earl of Bessborough, a past president of the European-Atlantic Group; Lord Home, former Conservative prime minister, and past chairman of the

---

[42] Publicity material, European-Atlantic Group, 6 Gertrude Street, Chelsea, London SW10 0JN.

Bilderberg Group; Edward Heath, former Conservative prime minister, Bilderberger, Trilateralist, and obsessively in favour of European union; Denis Healey; William Rogers, Bilderberger, former Labour minister, and one of the 'gang of four' who formed the breakaway Social Democratic Party, now the Liberal Democrats.

If the Royal Institute of International Affairs were not so shy about its membership list, you would find many names active within these two organisations involved at the RIIA also, I'm sure. The European Atlantic Group and the Atlantic Council are both part of the New World Order network.

THE TRILATERAL COMMISSION [43]

The next element of the secret government network was unveiled in 1972–1973 by David Rockefeller (Comm 300), the head of the Chase Manhattan Bank, leading Bilderberger, and leading manipulator of the Council on Foreign Relations, of which he was the long-time chairman. David Rockefeller is one of the most high profile, and most obvious, New World Order manipulators on the planet, although he is really a puppet of those above him in the pyramid. He created the Trilateral Commission which, as its name suggests, is made up of three groupings – the United States, Europe, and Japan. Rockefeller was partly inspired to do this by Zbigniew Brzezinski (TC, CFR, Bil), a professor at the Elite-controlled Columbia University. Brzezinski had also been researching the need for US-Europe-Japan cooperation at the Elite-controlled 'think tank', the Brookings Institute in Washington.

Brzezinski wrote a book called *Between Two Ages: America's Role In The Technetronic Era*, in which he described a new society "...that is shaped culturally, psychologically, socially, and economically by the impact of technology and electronics – particularly in the area of computers and communication".[44] He said in the book that "national sovereignty is no longer a viable concept" and suggested the movement, in stages, "toward a larger community of the developed nations...through a variety of indirect ties and already developing limitations on national sovereignty". In 1990, he wrote in the Elite's mouthpiece, the *New York Times*, that Europe should follow a policy "founded upon the grand concept of a trans-European commonwealth with the European Community at its core, but embracing Central Europe and being open also to eventual association with the Soviet Union". You can see

---

[43] Where I use the term (TC) or (CFR) after a person's name it denotes someone who is a member of those organisations, had been a member, or would later become one. As with the Bilderberg Group, it does not necessarily mean that these people all know what is going on. Many of them are probably being used without their knowledge. Those who know the real game plan are pretty obvious.

[44] Zbigniew Brzezinski, *Between Two Ages: Americas Role In The Technetronic Era*, (Viking Press, New York, 1970) p9.

where this guy is coming from. David Rockefeller was so impressed with Brzezinski that he made him director of the Trilateral Commission, which recruited members from all areas of influence and power in the United States, Europe and Japan. Many of those recruited were already members of the Council on Foreign Relations; some were Bilderbergers, too, and others, like Henry Kissinger, were linked to all of them and the Royal Institute of International Affairs as well. Among the seventeen people who met at the Rockefellers' estate (Pocantico Hills in Tarrytown, New York) to plan the Trilateral Commission on July 23rd and 24th 1972, were C. Fred Bergsten (CFR, Bil), Senior Fellow at the Brookings Institute and a former Assistant for International Economic Affairs to Henry Kissinger; and McGeorge Bundy (CFR, Bil), the President of the Ford Foundation and head of the National Security Council under both John Kennedy and Lyndon Johnson. The early funding for the Trilateral Commission came from David Rockefeller, the Ford Foundation, the Kettering Foundation, the Lilly Endowment, the Rockefeller Brothers Fund, and the Thyssen Foundation, with smaller amounts donated by organisations like General Motors, Exxon, Coca Cola, *Time* magazine, CBS, and the Wells Fargo Bank.[45] The Commission made its headquarters at 345 East 46th Street, New York.

One of the first ambitions for David Rockefeller and his Trilateral Commission was to put a commission member in the White House as President of the United States as soon as possible. He achieved this at the next election when Jimmy Carter, the Democrat peanut farmer from Georgia, beat Gerald Ford. Carter was selected for president by Rockefeller and Brzezinski and the whole Elite network of money, media, and dirty tricks were used to ensure he was elected. Carter was another puppet president controlled by the Elite. His speeches in his election campaign were written by Brzezinski and none could have been more insulting to the truth than his acceptance speech for the Democratic nomination. In the world of politics you don't tell people what you stand for; you tell them what they *want* you to stand for. When you look at Carter's background, what greater example of this could there be than when he spoke of:

> "...a political and economic elite who have shaped decisions and never had to account for mistakes nor to suffer from injustice. When unemployment prevails, they never stand in line looking for a job. When deprivation results from a confused welfare system, they never do without food or clothing, or a place to sleep. When the public schools are inferior or torn by strife their children go to exclusive private schools. And when the bureaucracy is bloated and confused, the powerful always manage to discover and occupy niches of special influence and privilege." [46]

[45] *Trilateralism*, p78.
[46] Quoted in *Trilateralism*, p197.

Sure, Jimmy, sure. He might have added at the end..."And quite right, too". Carter's administration was awash with Trilateral Commission members. Among its ranks were Walter Mondale, the vice president; Cyrus Vance, the secretary of state; Warren Christopher, the deputy secretary of state; Harold Brown (CFR), secretary for defense; W. Michael Blumenthal (CFR), secretary of the treasury; C. Fred Bergsten (CFR, Bil), assistant secretary of the treasury for international affairs; Henry Owen (CFR), the ambassador-at-large and the president's special representative for economic summits; Paul C. Warnke (CFR), chief disarmament negotiator; Andrew Young (CFR), ambassador to the United Nations, Paul A. Volcker (CFR, Bil), chairman of the Federal Reserve Board, and...Zbigniew Brzezinski (CFR, Bil), Carter's national security advisor. This was the Trilateral Administration. It became a standing joke among insiders that whenever Carter was faced with a decision or document involving foreign policy, he would say "Clear it with Brzezinski" or "Has Brzezinski seen this?"[47] Paul Volcker was made head of the Federal Reserve by Carter on the instructions of David Rockefeller. It is one of the most influential posts in the Elite network, with its power to control the American economy. Volcker became the North American chairman of the Trilateral Commission and was both a Bilderberger and member of the Council on Foreign Relations. He remained chairman of the 'Fed' until he was replaced during the Reagan administration by the present incumbent, Alan Greenspan, who is also a member of the TC, CFR, and Bilderberg Group. Just a coincidence, naturally.

The Trilateral Commission's influence became worldwide with its membership across the American, European and Japanese elites. Ireland was well represented on the executive committee of the TC in Europe through both Prime Minister Garret Fitzgerald (Bil) and the then little known Mary Robinson, who would go on to be the first woman President of Ireland. After I had spoken about these matters in a meeting at Totnes in South West England, a lady in the audience sought me out. "That's the first time I have heard anyone talk about this since my husband (who worked for the South African government) showed me a document which said that the Trilateral Commission had ordered Britain to pull out of Rhodesia", she said. The lady, like most people in the world, had never heard of the Trilateral Commission at the time she saw the document. Who was the British Foreign Secretary at that time, I thought, during the administration of Margaret Thatcher (Bil), when Britain left Rhodesia, now Zimbabwe? It was...Lord Carrington, Bilderberger and member of the Trilateral Commission. He was continuing a policy put into motion by the previous Labour government of Jim Callaghan (Bil), now a president, along with Lord Carrington and Lord Jenkins (TC, Bil), of the Royal Institute of International Affairs. And who was Callaghan's foreign secretary? David Owen, a soon-to-be member of the Trilateral

[47] *Los Angeles Times*, (January 23rd 1977) p1.

Commission who worked closely with Andrew Young, Jimmy Carter's ambassador at the United Nations, and member of the Trilateral Commission. I remembered also that when the European Community sent an 'ambassador' to negotiate 'peace' in Bosnia, they chose...Lord Carrington. When he 'failed', they sent...David Owen. Later an 'independent' peace negotiator arrived on the scene from America – Jimmy Carter. And, I thought, who was foreign secretary when the policies were decided that led to the Falklands War between Britain and Argentina in 1982? Lord Carrington. He resigned over what happened and was rewarded with the job of secretary general of NATO! Also deeply involved in the negotiations over Rhodesia and the transition from white dictatorship to dictatorship by Robert Mugabe, was Lord Soames, a director of N.M. Rothschild until 1979. I'm sure that all these coincidences must have an innocent explanation. Its just that I can't think of one.

THE CLUB OF ROME AND THE ENVIRONMENTAL MOVEMENT

The Club of Rome was launched publicly in 1968 by the Italian Freemason, Aurelio Peccei (Comm 300), who once said to his friend, the former US Secretary of State, Alexander Haig (TC), that he felt like Adam Weishaupt reincarnated.[48] Weishaupt was the man behind the modern Illuminati. Peccei was the chief executive of the Fiat Motor Company under its president and prominent Bilderberger, Giovanni Agnelli (Comm 300). The Club of Rome was created by meetings at the Rockefeller family's private estate at Bellagio in Italy.[49] It was, and is, the Club of Rome's role to issue propaganda about the environmental crisis and use this to justify the centralisation of power (problem-reaction-solution) and the suppression of industrial development in both the West and the so called Third World. It is also another 'justification' for population control (eugenics). Peccei was a passionate advocate of world government and his Club of Rome has produced plans for restructuring the world into five regions under the control of a central world authority. It has issued many 'reports', including *Limits To Growth* in 1972, sponsored by the Rockefellers. It was distributed as a 197-page paperback published in 18 editions and 23 languages. *Limits To Growth* has been widely quoted by the environmental movement to support their arguments, but they should consider the fact that anything that comes out of the Club of Rome is part of an Elite plan to direct human thinking and persuade people to accept the goals of the New World Order. So is the Club's "spiritual/arts" offshoot, the Club of Budapest, headed by Ervin Laszio, an associate of Aurelio Peccei. They might consider, too, the fact that Peccei later admitted that the computer used to produce their data and justification had been preprogrammed to produce the

[48] Quoted by Dr John Coleman in *The Conspirators' Hierarchy: The Story Of The Committee Of 300*, (America West Publishers, Bozeman, MT, USA, 1992) p15.
[49] Gary Allen, *The Rockefeller File*, ('76 Press, Seal Beach, California, 1976) p152.

desired result. He said this had been done because nations required 'shock treatment' if they were to accept population control.[50] The acclaimed economist, Gunnar Myrdal, said of the Club of Rome methods:

> *"The use of mathematical equations and a huge computer, which registers the alternatives of abstractly conceived policies by a 'world simulation model', may impress the innocent general public but has little, if any, scientific validity. That this 'sort of model is actually a new tool for mankind' is unfortunately not true. It represents quasilearnedness of a type that we have, for a long time, had too much of..."* [51]

It was under the influence and guidance of the Club of Rome and its 'data' that another report was produced which has had a fundamental effect on the acceleration of 'environmentalism'. This was a study ordered by the Trilateral Commission-controlled Carter administration. On July 24th 1980, in the last months of the Carter presidency, his secretary of state, Edmund Muskie (TC, CFR), presented the *Global 2000* report to the President. It painted a global picture of overpopulation, resource and food shortages, and environmental dangers which, it estimated, would cause the deaths of at least 170 million people up to the year 2000. This was followed six months later by another report, *Global Future: A Time To Act*, the work of the White House Council on Environmental Quality. This called for a series of measures to respond to the crisis set out in *Global 2000* and at the top of the list of responses was...population control through sterilisation and other means. Both reports called for, in effect, the restriction of scientific development and technological transfer to developing countries and soon these policies were being lauded around the world. Cyrus Vance (TC, CFR, Bil, Comm 300), Carter's secretary of state before Muskie, chaired the Committee for the Year 2000 for this purpose. Vance was the man who instigated both *Global 2000* and *Global Future* during his tenure at Carter's State Department. In his first official speech at the United Nations in 1977, Vance rejected calls from developing countries for changes to the International Monetary Fund and the unfairness of the economic system, and instead he suggested a "...new world order based on environmentalism".

I would have more confidence in the problems and solutions presented by the Club of Rome and these two US reports if the people behind them were not the very same politicians, bankers, industrialists, and academics who support and promote the policies of the Elite-controlled International Monetary Fund (IMF), Bank of International Settlements, and World Bank, which in turn, are responsible for the death, starvation, and suffering of

---

[50] *Executive Intelligence Review* Special Report, *Global 2000: Blueprint For Genocide*, p16.

[51] Julian L. Simon and Herman Kahn (editors), *The Resourceful Earth: A Response To Global 2000*, (Basil Blackwell Inc., New York, 1984) p34–35.

billions of people across the planet. One of the architects of the *Global 2000 Report* was Robert McNamara (TC, CFR, Bil), a former president of the World Bank, the policies of which have wreaked environmental and human genocide in the Third World! I would have more confidence if these 'environmental messiahs' were not the same people who suppress the introduction of known technologies, such as free energy technology,[52] which could in a few years replace today's fossil-fuel-burning environmental carnage. I differ from those who say there is no environmental crisis and that the whole thing is a propaganda creation. I think we are inflicting appalling wounds to Planet Earth and if we go on as we are there will be serious consequences, indeed there already are. What I feel, however, is that these wounds are being knowingly inflicted by the Elite, and no doubt in certain areas, exaggerated for propaganda purposes to create yet another global problem-reaction-solution scenario.

If those behind all this really cared about the environment and the lives of those who suffer so terribly from the present system, they would be releasing the suppressed technologies which would dramatically reduce the damage which is being wreaked upon the Earth. Reports like *Global 2000*, *Global Future*, and those produced by the Elite/Club of Rome, base their findings on what they call 'current trends'. But what are 'current trends'? They are only the result of the current policies of the Elite manipulators. Change the policies and you change both the 'trends' and the recommendations on how to react to the 'trends'. The rape of the Third World environment creates dependency by billions of people on the Elite-controlled economic system, as their ability to live sustainably without outside 'support' is destroyed. Environmental damage is therefore terrible for the mass of humanity, but an excellent tool for the Elite's ambitions. Change these policies and change the 'trends' (environmentally-created dependency) and you make irrelevant the 'solutions' suggested in Club of Rome reports. But funnily enough, such reports never call for an end to Elite policies, because these publications are part of them.

Most environmentalists are genuinely campaigning for what they believe to be right, but there are some who are knowingly working to the New World Order agenda and I must say I am less than convinced when I hear people like Al Gore (CFR), the vice president to Bill Clinton (TC, CFR, Bil), being presented as an 'environmentalist'. I would take his concern for the environment and humanity a little more seriously if he had not been one of the Democrats who voted with George Bush's Republicans in favour of the war in the Gulf in 1991, and had his environmental policies not come straight off the pages of Club of Rome and *Global 2000* reports. I was an

---

[52] Free energy technology harnesses the Earth's magnetic energy field and turns it into usable warmth and power. There are a number of versions of this – all suppressed. It would be virtually cost-free and require no electricity pylons or national grid. See *The Robots' Rebellion*.

environmental campaigner throughout the 1980s and became a national spokesman for the British Green Party, so I can see how many of the responses of the environmental movement resulted from the Club of Rome, *Global 2000*, approach to both problems and solutions. I am still an environmental campaigner, but now from a much, much, wider perspective and I can appreciate how the 'green movement' is being manipulated to promote the New World Order. When, for instance, the green movement presents wind power and wave power as alternative forms of energy to fossil fuels, this so lacks credibility that there appears to be no choice but to continue to exploit the planet and create pollution. This is helping to obscure the fact that free energy technology exists. I can also see today how the pressure for population control is, and always has been, promoted by the Elite to justify a policy of eugenics.

The theme of these various environmental reports is that economic growth must end, something with which much of the environmental movement would agree. So would I, in fact. As with everything, I feel, we need to look at the shades of grey if we are to find the truth of any situation. On one side you have the environmentalists who challenge growth and on the other you have some of those who are investigating the New World Order conspiracy, who say the environmental problems are all a hoax. I see the truth in the middle somewhere. Yes, there are environmental problems, but the questions we need to ask are these: Have the environmental problems been created deliberately, largely to produce a situation of problem-reaction-solution? And are at least *aspects* of the 'environmental crisis' being deliberately emphasised and exaggerated to quicken the problem-reaction-solution response by the public? I believe the answer to both questions is yes.

We can look in the same way at economic growth. Some say it has to stop, some say there are no limits to growth. But what is growth? It is merely the measurement of the amount of money that is spent for goods and services in any year. This figure is what we call Gross National Product (GNP) or Gross Domestic Product (GDP). Therefore 'growth' is the sum total of all the positive and negative events in the world every year that involve money being spent, that's all. The money spent on improving the quality of people's lives and that spent on wars, road accidents, and responding to oil tanker catastrophes are all measured exactly the same by this system, because all are adding to the economic tally – GDP. This is plainly farcical. What we call growth tells us nothing, except how absurd our economic indicators are. When we speak of an end to growth or we say there are no limits to growth, we have to ask "What kind of growth? And the growth of what?" Of course there are limits to growth if you are talking about the constant expansion of what we take from the planet and throw at her in pollution. But, when the true understanding of physics and technology is revealed and introduced in our everyday lives, we will see that this suppressed knowledge can give us the warmth and power we need for a comfortable life for *all* the peoples of the world without dismantling the planet. Under this system, the growth in take-make-and-throwaway and mine-burn-pollute can slow down and end, while – at the same time – everyone in the world has a *better*, not a more primitive standard of life. The end to growth in take-make-and-throwaway and the expansion of better living conditions for *all* are not a contradiction. They are made possible by ending the suppression of scientific knowledge that will solve the environmental and human 'problems' which have been engineered to control us. What is clear is that the use of environmentalism to justify centralised control continues apace. Working to this end alongside the Club of Rome is the United Nations. In February 1972, an advertisement sponsored by the Rockefeller/CFR-controlled World Association of World Federalists[53] appeared in the Humanist, the magazine of the American Humanist (this-world-is-all-there-is) Association. Note the use of words like problem and solution. It said:

> *"World Federalists believe that the environmental crisis facing Planet Earth is a global problem and therefore calls for a 'global' solution – a worldwide United Nations Environmental Agency with the power to make decisions stick. WAWF has submitted a proposal for just such an agency to be considered at the 1972 UN Environmental Conference to be held in Stockholm."*

The timing is interesting here. 1972 was the year of the publication of the Club of Rome's *Limits To Growth* report. The troops were being gathered for the battle. It was a battle to persuade the public that there was a global environmental problem in need of a global – centralised – solution. The momentum generated from that UN Environmental Conference led to just such an Environmental Agency, the UN Environment Programme (UNEP). The first executive director was a Canadian, Maurice Strong (Comm 300), a millionaire oilman and former trustee of the Rockefeller Foundation. He had been the secretary-general of the Stockholm conference and is a major voice in the Club of Rome. Strong and David Rockefeller wrote the foreword for a Trilateral Commission book, *Beyond Interdependence: The Meshing Of The World's Economy And The Earth's Ecology.*[54] Among the co-authors was Strong's friend and fellow Canadian, Jim MacNeill, who had advised him at Stockholm. They were also both members of the World Commission on Environment and Development and MacNeill, as secretary

---

[53] The World Federalists movement was formed in 1947 by two pillars of the CFR, James P. Warburg and Norman Cousins. Its slogan was "one world or none". The United World Federalists amalgamated three groups, the World Federalists, Student Federalists, and Americans United for World Government.

[54] Jim MacNeil, Pieter Winsemius and Taizo Yakushiji, *Beyond Interdependence: The Meshing Of The World's Economy And The Earth's Ecology*, (Oxford University Press, New York, 1991).

general of that organisation, played a leading role in writing the report called *Our Common Future*, another tome constantly quoted by the environmental movement. It is also known as The Brundtland Report, after the prime minister of Norway, Gro Harlam Brundtland, who put her name to it. She is an enthusiastic supporter of the European Union and population control measures. Her husband, Arne Olav Brundtland, is a Bilderberger. In 1992 came the much-heralded United Nations Earth Summit in Rio de Janeiro, Brazil, which brought together the heads of world governments and the best known environmentalists, such as Britain's Jonathan Porritt, the former head of UK Friends of the Earth and now advisor to Prince Charles. The secretary general of the Rio Summit was, well I never, ...Maurice Strong, David Rockefeller's green friend. Strong was advised by Rockefeller's other green buddy...Jim MacNeill. *Beyond Interdependence*, the Trilateral Commission's environmental offering, was published in preparation for Rio, as was *Global Economics And The Environment* by the Council on Foreign Relations. The theme was...centralisation of control to protect the world. Maurice Strong is President of the World Federation of United Nations Associations, co-chairman of the World Economic Forum, and a member of the Club of Rome, among countless other bodies steeped in the New World Order. He was later appointed as advisor to UN Secretary General, Kofi Annan. Strong is using the environment to justify centralisation of power.

Another well-known green face behind the Rio Summit was Lester R. Brown, the 'anti-establishment' head of the Worldwatch Institute in Washington. His dislike for the establishment does not, however, prevent him being a member of the CFR. His Institute publishes the annual *State Of The World* reports detailing the demise of the global environment. The 1989 version on my own bookshelf tells me that: "The Rockefeller Brothers Fund, Winthrop Rockefeller Trust, and the George Gund Foundation supply the backbone of financial support for the State of the World series". I can't claim to have been surprised. In his *State Of The World 1991*, Brown said:

> "...*the battle to save the planet will replace the battle over ideology as the organizating theme of the new world order...*[with] *the end of the ideological conflict that dominated a generation of international affairs, a new world order, shaped by a new agenda, will emerge.*" [55]

There had obviously been a mobilisation by the Elite to speak with the same voice and also to use those environmentalists – by no means all – who don't know they are being manipulated. David Rockefeller (Comm 300), Henry Kissinger (Comm 300), François Mitterand (Comm 300), Willy

[55] Lester R. Brown, *State Of The World 1991: A Worldwatch Institute Report On Progress Toward A Sustainable Society* (W.W. Norton, New York, 1991) p3.

Brandt (Comm 300), Mikhail Gorbachev, and so many more all parroted the party line on the environment, which, put succinctly, was global crisis = global solution. Gorbachev, well-schooled by his friends Rockefeller and Kissinger, suddenly began to speak passionately of the environment. He said:

> "*The ecological crisis we are experiencing today – from ozone depletion to deforestation and disastrous air pollution – is tragic but convincing proof that the world we all live in is interrelated and interdependent. This means that we need an appropriate international policy in the field of ecology. Only if we formulate such a policy shall we be able to avert catastrophe. True, the elaboration of such a policy poses unconventional and difficult problems that will affect the sovereignty of states.*" [56]

The *New York Times* columnist, Flora Lewis (CFR) welcomed Gorbachev's call to instigate a "plan for a global code of environmental conduct...[which would] have an aspect of world government, because it would provide for the World Court to judge states".[57] The secret government network has so many members in the media that there is never a problem finding support for its manoeuvrings from that direction. There are environmental problems, most of them due to Elite policies, but be very careful before you accept the propaganda of the environmental centralisers. It's your mind they are after. I would suggest that it is very much worth someone looking into the major funders of environmental organisations and the background to their front people to see if any links with the Elite network exist.

THE CLUB OF ROME AND POPULATION CONTROL

Another sinister aspect of the Club of Rome and the super dupers planning the Elite's 'green' campaign is their use of the environment to promote population control – eugenics. It is plainly true, as the New World Order promoters say, that there is a limit to the number of human beings who can live on this planet. You can't argue with that because when there is a human being for every square foot of the Earth, there will be clearly too many. So there are limits. But again we need to ask questions here. How many is too many? Would the comfortable carrying capacity of the Earth be far greater if the industrial and banking elite were not destroying the food-growing potential of the Third World and if suppressed scientific and technological understanding were made available to everyone? Have the projected future numbers been purposely exaggerated to justify a policy of global eugenics? The answers to those questions, I believe, are: more than we have now; yes; and yes. When you read the findings of the Club of Rome publications and

[56] Mikhail Gorbachev addressing the 1990 Global Forum Conference of spiritual and political leaders in Moscow, January 1990.
[57] "Gorbachev Turns Green", *New York Times*, (August 14th 1991).

others like *Global 2000*, and you look at the people behind them and their history of support for eugenics, its not hard to appreciate that these reports are really excuses for the culling of those areas of the world population considered to be of inferior stock, i.e. the non-white peoples and even those considered inferior among the whites. In political language it comes out something like this: "...the most fundamental point underlying all American foreign policy needs is overpopulation".[58] Those words were spoken by Robert McNamara (CFR, TC, Bil), one of the men behind the *Global 2000* report.

At the centre of all this is again the name Rockefeller. In 1952, after decades of funding and supporting eugenics, John D. Rockefeller III established his Population Council, which still exists today. This Elite-front has been calling for zero population growth in the United States and, in the words of its 1979 annual report: "the spread of government-supported family planning programs throughout the developing [ie. non-white] sector" and "the spread of the zero population movement and the Club of Rome's Malthusianism in the developed countries".[59] Malthusianism is named after Thomas Robert Malthus, the guy I mentioned in the last chapter. He was a paid agent of the British East India Company, which inflicted opium on the Chinese. His population theories were designed to justify the need to keep down the lesser genetic stock, whom he saw as little more than animals. Officials of the Population Council were strongly represented among the 'outside consultants' called in by the authors of *Global 2000* and *Global Future*.

The head of the *Global 2000* task force appointed by Cyrus Vance was Gerald O. Barney, the supervisor of another Rockefeller environment/population control study, *The Unfinished Agenda*. Other agencies which supported the preparation of the report included The World Wildlife Fund,[60] headed by Prince Philip (Bil) and backed by Prince Charles (Bil), Prince Bernhard (Bil), and the Hapsburg Family; the Institute for World Order, created by C. Douglas Dillon under the direction of Bertrand Russell (Comm 300); and the Draper Fund-Population Crisis Committee established by the eugenics promoter, William Draper; and the Elite-controlled Aspen Institute. In 1965, an organisation inspired by the Council on Foreign Relations was launched called the Agenda 2000 group. This produced a report co-authored by Zbigniew Brzezinski (TC, CFR, Bil) which called for an end to population growth in the Third World. The same year, George Ball (TC, CFR, Bil), the then Undersecretary of State for Economic Affairs in the Johnson Administration, appointed a task force to investigate the

[58] Quoted in the *Executive Intelligence Review* Special Report, *Global 2000, Blueprint for Genocide*, p3.
[59] Ibid p15.
[60] Now the World Wide Fund for Nature.

'problem' of population growth. Appointed to the task force, which later became the Office of Population Affairs, were...Cyrus Vance (TC, CFR, Bil, Comm 300), who instigated the *Global 2000* Report to the President, and Richard Gardner (TC, CFR, Comm 300) who would later become ambassador to Italy for Jimmy Carter and United Nations advisor to President Bill Clinton. Look how those demanding a New World Order of centralised global political and economic control are also those who want population control – eugenics. This is the thinking behind the Club of Rome and the *Global 2000* Report, which are so often quoted by the environmental movement!

Wars have been used blatantly and without mercy to enforce population control in non-white countries. Two of the main US military commanders in Vietnam were Maxwell Taylor and William Westmoreland, both members of the Population Crisis Committee-Draper Fund and committed to population control. The genocide by Pol Pot in Cambodia was one of the most obvious examples of the culling of a non-white population. Millions died as an estimated 32 per cent of the Cambodian population were murdered.[61] There were many people responsible for this, including Henry Kissinger, a winner of the Nobel Peace Prize. Kissinger, a legendary supporter of the Chinese communist regime, has been the key voice in American-Chinese relations since the time of Richard Nixon. His attempts to undermine the established order were highlighted in 1969 when he and his president authorised the illegal bombing of Cambodia. They used the excuse that they were attacking North Vietnamese troops stationed there during the Vietnam War.

This genocide was the subject of an article of impeachment against Nixon put to the House Judiciary Committee in 1974 in the wake of Watergate, but it was defeated. Kissinger always claimed the Khmer Rouge were the agency of the North Vietnamese when in fact Kissinger's Red China was behind them. Using the excuse of attacking the Khmer Rouge to stop their assault on the Cambodian capital, Phnom Penh, the US forces launched a campaign of terror bombing on that country. Nearly 80,000 bombing sorties by B-52s and F-111s have been officially confirmed and they dropped 539,129 tons of explosives. The number of Cambodian dead is estimated at anything at between 30,000 and 500,000.[62] But the biggest carnage was still to come because the devastation caused by the Kissinger-Nixon policy made the takeover by Pol Pot and the Khmer Rouge inevitable. The US 'ambassador' to Red China during this period, the man who communicated between the communist regime and his boss, Henry Kissinger, was George Bush.[63] Cambodia was, at least in part, about population culling, in my view.

---

[61] Russell R. Ross, *Cambodia: A Country Study*, (G.P.O., Washington, USA, 1990) p51.

[62] *Cambodia: A Country Study*, p46.

[63] The US did not have diplomatic relations with China at this time and 'ambassador' Bush, in fact, headed the US Liaison Office there. There was no US embassy.

Kissinger took over from Averell Harriman as the 'shuttle-diplomat' of the Elite. Kissinger is always flitting around, manipulating the American administration and foreign governments. In 1969 he was head of both the State Department and the National Security Council in the Nixon Administration. Nixon may have been officially president, but Kissinger ran the government. At his suggestion, Nixon named Laurance Rockefeller (TC, CFR, Bil) to lead a special commission on population growth. This recommended in 1972 that population control be introduced in America (i.e. among the 'lesser' stock). After discussions with the Club of Rome, of which he is a prominent member, Kissinger later established two other population control organisations within the departments of government which he controlled with an iron fist. In the years 1968 to 1977, the USAID programme for expenditure on health projects dropped by $40 million, while those directed at population control went up by $100 million. In 1974, Kissinger and the Rhodes Scholar, Brent Scowcroft (CFR, TC, Bil), supervised the production of the National Security Study Memorandum 200, called *Implications Of Worldwide Population Growth For US Security And Overseas Interests.* It has now been declassified and reveals some of the true motivations behind America's enthusiasm for population reduction in the developing world.

Continued population growth in these regions, the document said, would increase their political, economic, and military power in a number of these countries and would lead to an increase in demands for sovereign control of resources and to anti-imperial movements. This is a long-winded way of saying that these countries would wish to run their economies for their own benefit and not America's. Plans therefore had to be developed, it said, to remove opposition to population control. The countries the Kissinger-Scowcroft memorandum highlighted for special attention were India, Bangladesh, Pakistan, Nigeria, Mexico, Indonesia, Brazil, the Philippines, Thailand, Egypt, Turkey, Ethiopia, and Colombia. Look at what has happened in these countries since 1974.

In the Memorandum, Kissinger said that the truth behind the motivation for population control had to be kept secret from the leaders of these countries:

> *"It is vital that the effort to develop and strengthen a commitment on the part of less developed countries not be seen by them as an industrialised country policy to keep their strength down or to reserve resources for use by the 'rich' countries. Development of such a perception could create a serious backlash adverse to the course of population stability."*

In the early 70s, Kissinger asked the State Department's Office of Population Affairs to produce a study targeting Central/South America and Africa. This led, to a considerable degree, to the engineering of 'civil wars' in the countries of Central America and Africa which have caused so much famine, death, and suffering beyond imagination. It was a means to reduce the targeted population of the world, as are designer diseases. The US-Kissinger (Elite) policy was articulated by Thomas Ferguson, the Latin American case officer for the Office of Population Affairs. He said:

> *"There is a single theme in all our work – we must reduce population levels. Either they* [governments] *do it our way, through nice clean methods, or they will get the kind of mess that we have in El Salvador, or in Iran, or in Beirut* [all Kissinger engineered]. *Population is a political problem. Once population is out of control it requires authoritarian government, even fascism, to reduce it.* [Or rather, you need the 'problem' to justify fascism.]
>
> *"...The professionals aren't interested in lowering population for humanitarian reasons...We look at resource and environmental constraints. We look at our strategic needs, and we say that this country must lower its population – or else we will have trouble. So steps are taken. El Salvador is an example where our failure to lower the population by simple means has created the basis for a national security crisis. The government of El Salvador failed to use our programmes to lower their population. Now they get a civil war because of it. ...There will be dislocation and food shortages. They still have too many people there."* [64]

Some more of Mr Ferguson's little gems include:

> *"To reduce the population quickly you have to pull all the males into the fighting and kill significant numbers of fertile, child-bearing age, females...* [Speaking of the civil war in El Salvador he said] *You are killing a small number of males and not enough fertile females to do the job on population...If the war went on for 30 to 40 years like this, then you might accomplish something. Unfortunately* [sic], *we don't have too many instances like that to study."* [65]

I know it's horrible to know that anyone can see life in such terms, but Mr Ferguson is outlining very well the attitude of the Elite, its US State Department, and the Club of Rome. When prominent environmentalists stand in front of crowds of non-white peoples in the Third World telling television cameras that we must have population control, they are helping the Elite's agenda. Some will know that, many will not, but the effect is the same. I am in favour of all peoples having the choice not to conceive children if that is their wish. Choice, however, is not a word the manipulators can spell. Again look at the timing of the launch for so many of the population control

---

[64] *Executive Intelligence Review* Special Report, p28–30.
[65] Ibid.

initiatives by Kissinger and others: the late 60s and early 70s, just as the Club of Rome was getting started. Coinciding with the Club's beginnings in 1968, came the book by Professor Paul R. Ehrlich, *The Population Bomb*, which has sold upwards of 20 million copies. In that he said:

> *"Our position requires that we take immediate action at home and promote effective action worldwide. We must have population control at home, hopefully through a system of incentives and penalties, but by compulsion if voluntary methods fail... We can no longer afford merely to treat the symptoms of the cancer of population growth; the cancer itself must be cut out."* [66]

Ehrlich was a biologist at the Elite-controlled Stanford University and his wife, Anne, was a member of the Club of Rome.[67] He said that compulsory birth control could be imposed by governments via the addition of "temporary sterilants to water supplies or staple food".[68] Shortly, when we come to the "Report from Iron Mountain," you will see the even greater relevance of this statement. The 'brutal and tough-minded' decisions which Ehrlich said would be required are evident in Henry Kissinger's much-loved abode, China. It was here that the one-child-per-family policy was implemented and paid for directly, or indirectly, by the United Nations. Western and Chinese observers have spoken of seeing thousands of women "rounded up and forced to have abortions"; of women "locked in detention centres or hauled before mass rallies and harangued into consenting to abortions"; of "vigilantes abducting pregnant women on the streets, hauling them off, sometimes handcuffed and trussed, to abortion clinics". There are much worse stories even than those.

The United Nations network of organisations is awash with interlinked population control policies and eugenics. Behind them all is the Elite's secret government. When the UN secretary general, U Thant, started the UN Fund for Population Activities, it was administered by one Paul Hoffman (CFR, Bil), a US chief of foreign aid, trustee of the Institute of Pacific Relations and administrator of the Ford Foundation funds. He was also a member of the London-Wall Street financial clique. Professor Jacqueline Kasun, an outspoken opponent of UN population policies in her book, *The War Against Population*, revealed the network of agencies linked to the UN Fund for Population:

> *"Deriving its income from the United States and other governments, it provides support to numerous 'non-governmental organisations', including the*

---

[66] Dr Paul R. Ehrlich, *The Population Bomb*, 1st Edition (Ballantine Books, New York, 1968) Prologue.

[67] William Cooper, *Behold A Pale Horse*, (Light Technology Publishing, Sedona, Arizona, 1991) p71.

[68] *The Population Bomb*, p88, 135.

[Rockefellers'] *Population Council, the Population Action Council, Worldwatch, the Population Crisis Committee and Draper Fund, and the Centre for Population Activities. These organisations in turn make grants to each other and still other organisations."* [69]

The Elite's World Bank, which is supposed to make grants to help the development of the poorer countries, also has population control at the top of its agenda. In 1992, the World Bank President, Lewis Preston (CFR) said at the Rio Earth Summit that he would increase substantially the bank's support for population control – later pledging to double the money made available. The bank's International Safe Motherhood Initiative is a joint project with the International Planned Parenthood Federation, Family Care International, the Population Council (funded by US government aid programmes), and other agencies. These include several from the UN such as the Children's Fund (UNICEF) and the World Health Organisation (WHO). This 'initiative' involves forced birth control on pain of economic reprisals. As President Preston said, the Safe Motherhood agenda would be "integrated into the bank's policy dialogue with developing countries". Cut your population or you get no cash. There, Mr Preston, that's a simpler way to put it. Robert McNamara (TC, CFR, Bil), the head of the World Bank in the 1970s, is a vehement campaigner for population control. "The threat of unmanageable population pressures is very much like the threat of nuclear war" he said in the *Boston Globe* in 1982. This is the mindset of the organisation which controls 'development' funding in the Third World.

So the Club of Rome and its associated connections within the United Nations, the World Bank, the International Monetary Fund, and nation governments has the role in the network to promote the use of the environment to demand centralised control and eugenics. The Club of Rome was launched publicly in 1968, just a few years after a group of invited 'experts' met in the United States to prepare a report which, it is plain to see, was to inspire the sort of policies I've just described.

THE REPORT FROM IRON MOUNTAIN [70]

This was the secret report of the Special Study Group of fifteen people brought together during the Kennedy years. The proposal for the study group came around 1961 and it was established in August 1963. Among those assembled is claimed by some researchers to have been John Kenneth Galbraith (CFR), the Keynesian economist. The first and last meetings were at Iron Mountain, an underground facility near the town of Hudson, New

---

[69] Professor Jacqueline Kasun, *The War Against Population*, (Ignatius Press, San Francisco, 1988) p200–201.

[70] *Report From Iron Mountain On The Possibility And Desirability Of Peace.* With introductory material by Leonard C. Lewin (Pirate Press, England).

York. It is a place where important documents are stored and the base for the emergency corporate headquarters for corporations like Standard Oil of New Jersey (the Rockefellers, Exxon), Manufacturers Hanover Trust (Rothschilds), and Shell. The content of the report was revealed by one of the group who believed the public should know what it contained. This group member had the code name 'John Doe' and his friend, Leonard C. Lewin, produced a document summarising the Iron Mountain report. I have a copy of this.[71] It says that the idea for the study came from members of the Kennedy Administration like Robert McNamara (TC, CFR, Bil), McGeorge Bundy (TC, CFR, Bil), and Dean Rusk (TC, CFR, Bil). The brief was to study the implications of a world without war while still maintaining the control of the population wielded by war and the fear of war. Part of the report said:

> *"There is no question* [that] *a universal requirement that procreation be limited to the products of artificial insemination would provide a fully adequate substitute control for population levels. Such a reproductive system would, of course, have the added advantage of being susceptible to direct eugenic management. Its predictable further development – conception and embryonic growth taking place wholly under laboratory conditions – would extend these controls to their logical conclusion. The ecological function of war under these circumstances would not only be superseded, but surpassed in effectiveness.*
>
> *"The indicated immediate step – total control of conception with a variant of the ubiquitous 'pill', via water supplies or certain essential foodstuffs, offset by a controlled 'antidote' – is already under development."*

Remember this was the 1960s. More than thirty years have passed since then and such an 'indicated immediate step' was 'already under development'. So what the hell is going on today in our water supplies and essential foodstuffs, both of which are largely controlled by Elite companies? Also, just look again at what Professor Paul Ehrlich said in his book, *The Population Bomb*, published two years after this secret report was completed in 1966. He said that governments could enforce birth control by the addition of "temporary sterilants to water supplies or staple food...". Yet another amazing coincidence. The *Report From Iron Mountain* laid out the functions of war which new policies would have to replace:

1) Economic. *War has provided both ancient and modern societies with a dependable system for stabilising and controlling national economies. No alternate method of control has yet been tested in a complex modern economy that has shown itself remotely comparable in scope or effectiveness.*

---

[71] According to the foreword to the document I have, "John Doe" was a professor at a large university in the mid-west of America. His field of work was one of the social sciences.

2) Political. *The permanent possibility of war is the foundation for stable government; it supplies the basis for general acceptance of political authority. It has enabled societies to maintain necessary class distinctions, and it has ensured the subordination of the citizen to the state, by virtue of the residue war powers inherent in the concept of nationhood. No modern political ruling group has successfully controlled its constituency after failing to sustain the continuing credibility of an external threat of war.*

3) Sociological. *War, through the medium of military institutions, has uniquely served societies, throughout the course of known history, as an indispensable controller of dangerous* [free-thinking] *social dissidence and destructive antisocial tendencies.*

4) Ecological. *War has been the principle evolutionary device for maintaining a satisfactory ecological balance between gross human population and supplies available for survival. It is unique to the human species.*

Very nice, I'm sure. So what did these 'experts' suggest as alternatives to further world wars? Unite the people behind the controllers under the threat of war or some other form of destruction and keep them in a permanent state of fear, therefore dependent on their perceived 'saviours'. In the light of this need to control without world war, the *Report From Iron Mountain* proposed the following for consideration:

> *"An omnipresent, virtually omnipotent international police force* [a world army now called the United Nations Peace Keeping Force and NATO]*; an established and recognised extraterrestrial menace* [now being engineered with the themes of horrible aliens and a possible invasion of Earth?]*; massive global environmental pollution; fictitious alternate enemies; a modern, sophisticated form of slavery; new religions or other mythologies; a comprehensive programme of applied eugenics."*

All of these things have emerged since the report was completed. There you see the proposal for the environmental threat/eugenics scenario which was to follow very soon afterwards. The report called for the establishment of a secret War/Peace Research Agency using "unaccountable funds" which would study both the peace and war options. Among the research required, said the report, was the "...determination of minimum and optimum levels of destruction of life, property, and natural resources prerequisite to the credibility of external threat essential to the political and motivational functions" and "[the] frequency of occurrence, length of phase, intensity of physical destruction, extensiveness of geographical involvement, and optimum mean loss of life". This is the deeply imbalanced state of mind behind those who promote and manipulate into being the New World

Order, and conflicts are created to fit in with this plan – the war in the former Yugoslavia being another example.

In this chapter, I have described the network of Round Table-Royal Institute of International Affairs-Council on Foreign Relations-Bilderberg Group-Trilateral Commission-United Nations-European Union-Club of Rome, which together constitute a secret government of the world acting outside and above what laughably passes as the 'democratic process'. I have further shown that the members of these groups follow a long tradition of manipulators working from the same agenda of world government, central bank, currency, and army, and a genetically engineered, microchipped population. But the organisation behind the New World Order coup d'état is far wider and more complex than this network of front organisations. They are a vital part, but only a part, of the Pyramid of Deceit.

It is on that pyramid the spotlight will now be turned.

Chapter 9

Pyramid power

The covert network of control is but the physical version of the multidimensional prison, within which our lower consciousness has been, until now, entrapped for hundreds of thousands of years.

Those at the higher levels of the Elite-Illuminati-Brotherhood are, I believe, vehicles for the manipulation of the physical world by the Prison Warders of the Fourth Dimension. There are many connections between the Elite-Brotherhood and black magic, and once you get involved in that, it is easy for your consciousness to be taken over by an extreme negative force. Such ceremonies and ritual can conjure up very dark and malevolent energies, which can possess the people involved. Most Freemasons learn the lines of their ceremonies and go through the ritual without any idea of what they are playing around with and attracting to them. Most think it is just a gentlemen's club, but the ceremonial has been designed to attract extreme negative energies which allow a "possession" by the negative elements of the Fourth Dimension.

When I spoke at a spiritual-healing exhibition in Birmingham, I was surprised to find it was being held in the main Freemasons' centre in what is Britain's second city. The Freemasons rent part of the complex to outside organisations to earn money. I was delighted because it allowed me to study the subject in the heart of what must be among the largest centres of Freemasonry in the United Kingdom. By 'coincidence' while I was there, I managed to see the inside of some of the temples where the public are not allowed to go. The complex, called the Clarendon Suites, is built virtually without windows once you get through the main entrance. This is appropriately symbolic, I feel, of keeping out the Light. I walked into a temple of the Royal Arch branch of Freemasonry where the public are not allowed to go, and I will never forget the feeling of extreme negative energy hitting me the moment I stepped through the door. Goodness knows what they must do to attract that scale of malevolence! It took the breath away. And most of the members will not understand what they are doing. Once you synchronise vibrationally with that sort of energy, it can take you over and control you – especially if you have no understanding of what you are messing with. You can become a mental robot of the Prison Warders, without knowing it. This is how people are snared and pulled into the net. It won't happen to every Freemason because it depends on their intent and their own vibrational rate at the time, but it happens to those who are of a state of mind that is open to such possession.

Freemasonry, like the Elite network in general, can manipulate and deceive most of its own membership because it is structured like a pyramid. If you look at any organisation, from a small business to a multinational corporation, you will see the same pyramid structure. At the top will be a very few people who know everything there is to know about the organisation, its motivation, agenda, and the direction it wishes to go. The further you descend from the peak, you meet more and more people who know less and less about that overall picture. They are only aware of *their* part in the organisation and not everyone else's. This is a manipulator's dream and it is the means through which the Elite can control so many people and organisations across the world.

Most of those working for the New World Order agenda don't know they are doing so. The conspiracy couldn't exist if everyone involved was in on the plot. Manipulating the manipulators and controlling the controllers is essential to its success. Take the CIA. It has a policy of 'compartmentalisation'. Put more simply, the 'need to know' approach. At the top of the CIA are those who know the true nature of its agenda. The further down you go, the less the CIA employees are aware of this wider perspective. There can be many people within the CIA who do their daily tasks quite innocently. They might think that what they are doing is serving the United States and is not at all sinister. But they don't know how what they are doing connects with the work of others like them throughout the pyramid to produce a very unpleasant picture. Only those few at the top know that. It is in this way that the Elite control and manipulate. Each of the various elements, the Council on Foreign Relations, Freemasonry, etc are also structured as pyramids, and they are themselves all a part of a vast global pyramid with the Elite at the top. It may appear to be a mass of unconnected organisations and people, but there is a central controlling force that holds the structure together and unites it into a common cause and policy (*Figure 8 overleaf*).

THE GLOBAL ELITE

At the apex of this global empire are the Elite who are, I believe, solidly locked into the Fourth Dimensional Prison Warder consciousness which decides the policy and oversees its implementation. I don't know exactly the pecking order of power here, but I am confident about the various elements involved, at least. I believe that at the highest levels of the Global Elite are shadowy people who are not known to the public. I would say that the force behind the House of Rothschild is right up there, but I do not believe they are at the top. They too will be taking orders and maybe the Habsburg dynasty is above them in the hierarchy. The Elite's power stems from their misuse of the esoteric knowledge and their conscious connection to their

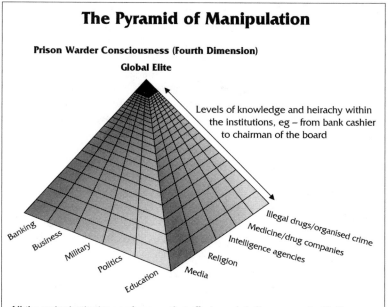

The Pyramid of Manipulation

Prison Warder Consciousness (Fourth Dimension)

Global Elite

Levels of knowledge and heirachy within the institutions, eg – from bank cashier to chairman of the board

Banking
Business
Military
Politics
Education
Media
Religion
Intelligence agencies
Medicine/drug companies
Illegal drugs/organised crime

All the major institutions and groups that affect our daily lives connect with the Global Elite, which decides the coordinated policy throughout the pyramid. People in the lower compartments will have no idea what they are part of.

Figure 8

'gods', the Prison Warders. Perhaps no-one I name in this book will be at that level. People such as Henry Kissinger, are yes-men, and super-gofers, albeit high-powered ones. Many of the others will be used without their knowledge, or full knowledge, of what they are part of. I am naming the pawns, the gofers and super-gofers, of this small group of people I call the Super Elite, the Black Magicians. These are the controllers of the All-Seeing Eye cult, which is the force behind the Global Elite and those who are manipulating the New World Order into being. Some researchers believe that the Rothschilds are at the peak of the Pyramid (I don't) and under them is a Council of Thirteen, a Council of Thirty Three, and then the Committee of 300, also known as the Olympians.[1]

The Global Elite as a whole is the group of people who are selected and initiated into the higher, sometimes highest, levels of knowledge in the whole human structure. While they will be working today to speed the emergence of the New World Order, they will also be looking for others who are deemed to be of the right calibre. Then, as the present personnel 'retire' or die, the reins of the conspiracy are handed to the next generation

---

[1] *Secret Societies*, pp294–295. See also Dr John Coleman's *Conspirators Hierarchy. The Story Of The Committee Of 300*.

of the Elite, just as Averell Harriman was replaced in his role by Henry Kissinger. In the same way Umberto Agnelli (Bil) is being prepared to replace his ageing father Giovanni Agnelli in the Elite hierarchy. So while the 'they' – the actual personnel – change with the generations, the agenda they are working from remains basically the same. It is like passing on a baton in a relay race and, because of the nature of the family structure of much of the Elite, the baton is often handed on across the generations of certain families. This becomes even more understandable because the parents indoctrinate the children from the earliest possible age and later introduce them to the same secret societies and ceremonial which synchronises them into the Prison Warders' vibration.

THE ILLUMINATI

Not every member of a secret society or the other organisations I name is part of the Elite. There is a difference between Freemasonry and what I will term 'Illuminised' Freemasonry, those parts of the order which have been infiltrated by Illuminati agents. The word Illuminati – 'the Illuminated Ones' – goes back into the ancient world. It is a covert force which has created or taken over groups and organisations to manipulate the world in the desired direction. The Illuminati's greatest weapon is the advanced esoteric knowledge it has passed on through its initiation ceremonies and the misuse and abuse of that knowledge. The most obvious expression of Illuminism was the Bavarian Illuminati officially created by the German professor, Adam Weishaupt, in May 1776, and controlled by the House of Rothschild, the bankers to endless revolutions and wars. It was Weishaupt who used his wing of the Illuminati to infiltrate and take over Freemasonry.

Weishaupt was trained as a Jesuit, which is short for the Society of Jesus. The founder of the Jesuits, the Spaniard, Ignatius Loyola, formed a secret society within this apparently Catholic order and the initiates were called the 'Alumbrados' which means the 'enlightened', the 'illuminated'. Conflict followed between the Jesuit 'illuminism' and Weishaupt's German version, battles which the traditions of Weishaupt mostly won although the Jesuit network is still very much a part of the Elite. Weishaupt created 13 degrees of initiation in his Illuminati and the key personnel were to be found in the top nine degrees. The Illuminati is a pyramid, too. The members were given special Illuminati names, inspired by ancient Rome and Greece. Weishaupt was called Spartacus. These people became members of other secret societies like the Freemasons and 'illuminised' them – took them over and used them to destabilise nations and hasten the New World Order. They did the same within governments, banking, commerce, the military, and the media, on behalf of the Elite.

So there is Freemasonry and Illuminised Freemasonry. The former manipulates at one level, but it too is being manipulated by another covert force, the Illuminati, which in turn answers to its Global Elite. There are organisations within organisations (say, the Freemasonry network within a government) and another organisation within *those* organisations (the Illuminati membership within the Freemasons). This Illuminised form of Freemasonry became known as The Grand Orient Lodges. It followed the modified Hegelian tradition of infiltrating two extremes and playing one off against the other to create the desired change. Using these methods, it was pledged to overthrow the rule of the monarchies, destroy faith in God, put an end to patriotism and nation states, abolish the ownership of property and dismantle traditional social order.

THE BLACK NOBILITY

The Illuminati interconnects within the Global Elite with what is known as the Black Nobility, an ancient grouping of 'blue bloods'. It has its base in Italy, particularly in Venice and Genoa. Both John Cabot (real name Giovanni Cabotto) and Christopher Columbus lived in Genoa before 'discovering' different parts of the Americas within four years of each other. Today another Giovanni is claimed by scores of researchers to be a member of one of the Black Nobility families. This is Giovanni Agnelli, longtime head of the Fiat Motor Company until 1996 and a leading Bilderberger. The Agnelli family dominates Italy and it is said, only half jokingly, that the main responsibility of an Italian prime minister is to "polish Agnelli's doorknobs".[2] Agnelli had a much publicised relationship with Pamela Churchill, Winston's daughter-in-law, before she married...Averell Harriman. She was a leading fundraiser for Bill Clinton and became US Ambassador to Paris. The Agnelli family were closely connected with Mussolini, and Giovanni's grandfather was made a senator for life by the fascist leader. Some families of the Black Nobility in Venice and Rome claim an ancestry back to the Roman Emperor Justinian, a man reputed to have taken references to reincarnation out of the biblical texts in the year 553. They have a desire to return to a system symbolised by the Roman Empire and they are a major force within the Global Elite. This 'noble' line would appear to go back at least a thousand years, probably far longer, and emerged in part through the Guelf and Ghibelline conflicts in Italy in the twelfth and thirteenth centuries.

Guelf came from Welf, a German prince competing for control of the Holy Roman Empire, and Ghibelline came from the name of the castle owned by his opponents, the Hohenstaufen family. The Guelfs supported the Pope and the Ghibellines supported the rule of the Hohenstaufen family. Great conflict followed, with the Guelfs triumphant in the end. The Guelfs (Black Nobility) became immensely powerful through their later control of banking and international trade. They set up great financial centres in Lombardy and they dominated the scene so much that Lombard became the name given to all Italian bankers in Florence, Genoa, Venice, and Milan.

[2] *The Sunday Times*, (December 17th 1995) p1, section 3.

Eventually they expanded their influence northwards to Hamburg, Amsterdam and London. Today the Black Nobility also control the financial centres of Switzerland where the spoils of the drug trade and other illegal activities are laundered behind the façade of Swiss respectability. The Black Nobility were at the heart of the slave trade from where the fortunes of many leading American and British families originated and they were behind the Orange Order which put William of Orange on the British throne, and led to the Bank of England and the National Debt. In more recent times, the Orange Order has been behind the Protestant wing of the conflict in Northern Ireland.

The Black Nobility includes, or is at least connected to, the Dutch Royal Family of Prince Bernhard, one of the founders of the Bilderberg Group. Its connections extend to London and the British 'establishment' families of the old aristocracy and the new 'money' aristocracies. Members of the European bluebloods which are closely linked with the British Royal Family are involved. The Swedish, Dutch and Spanish royal families are often represented at Bilderberg meetings. In the UK, Prince Philip and Prince Charles have attended Bilderberg meetings and Queen Elizabeth II is named as a member of the Committee of 300.[3] It is believed by researchers who have investigated the Black Nobility, that at this level the British Royal Family is subordinate to the Italian members who trace their ancestry back to the original Guelfs and beyond. I feel that the vicious personal attacks on Prince Charles and the taped telephone conversations released to the media, which have done so much to damage him, are no accident. Is it part of a coordinated campaign to undermine him? Is he a rebel they wish to destroy? It is possible. Charles and his brother Andrew, turned down the offer to become Freemasons, an organisation with close connections to the British monarchy over the years. The Illuminati/Black Nobility/Global Elite use many secret and less secret organisations in pursuit of their global tyranny and the most all-pervading of them is Freemasonry. Illuminised Freemasonry is the first level down from the Illuminati/Black Nobility, and you will find its membership involved in all the organisations in the network I described in the last chapter: the Royal Institute of International Affairs, the Council on Foreign Relations, the Bilderberg Group, and their like-minded brethren.

FREEMASONRY

The vast majority of Freemasons in the world never progress beyond the bottom three levels of degree (*Figure 9 overleaf*). But above them are another *thirty* higher levels in the Scottish Rite of Freemasonry, which owes its inspiration to the ancient Knights Templar. Even the 33rd degree is not the top because there are the Illuminati levels above that, and the 33rd degree

[3] *Conspirators Hierarchy. The Story Of The Committee Of 300.* See also *Who's Who Of The Elite* by Robert Gaylon Ross, Sr. (RIE, Spicewood, Texas, 1995).

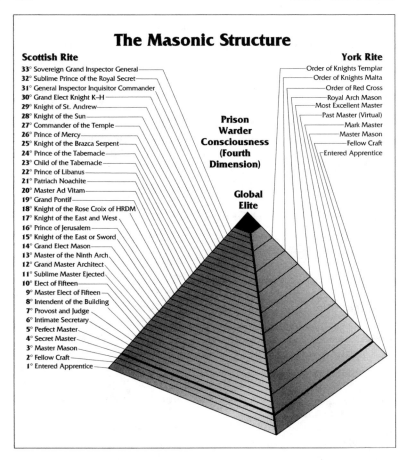

The Masonic Structure

Scottish Rite   **York Rite**

33° Sovereign Grand Inspector General
32° Sublime Prince of the Royal Secret
31° General Inspector Inquisitor Commander
30° Grand Elect Knight K–H
29° Knight of St. Andrew
28° Knight of the Sun
27° Commander of the Temple
26° Prince of Mercy
25° Knight of the Brazca Serpent
24° Prince of the Tabernacle
23° Child of the Tabernacle
22° Prince of Libanus
21° Patriach Noachite
20° Master Ad Vitam
19° Grand Pontif
18° Knight of the Rose Croix of HRDM
17° Knight of the East and West
16° Prince of Jerusalem
15° Knight of the East or Sword
14° Grand Elect Mason
13° Master of the Ninth Arch
12° Grand Master Architect
11° Sublime Master Ejected
10° Elect of Fifteen
9° Master Elect of Fifteen
8° Intendent of the Building
7° Provost and Judge
6° Intimate Secretary
5° Perfect Master
4° Secret Master
3° Master Mason
2° Fellow Craft
1° Entered Apprentice

Order of Knights Templar
Order of Knights Malta
Order of Red Cross
Royal Arch Mason
Most Excellent Master
Past Master (Virtual)
Mark Master
Master Mason
Fellow Craft
Entered Apprentice

Prison Warder Consciousness (Fourth Dimension)

Global Elite

Figure 9

itself is unofficially divided into two streams, one knowing far more than the other. At each stage, the initiate is told a little more about the true nature of Freemasonry and the real game plan. Those who have reached the 33rd degree are on a different planet in terms of what they know, compared with the Masons on the bottom three levels. Joseph Smith, the 'prophet' who founded the appalling Mormon 'church', was a 33rd degree Freemason. The men who go down to the local Freemasons' lodge in your town or city will not have a clue what their organisation is being used for. They have to be kept in the dark if the plan is to work and what better way of doing this than to use these distinct levels of initiation. Only those considered to be 'acceptable' progress to the higher levels and find out what is really going on. The vast majority of Freemasons are on the bottom three levels. They are the fodder and the front. Between the 4th and 33rd degrees, you find those of the 'right mind' who have influence in society, right up to presidents of the United States. Then you have the Illuminati levels, which you will not see mentioned in any Freemasons guidebook. Those are the people who actually run the show and they are the agents of the All-Seeing Eye cult. World Freemasonry is a massive pyramid of manipulation.

It was not always like this. It is said that Freemasonry was once a society that was exclusive to those who worked as stonemasons and builders on the churches and cathedrals. It was then called Masonry. Their lodges were like trade organisations some historians claim, and their secrecy and rituals were designed to protect their profession from unskilled outsiders. Most of the Masons' work came from the Catholic Church, ruled from Rome. The immense wealth of the Church, most of it stolen directly or indirectly, paid for the construction of the great cathedrals on which the masons' income largely depended. But disaster came when Henry VIII broke with Rome in 1534 and formed his own Church of England after the Pope refused him a divorce. This event had many implications for the future (see *The Robots' Rebellion*) and it ensured that many masons were made unemployed. Far from continuing the building programmes of Rome, Henry looted the monasteries and everything else he could get away with. He was broke, basically, and there were always wars to fight. One of his targets was the assets of the 'fraternities, brotherhoods and guilds'. The masonry societies collapsed in the wake of this royal mugging and the desperate lack of work for their members. Many of the lodges disappeared, along with their ancient records, and little is known about their true history.

The lodges (branches) which survived did so by opening their memberships to people who were not stonemasons, or so the story goes. These newcomers – the businessmen, merchants, landowners, and aristocracy – were called 'speculative' masons and soon they far outnumbered the original members. This was the Knights Templar/ Illuminati manifesting on the public stage in the guise of Freemasonry. The first recorded initiation of a speculative mason in England was in 1646 when Elias Ashmole (don't say it too quickly) joined a lodge in Warrington. He was an astrologer and indeed esoteric knowledge was to be an important part of the new Masonry at the higher levels of initiation. Masonry had become *Free*masonry and as the years passed, the only remaining connection with the stonemasons were the symbolic paraphernalia and names for the levels of initiation like apprentice, fellow craft, and master mason. The working tools of the stonemasons – the square, compasses, level, plumbline, gauge, gavel, and chisel – were still used in the bizarre ceremonies and rituals and the Freemason's apron was another throwback to the stone masons. But Freemasonry now had a very different agenda.

During the rituals which the founders of the new Freemasonry introduced, bare-chested initiates were blindfolded with a noose around their neck and a dagger held to their heart. They had to swear to serve the order and keep its secrets, on pain of a grotesque ritual death. The penalty for divulging the secrets of the Second Degree (the Fellow Craft Mason) is "having my left breast laid open, my heart torn therefrom, and given to the ravenous birds of the air, or devouring beasts of the field as a prey". In the Third Degree (Master Mason) it is "being severed in two, my bowels burnt to ashes, and those ashes scattered over the face of the Earth and wafted by the four winds of heaven, that no trace of remembrance of so vile a wretch may longer be found among men, particularly Master Masons".[4] Charming.

These are the sorts of ceremonies that conjure up the malevolent energies. At the same time, in public, Freemasonry is claiming to be a school of morality and it talks of fraternity and 'brotherly love'! The public apologists for Freemasonry will tell you that these rituals are only symbolic, but there is much evidence that not everyone thinks so, including the Freemason known as Jack the Ripper. The powerful ties of loyalty (and fear, too, when necessary) engendered in the membership makes sure that very few have dared to disclose the secrets, even after leaving the craft. In fact, while people may cease to pay their fees or turn up at the lodge, the oaths still apply. There is no mechanism by which a Mason, once initiated, can unswear his oath.

Such oaths were invented to create fear and control. They were not part of the rituals of stonemasons, as some of their few surviving rule books, the 'Gothic Constitutions' as they are called, have proved. The penalty for revealing the secrets in those days was to be thrown out of the lodge. It beats having your bowels burnt to ashes, for sure. The Freemasonry rituals and oaths are based on a piece of invention in the eighteenth century – the Freemason story of Hiram Abif. According to the Freemasonry invention, Hiram Abif was the architect of Solomon's biblical Temple. The Gothic Constitutions of the stonemasons make no reference to such a man, but he became the Freemasons' martyr figure. Invention has it that Hiram refused to betray the secrets to three fellow craft masons armed with masonic tools. They murdered him when he would not reveal his secrets, so the myth goes, and King Solomon ordered a search when Hiram appeared to be missing. Hiram's body was discovered 'indecently interred' and was reburied with 'all respect and reverence'. Solomon ordered those responsible for the murder to be executed and in some versions of the story, the killers, Jubela, Jubelo, and Jubelum, were so full of remorse that they asked to be put to death. Jubela asked for his throat to be cut and his tongue torn out; Jubelo chose to have his left breast torn open and his heart fed to the vultures; and

---

[4] After 1986, such dire penalties ceased to be spoken by the initiate during the ceremonies and are instead spoken by the Worshipful Master. What difference that is supposed to make I can't think. Purely cosmetic.

Jubelum was the one who asked for his bowels to be burned to ashes and scattered before the four winds of heaven. You can see where the Freemasons' rituals and oaths come from. Their rituals play out the story and death of Hiram Abif, baring their breast with their trouser legs rolled up to bare their knees.[5]

The story of Hiram Abif is a fantasy. The Freemasonic thought police have made great play of the ancient links with the building of King Solomon's Temple in Jerusalem. They have turned it into something akin to the Vatican – and then some. But the Bible from which the figure of Hiram was taken, describes a very different man. First of all his name was simply Hiram. The addition of Abif came from the founders of masonic myth. Abif's a miff, you might say. And what does the Bible say about this man? Does it say that he was "the most accomplished mason on Earth", as the Freemasons claim? Not quite. It says that he was neither a mason nor an architect, but a worker in brass. According to the Book of Kings, he arrived from Tyre *after* the temple was finished. The Book of Chronicles says he came *before* the Temple was built and was an ornamental metal worker. Any stone skills he had were in decoration, not construction. There is another Hiram in the Bible, the King of Tyre, who is not the same man. But he is also held in great esteem by Freemasonry because he is supposed to have supplied Solomon with Lebanese cedarwood for the Temple. And that's another thing. The Bible says the Temple was built mostly of wood and was no bigger than a church hall of today (30 by 90 feet). The last thing they needed was a stonemason architect. But while the story of Hiram Abif is a nonsense, it is possible that its themes originate in ancient Egypt when King Seqenenre was murdered for refusing to reveal the most secret esoteric knowledge to a rival. If so, this is yet further confirmation that the same stream of knowledge and manipulation stretches from antiquity into modern Freemasonry and the world today. My feeling is that the force that emerged as Freemasonry was, and is, the Knights Templar, which until then had been operating underground, following the papal purge. The pyramid structure allows the Elite, the few at the top of Freemasonry, to control the majority by misleading them and keeping them in the dark. *The Illuminati Protocols*, found in the last century, did – whatever people may say about their origin – describe brilliantly how Freemasons are used:

> *"We shall create and multiply Freemasonic lodges in all countries of the world, absorb into them all who may become or who are prominent in public activity, for in these lodges we shall find our principal intelligence office and means of influence. All these lodges we shall bring under one central administration [The Illuminati], known to us alone and to all others*

[5] I highly recommend Martin Short's, *Inside The Brotherhood*, (Grafton Books, London, 1990). This reference is from page 60.

absolutely unknown, which will be composed of our learned elders... In these lodges we shall tie together all revolutionary and liberal elements. Their composition will be made up of all strata of society. The most secret political plots will be known to us and will fall under our guiding hands on the very day of their conception. Among the members of the lodges will be almost all the agents of international and national police since their service is for us irreplaceable in the respect that the police is in a position not only to use its own particular measures with the insubordinate, but also to screen our activities and to provide pretexts for discontents..."
Protocol 15

The protocols describe the Masons on the lower levels of degree – the great majority – as a part of a 'show army' who are there only "to kick dust in the eyes of their fellows". Everyone is manipulating everyone else. Unless we know the secret society background of people employed by the controlling institutions, be it the police, politicians, doctors, military officers, editors and journalists, or government officials, and unless we know what that secret society *truly* stands for, how can we possibly know what agenda those who run a country or community are working from? These people pledge their total allegiance to their secret society in these ritual ceremonies, so what happens to their allegiance to the public they have been elected or appointed to serve? While people in the secret societies are allowed into such positions of control and influence without even having to acknowledge their membership, the whole system is open to the most outrageous corruption. And that is what happens. The system is outrageously corrupt. Not every member is corrupt; most are not. But it doesn't take many to have a terrific impact on society.

Once you have Freemasons in the top positions, who decide which people are recruited or promoted within an organisation, you can make sure that fellow Freemasons get into the key positions of power. One generation of Freemasons follows another as the baton is handed over. When you have achieved this you can run an organisation or a country almost as you like. Or a world. Freemasons also commit themselves to helping each other in distress. That sounds very nice, but what about those who are not part of the club, the 'Profane', as we are called? Does that mean we are subject to lesser consideration when faced with a Freemason in authority? In at least a number of cases, the answer is most certainly "yes". The Freemasons have a series of signs and words which allow them to recognise each other, including the funny handshake. These also include the Freemasons' sign for "grief and distress" (i.e. Get me out of trouble), the verbal version of which is: "Will no-one help the widow's son?" The widow's son is Hiram Abif.

These signs and signals come in very handy when you are arrested by Freemason police officers or appear in court before a Freemason judge. It doesn't always work, of course, but we are kidding ourselves if we think it doesn't happen. The political determination to tackle this dangerous injustice is simply not there, because either the politicians involved — of all parties — are Freemasons themselves or connected with the wider network, or they are frightened to act because their position depends on them not upsetting the secret society elite. Some leading politicians are high ranking Freemasons. Lord Palmerston, the British Prime Minister at the time of the opium wars against China, was the Grand Patriarch of the Grand Orient [Illuminati] version of the order. The former French president, François Mitterand (Comm 300), was also a Grand Master of the Grand Orient.[6]

Most of the names I have mentioned in the book, those involved with the Trilateral Commission, the Council on Foreign Relations, the Bilderberg Group, and all the rest will also be Freemasons or members of some connected secret society. But they are all answerable to the same master — the Global Elite. In most countries there is an elite Freemasonry 'cell' which is particularly powerful and which may be unknown even to some high ranking Freemasons. There are many cells linked to the Illuminati-controlled forms of Freemasonry, the Grand Orient Lodges. The French Revolution was partly hatched and coordinated by the Grand Orient Lodge in Paris. In Britain there are, according to some, an elite cell called the Parlour Club and a European elite group called the Club of the Isles.[7] In the US they have the the Skull and Bones Society, which is closely related to Freemasonry, and so is the Orange Order which is at the heart of the Northern Ireland conflict. The Round Table is designed on Freemasonic lines and links in with that network. The infamous Knights of Malta are another elite organisation which coordinates its covert activities with Illuminised Freemasonry and has enormous influence within the system. Its official head is the Pope! The best known of the Elite Freemasonry cells is the Propaganda Masonica Due Lodge (P2) based in Italy, but operating in other countries also. When this was discovered, it produced one of the greatest political scandals in history. If we look at the background of the P2, you will appreciate how these Elite Freemasonry cells operate in countries around the world and the methods they use.

PROPAGANDA MASONICA DUE (P2)

The P2 Lodge in Rome was founded in 1877 for those Freemasons who were visiting the capital from other parts of Italy. It had only fourteen members by the mid-1960s, but it was about to be launched into world prominence when it was 'restructured' by Licio Gelli at the request of the Grand Master of Italy, Lino Salvini. Once Gelli took over, the membership of the P2 Lodge soared within a few years to almost a thousand, although he was almost certainly the vehicle for other powers behind P2 who kept their control secret. Some researchers believe this hidden control to be the Alpine

---

[6] *Secret Societies*, p282

[7] If you know anything about these groups, please contact me.

Freemasons' Lodge in Switzerland, which has had among its membership, Henry Kissinger and the founder of the Club of Rome, Aurelio Peccei (Bil). Others say this was only the 'middle man' between P2 and its real controllers, the banking interests centred on the House of Rothschild. P2 initiation ceremonies took place at its headquarters in the Excelsior Hotel under the supervision of a former Grand Master of Italy, Giordano Gamberini, but the name most associated with P2 is Gelli.

Gelli was a fascist supporter of Mussolini during the war and helped to organise the "rat line" which smuggled Nazis out of Germany when the Allies invaded. He fled to Argentina some years later when his background came to light and he made many political friends there, including the dictator, Juan Peron (for whom he became an economic advisor), and Jose Lopez Rega, the man behind the Triple A death squads responsible for thousands of murders. Rega raised vast sums by smuggling cocaine into the United States. When Peron came out of exile to take power for the second time, he fell on his knees in public to thank Gelli. Many Nazis fled to South America after the war and P2 is closely connected with Nazi International. Gelli, as a committed fascist, would have been very much at home in such company. Indeed it was he who helped many Nazis, like Claus Barbie, escape to South America (which became a bigger version of Germany as it was under Hitler). Gelli was close to the Nazi dictator of Nicaragua, Somoza, and he was also connected with the Nazi paramilitary organisation operating in Italy called U Gladio (a CIA front).

Gelli returned to Italy in the mid-1960s as Argentina's honourary consul. He built a network of contacts in high places around him after he became a Grand Orient Freemason in 1965. This was helped by his membership in the Knights of Malta, which gave him an 'in' to the highest levels of the Vatican, a link he and P2 were to exploit so effectively. Gelli's friends in the United States Republican Party invited him to the inauguration of President Reagan in 1981. (Reagan would later lay a wreath on the graves of SS storm troopers during the 40th anniversary ceremonies of the Second World War, the symbolism of which would have been very powerful for the Nazi mentalities in the CIA and the Global Elite, the real controllers of the P2.) Gelli also attended the inaugurations of Presidents Carter and Ford, and he called himself a friend of George Bush.

In July 1981, Gelli's daughter was stopped at Rome Airport and documents were confiscated from the false bottom of her suitcase. They were copies of the United States document known as *Supplement B*. This was a supplement to the US Field Army Manual FM 30-31. It was dated March 18th 1970 and signed by General Westmoreland. It describes how to destabilise a country through infiltration of the controlling organisations and the use of agents provocateur.[8] This is precisely what Gelli and his controllers did.

---

[8] *Alternative Press Review*, (Fall, 1994, USA) p53.

Gelli worked successfully to win official recognition for Italian Freemasonry from the centre of world Freemasonry, the United Grand Lodge in London. Italian Freemasonry has a long history of controversy and involvement in politics. It was banned by Mussollini, as was German Freemasonry by Hitler, not the least because they were both helped to power by secret societies and realised their influence. After the war, the American OSS, the forerunner to the CIA, put pressure on the desperate Italian government to allow Freemasonry to return and the Mother Lodge in London conferred official recognition. In doing so, they had officially recognised an organisation that has the closest of connections with the Mafia. These ties go back to the 'Carbonari', an amalgamation of Freemasons, the Mafia, and the military, which was formed in the nineteenth century to oppose Napoleon. The Carbonari were also closely linked with the Guelphic Knights – the Black Nobility.

Through the 1970s, Gelli was recruiting some of the most powerful people in Italian society into P2 until he had created a state within a state, working from a common agenda. The names of the membership were known to him and maybe one or two others. Not even the other members knew all the names on the P2 membership list. Using the well-tested Elite structure, he divided the membership into two divisions and then subdivided them into a series of other groups. Only the leaders of these groups knew who their members were – and then only those in their particular group. P2 members were controlled by the terror of knowing the horrific penalties for not doing as they were told. When, in March 1981, Gelli's premises were raided by police they discovered 962 names on the P2 membership lists in his office safe and suitcase. There were three cabinet ministers, forty other MPs, forty-three generals, eight admirals and hundreds of civil servants and diplomats, heads of the security services, the chiefs of police in the country's four biggest cities, industrialists, financiers, TV stars, and twenty-four journalists. I believe strongly that something similar is happening in the United Kingdom and many other countries, which mirrors the methods and aims of P2. Henry Kissinger was believed by some to be a member of P2 or at least a major force in its policy and methods. P2 certainly has a powerful foreign membership, which gives it tremendous influence within European and US intelligence and banking. The Italian Prime Minister, Giulio Andreotti was close to Gelli. When Andreotti stood trial for involvement with the Mafia he named his character witnesses as the former United Nations Secretary General, Perez de Cuellar (a reputed P2 member), and…Henry Kissinger.[9] The journalist, Mino Peccorelli, a member of P2, said it was actually run by the CIA. He wasn't allowed to say it for very long, though. Peccorelli was murdered by a means acknowledged as a Mafia death-ritual for those who say too much. More evidence for the CIA connection came from former

---

[9] "A State Of Terror", by Ben C. Vidgen, *Nexus* magazine, (February/March 1996) p18.

CIA contract agent, Richard Brenneke, in an interview on Italian Television on July 2nd 1990. He said:

> *"We* [the CIA] *have used the assistance of these people* [P2] *to get in and out of the United States drugs and money, and to get in and out of Italy drugs and money. We used these people to create situations that would favour the explosion of terrorism in Italy and other European countries at the beginning of the 70s. The P2 is still alive and it is still used for the same purposes as at the beginning of the 70s. The CIA has financed the P2 to the tune of $1 million to $10 million per month...That CIA money was used for several purposes, one of them terrorism. Another purpose was to obtain support in smuggling drugs coming from other countries into the US. There also has always been a connection between P2 and the CIA."*

Brenneke was another who said that Licio Gelli was only the nominal head of P2 and the real control came via Switzerland and the United States. The 1970s and early 1980s were terrible years for Italy. Terrorism sponsored by P2 included the bombing at Bologna Railway Station, in which eighty-five people died in 1980. A terrorist group called The Red Brigade was blamed for many atrocities, including the kidnap and murder in 1978 of the Christian Democrat leader and former Prime Minister of Italy, Aldo Moro, in which five of his bodyguards also died. Terrorist groups like the Red Brigade and the Baader-Meinhoff Gang in Germany are not all that they seem. As with these two groups, their members are often trained by the CIA or other Elite organisations. They are part of the problem-reaction-solution process, a cover for the assassination of 'difficult' people, and a means to destabilise societies. At the hearing into the death of Aldo Moro, several members of the Red Brigade said they knew of high level US involvement in his murder. On November 10th 1982, the court heard devastating testimony from a close associate of Moro, Gorrado Guerzoni. He said that a top United States politician had threatened Moro that unless he changed his policies he would be dealt with. Moro wanted to stabilise Italy, the US politician wanted to destabilise her. Aldo Moro's wife, in her evidence, also said that a "high ranking United States political figure" had told her husband: "Either you stop your political line or you will pay dearly for it". Who was the man that Gorrado Guerzoni named in court?

Henry Kissinger.

This was widely reported in Italy, but not a single word appeared in the *New York Times* or the *Washington Post*, even though one of America's most famous people had been accused in a court of law with involvement in the death of a leading foreign politician kidnapped and murdered by a terrorist gang. Free press? Sure there is. When Moro was kidnapped, the Italian government refused to negotiate his release. This was strange because they had negotiated when others had been abducted. His family could not understand it at the time. It was as if the authorities didn't want him released. The truth was that they didn't. The Elite conspiracy does not have an allegiance to one country or political system. It has its members in all parties and countries and they cooperate for their common aims. To them borders and countries do not exist, except as a means to play one side against another.

Two significant names found on the P2 membership list were the financiers, Roberto Calvi and Michele Sindona. It was while investigating the fake kidnapping of Sindona and his work as financial advisor to the Vatican and the Mafia that the police uncovered Gelli's P2 scandal. The Roman Catholic Church had long outlawed Freemasonry within its ranks, although many of its clergy and officials are members. During the period of Gelli, however, when official Vatican hostility to Freemasonry was significantly reduced, the P2 Lodge took over the Papal State through the infiltration by Gelli, Calvi, and Sindona. The Pope through these years of P2 infiltration was Pope Paul VI and it was he who reduced the opposition to Freemasonry within the Roman Catholic Church. Interestingly, a Canadian publisher, Daniel Scallen, employed the Pinkerton Detective Agency of New York to investigate the Pope's behaviour. A detective went to Rome in 1973 and reported that there were *two* Pope Pauls in the Vatican! He reckoned that plastic surgery had been used to make an impostor resemble the Pope. When you see different close-up pictures of the Pope from this time, it is certainly feasible. There do appear to be distinct differences. Tapes of the Pope's speeches at Christmas and Easter were analysed by the FBI and found to be the voices of different people. During his investigations, the Pope's niece admitted to the detective that there was indeed an impostor, and his family (who visited the real Pope regularly at the Vatican) was aware of this, she said. The investigation ended when the detective was arrested in Rome and sentenced to four years in prison. He was later deported and then 'disappeared'. There were some who found it far-fetched when I said in *The Robots' Rebellion* that look-alikes were used for some public figures. It isn't, you know. It has now been shown that the Saddam Hussein we saw after the Gulf War was not the same man we saw before the war. It was a plastic-surgery-created look-alike.[10]

When the P2 scandal broke, top ranking Vatican officials were implicated, including the Secretary of State, Cardinal Villot. It was Villot, according to Stephen Knight's book, *The Brotherhood*, who many believe applied pressure on the Roman Catholic hierarchy to tone down its opposition to Freemasonry. He was also named, in another investigation by David Yallop

---

[10] "Saddam Double Fools The World", *Sunday Times*, (January 22nd 1995) p1 and section three, p1.

called *In God's Name*, as a prime suspect in the murder of Pope John Paul I, who died after only 33 days in office in 1978. This Pope perhaps knew something of what was going on, both in terms of Freemasonry infiltration and the stealing of Vatican wealth. The 'Christian' wing of the All-Seeing Eye cult wants to infiltrate and destroy Christianity in the same way its Jewish membership are working to undermine Judaism. Maybe Pope John Paul I was determined to act to bring an end to the manipulation, although others say he was an Illuminati Pope. Anyway, he was found dead, murdered by agents of P2, and this was covered up with lies about 'natural causes'. The doctors who were allowed to examine him appeared confused, with each suggesting a different cause – heart attack, cancer, and brain tumour. Take your pick. Many believe he was poisoned, but the truth was never investigated by the authorities. He was found dead at 5.30am and by 9.30am his body had been embalmed and his intestines removed and burnt. There was no post mortem. Standsfield Turner (CFR), the former CIA director, said that Pope John Paul's personal physician, one of the first to examine his body, was an asset of the CIA. Cardinal Villot himself died in 1979 before the P2 story was exposed. In the period leading up to his death, he said that he would reveal the story of the Pope's demise, but he never did. The doctors who were allowed to examine Villot gave the cause of death as bronchial-pneumonia...sorry, kidney trouble...no, hold on, hepatitis...no, er, internal haemorrhage. Remind me not to call the Vatican if I ever need a doctor.

Michele Sindona, the P2 member, financial swindler, money launderer, and later convicted murderer, became involved with the Vatican bank, L'Istituto per le Opere di Religione (IOR) and introduced his partner, Roberto Calvi, to the bank's chief, Bishop Paul Marcinkus. Calvi had his own bank, Ambrosiano, in which the Vatican bank became a major shareholder, thanks to the Freemasonic connections and Gelli's close relationship with the top officials and the Pope. A massive fraud ensued and when Banco Ambrosiano collapsed in 1982, it had debts of £800,000,000. The Vatican bank paid creditors £164,000,000 which created a cash crisis for the Roman Catholic Church, similar to the one faced by the protestant Church of England in more recent years.

Roberto Calvi, who became known, as did Sindona, as 'God's Banker', fled to Austria and then England, where he arrived on June 15th 1982. Two days later his secretary, Graziella Corrocher, who kept the books for P2, 'fell' from a fourth floor window at the Ambrosiano Bank. The following day Calvi was dead, too. He was found hanged from scaffolding under Blackfriars Bridge in London, with his pockets full of masonry, four miles from the Chelsea Cloisters where he was staying.

Even as his body was being found and reported, Italian police and other officials were chartering a plane to England. They need not have been so hasty, there were plenty of Freemasons within the London authorities who could cover up his murder. A City of London Inquest announced a verdict of suicide, which beggars belief. A man who wants to kill himself leaves his apartment, where the deed could have been done, travels to Blackfriars Bridge and despite suffering from extreme vertigo, he climbs down onto scaffolding underneath the arches which he could not have known was there. He then somehow rigs up the rope, fills his pockets with rubble, and hangs himself. Yeah, sounds feasible. A second inquest in June 1983 returned an open verdict, which at least was a little more sensible, though far from the outcome the evidence demanded.

There was certainly Freemasonic symbolism involved in his death and the Masons love their symbolism. Blackfriars was once the site of a friary church run by a Dominican Order who were called Blackfriars because of the black habits they wore. It was they who expanded the use of pulpits, hence the pulpit is a theme in the stonework on Blackfriars Bridge. Members of the P2 lodge dressed like Blackfriars for their rituals. Also, one of the masonic penalties talks of the victim being "...buried in the sand of the sea at low water mark, or a cable's length from the shore, where the tide regularly ebbs and flows twice in twenty four hours...". One tarot card depiction of death is also a man hanged beside water. Whatever the detailed background, Calvi was clearly murdered, either for what he had done or for what he knew about what had happened. It was probably both. And that is the penalty faced by many Freemasons who have outlived their usefulness.

It would be nice to think that the P2 scandal was an isolated case, but I do not believe that to be so. Yet to be uncovered in most countries (certainly in the most influential ones) are, I have no doubt, similar cells of elite Freemasons creating and controlling a state within a state. I do not accept, either, that even the P2 has ceased to exist, nor that the Elite's control of the Vatican has been purged. One other point is the name itself, P2. That indicates that somewhere there must be a P1. But where? Almost certainly the United States, or the United Kingdom, possibly both.

THE KNIGHTS OF MALTA

During the period of the Crusades in the twelfth and thirteenth centuries when the Pope tried to remove the Muslims from Jerusalem, a number of 'Knights' orders emerged. They included the Knights Templar (Knights of the Temple) and the Order of Knights Hospitaller of St John of Jerusalem. Both suffered persecution after the Crusades failed, but the Knights Templar survive to this day and their creed formed the basis of the Scottish Rite of Freemasonry with its 33 degrees. The Order of St John of Jerusalem changed its name with its changes of location. It became the Knights of Rhodes when it was given the island by the Pope and then the Knights of Malta, which it ruled as a sovereign state until the Order was removed by Napoleon in 1798. After a period of nomadic existence, or so their official history says, Pope Leo XII (a dogmatic Catholic extremist) established a new headquarters for the Order in Rome in 1834. Today they are called the

Sovereign Military Order of Malta and they enjoy all the diplomatic rights of a head of state. More than forty countries recognise their sovereignty and have full diplomatic relations with this official, and oh-so-accurately described, state within a state. By Papal Decree, the international head of the Order, the Grand Master, has the rank of prince, the importance of a cardinal, and the title Most Eminent Highness. The overall chief, officially at least, is the Pope.

The Knights of Malta are major powerbrokers within the Elite network, with close ties to the Black Nobility and world politics, not the least in the United States. Alexander Haig (CFR), the secretary of state in the Reagan administration, is a member and some believe Reagan may have been. Valérie Giscard d'Estaing, the former president of France, was also a member. It was d'Estaing (Bil) and former German Chancellor, Helmut Schmidt (Bil), who did so much together to promote European integration.[11] The Order has particularly close links with the security services like the CIA. In 1948, it gave one of its most prestigious awards of honour to General Reinhard Gehlen, who was Adolf Hitler's head of anti-Soviet espionage. After the war, Gehlen was hired by the newly created CIA to organise its operations in Europe! CIA directors known to be Knights of Malta have been John McCone and William Casey, and so was George Rocca, a deputy chief of CIA counter-intelligence. The Knights of Malta were almost certainly involved in the guns-for-drugs Iran-Contra affair in the US, which brought Oliver North to world public attention. North was represented at the hearings by the law firm of Bennett Williams, a Knight of Malta. One of the Americans who intervened to ensure that selected Nazi personnel escaped from Germany to the United States after the war was the industrialist, J. Peter Grace, the one-time American head of the Knights of Malta.

This Order is an ultra-extreme authoritarian organisation which connects with the highest levels of the Elite web. Research by the writer, Betty Mills, for her 1990 book, *Colonel North, William Casey, And The Knights Of Malta*, reveals that in the 1930s there was an attempted coup by the Order in America. At the centre of this was the Knight of Malta, John J. Raskob, but it failed when Marine General Smedley Butler refused to take part and instead produced evidence of the plan. He implicated Raskob, board chairman of the J.P. Morgan-controlled General Motors, and one of the thirteen founders of the Knights of Malta in the United States. Congressional hearings were held, but amazingly, or perhaps not so amazingly, Raskob was never called to testify. And, as Betty Mills says: "It is interesting and at the same time very disturbing to note that the 1930s plot to seize the White House is not to be found in history books or encyclopedias as far as we can

[11] *Treason At Maastricht*, p140.
[12] Betty Mills, *Colonel North, William Casey And The Knights Of Malta*, (Private Printing, 1990) p4.

tell".[12] Who controls the media and the official versions of history? Correct. Once more we see how the Knights of Malta cross-reference with the other pieces in the puzzle, including the media. William F. Buckley, the publisher and oilman, is a member of the Skull and Bones Society, the Council on Foreign Relations, and the Knights of Malta. Frank Shakespeare, another Knight, was president of CBS Television, vice-chairman of RKO, and the United States ambassador to the Vatican. Shakespeare has also served on the Elite-controlled Heritage Foundation under the ultra-right chairmanship of Paul Weyrich. This has links to the Habsburg family, one of the driving forces behind the Pan European Movement which led to the European Community, and a key family within the Global Elite. The social historian Stephen Birmingham says: "The Knights of Malta comprise what is perhaps the most exclusive club on Earth. They are more than the Catholic aristocracy…[they] can pick up the telephone and chat with the Pope".[13] I would go further than that and say they control the Vatican in league with other Elite elements and, far from being the Catholic aristocracy, they are not even Catholic. This is only a cover for their activities and they worship a very different version of 'god', the Luciferic Consciousness symbolised by the Pyramid and All-Seeing Eye. The Vatican was controlled by the Elite via the Knights of Malta before Gelli's P2 got involved. Indeed, Gelli was a member of the Knights of Malta.

The present Pope and official head of the Knights of Malta is the Pole, Karol Wojtyla, a former actor and employee of I.G. Farben. He has had one attempt on his life, which might have been a warning to "do as you're told or else". It's difficult to say. Certainly he carries with him the bent or broken cross, depicting the distorted figure of Jesus. This was an invention by Satanists in the fifth century and used by black magicians. It was outlawed in the Middle Ages. In 1978, the year that Pope John Paul I was murdered and Pope John Paul II took over the papacy, a set of Vatican stamps was issued featuring a pyramid and an all-seeing eye.

THE ORANGE ORDER AND SINN FEIN

Behind the ongoing conflicts in the world's trouble spots you will find the Global Elite secret society network manipulating both sides. The news is full of stories about "freedom fighters" and "arms struggles" around the world. Most of the people involved believe they are fighting for "freedom" in their country or community when they are really being used as part of a coordinated global revolution to destroy communities and nation states on the road to world government. In Northern Ireland, the arms struggle has cost the lives of 3,000 people on both 'sides' of the so called Catholic and Protestant Divide. At the lower levels, there is no doubt that two perceived 'sides' exist if only in the minds of those involved. But the Protestant political

---

[13] Quoted in the US Publication, *Matrix III*, p680.

and paramilitary groups are underpinned by a secret society, the Orange Order. This is the same secret society controlled by the Black Nobility that put King William of Orange on the British throne and imported the Dutch central banking system to Britain in the form of the Bank of England. The Catholic political and paramilitary wings are also part of the secret society network and far from "fighting for freedom", they are a Lansky-style organised crime syndicate. Why, at the highest level, can't they have been working together all along to play one side against the other in classic modified Hegel fashion while at the same time projecting at the public mind a belief in two deeply opposing forces? Pollard's *The Secret Societies Of Ireland* says that the force behind the revolutions of Europe had Ireland in its sights:

> *"These emissaries from France aimed at bringing England low, and spreading the doctrine of world-revolution by means of an alliance between the Catholic malcontents of the South and the Republican Presbyterians of the North."*

One vehicle for the Irish strand of the world-revolution was the Irish Brotherhood, later the United Irishmen, founded by the Freemasons, Wolfe Tone and Napper Tandy in 1791. The writer and researcher of the eighteenth and early nineteenth century, Robert Clifford, said that the Irish revolutionary network maintained contacts with similar international movements through the Illuminist Jacobin Club in Paris (a force behind the French Revolution), the Revolutionary Society in England, and the Scottish Committee of Reform. The Fenian Society, later the Irish Republican Brotherhood, was formed between 1857 and 1858 under the guidance of James Stephens who, from the start, saw this Brotherhood as a part of the much wider European revolutionary movement. Fenians travelled to Paris to study the methods of the Carbonari, the Italian Elite-Brotherhood network, very closely connected to the Black Nobility. In 1865, the Fenians joined the secret society network under Karl Marx known as the International Working Mens' Association and founded the Irish Brotherhood in London on September 28th 1864, which, with help from the American Fenian Brotherhood, was not primarily designed to win democracy, freedom and justice for the Irish people. It was created to exploit their thoroughly understandable sense of injustice to further the world (Elite) revolution. Marx saw Ireland as an important weapon to undermine England and it has been used that way ever since with the Irish people as the pawns of the manipulators on both 'sides'. Robert Clifford wrote:

> *"What unhappy deluded people then were the lower associates, who were informed of nothing, but were to be mere agents of rebellion and murder, and were hurried on into the abyss of horrors by a few political liberties who grasped at dominion, and wished to wade to the helm of the state through the*

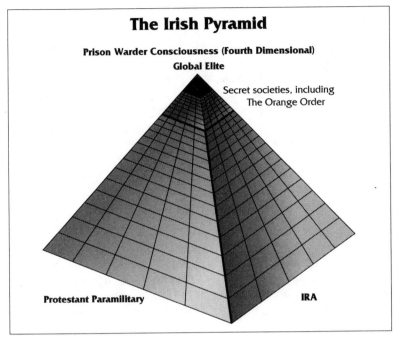

The Irish Pyramid

Prison Warder Consciousness (Fourth Dimensional)
Global Elite

Secret societies, including
The Orange Order

Protestant Paramilitary   **IRA**

Figure 10

blood of their countrymen! ...In those parts where the whole population was Catholic, hand bills were distributed, purporting to be the Constitution of the Orange Men, which was death and destruction to every Catholic; for, if the common people could once be stirred up to rebellion, it was easy to turn their minds against government as the centre of the Orange Men."

Meanwhile, you say something similar to the Protestants about the Catholic leaders and, bingo, you have the horror of Ireland throughout the twentieth century. It is classic modified Hegelianism or, you might also say, Kissingerism or Harrimanism (*Figure 10*). The secret society network in Ireland is phenomenal for such a small population and it is this which led to the creation of Sinn Fein in 1905, the political wing of the Irish Republican Army (IRA). This network is, in turn, connected to the web controlled by the Global Elite and it is through this that the well-documented links between the IRA and other terrorist groups have been coordinated. *The New Covenant Times* said in its January/March 1994 edition, that the loyalist paramilitary movement was deliberately backed by an MI5 operation called "Tara" with the intention of creating so much violence and tit-for-tat murder by both the IRA and Protestant loyalist paramilitary, that the UK Parliament would agree to allow Northern Ireland to be absorbed into the Republic of Ireland.

Some of the background to this came out in the story of Colin Wallace, the subject of a book by the journalist, Paul Foot, called *Who Framed Colin Wallace?* He was a part-time soldier and an outstanding public relations officer at the army headquarters in Northern Ireland. Later he was moved to another department under the control of MI5. It was a department dealing with the promotion of disinformation. Here Wallace became aware of the "Tara" operation and its links to the suppression over 20 years of the history of child sexual abuse at the Kincora Boys' Home. When Wallace asked to be removed from the project, he was immediately sent to England and charged with a 'security offence'. Later he was charged with murder. I have nothing in common with most views expounded by MP Enoch Powell (Bil) over the years, but on one thing I believe him to be entirely correct: that not only was Wallace framed by the establishment, his treatment implicated individuals at every level, from the Cabinet Office to junior policemen and civil servants. The conflict in Northern Ireland has a very much wider background than we have been led to believe[14] and a source within the UK establishment who worked on Northern Ireland related projects, told me that the catholic and protestant parliamentary leaderships meet to discuss strategies! I am sure something similar has been happening in the Middle East as the 'peace' negotiators, Arafat and the late Prime Minister Rabin, combined to offer the Palestinians the 'gift' of long-term slavery dressed up as 'freedom'.

THE SKULL AND BONES SOCIETY

This is an important society within the Elite pyramid which has tremendous influence within the United States. It is run with the strictest secrecy from its headquarters at Yale University, in a windowless mausoleum appropriately known as 'The Tomb' where the members meet twice a week during term time. The detailed history of the Skull and Bones is a mystery, but it is believed to have been introduced into the US more than 150 years ago as Chapter 322 of a German secret society and was also known at one time as the Brotherhood of Death. The Illuminati in disguise. The symbolism of the initiation ceremony would appear to indicate at least close links with Freemasonry. It was started in 1832–1833 by General William Huntington Russell and Alphonso Taft, a famous American family name. In 1876, Taft was to be the Secretary of War in the Grant Administration and his son, William Howard Taft, was the only man to be both President and Chief Justice of the United States. The Skull and Bones Society is deeply racist and was founded on the fortune made from illegal drugs. The society was incorporated in 1856 as the Russell Trust and by a special act of state legislation, its trustees are exempted from filing corporate reports to the Connecticut authorities.

The initiation ceremonies for the Skull and Bones still take place at Deer

---

[14] My thanks for the secret society background to Northern Ireland to *On Target* magazine. See bibliography.

Island in the St Lawrence River. The island is owned by the Russell Trust Association, along with most of the land on which Yale University stands. The Russell family made its enormous wealth from the opium trade in the nineteenth century through the drug syndicate known as Russell and Company. Its business was to take opium from Turkey and transport it illegally to China. Their only rivals were the Perkins syndicate, based in Boston, which had intermarried with other families of the British genetic line who had previously been involved in the slave trade.

The Russells eventually bought out the Perkins and became the centre of the US opium racket, in league with other 'blueblood' families like Coolidge and Delano (Comm 300 family designate), both of which produced Presidents of the United States. The head of Russell and Co in Canton while all this drug racketeering was going on was Warren Delano Jr, the grandfather of Franklin Delano Roosevelt. These American families also connected with British families involved in the opium trade like the Keswicks (Jardine Matheson) and many others supported by the British governments of Lord Palmerston, the symbolic head of Grand Orient Freemasonry. The Keswicks and Jardine Matheson have been members of the Committee of 300. Given the source of its creation, therefore, it was only right that the Skull and Bones Society was launched with a pirate's flag as its symbol.

The link between the Skull and Bones and the families of the Eastern Establishment named throughout this book was to continue to the present day…names like Bush, Rockefeller, Harriman, Whitney, Payne, Vanderbilt, Bundy, and so on. The writer, Anthony C. Sutton, acquired copies of Skull and Bones membership lists going back to 1832.[15] About 20–30 families, overwhelmingly from the Eastern seaboard, dominate the Order. Most claim ancestry with the British aristocracy or have a genetic line going back to the English Puritan families who arrived in America around 1630–1660. These families either secured financial power themselves or married into wealth via the sons of the moguls like the Rockefellers and Harrimans. One side had the money; the other had the genes from the perceived elite bloodlines of the 'Mother Country'. It is not only in Asia that they have arranged marriages. In these Anglo-American families it is done to protect or 'advance' the genetic lines of the pseudo-bluebloods who owe the origins of their inherited wealth and influence to drug running, slavery, and carefully chosen marriage partners. These intermingled families help and support each other in their quest for financial, political, and genetic dominance.

A big Skull and Bones family is the Lords of the well known New York law firm, Lord, Day, and Lord. Their present clients include the *New York*

Times and the Rubin Foundation, which funds the Elite's Institute for Policy Studies in Washington. Winston Lord (TC, Bil) became the chairman of the Council on Foreign Relations in 1983. The Bush clan are well represented, too, in the Skull and Bones. Prescott Bush was initiated in 1917 and then married into the family of financiers and wheeler dealers, the Walkers.[16] George Herbert Walker Jr was another Skull and Bones man. In 1948, Prescott's son, George Herbert Walker Bush, joined the Order, a move that would be exceedingly helpful in his climb to become head of the CIA and president of the United States. Pat Buchanan, one of Bush's challengers at the Presidential election, accused him of running "a Skull and Bones Presidency". Yale and the Skull and Bones are also recruiting grounds for the CIA and it was from his student days that Bush almost certainly began his career with the Elite-controlled spy agency.

His father Prescott Bush is most famous within the Order for raiding the grave of the Native American Apache leader, Geronimo. In May 1918, Bush and five other Skull and Bones members ransacked the grave at Fort Sill, Oklahoma. They took turns to stand guard while the others robbed the grave, and took away artifacts and Geronimo's skull. This was taken to Skull and Bones headquarters at Yale where it is used in their sick rituals and ceremonies. This horrible story is told in an internal history of the Skull and Bones Society. It was quoted to Ned Anderson, the Tribal Chairman of the San Carlos Apache Tribe, when he was negotiating to have Geronimo's remains returned to the tribe's custody. A 1989 article in the *New Yorker* said that "one Bonesman…recalled during the early 70s seeing perhaps 30 skulls, not all of them human, scattered about the Tomb".

This is the mentality which goes on to enjoy positions of power within the American administration – in George Bush's case, the presidency. Once again it is a mentality, a vibratory state, that can be locked into the Prison Warders frequency. Fifteen students a year are hand picked to join the Skull and Bones. They are selected in their junior year, but only become members in their senior year before they go off into the outside world. They can then continue to secretly promote the aims of the Skull and Bones in the worlds of politics, business, banking, the media, education, and all the other spheres of influence.

Fear and the threat of blackmail are weapons the society uses to keep its members in line. Part of the initiation ceremony is to lie naked in a coffin with a ribbon tied to their private parts while they masturbate and shout out details of their sexual experiences. I must say I have never seen George Bush in the same light since I realised that. Apparently these sexual discussions continue throughout the lives of Bonesmen, although only at the initiation is it done from a coffin. When a student is initiated, he is given his Skull and

---

[16] The famous golf trophy, the Walker Cup, is named after George Herbert Walker, the former president's grandfather.

Bones name. He becomes a 'knight' in the tradition of other secret societies like the Knights of Malta. The older knights in the S and B are called Patriarchs, and those of us on the outside – the masses – are called Gentiles, barbarians, and vandals.

If you look at the period of the Russian Revolution to the end of the Second World War alone, you can appreciate how the Skull and Bones has been a common theme throughout these years of conflict and manipulation. On the board of the Morgan Guaranty Trust Company which helped to fund the Bolshevik Revolution, maintain the Soviet dictatorship, and fund both sides in the two world wars, you find *nine* members of the Skull and Bones Society, including W. Averell Harriman, Harry P. Whitney, Knight Woolley, and Percy Rockefeller. On the board of W. A. Harriman (Brown Brothers, Harriman from 1933) were *eight* members of the Skull and Bones, among them W.A. Harriman, E. Roland Harriman, Knight Woolley, and Prescott Bush. Very obviously, the Skull and Bones Society was, and is, an important means of coordinating the Elite operations. Averell Harriman is a prime example of how Skull and Bones members have orchestrated the direction of the United States and the world, but many of the Americans I have mentioned in this book are members of the S and B. Its members have been behind the eugenics movement, the creation of the World Council of Churches, and the American Civil War (in which the Skull and Bonesmen worked with the Rothschilds, who had an agent on each side, Judah Benjamin and August Belmont).

I have in *Figure 11* (*overleaf*) fitted together the overall structure into the global pyramid of control. I do not claim for a moment that this is 100% accurate. We are talking of a force shrouded in secrecy and disinformation, after all. But it will give you some idea of how it fits together. It was constructed by the Elite with control of the following in mind: governments and politicians; political opinions of all shades; the economic system; the world military; the media; the intelligence agencies; public opinion manipulation; 'health' – the pharmaceutical industry; the illegal drugs network; population control – eugenics; education; food production; and so forth. These interconnecting elements hang together on a structure controlled from the top. It involves the covert infiltration of the authorities which guide the direction of society and the covert manipulation and coordination by key Elite satellites in the centre of the structure like the Round Table and the Royal Institute of International Affairs. All these threads and lines of command eventually feed into the United Nations and its ever mushrooming network of agencies and power. I do not wish to give the impression that this network is *all* powerful, nor that it manipulates without internal pressures and strife. The network can only control and manipulate the mass of the people if we cooperate with it. If we cease to concede our right to think for ourselves and stop cooperating with the controllers, their 'power' is no more. Also, the Elite do not always agree on

Figure 11

The Elite Network
(summarised version)

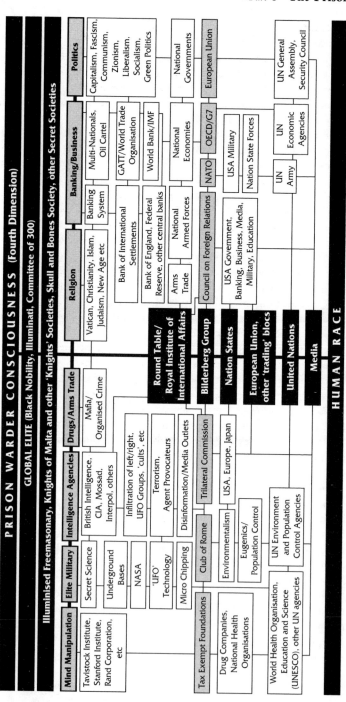

everything. One long-time researcher into the New World Order said the Elite were like a gang of bank robbers. They agree on the crime, but they argue over the methods and the division of the spoils. I think such pressures will play a major role in its imminent destruction.

One name in the diagram there which you may not have heard of is the Tavistock Institute of Human Relations, 120 Belsize Lane, London NW3 5BA, which, according to many books and investigators, tops the network of mass mind manipulation research establishments and its findings are used to direct the policies of the Global Elite network. In 1921, just as the Royal Institute of International Affairs and the Council on Foreign Relations were being formed, the Duke of Bedford, Marquess of Tavistock, gave one of his buildings for research into the effects of shellshock on British soldiers in the First World War. This was carried out under the direction of the British Army Bureau of Psychological Warfare under Sir John Rawlings-Reece (Comm 300). A student of Sir John Rawlings-Reece was Henry Kissinger. It was Tavistock, according to researchers like Eustace Mullins and others, that introduced the drug culture of the 1960s; and designed the mass bombing raids on civilians during the Second World War to break the spirit of the people. Mind manipulation and brainwashing will also be used on people useful to the Global Elite to 'encourage' them to see the world in the required manner.[17]

The Tavistock nexus has grown far and wide and links into the Club of Rome and the Bilderberg network. It connects with the Ditchley Foundation, which was founded in 1957 by Sir Philip Adams, a long time employee of the British Foreign Office, which is in turn controlled by the Royal Institute of International Affairs and the Bilderberg group. In the United States, the Tavistock network includes the Stanford Institute, the Institute for Social Relations, the Hudson Institute, the Heritage Foundation, the Hoover Institution, the Centre for Strategic Studies at Georgetown, and the Rand Corporation (which has Zbigniew Brzezinski among its number). This mind control network is itself linked (with the tax-exempt foundations) into the education system, including the business and banking schools which develop methods of controlling people through the financial system. Again the overwhelming majority of people involved will have no idea where the directives and policies really originate. The Brookings Institution in the US is responsible for developing policies to manipulate the population through the money system, and so is the Mont Pelerin Society. A leading light of this, and of the Hoover Institution, is economist Milton Friedman, the inspiration of the monetarism disaster introduced by those political puppets, Margaret Thatcher and Ronald

---

[17] For more detailed background to the Tavistock Institute, see Dr John Coleman's *Conspirators Hierarchy: The Story Of The Committee Of 300*, (Tavistock is mentioned extensively); Eustace Mullins, *The World Order, Our Secret Rulers*, p262–265.

Reagan, in the 1980s.

You'll note also that the whole structure not only connects from the top, down; the various elements connect crossways too. There are infinitely more link-ups and organisations involved than I have mentioned in the diagram. Within most of these organisations, the lower levels will not know what they are being used for and it is important to recognise that the system of compartmentalisation and the 'need to know' principle means that the different levels are following different agendas. At the lower levels within the CIA, British Intelligence, and the KGB, they would have been genuinely fighting the Cold War. Their agents in the field would have been spying on each other in the belief that East and West were sworn enemies. But at the higher levels, they had another agenda because they knew that the Cold War was a sham to serve Elite ambitions. These multidimensional agendas controlled by the all-knowing Elite continue within the economic, political, and military systems today and while most of the people involved in the Global Pyramid don't realise what they are part of, the mindset established at the top sets the agenda that filters down through all the levels. You could call this the 'culture of corruption' that we see so often in society, even in the lower echelons of business, the police, and politics.

Throughout this pyramid there is one common and all-pervading force, guide, and motivation. It decides the policy and holds the strings of those who manipulate our lives. This force is the guiding light, or rather darkness, which controls the thinking and the direction of those at the top of this Pyramid of Deceit. It is the Prison Warders' consciousness and its principal vehicle is known to us as black magic.

Chapter 10

The Super Elite – the black magicians

At the highest level of the Elite's human pyramid, I believe they do know that they are working with a Fourth Dimensional consciousness which has been known symbolically by many names (such as Satan, Set, Lucifer, the Devil, and – in this book – the Prison Warders). At this top level, they are knowingly interacting with this force, which probably takes many forms. There is evidence that many people involved over the years have believed they were working for extraterrestrial 'super men'. Some may have had face-to-face contact with a negative ET group from the Fourth Dimension.

To understand the true nature of the conspiracy, we need to appreciate its esoteric foundation. Esoteric knowledge, often called 'the occult', is not negative in or of itself. It is just the knowledge of the potential to harness the energies of Creation for good or ill, and the understanding of the human psyche and how it can be balanced, healed, or manipulated. It is not the knowledge that is good or bad; it is the way we use it. People at the highest levels of the Elite-Illuminati-Brotherhood network are often members of extreme sects based on ancient rites and Lucifer/Satan worship. Yes, Satanists run the world. If you infiltrated some of these bizarre gatherings, I am sure you would see some very famous faces. The security services such as the CIA and US Military Intelligence, are seriously infiltrated by sects that worship these various names for the Prison Warder consciousness. Lieutenant-Colonel Michael Aquino, a senior officer within US Military Intelligence, formed the Temple of Set, but when this was made public, the authorities said they saw no problem. During the Second World War, the Elite's esoteric tradition was at work on both sides.

President Roosevelt, who was a 33rd degree Freemason, also had the esoteric name, the Knight of Pythias, and wore the red fez of the Ancient Arabic Order of Nobles of the Mystic Shrine. This organisation claimed to be connected with the Illuminati.[1] Winston Churchill, the British Prime Minister, was a Freemason and had several meetings with the Satanist Aleister Crowley, another esoteric guru and a high initiate of many orders, including the Order of the Golden Dawn and the Order of Oriental Templars (more

---

[1] Enrique De Vicente, "The Occult Roots of the New World Order", *Exposure* magazine, Vol. 1, No. 2, p10.

on him later). Churchill's meetings with Crowley do not, of course, constitute proof that the British Prime Minister was a Satanist, but it does show that behind the scenes, esoteric knowledge in all of its forms is taken far more seriously than it is in public. This was the case during Elizabethan times and has been throughout human history.

The two greatest creations of the black magicians in the twentieth century have been the Soviet Union and Nazi Germany. If I take the example of Adolf Hitler and the Nazis you will get an idea of the mindset of those who control the Elite today. This story is not unique to Hitler's Germany. Behind the public faces, its themes could be told again and again within regimes, both authoritarian and 'democratic', across the world. Germany has long been a centre for esoteric thinking and the secret societies this knowledge seems to spawn. It was from this philosophical stream that Hitler and his crazed followers would emerge. One of the pre-Hitler 'prophets' was the composer, Richard Wagner, in the nineteenth century. His composition, *The Ride Of The Valkyries*, captures his obsession with the invading powers of evil. Wagner declared the imminent arrival of the Master Race. His work, *The Ring*, was the musical expression of his belief in German supermen bestriding the world stage like the ancient pagan gods Wotan and Thor. Hitler would later say that to understand Nazi Germany, one had to know Wagner. One of the students of master race fanatic Wagner was Gustav Mahler, whose studies with Wagner were funded by Baron Albert de Rothschild.

Adolf Hitler was officially born at Braunau-am-Inn, on the border of Germany and the Austria-Hungary empire, but the amazing story of who he *really* was will be told in a later book when I have compiled the evidence. The esoteric was to become a consuming passion for Hitler, especially in his rise to power. He was strongly influenced by the work of Helena Petrovna Blavatsky, who was born in the Ukraine in 1831. Some researchers claim she had connections with the secret society of Italian revolutionaries, the Carbonari, who were closely linked to the Black Nobility, and she was a member of the Egyptian society, the Brotherhood of Luxor, which she later denounced as "a den for disgusting immorality, greediness for selfish power, and money making". Madame Blavatsky arrived in New York in 1873 and, with the help of a Colonel Henry Olcott she founded the Theosophical Society two years later. This is still around today. Its doctrines are based on Blavatsky books such as *Isis Unveiled*, which was written in 1877, and *The Secret Doctrine*, published in 1888. She claimed to be in psychic contact with Hidden Masters or Supermen. These Hidden Masters, she said, lived in Central Asia and could be contacted telepathically by those who knew the secrets to the esoteric mysteries. Today we call this process of communication 'channelling'. There are many UFO sightings and much research which indicates that there are secret underground and underwater bases for extraterrestrials around the world, Central Asia among them. I am not saying that Blavatsky was negative, only that Hitler was influenced by her work.

The belief in the Masters and the Great White Brotherhood of discarnate entities promoted by people like the Theosophical psychic of the post-Blavatsky period, Alice Bailey,[2] is a theme that remains well entrenched in parts of what is known today as the New Age Movement. Alice Bailey claimed to 'channel' an entity she called "The Tibetan" and she produced a number of books, including *Hierarchy Of The Masters, The Seven Rays, A New Group Of World Servers,* and *New World Religion.* She said that her Tibetan Master had told her the Second World War was necessary to defend the plan of God. That sounds ridiculous to me, but there are many in the New Age field who believe that everything is meant to be and is the will of God, even a global holocaust. It seems like a great excuse to do nothing and a cop-out of mega proportions.

My own view is that the 'Masters', 'The Great White Brotherhood', and this whole concept is something to be very wary of. Whenever I hear the term 'master' I cringe. Two organisations linked to Alice Bailey's work, the Lucis Trust and the World Goodwill organisation, are both staunch promoters of the United Nations – almost UN 'groupies', such is their devotion. I will discuss these further in a later chapter. The more I go into this, it is interesting to see how the New Age has inherited 'truths' over the decades in the same way that conventional religion has done over the centuries. As the followers of Christianity have inherited the manipulated version of Jesus, so New Agers have inherited the 'Masters'. There is too little checking of origins, too much acceptance of inherited beliefs, I think. If the New Age isn't careful, it will be Christianity revisited. It is already becoming so. I believe this concept of Masters can be a means through which those who have (quite rightly in my view) rejected the status quo of religion and science can still have their minds controlled by the Prison Warders of the Fourth Dimension.

Another big influence on Hitler was the novel, *The Coming Race,* by the Englishman, Lord Edward Bulwer-Lytton (Comm 300), a British Colonial Minister heavily involved in imposing opium addiction on the Chinese. He was a close friend of Disraeli and Dickens, and Grand Patron of the English Rosicrucian Society which included Francis Bacon and John Dee in its earlier membership. Bulwer-Lytton is best known for his work, *The Last Days Of Pompeii,* but his passion was the world of esoteric magic and, as a British colonial minister, for running opium to the Chinese. In *The Coming Race,* he wrote of an enormous civilisation inside the Earth, well ahead of our own. They had discovered a power called Vril which, by the use of the psyche, could be used to perform 'miracles'. These underground supermen would, according to Bulwer-Lytton's novel, emerge on the surface one day

---

[2] Alice Bailey founded the Arcane esoteric school. Again, I am not saying that she was a negative force, but I think her name has been used by some of her 'followers' for purposes of manipulation.

and take control of the world. Many Nazis believed this. Lord Bulwer-Lytton is often referred to by Madame Blavatsky in her book, *Isis Unveiled*. The themes of underground supermen or hidden masters can be found in most of the esoteric secret societies. Certainly this was true of The Order of the Golden Dawn, formed in 1888 by Dr Wynn Westcott, a Freemason, and S.L. Mathers. They called their 'masters' the 'Secret Chiefs'. The theme of extraterrestrials living underground fits in with the 1960s survey of contactees which detailed the stories of the pure Melchedekan race with their blond hair and blue eyes. They were also said to be living inside the Earth.

Mathers devised a series of rituals and initiations and designed them to help his members access their full psychic and physical potential. He believed, however, that this gift was only for the few and he was a supporter of authoritarian government. These rituals, no doubt, would have attracted the dark energies which allowed vibrational synchronisation – possession – by the Warders. In the mid-1890s, there were temples of the Order in London, Edinburgh, Bradford, Weston-Super-Mare, and Paris, where Mathers made his home. The Order of the Golden Dawn also spoke of the vril force and one of the Order's secret signs was the salute which the Nazis would use when saying "Heil Hitler". The esoteric foundations on which Nazism was created continued to build. Mathers had known Madame Blavatsky and so had the master of the Order's London Temple, the poet, William Butler Yeats, who would go on to win a Nobel Prize. Yeat's view of Utopia mirrored that of Adolf Hitler or Josef Stalin. The poet spoke of:

> "...an aristocratic civilisation in its most completed form, every detail of life hierarchical, every great man's door crowded at dawn by petitioners, great wealth everywhere in few men's hands, all dependent upon a few, up to the Emperor himself, who is a God dependent upon a greater God and everywhere, in Court, in the family, an inequality made law." [3]

Remnants of the Order of the Golden Dawn continue to this day, but the original version splintered after a row between Yeats, Mathers, and Aleister Crowley, which split the membership into quarrelling factions. Other significant esoteric thinkers and groups which influenced the gathering Nazi philosophy included the Order of the Oriental Templars, which used sex as part of its rituals to create and harness the energy known as the vril, and two German esoteric 'magicians', Guido von List and Lanz von Liebenfels. In his summer solstice celebrations, List used wine bottles on the ground to form the symbol of the Hermetic Cross, also known as the Hammer of Thor. It was the Badge of Power in the Order of the Golden Dawn, and we know

---

[3] Quoted by Francis King in *Satan And Swastika*, (Mayflower Books, London, 1976).

this symbol as the swastika. Lanz von Liebenfels (real name Adolf Lanz) featured the swastika on the flag which flew over his 'temple' overlooking the Danube, and for these two black magicians it symbolised the end of Christianity and the dawning of the age of the Aryan supermen. They believed in the racial inferiority of those they called the "dark forces" such as the Jews, the Slavs, and the Negroes. Liebenfels recommended castration for these peoples. The two vons, List and Liebenfels, were to have a massive influence on Adolf Hitler. In 1932, with Hitler on the verge of power, von Liebenfels would write to a fellow believer:

> *"Hitler is one of our pupils…You will one day experience that he, and through him we, will one day be victorious, and develop a movement that will make the world tremble…"* [4]

Two others who would influence the thinking and beliefs of Adolf Hitler were the Englishmen, Aleister Crowley and Houston Stewart Chamberlain. Crowley was born in Warwickshire in 1875. He rebelled against a strict religious upbringing and was initiated into the Order of the Golden Dawn in 1898, after leaving Cambridge University. He left the Order after the row with its founders and then travelled to Mexico, India, and Ceylon, where he was introduced to yoga and Buddhism. He also became a record-breaking mountaineer. Buddhism replaced his interest in the occult until an experience in Cairo in April 1904. Crowley was asked by his wife, Rose, to perform an esoteric ritual to see what happened. During the ceremony, she entered a trance-like state and began to channel the words of a communicator. "They are waiting for you", she said to Crowley. The "they", she said, was Horus, the god of war and the son of Osiris, in ancient Egyptian belief. Crowley did not accept any of this and asked his wife a series of detailed questions in an effort to trick her. But Rose, who knew little of the esoteric, gave the correct answer every time. I believe the Prison Warders were on the line again.

The communicator told Crowley to be at a desk in his hotel room between noon and one o'clock on three specific days. He agreed and in these periods he wrote, via automatic writing, a document called *The Book Of The Law*. Automatic writing is when your arm and hand are guided by another force and often no-one is more surprised at what they are writing than the person involved. Crowley's communication said that the old age of Osiris was being replaced by the new age of Horus. But it said the old age would first have to be destroyed by barbarism and the Earth bathed in blood. There would be a World War, it said. *The Book Of The Law* talked of a race of supermen and condemned the old religions, pacifism, democracy,

---

[4] Quoted by J.H. Brennan in *Occult Reich*, (Futura, London, 1974) and by Francis King in *Satan And Swastika*.

compassion, and humanitarianism. "Let my servants be few and secret: they shall rule the many and the known" the 'superman' continued. The message went on:

> "*We have nothing with the outcast and the unfit; let them die in their misery. For they feel not. Compassion is the vice of kings; stamp down the wretched and the weak: this is the law of the strong: this is our law and the joy of the world...Love one another with burning hearts; on the low men trample in the fierce lust of your pride, in the day of your wrath...Pity not the fallen! I never knew them. I am not for them. I console not; I hate the consoled and the consoler...*
>
> "*I am unique and conqueror. I am not of the slaves that perish. Be they damned and dead. Amen...Therefore strike hard and low, and to hell with them, master...Lurk! Withdraw! Upon them! This is the law of the Battle of Conquest: thus shall my worship be about my secret house...Worship me with fire and blood; worship me with swords and with spears. Let the woman be girt with a sword before me: let blood flow in my name. Trample down the heathen; be upon them, O warrior, I will give you their flesh to eat...Sacrifice cattle, little and big; after a child...kill and torture; spare not; be upon them!*" [5]

If that sounds remarkably like some of the angry God stuff in the Old Testament, that's because it was almost certainly the same force on the Fourth Dimension which communicated to the ancients, to Crowley, and to anyone else on that vibration who would help to stimulate the conflict and the energy of human misery, on which the Prison Warders feed. This is the force that controls the consciousness of those which control the Global Elite-Illuminati-Brotherhood, and it is the focus of worship in the All-Seeing Eye cult going back to ancient times. The communicator said that Crowley was the "Beast 666" who had come to destroy Christianity, something his mother had said earlier in his life. He apparently tried to ignore what he had written with his guided hand, but it would not go away, and from 1909 on he began to take it seriously. Very seriously. He said:

> "*After five years of folly and weakness, miscalled politeness, tact, discretion, care for the feeling of others, I am weary of it. I say today: to hell with Christianity, Rationalism, Buddhism, all the lumber of the centuries. I bring you a positive and primeval fact, Magic by name; and with this I will build me a new Heaven and new Earth. I want none of your faint approval or faint dispraise; I want blasphemy, murder, rape, revolution, anything, bad or good, but strong.*"

---

[5] Verses from *The Book Of The Law*. Quoted by George C. Andrews in *Extra-Terrestrials Among Us*, p159–160.

Crowley left his former tutor, MacGregor Mathers, a broken man as he embarked on a psychic war against him. They both conjured up the 'demons' to attack the other, but Mathers lost out. Such psychic wars are very much part of the Brotherhood today. Crowley's communicator, the Prison Warder consciousness, would also take over the psyches of Adolf Hitler and the other architects of Nazism. Long after his death, Crowley would become a hero to many involved in the 'Flower Power' period of the 1960s, when the young were calling for love and peace. The irony is not lost. Crowley welcomed the First World War as necessary to sweep away the old age and usher in the new one. After going public with his revelations, Crowley was made the world head of the Germany-based Order of the Oriental Templars (OTO) and this gave him very significant influence among like-thinkers in Germany.

Houston Stewart Chamberlain (Comm 300) was born in England in 1855, but moved to Germany in 1882. He married Eva, the daughter of Richard Wagner, in 1908 and became a prestigious writer. His best known work was *Foundations Of The Nineteenth Century* which ran to twelve hundred pages and sold more than 250,000 copies. It made him famous throughout the country. He was, however, a troubled man who had a series of nervous breakdowns. He felt himself to be taken over by demons and his books were written in a trance and a fever, which suggests that he was locked into another highly negative consciousness. The Prison Warder consciousness again. In his autobiography, he said he did not recognise much of his writing as his own. The themes of his work are very familiar: all civilisation comes from the Aryan race and the Germans were the purest of all; Jews were the enemy who would pollute the Aryan bloodlines. Yawn.

Kaiser Wilhelm II and Adolf Hitler said Chamberlain was a prophet. Chamberlain became the principal advisor to Kaiser Wilhelm and urged the king to go to war in 1914 to fulfil the prophecy of Germany's world domination. When the war was over and Wilhelm had abdicated to an estate in Holland, he realised how he had been manipulated. He gathered together a mass of books on the occult and the German secret societies and he was convinced that they had conspired to create the First World War and cause Germany to be defeated. Chamberlain, who had been awarded the Iron Cross by the Kaiser, died in 1927 after years in a wheelchair, broken in body and spirit. But his influence was to live on in the mind of Adolf Hitler. Chamberlain, incidentally, was introduced to Hitler by Alfred Rosenberg, the refugee from Russia, and another satanist figure. "Satanism" is merely the worship of, and possession by, the negative manipulators on the Fourth Dimension. It was Rosenberg, despite his Jewish background, who gave a copy of the *Protocols Of The Learned Elders Of Zion* to Hitler via another occultist, Dietrich Eckart.[6] The All-Seeing Eye cult at work again.

---

[6] Quoted by Trevor Ravenscroft in *The Spear Of Destiny*, p106.

These were some of the people and beliefs that moulded the thinking of the man claiming to be a young Austrian born with the name Schiklgruber, but later rather better known as Adolf Hitler. "Heil Schiklgruber" would not have had the same ring to it, somehow. He hated school, the official story goes, and wanted to be an artist, an ambition which took him to Vienna. He spent hours in the libraries reading books on astrology, mysticism, and the religions of the East. He was fascinated by the books of Blavatsky, Chamberlain, List, and Liebenfels. He picked out bits from each of them to produce his preferred mixture, a cocktail of horror and hatred that would manifest as Nazism. His passion was the power of the will. The potential of willpower to achieve anything it desires was to be his focus and guide throughout the years that followed. Put another way, creating your own reality.

He practised the esoteric arts in his effort to access the level of consciousness he was convinced would turn him into one of the supermen he had read so much about and believed in so much. His psyche became locked into the Prison Warder vibration more powerfully than before. He was possessed, probably during some black esoteric ritual which opened his psyche to the malevolent vibration. You only have to look at his beliefs to see that he would have had 'vibrational compatibility' with this consciousness. It was now that an uncharismatic and ineffectual man would begin to exude the charisma and magnetism that would captivate and intoxicate a nation.

We talk of some people having magnetism and 'magnetic personalities', and that is exactly what they have. We are all generating magnetic energies and these attract to us the energies (people, places, etc) that relate to what is going on in our subconscious. Some people transmit powerful magnetism and others less so. Negative energies are just as magnetic as positive. Those connected to, and therefore generating, the extreme Prison Warder vibration will be very magnetic. You often hear highly negative people described as having a magnetic personality or a 'fatal attraction'. This is why. It is also where the magnetism and charisma of Adolf Hitler suddenly came from. When he was standing on a public platform with that contorted face and crazed delivery, he was channelling the Prison Warder/Luciferic Consciousness from the Fourth Dimension and transmitting this vibration to the vast crowds. This affected the vibrational state of the people attracted by it and turned them into equally crazed agents of hatred. It is the Pied Piper principle, using a vibration instead of a pipe. As the writer Alan Bullock said of Hitler:

> "His power to bewitch an audience has been likened to the occult arts of the African Medicine-man or the Asiatic Shaman; others have compared it to the sensitivity of a medium, and the magnetism of a hypnotist." [7]

---

[7] Alan Bullock, *Hitler, A Study In Tyranny*, (Pelican Books, London, 1960).

And Herman Rauschning, an aide to Hitler, said in his book, *Hitler Speaks*:

"One cannot help thinking of him as a medium. For most of the time, mediums are ordinary, insignificant people. Suddenly they are endowed with what seem to be supernatural powers which set them apart from the rest of humanity. The medium is possessed. Once the crisis is past, they fall back again into mediocrity. It was in this way, beyond any doubt, that Hitler was possessed by forces outside of himself – almost demoniacal forces of which the individual named Hitler was only the temporary vehicle. The mixture of the banal and the supernatural created that insupportable duality of which one was conscious in his presence…It was like looking at a bizarre face whose expression seems to reflect an unbalanced state of mind coupled with a disquieting impression of hidden power." [8]

Hitler was under the control of the Prison Warders and he appeared to live in perpetual fear of these 'supermen'. Rauschning told how Hitler suffered from terrible nightmares and would wake in terror screaming about entities who were invisible to all, but him. He once said to his aide:

"What will the social order of the future be like? Comrade, I will tell you. There will be a class of overlords, after them the rank and file of the party members in hierarchical order, and then the great mass of anonymous followers, servants and workers in perpetuity, and beneath them again all the conquered foreign races, the modern slaves. And over and above all these will reign a new and exalted nobility of whom I cannot speak…But of all these plans the militant members will know nothing…The new man is living amongst us now! He is here. Isn't that enough for you? I will tell you a secret. I have seen the new man. He is intrepid and cruel. I was afraid of him." [9]

After Hitler moved to Germany, he spent a lot of time in Bavaria, from where Weishaupt's Illuminati had sprung, and he returned there in 1918 after fighting in the war. Or at least that's the official line. The following year, he came across a tiny and rather pathetic political party called the German Workers Party. This was an offshoot of an esoteric secret society called the German Order, which was fiercely nationalistic and anti-Jewish. Out of this Order came other similar societies, including the infamous Thule Society. Thule was supposed to be an ancient lost civilisation of Nordic people with blond hair and blue eyes. Yet another foundation of the Nazi belief system can be seen to have an esoteric origin, as did the swastika, the Hitler salute, the idea of an Aryan Master Race, and the view of Jews.

---

[8] Hermann Rauschning, *Hitler Speaks*, (London, 1939).
[9] Ibid.

A founder of the Thule Society was Rudolf Glauer, an astrologer, who changed his name to the grand sounding Baron von Sebottendorff. His demands for a revolution against Jews and the Marxists turned the Thule Society into a focus for the anti-Jew, anti-Marxist, German Master Racers. Out of all this came the German Workers Party, which would one day become the Nazi Party.

Another committed occultist and friend of Sebottendorff now becomes highly significant. This was Dietrich Eckart, a heavy-drinking, drug-taking writer who believed he was here to prepare the way for a dictator of Germany. He met Hitler in 1919 and decided he was the one, the 'Messiah', he was looking for. It is Eckart who is credited with Hitler's advanced esoteric knowledge and probably the black magic ritual, or rituals, which plugged him so completely into the Prison Warder vibration. From now on, Hitler's power to attract support grew rapidly. Eckart wrote to a friend in 1923:

> *"Follow Hitler! He will dance, but it is I who have called the tune. We have given him the means of communication with Them. Do not mourn for me: I shall have influenced history more than any other German."* [10]

Hitler was also a member of another esoteric secret society, the Luminous Lodge or Vril Society. Vril was the name given by the English writer, Lord Bulwer Lytton, to the force which, he claimed, awakens people to their true power and potential to become supermen. In 1933, the rocket expert, Willi Ley, fled from Germany and revealed the existence of the Vril Society and the Nazis' belief that they would become the equals of the supermen in the bowels of the Earth by use of esoteric teachings and mind expansion. They believed this would reawaken the vril force sleeping in the blood. The initiates of the Vril Society included two men who would become infamous Nazis, Heinrich Himmler and Hermann Goering. Vril members were convinced they were in alliance with mysterious esoteric lodges in Tibet and one of the so called Unknown Supermen, who was referred to as The King of Fear. Rudolph Hess, [11] Hitler's Deputy Führer until he made his ill-fated flight to England in 1941, was a dedicated occultist and a member, with Hermann Goering, of the Edelweiss Society, a black sect which believed in the Nordic Master Race (Melchedekans?). Hess worshipped Hitler as The Messiah, although how he could do this when the Führer was hardly blue

---

[10] J.H. Brennan, *Occult Reich*.

[11] Rudolph Hess was supposed to have been kept at Spandau Prison until his death in 1987. But Dr Ewen Cameron, who became a CIA 'mind doctor', said that the CIA Chief, Allen Dulles, told him that the 'Hess' in Spandau was a look-alike. When Cameron tried to prove identification by examining 'Hess' and locating a First World War wound, he was not allowed to do so.

eyed and blond haired, is not clear. Hitler had the same problem in equating the two, but he would have found some ridiculous explanation for it, I'm sure.

Another Hitler obsession was the so called Spear of Destiny, the weapon alleged to have been use to pierce the side of Y'shua (Jesus) at the crucifixion. He stole what was claimed to be the spear when the Nazis annexed Austria in 1938, and it was taken to Nuremberg. The legend says that whoever has the spear and decodes its secrets will have control of the world for good or evil. The one that Hitler stole is now in the Hofburg Museum in Vienna, where there was a major fire in November 1992, seven days before the blaze which destroyed part of Windsor Castle.

Another obsessive occultist in the Third Reich was Heinrich Himmler. He was into all matters esoteric and he used his knowledge in the blackest of ways. He was particularly interested in the rune stones, a system of divination in which stones carrying symbols are thrown or selected and the choice or combination 'read' by an 'expert'. It was Himmler who formed the notorious SS and, as with the swastika, he chose an esoteric symbol for his horrific organisation: the double S or 'sig' rune, which looks like two flashes of lightning. The SS was a virtually self-contained body and the epitome of all of the esoteric knowledge in which the Nazis believed so passionately. Only those considered racially pure were allowed to join, and instruction in the esoteric arts, including the rune stones, was fundamental to their training. The SS was run and governed as a black magic secret society. Their rituals were taken from others such as The Jesuits and The Knights Templar. The highest ranking initiates were the thirteen members of the Grand Council of Knights (led by their Grand Master, Heinrich Himmler), and the black rituals were performed at the ancient castle of Wewelsberg in Westphalia. They celebrated the festivals of the Nordic pagans and the summer solstice. Here they worshiped Satan, Lucifer, Set, whichever name you prefer, the consciousness which was the Nazis and is the Elite today. Prince Bernhard, one of the founders of the Bilderberg Group, was in the SS.

Esoteric knowledge and black magic pervaded all that Hitler and the Nazis did, even down to the use of pendulums on maps to identify the positions of enemy troops. The original swastika symbol was right-handed which, in esoteric terms, means light and creation, the positive. Hitler insisted it be turned around to symbolise black magic and destruction. The mass rallies that Hitler used so effectively were designed with the knowledge of the human psyche and how it can be manipulated. In *Satan And Swastika*, Francis King says:

> *"Hitler's public appearances, particularly those associated with the Nazi Party's Nuremberg Rallies, were excellent examples of this sort of magical ceremony. The fanfares, military marches and Wagnerian music all*

emphasised the idea of German military glory. The massed Swastika banners in black, white and red filled the consciousness of the participants in the Rally with National Socialist ideology. The ballet-like precision of the movements of the uniformed Party members, all acting in unison, evoked from the unconscious the principles of war and violence which the ancients symbolised as Mars. And the prime ritual of the Rallies – Hitler clasping to other banners the "blood banner" carried in the Munich putsch of 1923 – was a quasi-magical ceremony designed to link up minds of living Nazis with the archetypal images symbolised by the dead National Socialist heroes of the past.

"The religio-magical aspects of the Rallies were emphasised by the fact that their high points were reached after dusk and took place in a 'Cathedral of Light' – an open space surrounded by pillars of light coming from electric searchlights pointed upwards to the sky. If a modern ritual magician of the utmost expertise had designed a ritual intended to 'invoke Mars' he could not have come up with anything more effective than the ceremonies used at Nuremberg."

And what applied then, applies now. The esoteric knowledge used by the Nazis for the mass hypnosis on the German people, is being used today to expand the global hypnosis on the human race. Symbols, words, colours, sounds, and techniques of which the public are not even aware are being used in the media and advertising to hypnotise us. The Propaganda Ministry of Joseph Goebbels was based on the esoteric knowledge of the human psyche. He knew that people will believe anything if you tell them often enough and if you can engineer events which create the "something must be done" mentality in the public mind. He used colours, symbols, and slogans to great effect. The slogans were used like mantras and repeated over and over again, hypnotising the mass psyche. All alternative views and information were censored and the people were programmed to respond as desired. What is the difference between that and the constant drip, drip, drip, of inaccurate and biased information that is fed to us and our children today? It may not have a swastika on it, but it is still mass hypnotism.

It would seem to be a contradiction that Hitler sought to destroy secret societies like the Freemasons and to prevent the use of esoteric knowledge in German society, but it isn't. He knew as much as anyone the power available to those with the understanding, and he wanted to keep that for himself. One man the Nazis wanted to destroy was the 33rd degree Freemason Dr Rudolf Steiner, an Austrian who understood the powers of creation and the way they can be used for good and evil. I have come across many conflicting views and claims about Steiner's intent and I've not yet developed an opinion. I feel, however, that he was not as positive as he's made out. He joined the Theosophical Society and the Order of the Oriental Temple, but later formed his own Anthroposophical Society.

Armed gangs began to break up Steiner's meetings and threatened the lives of those who listened to him. He fled to Switzerland and died in 1925, a year after his centre at Dornach was burned down by the Nazis. In 1934, all forms of fortune telling were banned in Berlin and later esoteric books were banned throughout Germany. Secret societies were disbanded and even the Thule Society and the German Order (which had together founded Nazism) were targeted. Astrologers were attacked and killed and people like Lanz von Liebenfels were prevented from publishing their work. This purge had two main motives. To distance Hitler and the Nazis from the occult in the minds of the public and other countries, and, most importantly, to pull up the ladder and stop anyone else from using esoteric knowledge against them as they were using it against others. This is one reason, too, why this knowledge has been suppressed and ridiculed throughout the Western world and hidden behind the smokescreens of this-world-is-all-there-is science, and one-life-and-then-heaven-or-hell religion.

The role of the esoteric in the rise of the Nazis has been thoroughly underplayed or ignored except in a few excellent books such as Gerald Suster's *Hitler And The Age Of Horus*.[12] Look deeper into any historical situation and you will usually find the esoteric. John Ruskin, the man who inspired Cecil Rhodes, Alfred Milner, and those who formed the Round Table secret society, was himself influenced by the esoteric writings of Plato and by Madame Blavatsky, the books of Lord Edward Bulwer-Lytton, and secret societies in the mould of the Order of the Golden Dawn. The murder of US President Abraham Lincoln has been explained by some as part of the struggle between competing secret societies, although I don't accept that. One of his close friends, Pascal Beverly Randolph, revealed that Lincoln was involved with a society called the Brotherhood of Eulis after being initiated into the secrets of "sexual magic" in the Middle East. Lincoln was also believed to be a high ranking member of the Hermetic Brotherhood of Luxor or of the Light.[13] Many of the famous political and economic faces of history and today are masks which hide their true nature and motivation. They are the apparently 'different' faces of the All-Seeing Eye network. We are watching actors on a stage and someone else is writing their script. Rasputin, the so called mad monk of the history books, was neither mad nor a monk in the conventional sense. He was a mystic who went through a massive spiritual experience while "searching for god" in Asia. His psyche was opened to some higher – or lower – consciousness and this Russian peasant was suddenly a different person. He was capable of healing and had an intense magnetism and legendary sexual drive. A few years after returning

[12] Gerald Suster, *Hitler And The Age Of Horus*, (Sphere, London, 1981).
[13] Enrique De Vicente, "The Occult Roots of the New World Order", *Exposure* magazine, Vol. 1, No. 2, (1993) p7.

to Russia, he had such a hold over the Tsar that he was, in effect, the ruler of the country.

Stories have come to light of the black esoteric basis of the KGB in the former Soviet Union. Today the KGB under other titles plays exactly the same role in 'free' Russia. Only its name has changed. One report highlights the manipulation within the Kremlin by General Georgy Georgievich Rogozin who, it is said, uses black magic to program the psyche of those he wishes to control.[14] He heads a highly secretive intelligence group in Boris Yeltsin's presidential team. The global intelligence network is founded on the misuse of esoteric knowledge. The Global Elite and those who abuse the esoteric knowledge also know that if you can control the key energy power points (acupuncture points and chakra vortexes) on the Earth's energy grid, you can massively affect the psyche of the people, as the human minds interact with the grid energies, the Earth mind.

We have seen how the United States of America was founded on esoteric principles and knowledge. The Great Seal of the United States is a mass of esoteric symbols, signs, and numbers, including the pyramid and all-seeing eye. This symbol was put on the dollar note during the presidency of Freemason Franklin D. Roosevelt. It is also no coincidence that the Declaration of Independence and the founding of Adam Weishaupt's Bavarian Illuminati both happened in 1776. Numbers and years represent energy vibrations, as do planets, sounds, colours, and symbols. We see some of these symbols in the crop circles and patterns. The genuine ones (those not hoaxed by the forces of disinformation), speak to our subconscious and help to awaken us in ways we cannot yet fully understand. At the higher levels of the Global Elite, this esoteric knowledge is used to decide when and where events will happen to give them the best chance of success.

You will find the same numbers and sequences throughout ancient texts and beliefs. The lists of sevens in Revelation have esoteric, not literal, meanings. The Bible is packed with such numerology, which the church has taken literally. Thirteen, or the 'twelve and one', has great esoteric significance under the laws of numerology and the vibrations they represent, and for other historical reasons, too. It means transformation, new birth, a new order. Hence you find Jesus and twelve disciples and the Grand Master Himmler and twelve other 'knights' in the Grand Council of the SS. It is the same knowledge, used with different intent. Osiris, the god of Egypt, had twelve followers according to legend, Buddha had twelve disciples, as did the Aztec god, Quetzalcoatl. There are the twelve knights of King Arthur's Round Table, twelve sons of Jacob, twelve princes of Ishmael, twelve tribes of Israel, twelve signs of the zodiac. The Bilderberg Group Steering Committee has 39 members (13 + 13 + 13) and it chooses its locations on

---

[14] "Black Magic Holds Sway Over a Paranoid Kremlin", *The European*, (May 11th–15th 1995) p4.

esoteric principles.[15] It is the same with the global institutions. Geneva, the home of the League of Nations and many other Global Elite fronts, is regarded by the secret societies as one of the planet's most important earth energy centres. You will find the numbers 13 and 33 in the symbols and logos of many institutions and companies named in this book. Francis Bacon's esoteric "code" number was 33 and it is used as code in the Shakespeare plays to indicate that Bacon was the real author (see the works of Manly P. Hall). The 33 represents the degrees in the Scottish Rite of Freemasonry. On the Great Seal of the United States and its depiction on the dollar note, you find 13 steps on the pyramid, the 13 degrees of the Illuminati. The pyramid has 33 stones. On the Great Seal the bald eagle (the phoenix until 1841) has 13 feathers on each wing, 13 arrows in the right talon and an olive branch with 13 leaves in the left. In his beak he has a scroll with the 13 letters of "E Pluribus Unum" – out of many, one. Around this are 13 stars in the shape of the Star of David. There is also a shield with 13 stripes which represent the original 13 states. On the United Nations logo, the map of the world is arranged in 33 segments within 13 ears of corn, and the UN building is sited over one of the most sacred springs (energy points) to the Native Americans. The Proctor and Gamble logo is an old masonic symbol with a bearded man in a circle alongside 13 stars. The combined Xs in the Rockefeller oil giant, Exxon (Esso), is another symbol of the Scottish Rite.[16] The symbolism is everywhere. The 'thinking' and the basic beliefs I have outlined from Nazi Germany are only a public manifestation of what is still going on in the secret world of the Elite today as they worship the All-Seeing Eye – the Luciferic Consciousness of the Fourth Dimension.

After the war, the Nazis moved their base to South America and the United States, at the invitation of the Nazi funder, Allen Dulles, and they helped him to form the Central Intelligence Agency, the CIA. This is a key part of today's global gestapo and the same black use of esoteric knowledge and the worship of the extraterrestrial 'gods' and 'supermen' remains at the core of the CIA and the Global Elite to this day. What was true of Hitler is true of the upper reaches of the Brotherhood network, even down to the appalling genetic experiments which have continued in the underground bases in the United States, (and other countries, too, no doubt, including the UK). We have this farce of a 'public debate' about the morality of genetic engineering while the most horrendous experimentation goes on in secret, I believe, using people (including children) who go 'missing'. After the first

---

[15] In 1965, for example, the Bilderbergers met alongside Lake Como in Italy, the ancient headquarters of the Order of Comocine, the forerunners of the Medieval Masons. I spent a lot of time at Lake Como in 1995 before later realising its esoteric significance. Among those attending the Bilderberg meeting at Lake Como in 1965 were Prince Philip and Lord Mountbatten of the British Royal Family.

[16] *Secret Societies*, p325.

edition of this book, a correspondent wrote to tell of an Argentine friend who said that Josef Mengele, the notorious Nazi geneticist, was set up with his own island after the war so that he could continue his sickening experimentation. The island is in a river delta in an area called Tigre, about 50 kilometres from Buenos Aires. Black use of esoteric knowledge under the guidance of the Prison Warder consciousness is at the peak of the Elite's human pyramid of global manipulation. I feel that people like Hitler were merely stooges, used to create conflict with other stooges like Stalin, and so bring about the desired post-war outcome. The Super Elite are well above the levels of people like Hitler and Stalin in the pyramid.

Given the background to the Nazi beliefs in the esoteric, the "Aryan supermen" and its possible connection with the stories of the Melchedekans, I was interested to come across an organisation called the Raëlian Foundation. It is based in Geneva, Switzerland, with branches around the world. This is the creation of a former French motor racing journalist called Claude Vorilhon Raël (rail) who claims to have met an extraterrestrial group which he says are the Elohim of the Old Testament. Raël says he was taken to their planet and he was told that the Elohim genetically engineered the human race. According to the stories told in the secret 1960s survey of contactees, the ones known as Elohim were the Melchedekans. Raël claims to be the "messiah" of the Elohim, the "Guide of Guides", and they instructed him, he says, to tell people that they must do everything he says. Oh really, Raël? My reply to the Elohim and to Claude would be unsuitable for a family audience. Raël (the messiah, Guide of Guides), says the Elohim are preparing to return to take over the world. Fascinating how close that is to the Nazi belief in the return of the supermen. And what was it that Raël says that the Elohim desire? A world government and currency; for the armies to stop fighting each other and come together as a world police force; and for only those scientifically assessed as the intellectually brightest to be allowed to run for political office. What's more, only those who pass an intellect test devised by scientists should be allowed to vote and the masses should simply do as they are told with no rights to decide who governs them.

I had never heard of Raël or his followers until I was told by a source close to the British intelligence network that some of those behind the campaign to discredit me as a "neo-Nazi" after the first edition of this book were connected with the Raël Foundation in the UK. That same day someone else gave me a book by Claude Raël called *The Message Given To Me By Extra-Terrestrials. They Took Me To Their Planet*.[17] The Raël Foundation appeared to be suddenly very shy about the symbol on the front of the book which Raël said was the symbol of the Elohim. A sticker with another

---

[17] Claude Vorilhon Raël, *The Message Given To Me By Extra-Terrestrials. They Took Me To Their Planet*, (AOM Corporation, Tokyo, Japan, 1986. Fifth printing, 1992).

The new sticker on the front of Raël's book

When the sticker was peeled off, this is the symbol that it was hiding

Temporary Sticker   **Swastika within Star of David**

Figure 12

symbol had been used to cover up the original one on the cover. You will perhaps appreciate why when you look at *Figure 12*. The esoteric knowledge and the themes of extraterrestrial master races pervade the Elite pyramid and have done for thousands of years right into the modern world.

But I cannot stress too powerfully that esoteric knowledge is neutral. It is not the knowledge we need to challenge, but its negative use. It can, and is, used to very positive effect. When I hear Christian investigators of the New World Order condemning all esoteric thinkers and groups as the 'evil occult' and 'Devil worshippers', it reveals a serious misunderstanding of reality, in my view, and a bigotry that ill becomes them. As I shall discuss in more detail towards the end of the book, the positive use of spiritual knowledge is crucial to building the better world we seek and which we *are* making a reality, have no fear. It is built on the foundations of love and respect, the emotions – the energies – which are sweeping away the blackness of hatred and misunderstanding.

In these last three chapters I have outlined the structure within which the manipulation is coordinated, the means through which the dark force controls it, and the mindset that motivates its behaviour. Now we can examine how this is expressed in the world around us and how it affects our lives every day.

Chapter 11

The debt scam

It is impossible to understand the global conspiracy unless we appreciate the background to the world money system. This is not taught in the schools and no smart-suited economist or correspondent on the television news will tell you the truth, either. Some of them don't know what is going on because they have been programmed to believe nonsense by the education system, while others simply don't want you to know. The foundations of the manipulation toward a world government, army, bank and currency are built on the fantastic con trick we call the banking system. Once people understand the way this works, it is easy to see how a few can control the lives of everyone else. It is worth repeating and expanding here on what I said in *Chapter 3*.

The banks are given the power to 'create' money, by which they mean 'creating' non-existent money known as credit. This costs them nothing, but the moment this credit is brought into theoretical existence the banks can start to charge interest on it. This is the system that controls everyone's life. But it goes further than that. When you take out a loan, the bank 'creates' credit for the size of the loan, say £20,000. If only in theory, that is 'new' money. But you are not going to pay back only £20,000, because you have to pay interest on that loan. The interest has not been 'created' by the bank, but it still has to be found from somewhere. So where? From the wealth and credit already circulating in the world.

In this way, since this crazy banking system began, the real wealth of the planet has been sucked into the banking system as the interest paid on every loan to every person, business, and government. This has allowed them to lend even more non-existent money on the back of that and get the world even deeper in debt. The wealth and credit-loaning capacity they have accumulated is beyond comprehension, far more than that of the United States, the richest country in the world. In fact, they *own* the United States, as they own almost every other country in the world. The bankers have used this wealth and credit mountain to buy and control the global oil companies, multinationals of every kind, the media, the armament companies, the drug companies, the politicians, the political 'advisors', and virtually everything else they need to control the world. The same few people and families own the lot! They hide this truth behind the front organisations, the nexus of companies, and the puppet directors, and they are supported in their desire for secrecy by the pathetic media and the education system. The Rockefellers and Rothschilds alone control a fantastic network of banks, oil companies, multinational corporations, airlines, and scores of other organisations. The Rockefeller/Rothschild Chase Manhattan Bank has enough power by *itself* to stimulate a global financial panic. In 1995 the Chase merged with Chemical Bank which had already absorbed Manufacturers Hanover. The concentration of power is incredible. But the true controllers of these empires are hidden from public view by frontmen, trusts, foundations, and companies. The Rockefellers' ability to hide the extent of their power is phenomenal. But with the Rothschilds it borders on genius. Particularly since the second World War, they have sought to promote an image of a declining power operating outside of the big league. Nonsense. They *are* the big league along with other elements of the Global Elite.

According to the New World Order researcher, Eustace Mullins,[1] the Rothschilds use the code 'City' and 'First City' in North America to indicate banks under their influence from the City of London. He says these include First City Properties, First City Financial Corporation of Vancouver, First City Trust of Edmonton, and First City Development Ltd, which are all headed by Samuel Belzberg. Much of the coordination is communicated through Rothschild Inc., of Rockefeller Plaza, New York, according to Mullins. The Rothschilds also operate through a Canadian company known as PowerCorp which in turn connects with the Hollinger Group, the Canadian publishing empire owned by the elite Bilderberger, Conrad Black. The Hollinger Group controls a stream of publications worldwide, including the London-based *Telegraph* newspapers, and its international advisors are Henry Kissinger and Lord Carrington, chairman of the Bilderberg Group, former British cabinet minister, and a cousin of the Rothschild family. (These two formed their own company, Kissinger Associates.) This covert interlinking of power in banking, politics, and the media allows the same few individuals to promote the same policy through a host of apparently unconnected institutions and organisations.

By controlling the creation of credit, the bankers can cause booms and busts, nationally and internationally, whenever they wish to further their ambitions. An economic depression is not caused by a collapse in the demand for goods and services. People do not decide that they no longer want jobs done or articles produced. An economic depression is caused when there are not enough pieces of paper and electronic 'money' in circulation to *pay* for those goods and services. And who controls the amount of money-credit in circulation? The banks. If they want to cause a depression for ulterior motives, as in pre-war Germany and the US, they take

[1] *The World Order, Our Secret Rulers*, p60–61.

measures which reduce the amount of money in circulation. They reduce the number of loans they make and raise interest rates.

This also reaps a colossal reward for the major (Global Elite) banks. People still have to pay the interest on loans taken out before the manufactured economic collapse and if they default, the banks take their property and increase by hundreds of thousands the number of farms, businesses, and homes they own. And with every payment of interest by those who continue to pay their loans during a depression, more money is being taken out of circulation and not recycled back into the economy, thus increasing the depression.

This process of reducing the money in circulation and causing a depression can be seen all the time. The economists and their poodles, the politicians and economic correspondents, call all this part of the 'economic cycle'. Baloney. In the 1930s that terrible depression, in which men, women, and children starved in a world of plenty, was caused by the banks withdrawing money from circulation by refusing loans. It wasn't that people didn't want to eat; they simply could not afford to buy the food because money had been artificially taken out of circulation. I will leave it to an 'insider' to sum up the situation I have described. Robert H. Hemphill, a credit manager at the Federal Reserve Bank in Atlanta, said:

> *"This is a staggering thought. We are completely dependent on the commercial banks. Someone has to borrow every dollar we have in circulation, cash or credit. If the banks create ample synthetic money we are prosperous, if not, we starve. We are absolutely without a permanent money system. When one gets a complete grasp of the picture, the tragic absurdity of our hopeless position is almost incredible, but there it is. It is the most important subject intelligent persons can investigate and reflect upon. It is so important that our present civilisation may collapse, unless it becomes widely understood and the defects remedied very soon."* [2]

There was no money, people were told, to build houses and feed the population. But suddenly, when it was time for the Global Elite's war, the money available to finance Hitler, Japan, and the war effort in the United States and Great Britain was limitless. People often say that there always seems to be money available to fight wars. Of course there is, because the bankers who control the world economic system *want* those wars. They do not want people well-housed with full bellies and a proper education because then they would be much harder to control. It was not the much-hyped 'New Deal' policies of Franklin Roosevelt which ended the 30s depression, it was the banks putting money back into circulation to finance the war they were creating. Here is a reality of life on Earth:

---

[2] Sheldon Emery, "Billions for the Bankers, Debts for the People" – a *Spotlight* newspaper reprint, (February 3rd 1986) p8. This article was a summary of Emery's book of the same name.

There is no need for anyone to be cold, hungry, homeless or in poverty. All these things are caused by the lack of pieces of paper and electronic numbers called money circulating in the world and by the charging of interest on them. We could change that today if the desire was there.

The world financial system and policies of boom and bust are controlled by just *thirteen* people – the members of the International Banking Commission in Geneva, Switzerland, which was set up by David Rockefeller on behalf of the Elite in 1972. The Commission is made up of two members each from the US Federal Reserve, the Bank of England, the central banks of Germany, France and Switzerland, and one member each from the Netherlands, Austria and Scandinavia. It has its own intelligence agency known as Four-I, the International Intelligence Information Institute. This banking Elite is controlled by families like the Rothschilds, Rockefellers (Rockenfelders), Bilts and Goldbergs. Connecting with the Commission is the Bank of International Settlements, also in Switzerland, the country at the centre of the Elite financial network. The BIS helps to coordinate the policies of the national central banks, like the United States Federal Reserve, the private banking cartel which decides the economic and interest rate policies of the United States, no matter what the puppet presidents and politicians think about it (*Figure 13 overleaf*). The 'Fed' does not have board membership of the BIS, but it is the coordination that goes on unofficially that matters. The Federal Reserve sends representatives to all its meetings and subscribes to the shares of the BIS.[3] Most people in America don't even realise the Federal Reserve is a private organisation. They think (a) the government would not be stupid or corrupt enough to allow a private banking cartel to run the country (wrong!) or (b) that the word 'Federal' means that it must be part of the government (equally wrong).

The term Federal is used for many Elite organisations in the US to give the illusion of government ownership. In the United Kingdom, we are sold the illusion that the Bank of England is nationalised and therefore under the control of the government. The Bank of England is one of the focal points of the Elite financial network. It was controlled by the Rothschild Empire when it was an officially private bank, and it has continued to be controlled by the Global Elite since it was nationalised by the post-war Labour Government and it became an *unofficial* private bank.

Significantly, the British Labour Party suggested in opposition that it would give the Bank of England, not the government, control over interest rates, and so mirror the Federal Reserve.[4] Within days of taking office, Labour Chancellor, Gordon Brown (Bil), did precisely that. Eddie George,

---

[3] Source: The United States Embassy, London.
[4] "Labour Hints At Bank Freedom", *The Times*, (May 18th 1995).

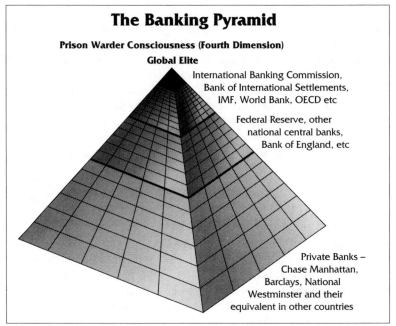

Figure 13

the Bank of England Governor, is a former executive of both the Elite-controlled Bank of International Settlements and the International Monetary Fund (IMF).

The whole house of cards, and the control of the human race, is based on the charging of interest on money. The subject of interest is crucial. There is nothing wrong with money if it is used only as a measure of exchange for goods and services. It is when you can charge interest on money, most of which doesn't physically exist, that enormous dangers arise. You can then make more money from manipulating pieces of paper and electronic numbers than you can from producing essential goods and services for people who need them. With the charging of interest, the money chases those who already have money and ignores those who have not. The cataclysmic social and financial divisions in the world are caused by the charging of interest on money. Production is geared to greed, not need, and the rich get richer and the poor, poorer. Often it is not the cost of a house that prevents people from buying a home, it is because we have to buy three or four for the right to live in one!

A mortgage leaflet put out by the National Westminster Bank tells me that if I take out a loan of £50,000, I will actually pay them back £152,000, the price of three houses to buy one. And on the front of the leaflet they have the nerve to claim: "The National Westminster Bank. We're here to make life easier". Imagine the transformation that would occur if people only had to repay the *capital* (with no interest) on their house over a period of 25 to 30 years. The cost of a mortgage and a basic human right (a home) would plummet immediately by two-thirds. The builders would still get paid because they are paid from the capital price. The suppliers of the materials would still get paid for the same reason. The only person who would not make the killing of today would be the banker who currently makes a fortune from every house purchase. Builders go out of business and people sleep in the streets to allow a few bankers to grow fatter and richer, and ever more powerful.

There is no reason whatsoever why a government cannot print its money interest-free and lend it interest-free to the people to buy a home, with perhaps a small one-time charge to cover administration costs. The only thing stopping this is the lack of will to do so by politicians of all parties controlled directly by the Elite or by its economic manipulation. Look at how taxation could be reduced dramatically, or even removed, if our governments – the people, in other words – were not paying back phenomenal sums in interest on money 'borrowed' from the banks. A friend in the financial business reckons that for every pound or dollar that exists as cash, another 30 *million* exists (or rather doesn't!) as electronic "credit". Pastor Sheldon Emery described this system of government debt-creation very well in his book, *Billions For The Bankers, Debts For The People*:

> *"The Federal Government, having spent more than it has taken from its citizens in taxes, needs, for the sake of illustration, $1 billion. Since it does not have the money, Congress has given away its authority to 'create' it, the Government must go to the 'creators' for the $1 billion. But the Federal Reserve, a private corporation, doesn't just give it away! The bankers are willing to deliver $1 billion in money or credit to the Federal Government in exchange for the Government's agreement to pay it back – with interest! So Congress authorises the Treasury Department to print $1 billion in US Bonds, which are then delivered to the Federal Reserve Bankers. The Federal Reserve then pays the cost of printing the $1 billion (about $1,000) and makes the exchange. The Government then uses the money to pay its obligations. What are the results of this fantastic transaction? Well, $1 billion in Government bills are paid all right, but the Government has now indebted the people to the bankers for $1 billion on which the people must pay interest! Tens of thousands of such transactions have taken place since 1913 [when the Federal Reserve was created] so that by the 1980s, the US Government is indebted to the bankers for over $1 trillion on which the people pay over $100 billion a year in interest alone with no hope of ever paying off the principal. [It is far more today]. Supposedly our children and following generations will pay forever and forever!*
>
> *You say, "This is terrible!" Yes, it is, but we have shown only part of the sordid story. Under this unholy system, those United States Bonds have now become 'assets' of the banks in the Reserve System which they then use as*

'reserves' to 'create' more 'credit' to lend. Current 'reserve' requirements allow them to use that $1 billion in bonds to 'create' as much as $15 billion in new 'credit' to lend to States, Municipalities, to individuals and businesses. Added to the original $1 billion, they could have $16 billion of 'created credit' out in loans paying them interest with their only cost being $1,000 for printing the original $1 billion! Since the US Congress has not issued Constitutional money since 1863, in order for the people to have money to carry on trade and commerce they are forced to borrow the 'created credit' of the Monopoly Bankers and pay them usury-interest!" [5]

The term 'constitutional money' is a reference to the United States Constitution, which says, "Congress shall have the power to coin money and regulate the value thereof." Unfortunately, either by accident or design, it does not say that Congress shall always coin money and regulate the value thereof, and that no-one else will ever do so. The consequences of this have been quite dreadful for America and the world: in 1910, the Federal debt was only $1 billion, or $12.40 per person. State and local debts were very small or non-existent; by 1920, just seven years after the Federal Reserve was launched, the US Government debt was $24 billion, $228 for every citizen; in 1960, the national debt was $284 billion or $1,575 per head; by 1981, the debt passed $1 trillion and has gone on soaring ever since. If the whole of the United States were handed to the bankers to pay back the debts, they would still be owed another two, maybe three Americas! [6] It was not without reason that Thomas Jefferson, one of the founding fathers, said:

"If the American people ever allow private banks to control the issue of their money, first by inflation and then by deflation, the banks, and the corporations that will grow up around ...[the banks]..., will deprive the people of their property until their children will wake up homeless on the continent their fathers conquered." [7]

In the United Kingdom, the government was paying £1 billion a year in interest on borrowing after the end of the 1960s. By 1993 it had soared to £24.5 billion. The government has borrowed to pay interest on previous loans while the capital has remained unrepaid. Contrast that £24.5 billion in interest payments with the £33 billion spent on health that year and the £11 billion awarded to education. [8] Don't complain about a lack of school books or crumbling buildings. The bankers have got to eat, you know.

[5] Sheldon Emery, *Billions For The Bankers, Debts For The People*, p2–3.
[6] Figures from *Billions For The Bankers, Debts For The People*.
[7] Ibid p1.
[8] Dr Kitty Little, submission to the Committee on Standards in Public Life, (January 1995) p15, paragraphs 53 and 54.

The creation of debt through interest charges also sets up the structure through which the takeover of the world by the few becomes possible. The bankers can accumulate and manipulate businesses by accepting, or refusing, loans. One regular takeover scenario is for the Elite bankers, in concert, to deny loans to a target business or multinational corporation. This depresses its value on the stock exchanges. At this point, with the price of the stock falling, the bankers buy large blocks of shares at bargain prices. The bankers then have a sudden change of heart and approve the loan, thus increasing the company's share value. The banks either sell the shares and make a handsome profit or they retain their increased control in the boardroom. When the banks gain control, what do they do? They ensure that the company borrows more and more from the banks until they are so much in debt that the banks own everything.

It is in this way that the same few people have come to own all the major businesses, the media, and so on. Once they owned the media, of course, it became easy to keep the truth from the people and feed us the lies that are necessary to mislead and confuse us. If you are a journalist or a bank employee, go and find a mirror and ask it some questions. Your children are going to face the consequences of the New World Order like everyone else's, unless you wake up. Nothing would improve the lives of people quicker than an end to the charging of interest on money and for governments to print their own money, interest free, or to make the banks pay interest to the government. President Abraham Lincoln began to do this with his so called 'greenbacks'. He was murdered soon afterwards by John Wilkes Booth, an alleged agent of the House of Rothschild, in 1865. President John F. Kennedy proposed to do it and some of his interest-free notes are still in circulation. He was murdered by the Elite in Dallas, Texas, in 1963.

Another money confidence trick is that of inflation. We are told that inflation is caused by too much money in circulation chasing too few goods. This is used to justify the removal of money from circulation, which leads to an economic 'depression'. This was a ruse used by the Volcker-Reagan-Thatcher trio in the early 1980s when the 'in' phrase was "squeezing inflation out of the system". How can inflation be caused by too much money chasing too few goods when in any boom or depression the shops are full of goods on the shelves left unsold? And if more goods are being sold and production is increased, why don't the so called economies of scale bring prices down? Greed is part of this, for sure, but there are actually too *many* goods chasing too *little* money in circulation. Interest on money massively inflates prices and it does so while ensuring that there is too little money to spend on goods.

Each time a bank creates a loan, it is creating more debt than the amount of the loan itself. Take the example of the £50,000 loan from the National Westminster Bank I mentioned earlier. The loan is worth £50,000, but the debt created at the same time is £102,000. To pay this back, the borrower has to find more money – double, in this case – than he has borrowed. The only way he can do this is to earn money that *someone else* has borrowed into existence. The debt of people and government explodes in this way, but there is still a scarcity of money to spend on goods because so much of the money in circulation is spent on servicing debt.

We are told in these circumstances that the supply of money in circulation must be reduced because prices are being inflated by too much money in the system. The main reason prices go up is because they are reflecting the amount of debt that has to be serviced. The more debt, the higher the prices throughout the system from material suppliers to transportation to advertising to shops. The cumulative effect of all this debt is reflected in the price of a product on the shelf. Whenever you buy anything, from a loaf of bread to a Rolls Royce, you are paying back someone else's debt to the banks. How do the economic 'experts' react to higher prices caused by the need to service debt? They raise interest rates to discourage more borrowing and reduce the amount of money in circulation. And what effect does that have? It creates more debt among those people already servicing loans and ensures that there is even less money to spend on goods. Whichever situation you have, there is never too much money chasing too few goods, except among certain products and commodities from time to time due to a host of other factors, including greed. Generally it is always the other way round, too little money for too many goods. The only difference in this situation during a boom or bust is that of degree. The end of charging interest on money will lower prices and transform the lives of everyone on the planet. So what are we waiting for?

THE GOLD MOUNTAIN

One point to emphasise is the extent of the wealth accumulated by the Elite through the debt-interest system, and by stealing the world's gold. A contact who has studied and worked within the global financial system, says that gold stolen by the Elite, from Russia after the war and from Japan, the USA and other sources, totals some $60 *trillion*. This, he says, is held at the Clouten precious metals depository near Zurich, and similar depositories at Umbrea near Geneva, in Vienna and at the Rhein – the main airbase in Frankfurt. During the war, he says, the Elite's gold was guarded by the US military at various locations and he claims to have proof of this.

THE MONEY POLICE

After the Second World War, with the nations of Europe devastated by conflict and debt to the Elite's bankers, the next stage in the global domination of money and credit was installed through groupings like the Organisation for Economic Cooperation and Development (OECD), the World Bank, the International Monetary Fund (IMF), and the General

Agreement on Tariffs and Trade (GATT). The World Bank, IMF, and GATT were all agreed upon by British and American negotiators at a conference in Bretton Woods, New Hampshire, in 1944. Most influential in these agreements were the economist, Lord Keynes, from Britain, and the US Treasury Secretary, Harry Dexter White (CFR), who, with Alger Hiss, the secretary general at the launch of the United Nations, would later be exposed as communist spies. The technical secretary at Bretton Woods was Virginius Frank Coe, an official of the US Treasury. He was appointed secretary of the new IMF until it was revealed in 1952 during congressional testimony that he was also a member of Dexter White's communist ring! These were the guys who created the IMF, World Bank, and GATT.

The role of the World Bank (not to be confused with a world *central* bank) is to make loans to governments for large capital projects. These have been used, as intended, to finance projects in poor countries designed to meet the needs of the multinationals. These include policies forcing people from the land, thus destroying self-sufficient lifestyles and creating dependency on the Elite's global economy. Much of the destruction of the rainforests has been done with loans from the World Bank, which, as we have seen, is always headed by appointees from the CFR, TC, Bil, establishment, and has eugenics as a key pillar of its policy. This subsidised environmental destruction has another plus for the Elite. It helps them to justify world control by the need to 'save the planet'.

A role of the World Bank and other global economic 'agencies' is to make a fortune for the multinational construction companies like the Bechtel Group. This is normally done by making loans to Third World countries for mega construction projects which are irrelevant, even disastrous, for the needs of the local people. In April 1995, President Bill Clinton successfully nominated James Wolfensohn[9] to be the new president of the World Bank. Wolfensohn, an Australian-born, naturalised American, has the perfect background for the post. In the 1960s, he worked for the J. Henry Schroder Bank in London and went on to serve on the Rockefellers' 'population control' organisation, the Population Council. Other Global Elite groups he has served include the Rockefeller Foundation, the Institute of Advanced Studies at Princeton, and the Brookings Institute. Add to that his position on the steering committee of the Bilderberg Group and his membership in the Council on Foreign Relations and Trilateral Commission, and you have the perfect man to head the Global Elite's World Bank. I'm sure none of this influenced Bill Clinton's 'decision' to nominate him! In 1992, Wolfensohn joined forces with Lord Rothschild to form J. Rothschild, Wolfensohn, a business advice consultancy. As chairman, they appointed Paul Volcker,[10] the former chairman of the Federal Reserve Board and leading member of the

[9] *Jewish Chronicle*, (April 17th 1995).
[10] *The Financial Times*, (March 3rd 1992).

Council on Foreign Relations, Trilateral Commission, and Bilderberg Group. Volcker was the man who launched the devastating economic policies in the United States and the UK in the 1980s which were fronted by Ronald Reagan and Margaret Thatcher.

The International Monetary Fund (IMF) is there to intervene when poor countries in Africa, Asia, and the rest of the developing world get into Elite-engineered financial trouble. The idea has been to encourage and bribe the politicians in these countries into relinquishing self-sufficiency in food and into opening up their lands to the multinational food and chocolate giants. These countries began to export luxury cash crops to the rich nations and to use that money to pay for imported food from those same rich countries. Also, the developing nations would export natural resources to the rich nations at knock-down prices and then buy back (at inflated prices) the luxury products the industrialised countries made with those natural resources. However, these luxury goods only go to the tiny, corrupt, political and economic clique in these developing countries. The majority of the population go hungry because the food-growing land is occupied by the multinational corporations. The Elite's policy was to submerge the poor countries in debt and take them over in the same way they had with the multinationals and the industrialised nations. When these governments find themselves in financial trouble and unable to meet their debt repayments, in goes the IMF to 'restructure' the repayments or offer more loans to pay the interest on the previous ones. But, in return for imposing more debt, the IMF insists that its (Elite) economic policies are followed. These involve cutting food, health, and education subsidies, and the exporting of more resources and cash crops. The IMF tells all the developing countries to do this and thus creates a glut on the world market for these commodities and the price collapses. More is exported at the expense of food-growing land for the poor, but no more is earned. The winners are the rich nations who get their resources and commodities cheaper. As a result you have the sight of hundreds of thousands of Brazilian children dying through hunger-related disease when Brazil is the second biggest *exporter* of food in the world. But what a wonderful form of eugenics and culling of the non-white population! A third of the Brazilian population lives below the poverty line and seven million abandoned children beg, steal, and sniff glue on the streets. This, in a country that should be among the most prosperous in the world, with no problem of feeding itself. Its problems are not natural. They are, like those throughout the Third World, manufactured for the benefit of the Elite. Don't be kidded by all this stuff about compassionate 'overseas aid'.

Every year vastly more wealth is transferred from poor countries to rich than goes the other way. We are bleeding them to death. And the overseas aid that is made available is not aimed at helping developing countries. It is used to bribe corrupt politicians, to build the infrastructure needed by the multinationals, or to subsidise industries in the rich countries, like Bechtel, who carry out the work as part of the aid deal. Another reality of life on Earth:

There is no need for starvation and horrific suffering in Africa, Asia and Latin America. It is not the result of 'natural disasters', but of coldly calculated design.

'FREE' TRADE

The GATT policy is there to create dependency on the world economic system by forcing countries to drop their barriers to trade. This concept of 'free trade' was advocated in the last century by the Scottish economist, Adam Smith, and it was designed, at least in part, to justify Britain's refusal to stop the exports of opium into China. Pressure for Adam Smith's – Elite-supported – view led to the repeal of the Corn Laws in May 1846, which removed protection for British agriculture from overseas imports. It was a disastrous policy, just as its architects (such as the Elite-controlled Bank of England and the Baring Brothers Merchant Bank) intended it to be. 'Free' trade has come a long way since then. GATT is now coordinated by the Elite's World Trade Organisation, based in its stronghold of Switzerland. It makes sense for the coordination of Elite banking and trade policies to be based in the same country, I suppose. Countries which add tariffs to imported goods to protect home producers are bad news for the New World Order. Such countries are far less dependent on the global system because they produce for themselves what their population needs. Trade in this sense is based on mutual benefit, not winner takes all.

In the early years of the United States, the government's main income was from tariffs. If goods were going to be imported, all the people should benefit, it was believed. GATT, the European Union, the North American Free Trade Area, and the new Asian-Pacific free trade area (APEC), are designed to destroy this protection and create dependency on the global system which the Elite control. Over recent years the momentum has increased to destroy the diversity of production in all countries and make them dependent on importing essential goods.

The British Conservative Governments of Margaret Thatcher and John Major played their part to perfection in this. The suicidal 'monetarism' of the Thatcher-Reagan years destroyed the diversity of home production while the wave of 'privatisations' in the UK and elsewhere has handed the power over essential services like water, electricity, and gas into Elite hands – often with big government subsidies, to boot. The consequences of this can now be seen by all but the most dedicated idiot. But the media promotes 'free trade' as a good thing and 'protectionism' as bad. They have bought the line sold to them by economists, politicians, and university lecturers, and they sell it to everyone else – the public.

I remember when the latest GATT agreement was being negotiated (the so called Uruguay Round), how the famous news presenters in Britain summoned their most concerned and ominous voices to announce to their nightly audience of millions that the negotiations had broken down. We should all be very worried, we were led to believe, because if the new GATT was not agreed upon, an economic nightmare would ensue. In truth, a nightmare for the Global Elite, not for the people. The Director General of GATT, Peter D. Sutherland (Bil, TC, Comm 300), was wheeled out to tell the world how important it was that the governments reached agreement.

Sutherland, a former member of the European Commission and chairman of the Elite-controlled Allied Irish Banks, was well briefed with the Bilderberg Group's views on the matter. He attended their meeting in Finland in June 1994, and again in Switzerland in 1995. Of course, in the end GATT was agreed and passed through Congress and parliaments by governments and 'oppositions' alike, because the overwhelming majority of politicians of all parties are either too naïve to see beyond the end of their noses (most of them) or they know what the game plan is (the relative few). The World Trade Organisation has the power to impose sanctions on countries which erect barriers to the flow of 'free' trade. The Elite must have gone into orgasm when this lot was agreed. What a tool to control the world!

'Free' trade is the freedom of the strong to exploit the weak. It is the means through which multinationals, subsidised by their governments via the overseas aid budgets and other hidden channels, operate 'cartelism' against the interests of the general population. It is the freedom to create dependency on a system which only the few control, and to use that dependency to manipulate at will. The freedom to move production from high wage industrialised countries to the sweat shops of the Third World, savagely exploiting the native population. The freedom to steal their food growing land and to destroy the industries and incomes of those in the developed world, also. In doing this, the Elite create anger, despair, and division, the perfect combination for manipulation. That, my friends, is the 'free' trade the economists, politicians, and news correspondents tell us we desperately need more of. The word in my head at this moment does not bear repeating.

THE SEVEN SISTERS OIL CARTEL

Working alongside the banks, and owned by the same people, are the oil companies. These are responsible for countless coups and conflicts and the grotesque manipulation of sovereign countries. As late as 1882, oil had little commercial value. It was used in lamps and not much more. William "Doc" Rockefeller also peddled oil at $25 a pint as a cure for warts, snake bites, cancer, and impotency.[11] In 1853 his son, John D. Rockefeller, formed the infamous Standard Oil Company to supply the fuel for the growth in oil

---

[11] Gary Allen, *The Rockefeller File*, p20.

burning lamps and to exploit the much greater potential claimed for the substance seeping through the rocks and fissures of the Earth. With the development of the internal combustion engine, the value of oil was transformed. So were the economy and politics of the world. The British Admiral, Lord Fisher, was one of the first to see the military significance of oil and later, as First Sea Lord, he led the debate on how to secure supplies for the British Navy in a country which, at that time, had no oil of its own. As usual, the answer was: If we don't have any, we'll take someone else's. An Australian engineer, geologist, and devout Christian called William Knox d'Arcy had found oil north of the Persian Gulf, in what is now Iran. He had bought the rights to exploit it from the Shah for $20,000 and agreed to pay a 16% royalty on sales. The contract granted him and all his "heirs, assigns, and friends" exclusive rights to Persian oil until 1961. The British Secret Service, on behalf of the government, dispatched the 'ace of spies', Sidney Reilly, to dupe d'Arcy into handing over his rights to the British. Reilly (real name, Sigmund Georgjevich Rosenblum from Odessa, Russia) posed as a priest and persuaded d'Arcy to sign over his exclusive rights to Persian oil to a 'Christian' organisation, the Anglo-Persian Oil Company. In early 1913, at the urging of Winston Churchill, Fisher's successor as First Sea Lord, the Asquith government secretly bought a controlling interest in Anglo-Persian Oil. We know this company better today as British Petroleum – BP. The wealth of this company is founded on the work of an agent of the British Secret Service, the notorious spy, Sidney Reilly, who lied to, and hoodwinked, a gullible man by manipulating his devout Christian beliefs. Given the behaviour of BP over the years, that is rather appropriate, really.

For years, the competition between oil companies and countries seeking to dominate world oil supplies, led to conflict throughout Europe and the Middle East. Britain was responsible for stimulating wars in the Balkans, Turkey, and Bulgaria before 1914 to disrupt and sabotage the building of Germany's 'Berlin to Baghdad' Railway, which threatened Britain's grip on the Middle East. The British used their control of Kuwait to prevent the completion of the railway from Baghdad to the Persian Gulf. Using force and corrupt sheikhs, the British Government ruthlessly seized control of Arab countries and their oil supplies. It was to set the scene for the conflict we have witnessed in the Middle East ever since, and the creation of the State of Israel was part of the divide and rule policy based on the control of oil. Can you understand why the Arabs today get so angry at what they see – quite rightly – as Western imperialism? They have had it up to here.

The other oil company controlled by the British government was Royal Dutch Shell,[12] outwardly run by the Dutch-born, Sir Henry Deterding

---

[12] Royal Dutch Shell is the amalgamation of Deterding's Royal Dutch Oil Company and the Shell Transport and Trading Co, owned by the shipping magnate, Marcus Samuel (Lord Bearsted).

(Comm 300), a naturalised Briton. In fact, it was controlled by a group of parties who voted on behalf of the British Government. The covert support and guidance of the British government turned Shell into a global company which challenged the Rockefeller's Standard Oil, even on its own ground in America. Deterding is another man often linked with the secret funding of Adolf Hitler and a future major shareholder of Shell Oil would be Prince Bernhard, a chairman and founder of the Bilderberg Group. In May 1933, Deterding entertained Hitler's representative, Alfred 'Protocols' Rosenberg, at his estate near Windsor Castle. Researcher Oswald Dutch claims that in 1931, Deterding and his backers (the Samuel family) gave Hitler £30,000,000. Eventually the 'oil wars' between the rival companies ended in the late 1920s with an agreement finalised at Achnacarry, Sir Henry Deterding's Scottish Castle. This created the Anglo-American oil cartel which became known as the Seven Sisters. The meeting between Deterding, John Cadman of Anglo-Persian Oil (BP), and Franklin D. Roosevelt's close friend, Walter Teagle, of the Rockefellers' Standard Oil (Exxon), was held secretly under the cover story of a grouse shoot. The Seven Sisters cartel has worked as one unit since then to control price and supplies to suit its sordid ambitions. The ultimate control is with the Elite. The Seven Sisters is comprised today of Shell, BP, Esso/Exxon (Standard Oil of New Jersey), Gulf, Mobil, Standard Oil of California (SOCAL), and Texaco. This virtual amalgamation of interests and policy mirrored to an extent the post-war banking mergers which created giants like the Rockefellers' Chase Manhattan, the amalgamation with the Kuhn Loeb (Rothschilds), Bank of Manhattan. The oil industry, too, was divided between the Rockefellers (Rockenfelders) and the Rothschilds.

Shell and BP were part of a power structure which included the British government, the Foreign Office, and the intelligence agencies. This remains so today. There are countless examples of this government/oil company/intelligence agency connection at work. In 1941, the British and the Russians invaded neutral Iran on the nonsensical pretext that a few German engineers were there. Controlling the oil supplies of Iran had nothing to do with it, naturally. The troops, backed up by smaller Indian and American forces, took over the country's food supplies, causing the deaths of tens of thousands of Iranians through starvation. Typhus and typhoid killed yet more, as did the use of the railway for shipping lend-lease supplies to Russia which stopped heating oil from reaching the Iranian people in the terrible winter of 1944–1945. These were the countries who sat in judgement of war crimes at Nuremberg.

In response to this, the Iranian nationalist leader, Dr Mohammed Mossadegh, became prime minister in April 1951. He instituted a policy of nationalising all oil production, with appropriate compensation to the foreign oil companies. The Iranian government also guaranteed supplies to Britain as before and the employment of British workers in Iran. The British

Government responded by imposing an economic stranglehold on Iran, freezing her assets held in British banks, introducing full sanctions and an embargo on Iranian oil. This was supported by other members of the Seven Sisters cartel. Mossadegh went to the United Nations to plead his case in 1953, but the Security Council, dominated by the US and Britain, did not want to know. He then went to Washington for help, but again got nowhere. The US sent a 'mediator' to Iran with a delegation full of people connected to the American oil companies. Who was this 'mediator'? It's that man again...W. Averell Harriman. His view was that Iran should accept the British position of Prime Minister Winston Churchill, his old friend. I never would have guessed that, would you?

While the British and American press assassinated Mossadegh's character and grossly misrepresented the situation, Iran did win its case, thanks to Mossadegh's eloquence at the World Court. But by now his downfall was well-advanced. Appeals for economic aid from the US were turned down by President Dwight Eisenhower (CFR) on the advice of his Secretary of State, John Foster Dulles (CFR), and his brother, the CIA chief, Allen Dulles (CFR). The Dulles brothers, in concert with British Intelligence, persuaded Eisenhower that Mossadegh had to be overthrown. Seventeen key members of the Eisenhower administration were members of the Council on Foreign Relations.

Norman Schwartzkopf senior, the father of 'Stormin' Norman' of Gulf War fame, had made many contacts in the Iranian army when he trained some of their generals during the war. He offered these people power if they overthrew Mossadegh. A coup, organised by British Intelligence and the CIA with the code-name, Operation AJAX, removed Mossadegh in August 1953. The Shah of Iran was installed as a puppet of Britain and the USA until he was, himself, removed by those same forces twenty-five years later and replaced by the Ayatollah Khomeini. This was part of the Elite's 'arc of crisis' policy in the Middle East, which has ensured the Arab nations have remained divided and ruled. The Shah reversed Mossadegh's policy and denationalised the Iranian oil industry. He and the CIA also established SAVAK, one of the most vicious intelligence agencies in the world. Its operatives were trained by the CIA and subjected their victims to sickening torture and imprisonment without trial. From about 1957 SAVAK began a close relationship with the Israeli/Global Elite intelligence arm, Mossad, which also trained SAVAK personnel. You thought Israel and Iran were different sides? Not at the top level they aren't.

Another brave man to take on the Seven Sisters cartel was Enrico Mattei, the leader of Italy's biggest non-communist resistance organisation in the Second World War. It was Mattei who coined the term Seven Sisters. He wanted a self-sufficient Italy which was independent of the Anglo-American oil cartel. As head of the State energy company, ENI, he established a network of petrol stations across Italy which rivalled those of Shell and Esso.

This expanded into refineries, a vast chemical plant, a tanker fleet, and an engineering subsidiary. He began negotiations with Egypt's Gamal Abdel Nasser and the Shah of Iran, to whom he offered 75% of all profits. Mattei was challenging the Seven Sisters monopoly like no-one had before and his competition forced down petrol prices in Italy by a quarter. The last straw for the Seven Sisters came in October 1960 when Mattei went to Moscow to negotiate a deal to access the massive oil fields of the Soviet Union. Two years later to the month, as the pipelines were being constructed to exploit the Soviet reserves, Enrico Mattei was killed when his private plane crashed on a flight from Sicily, the home of the Mafia, to Milan. Charges of deliberate sabotage continue to this day. The head of the CIA station in Rome, Thomas Karamessines, who would later help to organise the coup against the Chilean leader, Salvador Allende, left Italy immediately after the crash without explanation. The CIA chief at the time, the Knight of Malta, John McCone, owned more than $1 million worth of shares in Standard Oil of California, better known as Chevron. At the time of his death, Mattei was arranging to meet President Kennedy, who, according to some researchers, was pressuring the oil cartel to reach agreement with the Italians. A year later Kennedy himself was assassinated.

The oil companies, governments, intelligence agencies, the banks, the multinationals, the media: all of these are indivisible because all are owned or controlled by the same forces. The intelligence agencies work for the interests of the oil companies and vice versa. Sir Henry Deterding was known to have been connected with British Intelligence as was Weetman Pearson (later Lord Cowdray), who sold his Mexican Eagle oil interests to Deterding's Shell. Pearson (Comm 300) used the profits to establish the Pearson Trust, which owns *The Economist* magazine and the London *Financial Times*. It also holds a substantial share of the international merchant bank, Lazard Freres. *The Economist* was launched in 1843 to press for the abolition of the Corn Laws and the advent of 'free' trade.

THE OIL PRICE SHOCKS

The Elite coordinate a single overall policy through the many and various elements in the pyramid and nothing reveals more obviously how the banks, oil companies, and politicians work in concert than the oil price shocks of the 1970s. Part of the Bretton Woods Agreement of 1944 was to make the dollar the world's premier currency and link its value to gold. It was decided that $35 would equal an ounce of gold and that US gold could be redeemed for dollars. The United States government, however, found itself in serious trouble by the early 1970s, as so many dollars were exchanged for gold that US reserves couldn't cope. An American financier friend, who has many contacts at high levels in the States, says that since this time there has been little or no gold in Fort Knox, although this is obviously covered up. President Richard Nixon decided to suspend the policy of exchanging dollars for gold. This sent the world financial system (those who didn't know beforehand) into chaos. Nixon was acting on the advice of his chief Budget Advisor, George Shultz (CFR, TC, Bil, Comm 300 and later Kissinger Associates), Paul Volcker (CFR, TC, Bil, and future head of the Federal Reserve), and Jack F. Bennett, a future director of the Rockefellers' Exxon Oil. On Nixon's shoulder at this time was Henry Kissinger, of course. The other architects of Nixon's policy were the financial institutions and merchant banks in the City of London.

The 'City' is alive with Freemasonry and it is no coincidence that such a small country can have so much influence, via the City institutions, on the world economy. The Freemasons, and more particularly Illuminised Freemasonry, run the City and the UK Government, regardless of which party is nominally 'in power'. Among the main characters in the manipulation of Nixon at this time were the merchant bankers, Sir Siegmund Warburg, Edmond de Rothschild, and Jocelyn Hambro (Comm 300).[13] The dollar was revalued at $38 an ounce, but this was now only theoretical, because dollars could not be redeemed for gold. This created the so called Eurodollar market to handle the investment of the huge flow of dollars in Europe which once bought US gold. This Eurodollar market was based on London's financial centres which made colossal profits from their 'accidental' windfall. Lord Roll of Ipsden (then Sir Eric Roll), was one who exploited this situation to great effect and made vast sums for S.G. Warburg. Roll is a former chairman of the Bilderberg Group, a Trilateralist, a member of the Committee of 300, and a board member of Kissinger Associates.

The value of the US dollar plummeted as a result of these events, but delinking the dollar from its exchange for gold was only the first stage in the Elite strategy. In May 1973, the Bilderberg Group met on an island at Saltsjoebaden, Sweden, owned by the Swedish banking family, the Wallenbergs (Comm 300). Under the chairmanship of Prince Bernhard, the meeting brought together 84 leading financial and political manipulators. They included: Lord Roll of Ipsden from S.G. Warburg; Henry Kissinger; Robert O. Anderson, owner of Atlantic Richfield Oil; Sir Eric Drake, the chairman of BP; Sir Dennis Greenhill, a director of BP; Rene Granier de Lilliac, of French Petroleum; Gerrit A. Wagner, president of Royal Dutch Shell; Olof Palme (Comm 300), the later assassinated prime minister of Sweden; George Ball of Lehman Brothers; David Rockefeller of Chase Manhattan Bank; Zbigniew Brzezinski, director of the newly formed Trilateral Commission and future national security advisor to Jimmy Carter; Giovanni Agnelli, head of Fiat; Helmut Schmidt, the German Finance Minister; Otto Wolff von Amerongen of German Chambers of Commerce; and Baron Edmond de Rothschild. Also representing Britain were Denis

---

[13] F. William Engdahl, *A Century Of War*, (Dr Bottiger Verlags-GmbH, Germany, 1993) p147. A superb exposé of Anglo-American oil politics and its place in the New World Order.

Healey of the Labour Party and the Conservative, Reginald Maudling, another regular Bilderberger in the 1960s and '70s. The meeting was organised by Robert D. Murphy, who, as US Consul in Munich, sent back favourable reports about Adolf Hitler in the 1920s.[14]

At this meeting, a presentation was made that was to affect the entire world. Walter Levy, the US Government's official oil economist for the Marshall Plan after the war, announced a proposal to increase the price of oil by 400%.[15] Just five months later, in October 1973, came the 'Yom Kippur War'[16] when Egypt and Syria unsuccessfully invaded Israel. It was this excuse that the Arabs used to massively inflate the price of oil, cut production, and announce an oil embargo against the USA for supporting Israel. Yet again the world economy was thrown into a frenzy of pain and turmoil. In Britain, there was a three-day working week to preserve fuel stocks and millions lost their jobs and livelihoods throughout the world. The poor countries of the Third World were devastated, making them open to the next stage in the strategy – unrepayable debt. The architect of the Yom Kippur War was the US National Security Advisor and Secretary of State, Henry Kissinger. The 'shuttle diplomacy' for which he became famous and much revered was, in fact, a policy of misrepresenting each side's position to the others, thus making war inevitable. This is what Kissinger did via the Israeli Ambassador in Washington, Simcha Dinitz, and his diplomatic contacts in Egypt and Syria.[17] Look at the wars and terror that Kissinger has been responsible for and then remember this: in this same year, 1973, Kissinger was awarded the Nobel Peace Prize! There's nothing like a Nobel Peace Prize to hide what is really going on. Look at some of the other recipients and the timing. How do you win a Nobel Prize? Start a war secretly and then get the credit for stopping it. How appropriate that Alfred Bernhard Nobel, after whom the peace prize is named, made his fortune from the discovery of dynamite and the manufacture of explosives!

The Bilderberg Group had secured its enormous rise in the price of oil and so well had it been done, the manipulators also had someone else to blame for it – the Arab oil-producing countries. This is a vital ingredient in every Elite strategy. Make events happen, but find someone else to blame for them so that you, the 'innocent party', can step forward with the 'solutions' to the problems you have covertly created. All of this had been long planned. Look at the sequence of events: through 1972 and 1973 before the Yom Kippur War, the multinational oil companies in the US, like the

[14] *A Century Of War*, p150.
[15] Ibid p149.
[16] Before the previous Arab-Israeli war in 1967, there was considerable UFO activity over Israel and the Golan Heights. This is often reported in war zones before and during the conflict. See *Extra-Terrestrial Friends And Foes*, by George C. Andrews.
[17] *A Century Of War*, p150.

Rockefellers' Exxon, had been cutting back on the domestic supply of crude oil, reducing stocks to alarming levels in time for the Arab Oil embargo and soaring prices they knew were planned in late 1973. The oil companies were given a free hand to do this by Nixon on the advice of his aides, who included Henry Kissinger and George Shultz. In February 1973, Kissinger, Shultz, and John Ehrichman (who was implicated in Watergate) were appointed by Nixon as an 'energy triumvirate' and they effectively controlled US energy policy. Three months later came the Bilderberg meeting which agreed to the 400% oil price rise. Five months after that came the Yom Kippur War and the price rise and oil embargo on the USA. With domestic supplies so low, the US economy collapsed. All these events dovetailed perfectly.

We should not underestimate the role of Britain in this story. Diplomatic sources quoted in *A Century Of War* say that the British and Kissinger worked hand in hand in countless covert projects to manipulate events in other sovereign states. "The British, you know, were very clever" the sources said. "They were willing to let the Americans do the public dirty work and take the blame, while they worked very effectively on a more discreet level...(through)...Chatham House..."[18] And look at what Kissinger himself said in a speech to the Royal Institute of International Affairs at Chatham House on May 10th 1982. Speaking of the Anglo-American special relationship, he said:

> *"Our postwar diplomatic history is littered with Anglo-American 'arrangements' and 'understandings', sometimes on crucial issues never put into formal documents...The British were so matter of factly helpful that they became a participant in internal American deliberations to a degree probably never before practised between sovereign nations. In my period in office, the British played a seminal role in certain American bilateral negotiations...In my White House incarnation, then, I kept the British Foreign Office better informed and more closely engaged than I did the American State Department.*
>
> *"In my negotiations over Rhodesia, I worked from a British draft with British spelling even when I did not fully grasp the distinction between a working paper and a Cabinet-approved document. The practice of collaboration thrives to this day..."*[19]

---

[18] *A Century Of War*, p180–181.

[19] Henry A. Kissinger, *Reflections On A Partnership: British And American Attitudes To Postwar Foreign Policy*, (Royal Institute of International Affairs, Chatham House, London, May 10th 1982). In June 1995 Kissinger was given an 'honourary knighthood' by the Queen for "services to Anglo-American relations"! He became an Honourary Knight Commander in the Most Distinguished Order of St Michael and St George (KCMG) in a ceremony at Windsor Castle. The Honour was bestowed on the recommendation of the Foreign Secretary, Douglas Hurd (London *Daily Telegraph*, June 14th 1995).

The British Foreign Secretaries involved in the negotiations to pull the UK out of Rhodesia were David Owen, then of the Labour Party, and member of the Trilateral Commission a year after leaving office, and...Lord Carrington, now chairman of the Bilderberg Group, a Trilateralist, and founding board member of his close friend's company, Kissinger Associates. Another consequence worthy of note is that the leap in the price of oil suddenly made it far more financially viable to exploit the UK oil reserves in the North Sea by BP, Royal Dutch Shell, and others. In January 1974, Kissinger's reluctant puppet, The Shah of Iran, demanded and achieved another 100% increase in the price of oil by the Organisation of Oil Exporting Countries (OPEC). The 400% increase decided upon by the Bilderberg Group had been achieved.

THIRD WORLD DEBT

So what did the Elite bankers and oil companies gain from the oil price shocks? Money, power, and manufactured dependency for great swathes of humanity. The economic collapse allowed the banks to accumulate yet more land, businesses, people, and control, and their oil companies flourished. In 1974, the Rockefeller-owned Exxon replaced General Motors as the biggest American corporation. But the real motivation went well beyond that. Part of the deal behind the scenes with the Arab oil producers was that a large percentage of the billions of dollars the Arabs were receiving in extra revenue would be invested in the global Elite banks. The main recipients were Chase Manhattan, Citibank, Manufacturers Hanover Trust, Bank of America, Barclays, Lloyds, and Midland. They then set about 'investing' these enormous revenues in the poor countries of the world in Asia, Africa, and South America, who were forced to borrow to prevent starvation in the wake of the oil price shocks. The Rothschild-controlled Manufacturers Hanover Trust of New York, led the way in this.[20] Millions of men, women, and children suffered and died from this callously created depression.

These loans which caused the debt crisis of the 70s, 80s and 90s were the Bilderberg Group's 'petrodollar recycling' strategy at work. The deal with the Arabs was that oil would only be purchased in dollars, and that created another killing for the holders of dollars and Eurodollars in the USA and London. Kissinger ensured that the Saudi Arabians were well supervised. David Mulford, the head of the London eurodollar operations of White Weld and Company, was made director and senior investment advisor to the Saudi Arabian Monetary Agency, the country's central bank. In 1974, 70% of OPEC profits were invested in stocks, bonds, and land overseas. Sixty per cent of this ($57 billion) went to the financial institutions based in New York and London in one year alone.

---

[20] *A Century Of War*, p206.

But even these incredible sums were nothing compared with the figures the recipient banks were actually *lending* to the Third World. Banks are allowed to 'create' new money (non-existent credit) many times in excess of the wealth they have deposited in their vaults and on their computer screens. If they lent only ten times the money they received from the Arabs in one year, 1974, they would have loaned (and charged interest on) $570 billion. But thanks to a banking scam called fractional reserve lending, they could loan 26 times the funds they had on deposit and, in some cases, 66 times! This is the 'debt' that has caused such untold famine, poverty, and death in what we call the Third World. It is credit that does not, in reality, exist. A third fact of life on Planet Earth:

The so-called third world debt which is crucifying great swathes of our fellow humanity across Africa, Asia, and Latin America, causing unspeakable misery, is debt on money that has never, does not, and will never exist!

The banks sent out representatives in droves across the Third World, lending money like confetti and looking especially for corrupt and incompetent politicians who they knew would waste it. Why would they do that? Because it was the land and natural resources of these countries the Elite are after, and still are. They *want* them to default on their debts, that's the idea. The plan was to offer them a forgiveness of debt in return for rights over those countries' natural resources *for all time*. This is happening today and those leaders who refuse are being removed in 'people's revolutions' and assassinations. The non-existent money was lent to the Third World at flexible interest rates. If world interest rates went up, the repayments increased. So, lend them the money when interest rates are relatively low, and then hit them with the sting.

Enter Paul Volcker, Margaret Thatcher, and Ronald Reagan at exactly the right time during the 1980s to launch the madness called monetarism which sent interest rates, and so Third World debt, through the roof. This policy, decided by the Elite's International Banking Commission in Geneva, which swept across the world from London and Washington in the 1980s, began with the appointment by President Carter of Paul A. Volcker as head of the Federal Reserve Board. The President's right to appoint the chairman of the 'Fed' is another little ploy to kid the people that the Federal Reserve is part of the government. Carter was told to appoint Volcker by his puppeteer, David Rockefeller. Reagan said during his election campaign that he would replace Volcker. Reagan was elected, but Volcker stayed put. Volcker is a high ranking member of the CFR, the Trilateral Commission, and the Bilderberg Group. So is his successor, Alan Greenspan. You get the picture? Monetarism, the oil price shocks, the Yom Kippur War, and Third World debt are all interconnected and part of a coordinated Elite policy to take over the planet on behalf of the Prison Warders.

Across the world in the 1980s, the regulation of the stock markets, banks, and financial centres, was dismantled in the name of 'freedom'. The Elite's control of the world financial system reached new heights. Companies which had served the community for a hundred years and offered sound employment to thousands were taken over on borrowed money by manipulating the share price and then asset-stripped and destroyed. We heard the new wisdom of "You can't buck the markets" and "Set the people free". They forgot to add "...and hand them over to the Elite cartels". In the United States, Ronald Reagan deregulated the savings and loans system through the Garn-St Germain Act of 1982. This opened the doors for the funds of these businesses to be looted by the CIA, the Mafia, and other organised crime. One of them, the Silverado Bank Savings and Loan, was a CIA operation.[21] It crashed to the tune of billions of dollars which the American taxpayer is having to replace. On the board of Silverado Savings and Loan and its most prominent director, was Neil Bush, the son of George Bush (who had been at the forefront of deregulation).

This was the period of the yuppie, young people who could make hundreds of thousands of pounds and more in a week by guessing the future price of commodities desperately produced for export by the starving Third World. The effect in Africa, Asia, and Latin America, was beyond words. With each percentage rise in world interest rates, the repayments and the debts themselves soared. All this and more continues today. Yet despite all this suffering, the interest rate policies of the Elite and its political stooges, meant that at the end of each ever more desperate year, these countries owed more than they had owed twelve months before, without borrowing a single extra cent. Meantime, the Elite banks like Citicorp, the Rockefeller/ Rothschild Chase Manhattan, and the major British banks were reporting record profits.

The impression is given that all this debt was the result of stupid and corrupt politicians in these countries. Yes, there are stupid and corrupt politicians in the Third World, as there are in the House of Commons and the Congress, and the Elite are quick to seek them out and often promote them into positions of power. But many politicians in the Third World are neither corrupt, nor stupid. Their difficulty, once again, is that the banks, multinationals, intelligence agencies, the media, and governments, work as one entity to an agreed-upon policy. Because of compartmentalisation, most people involved in these organisations don't even realise that this is the case. In August 1976, the heads of 85 non-aligned countries (those not involved with the USA or USSR), met in Colombo, Sri Lanka, to discuss the mounting debt crisis. Their declaration called for a restructuring of the global economic system to remove the rigged, built in, subservience of

---

[21] Rodney Stich, *Defrauding America, A Pattern Of Related Scandals*, (Diablo Western Press Inc., Alamo, California, 1994) p176.

developing countries to the industrialised world. It also demanded a resolution to the debt crisis which was swamping these countries in hunger and disease. The United Nations did nothing. And one by one the leaders who signed and promoted the Colombo Declaration were removed from office. Frederick Wills, the representative from Guyana, was among them. He told the authors of *A Century Of War*:

> *"The only Third World raw material that did well in the economic arena was oil, but the large oil reserves were centred on the Middle East, and manipulation of inter-Arab and Arab-Israeli conflicts, together with inculcation of penchant for prestige projects meant that Third World oil reserves could not be used as factors in Third World development. One by one Third World countries were gripped by inflation and starvation, by low life-expectancy and high infant mortality. The Old Order of Canning, Castlereagh, Pitt, and Disraeli remains."* [22]

Note another reason for these policies. The culling of Third World, non-white people. Eugenics. The Castlereagh mentioned there was a nineteenth century British Foreign Minister who handed over Europe to the New World Order bankers, particularly the House of Rothschild, at the Congress of Vienna in 1815. A devout student of this man's methods was...Henry Kissinger. It was Kissinger who blackmailed and threatened other developed countries into ignoring the appeals from the Third World and it was he, too, who set in motion the events that would remove those leaders, among them Indira Gandhi in India. This was done, as in many other cases, by sending in the IMF to enforce policies of such austerity that the leader was blamed and thrown out. By now he had formed his own 'consultancy' called Kissinger Associates, the board members of which were Kissinger, Lord Carrington, Lord Roll of Ipsden, and Robert O. Anderson of Atlantic Richfield. All except Carrington attended the Bilderberg Group meeting in Sweden which agreed the 400% increase in the price of oil. IMF debt restructuring became the buzz words for increasing the debts without lending another dollar. As a result the people of the Third World continue to suffer and all the Live Aids in the world will not change that unless we address the cause – Elite exploitation with the aim of owning the planet and everything upon it, and the way the people of the Third World are programmed to expect and create that reality.

Charity events like Live Aid, Band Aid, and Comic Relief are wonderful in that they help to highlight the plight of the developing countries. But we need to be addressing the cause, so that such charities are no longer needed. Charities are a symbol of a global imbalance. They only exist because of that imbalance. It is not gifts of charity which the Third World needs as a first

---

[22] *A Century Of War*, p179.

priority, it is the dismantling of the system in which the rest of the world live off their backs and bleed them dry with the net *outflow* of funds and resources to the industrialised countries (read banks) every year. The greatest gift we can give those people is a new vision of what they can achieve and what life can be like if they are determined to grasp it and create that reality. If you were born in unthinkable poverty and despair and in an apparently hopeless situation, you, like everyone else, would believe that life will always be like that. A day-to-day struggle, just to survive. Such a mindset will create, and continue to attract, that reality. Breaking the spiral of despair is vital to the creation of another and positive reality. There are many ways this can be achieved, but giving people a belief in their own potential and how they can change their lives for the better is at the heart of any solution.

STEALING THE PLANET

Today we continue to see the next stage in the Elite/Third World debt strategy: to forgive or restructure the debt in return for land and resources. The environmental movement is playing a part, mostly unknowingly, in this. One of the initiatives supported by many in the environmental movement is known as 'debt for equity'. Under this proposal, the international debt of Third World countries is forgiven in return for handing over areas of wilderness and 'environmentally sensitive' lands. It is promoted as a system that wins both ways. The debts of poor countries are reduced and these wilderness and other lands are protected. Unfortunately, the green movement in general has a very poor record of looking behind the smokescreens thrown up by the New World Order crowd. Firstly, the scheme would not reduce debt; it would change the nature of it and steal the lands of these countries. And secondly, who is behind the idea? Ladies and gentlemen let's hear it for...David Rockefeller and Baron Edmond de Rothschild! One example of this was something called The World Conservation Bank (WCB), which was apparently initiated at the Fourth World Wilderness Conference, held on September 13th 1987 at Denver, Colorado, and continued over the following four days at the notorious Aspen Institute for Humanistic Studies. James Baker, the US Treasury Secretary and long time buddy of George Bush, made a speech in support of the World Conservation Bank. The official host of the World Wilderness Conference was George W. Hunt, an accountant and investment consultant, who had done some reading about world conspiracy 'theories'. This helped him to realise what was going on before the eyes of some genuine environmentalists who had no idea how they were being manipulated. An interview with George Hunt appeared in *Moneychanger* magazine in the United States. In that, he explained how the World Conservation Bank was being designed as a world central bank to create yet more debt in the Third World and steal the lands of the poor while trumpeting its success in reducing debt and 'saving the environment'. He said:

"...the banker Baron Edmond de Rothschild was at the meeting for six days. Edmond de Rothschild was personally conducting the monetary matters and creation of this World Conservation Bank, in the company of I. Michael Sweatman of the Royal Bank of Canada. Those two were like Siamese twins, and that's why I say that it appears they were running at least the money side of this conference and I would say the conference was primarily to get money. Also, David Rockefeller (of Chase Manhattan Bank) was there and gave a speech on Sunday..." [23]

The scam was to transfer the debts from the Third World countries to the World Conservation Bank and, in return, those countries would give land to the WCB. Should the WCB collapse or get into repayment difficulties on the debts, it would then owe its assets to the global bankers, who would be at liberty to seize the lands of the Third World. Alternatively, in the ever-gathering centralisation, there could be a 'takeover' of the WCB by the United Nations, thus giving control over the lands to this New World Order front. As the fact sheet published by the Secretariat of the Wilderness Conference said:

"...plans for the WCB propose that it act as an intermediary between certain developing countries and multilateral or private banks to transfer a specific debt to the WCB, thus substituting an existing 'doubtful debt' in the bank's books for a new loan to the WCB. In return for having been relieved of its debt obligation, the debtor country would transfer to the WCB natural resource assets of 'equivalent value'."

Problem-reaction-solution. If accepted, this would give the World Conservation Bank control over 30% of the Earth's land surface through this means alone, never mind all the rest that the Elite own. When George Hunt delivered a written protest to David Rockefeller via the 'great man's' bodyguard, Hunt says he received a warning from Rockefeller's office saying that: "I'd better stay out of politicking or I'd regret it."

Note also that while the manipulators are quite happy for loans from other countries to be, in effect, forgotten – 'retained in-country' for environmental projects – the loans from the Elite banks would not be forgotten. They would be transferred from the Third World Countries ('doubtful debts') to the World Conservation Bank, which would guarantee the repayments in money or Third World land. Another well known face at this conference which initiated the WCB was the Social Democrat Prime Minister of Norway, Gro Harlem Brundtland. This was appropriate because she recommended an organisation like the WCB in the UN-sponsored Brundtland Report on the environment called "Our Common Future".

---

[23] *Moneychanger* magazine, (December 1987, Memphis, Tennessee).

This was compiled in league with David Rockefeller's 'green' associates, Maurice Strong (Comm 300) and Jim MacNeill, two leading lights in the UN Commission on Environment and Development and the 1992 Earth Summit in Brazil. Same names, same agenda; on and on it goes. If it wasn't so tragic, it would be funny. In fact, some of it is anyway. In the *Moneychanger* article, George Hunt reported the contribution to the environmental debate made by Baron de Rothschild:

> *"He said innovation is the key to the pollution problem. We need growth and development. For instance, we have a CO_2 problem.* [Baron de Rothschild proposed] *that we create large dry ice machines that will absorb CO_2 from the atmosphere, and then take the dry ice that we create up to the polar ice cap to keep it from melting."*
>
> *Moneychanger interviewer: "Oh, come off it."*
>
> *"No, I'm not kidding. I said to myself, this guy has either lost his mind or...*
>
> *(Moneychanger interviewer in fits of uncontrollable laughter)*
>
> *"...or he is just laughing at us. Isn't that something? And by the way I've got the whole conference on tape."*

I tried to track down the World Conservation Bank in 1995 and no-one seemed to have heard of it. I rang Friends of the Earth, Greenpeace, and the British Government's Environment Department, and they all scratched their heads. I rang the United Nations Environment Agency and at first they acknowledged the name before returning to the phone to say that they, too, had never heard of it. Maybe it never got started or maybe it is working quietly out of the public eye, I don't know. I do hope the first one is the case. If you know what happened to the WCB, please let me know.

THE NUCLEAR POWER 'STING'

One effect of the oil price shocks which the Elite oil cartels had to suppress was the move to nuclear power. I have great reservations about nuclear power and I feel it is just a middle stage before we realise it is possible to harness the natural energies of Planet Earth to give us all the safe, non-polluting, warmth and power that we need. What is clear, however, is that there has been a well-organised campaign by the oil cartels to discredit and destroy nuclear power as a credible alternative to oil. What follows will provide more cause for reflection by the environmental movement, and give you another example of how the network of banking/oil-business/political interests work together to deceive and use people of genuine intent.

In December 1971, McGeorge Bundy (CFR, TC, Bil), the head of the Ford Foundation, arranged for the $4 million funding of a study called *A Time To Choose: America's Energy Future*. This made its report in 1974, amid the energy debate stimulated by Henry Kissinger's oil price hike. Bundy was Kissinger's former dean at Harvard University and his boss for a short time when Kissinger was a consultant to the National Security Council of John F. Kennedy. The Ford Foundation report pressed for 'alternative' energy sources like wind and solar power, and dismissed nuclear power. The oil cartel is quite happy with the conventional green 'alternatives' because they do not have the credibility to replace oil. They fear other alternatives, however, like nuclear power and, especially, the free energy technology which uses the Earth's energy field. This is why the latter has been so soundly suppressed.

The expansion of nuclear power was another reason for the environmental agenda which was being stimulated in this same period via the Club of Rome and other Elite fronts. Here again we meet one of the oilmen at that infamous Bilderberg Group meeting which agreed to the oil shocks, Robert O. Anderson, owner of the Atlantic Richfield Oil Company and a board member of Kissinger Associates. He channelled large sums through his Atlantic Richfield Foundation to organisations opposed to nuclear energy. One was to become a front-runner in the environmental movement: Friends of the Earth. It was set up with the help of a $200,000 dollar grant from Anderson.[24] He also donated to the Friends of the Earth campaigns against the German nuclear programme in the mid-to late-seventies by people like FoE leader, Holger Strohm. The CFR/Rockefeller-controlled Ford and Carnegie Foundations poured millions into the environmental campaigns and pressure groups, as did the Rockefeller Brothers Fund, the Rockefeller Foundation, the Rockefeller Family Fund, and the Rockefeller-connected Mellon Foundations (Gulf Oil).[25]

The French Friends of the Earth director, Brice LaLonde, was a partner in the Rockefeller law firm, Coudert Brothers, in Paris. LaLonde was appointed Environment Minister in 1989 by the Freemason, François Mitterand (Comm 300). Robert O. Anderson, the multimillionaire oilman, was chairman of his own creation, the Aspen Institute for Humanistic Studies. Where was most of the Wilderness Conference held which discussed the World Conservation Bank? ...the Aspen Institute. Anderson has used Aspen as part of his anti-nuclear power strategy and to highlight the environment as a global problem in need of a global – centralised – solution. Aspen is partly funded by the Rockefeller Brothers Fund. Some of the trustees of the Aspen Institute were Robert McNamara (CFR, TC, Bil and World Bank President), Richard Gardner (CFR,TC, Bil, Comm 300), Lord Bullock of Oxford University,

[24] *A Century Of War*, p159.
[25] Gary Allen, *The Rockefeller File*, p146–147.

Russell Paterson of Lehman Brothers, Kuhn, Loeb Inc., and oil executives of Exxon, Gulf, and Mobil. Anderson appointed Joseph Slater from the Ford Foundation as Aspen President. Here we had a close knit and cosy bunch of pro-oil, New World Order manipulators. Surely there would not be an environmentalist to be seen in such company!

But wait, who's this? There is a Maurice Strong named on the Aspen Institute Board. It couldn't possibly be the *same* Maurice Strong I mentioned earlier as the friend of David Rockefeller, could it? The Maurice Strong who was the first head of the UN Environment Agency and 'Mr Green' at the 1992 Earth Summit in Rio? The advisor to UN Secretary General, Kofi Annan? It surely could. Given that this 'environmentalist' is a Canadian oil man, he would have had a lot in common with his fellow directors.

Aspen financed an international network linked to the UN called the International Institute for Environment and Development and on its board were Anderson, Strong, McNamara, and Roy (Lord) Jenkins, from Britain, the Labour cabinet minister, founder of the Social Democratic Party, head of the European Commission, Bilderberger, member of the Trilateral Commission, and a president of the Royal Institute of International Affairs. Anderson's strategy was timed to be ready to attack the nuclear power industry when its credibility was at its peak – the period following the leap in oil prices. Atlantic Richfield and the Rockefellers funded the anti-nuclear 'green' lobby, including the World Wildlife Fund, chaired by the Bilderberg Group's Prince Bernhard, and later by Trilateralist and Rockefeller associate, John Loudon, an executive of the company of which Bernhard was a major shareholder, Royal Dutch Shell.

Today the WWF, now called the Worldwide Fund for Nature, is headed by Prince Philip (Bil), the environmentalist with a love of shooting birds from the sky. It is not only Prince Philip who can be seen to have a smoking gun in his hand. So can many who have shaped the environmental debate and the 'solutions' to Third World debt. It really is time for those in the green movement who genuinely care for the planet – the majority – to wake up and take another look at what they are involved in. There is one heck of a confidence trick going on.

Researcher, Dr Kitty Little, suggests another reason for the Elite's attack on nuclear power. Dr Little worked at the British Atomic Energy Establishment at Harwell between 1949 and 1958, and she has been a major contributor at the public inquiries into the nuclear power complexes at Windscale (Sellafield) and Hinkley Point. Her research and contacts over more than 50 years led her to believe that the French arm of the House of Rothschild is seeking to monopolise uranium and nuclear power technology, together with the technology for reprocessing spent fuel. Dr Little says they are planning to achieve this monopoly by the time gas and oil supplies are running out. In pursuit of this, they are using environmental concerns and political manoeuvring to destroy the coal industry and to stop the development of nuclear power and reprocessing by national governments. They want to hoard the rights to this know-how themselves for when the world is running out of energy. The privatisation of the British electricity industry was part of this strategy of controlling energy supplies, Dr Little says. Who privatised British electricity and helped to run down the coal industry? Lord Wakeham. Who did he work for after he left the government? N.M. Rothschild. Who advised the government on the privatisation of electricity, coal, and gas? N.M. Rothschild. Who advised the Hanson multinational in its efforts to acquire the privatised Eastern Electricity in August 1995? N.M. Rothschild. The alleged KGB spy Donald Maclean was, in fact, feeding geology reports to Guy Rothschild in France, detailing where resources had been located, including uranium. Maclean had access to these reports in his job at the Foreign Office. According to Dr Little, the Rothschilds now control 80% of world uranium supplies.[26]

I stress that I am not attacking Friends of the Earth, Greenpeace, and the environmental movement in general. They have done some good work overall. I am merely pointing out that they can, and are, used to promote the New World Order, mostly (though certainly not in every case) without their knowledge. Again the Elite are not 'pro' or 'anti' the environmental movement. They will use it when it suits their interests and undermine it when it doesn't. The British Friends of the Earth campaigns director, Andrew Lees, a man I met and had great respect for, was found dead in Madagascar in January 1995 where he was filming the site of a proposed two billion pound mine, a joint venture between a subsidiary of the London-based multinational, Rio Tinto Zinc (RTZ), and the Madagascar government. The official verdict of a 'heart attack' sounds very convenient and coincidental to me. When environmentalists can be duped into advancing the New World Order agenda, they are supported, congratulated, and patted on the head. When they are behaving in ways that oppose the plans of those in power, quite another approach is used towards them. So it is with all people and all subject areas.

When Pakistan's Prime Minister, Ali Bhutto, proposed an expansion of his country's nuclear power programme, he came under tremendous pressure from Henry Kissinger by August 1976 to drop the plan. Independent power supplies of whatever kind are not good for control and what the Elite fear more than anything is someone setting a good example that others will follow. What happened to Bhutto also fits in with Dr Little's contention about the monopoly of nuclear technology. According to some Pakistani sources, Kissinger said that unless the policy was changed he would "make a terrible example of Pakistan."[27] Bhutto still refused and by 1977 he was

---

[26] Submission to the Nolan Committee on Standards in Public Life, p37–38, paragraphs 130–134.
[27] *A Century Of War*, p182.

overthrown in a military coup led by General Zia Ul-Haq, who reversed Pakistan's policy of independence from the US Bhutto named Kissinger as the force behind the coup and, because he knew too much and was prepared to say it, the controlling world community sat on its hands while Bhutto was hanged. From his prison cell, Bhutto wrote:

> *"Dr Henry Kissinger, the Secretary of State for the United States, has a brilliant mind. He told me that I should not insult the intelligence of the United States by saying that Pakistan needed the Reprocessing Plant for her energy needs. In reply, I told him that I will not insult the intelligence of the United States by discussing the energy needs of Pakistan, but in the same token, he should not insult the sovereignty and self-respect of Pakistan by discussing the plant at all. I got the death sentence."* [28]

The list continues to mount. Even the campaign against nuclear power leads to the same people and the same agenda. And by the way, it was the Elite-puppet, General Zia Ul-Hag, who was used to trigger the war in Afghanistan.

WHAT NEXT?

What can we expect the banking-business manipulators to do from this point on? The Elite want the introduction of a world central bank that would run the planet as the Federal Reserve now runs America. All banks and money-flows would be controlled by the handful of people who would control the World Central Bank. The idea is to concentrate power into regional centres, as with the European Central Bank, and then fuse them together as one. The present World Bank and IMF would be absorbed into this centralised global financial dictatorship. In the same way, the proposed European currency is a stepping-stone to the planned one-world currency. The momentum towards this centralisation will be furthered by increasing pressure to allow the United Nations to levy taxation via tariffs on all air travel, cross-border trade, or other means, to give it an income independent of the sovereign states it is supposed to be serving. It can then fund its own empire and the world army, which is being created by fusing NATO with the UN 'peacekeeping' forces. The world army is designed to ensure that no nation refuses to concede to the global dictators. The manipulation is seeking to intertwine all economies and governments into a global system, from which even those who eventually see what is going on will find it very difficult to delink. You only have to read the newspapers and the Elite publications to see what is afoot. In 1984, Professor Richard N. Cooper (CFR, TC) said in the CFR's Foreign Affairs propaganda sheet that the world required a new monetary system:

---

[28] Benazir Bhutto, *Tochter Der Macht: Autobiographie*, (Droemer Knaur, Munich, 1989).

"...I suggest a radical alternative scheme for the next century; the creation of a common currency for all the industrial democracies [sic], with a common monetary policy and a joint Bank of Issue to determine that monetary policy. ...The key point is that monetary control – the issuance of currency and of reserve credit – would be in the hands of the new Bank of Issue, not in the hands of any national government. ...A single currency is possible only if there is in effect a single monetary policy, and a single authority issuing the currency and directing the monetary policy. How can independent states accomplish that? They need to turn over the determination of monetary policy to a supranational body." [29]

This has been the Global Elite's game plan for centuries. The manoeuvrings and the politic-speak can be observed every day. Look at what President Bill Clinton and the other heads of the elite Group of Seven (industrial nations), said in the summer of 1994. Under the headline "G7 reaches out for new order – UN and finance reforms urged", the London *Guardian* reported on July 11th:

"The West's leading industrial powers yesterday took the first tentative steps towards the creation of a post-Cold War economic and political order, calling for a fresh look at the Bretton Woods financial institutions and a revitalised United Nations...

"...At the initiation of President Clinton and with the support of President Mitterand, the Group of Seven pledged itself to a revamp of the International Monetary Fund, World Bank, and the G7 itself. The world needed new global economic institutions to 'ensure the future prosperity and security of our people', Saturday's communiqué said."

The global currency is not intended to be physical money. It will be entirely credit, figures on a computer screen. The plan is to replace all paper money and coins, and even credit cards, with a bar code inserted under the skin of every human being. This barcoding would be programmed with all the details about us, including our financial assets. You would go into a shop and pay for the goods by holding the bar code, probably in your wrist, over a beam at the check out. This will read the bar code, check that you have enough credit, and reprogramme your under-the-skin bank statement to remove the amount you have just spent.

This offers enormous potential for control. At present, if you go into a shop and the computer refuses your credit card, you can pay with cash. But what happens when cash no longer exists and the computer says no to your barcoding? You have no means to purchase anything. And, naturally, those who campaign against the (by then) global fascist/communist dictatorship,

---

[29] *Foreign Affairs* magazine, (Autumn 1984 edition).

will find that the computer doesn't want to know. Far fetched? Not in the least. The technology already exists and it is only a case of bouncing public opinion into accepting it. We will be told that this system will end all tax evasion (no 'readies' to avoid taxation), stop credit card fraud, and help to fight the 'war on drugs', a classic problem-reaction-solution scenario, because the Elite control the illegal drugs market. Credit cards are a stepping-stone to lead us along the road to barcoding and the end of cash, just as microchipped identity cards are also stepping-stones to the under-the-skin microchip which will connect us permanently to a central computer – if we don't wake up and stop it.

The day I completed a draft of this chapter, or thought I had, I went into the next room to read the newspaper. It was the London *Times* of January 6th 1995, and in there I found an article by writer Paul Penrose, headed "Will plastic smart cards be Europe's common currency?" All that I had been writing that day, and had outlined in *The Robots' Rebellion*, was there before me. The best banking brains of the European Union are designing the money of the future, the article said. It made the point that the introduction of the planned European currency would be very costly for governments and businesses with all the new notes and coins involved. So there was a problem. What could the solution be, one wonders expectantly? It couldn't just be..? Oh yes it could. I quote:

> "One novel solution is to phase out physical cash altogether. Under this scenario, electronic money [credit] loaded into a microchip embedded in a plastic card would become the symbolic common currency of a united Europe. In the Federal superstate of the next millennium, there may be no rustle of Euro-notes, no jingle of Euro-coins, just the battery operated blip of machine-readable data changing hands."

And, of course, something will be found to be less than perfect about this system once it is introduced and the cash has gone. The solution to this 'problem' will be the barcoded human being. What is clearly planned to hurry along the world central bank and one world currency is a global crash and currency chaos, using the tried and trusted methods. For that to work and the public mind to be conned, the Elite will need to find a scapegoat for the crash, so the bankers and politicians can appear over the horizon on their white horses to offer the solution.

An Englishman called Jonathan May, who worked in financial and oil circles for many years, realised what was going on and began to tell anyone who would listen. He tried to form a group of wealthy people who could construct an alternative money system to the one the Elite controlled. Threats were made on his life in England and he moved to America to continue his work. When he tried to introduce a non-interest credit system for Minnesota farmers struggling under a mountain of debt, it was crushed by the Federal Reserve. He was charged with fraud and jailed for 45 years.

May says that not only did he not commit the crime – no crime actually took place! May's view is that the oil price shocks of the 1970s and the tidal wave of petrodollars channelled from the Arabs, through the Elite banks, to the Third World, were part of the plan to crash the global economy at some future date. The Arab oil producers, especially Saudi Arabia, didn't realise what they were being used for, May says, nor that the global oil and banking cartels were owned by the same people. He believes the plan is to forgive the debt of the Third World countries when the time is suitable in return for the rights to their natural resources forever. This, says May, would mean the Arabs would lose their petrodollars held on deposit for a fixed term in the global banks (or rather, held by the companies created at arms' length from these banks to protect them from the consequences of such action). Arab nations would then have to raise cash flow by selling off enormous amounts of their shares, land holdings, property, and businesses throughout the United States and the industrialised world. This, May's scenario continues, would collapse the global economy and the 'greedy' Arabs would get the blame for it. The bankers and politicians of the Elite in the midst of the chaos and turmoil would step forward with the solution…the end of cash and a one world credit currency administered by a world central bank.

I don't know if that is precisely correct, but Jonathan May was obviously saying something the Elite didn't want the people to hear. I am sure the plan involves events similar to this in outcome, if not in detail. May also reveals that the whole confidence trick is made possible by the unique privileges enjoyed by the banking trusts set up by the original John D. Rockefeller. Such trusts have since become illegal, but the ones already created have been allowed to continue. May says that the ownership of these trusts was vested in thirteen long-established banking families, most of which will have been mentioned in this book.

THE FOOD BANK

Another aim of the Elite is to control the land and production of food at every level of the process. The natural crop seed varieties are being systematically destroyed and replaced by genetically-engineered seeds, which a handful of Elite-controlled multinational companies are patenting. Under Plant Breeder's Rights legislation, anyone using these seeds must pay a royalty to these companies or face a six-month jail sentence or fines of up to $250,000. This applies to anyone from a Western farmer to a poverty-stricken peasant in Bangladesh. The same 'patents' are being applied to all plants, animals, fungi, genes, and viruses, that have been genetically tampered with. The Uruguay Round of the GATT agreement has increased the hold that companies like Britain's ICI (supported by BP) and the US giants have over global seed varieties. This is giving them control over what we eat and even *if* we eat. This was the GATT agreement that the politicians, the media, and the big-name news presenters were telling us was so vital to our economic well-being!

The 'Green Revolution' of the 1960s and 70s which was sold as a means to feed the poor countries of the world was, in truth, a means to steal the natural plant varieties used there and replace them with hybrids dependent on chemical inputs which the same companies monopolise. The chemical inputs are killing the land and the body, in another form of population control. Control and dependency was the plan. The Rockefeller Foundation collected the seeds from 95% of the world's major cereal crops in the years leading up to the GATT Agreement and the Plant Breeder's Rights Bills. The multinationals are phasing out the varieties they do not have rights to and making the world dependent on those that they do. UN statistics estimate that 75% of genetic diversity in agricultural crops has been lost in this century and what is left is now in great danger. More than 1,500 varieties of vegetable seeds were withdrawn from use in England in the first few years after a national list of 'approved' species was established. The costs of registering seed varieties is so high that only the multinationals can do it and yet genetically-engineered varieties forced upon Third World countries are often useless in those environments. This adds to the hunger and debt. In India, a million farmers took to the streets when a US patent was awarded for the active genes of the neem tree, which has been used for centuries as a herbal remedy. No-one should own the patent to any seed or animal and especially not the mindset that controls the multinationals.

The farming policies of the European Community and those demanded by GATT have been designed to destroy the small and medium-sized farmer and allow the land and the market to be taken over almost entirely by the multinational corporations across the world. Over-production in agriculture, the butter 'mountains' and the wine 'lakes', has not been caused by stupidity. It has been calculated to destroy smaller farms. What is happening to the smaller farmers in the industrialised countries is only a continuation and expansion of the policies used to steal the land of the Third World farmers. Ninety per cent of the food trade on this planet is in the hands of five multinationals. Half of our supplies are controlled by two of them, the Anglo-Dutch giant, Unilever (controlled by Bilderberg group clones), and the Nestlé corporation in the Elite stronghold of Switzerland. Once again we see that 'free trade' is really cartelism, the means through which the vast destroy the small and get paid for doing so with public money. As John D. Rockefeller Jr once said: "Competition is a sin." [30] In the European Union it is estimated that the multinationals receive between 10 and 12 billion German marks every year, merely for transporting goods and raw materials across national borders to repackage them and give the goods a 'national

---

[30] Gary Allen, *The Rockefeller File*, p19.

image'. The biggest beneficiary is Unilever, which has close family ties to the Sainsbury Supermarket Empire. Unilever increased profits in one year by 25.6%, at the same time that farming incomes in Denmark dropped by 35.3% and in Germany by 27.5%. Such are the profits to be made for the corporations that even car companies like Volkswagen and Daimler Benz entered the cattle-breeding market, a business which has led to the destruction of enormous swathes of rainforest.

This all fits into the global plan for dependency and control of every aspect of our lives. They want us literally to be robots, programmed to do as we are told, and the banking/business system is the backbone of this strategy. As with the wars and conflicts, I hope you can see that there is no need for all the poverty and economic suffering that we can hardly bear to witness on our television screens. This doesn't have to happen. We *allow* it to happen. There is enough for everyone – enough food, enough warmth, enough for all we need for a good life – yes, even with the number of people currently occupying Planet Earth. The suffering and poverty are there by design to control us, to divide and rule, and to create the fear within us that if we don't conform and play the game by the rules of the Elite, we will end up in dire straits, also. Everyone for themselves. Winner takes all. It is a battle called survival, a battle to the death. The collective human mind has taken on those thought patterns and created this reality.

But remember, remember, remember. It doesn't have to be like this. This doesn't have to be the future. We are creating the future with every thought and act. If what we think and do changes, so will the future. If you summon your courage and get off your knees, we can leave our children a world that is truly, truly, free. There is nothing and no-one who can stop us, if enough people demand an end to this manipulation and are prepared to work unceasingly to that goal. No, not even the Global Elite.

Chapter 12

The hidden hand

"He who gains most advantage from a crime is the one most likely to have committed it."
The Roman playwright, Seneca

The covert force which is responsible for all those apparently unconnected economic events is also at large in the national and global political arena. The hidden hand of the Elite and its pyramid of deception can be shown to be behind a stream of officially unconnected political assassinations and scandals.

For instance, what apparent link can there be between the assassination of President John F. Kennedy in 1963, the Oklahoma bomb in 1995, the Vietnam War, and the drugs-for-arms operation during the Reagan-Bush administration in the 1980s, known as Iran-Contra? What could be the connection between the assassinations of Martin Luther King and Malcolm X, the Watergate scandal which brought down Richard Nixon, the Bay of Pigs invasion against Castro's Cuba in 1961 which did much to discredit John F. Kennedy, the removal of Margaret Thatcher as Prime Minister of the United Kingdom in 1990, and the suppression of information about the UFO phenomenon which has been identified since the war? The answer is the Elite and the cult of the All-Seeing Eye.

The same force has been behind all of these events and countless others which, on the surface and in the media, are not connected in any way. In this chapter, I'm going to show how these political assassinations and events were part of the same ongoing plan, which removes anyone who gets in the way, either by physical or character assassination. Understanding this is important because one method through which the human mind is diverted from seeing these connections is for each event to be promoted as a 'one-off'. This is done by the 'lone assassin/no conspiracy' approach. The same strategy is used when each national civil war and revolution is said to be confined only to that country, and not part of a world revolution instigating trouble across the planet toward a common end.

THE VIETNAM WAR

So many events and implications were triggered by the war in Vietnam. The United States embarked on that debacle, the public were told, to challenge

274

the spread of 'communism'. We have already seen that 'communism' was the creation of the same Elite who publicly promote 'capitalism'. There is, therefore, another reason behind a war that killed so many on both 'sides'. Retired Air Force Colonel L. Fletcher Prouty was chief of special operations for the Joint Chiefs of Staff during the Kennedy years and he was directly in charge of the global system providing military support for the covert activities of the CIA. He wrote a book called *The Secret Team* and in the film, *JFK*, the character Colonel X was apparently based on Prouty who advised the film-makers.[1] On April 13th 1995, Prouty talked on Radio Free America about the background to the Vietnam War. He said that on January 29th 1954, the CIA Director, Allen Dulles, secured approval during a meeting at the White House for the creation of an organisation called the Saigon Military Mission. The man selected to head this 'Mission' was the then Colonel Edward Lansdale, who had been working with the CIA to overthrow the government of the Philippine President, Ramon Magsaysay. The idea was to move Lansdale to Vietnam to do the same sort of work there. Vietnam at that time had been divided at the 17th parallel into North and South Vietnam by something called the Geneva Agreement. There were to be elections and either Ho Chi Minh in the North or Ngo Dinh Diem in the South would be elected to rule over all of the country. That was the theory, anyway.

The Elite wanted a war instead. This would provide massive profits for the banks and arms companies (the same people), help to destabilise American society, create divide and rule in the Far East, and provide a cover for an enormous trade in hard drugs. Prouty said that to create the appearance of an enemy to justify a war, the Saigon Military Mission (Allen Dulles and the CIA) embarked on "psychological warfare" – terrorism. They moved more than a million Vietnamese from the North to the South between 1954 and 1955. American Navy transports carried more than 657,000 of them and CIA airlines transported 300,000. Hundreds of thousands of others were persuaded to walk. These people had no food or money and they began to form into gangs of bandits to steal what they needed to survive. As this began to grow, the Americans who had purposely created the problem, dubbed these bandit gangs "insurgency movements" from the North and they were given the name the "Viet Cong". Thus the 'justification' had been created (problem-reaction-solution) for the Vietnam War.

Robert McNamara (CFR, TC, Bil), Kennedy's defense secretary at the time of Vietnam, and later head of the World Bank, has now publicly confessed that Vietnam was a war that should never have been fought. He said that it was a war that the United States could not win and never even tried to win. Indeed, he might have added that it was a war that was never officially declared. McNamara's middle name is "Strange" and it was an inspired choice

---

[1] There is more to know about the *JFK* film and Oliver Stone, as we shall see shortly.

given his immense record of manipulation. He was the man behind the jungle clearances using the notorious Agent Orange. Quite why he has chosen to 'reveal all' now is not clear. Both McNamara and Prouty agree that President Kennedy wanted to withdraw from Vietnam and end the war. Prouty says that Kennedy approved a document called *National Security Action Memorandum 263*. This said that all US soldiers and other personnel would be out of Vietnam by 1965. This followed a stream of meetings called by the president to discuss Vietnam, most of which are recorded in the Government Printing Office publication, *Foreign Relations Of The United States 1961–1963 (Volume IV): Vietnam* (August to December 1963). McNamara says that Kennedy also refused to endorse the introduction of US combat forces in Vietnam. The Elite, however, did not want the war over that quickly and after Kennedy was assassinated in 1963 there was no withdrawal. According to McNamara, the successor to Kennedy, Lyndon Johnson, released false reports about a North Vietnamese attack on US destroyers in the Gulf of Tonkin. No such attack took place, McNamara says, but thanks to the unquestioning reporting of this 'fact' by the media, it further "justifed" the escalation of the war.[2] Throughout the 1960s, employees of the Morgan banking empire were officials in the military arms of government.

On July 4th 1971, a group of young Americans gathered in Detroit, Michigan, to issue a formal indictment against a list of people they said were responsible for the carnage called Vietnam. The men they named were: William F. Buckley Jr; Daniel Ellsberg; Henry Kissinger; Henry Cabot Lodge; Robert McNamara; Andre Meyer; David Rockefeller; Nelson Rockefeller; Dean Rusk; Walt W. Rostow; and Maxwell D. Taylor. Those names abound with members of the Council on Foreign Relations and the Bilderberg Group. To tell the full truth, that list needs to be very much longer. Vietnam was just another engineered human catastrophe. It happened only because it was *made* to happen in pursuit of the New World Order. Yet if you recall, the boxer Muhammed Ali was jailed for the 'crime' of refusing to take part and American men are still looked down upon for "avoiding the draft" to Vietnam. Being someone else's cannon fodder makes you a 'man', does it? Others were treated like lepers when they came back from Vietnam because of the way American 'pride' had been damaged by failing to win. My God. My God.

JOHN F KENNEDY

President Kennedy's alleged 'lone assassin', Lee Harvey Oswald, was an asset of the CIA who was set up to take the blame. He was the 'patsy', as they say in America. Investigations by New Orleans District Attorney, Jim Garrison, showed that Oswald could not possibly have been responsible. Anyway, as the cine film taken by onlooker Abraham Zapruder proves, Kennedy was killed

[2] *The Spotlight*, (December 11th 1995) p3.

by shots from the front of the car, not the back where Oswald is supposed to have been shooting from a book depository.[3] The assassination was the work, not of one man, but of a highly trained and coordinated squad of professionals. Oswald, who realised he'd been set up and was prepared to say so in court, was taken through a public place where the nightclub owner Jack Ruby killed him. Ruby himself later died very conveniently or at least disappeared. The plan was complete. It was a lone assassin and the lone assassin was now dead. End of story. Long live President Johnson.

District Attorney Jim Garrison, the man featured in the film, *JFK*, is still the only person to have tried a suspect with the murder of the president. This was Clay Shaw. Garrison's case against Shaw was severely damaged by the intimidation and murder of his main witnesses and Shaw was found not guilty. Later it became known that Shaw had been working for the CIA all along. Shaw was also a director of Permindex, a Mossad front company which operated as an assassination bureau. Garrison established that witnesses to the assassination were threatened when they gave a version of events that did not match the official line. Many people who gave evidence to the Warren Commission which 'investigated' the assassination said that their statements were altered in the report and in some cases their signatures were forged on statements they did not make. There were so many obvious indications of official murder and official cover-up. Kennedy's body was rushed out of Dallas for a 'post mortem' in Washington, under military control. The pathologist was surrounded by officials while the examination took place and he was told what to find. The president's brain, the examination of which would have shown the direction of the bullets that killed him, went 'missing' and has never been found. Scores of other people who clearly knew something about the assassination went to an early death by car crash, shooting, or the Global Elite classic, the faked 'suicide'. The events in Dallas, Texas, on that tragic day, November 22nd 1963, were an Elite coup on the United States of America. It was so well done that very few even noticed that a coup had indeed taken place.

There has been endless speculation about who killed Kennedy. Was it the CIA? The Mafia? Who? As usual, much disinformation has been spread to confuse and divert, but when you look at the pyramid nature of the manipulation, it probably involved many different agencies who were controlled by the Elite. This way there could be coordination between elements within the CIA, the FBI, the organised crime syndicate, the Dallas police department, the military, the 'Justice' Department, the media, the

---

[3] When CBS News presenter, Dan Rather, saw the Zapruder film for the first time, he raced to the CBS studio to appear live on the news and announce to the nation that it confirmed the official view of events. In fact, it quite clearly does the opposite. Either Rather (CFR) was in urgent need of an optician or he had another agenda that had nothing to do with telling his viewers the truth.

incoming President Johnson, and many others. Freemasonry was certainly a thread in this, too. Near the site of the killing today is an obelisk monument to Freemasonry with the flame of Lucifer positioned on the top. Mossad and the CIA were the prime agencies involved, I believe, right down to the driver of Kennedy's car, agent William Greer. The basic training of all drivers in intelligence agencies and security firms all over the world is: If you hear shots, your right foot hits the floor, and you get the hell out of the area as fast as the car will move. Greer stopped! Maybe he was a reincarnation of the guy who drove the Archduke Ferdinand.

John and Bobby Kennedy were clearly bad news for the Elite for some reason, probably more than one. JFK's was a Bilderberg Group presidency, as Carter's was a Trilateral Commission administration. Kennedy, as far as I know, was not a Bilderberger, but many of his leading staff were. Dean Rusk, George W. Ball, McGeorge Bundy, Arthur Dean, Walter Roscow, George McGhee, Robert McNamara, and Paul Nitze were all Bilderbergers. His assistant secretary and undersecretary of state, was... Averell Harriman, one of the main architects of the Vietnam War. Kennedy had asked the Brown Brothers, Harriman partner, Robert Lovett, to give him a list of possible candidates for his Cabinet! He also accepted the advice of Nelson Rockefeller to appoint Dean Rusk as his secretary of state, a man he had never even met.[4] Rusk took leave of absence from his job as head of the Rockefeller Foundation, to accept the job. Kennedy (CFR) also 'chose' Douglas Dillon (CFR) to be secretary of the treasury. Dillon was a trustee of the Rockefeller Brothers Fund. Rockefeller-connected place men have also held the treasury post under Eisenhower, Johnson, and probably every other president of modern times.

It is worth looking at the Kennedy assassination in some detail because it offers a superb example of the methods used by the Elite and the extent of their influence on events. I am indebted in parts of this section to the brilliant book by Michael Collins Piper called *Final Judgement, The Missing Link In The JFK Assassination Conspiracy.* John F. Kennedy was the son of Joseph P. Kennedy, the US Ambassador to London at the time that Tyler Kent was being jailed for revealing the shocking pre-war cables between Roosevelt and Churchill. Joe Kennedy was a sinister character who operated in the criminal underworld and made a fortune out of running booze during the prohibition era. He apparently had no love for Jewish people to say the least and he became a bitter enemy of Meyer Lansky, the head of the Organised Crime Syndicate. There were two main groups within organised crime, La Cosa Nostra, better known as the Italian Mafia, and the Jewish operation dubbed the "Kosher Nostra". Lansky led the latter and, contrary to popular myth and media stories, it was he, not the Italians, who was the "boss of bosses" in organised crime. Joe Kennedy's bitter relationship with

---

[4] *The Rockefeller File,* p157.

Lansky worsened still further, it would appear, after Lansky's men highjacked one of Kennedy's consignments of bootleg whisky from Ireland.[5] According to the family of Chicago Mafia boss, Sam Giancana, the "Jewish Mafia" in Detroit, the so called Purple Gang, issued a contract on Joe Kennedy's life for operating his liquor activities through their territory. Kennedy, the Giancanas' say, went to Chicago to plead for his life with the Mafia bosses and their influence saved him.[6] This was the background from whence emerged John F. Kennedy, the 35th president of the United States.

When JFK turned his eyes to the presidency he had a number of hurdles to overcome, especially the Kennedys' deep animosity with the Jewish lobby in the US and the Meyer Lansky Crime Syndicate. Kennedy needed the money and support of both the Jewish lobby and organised crime if he was to have any chance of winning. In 1957, he further enraged Israel (the Rothschilds/Global Elite) and its massive network in the US when, as a young senator, he supported the demands by Algeria for independence from France. Israel bitterly opposed this. But father Joe Kennedy decided to swallow his pride and put aside his feelings to make sure his son became president. According to DeWest Hooker, a New York entertainment executive, he once approached Joe Kennedy with a business proposal to set up a television network independent of Jewish money and control. Hooker says of the meeting:

> *"Joe admitted that when he was ambassador to England that he had been pro-Hitler. However, in Kennedy's words, 'we' lost the war. By 'we' he didn't mean the United States. When Kennedy said 'we', he meant the non Jews. Joe Kennedy believed that it was the Jews who had won World War II.*
>
> *"Kennedy said: 'I've done everything I can to fight the Jewish power over this country. I tried to stop World War II, but I failed. I've made all the money I need and now I'm passing everything I've learned to my sons'.*
>
> *"I don't go with the 'loser', Kennedy told me. 'I've joined the "winners." I'm going to work with the Jews. I'm teaching my boys the whole score and they're going to work with the Jews. I'm going to make Jack the first Irish Catholic President of the United States and if it means working with the Jews, so be it. I have sympathy with what you're doing Hooker', Kennedy said 'but I'm not going to do anything that will ruin Jack's chances to become president'."* [7]

Events certainly support Hooker's claims. Joe Kennedy arranged for planted 'news' stories to appear claiming Nazi support for his son's opponent, Richard

[5] Michael Collin Piper, *Final Judgement, The Missing Link In The JFK Assassination Conspiracy*, (The Wolfe Press, Washington D.C., 1995) p32.

[6] Sam and Chuck Giancana, *Double Cross: The Explosive Inside Story Of The Mobster Who Controlled America*, (Warner Books, New York, 1992) p75.

[7] Interview with Michael Piper Collins on January 20th 1992 for *Final Judgement*.

Nixon, and JFK began a series of meetings with the Jewish lobby, particularly Abraham Feinberg, the president of the Israel Bond Organization who, unbeknown to Kennedy at the time, was raising private money for Israel's secret nuclear programme headed by Victor Rothschild.[8] Kennedy assured him that he would be good for Israel and the US Jewish lobby. Feinberg said of Kennedy: "My path to power was cooperation in terms of what they needed – campaign money".[9] Feinberg apparently produced a donation of $500,000 from Jewish sources. Privately, however, Kennedy was appalled at what he was seeing. The newspaper columnist, Charles L. Bartlett, said that Kennedy, a close friend, had driven over to see him after the meeting with Feinberg and company. Bartlett said: "As an American citizen he was outraged to have a Zionist Group come to him and say: "We know your campaign is in trouble. We're willing to pay your bills if you'll let us have control of your Middle East policy".[10]

Bartlett said Kennedy had pledged that if he became president he would end the power of special interest groups, particularly foreign ones, to dictate the outcome of election campaigns and foreign policy through their financial and political manipulation. In the meantime he had clearly decided that he needed their money to win power in the first place, as he did with Meyer Lansky and the Mafia. Joe Kennedy went back to Sam Giancana of the Chicago Mafia, who saved his life when the Jewish mobsters put a contract on him. Giancana's family say that Father Kennedy begged Giancana to support his son in the election and agreed a deal. When Giancana said he was not convinced that Kennedy could offer him anything for his help, father Kennedy is said to have replied:

> "I can. And I will. You help me now, Sam, and I'll see to it that Chicago – that you – can sit in the goddamned Oval Office if you want. That you'll have the president's ear. But I just need time…My son, the President of the United States, will owe you his father's life. He won't refuse you ever. You have my word." [11]

JFK, meanwhile, was making his own deals with the mobsters. FBI phone taps and documents reveal that John "Jack" Kennedy had "direct contact" with Meyer Lansky during the 1960 presidential campaign.[12] So here we had a situation in which the Kennedys' had agreed pacts with the Israeli lobby

---

[8] *Final Judgement*, p35.
[9] Quoted by Seymour M. Hersh, *The Samson Option: Israel's Nuclear Arsenal And American Foreign Policy*, (Random House, New York, 1991) p94.
[10] Ibid p97.
[11] *Double Cross: The Explosive Inside Story Of The Mobster Who Controlled America*, p230.
[12] C. David Heymann, *A Woman Named Jackie*, (New American Library, New York, 1989) p151.

(Israel and the Rothschilds in effect) and organised crime. In return the Israelis/Rothschilds wanted control of President Kennedy's Middle East policy and the mob wanted to be left alone to operate their international crime syndicate, headed by Meyer Lansky, without interference from the government law enforcement agencies. They were in for a shock on both counts. Kennedy double crossed them and they were beside themselves with rage and resentment. Both would be involved in Kennedy's assassination.

As Michael Collins Piper reveals so superbly in his book, *Final Judgement*, there are key elements to the Kennedy story that have been suppressed because of where that knowledge would lead – Israel. Kennedy won the 1960 election by just 100,000 votes, the smallest margin in American history, a confirmation of how crucial the financial and political support from the Israeli lobby and organised crime turned out to be. But JFK had no intention, it would seem, of giving them what they paid for. Quite the opposite. Almost from his inauguration, Kennedy waged a secret war with Israel and it's prime minister, David Ben-Gurion, over American policy in the Middle East and Israel's nuclear weapons programme.[13] Kennedy decided on a "no favourites" policy in the Middle East to ensure American influence in all those countries and he was horrified when he heard of Israel's development of a nuclear bomb. Ben-Gurion denied his country had such a programme, but as history has shown, he was lying. Abraham Feinberg, who arranged for Kennedy's election funding from the Israeli lobby, told the president that his demands for inspections of Israel's nuclear plant at Dimona, could "result in less support in the 1964 presidential election".[14] In 1962 and '63, Kennedy also introduced a total of seven bills to Congress to reform the laws over campaign financing by special interest groups. All of them were crushed by the lobbying of those same groups. Kennedy was becoming seriously unpopular with the thugs and terrorists who controlled, and control, Israel at the expense of Jewish people as a whole.

Kennedy further increased the tension with his support for a just solution to the problem of Palestinian refugees displaced by Israel. He pressured Israel at the United Nations to conform to a UN resolution demanding justice for the refugees, but Israel's foreign minister, Golda Meir (a later prime minister) described her "astonishment and anger" at Kennedy's policy. All this added massively to the hostility with Ben-Gurion and, on the Israeli's part at least, the animosity developed into a fierce hatred of Kennedy. On June 16th 1963 Ben-Gurion resigned as prime minister and defence minister. While other official reasons were offered for his decision, behind the scenes he believed that Kennedy's even-handed policy in the Middle East threatened the very existence of his beloved Israel. He could not change Kennedy's mind and so he wished someone else to try. In one of his last exchanges with Kennedy, he

---

[13] *Final Judgement*, p46.
[14] *The Samson Option: Israel's Nuclear Arsenal and American Foreign Policy*, p108.

said: "Mr. President, my people have a right to exist…and that existence is in danger".[15] According to the research of Michael Collins Piper in *Final Judgement*:

> "…in his final days as prime minster, (Ben-Gurion) ordered Israel's Mossad to orchestrate the assassination of John F. Kennedy. Based upon additional evidence uncovered, we believe that Mossad took the necessary steps and achieved that goal." [16]

Mossad certainly had many close connections with others who wished to see an end to Kennedy, especially the CIA and Meyer Lansky. Kennedy had both of those in his sights also. While Kennedy had accepted campaign money from Lansky and the Mafia, he really wanted to destroy them. Once in office he appointed his brother Bobby as attorney general and he began a massive drive against the organised crime syndicate. Lansky and the Mafia were outraged at what they saw as a double cross. With his close ties to the CIA and Mossad, Lansky had previously been untouchable, but now he and his international operation were under threat. Kennedy also realised that the CIA was out of control and operating its own agenda. It had set him up for tremendous criticism in the Bay of Pigs disaster, the failed attempt to remove Castro from Cuba. Lansky's crime network was also involved in that because their casino and prostitution rackets in Cuba were destroyed by the arrival of Castro. Kennedy sacked Allen Dulles, the head of the CIA and funder of Adolf Hitler, and pledged to "splinter the CIA in a thousand pieces and scatter it to the winds".[17] The CIA, like Lansky and the Israeli lobby, knew that the survival of their power structure was threatened by John and Bobby Kennedy. Any one of these groups had the power and organisation to have Kennedy removed and here he was taking on all three.

More than that, he had decided to withdraw the United States from the Vietnam War, much to the dismay of Lansky, Mossad, and the CIA who were using the conflict as a cover for their drug running operations in South East Asia, and to Israel who believed that while the attention of the US was concentrated on Vietnam, it could not keep a close eye on what was happening in the Middle East. The arms manufacturers and global banks also wanted the war to continue, of course. And there was yet another reason why Kennedy was deeply unpopular with the Global Elite as his presidential policies became clear. He wished to destroy the power of the Federal Reserve Board by issuing interest-free money. In fact he had already made a start with that before his death and some of his interest-free notes are still in circulation today. This was the Elite's worst nightmare.

[15] Dan Kurzman, *Ben-Gurion: Prophet Of Fire*, (Simon and Schuster, New York, 1983) p 121.
[16] *Final Judgement*, p57.
[17] Mark Lane, *Plausible Denial*, (Thunder's Mouth Press, New York, 1992) p93.

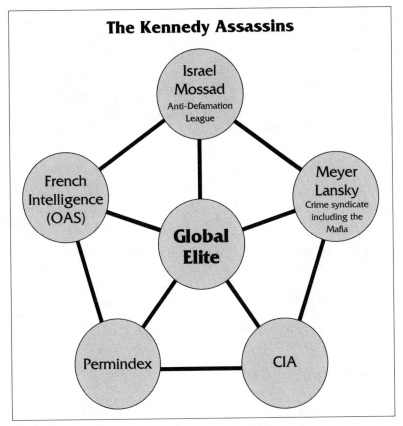

Figure 14

The last president to issue interest-free money had been Abraham Lincoln and look what happened to him. The forces ranged against Kennedy by 1963 were simply enormous. Indeed, when you look behind the façades, they were all the *same* organisation controlled by the few. This will become clear as we look at the organisations working together to assassinate John F. Kennedy (*Figure 14*).

ISRAEL, MOSSAD, AND THE ANTI-DEFAMATION LEAGUE

Israel is not a home for Jewish people. Let us not mince words here. The time for pussyfooting around is over. Israel is a base for the terrorists who created and control that state to operate, on behalf of the House of Rothschild and the Elite, a global terror and manipulation network. That is why it was created after the war and the influence of its intelligence arm, Mossad, is so vast for such a tiny country because Mossad is really the intelligence agency of the Rothschild-Rockefeller-Global Elite, while genuine Jewish people who live in Israel (the vast, vast majority) are used as an innocent front, a smokescreen, for this. So, too, is the suffering of Jews in Nazi Germany which resulted from the manipulating of the Nazis into power by, among others, 'Jewish' financial and political forces. The way Jewish people have been stitched up is astonishing. It is no good some writers condemning the whole thing as a Jewish plot. It is not. The mass of Jewish people are victims, not perpetrators of the events I describe. It is those who control Israel who are among those behind the plot, not Jewish people, as at least some brave rabbis and other Jews have had the guts to point out.

Mossad, like the State of Israel itself, was created by groups such as the Stern Gang and others, which terrorised Palestine out of existence after the war, under the financial and political direction of the House of Rothschild. Lord Victor Rothschild, the former British intelligence officer and KGB spy, was at the forefront of this. According to Simon Schama's book, *Two Rothschilds And The Land Of Israel* (Collins, London, 1978), the House of Rothschild had acquired 80% of the land of Israel. They also paid the expenses of the early settlers, manipulated into being the 1917 Balfour Declaration which recognised Israel as a Jewish homeland, funded the Nazis and created Mossad and the terrorist underground in Palestine. Israel was founded by, and has always been controlled by, the Rothschilds and the rest of the Elite. The "Jewish homeland" scam is just a smokescreen and Jewish people are pawns in the game. The leaders and participants in this terror network later became leaders and prime ministers of the new Israel. People like David Ben-Gurion, Menachem Begin, Yitzhak Rabin, and Yitzhak Shamir, the head of the Mossad assassination squad at the time of Kennedy's murder. The Anti-Defamation League is a Mossad (Rothschild) front in the United States and further afield. As we have seen, it evolved from an organisation set up before the First World War to brand as "anti-Semitic" the New York police commissioner who was determined to destroy the mobsters. To this day the Anti-Defamation League (ADL) works, mostly covertly, to condemn as "anti-Semitic" anyone getting close to the truth. The former Mossad agent, Victor Ostrovsky, has confirmed all this in his books, *By Way Of Deception* and *The Other Side Of Deception*, which massively expose the extent of Mossad's world-wide operations and what he calls the "Judeo-Nazis" who control Israel and the Mossad. The ADL has tremendous influence, even control, of the mainstream media via other parts of the Elite network. As with Mossad, it prefers to use other people and organisations as fronts for its activities, so no-one knows where the motivation for stories, attacks, and assassinations is really coming from. Mossad ("The Institution for Intelligence and Special Tasks") has a genius for diverting attention from its own responsibility by producing "patsies" to take the blame – "false flags" as they are called in intelligence parlance. The ADL, which is part of B'nai B'rith, is based at United Nations Plaza, New York. B'nai B'rith means "Sons of the Alliance" and was established in

1843. Many of its speakers openly supported slavery during the American Civil War and it covertly supports and controls the Ku Klux Klan. Today this same B'nai B'rith seeks to label leading blacks as "anti-Semitic" and racist![18]

THE MEYER LANSKY CRIME SYNDICATE

Meyer Lansky was devoted to Israel and therefore the Rothschilds. His network played a crucial role in supplying guns and funds to the terror groups of Rabin, Begin, Ben-Gurion, Shamir, and others, as they shot and bombed the State of Israel into being. He then became a major supplier of the same to Israel. Lansky, Mossad, the Anti-Defamation League, and Israel were as one. Morris Dalitz, an intimate of Lansky in his gangster network, was given the Anti-Defamation League's annual Torch of Liberty award. His terror activities were not deemed as important as his contributions to Israel and the ADL. Indeed, his terror activities on behalf of the ADL may well have swung the voting.

Whenever the heat was on in the United States, Lansky would run to Israel and he eventually settled there. Lansky (Israel) was trailing John Kennedy for a long time and, of course, Lansky hated the Kennedy family because of his conflict with Father Joe. It was a Lansky henchman on the West Coast called Mickey Cohen who was behind the introduction of Kennedy to the film star, Marilyn Monroe, after which they began a now much publicised relationship. The vehicle for this meeting was Cohen's close friend, the entertainer Joey Bishop, who was a member of the Frank Sinatra clique known as "The Rat Pack". The idea was to use Monroe to pump Kennedy for information about his attitute to Israel, should he become president. She was, of course, later murdered, although it was made to look like "suicide". Those who killed her also killed Kennedy. Mickey Cohen was Lanksy's man in Hollywood where the film industry had long been a propaganda machine for the Elite's agenda and version of 'history'. It still is today, only the names have changed. Cohen also specialised in compromising screen stars sexually and then blackmailing them. Nice man. He was another financer and political manipulator on behalf of the Jewish terror groups and the State of Israel. Still, I'm sure "God" would have approved. One of Cohen's close associates was...Menachim Begin, then head of the terrorist group, Irgun. Jimmy "the Weasel" Fratianno, a leader of the West Coast Mafia, told of a meeting he attended in Bel Air to raise money for Begin's terrorists:

> *"After (Cohen's) little speech, we start moving around the room and Mickey's rabbi introduces us to a guy called Menachim Begin, who's the boss of Irgun, an underground outfit in Palestine. This guy's wearing a black*

---

[18] *Secret Societies*, p128.

armband and he tells us he's wanted back there for bombing a hotel that killed
almost a hundred people. He's a fucking lamster (on the run)." [19]

Begin, as Prime Minister of Israel, later won the Nobel Peace Prize! Gary
Wean, a detective sergeant in the Los Angeles Police Department, had the
job of monitoring Cohen's activities. In his book, *There's A Fish In The
Courthouse*, Wean confirms the story about Marilyn Monroe and the Cohen-
Begin connection:

> " *At the time the rabbis were pushing them hard as hell to squeeze every*
> *bit of dough they could get out of Hollywood for Israel. Begin was spending*
> *more time hanging around Cohen in Hollywood than in Israel. Begin*
> *desperately wanted to know what Kennedy's plan was for Israel if he became*
> *president."* [20]

Another of Cohen's associates and a leading errand boy and operative for
Meyer Lansky was Jack Rubinstein. He's better known today as…Jack Ruby,
the man who killed the Kennedy "patsy", Lee Harvey Oswald.

THE CIA

The connections between the CIA, the organised crime syndicates, and
Mossad are endless, not least with the global drug running operations in
which the three of them cooperate. During the war the Americans used
Meyer Lansky and the Mafia in a plan known as Operation Underworld and
it is common knowledge that they were also used in plots to remove Fidel
Castro in Cuba, an operation in which Jack Ruby also played a part. The
Global Elite elements within the CIA and the Global Elite's wholly-owned
subsidiary, Mossad, are the same organisation. Before, during, and after the
assassinations of both John and Bobby Kennedy, the key coordinator of these
connections was one James Jesus Angleton, who was educated in his early
years in England at Chartridge Hall House in Buckinghamshire and Malvern
House in Worcestershire. He was recruited by the CIA's predecessor, the
Office of Strategic Services (OSS), after leaving the Skull and Bones
university of Yale. In 1947, he joined the new CIA and progressed to the
highly sensitive and pivotal post of head of CIA counter-intelligence.
According to his biographer, Tom Mangold, his major patrons were Allen
Dulles, the CIA director fired by Kennedy, and Richard Helms, who was
appointed CIA director by Lyndon B. Johnson after Kennedy's assassination.
Mangold says that, in effect, Angleton was given such a free reign to pursue

---

[19] Ovid Demaris, *The Last Mafioso*, (Bantam Books, New York, 1981) p32. Also quoted in
Final Judgement, p159.
[20] Gary L. Wean, *There's A Fish In The Courthouse*, (Casitas Books, Oak View, California,
1987) p679.

his own agenda that there was virtually no monitoring or control of his activities. He was a law unto himself. This becomes very significant to the story when we realise that one of Angleton's key roles was the official CIA liason with Allied foreign intelligence agencies...particularly with Mossad (Rothschilds). He was the head of the CIA's Israel desk! More than that he had long and intimate ties with David Ben-Gurion, the Israeli Prime Minister, who despised Kennedy and saw him as a threat to the existence of Israel. Kennedy's war with the CIA also threatened the existence of Angleton's job and power base. Angleton had many reasons to want Kennedy out of the way, but the most important was his connection to, and likely control by, Israel, which then, as now, controls much of the CIA operation. Wilbur Crane Eveland, a former advisor to the CIA and member of the policy-planning staff at the White House and Pentagon, said:

> *"Stemming from his wartime OSS liaison with Jewish resistance groups based in London, James Angleton had arranged an operational-intelligence exchange agreement with Israel's Mossad, upon which the CIA relied for much of its intelligence about the Arab states."* [21]

My goodness, I bet those intelligence reports were unbiased!

LORD VICTOR ROTHSCHILD

There is also the British connection to consider here. While working in London for the OSS, James Angleton became a close friend of the spy, Kim Philby, and worked with Lord Victor Rothschild, the "fifth man" in the spy network of Philby, Burgess, Maclean, and Blunt. Lord Rothschild, the friend of Winston Churchill, was in fact far more than the "fifth man". He was the string puller of British Intelligence, a controller of, and agent for, Mossad[22], and a dedicated manipulator for the House of Rothschild and the Global Elite. When Angleton was posted to Rome in 1944 by the OSS, it was Rothschild who gave him contacts in the Jewish underground there.[23] Angleton was also a friend of the British Intelligence operative, Peter Wright, the man behind the books, *Their Trade Is Treachery* and *Spycatcher*, which were suggested and organised by Lord Rothschild. The books named the former MI5 chief, Sir Roger Hollis, as the "fifth man", so diverting attention from Rothschild. Wright's contention that Hollis was the Soviet spy was supported by Angleton on Rothschild's behalf. Angleton was in Rothschild's debt for earlier favours and support. The British (Rothschild)

[21] Wilbur Crane Eveland, *Ropes Of Sand: America's Failure In The Middle East*, (W.W. Norton and Company, 1980) p95.
[22] Roland Perry, *The Fifth Man*, (Sidgwick and Jackson, London, 1994) p223.
[23] Ibid p129.

connection to Angleton and the CIA/Mossad clique was fundamental. It was Rothschild who had powerful connections with all the parties involved, British Intelligence, Mossad, the CIA with it's head of counter-intelligence James Jesus Angleton, and other contracts at the highest Elite levels in the United States.

Crucially, it was Lord Victor Rothschild who masterminded the Israeli nuclear weapons programme which Kennedy wished to stop. Within months of Israel's formation, Rothschild and his close friend, Chaim Weizmann, set up a special nuclear physics department at Rehovoth. It was named after Weizmann, the head of British Zionism and the first president of the new Israel. Weizmann had also been a key manipulator behind the Balfour Declaration, the letter sent by British Foreign Secretary Arthur Balfour to Victor Rothschild's uncle, Walter, in 1917, confirming British support for a Jewish state in Palestine. Victor Rothschild covertly gathered information for the nuclear scientists at the Weizmann Institute from researchers and experts all over the world, including Albert Einstein, members of the British Atomic Scientists Association, and the mathmatician and philosopher, Bertrand Russell, who, with Einstein, helped to create the Pugwash Conferences on nuclear weapons.[24] Roland Perry writes in his book *The Fifth Man*:

> *"The dream of an Israeli bomb was ambitious indeed, but it spurred Rothschild to keep abreast of all things nuclear so he could pass on data to the Weizmann Institute, which was planning a nuclear reactor at Dimona in the Negev Desert. Under a modified guise of concern about the spread and dangers of nuclear weapons, he was able to keep contact with appropriate scientists around the world."* [25]

In this way, Rothschild had access to the Manhattan Project which led to the atomic attack on Japan, and he was an associate of Klaus Fuchs, the German physicist who was later jailed for giving nuclear secrets to the Soviet Union. Rothschild, who did the same, got away with it. His leading role, with money and information, in the creation of the Israeli nuclear weapon was publicly rewarded in 1962 when Rothschild was made an Honorary Fellow of the Weizmann Institute. Shimon Peres, who became Prime Minister of Israel following the murder of Yitzhak Rabin in 1995, worked with Rothschild to persuade the French to build the nuclear facility at Dimona. The French wing of the House of Rothschild would have had enormous influence on the French Government. Peres, then director of the Defence Ministry, promised in return to support the French and British in their efforts to retake the Suez Canal from Egypt's President Nassar,

---

something Israel wanted to happen anyway![26] Peres and Asher Ben-Natan, a Mossad agent at the Defence Ministry, signed a top secret agreement with the French and her prime minister, Bourges Maunoury.[27] Roland Perry writes:

> " In it, the French promised to supply a powerful 24 megawatt reactor, the technical know-how to run it, and some uranium. The secret deal was only known to about a dozen individuals, including Rothschild, and with good reason. The fine print of the document allowed for the inclusion of equipment which would permit the Israelis to produce weapons-grade nuclear fuel.
>
> "In 1957, French engineers began building the two-storey reactor facility at Dimona on the edge of the Negev Desert, which secretly went down six levels below ground. The subterranean construction would be the place where nuclear weapons would be built." [28]

This was the nuclear programme, the very creation of Rothschild, which President Kennedy wanted to end. So here was Lord Victor Rothschild (the man behind the use of Regulation 18b to jail people without trial for exposing the Second World War as a scam) with a stream of reasons to want Kennedy out of the way. He was also closely connected to all the people and organisations which assassinated the president. At the time of Kennedy's death, Rothschild was working for Shell Oil, but this post was a front for his covert manipulation and wheeler-dealing within British intelligence on behalf of the Elite. The House of Rothschild was deeply involved in the Kennedy assassination, of that I have no doubt.

PERMINDEX

This company was a central part of the coordination between Mossad, the CIA, and the Lansky Syndicate. Serving on its board was Clay Shaw, the CIA operative indicted for Kennedy's murder by New Orleans District Attorney, Jim Garrison, as highlighted in the film, *JFK*. It was because Shaw was linked to Permindex, the pivotal vehicle in the whole plot, that so much dirt was thrown at Garrison. Shaw was also managing director of International Trade Mart and on the board of that company was Edgar Stern Jr, whose parents were leading financial supporters of the US Israeli lobby.[29] The Sterns were among Shaw's closest friends and he was also connected to the Lansky syndicate.

Permindex (short for Permanent Industrial Expositions) was a subsidiary of a company called CMC, founded in 1961 by an Eastern European Jew,

---

[26] *The Fifth Man*, p224.

[27] Ibid.

[28] Ibid.

[29] *Final Judgement*, p90.

Georges Mandel, who called himself Giorgio Mantello. Its cover operation,
like that of Permindex, was presenting business exhibitions. One of its chief
shareholders was the Banque De Credit International (BCI) based in the
Elite stronghold of Geneva. This bank was established by Rabbi Tibor
Rosenbaum, the longtime director of finance and supply for Mossad.[30]
Rosenbaum was also an international vice-president of the World Jewish
Congress, a co-founder of the World Zionist Congress, and a director of the
Jewish Agency in Geneva, successor to the Palestine Liberation office, a
coordinator of Jewish terrorism against the Arabs and the British in Palestine.
The newspaper, Ha'aretz, once declared that "Tibor Rosenbaum is Israel".
He worked closely with the Rothschilds (including Lord Victor for sure) and
together with Baron Edmond de Rothschild, the French aristocrat, he set up
the Israel Corporation which sought money abroad for Israel's development
projects, so allowing her tax money to be spent on funding the military.[31]

Among the names that Rosenbaum sponsored was the 'financier' and
Lansky drug money-launderer, Bernie Cornfield.[32] It was through
Rosenbaum's bank that the Lansky Syndicate laundered most of its money in
Europe. So did Mossad and the CIA.[33] The chairman of Permindex was
Major Louis M. Bloomfield, a devoted supporter of Israel. Permindex was
based in his home city of Montreal, Canada, before being relocated to
Rome, where the CIA's James Angleton had endless intelligence and
underworld connections. Bloomfield was involved in Operation
Underworld, the joint American intelligence operation with Lansky and the
Mafia, while he served with Britain's counter-intelligence elite during the
war, the Special Operations Executive (SOE). Operation Underworld was
run from the Rockefeller Center in New York. Bloomfield's boss was Sir
William Stephenson, who set up British intelligence operations in the
United States before the war and was also connected with Lansky, Mossad,
and the Rockefellers.[34] Stephenson is said to have been the character on
which James Bond is based. Operation Underworld later became a centre for
gun-running operations to the Jewish terrorist underground in which
Stephenson, Bloomfield and Victor Rothschild played crucial parts. Working
with Bloomfield in this were Meyer Lansky and Samuel Bronfman of the
Canadian underworld family.

It was a company set up by William Stephenson's Special Operations
Executive that we know today as the Hollinger Group, controlled by the
Canadian and leading Bilderberger, Conrad Black, the owner of the global
media empire which includes the London Telegraph Newspapers and The

[30] *Final Judgement*, p89.
[31] Ibid p191.
[32] Ibid p187.
[33] Ibid.
[34] For more details of his Lansky-Mossad connections, see *Final Judgement*.

Jerusalem Post. On the board of the Hollinger Group are a stream of Bilderbergers and CFR/TC members, including Henry Kissinger and Lord Carrington. This is even more interesting when you think that the Permindex chairman and SOE operative, Louis Bloomfield, was really a frontman and attorney for the Canadian Bronfman family, who made their fortune from running booze during prohibition and from general gangster activities. The Bronfman gang were close to Conrad Black's father, another booze merchant and intelligence operative with the SOE, and the Bronfman's are long term financial supporters and members of the Mossad front, the Anti-Defamation League.

Bloomfield first met Clay Shaw during the latter's service with the Office of Strategic Services (OSS) during the war, an organisation to which Bloomfield was also assigned. Shaw was based in London and became a friend of Prime Minister, Winston Churchill (Comm 300), whose personal advisor was...Sir William Stephenson. Also serving with the OSS in London at this time was James Jesus Angleton, the CIA's head of counter-intelligence and the Israel desk when Kennedy was killed. And who was the man controlling British Intelligence at this same period? Lord Victor Rothschild, another close friend of Churchill, the man behind Israel's nuclear weapons project and one of the key people behind the creation of Israel. Rothschild knew Shaw, Bloomfield, Stephenson, and Angleton, who were all part of the team which conspired to kill Kennedy. Either directly, or through this group, Rothschild would have known, or had the means to communicate with, Meyer Lansky. Rothschild's connections with Mossad and Israel were fundamental. He was at the heart of the Jewish terror and intelligence groups which brought Israel into existence. One of these intelligence groups, the Hananah or Hananah "B", the terrorist wing, became what we know as Mossad.[35] The Rothschilds' own "in house" intelligence agency, which had been operating since the early days of the Rothschild dynasty, also fused with Mossad.

Bloomfield and Shaw came together again on the board of Permindex and worked together on its cover operation, the setting up of trade exhibitions around the world. On November 22nd 1963, President Kennedy was on his way to speak at the newly created Dallas Trade Mart when he was assassinated. It was that appointment at the trade mart which led his motorcade to pass through Dealey Plaza where the fatal shots were fired. A coincidence? I don't think so, somehow.

FRENCH INTELLIGENCE
The death of President Kennedy and the many attempts on the life of the French President, General Charles DeGaulle, were orchestrated by the same organisation – the Rothschild-controlled, Mossad. One of the assassination

---

[35] *The Fifth Man*, p79.

attempts on DeGaulle was immortalised by the Frederick Forsyth 'novel', *The Day Of The Jackal*. Interestingly, in this same period there was a terrorist group known as the Jewish Anti-Communist League or JACL,[36] and this group cooperated with a renegade "cell" within French Intelligence called the OAS.

The Israeli–CIA backed OAS was the group directly behind the attempts on DeGaulle's life. They opposed him for what they saw as his betrayal of France in giving independence to Algeria. Also opposed to this were Israel and Mossad, and the issue was one of the many conflicts they had with Kennedy, who supported Algerian independence as a young senator. Once again the endless connections unfold. During World War II, the CIA's head of the Israeli desk, James Jesus Angleton, served as American intelligence liason with French Intelligence, the SDECE, and maintained many contacts with their operatives who shared his love of Israel. He also had strong connections with the Corsican Mafia in France which worked with the Lansky Syndicate. Drugs produced in the laboratories of Marseille by the Corsican Mafia were transferred to the streets of America by Lansky and Angleton's CIA. Israel and Mossad rarely do their dirty work themselves, nor the CIA come to that, and a former French Intelligence agent and diplomat told Michael Piper Collins, the author of *Final Judgement*, that Mossad used a French team to assassinate Kennedy:

> *"Even the CIA contract the services of the intelligence community (they like the French style) to wash dirty linens. The right hand does not know what the left did. The cover-up team doesn't know who execute. And the executioners are not interested in the aftermath of their mission. They don't care less."* [37]

The intelligence officer said that Yitzhak Shamir, the then head of the Mossad assassination unit and later Israeli Prime Minister, arranged for the French team to kill Kennedy in collaboration with Colonel Georges deLannurien, the deputy head of French Intelligence. As Collins' informant said:

> *"It was no coincidence that on the very day of the execution of the president by the French team, that (deLannurien) was at Langley (CIA headquarters) meeting with James Jesus Angleton, the Mossad mole."* [38]

Funny how Shamir doesn't mention any of this in his 'autobiography', *Summing Up*. In that he says that Mossad stood for "honesty" and "moral

[36] *The Fifth Man*, p79–80.
[37] *Final Judgement*, p245.
[38] Ibid p241–242.

standards".[39] No I'm not kidding. Shamir also says that he heard of the Kennedy assassination with "stunned disbelief" and somehow knew that everything would now be different.[40] Ahem, excuse me Yitzhak, but wasn't that the whole idea?

NEW ORLEANS

The City of New Orleans was important in the plot. From there a man called Guy Bannister, a former FBI and Naval Intelligence operative, ran a 'detective agency', a cover story for it's CIA intelligence work. According to the former CIA contract agent, Robert Morrow, who was close to the New Orleans operation, the immediate CIA superior of Bannister was...Clay Shaw, the Permindex director, and the only man to face trial for the murder of Kennedy, a charge he survived thanks to the murder and intimidation of key witnesses. One of Bannister's close friends was A.I. Bosnick, a leading figure in the New Orleans office of the Mossad-front, the Anti-Defamation League. Bannister's office at 544 Camp Street in New Orleans was also an informal branch of the renegade French intelligence cell, the OAS, which provided the actual assassins for Mossad and the CIA in Dallas. An OAS representative working out of Camp Street was the mercenary, Jean Souetre, who had ties with Meyer Lansky's allies in the Corsican Mafia. A CIA document discovered in 1977 by Dallas researcher, Mary Ferrell, revealed that French intelligence were trying to locate Souetre, an OAS terrorist, because he was considered a threat to the life of Charles DeGaulle. The document, dated April 1st 1964, listed some known sightings of Souetre. It said that he was in Fort Worth on the morning of November 22nd 1963 (so was Kennedy) and that he was also in Dallas that same afternoon when Kennedy was shot. Within 48 hours of the assassination, the document said, Souetre was picked up in Texas and expelled from the United States.[41] Souetre said that the man referred to in the document was really another French assassin called Michel Mertz who, he claimed, used his name.

It was through Bannister's office that Lee Harvey Oswald, himself a CIA asset, was unknowingly set up as the patsy. He was given a false story and told to pose as a pro-Castro communist by the CIA without realising why. It seems that plan A was to persuade the public that Oswald killed Kennedy out of support for Castro. It is possible that Oswald was funded by the Anti-Defamation League. Certainly the plan to give Oswald a pro-Castro public personna was supported by the ADL-controlled media. The NBC television and radio affiliate in New Orleans, WDSU, interviewed Oswald about his "pro-communist, pro-Castro" views in August 1963 and then turned the

[39] Yitzhak Shamir, *Summing Up, An Autobiography*, (Weidenfeld and Nicholson, London) p81.
[40] Ibid p13.
[41] Henry Hurt, *Reasonable Doubt: An Investigation Into The Assassination Of John F. Kennedy*, (Holt, Rinehart and Winston, New York, 1985) p417–419.

tape over to the FBI. They also invited him to a debate about Castro and filmed him handing out pro-Castro leaflets in Dallas.Why so much airtime for Oswald in the months leading up to the Kennedy assassination? Maybe the fact that WDSU was owned by the Stern family, very close friends of Clay Shaw, and major contributers to Israel and the Anti-Defamation League, would answer that question. After the assassination, the WDSU interviews with Oswald were immediately broadcast nationally by NBC, so providing support for the idea that Oswald was a "lone nut" who killed Kennedy in support of Castro. (Johann Rush, the young camerman who took the film of Oswald handing out the leaflets, emerged 30 years later as the "expert" whose "enhancement" of the Zapruder film was supposed to have "proved" that Oswald was the lone assassin!) [42]

THE STING

It appears from the excellent research in *Final Judgement* that Dallas and Dealey Plaza was full of different people and groups who, after the event, could be linked by investigators to the assassination. This was done to provide so many possible assassins and senarios for investigators that the waters would be seriously muddied. It is a classic diversion tactic. Only a tiny few at the scene, the assassins in the Mossad-CIA-OAS ZR-Rifle Team, knew that the plan was to kill Kennedy. The others were there for other reasons and among these groups, it seems, was a CIA team who believed the plan was to fake an assassination attempt on the president. The idea, they believed, was to blame the attempt on Castro and cause so much outrage in America that Kennedy would drop his plan to make some kind of peace with Cuba or, ideally, he might even be pressured to launch an invasion and remove Castro. It is probable that the CIA's E. Howard Hunt, with his connections to the Bay of Pigs disaster and the anti-Castro Cuban resistence groups, was one of this CIA "fake assassination" team, possibly its leader. If the story is true, no-one would have been more surprised than Hunt and his colleagues when Kennedy was actually shot and Hunt's CIA team almost certainly included one Lee Harvey Oswald. This is the mission Oswald would have been told he was assigned to before he began to promote himself so publicly as a pro-Castro communist when he was nothing of the kind. The story about the CIA "fake" team in Dallas was told to Gary Wean, formerly of the Los Angeles Police criminal intelligence squad. Wean met his informant through the Dallas Sheriff, Bill Decker, who had said:

> *"There's a man in Dallas I've known for a long time. He knows the entire truth about Oswald's involvement. He's scared to death to go to the Dallas Police Department or FBI. There has been a terrible double cross somewhere and everybody is scared shitless of everybody else.*

---

[42] *Final Judgement*, p255.

"You wouldn't believe the crazy suspicions and accusations heaped on all law enforcement in the South by imbeciles in D.C. and the chaos it has created." [43]

Later Wean met with Decker's informant and he referred to him only as "John". Wean was told that E. Howard Hunt (who would later be one of the Watergate burglars) had informed Oswald that Kennedy himself was not aware of the fake assassination plan, but high-ranking cabinet officers did know about it. Oswald was told that he would flee the country after the fake 'assassination', but he would be allowed to return once Castro had been dealt with.[44] So Oswald thought the assassination was designed purposely to fail and he certainly realised immediately after Kennedy was killed that he had been set up to take the blame. Intelligence agencies do not operate as one entity, they use compartmentalisation to ensure that different elements have no idea what the others are doing. Gary Wean did not reveal the identity of "John" for obvious reasons, but after 1991 he was safe to do so. "John" was Senator John Tower, who in 1961, had become the first Republican this century to win a senate seat in Texas. Tower was a strong supporter and ally of the CIA throughout his career and would later help to cover up George Bush's fundamental involvement in the Iran-Contra arms-for-drugs scandal. On April 5th 1991, John Tower died when his plane exploded.

THE COVER UP

The cover up began from the moment the fatal shots were fired, indeed the cover stories were arranged well before. Oswald was presented across the world as a lone assassin who did it for Castro and Cuba. Oswald, however, said after his arrest that he had been set up. He wasn't going to go quietly, so he had to go physically. Step forward Jack Ruby (Rubenstein), who shot Oswald at point-blank range as police "escorted" him through a public place after his arrest. Ruby was portrayed as a Dallas night club owner who killed Oswald to avenge Kennedy's death. Er, I don't think so, somehow. Ruby's first phone call after his arrest was to Al Gruber, a close associate of Mickey Cohen, the Meyer Lansky henchman in Hollywood. It was Cohen who worked with Menachim Begin to set up the John Kennedy-Marilyn Monroe connection which ended in the film star's murder by the same crowd. Gruber had arrived in Dallas shortly before the Kennedy assassination to visit Ruby, a man he hadn't seen for ten years.[45] Ruby's lawyer at his trial was Melvin Belli, the friend and attorney of Mickey Cohen.[46] At least one meeting has been confirmed between Belli, Cohen, and Begin.[47]

[43] *There's A Fish In The Courthouse*, p695.
[44] Ibid p699.
[45] *Final Judgement*, p166.
[46] Ibid p178.
[47] Ibid.

Jack Ruby worked for Al Capone and spent most of his life operating within the organised crime syndicate, especially for it's boss of bosses, Meyer Lanksy. Ruby has been portrayed as a Mafia man to divert attention from his real employer – Lansky. His association with Lansky led to Ruby's connections with the CIA, Israel, and the anti-Castro groups. Marita Lorenz, a former CIA operative, said at a libel hearing involving E. Howard Hunt of the CIA and *The Spotlight* newspaper, that the day before Kennedy's assassination she met in Dallas with Hunt and a group of other CIA operatives including...Jack Ruby. Hunt, she said, was the paymaster for a top secret operation, the purpose of which she had no idea. She was told that her part was to act as a "decoy".[48] Instead she left Dallas and didn't take part. It seems likely that Ruby, like Oswald, eventually realised that he had been set up. His family fired his lawyer, Melvin Belli, after Ruby was convicted and sentenced to death. But before his appeal could be heard, Ruby conveniently died in jail.[49] Ruby's demise, or at least disappearance, came after he made it clear he had some very important things to say about Kennedy's death. He asked Earl Warren, the head of the commission investigating the assassination, to be transferred for his own safety from Dallas to Washington to tell his story. Warren refused and the story was never told. I wonder why?

In the light of what you have read in this book and in particular in the last few pages, let us look at the make up of the Warren Commission which decided that yes indeed Lee Harvey Oswald had worked alone. The Warren Commission was appointed by Lyndon Baines Johnson, the man who became president as a result of Kennedy's death. If you apply the question of: Who benefits? to the Kennedy assassination then Johnson is high on the list. What's more, he was closely connected to all the other players who benefited massively from the killing. Johnson had longtime connections with Meyer Lansky and had been taking bribes from the syndicate in return for political favours since he became a Texas Senator. Johnson, as *Final Judgement* makes clear, was a megacrook and only by using the Elite networks did he avoid going to jail for a very long time. When Johnson replaced Kennedy, the adminstration's war on organised crime was immediately disbanded. Johnson was also a favourite and keen supporter of Israel. Again, after Kennedy was gone, Johnson quickly reversed America's neutral policy in the Middle East to one of virtually unlimited financial and political support for Israel. Researcher and author Stephen Green wrote of the Johnson period in his study of America-Israel policy:

> "...during this time US financial support for Israel far exceeded that given any other nation in the world, on a per capita basis. And US

---

[48] Ibid p213.

[49] Or did he die? At least one person who knew Ruby well has said that she saw him boarding a plane for Israel *after* he was supposed to have died (*Final Judgement*, p183).

diplomatic support for Israel in the UN and elsewhere was no less generous." [50]

Johnson also reversed Kennedy's policy of withdrawing from Vietnam and that war escalated to the enormous benefit of the Lansky-CIA-Mossad drugs operation in South East Asia and the coffers of the arms manufacturers and bankers. Johnson quickly halted the Kennedy plan to issue interest-free money and curtail the power of the Federal Reserve banking cartel. Lyndon Johnson, yet another crook to occupy the White House, gave all the participants in Kennedy's murder everything they asked for after becoming president in the wake of JFK's death. Johnson was the man whose very survival depended on the truth about the assassination (and his own involvement) never being publicly known. This was the same man who appointed the Warren Commission to establish the killer! Among it's members were:

Chief Justice Earl Warren: 33rd degree Freemason and a man under the control of the organised crime syndicates, according to some researchers. That would certainly fit the picture. Warren was also a close friend of the leading newspaper columnist, Drew Pearson, and, through him, another columnist, Jack Anderson. It was Pearson who wrote stories aimed at diverting attention from the real assassins. He supported Israel slavishly through his columns and his biographer wrote that: "Over the years the Anti-Defamation League had helped Pearson enormously. It provided information he could not obtain elsewhere, backed his lecture tours, even assisted in the circulation of his weekly newsletter".

Allen Dulles: The head of the CIA fired by Kennedy. Dulles helped to fund and support the Bolsheviks and Adolf Hitler, and the Dulles law firm handled the US affairs of the Nazi cartel, I.G. Farben. He headed the CIA during its gruesome mind-control project, MKUltra, and was a member of the Council on Foreign Relations and the Bilderberg Group. Dulles was a Nazi in his attitudes and a keen supporter of eugenics.

John J. McCloy: At the time of Kennedy's death and the Warren Commission, he was chairman of the Council on Foreign Relations. McCloy was also a chairman of the Ford Foundation and of David Rockefeller's Chase Manhattan Bank. He was a US delegate at the founding of the United Nations, a member of the Committee of 300, and helped Jean Monnet (Comm 300) to create the European Community. During the war he opposed a policy of accepting the Japanese surrender without dropping

[50] Stephen Green, *Taking Sides: America's Secret Relations With A Militant Israel*, (William Morrow and Co, New York, 1984) p243–244.

the atomic bombs. After the war, he ordered the release of Hitler's banker, Hjalmar Schacht, from his sentence for war crimes, as he did with other Nazis.

J. Edgar Hoover: 33rd degree Freemason. Legendary manipulator and director of the FBI. He hated Kennedy, who planned to remove him after the 1964 election. Hoover was connected to both Meyer Lansky and the Anti-Defamation League. Michael Milan, a former Lansky associate and undercover FBI operative, said: "I also knew that (J. Edgar Hoover) and Meyer Lansky sometimes broke bread together. Mr L. was never rousted, was rarely served with federal subpoenas, and was generally left alone to conduct business".[51] Hoover had very close links with the Mossad-front, the Anti-Defamation League. In 1947 a foundation was set up in his name thanks to money from the ADL. The Hoover Foundation's first president was Rabbi Paul Richman, Washington director of the ADL.[52] Hoover was also a close friend of Louis Bloomfield, the head of the Mossad assassination front, Permindex!

Gerald Ford: 33rd degree Freemason, member of the CFR, the Bilderberg Group, and the Rockefeller-Elite-controlled Eastern Establishment. Vice president to Nixon at the time of Watergate. Nixon's forced resignation gave Ford the presidency and he appointed Nelson Rockefeller to head a 'commission' on the security services after Watergate to ensure that nothing of substance was done. It wasn't. While president, Ford would write to Senator Frank Church, chairman of the Senate Intelligence Committee, demanding that the committee's report on US assassination plots, including that of JFK, be kept secret.[53]

These, then, were the men who decided that Oswald was the lone killer! More than that, the CIA department given responsibility for dealing with the Warren Commission 'investigation' was the counter-intelligence department controlled by...James Jesus Angleton, the Mossad mole and a prime organiser of the assassination. The FBI-Warren Commission coordinator was William Sullivan, a close friend of...James Jesus Angleton.

The cover up has continued to this day with books and magazines funded by the assassins and their successors claiming that the Mafia, Castro, the KGB, etc. etc. killed Kennedy. Each one is designed to further obscure the real culprits, the Israel-CIA-Meyer Lansky-OAS network operating together

---

[51] Michael Milan, *The Squad: The US Government's Secret Alliance With Organised Crime*, (Shapolsky Publishers, New York, 1989) p206.

[52] *Final Judgement*, p81–82.

[53] Letter sent by Ford on October 31st 1975. The contents were revealed by Church and quoted in *George Bush, The Unauthorised Biography*, p291–292.

under a central command, probably the House of Rothschild. Do you think the media is not controlled enough to keep the truth from the public for more than thirty years? As the former Mossad agent, Victor Ostrovsky says:

> *"(I realised) that the occupation of the North American media is complete. In subjects dealing with the Middle East in general and Israel in particular, there is no longer a free press…I had always known there was a double standard when it came to dealing with subjects that were dear to the Jewish community. I had not known, however, how hypocritical that community and the media that lie at its feet can be. I had known that it had all but taken over the film industry and has a strong grip on Washington…Now through intimidation and double dealing, it obviously has taken over large portions of the American media. To all those who knew this all along, and were silent, and to those who remain silent now – shame on you."* [54]

The editor of *Life* magazine, Richard Billings, ran a vehement campaign to discredit Jim Garrison's investigations into the assassination, as Garrison has documented. Billings would later serve on the staff of the House Assassinations Committee, alongside it's director, G. Robert Blakey, an associate of Meyer Lansky's friend, Morris Dalitz. The committee decided the "Mafia did it". The Time-Life organisation later merged with Warner to create the Time-Warner media empire. This is an Elite-controlled organisation which now owns Turner broadcasting and its global 'news' channel, CNN. Warner Brothers was absorbed by a company called Seven Arts set up by a Meyer Lansky operative, Louis Chesler, and used to launder syndicate money. When Seven Arts won control of Warner Studios, major blocks of shares in the company were owned by the Investors Overseas Service of Bernie Cornfield, the frontman for the Rothschilds and Mossad's Rabbi Tibor Rosenbaum, the funder of Permindex. In 1993, the Bronfman's (the gangster family who controlled the Permindex chief, Louis M. Bloomfield) bought a controlling interest in Time-Warner. How facinating, then, that Oliver Stone's 'exposé' of the Kennedy Assassination, *JFK*, was distributed by Warner Brothers. Stone's film, a mixture of fact and fiction, blamed the military-industrial complex and the CIA and not the real conspirators, Mossad. Stone has since done a similar diversion job on Richard Nixon. The executive producer of *JFK*, the man responsible for finding the money for the film, was Arnon Milchan, who was identified as a major arms supplier and undercover operative for Israel. Journalist Alexander Cockburn wrote in The Nation on May 18th 1992 that Milchan "was identified in one 1989 Israeli report as 'probably' (Israel's) largest arms dealer. A company he once owned was caught smuggling nuclear weapons fuses to

---

[54] Quoted in the Australian spiritual/conspiracy research magazine, *New Dawn*, (November/December 1995) p20.

Iraq". The public relations company hired by Stone to handle publicity for the *JFK* film was Hill and Knowlton in Washington D.C., the firm which coordinated the propaganda supporting America's involvement in the Gulf War. The Hill and Knowlton executive who headed the *JFK* publicity was Frank Mankiewicz, who began his career with the Anti-Defamation League in Los Angeles.

To this day, the Kennedy assassination continues to stink.

John Kennedy realised from his experiences before and after he became president that a Hidden Hand controlled the United States. Ten days before his death, he said at Colombia University:

> *"The high office of President has been used to foment a plot against the American people. Before I leave office, I must inform the citizen of his plight."* [55]

Unfortunately, he never had the chance to do that.

In his book, *Defrauding America*, Rodney Stich also reveals further evidence of CIA involvement in the Kennedy assassination and its cover-up. Stich, a former federal inspector, uses his own knowledge, experience, and informants from within the intelligence network, to reveal the web of interconnected corruption throughout the US government. One of his contacts was Colonel Trenton Parker, a former high level CIA operative, who was connected with the agency's counter-intelligence unit known as Pegasus. Parker said that the Pegasus group had tape recordings of people planning the Kennedy assassination. He named them as "Rockefeller (which one, I wonder), Allen Dulles, Johnson of Texas, George Bush and J. Edgar Hoover". Parker went on:

> *"I don't have the tapes now, because all the tape recordings were turned over to [Congressman] Larry McDonald. But I listened to the tape recordings and there were conversations between Rockefeller and Hoover, where Rockefeller asks: 'Are we going to have any problems? I checked with Dulles. If they do their job, we'll do our job.' There are a whole bunch of tapes, because Hoover didn't realise that his phone had been tapped."*

Parker said that the Pegasus group had also given files to Congressman McDonald about CIA criminal activities between 1976 and 1982. McDonald, a member of the Joint Armed Services Committee, let it be known that he was going to reveal startling evidence about CIA and government corruption when he returned from a trip to the Far East. But he

---

[55] Quoted in *Extra-Terrestrials Friends And Foes*, p289.

did not return. He was on the Korean Airlines flight 007 shot down by the 'Soviet Union'. The plane's flight computer was reprogrammed to divert the aircraft into Russian airspace and they were waiting to shoot it down.[56] Two 'sides' – same masters.

BOBBY KENNEDY

JFK's death triggered a spate of political assassinations in the United States during the 1960s as the New World Order imposed itself. His brother Bobby Kennedy, the attorney general who led the challenge to the Lansky syndicate, was murdered in 1968 after making a speech at the Ambassador Hotel in Los Angeles as part of his campaign for the Democratic presidential nomination. It is said he was killed by another "lone assassin", Sirhan Sirhan. Bobby's death benefited Richard Nixon, who had been supported in his political career by Prescott Bush, father of George. Nixon eventually became president at the election in which he would have faced serious opposition from Bobby Kennedy. Nixon's director of security in his 1968 election campaign was James Golden, who took leave from his job as director of security at the Lockheed Corporation. Coincidentally, it was a guard from Lockheed, Thane Eugene Caesar, who was standing right alongside Bobby Kennedy when he was shot. Caesar, an employee of the Lansky syndicate, worked at Lockheed's Burbank centre in the top secret area reserved for the CIA's U-2 spy plane project. Lee Harvey Oswald was also affiliated with the U-2. Another employee of Lockheed was Richard Gernt Butler an associate of the neo-Nazi, Keith Gilbert. This same Keith Gilbert, was charged with the failed attempt to assassinate the black civil rights leader, Martin Luther King, in February 1965, four days after another black leader, Malcolm X, was murdered. Gilbert said in prison that he was supported by some powerful forces and it later emerged that he was funded by another white supremacist, Loren Eugene Hall. In turn, Hall had been a witness for Edwin Meese, the legal counsel for Ronald Reagan (then governor of California), in a case linked to the JFK assassination. District Attorney, Jim Garrison, issued an extradition request to Reagan for the California resident, Edgar Eugene Bradley, in connection with the death of JFK, and Reagan asked Meese to handle it. In the course of this, Loren Hall was among his informants. Reagan delayed Garrison's request until Nixon became president and then refused it without comment. Meese would later become US attorney general, the nation's chief law officer, under President Reagan. Loren Hall and his son Loren Junior would be indicted for running a drug ring in Oklahoma in 1989. Loren Junior called a press conference to say that the drug operation was being used to raise funds for the Contras in Nicaragua, so beloved of Ronald Reagan and George Bush.

[56] Rodney Stich, *Defrauding America*, (Diablo Western Press, Alamo, California, 1994) p316–317, 615.

Behind the scenes, those who killed JFK also killed Bobby. It was becoming increasingly likely that Bobby would win the Democratic nomination and he had an excellent chance of becoming president. This would have renewed JFK-style policies in relation to the Middle East and Organised Crime. Just as important, with Bobby in the White House the opportunity was there to blow the lid off the JFK assassination. Therefore Bobby was murdered using a mind-controlled assassin and if the former CIA operative, Robert Morrow, is to be believed, Mossad and the CIA used SAVAK, the Iran (Mossad-CIA) secret police force to do their dirty work this time.[57] It is certainly true that in the weeks before the murder, the Bobby Kennedy campaign had been infiltrated by Khyber Khan, a high ranking member of SAVAK, who used a cover story about falling out with the Shah. Bobby Kennedy believed him after previous experiences with Khan, but Khan brought in more SAVAK operatives to join him at Kennedy campaign headquarters.

Lord Victor Rothschild, who was a close friend of the Shah, was involved along with the CIA's James Jesus Angleton, in the overthrow of the Iranian leader, Mohammed Mossadegh, in 1953 which led to the creation of SAVAK. The patsy they used for the assassination of Bobby Kennedy was an Arab, Sirhan Sirhan. In the weeks before he killed Kennedy, Sirhan Sirhan, joined the Ancient Mystical Order of the Rosicrucians and followed their mail order course on "how to control your mind waves". He learnt how to put himself into a trance by staring into his own eyes in a mirror. During these trances, he began to write incoherent threats of violence and assassination. He didn't remember doing this, but afterwards he recognised the handwriting as his own. Sirhan apparently worshipped Bobby Kennedy, but, it is said, he felt betrayed when Kennedy supported the deployment of 50 war planes to Israel. Sirhan had hated Jews since he was bombed and shelled by the Israelis as an Arab boy in Palestine in 1948, the story goes. After this perceived betrayal in the two weeks before he shot Kennedy, Sirhan's trance experiences became more and more extreme. He thought he saw Kennedy's face come out of the mirror towards him and he wrote "Kill Kennedy" in his trance notebook. "Kennedy must be assassinated before June 5th 1968" it said. June 5th was the anniversary of the Israeli victory over the Arabs. The question is: Who was in control of Sirhan's subconscious mind? Himself or someone else? In the view of Sirhan's psychiatrist, Bernard L. Diamond, he self-programmed himself to kill Kennedy.[58] Pardon? Yeah, sure he did.

Let us consider the remarkable 'coincidences' which allowed this 'self-programmed' man to complete his mission. On the night of the killing, June 4th, Sirhan said he met a friend for dinner and intended to go on to a

[57] Robert D. Morrow, *The Senator Must Die: The Murder Of Robert F. Kennedy*, (Roundtable Publishing, Santa Monica, 1988).
[58] *Psychology Today*, (September 1969) Vol 3, No 2.

Rosicrucian meeting. But his 'friend' had a newspaper in which Sirhan saw an advertisement for a parade celebrating the anniversary of the Israeli victory. The ad said the event was "this evening", but what Sirhan didn't realise was that he had somehow been given a copy of the *next* day's paper. The parade was actually the following night, the 5th. Ignorant of this, Sirhan changed his plans for the evening and went off to the parade. Of course, he didn't find it. According to the account given by Sirhan under hypnosis by Bernard L. Diamond,[59] he now felt lonely and just happened to remember a girl he knew from high school who, he thought, could be found at the Ambassador Hotel where, purely by 'chance', Bobby Kennedy's event was taking place that same night. Sirhan drifted around the hotel for some hours getting himself drunk. At about eleven o'clock he decided to go home – his last conscious memory of the night. Under hypnosis, he then described walking out to his car, but he felt too ill and drunk to drive. He noticed his gun on the back seat and, concerned it might be stolen, he hid it in the top of his trousers. Back in the hotel he drank coffee with a "dark, attractive" (never identified) woman. On the way to buy another coffee, he said he found himself in an alcove with "dazzling lights and mirrors". He felt dazed and bewildered. Mirrored doors led to the hotel kitchen, but he didn't go through them. Instead he went to the kitchen by a longer route. Sirhan found himself in a hypnotic trance like those he experienced with the Rosicrucian course. He told Diamond of how he leaned on a table feeling sleepy and unsure of where he was. Suddenly he looked up to see a group of people coming towards him. He noticed that one of them was Bobby Kennedy and in his conscious mind he decided to shake his hand. Instead he pulled out the gun and started shooting. As psychiatrist Diamond said: "Sirhan executed the crime in a twilight state, knowing next to nothing about what was happening".[60]

And so how come Bobby Kennedy was walking through the hotel kitchen at exactly the wrong time? He had wanted to walk through the crowds after his speech, but his 'minders' insisted that he leave via the kitchen to avoid possible danger! The man most insistent that Kennedy go through the kitchen was...Frank Mankiewicz, the former public relations man for the Anti-Defamation League who handled the publicity for Oliver Stone's film, *JFK*![61] Also alongside Kennedy was Thane Eugene Caesar, the 'security guard' employed at the last minute, and a man connected with the Meyer Lansky Syndicate. Lone assassin? No conspiracy? You must be joking. To make sure there were no mistakes, according to the CIA's Robert Morrow, a Pakistani-American also shot Kennedy with a CIA handgun disguised as a

[59] *Psychology Today*, (September 1969) Vol 3, No 2.
[60] Ibid.
[61] Private interview for *Final Judgement* with one of the Kennedy campaign volunteers who was present when Kennedy was shot.

camera. In his book *The Senator Must Die*, Morrow shows a picture of the Pakistani with his "camera" seconds before Kennedy was killed. Other researchers suggest that no bullets fired by Sirhan Sirhan actually hit Kennedy and that the real killer was Thane Eugene Caesar.

Whatever precisely happened, Bobby Kennedy was murdered by the same forces that killed his brother and they used a mind-controlled assassin who has remained programmed and mentally scrambled ever since. It is by this same method of hypnotic mind control that many computer programmers in the UK defence industry have suffered bizarre "suicides" and other deaths. Many victims have worked for the General Electric Company and its subsidiary, Marconi, and yet another cover up has suppressed the truth.

One other name I believe was associated with the murders of both John and Bobby Kennedy was the Greek shipping magnate Aristotle Onasis who made an incredible fortune by using his ships to transport drugs. Interestingly, it is a Greek custom that if you kill a man, you have to look after his wife and family. Onasis married Jackie, John Kennedy's widow.

MALCOLM X

Malcolm X was murdered while speaking at the Audubon Ballroom in New York. All the other speakers at the event pulled out at the last minute. Across the street was the Columbia Presbyterian Hospital, but they refused to respond. In the end Malcolm's aides had to run over to the hospital, grab a stretcher, and carry him there themselves. One of his close aides, Leon 4X Ameer, went to the FBI to say that elements within the government and the black organisation, the Nation of Islam, had been involved. A few days later, at the age of 32, he was dead. The cause of death was given as suicide, then a drugs overdose, and finally natural causes. I wonder if his doctor was trained at the Vatican! The black consciousness movements had long been infiltrated by the FBI and CIA and assassinations could be arranged from inside as well as outside of these black organisations. This FBI operation was called COINTELPRO and was headed by...William Sullivan, the friend of the CIA's Mossad mole, James Jesus Angleton! Sullivan was the liaison between the FBI and the Warren Commission and his COINTELPRO operation relied heavily on information from the Anti-Defamation League.[62] (The Elite's control and manipulation of black groups equally applies to anti-black groups like the Ku Klux Klan. The Klan was an Elite creation, founded by the Satanist Albert Pike, the Sovereign Grand Commander of the Ancient and Accepted Rite of Scottish Freemasonry in the American South. He was an associate of Guiseppe Mazzini, the leader of the Bavarian Illuminati after the death of Adam Weishaupt.[63] A statue of Pike still stands today in Washington DC in honour of his work on behalf of the Elite.) The FBI used

---

[62] *Final Judgement*, p83.
[63] *Secret Societies*, p125.

an anti-communist group called BOSSI to infiltrate the Nation of Islam and Malcolm X's breakaway group, the Organisation of Afro-American Unity. The head of BOSSI was Anthony Ulazowitz and his chief operative was John Caulfield. Both were publicly exposed during the Watergate scandal as two of the main characters in Richard Nixon's dirty tricks department. Caulfield had been used by the Warren Commission to 'investigate' an anti-Castro group. Common names and ties can be identified between the killings of the Kennedys, Malcolm X, and Martin Luther King, the Watergate scandal, and a stream of lesser known murders and events.

MARTIN LUTHER KING

Martin Luther King's campaign for black rights and against the Vietnam War cost him his life on April 4th 1968. A former FBI agent would later tell the House Select Committee on Assassinations how staff in the Atlanta FBI office cheered when the news of the shooting came through. "They got him," one man said. "They got Zorro" – the FBI code name for King. "I hope he dies, the son of a bitch" said another. The former agent burst into tears as he recalled the story. Dr King was also a target of William Sullivan's COINTELPRO operation at the FBI. Same names, same people, same force.

Before Dr King's arrival at the Lorraine Motel in Memphis, Tennessee, a man approached the reception desk and said he was an 'advance man' for Dr King. He insisted that King's room be changed because, said the 'advance man', "he would like to have a room on the second floor overlooking the swimming pool".[64] Staff at the motel said they didn't think he was a black man, but a white man wearing black face makeup. This is a ploy used by intelligence services for agents provocateur who cause trouble at black demonstrations and make the blacks take the blame for it. This character certainly had nothing to do with Martin Luther King because he didn't have any 'advance men'. King was shot dead when he walked out onto the balcony to talk with his driver.

The black police officer in charge of the security for Dr King was sent home against his will hours before King was killed and by then the security team had been reduced from eight men to one lone policeman. The only two black firemen at the station next to the motel were sent to other stations just for that day and when King was shot, the ambulance was delayed because it was blocked in by appliances from the same fire station. As retired Air Force Colonel L. Fletcher Prouty said: "No-one has to direct an assassination – it happens. The active role is played secretly by permitting it to happen...This is the greatest single clue...who has the power to call off or reduce the usual security precautions...".[65] That is what happened with

---

[64] David Emery, *Conspiracy Nation*, Vol. 1, No. 88.
[65] Jim Marrs, *Crossfire: The Plot That Killed Kennedy*, (Carrol and Graf Publishers, New York, 1989) p582.

Martin Luther King as it did with Yitzak Rabin, the Israeli premier, in 1995. According to the Israeli press, Rabin had a number of secret meetings with Henry Kissinger in the weeks before his assassination. Israel's security is fantastic as I have witnessed myself at Tel Aviv airport and no-one could kill an Israeli prime minister in the way it happened unless it was allowed to happen.

Witnesses said they were sure that the shots that killed Dr King came from the ground and not from the second floor of the rooming house where another 'patsy', James Earl Ray, was staying. The point where the bullet entered and left Dr King confirmed this. James Earl Ray could not have done it. A former FBI ballistics expert said that part of the rifle would have needed to be buried six inches into a wall for Earl Ray to have shot Dr King from where he was supposed to be. But James Earl Ray was convicted. Just another lone assassin. No conspiracy. Sure.

A central character in the King assassination appears to have been Jack Youngblood, a US Intelligence operative, who has been named by some researchers as the "Eggs and Sausages Man", because he began to appear regularly at a cafe close to the rooming house where James Earl Ray was staying. When shown a picture of Youngblood, James Earl Ray confirmed that it was the man who had been following him prior to the King assassination. One of Youngblood's associates was Frank Fiorini, who later changed his name to Frank Sturgis. This man was one of the Watergate burglars.[66]

The journalist, Lewis Lomas, investigated the King and Malcolm X assassinations and wrote a book, *To Kill A Black Man*. He revealed that John Ali, the treasurer of the Nation of Islam organisation to which Malcolm X was connected for some time, worked for the FBI. At one point, Ali was the most powerful man in the Nation of Islam. Lomas was following leads which could have linked the murders of JFK and Martin Luther King, particularly through the Guy Bannister 'Detective' Agency in New Orleans which played a key role in the JFK assassination. Lomas intended to implicate the intelligence agencies in Dr King's death in a film he had been contracted to make. A few days into the filming, the brakes failed on his car and he was killed. The summer after the Memphis assassination, Dr King's brother was mysteriously drowned in his swimming pool. Neighbours heard screaming, splashing, and then silence. Two years after that, Dr King's mother was murdered when a 'lone nutter' walked into her church and opened fire. It is a matter of public record that all these events took place at a time when the FBI of J. Edgar Hoover was plotting to stop the black civil rights movement and those opposing the Vietnam War. So was the Anti-Defamation League on behalf of the terrorists who control Israel.

Another famous name pops up here, too. Jesse Jackson. He has become the best known black man in America and he was featured on Christmas Day 1994 on the British network television station, Channel Four, giving an 'alternative Queen's Speech' to the one being delivered by Queen Elizabeth II on other channels at the same time. Quite an honour, if you like that sort of thing. Jackson was in the Dr King party when King was killed, although King had told his aides that he intended to part company with him. Immediately after the assassination, Jackson turned up at a press conference in a blood-stained shirt and told the story of how he held the dying Dr King in his arms. It made Jackson famous. This greatly angered other people at the scene because they knew it wasn't true. Nearly twenty years later, Jackson admitted on the Phil Donahue TV Show that he had lied. He had not held King's head in his arms at all. Where the blood on his shirt had come from has never been credibly explained. After George Bush (CFR) was elected president in 1988 he and Jackson (CFR) held a joint press conference in which Jackson endorsed the view that James Earl Ray should not be released from jail on parole. This from a man who was there when Dr King died and who has said many times that it was not the work of a lone assassin. What goes on?

The 1960s were a particularly bloody period for assassinations in the United States, but they continue today right across the world, to oust those who are not playing the Elite game and replace them with those who will. There are scores of cover stories to hide the real instigators of these murders. It could be a 'lone nutter', an Elite-controlled 'terrorist' group, a plane crash (it's easy to destabilise a small plane with the technology they have today), suicide, induced heart attacks, and so many other little 'accidents'.

WATERGATE

On the global stage, one of the finest exponents of the art of political manipulation in modern times is the Elite's Ambassador-at-Large, Henry Kissinger, who has used a series of frontmen to do his bidding. One of the best known is George Bush. From Watergate and the early 1970s, these two names began to turn up everywhere. Kissinger was not born and bred in the United States. He was born in Germany in 1923 and grew up as a Jew under Adolf Hitler. He arrived in the United States on September 5th 1938, and later became a naturalised American. In 1972 the Polish KGB agent, Michael Goleniewski, told the British government that KGB documents he saw prior to his defection in 1959 included the name Henry Kissinger as a Soviet Union asset. According to Goleniewski, Kissinger was recruited by the KGB into an espionage cell called ODRA. He was given the code name BOR or COLONEL BOR, Goleniewski claimed. Kissinger built his power-base and reputation at Harvard before becoming a leading figure in the New World Order.

US foreign policy under Kissinger followed the tried and trusted British approach for centuries – maintain the balance of power under the rule which says "My enemy's enemy is my friend". It was this approach which, in part, was behind the strategy of the Kissinger-Nixon Administration of forging links with communist China. During this time, before and after Watergate,

Kissinger (Comm 300) was in close contact with his friends in British Intelligence circles whom he worked with over the decades. These have included other Committee of 300 members like Sir Eric Roll (Lord Roll of Ipsden), and Lord Victor Rothschild the manipulator of British intelligence and Mossad, and Soviet spy along with Philby, Burgess, Maclean, and Blunt. Blunt left the staff of the Warburg Institute to work for MI5.[67] Kissinger had close connections with Britain and I have no doubt that British elements including Victor Rothschild were involved in the Kennedy assassinations, Watergate and the removal from office of Richard Nixon. Kissinger himself has admitted in a speech at Chatham House which was supposed to remain private, that he was often closer to the British Foreign Office than his own US State Department.[68]

Kissinger had an enormous influence on George Bush and some Bush biographers describe him as little more than a 'Kissinger clone'. Bush was born into the heart of the New World Order conspiracy as the son of Prescott Bush and was given all the background and experience he needed to be its frontman. He was a member of the Skull and Bones Society, a 33rd degree Freemason, member of the Committee of 300, Council on Foreign Relations and the Trilateral Commission, oilman, ambassador to China and the United Nations (both under Kissinger), chairman of the Republican Party National Committee, CIA operative before, during and after the JFK assassination, head of the CIA, vice president, and then the prize he had been groomed for since he was a boy, president of the United States.

After Richard Nixon was returned to office in November 1972, he made Bush the chairman of the Republican Party National Committee. Bush took over, 'coincidentally', in January 1973, during the trial of the Watergate burglars. They had entered the headquarters of the Democratic Party in the Watergate Building in Washington on the night of June 17th the previous year. These were the so called 'Plumbers', a White House surveillance team spying on the Democrats in the run up to the election. Or so we are led to believe. In reality, they made a botched job of it because they were meant to be caught. That was the idea.

Behind this 'scandal', many researchers now believe, and I certainly agree with them, was Henry Kissinger, the frontman for the Rockefellers and the Rothschilds. Kissinger left his executive job at the Council on Foreign Relations to join the Nixon administration, which contained more than 115 members of the CFR.[69] Nelson Rockefeller, who became vice-president as a result of Watergate, said that Kissinger took the job because he asked him to.[70] Watergate was a setup to give total power to Kissinger, and therefore the

[67] *The World Order, Our Secret Rulers*, p80.
[68] Chatham House, London, May 10th 1982.
[69] *The Rockefeller File*, p158.
[70] Ibid p180.

Elite. This was a crucial period in the global manoeuvrings by the New World Order manipulators to remove what shreds were left of government for the people, by the people. Watergate and the removal of Richard Nixon was another coup d'état on America. Nixon was no political angel, but he was just another stooge. George Bush became chairman of the Republican Party National Committee at exactly the time the Watergate story was really breaking and his mentor, Henry Kissinger, was both national security advisor and secretary of state, the only man in American history to hold those two posts at the same time. Bob Woodward and Carl Bernstein, the journalists from the Elite-controlled *Washington Post*, were given Watergate 'clues' from their informant 'Deep Throat', and turned them into front page headlines. The owner of the *Post*, Katharine Graham (CFR, TC, Bil), must have been delighted with their well-informed journalism. Their stories put so much pressure on Nixon that he had no time to oversee the government of the country. So Graham's friend Henry Kissinger did that instead.

It is public knowledge that it was Kissinger who persuaded Nixon to create the White House Special Investigations Unit (the Plumbers) with the job of stopping White House leaks. Kissinger cited to Nixon the leaking of the 'Pentagon Papers' in 1971 to justify the need to set up the unit. It emerged later that one of the Watergate burglars, E. Howard Hunt, a CIA planner of the Bay of Pigs invasion which discredited Kennedy, and a man involved at some level in the Dealey Plaza operation, had been to the Miami CIA station to recruit people for Kissinger's White House Unit two months *before* the Pentagon Papers were leaked.[71] Create the problem, then offer the solution. The White House Unit was full of CIA and other intelligence operatives and it was funded by Bill Liedtke, the president of the George Bush company, Pennzoil, and a close friend of Bush, the Republican Party chairman. Wright Patman, the chairman of the House of Representatives Banking and Currency Committee, confirmed that one of the Watergate burglars was sent $100,000 by the chairman of the Texas committee of the Campaign to Re-elect the President, known, appropriately, as CREEP. The burglar who received the money was Bernard Barker, a CIA man since the Bay of Pigs invasion. The man who sent the money was...Bill Liedtke, George Bush's business partner and one of his closest friends.[72] Congressional investigator, Wright Patman, established that the $100,000 was actually donated by Robert H. Allen, who was Liedtke's chief financial officer at CREEP in Texas. The money went from Houston into Mexico to be laundered and then back via Liedtke to Watergate burglar, Bernard Barker.[73] In 1982, Robert H. Allen was given the Torch of Liberty Award by the Anti-Defamation League (ADL), the dreadful Elite–Mossad front supported so vigorously by Henry Kissinger.

[71] *George Bush, The Unauthorised Biography*, p250.
[72] Ibid p247–247.
[73] Ibid.

Another business partner and close friend of Bush, Robert Mosbacher, was also implicated in the CREEP money laundering policy. Yet Bush said he knew nothing of what was going on! Are we really expected to believe that George Bush, the chairman of the Republican National Committee, a man with fingers in more pies than a bakers' convention, did not know that his closest friends and business associates were involved in laundering contributions to CREEP and channelling it to Watergate burglars? Are we really? Senator Patman was getting close to implicating some famous names in the Watergate break in, but he was unable to continue his investigation. His committee, which had a *Democratic* majority, ordered him to stop and the plan to subpoena twenty-three CREEP officials to testify before Congress was cancelled. Why would they do that? Perhaps the Kentucky Democrat, William Curlin, had the answer when he said:

> "...*certain members of the committee were reminded of various past political indiscretions, or of relatives who might suffer as a result of a pro-subpoena vote.*" [74]

A vicious attack on Patman and his investigation was led by the House Republican leader, Gerald Ford (CFR, Bil), the 33rd degree Freemason, member of the Warren Commission, and puppet of the Rockefeller-Morgan-Harriman-Mellon empires of the Eastern Establishment. When Nixon was forced to resign over Watergate, Gerald Ford became president. Nixon was doomed after the release of the infamous 'smoking gun tape', the recording of a conversation between himself and his chief of staff, H.R. Haldeman on June 23rd 1972, in which he discussed ways to frustrate the Watergate investigations. When Bush heard the tape had been released, he was extremely disturbed. He knew that "the Texans" mentioned on the tape was a reference to himself and his close associates, Bill Leidtke and Robert Mosbacher. In the Woodward and Bernstein book, *Final Days*, they report a conversation about Bush's reaction between William Timmons, the White House Congressional Liaison, and Dean Burch, a White House counsellor:

> "*Dean, does Bush know about the* [smoking gun] *transcript yet?*"

> "*Yes.*"

> "*Well, what did he do?*"

> "*He broke out into assholes and shit himself to death.*"

---

[74] *George Bush, The Unauthorised Biography*, p249.

But Bush could breathe easy. He would not be exposed by the tape to the wider public. Robert Mosbacher survived unscathed, too, and was to become Secretary of Commerce in the Bush presidency. Kissinger's conversations at the White House were not recorded, but those of Nixon always were. The man in charge of the recordings and the tapes which condemned Nixon was David Young, a Wall Street lawyer appointed by Kissinger and a man who had worked for the Rockefellers. The existence of the "Smoking Gun Tapes" was revealed by Alexander Butterfield, the White House liaison with the secret service. The overall head of the secret service was Kissinger. Another Kissinger appointee very significant in the demise of Nixon was Rockefeller-puppet and Knight of Malta, Alexander Haig (TC) (CFR), who would go on to be military head of NATO and Ronald Reagan's secretary of state. Nixon still refused to resign despite the tapes, and the nightmare for Kissinger, Haig and their fellow conspirators, was for Nixon to appear before an impeachment trial at which the whole plot could be exposed. Eventually pressure from Bush and Kissinger forced his hand.

Ford (CFR, Bil) took over as Kissinger's frontman (using the title President of the United States), and he pardoned Nixon for any offences he may have committed, thus avoiding further investigations or trial. Ford named Nelson Rockefeller (CFR, Bil) as his vice-president and made him head of an 'investigation' into the activities of the intelligence agencies in the light of Watergate. Also on the Rockefeller Commission was Ronald Reagan. It found nothing of worth and did nothing of substance. The Elite now had complete control of the United States administration. With the help of Ford and Rockefeller, and supervised by Kissinger, the nature of government administration was to become a fully-fledged dictatorship. That has continued to this day, through the political and economic cartels which have chosen and controlled the presidents who have followed: Carter, Reagan, Bush, and Clinton. Whoever follows Clinton will be chosen in the same way. Watergate was more than just a break-in. It was the destruction of what was left of the democratic process and all the main people behind it escaped prosecution.

IRAN-CONTRA

After a period as the United States representative in China while the Chinese and Henry Kissinger were supporting Pol Pot in Cambodia, George Bush returned home in 1975. He received a telegram from Kissinger saying that he was being nominated by Ford (Kissinger) to be the Director of the CIA. This is a major Elite organisation, as is British Intelligence, which is probably above the CIA in the Elite pyramid. It was British Intelligence that helped to set up the CIA after the war. The familiar names step forward again. A key figure behind the formation of the Office of Strategic Services, later the CIA, was General William J. Donovan. He studied law at Columbia University under Professor Harland F. Stone, who would later become US

Attorney General and appoint Donovan as his assistant. Another of Stone's protégés was J. Edgar Hoover, who would be head of the FBI, and one of Donovan's classmates was Franklin D. Roosevelt, the future President. In the First World War and between the wars, Donovan accepted a number of intelligence assignments from the New World Order brigade, including J.P. Morgan, the Rockefellers, and the Rothschilds, and on one occasion he spent an evening with Adolf Hitler. In 1941 he was appointed head of the new OSS intelligence agency by his friend from Columbia, Franklin Roosevelt. Donovan was assisted by James Paul Warburg, the son of Paul Warburg. It was James Warburg who said: "We shall have a world government whether or not you like it – by conquest or consent."[75] However, it seems Donovan was not actually in charge of the OSS. According to Eustace Mullins in *The World Order, Our Secret Rulers*, Winston Churchill's military secretary, Colonel E.I. Jacob, was told by Major Desmond Morton Church, the Prime Minister's liaison with British Intelligence, in September 1941:

> *"Another most secret fact of which the Prime Minister is aware is that to all intents and purposes US Security is being run for them at the President's request by the British. A British officer sits in Washington with Mr Edgar Hoover and General Bill Donovan for this purpose. It is of course essential that this fact should not be known."*

The leading British coordinator of the OSS and its policy was William Stephenson, the head of the Special Intelligence Section of the Secret Intelligence Service (SIS) and he was given a floor of the Rockefeller Center rent free. From there he ran a network of British agents in the United States which, according to Mullins, were involved in the murders of German sailors in New York, acts designed to entice Hitler to declare war on America. Stephenson and Louis Bloomfield, the head of Permindex, also ran Operation Underworld with the Lansky syndicate. Mullins suggests that three other members of the British Chiefs of Staff behind the creation of the OSS were: Lord Louis Mountbatten (Comm 300, Bil), a cousin of the King and related to the Frankfurt banking families, Rothschild and Cassel; Charles Hambro, director of Hambros Bank and the Special Operations Executive; and Colonel Stewart Menzies, head of the Secret Intelligence Service (SIS). Lord Victor Rothschild was also at the heart of it.

OSS agents in Europe were trained at the British espionage headquarters at Bletchley Park, close to Woburn Abbey, from where Sefton Delmer (agent to Committee of 300 newspaper tycoon, Lord Beaverbrook) operated a British dirty tricks department. Woburn was the home of the Duke of Bedford, Marquess of Tavistock. The British Bureau of Psychological Warfare became known as the Tavistock Institute. After the war, Donovan was special assistant to the US prosecutor at the Nuremberg Trials to ensure that British and American involvement with the Nazis was not revealed. President Truman disbanded the OSS in 1945, but it was reformed as the CIA in 1948 under the control of Allen W. Dulles, a major funder of Adolf Hitler. Appropriately, Dulles, a director of Hitler's bankers, J. Henry Schroder (Comm 300), chose them to handle CIA funds. The CIA is an arm of the tax-exempt foundation syndicates controlled by the Rockefellers/Rothschilds, like the Rockefeller Foundation, the Ford Foundation, and the Carnegie organisation, through which much of the CIA policy is decided.

But although the CIA is extremely important to the New World Order, the real power in American intelligence circles is the National Security Agency (NSA), an organisation that keeps its head down while the CIA does its dirty work. So while Bush was head of the CIA and even when he was president, he would be answerable to higher masters within the Elite. In his book, *The Matrix*, Valdamar Valerian reports the following conversation with a man claimed to be a CIA operative:

> *"Don't kid yourself...the CIA is just a whipping boy. NSA are the ones with the hit teams. Look into their records – you won't find a thing. Look into their budget – you can't. The CIA is just a figurehead, but as far as intelligence goes, the NSA's far superior to them – far in advance in the 'black arts'. The CIA gets blamed for what the NSA does. NSA is far more vicious and far more accomplished in its operations. ...The CIA gets the information, but the military heads the show...*
>
> *"There are about 18 or 20 people running this country. They have not been elected. The elected people are only figureheads for the guys who have a lot more power than even the President of the United States.*
>
> [Valerian]: *You mean the president is powerless?*
>
> *"Not exactly powerless. He has the power to make decisions on what is presented to him. The Intelligence agencies tell him only what they want to tell him."* [76]

Bush was not heading an independent CIA, but an element within the so called 'Inner Fed' of the secret government which consists of the CIA, NSA, FBI, NASA, and the Federal Reserve. Much of the funding for this cartel of manipulation comes from its involvement in the hard drugs trade.

Many of the people involved in the Bay of Pigs invasion in the early 1960s, who would also turn up in the 1980s in the Iran-Contra drugs-for-arms scandal, would be employed by George Bush during his period at the CIA.

---

[76] Valdamar Valerian, *The Matrix*, (Arcturus, 1988).

Bush was not new to the intelligence game and I believe his connections with the CIA go back to the 1950s. In *The Immaculate Deception,*[77] Russell S. Bowen names him as a top CIA agent since before the Bay of Pigs invasion, when he worked with Felix Rodriguez and other anti-Castro Cubans. Intriguingly, the top secret code name for the Bay of Pigs Invasion was "Operation Zapata".[78] Bush's oil company was called Zapata Oil.

Rodriguez would turn up again in the Iran-Contra scandal during the Reagan-Bush administration, which made more hard drugs available to the young people of the United States. When you look at the personnel in the Plumbers group involved in the Watergate break-in, a remarkable number of them were also involved in the Bay of Pigs. A CIA coordinator, William Buckley said that if he told what he knew about the Bay of Pigs and the Kennedy assassination "it would be the biggest scandal ever to rock the nation."[79] Buckley would later be assassinated in the Middle East. There is plenty of documented evidence that George Bush was a long-time CIA asset, since before the Kennedy assassination when the family friend, Allen Dulles, was head of the CIA. There is evidence that Bush was closer to the Kennedy assassination than people have believed.[80]

From his office at the CIA headquarters in Langley, Virginia, Bush put together his team. Among them was the infamous Theodore Shackley, whom Bush named as the CIA's associate deputy director for covert operations. Shackley had been head of the CIA Station in Miami during the early 1960s, from where E. Howard Hunt and his Watergate burglars would emerge. Shackley went on to head the CIA station in Saigon during the Vietnam War, where he masterminded Operation Phoenix. This involved the deaths of tens of thousands of Vietnamese civilians who were 'suspected' to be working for the Viet Cong. Just being able to read and write was enough to invite this suspicion, apparently. Oliver North, the 'star' of Iran-Contra, worked with Shackley on Operation Phoenix, which is reputed to have murdered 40,000 South Vietnamese villagers for Meyer Lansky and the CIA. Shackley ran a huge assassination and drug operation in South East Asia in the 1970s in which two other Bush men, Donald Gregg (Bil) and Felix Rodriquez, were involved. This operation was threatened by John Kennedy seeking to withdraw from Vietnam. This same Theodore Shackley was now appointed to an important position in Bush's CIA and he would later be recruited as Bush's 'speech writer' during the 1979-80 election campaign.

The idea that someone like Shackley would be hired to write Bush's speeches defies the imagination. No doubt his other 'talents' were the real

[77] Russell S. Bowen, *The Immaculate Deception, The Bush Family Crime Exposed,* (American West Publishers, Carson City, USA, 1991) p30–31.
[78] *The World Order, Our Secret Rulers,* p123.
[79] *The Immaculate Deception, The Bush Family Crime Exposed,* p30–31.
[80] See *Final Judgement,* p306–313.

reason for his presence. Today Shackley apparently lives in Medellin, Colombia, the home of the drug cartel. How thoroughly appropriate. Thomas Clines, a former second-in-command at the CIA station in Miami, was another Bush appointee to his CIA administration who would be involved in Iran-Contra, a scandal Bush was to say he knew nothing about. During Bush's tenure in the CIA, the operatives knew that they could virtually do as they liked because their director had a gift for looking the other way. The power over the US Intelligence operations was concentrated in Bush's hands as a result of a series of measures by President Ford. In the words of the Elite's *New York Times*, Ford: "…centralised more power in the hands of the Director of Central Intelligence than any had had since the creation of the CIA".[81]

Bush turned the screw on journalists who asked unpleasant questions while, at the same time, he was paying other 'journalists' to be CIA informants. One reporter who suffered from Bush's wrath was Daniel Schorr (CFR) of CBS. Bush was pictured on the front page of the *Washington Star* angrily remonstrating with Schorr on Capitol Hill for leaking information which put the CIA in a less than good light. Schorr, who was on Nixon's list of 'enemies' during the Watergate affair, was sacked by CBS. The late owner of CBS, William Paley (Comm 300), owed much to the Bush family. The credit which enabled him to buy the TV network was personally arranged by Prescott Bush, who was a CBS director in the 1950s.

The contacts George Bush made at the CIA would be invaluable when he became vice-president to Ronald Reagan on January 21st 1981. Reagan's personal fortune dates from a time shortly after becoming governor of California when he bought some land cheaply and sold it at a vast profit to a group of benefactors who have never been publicly identified.[82] (I bet I could have a decent shot at who they were!) He was, at 70, the oldest man to be inaugurated as president. His mind was failing and he needed long afternoon naps each day. Almost every word he spoke, even in relatively off-the-cuff situations when greeting foreign leaders, was written for him on cards by his aides. George Bush was president in fact, if not in name. After an assassination attempt on Reagan by another 'lone nutter', John Hinckley,[83] his sharpness of mind further deteriorated and his need for sleep increased. This gave George Bush almost complete control of affairs and in the background would have been hovering his mentor, Henry Kissinger.

Bush built a network of organisations within the government with himself at its head. These were the Standing Crisis Pre-Planning Group, the Crisis Management Centre, the Terrorist Incident Working Group, the Taskforce

---

[81] *The New York Times*, (February 18th 1976).

[82] George C. Andrews, *Extra-Terrestrials Among Us*, p173.

[83] Journalists and investigators have identified at least circumstantial connections between the Hinckley and Bush families.

on Combating Terrorism, and the Operations Sub-Group. These were all subordinate to, and controlled by, the Special Situation Group chaired by Bush. If ever there was a line-up of problem-reaction-solution and 'managed crisis' organisations, then this was it. Through this network would come the arms-for-drugs operation, Iran-Contra.

Bush hired his former CIA associate, Donald P. Gregg, as his main advisor on national security and Gregg brought with him a 'former' CIA assassinations manager, Felix I. Rodriguez, whom Bush had known back to the time of the Bay of Pigs invasion and during his period as head of the CIA. Gregg and Rodriguez were involved with Theodore Shackley in the assassination and drug-running operation in Southeast Asia, and the two now worked out of George Bush's office! It was strictly illegal under US law for the government to supply arms to Iran or to supply the Nicaraguan 'freedom fighters', the Contras, in their war with the Sandinista government. It was certainly illegal to accept payment with drugs in return. The Reagan-Bush administration would do all of these things.

One of the ways the US government secretly undermined the Sandinistas was by mining harbours in Nicaragua. This was done by a company called Continental Shelf Associates Inc which is based on Jupiter Island, Florida. Jupiter Island is an interesting place. It became the feifdom of the Harriman set...including George Bush, who has a home there. Jupiter Island has been a base for generations of New World Order families. Continental Shelf Associates (CSA) lists many oil companies and government agencies among its clients. They include the Rockefellers' Exxon and the Bush-Leidtke company, Pennzoil.

CSA was used by the US military for coastal mapping and reconnaissance in Grenada before the invasion in October 1983 and during US operations in Lebanon. The company was run by Robert 'Stretch' Stevens, a close associate of Theodore Shackley and Felix Rodriguez when they were all involved in Vietnam and the Bay of Pigs. A CSA company at the same address is Acta Non Verba, which means 'action, not words'. A high level CIA officer quoted in *George Bush, The Unofficial Biography*, said of this CSA subsidiary:

> "*Assassination operations and training company controlled by Ted Shackley, under cover of a private corporation with a regular board of directors, stockholders, etc, located in Florida. They covertly bring in Haitian and South East Asian boat people as recruits, as well as Koreans, Cubans, and Americans. They hire out assassinations and intelligence services to governments, corporations, and individuals...*" [84]

The bombs planted in the harbours of Nicaragua caused such a row in the US that the laws against such action, the Boland laws as they were called,

---

[84] *George Bush, The Unofficial Biography*, p397

were still further strengthened. But at a secret meeting of the National Planning Group on June 25th 1984, Reagan, Bush, Casey, and other top officials decided to ignore the law. They would fund the Contras through Honduras, just as they had used El Salvador against the Sandinistas. Bush and Oliver North, an official of the National Security Council, travelled together to El Salvador. While Bush is so keen in public about "Wars on Drugs", the smuggling of hard drugs gets uncomfortably close to him time and again. On January 18th 1985, Felix Rodriguez is known to have met his namesake (but not thought to be a relative), Ramon Milian Rodriguez,[85] an accountant and money launderer who worked for the Medellin cocaine cartel in Colombia. From his prison cell in Butner, North Carolina, Ramon told the investigative journalist, Martha Honey:

> "...[Felix offered] *in exchange for money for the Contra cause he would use his influence in high places to get the* [cocaine] *cartel US goodwill...Frankly one of the selling points was that he could talk directly to Bush. The issue of good will wasn't something that was going to go through 27 bureaucratic hands. It was something that was directly between him and Bush."* [86]

This could easily be done, given that Felix Rodriguez was working from Bush's office. A memo in early September 1986, sent to Oliver North by retired Army Major General, John K. Singlaub, said that Rodriguez was talking of having 'daily contact' with Bush's office and this, said the memo, could damage President Reagan and the Republican Party. Oliver North would also write in his notebook that "Felix has been talking too much about the VP [vice-president]".[87] In his 1987 book, *Out Of Control*, Leslie Cockburn presents devastating evidence of Bush's involvement in Iran-Contra and the drug running. He says that planes chartered by the CIA and packed with cocaine flew directly into the Homestead Airforce Base in Florida using a CIA code signal.

In 1986, the Reagan-Bush administration admitted that Adolfo Chamorro's Contras, who were supported by the CIA, were helping a Colombian drug trafficker transport drugs into the United States, and the testimony of John Stockwell, a former high ranking CIA official, revealed that drug smuggling was an essential component of the CIA operation with the Contras. George Morales, one of South America's biggest traffickers,

---

[85] This meeting was confirmed by Felix Rodriguez and reported in the *Miami Herald* on June 30th 1987. Ramon Rodriguez, a notorious drug money launderer, was invited to Ronald Reagan's Inauguration Ceremony in 1981. He would have had much in common with another guest, Licio Gelli of the P2 Freemasonry Lodge.

[86] *George Bush, The Unoffical Biography*, p399.

[87] Entry in North's diary for January 9th 1986. Revealed in a court hearing in April 1988.

testified that he was approached in 1984 to fly weapons to the Contras. In return, he says, the CIA helped him to smuggle thousands of kilos of cocaine into the United States via an airstrip on the ranch of John Hull, a self confessed CIA agent, and associate of Oliver North. At the time, George Bush was having a war on drugs – for public consumption only.

Meanwhile, the other wing of Iran-Contra was continuing, the arms-for-hostages-deal with Iran. Oliver North was heavily involved in the supply of arms to Iran, via Israel, in return for hostages. The release of the hostages was explained, in part, by the efforts of Terry Waite, the representative of the Archbishop of Canterbury. Waite was being used without his knowledge by North who was quite happy for him to take the credit for releases which were, in fact, the result of arms sales via Israel. Waite would eventually be taken hostage himself. Bush, who as George Shultz publicly confirmed, supported the arms-for-hostages policy, was telling the nation: "We will make no concessions to terrorists". The money and drugs involved in the arms transfers to Iran were laundered through Switzerland, that centre for Global Elite activities. Jean Ziegler, a member of the Swiss Parliament, writes in his book, *Switzerland Washes Whiter*:

> "The Commerce developed by North and his accomplices was as simple as it was lucrative. With the expert assistance of the Swiss magnates, as well as some discreet help from the Swiss Secret Service, they delivered American and Israeli weapons to the Imam Khomeini. The Imam paid for some of the weaponry in dollars, but for most of it in drugs [morphine base and heroin]. The godfathers of Turkish and Lebanese networks installed in Zurich turned the drugs into cash on the international market. After taking their cut of the profits, the godfathers deposited the remainder in numbered accounts that had been opened in the main banks and financial institutions of Geneva and Zurich."

In an interview for Italian Television in May 1990, the CIA agent, Ibrahim Razin, said that he had learned from a leading Mafia boss that Licio Gelli of the P2 Freemasonary Lodge had sent a telegram in February 1986 to Phil Guarino, a close associate of George Bush. According to Razin, the telegram said: "Tell our good friend Bush that the Swedish tree will be felled". Three days later, the Swedish Prime Minister and Bilderberger, Olof Palme, was assassinated. Razin, who went into hiding in fear of his life, said that Palme was killed because he knew too much about the American arms trafficking to Iran which, Razin said, P2 had been involved in. Part of the reason for the arms to Iran, he said, was the payback from Bush and his colleagues for the Khomeini regime *delaying* the release of American hostages in the so called "October Surprise". This was when the Reagan-Bush campaign had negotiated with the Iranians not to release American hostages until after the election against Jimmy Carter to prevent Carter getting the credit, and therefore the votes, for their release. The plane which flew 51 of the 52 hostages home left Iran as Reagan and Bush were being inaugurated.

While all the leading politicians are implicated with, or controlled by, the Global Elite network, there is great rivalry between some of them and this allows the Elite to play them off against each other. Even at the higher levels of the pyramid, the personnel are being manipulated by those even nearer the top. George Bush flew to Paris to meet with Iranian officials, including Ayatollah Mehdi, at the Hotel Ritz on October 19th 1980. Among those accompanying Bush were William Casey, the soon-to-be head of the CIA; Donald Gregg, the CIA operative; Robert McFarlane, who had been a member of President Carter's National Security Council; Senators John Tower and John Heinz; and a long-time CIA and Office of Naval Intelligence operative, Gunthar Russbacher. It was John Tower, a Texas senator at the time of the Kennedy assassination, who told the CIA's police detective Gary Wean about the CIA's "fake" assassination plot involving E. Howard Hunt. Russbacher described the event in intricate detail to Rodney Stich, a former federal inspector and author of the book, *Defrauding America*. Russbacher claims he flew Bush back to the States in a two seater SR-71, which allowed Bush to arrive in time to make a speech at the Washington Hilton. This event was used to deny the Paris meeting on the grounds of time and logistics. But Ari Ben-Menashe, an agent with Israel's (and the Rothschild's) Mossad, also confirms the meeting took place. He was there because Israel was the middleman for the arms deal between the US and Iran. Bush has always denied being in Paris or that he knew anything about the October Surprise and arms shipments to Iran. *Defrauding America* includes copies of a number of letters from the National Security Agency which describe the Iran operation. Each is marked…"Copy to V.P. George Bush." Poor old George needs to consult one of those mail order books you see: *How To Improve Your Memory*.

It may seem hard to believe that a drug-for-arms operation run illegally from George Bush's office could be covered up so well that he would then be elected president, but the extent of media control should not be underestimated. Cover ups are the daily bread of the Elite. They can't cover up everything, just as they cannot control everything, and they have had some spectacular failures on both counts. But as a rule they are extremely effective in keeping information that would expose the game from the public.

In late 1986, the Iran-Contra scandal blew. On October 5th, a plane left the Ilopango air base in El Salvador with arms and ammunition for the Contra terrorists in Nicaragua. The flight had been coordinated by officials within George Bush's office. As the plane came low to make the drop, it was grounded by a Sandanista missile. Three people died in the crash, but cargo handler, Eugene Hasenfus, parachuted into the hands of the Sandanistas. Bush was alerted in a call to his office by drug-runner Felix Rodrigeuz. The truth was out. Or some of it was.

The power of the Elite channels can be the only explanation of how, despite the overwhelming evidence against him – far, far, more than I have outlined here – Bush evaded prosecution, even though Buz Sawyer, the pilot of the crashed plane, was found to have the private phone number of George Bush's office in his pocket! Hasenfus also stated that George Bush knew about the whole thing. But Bush denied any involvement or knowledge of what happened, and subordinates like Don Regan, Admiral John Poindexter, Oliver North and Major General Richard Secord were sacrificed and scapegoated. They were heavily involved, of that there is no doubt, but Bush got away with it, as did Reagan and his Secretary of Defense, Casper Weinberger (CFR, TC). North, who was up to his eyes in the intrigue, faced hearings and, given the evidence, it was staggering that he should not only escape punishment, but emerge as almost an American hero. Of all the peoples in the world, certain expressions of the American psyche have been the easiest to dupe. Others involved, like CIA Director William Casey, had health problems. In the aftermath of the Iran-Contra revelations, Casey (who knew the whole story) literally could not speak following an operation for a 'brain tumour' that took away his ability to talk. Two months later he was dead. In his presidential election campaign, Bush pledged to build a 'kinder, gentler' America.

The Tower Commission was appointed to investigate the Iran-Contra affair, chaired by our old friend, the Texas Senator, John Tower. This is the same John Tower who, according to CIA man Gunthar Russbacher, was on the plane with Bush when he flew to Paris for the October Surprise meeting with the Iranians! The John Tower who knew the real story of Lee Harvey Oswald. Also on the Tower Commission was Brent Scowcroft (CFR, TC, Bil), a Kissinger 'yes man' and an executive of Kissinger Associates; and Ed Muskie, another do-as-you're-told politician who could be twisted to suppress the truth. Muskie was himself implicated in both the October Surprise and Iran-Contra. As you can see, the Commission was thoroughly independent. It cleared George Bush of all blame and involvement. When Bush became president he made John Tower his secretary of defense. Tower was asked by reporters if this appointment was a pay-off from Bush. His response?

> "As the Commission was made up of three people, Brent Scowcroft, and Ed Muskie in addition to myself, that would be sort of impugning the integrity of Brent Scowcroft and Ed Muskie…We found nothing to implicate the Vice President…I wonder what kind of pay-off they're going to get?" [88]

I can tell him. Bush appointed Brent Scowcroft as his National Security Advisor. The Senate refused to accept Tower's appointment and he began to

---

[88] *The New York Times*, (March 2nd 1989).

speak of the injustice he believed had been done to him. He died in a plane crash on April 5th 1991. When the Senate turned down Tower, a decision Bush probably engineered, he selected Dick Cheney (CFR) as defense secretary. Cheney was the senior Republican member of another committee which cleared Bush of involvement in Iran-Contra, the House Select Committee to Investigate Covert Arms Transactions with Iran. A group of other people, including former defense secretary, Casper Weinberger, were given a pardon by Bush for their involvement in Iran-Contra. This came on Christmas Eve 1992, a matter of weeks before they were due to face a trial which would have implicated Bush. In January 1993, he then passed over the presidency to Bill Clinton who continued the cover-up because – as we shall see in the next chapter – he was involved too! The *Washington Post* and the rest of the mainstream media which had turned a comparatively minor break-in at the Watergate building into a scandal that dethroned Richard Nixon, kept their heads down as the United States government sold arms to terrorists in exchange for drugs for American children. It is actually possible to coordinate a drug running and arms running operation from the White House and get away with it. Unbelievable, maybe, but true all the same.

THE OKLAHOMA BOMB

On April 19th 1995, I believe that the Global Elite, via elements within the US government, the CIA and Mossad, murdered some 168 men, women and children in the bombing of the Alfred P. Murrah Federal Building in Oklahoma City.

I do not agree with the approach of the 'people's militias' which have expanded enormously across the United States in the face of the evidence that the New World Order agenda includes a coup d'état on dissidents who oppose the tyranny. The militias arm and train themselves in readiness for what they see as the inevitable day when the New World Order troops will arrive on their doorstep. Meeting violence with violence is not my scene. I would not pull a trigger if my life depended upon it. What would be the point? I wish to see an end to violence, not add to it, and my own view of life and creation could hardly be more at odds with that of the 'Christian Patriotism' at the heart of the militias' belief system. But for months before the Oklahoma bombing, I was reading reports from America of how the government was targeting these militias and hounding them, not the least because they were having some considerable success in circulating information about the plans of the Global Elite. Then, suddenly, came that horrific bomb and the blame was dumped not only on a few people, but on the whole of the militia movement.

What was Bill Clinton's response and that of his attorney general, Janet Reno, the subject of much criticism by the militias? To use the bombing as an excuse to increase the powers of the FBI to infiltrate and attack these groups and, as Clinton put it, to "ease the restrictions on the involvement of the military in domestic law enforcement". This is similar to the policy of UK Prime Minister John Major, when he allowed the MI5 intelligence agency to become involved in domestic law enforcement. The idea is to turn the intelligence agencies and the military into the world police who will enforce the New World Order. Clinton also used Oklahoma to urge the media to ban "anti-government extremists" from their papers, screens, and microphones and attacked the talk radio shows which involve the public and offer a rare opportunity to communicate information which differs from the official line. A former official of the Bureau of Alcohol, Tobacco, and Firearms (BATF) was harangued and accused of stirring up the climate of opinion that led to Oklahoma. How was this man supposed to be doing this? By saying that the BATF, which was responsible for the Waco massacre, was rotten to the core when he worked for it and remained so today.

I wonder how many Americans saw the irony of a president denying that America was becoming an authoritarian state while at the very same time he was using the bombing to push it closer to exactly that. And who supported the 'Democrat' president in this? His chief 'opponent', Newt Gingrich, the 'Republican' Speaker of the House. What a surprise. Ford, Carter, Reagan, Bush, Clinton, Gingrich, are all stooges for the same One Party State in which the same force controls both the Republicans and their 'opponents', the Democrats.

The Oklahoma bombing could well have been problem-reaction-solution of the most grotesque kind. Do you think that a force which creates wars that cost tens of millions of lives, kills presidents, and blows passenger aircraft out of the sky, would not sacrifice the lives of children for their sick ambitions? If only that were so. The FBI and the Bill Clinton/Janet Reno Justice Department claims that one explosion destroyed the Alfred P. Murrah Federal Building, and that the bomb was concocted by the former soldier Timothy McVeigh and Terry Nichols from fertiliser and fuel oil. McVeigh has said that he was microchipped while serving in the US forces. This is done to many US soldiers and, as you will see in a later chapter, a microchipped person can be used to do almost anything. For an event like the Oklahoma bomb, however, they would require support from powerful sources. Ted Gunderson of Santa Monica, California, a man of 28 years experience with the FBI, believes the official explanation of the bomb to be both ridiculous and impossible.[89] Gunderson, and other contacts within the FBI, believe that the blast was caused by an electrohydrodynamic gaseous fuel device known as a barometric bomb. To know how to make such a bomb you would require security clearance at the highest levels of the government/military and have access to a wide range of chemicals and electronic technology. The barometric bomb has "Q" clearance, which puts it on a level of security and

---

[89] *The Spotlight*, (Washington D.C., May 15th 1995) p1, 12, 13.

secrecy with nuclear weapons components. If Gunderson is correct, someone like McVeigh and others charged with him, could not possibly have such knowledge or resources. The very idea would be ludicrous.

Gunderson says he spoke to one of the inventors of the barometric bomb and was told that the devastation caused to the building was exactly in line with what such a device would achieve. The bomb works like this. There is a first explosion using an explosive known as PETN and this releases a lethal cloud of chemicals, ammonium nitrate, and aluminum silicate. The cloud, Gunderson says, is energised with a "high potential electrostatic field". There then follows a second blast a few seconds later using another explosive called PDTN which ignites this cloud and creates an explosion of greater magnitude than TNT. To confirm that a top secret barometic bomb was used in Oklahoma there would need to be traces of the appropriate chemicals and there had to be two explosions a few seconds apart and not just one, as the Clinton administration and the FBI are claiming. At a court hearing in El Reno, Oklahoma, on April 28th 1995, the FBI Special Agent, John Hersley, said a shirt that McVeigh was wearing when arrested was found to contain traces of the explosive PDTN.[90] And when Gunderson checked with the seismographic record at the Oklahoma Geological Survey at the University of Oklahoma, it revealed that there had been...two explosions, ten seconds apart. The first went off at 9.02 am and 13 seconds and another followed at 9.02am and 23 seconds. That could not possibly happen with a fertiliser bomb, a claim for which there is no credible evidence anyway. Other bomb experts have suggested different devices to the one described by Gunderson, but they agree with him that the government 'explanation' is ridiculous. Rubble from the Murrah building was piled up against the general records office across the street on the *other* side of the truck which supposedly exploded with the fuel-fertiliser bomb. The only way the rubble could have blown in that direction was by an explosion inside the Murrah building. Very conveniently, the building was demolished by the authorities and the debris removed before it could be properly investigated.

There is an excellent chance that elements of the US government and its agencies blew up its own building and killed some 168 men, women and children, to further the goals of the New World Order under problem-reaction-solution. Stunned? Who wouldn't be? I think, however, that this is a bomb too far for the Elite. I believe the truth will eventually come out and reveal a much wider picture.

The government has consistently increased the size of the 'fertiliser' bomb it claims was built by McVeigh and co, because the size of the bomb and the extent of the devastation are clearly at odds. It was first announced that the 'fertiliser' bomb weighed 1,000 pounds, but this has since increased in stages to reach some 4,800 pounds. As a result, the description of the vehicle used

[90] *USA Today*, (April 28th 1995) p3A.

to carry it has had to change in line with the ever greater weight involved. The bomb was first carried in a delivery van, according to government announcements, but now it has changed to a removal van. Stand by for the articulated truck to make an appearance! As Michael J. Riconosciuto, the designer of the barometric bomb said, a fertiliser bomb would have scattered fertiliser all over the site. This did not happen at Oklahoma.[91] Many government officials who would normally have been in the building that day were not there, including some of those from the Bureau of Alcohol, Tobacco and Firearms (BATF), who were supposed to have been the target of the bomb because of their genocide at Waco. Also, Michael J. Riconosciuto revealed to *Spotlight* that records and components of his barometric bomb were stolen in two raids on a well-guarded warehouse in Aberdeen, Washington State, in 1988. On the first occasion, he said, those involved were set free by police without charges and on the second the police watched the robbers carry out the raid and yet did nothing![92] The whole thing stinks and yet the American people have allowed themselves to be so duped that they have permitted, and even demanded, the increased powers of the government to open mail, tap phones, search homes, and take away papers and documents at will. These powers have been achieved by using the excuse of a bomb which elements within the government are almost certainly responsible for. Problem-reaction-solution. I believe that the Anti-Defamation League will prove to be seriously implicated and we can expect more 'set-ups' of this nature to discredit those who expose the truth.

Wake Up America... Wake Up World!

All this has happened so many times before. The Kennedy assassination was used by his successor, Lyndon Johnson, to increase the powers of the State, as have other such engineered events and 'problems'. The CIA, often in league with Mossad, has been responsible for some horrific terrorist outrages abroad involving the murder of children, thousands of them if the full truth be told. In Beirut in 1983, a car bomb planted by the CIA-Mossad went off. It failed to kill its intended target, a muslim cleric, but instead murdered 91 passers-by, a story later revealed by the former CIA operations analyst in Vietnam and Latin America, Gordon Thurlow.[93]

We are dealing here with a consciousness working through these people that knows no scale of horror it would not use to achieve its end and, as we saw in Oklahoma, it is supported by a media peopled by a combination of the few who know what is going on and the many who are nothing more

---

[91] *The Spotlight*, (June 5th 1995) p5.
[92] Ibid p3.
[93] *The Spotlight*, (May 8th 1995) p4–5.

than manipulators' mouthpieces, while having no idea that this is so. The way the 'journalists' and television 'correspondents' simply repeated the government's version of events without question was incredible. Anyone who suggested that the New World Order was happening was dismissed as 'paranoid' and yet at least 99.9% of those reporters will never have read a single word about the conspiracy. Nice to know that those who inform us are so informed themselves!

MARGARET THATCHER

The sort of methods of covert manipulation and cover-up I have mentioned here are happening around the world every day. Even the demise of Margaret Thatcher as Prime Minister of the United Kingdom in 1990 is also linked with the stories I have outlined here.

Assassinations can become a problem when investigators won't let them go away, as with the JFK killing in particular, and it is easier and 'cleaner' from the Elite point of view to remove people more subtly by creating events, often economic in nature, which undermine leaders and cause them to be removed 'democratically'. Margaret Thatcher, a Bilderberg attendee, was an Elite choice who served the cause well economically during the 1980s when she and Ronald Reagan set the themes for the decade under the control of Paul Volcker, the head of the Federal Reserve and the International Banking Commission. One of the people who did most to ensure that Margaret Thatcher became conservative party leader in the 1970s was Sir Alfred Sherman, who would later be advisor to the Serbian leader Radovan Karadzic, the man responsible for so much suffering and horror in the civil war in the former Yugoslavia. Thatcher was selected by the Elite, possibly without her knowing what was really going on. But politicians are only there to be used as appropriate to the plans of the Global Elite and she outlived her welcome when she continued to oppose the removal of national sovereignty by the European Community through a European currency and central bank. In May 1989, *The Spotlight* newspaper reported that the Bilderberg Group meeting on La Toja Island off Spain in that same month, had decided she had to go. A year later she was removed by her own MPs while still in office.

Mrs Thatcher would not have been removed by people going to Conservative MPs and saying: "Hey, the Bilderberg Group says she's got to go." It is much more covert. The media is used to undermine the target, drip, drip, drip style, and unrest, doubts, and fears, are stimulated among ministers and MPs who want to keep their jobs. The threat of losing their privilege because "We will never win the next election with Margaret Thatcher as leader" is a wonderful way to concentrate the minds of politicians to believe that "something must be done". A momentum is created which in the end makes the target politician's removal inevitable. When, in Britain, we hear of the "men in grey suits" who decide when the leader of the Conservative Party will come and go, we are looking at Elite/Brotherhood representatives within that party. Not top of the pyramid people, or anything like, but those who do as they are told when a change is demanded. The same with other parties in other countries. There are so many world events I could list over the last 40 years that would all come back to the same group.

THE UFO COVER-UP

Throughout the period since the war, reports by the public of UFOs have been continually dismissed by the authorities. They don't exist, we are told. About the same time that the Warren Commission reported its covered-up version of the Kennedy assassination, the Condon Report came out which did a similar job on UFOs. It said there was nothing about the phenomena worth investigating. If that is the case, why are the files on UFO reports designated at 'above top secret'? Because this is probably the biggest cover-up of them all, that's why. A cover-up of the truth that the American elite have flying saucer, anti-gravity technology which makes the Space Shuttle look like an antique, and to smokescreen the fact that extraterrestrials are visiting this planet from the Fourth Dimension. This whole area is a minefield of disinformation and we need to keep a very open and flexible mind here, especially as the UFO investigation field will have been seriously infiltrated by those who wish to deflect us. But there are now an average of 150 reported UFO sightings *a day*. If you accept the claim that only ten per cent of sightings are reported, that's more like 1,500 a day, across the world. They can't all be flown by Earth humans and while the Elite could use their craft to set up specific events to manipulate the human mind, there are, in my view, also increasing numbers of true extraterrestrials operating on this dimension. Some are here to help, others to hinder the transformation of humanity and Planet Earth. The latter are linked with the Global Elite, either by face-to-face contact, or via channelling and consciousness control.

I have presented a lot of evidence relating to UFOs in *The Robots' Rebellion*, but there is much more available for those who wish to research further. What's for sure is that there is a whole library of information about UFOs and extraterrestrials which the public is not being told about, including the background to human abductions and the mutilation of cattle and other farm animals all over the world, in ways that can only be done by technology not known in the public arena. Either it is the work of extraterrestrials or of the human scientific elites at the underground bases in the United States (at places like Area S-4 near Groom Lake in Nevada and the Dulce facility in New Mexico). John Lear, a one-time pilot for the CIA, told a Dallas UFO Group in 1988:

> *"The nation has been brainwashed by a CIA mind-control operation based on fear of ridicule. There have been at least one million abductees in the US*

since 1947. In the last 13 years, there have been over 40,000 cattle mutilations in the US. There are approximately 70 alien civilisations known to be visiting us at the present time.

"Gordon Cooper, one of our very best astronauts, lost his chance to go on the Apollo flights because he dared to speak out about UFOs in a letter to the United Nations. During the past few years, there has been a steep increase in the number of missing persons. It is estimated that there are about ten million of the Grays [an alleged ET race] in bases on the Earth and Moon, but it is not known whether they are able to return to their home base. They enter and exit their underground bases through interdimensional transference, a hyperspace manoeuvre which accounts for the apparently nonsensical stories of UFO witnesses who report having seen UFOs going in or out of mountains. Those witnesses are truthfully describing a manoeuvre that is at present incomprehensible to our science.

It was President Eisenhower who allowed the reins of power to pass from the hands of the President into the control of the Pentagon. Ever since Eisenhower, the real rulers of this nation have been a military junta." [94]

Again Lear's claims may be disinformation. But the themes cross-check with an enormous number of other reports (which, of course, might also be disinformation). I am now certain to my own satisfaction that the human form was created by extraterrestrials; that negatively-inspired ETs from the Fourth Dimension have sought to control this planet throughout known history by actual appearances and (mostly) by controlling the consciousness of those humans operating within a negative frequency range; that those who have conspired to install the New World Order since ancient times have been puppets of these beings (quite possibly, in part, the "Melchedekans" or "Elohim") and the same applies to the Global Elite of today. I feel that contact has taken place between the Elite and certain negative ET races, and the most unspeakable genetic experiments are being carried out in the underground bases around the world, especially in the United States, on those who are written off as 'missing persons'. The Nazi mentality is alive and well and controlling America under the direction of an extraterrestrial consciousness which *is* the Nazi mentality. I believe that these ETs of the Fourth Dimension feed off negative human emotion. They feed off the energies of fear, guilt, and misery, and therefore seek to increase our pain and sense of fear and hopelessness, both for nourishment and to diminish our sense of worth and potential, thus making it easier to control the vibratory prison. When we love and respect ourselves, we cut off the food supply and open our minds and hearts to breach the blocking vibration. This we can and *will* do.

The reason for the UFO cover-up is to keep information from us about other civilisations and worlds that would open people to a far greater

---

[94] Dallas MUFON group meeting, August 10th 1988.

perspective of life and Creation, and to keep hidden the Global Pyramid of manipulation which (at its highest levels) is knowingly in contact with – and guided by – a negative force from another dimension. The number of scientists and computer programmers in the UK and the USA working with advanced technology who have met strange, unexplained, deaths is ridiculous. Most have been written off as…'suicide'. One after the other has died, many of them linked to the Star Wars project and Marconi, a subsidiary of General Electric in the UK. If the Elite do have 'flying saucer', anti-gravity craft (and I believe they certainly do), or technology in the 'defence' field they wish no-one to know about, it is just such scientists and computer programmers who might know about it, either by accident or design. Maybe they found out too much about that or the technology linked to Star Wars, which may really be part of the global electronic communications network designed to monitor billions of microchipped people. Each mysterious death has been claimed to be unconnected to the others, under the familiar lone-assassin-no-conspiracy-type approach. Secret technology is put together under the rules of compartmentalisation. Each company or scientist only works on *part* of the project. Only a tiny few know how each part fits together to produce the finished article.[95]

One of the most famous scientific victims of the Elite was Dr Wilhelm Reich, who died in a federal penitentiary in 1957 while the authorities destroyed all his work they could find. His organs were removed at an 'autopsy' and were never seen again. Reich's last book was called *Contact With Space*, which detailed his UFO research. He understood how the Earth reflects the human mind and he recognised the barrenness and desertification of once beautiful landscapes as the result of humanity's emotional barrenness. He identified the lifeforce energies, which he termed orgone energy. He labelled positive energy 'OR' and the negative 'DOR'. Reich believed that a particularly virulent form of negative energy, which he called Melanor, was emitted by some of the extraterrestrial spacecraft he said were visiting the planet. This Melanor took the form of a black powder-type substance which "smelled like dead bodies". This has been mentioned in a number of stories by people claiming to have seen UFOs.

Reich said that by using the knowledge of positive orgone energy, the lifeforce, he and his small team had grown grass to knee height in the Arizona desert, where it had never grown before in modern times. He also realised that this energy could be harnessed to provide 'free energy' for all the warmth and power we need, without pollution and (virtually) cost free.

This is what could be happening all over the world if the knowledge of how to do it were not suppressed. The 'unsolvable' problems of this world are only unsolvable because the solutions are kept from us. Throughout his

[95] See *Open Verdict* by Tony Collins, an investigation into 25 mysterious deaths among people working in the defence industry, (Sphere Books, London, 1990).

career in the United States after fleeing Nazi Germany, Reich was harassed by what he called the 'hoodlums in government', the 'higs'. He developed a weapon which, he said, made UFOs disappear and he discovered how to change the weather and make it rain in the desert. This was only a technological extension of what the Native Americans could do with their rain dances. They were both utilising the same energies. In *Contact With Space*, the book that helped to speed the end of his life, Reich was getting close to the truth. He wrote:

> *"Am I a spaceman? Do I belong to a new race on Earth, bred by men from outer space in embraces with Earth women? Are my children offspring of the first interplanetary race? Has the melting pot of interplanetary society already been created on our planet, as the melting pot of all nations was established in the USA 190 years ago? Or does this thought relate to things to come in the future? I request my right and privilege to have such thoughts and to ask such questions without being threatened to be jailed by any administrative agency of society...In the face of a rigid, doctrinaire, self-appointed, ready-to-kill hierarchy of scientific censorship it appears foolish to publish such thoughts. Anyone malignant enough could do anything with them. Still the right to be wrong has to be maintained. We should not fear to enter the forest because there are wild cats around in the trees. We should not yield our right to well-controlled speculation. It is certain questions entailed in such speculation which the administrators of established knowledge fear...But in entering the cosmic age we should certainly insist on the right to ask new, even silly questions without being molested."* [96]

Sadly, for Reich, the freedom he so rightly proclaimed was denied to him, as it has been for so many others who have been killed for the crime of acquiring knowledge of science and UFOs which the Elite and their extraterrestrial/Luciferic masters wish to remain hidden. His fellow 'scientists' looked on as he was crucified. It is even speculated that another reason President Kennedy was killed was that he found out about the ETs and pledged to make the information public. In 1965, a leading journalist, Dorothy Kilgallen, was investigating both the UFO cover-up and the Kennedy assassination. She said in her column in the *Los Angeles Examiner* of May 22nd 1965, that she had met "a high British official of cabinet rank" in London who had told her that British scientists had examined a crashed UFO crewed by small men, less than four feet tall.[97] In the same year, she interviewed Jack Ruby in a Dallas jail. Ruby, the man who killed the 'patsy', Lee Harvey Oswald, told her something which, she told close friends, "would blow the Kennedy case sky high." Within days she was found dead.

---

[96] *Contact With Space*, quoted in *Extra-Terrestrials Friends And Foes*, p47.
[97] *Extra-Terrestrial Friends And Foes*, p238.

Verdict: suicide. Her friends searched her apartment for the notes of her meeting with Ruby. None were found.[98]

The UFO scene is awash with disinformation and that means there is something going on which those in power don't want the public to know. I believe there is a scenario in which a threat from an extraterrestrial force is hyped up by the Global Elite to the point where public terror will allow them to install a world government and army. This was one of the suggestions in the *Report From Iron Mountain*. I have no doubt, as I said in *The Robots' Rebellion*, that at least some abductions attributed to 'aliens' are actually carried out by humans as part of a mind manipulation and microchipping operation. The Rockefellers (via billionare Laurance Rockefeller) have been linked with the 'research' into extraterrestrials.[99] As this book was being completed, I was approached with information about what was claimed to be a mass mind manipulation policy on the people of the United Kingdom, headed by the National Security Agency (NSA) in America with the blessing of the British authorities. This has involved among other things the staging of 'UFO' sightings, 'alien' abductions, and the microchipping of people, including some of those involved in UFO research. I want to know a lot more about this to see if it checks out. If you know something and you would like to talk to an open mind, please contact me.

One thing's for sure from where I am sitting: there is an underground facility connected with RAF Rudloe Manor in Wiltshire, England, which the British people ought to know about, and the same goes for places like the top secret Mount Weather underground city near the little town of Bluemont, Virginia, about 46 miles west of Washington D.C. Some of the things you see in the James Bond films are not all fiction. Neither of these facilities, or the others, are operating in the interests of the people. Mount Weather is likely to be a centre from where the parallel government of the United States, the one that *really* runs the country, coordinates its operation. It is also the place which supervises the surveillance of Americans who challenge the tyranny. Congress, the 'elected' representatives of the people, has been refused any information about what goes on there. Yes, ladies and gentlemen, this is the free world.

The same Hidden Hand which was behind the Bay of Pigs, Vietnam, the Kennedy, King and Malcolm X assassinations, Watergate, Iran-Contra, terrorist bombings, and the demise of Margaret Thatcher, is also responsible for the disinformation and cover-ups over UFOs and extraterrestrials. On the surface, these often very different subjects and events appear to be unconnected, while they were – and are – coordinated by one force: the

---

[98] Story reported by Richard Deacon in *The Truth Twisters*, (MacDonald, London, 1987).

[99] "Watching For Aliens", *The Spotlight*, (September 25th 1995) p2. It reveals Laurance Rockefeller's support for the Center for the Study of Extra-terrestrial Intelligence.

Global Elite, controlled by the Fourth Dimensional Prison Warders of the Luciferic Consciousness. But the truth about UFOs, whatever that may turn out to be, is not far from being known, and the veil is lifting on so much that has been kept secret across the generations. This is the time when the hidden will be revealed and the cause of the manipulation removed.

When the Elite network has been dismantled in our lifetimes, what a different world this will be. For it is this which is behind the global conflicts, the trafficking in hard drugs to young people, and the minute-by-minute abuse of what we call democracy and freedom. Yet still the mass of the people allow their minds to be misled like bewildered rabbits caught in the headlights of an oncoming car.

I have sketched out the mere bones (or should I say the skull and bones) of George Bush's career up to 1989. I have not even mentioned his endless business dealings, or the number of times his business associates found themselves appointed to the government payroll. That would take many chapters in itself, but the information is all there and I recommend the book, *George Bush, The Unauthorised Biography*, if you wish to know more. He has been a constant theme in the New World Order for over forty years. You have read some of his background and the way his hand was symbolically holding a smoking gun when some terrible events were unfolding. So what did the American people do about it? I'll tell you.

They made him president.

Chapter 13

The One Party States

I saw a television programme a few years ago about research into animal behaviour and it featured a rather unpleasant experiment in which a mouse was placed in a network of glass tubes. Every few seconds it came to a junction and had a choice of going left or right. The mouse thought it was free to go wherever it wished, but in fact the choices were strictly controlled. Its freedom was an illusion.

The human race today has allowed itself to be like that mouse in the tubes. The multidimensional manipulators are very clever in their use of buzz words. They link them together to create an accepted meaning, which is often the opposite of the real situation. If you say something often enough, people will believe it. The word 'freedom' has been equated with 'democracy', and democracy is equated with the parliamentary systems of government in the 'free world'. We are programmed to see the three elements of freedom-democracy-parliament as the same thing. They are not. The 'democratic' systems are part of the smokescreen designed to fool us. If you know you live in an authoritarian regime which controls your thoughts and behaviour, the media, and the economic highs and lows, the desire for freedom in the human heart will eventually rebel against this. People are much easier to control and suppress if this is done while they go on *thinking* they are free. Such is the nature of our 'democracy'.

We can take the example of Westminster, this Mother of Parliaments, to see what a phoney democracy we have. Most Members of Parliament are not elected by the people, but by the committee or members of their constituency party! The United Kingdom parliamentary system is made up of constituencies which return an MP to parliament at the General Election. But only a relative few of these constituencies are 'marginal' in that the outcome is in doubt. Most are either overwhelmingly Conservative or Labour. The public are mind-controlled to believe that their income should decide whom they vote for. The Conservatives have the 'image' of low taxation and voting Conservative is, for many – depressingly many – just another part of their social status. Detached house, two cars, vote Tory. In the poor and deprived areas, many of which have been devastated by the people-are-numbers housing policies of Labour governments and councils, the majority vote Labour because "they're the party of the working classes".

Yes, they are the party which sees economic success as more people standing for eight hours a day next to a factory machine, or a mile underground in a coal mine. These rigid mindsets mean that constituencies which are mostly affluent return Conservative MPs, no matter how competent or otherwise the person with the blue rosette may be; and in the poor areas, the one with the red rosette, whoever he or she may be, will become the Member of Parliament.

In these constituencies – the overwhelming majority – the would-be MP only has to persuade the local party members to select him or her to stand at the election and they are virtually certain to be elected to Parliament. It is what they call being selected to stand in a "safe seat". So if the Elite want someone to be elected to further the New World Order, it is no problem. Find them one of the endless safe seats and they are in. Even if an MP with his or her own mind slips through the net, they will be told how to vote by their party or face sanctions against them, like a block on their advancement or, as in the case of the Conservative MPs opposed to further integration into the European Union, suspension from the party. This is democracy, Elite-style, because it was they who created the parliamentary structure after the power of the monarchies was curtailed or removed by the 'people's' revolutions. If our new MP does as he or she is told, they may advance into government or even be Prime Minister. More than that, if they are clones of the Elite, the advancement can be very quick.

In the United States, I understand, there are still some people who believe that the public select the president. If only it were true. Two things select the president: money and the media. The Elite controls both. You need fantastic amounts of money to run for the presidential nomination within your own party, never mind the presidency itself. To do that you need silly money. Only the banking/business establishment has those resources and their money goes to the one they want. Sometimes it also goes to a candidate they know has no chance of winning because that makes sure that his opponent – the one they *really* want – will be the next occupant of the White House. Add to this the media coverage which supports one candidate and undermines the other, and you have a rigged election promoted as the democratic process. Once the candidate is elected, it is pay back time. They who pay the piper call the tune.

Certain legislation and an agreement to select certain people in the main positions within the administration are arranged before the election funds begin to flow. Give David Rockefeller a call and ask him who the next president is going to be. He'll know by now. The background staff are far more powerful than a prime minister or president if they work in concert. They don't have to be popular because the public don't know they exist or what they do. But the politicians do have to court popularity, particularly at election time. This makes them easy prey for those in the background. We have a television comedy programme in the UK called *Yes, Minister*, which involves a civil servant manipulating a minister to do exactly as he wants. It is very funny, but in the reality of the political system, such manoeuvring is deadly serious.

The politicians and the media perpetuate an illusion and so divert attention from those who truly run the world. The politicians give the impression that *they* have the power, and the media supports this gigantic myth by reporting events and decisions *as if* the politicians were the ultimate sanction. Hour by hour we have the presidents, prime ministers, and their underlings, pictured and quoted. We see them meeting at 'summits' and issuing statements about events over which they have little or no power. But the public have to be persuaded by the media that 'elected' politicians are the global decision makers. If we don't accept that illusion, we start to ask questions about who does, therefore, control events. The media report the world as if politicians are at the top of the pyramid, when they are only the puppets, trigger-pullers, and mouthpieces for those who are *really* at the top. As a result, those who control our lives can stay in the shadows while those who only appear to be in power are constantly in the spotlight. The diversion is brilliantly orchestrated.

It is vital for those of us who live in the 'democracies' to realise that we do, in truth, live in a One Party State. When we appreciate that, we will stop looking to politicians to tell us what to do and start thinking and acting for ourselves. We will stop believing that by voting for a different party at election time we will change anything of substance. Politicians of whatever party are not going to change the world because they are just pawns. We all have to take that responsibility and stop handing it over to "them", the politicians, economists, and anyone else who will have it. The illusion that we have a 'choice' of who governs us will continue to persuade us to give our responsibility away unless we get wise to the fact that we don't have that choice.

All political movements are controlled by the same force (*Figure 15*). If you have two main parties from which the government is chosen each time and they vote the same way on all the legislation that really matters, there is no 'choice' for the elector. This is the case with the Democratic and Republican Parties in America. The USA, this home of 'freedom' as the presidents are constantly telling us, is a One Party State. So is the United Kingdom. There is no fundamental difference between the Labour and Conservative Parties. It is impossible to vote for a party in Britain which has any chance of forming a government that is not in favour of further centralisation of power in Europe, with one currency and a central bank. I am sure you will find the same themes all over the world. When people point to other, smaller, parties, offering an apparent alternative, they are missing the point. If the parties who have any chance of winning agree on the fundamentals, elections become an irrelevance, a farce.

What confuses people is the way that politicians who are working to the same ends appear in public and even privately among their colleagues and

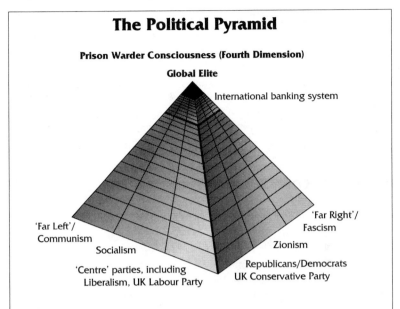

The Political Pyramid

Prison Warder Consciousness (Fourth Dimension)

Global Elite

International banking system

'Far Right'/
Fascism

'Far Left'/
Communism

Zionism

Socialism

Republicans/Democrats
UK Conservative Party

'Centre' parties, including
Liberalism, UK Labour Party

This is a generalised summary of how all political movements connect to the same source. There are, however, elements of communism/fascism within all of them – some more than others. The spectrum is really a circle with fascism and communism operating on the same thought pattern – **authoritarianism**

Figure 15

friends, to be promoting very different, sometimes opposite, attitudes to life. This allows them to appear to be opponents when they are really on the same side. Dr Kitty Little, a researcher into the infiltration of British politics and intelligence agencies for more than 50 years, explained the technique in her booklet, *Treason At Westminster*:

> *"It is probable that some of those infiltrators who have in the last 20 years reached the top of the Labour and Conservative parties, had training in the art of concealing their true opinions. Fuchs* [the German physicist who worked on the atomic bomb project] *has described his formal instruction in what he called 'controlled schizophrenia', and even boasted that when drunk he could retain his assumed character with the political opinions of those with whom he worked. Similarly another member of the* [subversive] *organisation, Philby* [Kim Philby, the spy] *wrote: 'I will conclude by mentioning a factor which has unnecessarily puzzled some western commentators on my case. That was the liberal smokescreen behind which I concealed my real opinions. One writer who knew me in Beirut has stated that the liberal opinions I expressed in the Middle East were 'certainly' my true ones. Another comment from a personal friend was that I could not have*

maintained such a consistently liberal-intellectual framework unless I had really believed in it. Both remarks are very flattering. The first duty of an underground worker is to perfect not only his cover story, but his cover personality.'" [1]

When we look at the apparently 'different' political views, we are so often looking at a façade. A series of people wearing masks to hide their real intentions and opinions. Behind the mask are the Global Elite and the All-Seeing Eye, and it is this 'democratic' masquerade[2] which acts as the smokescreen for the One Party States.

AMERICA'S ONE PARTY STATE

Nothing makes this more obvious than the example of George Bush and Bill Clinton, two apparent 'opponents'. One is a Republican, the other a Democrat, but both are controlled by the same group. Both are frontmen for the One Party State and they are connected by the Council on Foreign Relations, the Trilateral Commission, Freemasonry, drugs, murder, Iran-Contra, the Bank of Credit and Commerce International (BCCI), their support for the invasion of sovereign states, centralised institutions, the GATT agreement, the North American Free Trade Area (NAFTA), the Gulf War...on and on it goes.

Bush swept to victory against Michael Dukakis in 1988 on a tidal wave of Elite money. Henry Kissinger's presence was again at the heart of the Bush government with two members of his company, Kissinger Associates, taking leading roles. They were Brent Scowcroft, head of the Kissinger Associates Washington office, and Lawrence Eagleburger, the president of the company. Scowcroft was director of the national security council and Eagleburger, the undersecretary at the State Department. A founding board member of Kissinger Associates, Lord Carrington, was Secretary-General of NATO from 1984 to 1988. Quite a line up for one company! Bush also promoted the Elite strategy of 'saving' the environment, just as Bill Clinton (CFR, TC, Bil) and Al Gore (CFR) would do. On the other side of the Atlantic, exactly in tandem, Margaret Thatcher (Bil), turned a mental somersault and began to proclaim the need to protect the environment after once calling

---

[1] *Treason At Westminster.* Text of a memorandum submitted in October 1978 to the Royal Commission on Criminal Procedure by Dr Kitty Little (p3). The Philby quote comes from his book, *My Silent War.* Dr Klaus Fuchs left Germany before the war and, thanks to Lord Victor Rothschild, travelled to the United States to work on the Manhattan Project which produced the atomic bombs that were dropped on Japan. He was later jailed for giving British and American atomic secrets to the Russians.

[2] *The Concise Oxford Dictionary* defines the word masquerade as: "masked ball; false show; pretence; appear in disguise; assume false appearance". This is what you are observing in the parliaments and governments of the world.

environmental campaigners "the enemy within". The word "drugs" is also a constant theme which links the Bush and Clinton presidencies. Drugs are a massive form of income for the Elite and a front-line weapon in the destabilisation of society. We shall look first at the Republican wing of the One Party State in the form of Mr George Bush.

THE INVASION OF PANAMA

The Bush attack on Panama on December 20th 1989, was connected with drugs, though not in the way it was portrayed by the government and the media. This is another fine example of how the truth of a situation is submerged in political rhetoric and media camouflage. We are told that American troops invaded Panama and abducted President Manuel Noriega because of his drug running activities and to save American children from the evil of drugs. There is a chance that the very opposite is the case. Noriega was on the payroll of the CIA while Bush was the Director and he was being paid some $110,000 a year for his 'services', which included running drugs. When Bush was challenged about this after the invasion of Panama, he said he had never met Noriega, but then suddenly remembered the meeting. Noriega was involved in the drugs market and rigged elections, but the American government and the CIA knew that when they employed him. The 1984 Panama election was won by Arnulfo Arias, but Noriega took power with a mixture of extreme violence and fraud. President Ronald Reagan then dispatched Secretary of State George Shultz (CFR, TC, Bil, Comm 300), to give legitimacy to Noriega and even to declare that Panama's democratic principles were a lesson to the Sandinista government in Nicaragua!

The Bush-Noriega relationship began to change during the Iran-Contra period, according to Noriega, when he was visited by Admiral John Poindexter, the head of the National Security Council, on December 17th 1985. Poindexter was prosecuted for his part in Iran-Contra. Noriega told CBS reporter Mike Wallace that Poindexter demanded that he support the US war against the Sandinista government in Nicaragua. When he refused, Poindexter threatened economic warfare and the destabilisation of Panama. What Poindexter wanted was for Panama to invade Nicaragua with American support, Noriega said.[3] At no point was Noriega's alleged involvement in drugs mentioned. But the US Drug Enforcement Administration (DEA) did contact him about drugs. They wrote to congratulate him on helping them to stop Panama being used as a drug and drug-money-laundering centre![4] Just one month later, the Reagan-Bush administration demanded that Noriega be removed on the grounds of drugs, corruption, and lack of democracy. The need for 'democracy' in Panama is an insult. Again Noriega was certainly no saint, but the CIA have supported,

---

[3] "Panama: Atrocities of the 'Big Stick'," *American Leviathan*, p39–40.
[4] *American Leviathan*, p41–42.

and imposed, some of the most grotesque far Right dictatorships across the world to suit their own agenda, including the financing of terrorists to murder women and children by the thousands.

It is not easy working out the motivations of the Drug Enforcement Administration, because within it are people committed to stopping the flow of drugs into America and others equally determined to increase it. A number of DEA and CIA operatives have described how some officials of the Drug Enforcement Administration are involved in expanding the availability of hard drugs in the United States. Noriega's former chief advisor, Jose Blandon, has claimed that the DEA has protected the biggest players in the drug empires and that DEA officials paid Noriega $4.7 million to keep quiet. In February 1988, Noriega was indicted on drugs charges, all but one of which related to activities before 1984, when he was on the CIA payroll! Economic sanctions against Panama followed – the economic warfare which Poindexter had promised. If Noriega had agreed to support the US war with Nicaragua, or hadn't fallen out with Bush in some way, he would still be dictator of Panama instead of being in a US jail.

When Bush became president, he made the ludicrous statement that Panama posed an "unusual and extraordinary threat" to US national security and foreign policy. *US News And World Report* said on May 1st 1989 that Bush had authorised $10 million in CIA expenditure on projects against the Panamanian government. Some of the money was delivered by the CIA's Carlos Eleta Almaran, who had recently been arrested for drug trafficking. Those charges were ordered to be dropped by Bush after Noriega was ousted. By December 20th 1989, with Noriega still there despite the CIA's best efforts, US forces invaded Panama. Hundreds, perhaps thousands of civilians, including children, were killed. Noriega was abducted to America for trial and sentence on drug charges. The rest of the 'free' world, including Britain's Margaret Thatcher, offered not a word of protest. The judge at his trial refused to allow any CIA documents to be seen in his defence and he was sentenced to 40 years for running drugs.

What would the government and CIA officials get if they came to trial! They'd have to reincarnate a number of times to complete the sentence. When you observe the background to Noriega's arrest, it is extremely relevant to know that the men the Bush regime imposed on the people of Panama to replace Noriega were closely connected with the money laundering, drug trafficking, business. The new president, Guillermo Endara, was an official of at least six banks involved in drug-money-laundering. The money laundered through these sources came from the Colombian drug smuggling ring led by Augusto Falcon and Salvador Magluta, who were reported to be smuggling one ton of cocaine a month into Florida from the late 1970s until 1987.[5] The new vice president of Panama installed by Bush was Ricardo Arias Calderon,

[5] *George Bush, The Unofficial Biography*, p537.

whose brother was president of the First Internamericas Bank when it was controlled by the Cali drug cartel. Official figures show that drug trafficking and money laundering in Panama after Noriega has been greater than it was when he was there. One of those captured by the invading US forces was the Mossad agent, Michael "Freddy" Harari, who, with other operatives like David Kimche, worked with the CIA on behalf of Mossad with the Medellin and Cali drug cartels. He was allowed to escape in an Israeli jet because, if he had been put on trial, the whole CIA-Mossad drug operation would have been blown.[6]

THE WAR ON DRUGS

George Bush became America's 'Mr War on Drugs'. Hard to believe when you see the company he kept and the operations he was involved in during Iran-Contra and the invasion of Panama. Bush is a global drug trafficker!

He led 'anti-drug' campaigns during the Nixon and Reagan presidencies and another during his own. None of them worked, and, in the words of Congressman Glenn English, his war on drugs was "little more than lip service and press releases". One of these claimed that his South Florida Task Force, set up under Reagan, had ended the marijuana trade in South Florida. This was an outrageous claim, but when Francis Mullen Jr, of the Drug Enforcement Administration (DEA), challenged the statement, he was sacked. Bush even used the CIA to arrange drug 'busts' that were designed to give the public the impression that he was succeeding. CIA operative, Trenton Parker, has told how the Colombian drug dealers each donated cocaine which was landed at Miami International Airport in March 1980 and left in a place where it would be found by customs officials.[7] This is often done to give the illusion of success. On other occasions the small fry are targeted while the major players, with their links to the highest levels of world politics and intelligence, are allowed to ply their trade unmolested. Only rarely do genuine officials apprehend the big names. Even then it can be because they have outlived their usefulness to the manipulators. Parker also described how it was the CIA who called together the top Colombian drug dealers for two meetings in late 1981 under the Reagan-Bush administration to form a cartel to improve the shipment of drugs into the United States. The first meeting, he said, took place at the Hotel International in Medellin, attended by about 200 drug dealers. The now infamous Medellin Cartel was officially created in December 1981.[8] The CIA formed the Colombian drug cartels? Yes. But, then, what is amazing anymore?

Nothing of substance that Bush promised in his various drug 'campaigns' was ever delivered and, more than that, the revelations of his links with drug

---

[6] *Defrauding America. A Pattern Of Related Scandals*, p512.

[7] Ibid p312–313.

[8] Ibid p306–307.

dealers continue to mount, as they do with Jimmy Carter and Bill Clinton. We have already seen the Shackley-Gregg-Rodriguez connections through the Iran-Contra arms-for-drugs scandal when more – not fewer – hard drugs were brought into the United States to further destabilise American society. For fourteen years Bush was also a friend of Don Aronow, who (according to one published account[9] and a number of other researchers) was connected with the Meyer Lansky crime syndicate, drug running and drug money laundering. Then there is the Zapata Oil Corporation, which was set up by George Bush. This company was a CIA front and that its subsidiary, Zapata Offshore, was implicated in drug smuggling while Bush was its top man. Michael Maholy, who worked for the State Department and the CIA for two decades, said that drugs were brought by sea to the Zapata Offshore rigs, unloaded, and then flown ashore in the helicopters, constantly carrying goods and personnel between the rigs and the American mainland. He said he saw this happening and confirmed it through the cables that he handled. Maholy said the ships of a company called Pacific Seafood were used to ferry the drugs between countries.[10]

It is a big mental leap, I know, to appreciate that the world market in illegal hard drugs is controlled and supervised by Elite elements within organisations like the CIA and British Intelligence, which are supposed to be there to protect society from the consequences of hard drug addiction. But there it is. Nothing is ever what it seems. It has been accepted that the CIA experimented with LSD before it was promoted as the 'freedom' drug of the 1960s. The Elite have been involved in the manipulation of society through drugs for a very long time. It goes back many centuries and reached a new peak with the Opium Wars against China in 1840 and 1858, when Chinese efforts to stop the flow of opium into their country were thwarted by the might of the British Empire. Queen Victoria's Prime Minister, who was involved in both wars, was Lord Palmerston, the Grand Patriarch or Master of Grand Orient (Illuminati) Freemasonry and a member of the Committee of 300. The vehicle for this trade in opium from India to China and elsewhere was the East India Company, a group of Scottish merchants who were aligned with the Knights of St John of Jerusalem and the Society of Jesus (the Jesuits). Some researchers believe that the company's real masters were the banking families of northern Italy, the Black Nobility.[11]

The strategy used by the British in China has become a blueprint for invasion-by-drug-addiction ever since. They sponsored a mass addiction to opium until Chinese society and vitality was torn asunder. The British

---

[9] Thomas Burdick and Charlene Mitchell, *Blue Thunder*, (Simon and Schuster, New York, 1990).

[10] *Defrauding America*, p312–314.

[11] *The World Order, Our Secret Rulers*, p279.

government used a network of terrorism and organised crime, like the Triads, the Hong Society, and the Assassins, to carry out the trade on their behalf. When the Chinese rulers reacted to stop the supply, the British used their military and naval might to defeat them. And the 'peace' treaty after the conflict then gave the British a guaranteed right to increase the flow of opium; to be paid compensation for the opium the Chinese rulers had confiscated; and to have sovereignty over strategic ports and offshore islands. This is how Hong Kong came under British rule. It was used as the centre for Far East drug trafficking and that is still its role today.

Most of the gold and money transactions on the Hong Kong financial markets are the pay-offs and money laundering of the drug trade. The Treaty of Nanking of 1842 gave Britain control over Hong Kong, plus $21 million in silver. It was written by the colonial minister, Edward Bulwer-Lytton (Comm 300), whose writings were to so inspire Hitler, the Nazis, and others such as Madame Blavatsky. His son was the Viceroy of India at the height of the opium trade between India and China, a period camouflaged by the writings of Rudyard Kipling about the British Raj (British drug runners). In the book, *The Opium Clippers*, Basil Lubbock names the owners of the British vessels engaged in the opium trade as the East India Company; Jardine Mathieson; Dent and Co; Pybus Bros; Russell and Co; Cama Bros; Duchess of Atholl; the Earl of Balcarras; King George IV, The Prince Regent; The Marquis of Camden; and Lady Melville. It was Lady Melville's ancestor, George, who welcomed William of Orange to the throne and was made Lord Privy Seal.

After the second opium war, which ended in 1860, the British merchant banks and trading companies established the Hong Kong and Shanghai Corporation as the central bank of the Far East drug industry. According to all research I have read about the drug network, the Hong Kong and Shanghai Bank, with its global connections, continues to be a financial centre for the drug industry to this day.[12] So was the Nugan Hand Bank (based in Sydney, Australia), another CIA/Mossad operation run by Francis Nugan and Michael Hand, a Green Beret and a colonel in the US Army assigned to the CIA. Hand was in frequent contact with George Bush after his election to vice president, according to CIA operative, Trenton Parker.[13]

Look at some principal officers of Nugan Hand: Admiral Earl F. Yates, President, chief of staff for strategic planning of US forces in Asia and the Pacific during the Vietnam War; General Edwin F. Black, President of the Hawaii branch, the commander of US troops in Thailand during the Vietnam conflict; George Farris, operative with the Washington and Hong Kong branches, a military intelligence specialist; Bernie Houghton, the Saudi

---

[12] "State Organised Crime", the presidential address by William J. Chambliss to The American Society of Criminology, 1988.

[13] *Defrauding America*, p355.

Arabia representative, a US Naval Intelligence undercover agent; Thomas
Clines, of Nugan Hand in London, a director of training in the CIA's
clandestine service who was involved in Iran-Contra and operated with
Michael Hand and Theodore Shackley during Vietnam; Dale Holmgreen, of
the Taiwan office, flight service manager in Vietnam for Civil Air Transport
which later became the infamous CIA airline, Air America; Walter
McDonald, head of the Annapolis, Maryland, branch, the former deputy
director of CIA economic research; General Roy Manor, the Philippine
branch, the chief of staff for the US Pacific command and the US
government's liaison with President Ferdinand Marcos; William Colby,
Nugan Hand's lawyer, a former director of the CIA.[14]

Just the kind of people you would expect to be running a bank, eh? Well, at
least they would be, if you wanted your bank manager to give you advice on
running covert operations and training terrorists. A director of Nugan Hand,
Donald Beazley, was chairman of City National Bank of Miami, which
handled funds for the Anti-Defamation League.[15] Michael Hand was found
dead in his Mercedes Benz in the late 1970s on a remote road outside Sydney.
He had 'shot himself'. It was a remarkable suicide in that he had pulled the
trigger and then, before he died, he must have wiped all his fingerprints off
the gun because none were found. An Australian government investigation
revealed that millions of dollars in Nugan Hand records were unaccounted for
and that it was serving as a money laundering operation for drug traffickers.
These profits were being used by the CIA to finance gun smuggling, and
illegal covert operations around the world. There was also evidence that the
CIA was using the bank to pay for political campaigns against politicians in
many countries, including Australia, to ensure the voters supported the CIA
choice. Yes, this is still the 'free' world we are talking about.

Banks with household names across the world are vehicles for laundering
drug money as it passes from account to account until its origins are lost in
the web of transactions. The gold and diamond industries, dominated by the
Rothschilds and the Oppenheimers through companies like DeBeers, are also
used to wash drug money. The money buys gold or diamonds from those
companies and then they are sold to produce 'clean' money. The network of
interconnecting Anglo-American families in the Elite web of manipulation,
who have been responsible for the engineering of conflict and economic
depression through the generations, are also behind the world illegal drugs
market.[16] Some of the most famous names, merchant banks, and companies in
the world are making a good slice of their fortunes directly or indirectly from

---

[14] *Defrauding America*, p355.

[15] *Final Judgement*, p92.

[16] For a detailed explanation of the global drug industry and who is behind it, see *Dope Incorporated. The Book That Drove Kissinger Crazy*, by the editors of *Executive Intelligence Review*, (Washington D.C., 1992).

the drug addiction of the young. We are entering the time when those people will have to face that responsibility publicly as part of their eternal evolution and the public are going to be astonished at some of those involved.

The same families and organisations were responsible for the slave trade and alcohol prohibition. The latter was a means to create the massive network of organised crime in the United States. The structure thus produced was perfect, as intended, for drug trafficking once Prohibition was over. The main groups campaigning for Prohibition and an end to the "evils of drink", groups like the Women's Christian Temperance Union and its Anti-Saloon League, were financed by the Rockefellers, Vanderbilts and Warburgs via the Rockefeller Foundation, the Russell Sage Foundation, and similar tax-exempt foundations. Prohibition was another con by the Elite used for longer-term motives. Incidentally, it also made a fortune for Joseph Kennedy, the father of JFK.

Professor Alfred McCoy's 1972 classic, *The Politics Of Heroin In South East Asia*, and his 1991 update, *The Politics Of Heroin – CIA Complicity In The Global Drug Trade*, tell of how CIA helicopters in Vietnam were carrying drugs from the fields to the distribution points, when the American public thought they were there to fight 'communism'. He describes how a Pepsi Cola bottling plant was used for this trade and how the media suppressed this information. 58,000 Americans and goodness knows how many Vietnamese were killed in that conflict and nothing sums up more powerfully the lack of respect this mindset has for human life than the way the CIA smuggled drugs into America in plastic bags hidden in the body cavities of the dead soldiers being returned home for burial from Vietnam. CIA operative, Gunthar Russbacher, has told how some bodies were gutted and filled with drugs for shipment back to the States.[17] The bodies carried secret codes which allowed those carrying the drugs to be identified on arrival at West Coast airbases, particularly the Travis Air Force Base in California. The drugs were then removed and made available for the young people of America.

One man who had his eyes opened to all this during the Bush presidency was Lieutenant Colonel James "Bo" Gritz, one of America's most decorated soldiers, with sixty-two citations for valour, five Silver Stars, eight Bronze Stars, two Purple Hearts, and a Presidential Citation. My outlook on life and that of Bo Gritz could hardly be further apart, but his experiences deserve to be heard by anyone who thinks that government is still – or ever was – 'for' and 'by' the people. In an address to the American Liberty Lunch Club, recorded on the video, *A Nation Betrayed*, Gritz describes how he twice visited a man called Khun Sa, who was the recognised "overlord" of heroin trafficking in the Golden Triangle of the Far East. Heroin is a derivative of opium. Gritz became involved when he was told that the release of US prisoners of war (still being held after the conflicts in Laos) was being stopped by American government officials involved in drug trafficking. He

[17] *Defrauding America*, p295.

found this to be correct. The government did not want the prisoners released because they knew about their officials' involvement in the drug trade and might talk about it when they returned home. Kuhn Sa and his operatives in the Golden Triangle told Gritz about some of the Americans they had worked with in the past. They named Theodore Shackley, whom George Bush appointed to a top job in the CIA and used as a 'speech writer'. They also listed Richard Armitage, then a US Embassy official and later on the campaign staff of Ronald Reagan, who appointed him the assistant secretary of defense. No wonder there was so little interest in releasing US prisoners of war who could blow the whole thing. Armitage is reported to be a close friend and advisor to Colin Powell, the US Chief of Staff during the Gulf War, who was presented as a possible presidential candidate, standing as a self-styled "Rockefeller Republican".[18]

The Elite are involved in drugs for three main reasons. First to make unthinkable amounts of money – billions per year – to finance covert operations against elected governments and society in general. Drug profits produce money which does not need to be channelled from government sources where it could be traced. Secondly, the 'problem' of drugs has produced (understandably) such a reaction of "something must be done" that people are agreeing to the erosion of rights and freedoms in a way that they never would unless there was a 'solution' required to 'stop' the supply of drugs and its terrible effect on the structure of society. It also provides the US (Global Elite) with an excuse to intervene in the affairs of other countries. Thirdly, we have the opium-to-China syndrome. If you want to divide and rule and stop people manifesting their full potential, what better way of doing it than to get a significant section of the young generation (and many others besides) hooked on hard drugs? What the British provably did to the Chinese is what the Elite is seeking to do to the young people of the world, to sap their natural vitality, their sense of worth, and the knowledge of their infinite potential to achieve anything they wish to achieve. The war on drugs is another phoney war. As Bo Gritz put it:

"No president that's ever declared a war on drugs has ever fought one." [19]

And Michael Levine, a former agent with the Drug Enforcement Administration, said that the war on drugs was the:

"...biggest, whitest, and deadliest lie ever perpetrated on US citizens by their government." [20]

[18] *The Spotlight*, (May 8th 1995) p2.
[19] The video, *A Nation Betrayed*.
[20] Michael Levine and Lauri Kavanau-Levine, *The Big White Lie*. Also quoted in *Defrauding America*, p293.

And who have been the two frontmen for every "war on drugs" since the Nixon administration? George Bush and Bill Clinton. We'll hear more of Clinton's drug activities shortly.

THE GULF WAR

George Bush is an oilman. Much of his colossal fortune comes from oil and those companies provided the bulk of his election funds. When Bush policies led to a rise in the price of oil, both his income and that of the oil cartel went up by enormous amounts. It was the same for another oilman, James Baker, Bush's secretary of state. In the wider sense, the more the Arab oil producers could be divided, the more power the United States, the British, and other industrial countries would have over them. Conflict in the Middle East, which raises the price of oil and causes turmoil and hostility within the Arab world, is good for oilmen and good for divide and rule. If you can arrange such conflict to involve a group of countries fighting under the United Nations flag, you are accelerating the move to a world army under central global control – one of the fundamental aims of the New World Order. The Gulf War did all of these things. If Saddam Hussein, a close friend of Bush for many years, was not in on the plot, then he was brilliantly set up.

In July 1990 Bush attended the NATO Summit at Lancaster House in London, chaired by the NATO Secretary General, Manfred Wörner, who (like his predecessor, Lord Carrington) was a Bilderberger. Some researchers established that the possibility of a new Middle East War was discussed and so was the deployment of NATO forces outside their designated region, the so-called "out-of-area" deployment. From this Summit came the London Declaration which called for closer cooperation between NATO and the countries of the former Soviet Union. This has since evolved, as was always intended, into the policy of absorbing those countries into NATO as part of the world army strategy. The Elite is obviously anxious to make sure this absorption policy is adopted, because once NATO begins to expand and operate outside Europe and the North Atlantic, it gets ever closer to being a world army. The idea is to extend NATO's area of operations by inviting more countries to join and to engineer events using the problem-reaction-solution strategy which lead to a fusion of NATO and the UN 'peacekeeping' forces and the formation of the world army. This is the background from which the Gulf War needs to be viewed.

Disputes between Iraq and Kuwait are not new. Kuwait has been under British and Elite control back to the days when the economic potential of oil was discovered. It is a dictatorship, an unpleasant one, and the idea that the Gulf War was to 'free' Kuwait is just ridiculous. If Kuwait is to be freed, the dictators of the Royal Family elites need to give up their power and the British manipulation of that country and its people has to end. Saddam Hussein was encouraged by the Americans and the British to go to war with Iran in 1980. If the findings of some researchers are accurate, Saddam was led to believe by British and American Intelligence that the Khomeini regime was in such chaos, the war would be over quickly. They lied. It dragged on for eight years amid appalling suffering and loss of life. But it was good for the oil companies, the banks, the armament companies, and divide and rule.

The British government armed both sides in this conflict and some (but only some) of this scandal has surfaced through the Scott Inquiry into illegal arms sales to Iraq. I wonder if this inquiry has heard of a company called Midland Industrial Trade Services, which is claimed to be the Midland Bank's secret arms operation. This is based, I am told, behind the façade of an 'ordinary' branch of the Midland in Victoria Street, Westminster, London SW1H 0NJ. I wonder also if the Scott Inquiry has heard any allegations that Midland Industrial Trade Services were introduced to the Iraqis by Kissinger Associates? I'm sure there is nothing whatsoever in these rumours from very well informed sources. The Midland Bank, that pillar of respectability, involved in secret arms sales? The very thought is ridiculous. Isn't it?

The Iran-Iraq war is a grotesque example of modified Hegelianism. The CIA looked after Khomeini during his exile in Paris to ensure he was ready and waiting to take over when the Shah, another CIA puppet, had outlived his usefulness. At the same time, as *The Wall Street Journal* of August 16th 1990 reported, it was the CIA in 1968 who supported the Baath Party in Iraq and installed Saddam as dictator. Now Saddam would be used again, knowingly or otherwise, to start up another war in the Gulf, another war planned long before. George C. Andrews reports in his book, *Extra-Terrestrial Friends And Foes*:

> "*A little known fact about the Gulf War is that one month before our Declaration of War on December 15th, 1990, Secretary of State, James Baker, signed the US Army report from the 352nd Civil Affairs Command on the New Kuwait* [unclassified, and therefore available to those interested]. *This report describes in detail how extensively Kuwait will be destroyed, how the oil wells will be set on fire, and then how it will all be rebuilt 'better than before', with despotism, instead of democracy, even more strongly entrenched than it had been before. The report includes a list of US corporations who are to be assigned the profitable task of rebuilding Kuwait and extinguishing the oil well fires, as well as the Arab names they will be operating under.*
>
> "*Why have none of his political opponents thought of asking the obvious questions: How did George Bush's so called 'blind trust' make out during the time frame of the Gulf War? Why are the huge business deals between Bush and Hussein still off-limits to the public's right to know?*" [21]

---

[21] *Extra-Terrestrial Friends And Foes*, p288.

To readers of this book, the answers to those questions will be obvious. The 'blind trust', by the way, is the farce which insists that presidents must hand over all their business dealings to a trust during their term in office, which is supposed to make sure that they can't make political decisions which affect their own investments and companies. Do you believe it works like that? No, nor me. Bush's 'blind trust' was controlled by William Farish III, his close friend and grandson of William Farish, the President of Standard Oil of New Jersey when they were working with I.G. Farben and supplying Adolf Hitler. I will come to Bush's business links with Saddam shortly.

American reconnaissance advised President Bush around July 16th and 17th 1990 that Iraqi troops were assembling along the border with Kuwait. Nothing was done. On July 25th Saddam Hussein met with the US Ambassador in Baghdad, April Glaspie, who told him she was acting on the instructions of President Bush. She said that the Bush government had "no opinion on the Arab-Arab conflict, like your border disagreement with Kuwait." [22] I wonder if the Argentine government were told something similar before they invaded the Falklands? Glaspie added that she had instructions from the President to seek better relations with Iraq. She then left for a summer holiday, another indication to Saddam that the Americans were disinterested in the whole thing.

That date of July 25th is most significant because it was in the days before that, according to CIA and Naval Intelligence operative, Gunther Russbacher, that George Bush, Brent Scowcroft (Kissinger Associates), and other close advisors drew up an agreement to be submitted to President Gorbachev, through which he would agree not to intervene if the United States invaded Iraq. Remember this was *before* Glaspie met with Saddam and while Bush was ignoring the Iraqi troop buildups. Russbacher says he was briefed on the plan in mid-July by Scowcroft and Bush's CIA chief, William Webster. Russbacher was one of the pilots of four CIA SR-71s which flew to Moscow on July 26th from the Crows Landing Naval Air Station in California, refuelling twice on the way. On board were Scowcroft and Webster. Russbacher, who spoke Russian, met with Gorbachev who signed the agreement. [23]

While all this was going on, Bush still had nothing to say in public about the troops' buildup along the Kuwaiti border. By July 31st perhaps 100,000 troops were involved. Still Bush was silent. Two days before the invasion, John Kelly (CFR), an assistant secretary of state, was asked by a congressional hearing if the US would defend Kuwait in the event of an attack. He replied: "We have no defense treaty with any Gulf country". [24] On August 2nd,

---

[22] Transcript of the meeting released by the Iraqis and quoted in *The Immaculate Deception. The Bush Family Crime Exposed*, p146–147.

[23] *Defrauding America*, p433.

[24] *Extra-Terrestrial Friends And Foes*, p287.

Saddam invaded Kuwait. That same day, and again on August 6th, Bush met with Margaret Thatcher at Aspen, Colorado, and at the White House. The British prime minister was, as usual, highly belligerent about the need to teach Saddam a lesson. Henry Kissinger was behind the scenes, too, in the form of Brent Scowcroft, the national security advisor, a long-time Kissinger aide back to the days of the Nixon presidency, and an executive of Kissinger Associates. Scowcroft was urging military intervention. The Bush tone began to change. The Saudi Arabians were told by the Americans that Saddam was likely to invade their country next – utter nonsense – and Bush ordered US troops to assemble along the 'threatened' Saudi border. There would be no intervention, the world was told. The US forces were only there to protect Saudi Arabia, Bush said. Economic sanctions were to be the weapon used against Saddam. The Saudi Arabians, Germans, and Japanese would be badgered into contributing large sums towards American costs.

But sanctions were never going to be the real weapon. The rhetoric became ever stronger. Bush labelled Saddam "the new Hitler" and he said that the Second World War had shown that appeasement of such people was not the answer. He might have added that it also was not the answer to fund both sides at the same time and to help finance Hitler's war machine, as his father had done. For those who knew the game plan, it was easy to see what was happening. On August 23rd, Kissinger's man, Brent Scowcroft, said it all: "We believe we are creating the beginning of a new world order out of the collapse of the US-Soviet antagonisms".[25] The term, the New World Order, would now be used by Bush and enter into political-speak around the world to the point of tedium. Bush (Comm 300) received enthusiastic support from Margaret Thatcher and the Freemason President of France, François Mitterrand (Comm 300), who both sent forces to the Gulf to support the Americans. They presented themselves as a United Nations force. In effect, a world army. Bush said in a speech to Congress on September 11th:

> *"Clearly no longer can a dictator count on East-West confrontation to stymie concerted United Nations action against aggression. A new partnership of nations has begun, and we stand today at a unique and extraordinary moment. The crisis in the Persian Gulf, as grave as it is, also offers a rare opportunity to move toward an historic period of cooperation. Out of these troubled times, our fifth objective – a new world order – can emerge..."* [26]

For 'fifth' read 'first'. On November 8th, Bush announced that the forces in Saudi Arabia would be substantially increased. The 'defensive' force was now to switch to offensive mode. A week later Bush left on a tour of Europe

---

[25] Bush's talk of a "New World Order: Foreign Policy Tool or Mere Slogan?", *Washington Post*, (May 26th 1991).

[26] *Washington Post*, (September 12th 1990).

and the Middle East gathering support for the invasion. He met for three hours with President Assad of Syria, a tool of the Elite, who pledged to increase his contribution to Bush's forces to 20,000 men. The Bush 'UN' forces attacked on Wednesday, January 16th. 120,000 air sorties were unleashed on Iraq, mostly, it turned out, against civilian areas. The operation was headed by Bush's chairman of the Joint Chiefs of Staff, Colin Powell, a member of the Council on Foreign Relations, who has ancestral links with many old American and British families. Every allied supreme commander and US secretary of defense since the Second World War has been a member of the CFR. The number of dead and injured from the bombing of Iraq, the resulting disease, and the continuing economic sanctions can hardly be comprehended. Conditions for the innocent civilians in Iraq are terrible under the economic stranglehold, but the West looks on. So this is the United Nations in all its glory, this is the bastion of jaw, jaw, not war, war. This is the promoter of peace. This is the New World Order. The future president, Bill Clinton, supported the Gulf War and the United Nations policy. There is another stunner in all this, too. The United States government funded Saddam Hussein to fight the war against the United States and UN forces! It was done through a branch of the Banca Nazionale del Lavoro (BNL) in Atlanta. Congressman Henry Gonzalez exposed the BNL scandal in 1991 after he noticed that this little branch of the Italian government bank had loaned Iraq $5 *billion*. This came after November 1989 when the White House guaranteed bank loans to Iraq if they were used for the purchase of US farm products. If Saddam defaulted, the US taxpayers picked up the tab for the loan and since he was always defaulting, that was obviously going to be the outcome from the start. Instead of buying food, Saddam spent the money on arms, including purchases from the Matrix Churchill machine tool company in England (which was the subject of a court case in which the British government was implicated, and this led to the Scott Inquiry). Although many US investigators warned Bush that the money was being used for arms, the loans were allowed to continue.

The scam was so obvious, when you look at the other evidence. Son George was doing the same as Father Prescott did with Hitler. Funding an aggressor so you can start a war with him. Some of the money was spent on buying poison gas from a CIA front called Cardeon Industries in Chile.[27] When the war started, Saddam defaulted on the loans and the US taxpayers are now paying for the money spent by Iraq to fight their own sons and daughters. The cover-up of this, as usual, led to the scapegoating of the small fry. The whole thing was blamed on the bank manager at the BNL's Atlanta branch, Christopher P. Drogoul, who could never have sanctioned that sort of money without the highest authorisation. US District Judge, Marvin Schoob, said the claim that the Atlanta branch could loan $5 billion without the approval of the head

---

[27] *Defrauding America*, p426.

office in Rome could only come out of "never, never land." The judge said
that Drogoul and four other employees at the branch:

> "...*were pawns or bit players in a far larger and wider-ranging sophisticated
> conspiracy that involved BNL-Rome and possibly large American and foreign
> corporations and the governments of the United States, England, Italy and
> Iraq...Smoke is coming out of every window. I have to conclude that the
> building is on fire.*" [28]

This is the last thing the Bush administration and the Global Elite wanted
to hear. Judge Schoob was removed from the case and replaced by Judge
Ernest Tidwell, who refused to allow any evidence to be presented about the
CIA or Bush White House involvement in the bank. Drogoul was persuaded
by his attorney, against his better judgement, to plead guilty. The funding of
the Iraqi arms build up before the Gulf War and its prosecution by the UN
was a calculated plan to trigger the conflict, and it involved the Bush
administration, the British government of John Major, the Italian
government, the Soviet Union, and the other leading governments controlled
by the Global Elite. It also involved a familiar name: Henry Kissinger.

As early as 1984, Kissinger Associates were arranging loans from the BNL
to Iraq to finance its arms purchases from a little known subsidiary of Fiat,
the Italian car makers (headed by leading Bilderberger, Giovanni Agnelli).
Charles Barletta, a former Justice Department investigator, was quoted about
this in the *Spotlight* newspaper of November 9th 1992. The report said:

> "*Barletta added that federal probers had collected dozens of such
> incriminating case histories about the Kissinger firm* [director, Lord
> Carrington]. *But Henry Kissinger seems to possess a special kind of
> immunity. I'm not sure how he does it, but Kissinger wields as much power
> over the Washington national security bureaucracy now as in the days when he
> was the Nixon administration's foreign policy czar. He gets the payoff; others
> get the blame. Kissinger will remain unscathed until Congress finds the
> courage to convene a full-dress investigation into this teflon power broker.*"

Hear, hear.

THE BANK OF CREDIT AND COMMERCE INTERNATIONAL (BCCI)

The Bush (Republican) and Clinton (Democrat) wings of the One Party
State have another mutual connection, the Bank of Credit and Commerce
International, which had close links with the Italian BNL. The BCCI was
formed in the early 1970s and expanded rapidly to boast 400 branches in 78

countries. Its name is remarkably similar to the Banque De Credit International (BCI) of the Mossad agent, Rabbi Tibor Rosenbaum, which was used to fund Permindex and launder syndicate CIA and Mossad drug money at the time of the Kennedy assassination. Its "successor", the BCCI, was a major player in the drug money laundering network and was used for this purpose by the Elite elements within the CIA, British Intelligence, Israel's (or the Rothschild's) Mossad, and others, who control the world market in illegal drugs. Money to fund covert operations, terrorist groups like Abu Nidal, coups throughout the world, and the financing of Iran-Contra and Saddam Hussein, was also channelled through the BCCI. Money could be transferred between apparent enemies through this network, as with Saudi Arabian money which found its way to Mossad. In this case, Saudi and other Gulf money was laundered through the BCCI and transferred to CenTrust in Miami, which was later seized by federal investigators. The BCCI owned 28% of CenTrust. Allegations emerged that Robert Gates, the man Bush had nominated as his Director of the CIA, had obstructed an investigation into drug money laundering by the BCCI. Gates withdrew his nomination to be CIA Director, as he had once before, when implicated in Iran-Contra. The BCCI crashed amid a worldwide scandal in 1991. It was the world's biggest banking collapse and cost investors billions of dollars. Three years before the crash, Robert Gates was describing the BCCI as the Bank of Crooks and Criminals.[29]

The BCCI began to operate in Pakistan in 1972 with most of its funding provided by the Bank of America and the CIA. Bank of America also loaned money to people to buy stock in BCCI, probably to hide the scale of its control, and the B of A knew all about money laundering. In 1986, it was fined $7 million for 17,000 acts of washing dirty money. Some researchers say that the Bank of America is owned by the Rothschilds. At the hub of Rothschild involvement in the BCCI was Dr Alfred Hartmann who, at the same time, was the managing director of the Swiss branch of the BCCI; the head of the Zurich Rothschild Bank A.G.; a board member of N.M. Rothschild in London; and a director of...Italy's BNL.[30] The involvement of the Rothschilds at the heart of the BCCI was never mentioned or investigated by the lap dog media, nor the alleged involvement of the Rothschild 'gofer', and currency speculator, George Soros (Bil).[31] George Bush and Bill Clinton both had considerable connections with the BCCI, among them one Jackson Stephens, owner of Stephens Incorporated, a big investment bank based in Little Rock, Arkansas, the home of Bill Clinton. Stephens was one of the founders of the BCCI. He had connections with a company called Harken Energy and

---

[29] A statement made by Gates to the Head of Customs, William von Raab, in 1988. *Defrauding America*, p416.

[30] *Secret Societies*, p287.

[31] Ibid.

arranged a loan for them from a Swiss Bank affiliated with the BCCI. This would have greatly pleased George Bush Junior, the president's son, who sat on the Harken board. Another son, Jeb Bush, also had numerous dealings with the BCCI. He was often seen in the bank's Miami office[32] and George Bush's deputy campaign manager, James Lake, worked for a major owner of the BCCI at the same time. When Bush's 'opponent', Bill Clinton, ran for president, his main financial backer was Jackson Stephens who made the donations via his Worthen National Bank which was connected to the BCCI. Stephens was implicated in deals in which the BCCI secretly and illegally took over the First American Bank of Washington and others. This was the man who funded the president.

George Bush's involvement with the BCCI was considerable, according to the Chicago journalist, Sherman Skolnick, who made a detailed study of the bank. He has claimed publicly, including an interview on Radio Free America, that Bush, Saddam Hussein and others, used the BCCI to split $250 billion in oil "kick backs", the skimming off of money paid by western oil companies in the Gulf. He claims the records implicating Bush in deals with Saddam and Manuel Noriega were in the hands of the Bank of England and that the money was channelled through the BCCI and Banca Nazionale del Lavoro (BNL), branches in the USA. Henry Gonzalez, the chairman of the House Banking Committee, identified links between the BCCI and BNL. Skolnick told interviewer, Tom Valentine, on Radio Free America:

> *"The bulk of the money went through BCCI. That bank was formed in the 1970s with seed money from the Bank of America, the largest shareholders of which are the Rothschilds of Chicago, Paris, London, and Switzerland...The bank is also linked to the financial affairs of former President Jimmy Carter, and his friend and one-time budget director, banker Bert Lance.*
>
> *"Some of the...Democrats who have been involved in this whole affair have been published, for example, in the May 3 issue of* The Wall Street Journal. *During the 1988 presidential campaign, additionally, BCCI was one of the major financiers of the Michael Dukakis campaign. ...BCCI financed the Democratic Party in the United States and arranged deals for Republicans outside the United States."* [33]

Jimmy Carter personally dedicated a number of BCCI branches and they made an $8.5 million donation to one of his favourite charities. Carter's foreign travel after he left the White House was paid for by the BCCI and his banker friend, Bert Lance, was bailed out of big financial difficulties by a

---

[32] *Defrauding America*, p410.
[33] Quoted in *The Immaculate Deception*, p165.

man called Ghaith Pharaon, a front man for the BCCI.[34] This would fit with a contact's suggestion that the man behind the BCCI was an Arab, Gaph Feherton, a major funder of Jimmy Carter's presidential campaign. Andrew Young, Carter's former United Nations ambassador and a fellow Trilateralist, had a loan of $160,000 written off by the BCCI and he was paid to promote the bank to individuals and governments in Africa and Central America.[35] The Republican senator for Utah, Orrin Hatch, was making stirring speeches in support of BCCI even while it was being indicted for drug money laundering. The Democrat Clark Clifford and his law partner Robert Altman, the BCCI's lawyers, were at the centre of the story, also. Price Waterhouse, the BCCI's auditors for nearly 20 years, were giving the bank a largely clean bill of health while all the corruption was going on. Skolnick said records detailing the alleged Bush-Saddam deals were held in the Chicago branch of the BCCI, which was seized by the Reagan-Bush Administration in 1988 (along with other BCCI assets in the United States). Skolnick went on:

> *"The same bank has records showing joint business ventures between General Manuel Noriega, former dictator of Panama, and George Bush. In January of 1990, the federal prosecutor in Tampa had former top officials of Florida's branch on trial. They were allowed to escape prison with only a slap on the wrist and a small penalty. Here's why: they told the Justice Department that if they were going to prison, they had documents from their bank showing that George Bush had private business ventures through their bank with a series of dictators including not only Saddam and Noriega, but others as well...*
>
> *"...Saddam's oil was shipped to Texaco. In 1985 a Texas jury, at the behest of Pennzoil, issued the largest damages verdict in American history against Texaco. Pennzoil claimed that Texaco damaged them in a deal with Getty Oil. Who owns Pennzoil? George Bush and his friends* [the Liedtke brothers referred to earlier, in relation to Watergate]. *...As a result Texaco fell under the domination and supervision of Pennzoil. Where did the kickbacks to Saddam reportedly come from? They came from the deals between Texaco and its subsidiaries purchasing oil from Iraq."* [36]

If you placed end to end all the questions that George Bush needs to answer, but won't, they would stretch from Washington to Baghdad. Via Panama City. An official investigation was ordered to expose the BCCI scandal. It was chaired by Democrat senator, John Kerry, of Massachusets. It exposed nothing. Senator Kerry was chairman of the Democratic Senate

---

[34] *Defrauding America*, p408–409.
[35] Ibid.
[36] *The Immaculate Deception*, p166.

Campaign Committee, which received large contributions from the BCCI. Senator Kerry is also a member of the Skull and Bones Society, as is George Bush. The corruption across American politics, media, and business, is staggering and so it is in the United Kingdom wing of the Global Elite operation, where the BCCI had its main base.

The report on the bank by Lord Justice Bingham decided that the collapse was due to "a tragedy of errors, misunderstandings, and failures of communication." For goodness sake, it was one of the biggest drug money and illegal arms money laundering operations the world has yet seen. It implicated some of the biggest names in global politics, banking, and business, and financed terrorists, drug cartels, and covert operations by the CIA, Mossad, and others. The Bank of England completed the cover-up through an arrangement with the bank's principal owners at the time of the collapse, Abu Dhabi. This agreement allowed important records and witnesses to leave Britain. How convenient. In his review of *Dirty Money*, a book about the BCCI, the journalist Robert Sherrill said:

> "Dirty Money *clearly leaves the impression that many officials are less than enthusiastic about digging deeper into the scandal. Could it be because of that rumoured list of 100 politicians that the BCCI paid off? Or because 'key investigators' have indicated that if they continued their probe it might take them 'into the highest levels of political power around the world' in ways that would dwarf even the wildest conspiracy theory? Whoa! That would never do.*" [37]

On that note we will take our leave of George Bush and welcome Mr Bill Clinton. He defeated Bush, with support from the *Washington Post* among many others, and on January 20th 1993 he officially became the 42nd president of the United States. George Bush (CFR, TC, Skull and Bones Society, 33rd degree Freemason, and Republican), was replaced in the White House by Bill Clinton (CFR, TC, Bilderberger, Rhodes Scholar, 33rd degree Freemason, and Democrat). The names changed, the controllers did not. The One Party State rolled on.

BILL CLINTON

William Jefferson Clinton was born in Hope, Arkansas, and brought up in Hot Springs. His Rhodes Scholarship to Oxford University gave him a grounding in the World government philosophy and he knew what was required for political advancement from an early age. Clinton said in an interview in 1994 that he knew from Carroll Quigley's books that a

[37] *Washington Post* National Weekly Edition, (April 13th–19th 1992) p34: Mark Potts, Nicholas Kochan, and Robert Whittington, "Dirty Money. BCCI: The inside story of the world's sleaziest bank".

permanent shadow government of bankers and government officials existed which controlled the political agenda from behind the scenes. He said that, while still a young man, he realised that it was necessary for him to gain access to this inner circle if he was to become part of the decision-making process that shapes the world.[38] That is exactly what he did. His desire for high office was no doubt fired when he shook hands with John Kennedy as a boy. He was another product of the Global Elite production line of presidents: easily manipulated, knows how to do as he's told, and with a mountain of unpleasant information about him waiting to be revealed if he steps out of line. "We'll give them a Democrat president this time, just to let them think they still have a choice", you can almost hear the manipulators say. David Rockefeller, the Kingmaker of America, had met with Clinton in the mid-1980s at Winrock, the farm built by Winthrop Rockefeller, a former governor of Arkansas.[39] The state of Arkansas is an Elite centre. The southern wing of the Scottish Rite of US Freemasonry is based there and it was from this organisation that the Ku Klux Klan emerged. The Klan's emblem is the Maltese Cross, the same as the Knights Templar, the Knights of Malta and the Knights of the Golden Circle, which played a major role in the Rothschild manipulation of the American Civil War. The Ku Klux Klan is the old Knights of the Golden Circle under another name, controlled by the same force. It is said to be funded today by Mossad.[40] According to the German magazine *Neue Solidaritat*, the guru and foster-father of Bill Clinton was Parson Wo Vaught, a 32nd degree initiate in the Scottish Rite.[41]

If you think the background to George Bush is amazing, well old Bill has a few surprises in store, also. Indeed, these 'opponents' have so much in common. He progressed politically and became governor of Arkansas, the position he held when he was summoned by David Rockefeller to the Bilderberg Group meeting in Baden Baden, Germany, in 1991. The invitation came after the controllers had decided that he would be the next president of the United States.

Bill Clinton, according to the American Freedom Network, is a member of many secret societies, including an Illuminised Freemasonry order which claims allegence to the martyred Knights Templar leader, Jacques de Molay. In Arkansas, Clinton sat at the head of a complex network of drug running, money laundering, and general corruption. His biggest financial backer when he ran for president was, as we've discussed, Jackson Stephens, one of the founders of the BCCI. The Citizens for Honest Government organisation produced an investigative video into Bill Clinton's background in 1994 and

---

[38] Interview with James K. Kilpatrick of *The Wanderer*, Also reported in *Don Bell Reports*, (No. 15 on August 1st 1994).

[39] *Arkansas Democratic Gazette*, (May 21st 1995).

[40] *Secret Societies*, p128.

[41] Ibid p130.

they interviewed a former friend of Clinton in the Arkansas days, Larry
Nichols. It would appear that Clinton misjudged Nichols. He thought he
could be trusted to keep quiet and take the perks. Clinton gave him the job of
Marketing Director of the Arkansas Development Finance Authority (ADFA).
It was a State-run operation created by Clinton to, he said publicly, invest tax
money in low interest bond loans to local businesses, colleges, schools, and
churches. It would stimulate jobs, he said. When Larry Nichols took up his
post, he saw the truth. Nichols said:

> "...I'd been there about a month and I realised that I was at the epicentre of
> what I'd always heard about all my life...I was literally working, sitting, in the
> middle of Bill Clinton's political machine. It was where he made his pay offs,
> where he repaid favours to people for campaign support. I was in an interesting
> seat and I knew it. If you needed a million dollars, you had to get your
> application handled by the Rose Law Firm and pay them $50,000. There were
> five other companies in the state of Arkansas that were actually more qualified in
> bond structuring and applications, but the Rose Law Firm got 'em all." [This,
> by chance, was the law firm run by Hillary Clinton (CFR)]
> "I started checking around, and I kept asking...the comptroller, Bill Wilson.
> ...how did people make payments on these loans? He looked at me and said:
> 'They don't.' He thought I knew. Well, that blew my mind. And this is about
> two months in. It was getting tough then. So I started gathering documents. After
> everybody left I would stick around as if I was working on the annual report. That
> would give me access to the documents and I made copies of them all."

Nichols established that Bill Clinton's Arkansas Development Finance
Authority was laundering drug money! ADFA was a front for giving loans to
his business friends, who would then fund his election expenses, while at the
same time it was also used to launder drug profits. Nichols went on:

> "There was a hundred million a month in cocaine coming in and out of
> Mena [an airstrip] in Arkansas. They had a problem...you create a problem
> in a little state like Arkansas. How do you clean one hundred million dollars
> a month? ADFA until 1989 never banked in Arkansas. What they would
> do is...ship the money down to...a bank in Florida which would later be
> connected to BCCI. They would ship money to a bank in Georgia, which
> was...later connected to the BCCI. They'd ship to Citicorp in New York,
> which would send the money overseas." [42]

At the centre of this operation was Clinton's closest friend, Dan Lasater,
who would be jailed with the president's brother, Roger Clinton, for cocaine

---

[42] *The Clinton Chronicles*, produced in 1994 by Citizens Video Press, a division of Citizens For
Honest Government, PO Box 220, Winchester, CA 92596.

offences. Doc Delaughter, the police investigator in charge of the Lasater case, said he gathered detailed statements from people connected with Clinton's friend and his use of drugs to get young girls hooked and under his control for sexual favours. The policeman revealed how he suffered harassment from his own police department during his investigation and, he said, he knew that was because of the connection between the state police and Governor Clinton's office. Lasater spent less than a year in a minimum security prison for his drug offences and when he was released, Bill Clinton granted him a full pardon. Legislation enacted by Governor Clinton helped Tyson Foods to become the biggest company in the state. The owner, Don Tyson, was given $10 million by ADFA and never paid a cent of it back. He did, however, put $700,000 into Clinton's election campaign. Doc Delaughter said he had enough evidence on Tyson to launch an investigation into a possible drug distribution racket. The interconnected corruption was astonishing. Larry Nichols said:

> *"The first loan made at ADFA was to Park-O-Meter...As I started looking, I found that the secretary-treasurer was Webb Hubbell...Guess who drafted the legislation... which created ADFA? Webb Hubbell. Guess who introduced the legislation to our legislators and got it passed through our house? Webb Hubbell. Imagine this. Guess who did the audit and the evaluation on the (Park-O-Meter) application. Rose Law Firm, you guessed it. Who signed it? Webb Hubbell, Hillary Clinton."* [43]

Nichols said that when reporters made inquiries about the Park-O-Meter loans, they found that instead of making parking meters, Park-O-Meter was actually building retrofit nose cone compartments that were being shipped to Mena. The nose cones were being used to smuggle drugs back into the country and onto the streets of America! Nichols went on:

> *"Webb Hubbell, the Rose Law Firm, are guilty, I say to you, of conspiring to defraud the state of Arkansas, the Federal Government, and conspiring to solicit the sales and the laundering of money for illegal drugs. This is your president. This is his circle of power. These are the people when he got elected president...he took them straight to Washington with him."*

Webster "Webb" Hubbell was named acting US attorney general by Bill Clinton when he was elected to the White House! Hubbell was soon back in Arkansas, however, to plead guilty to charges of defrauding clients at Hillary Clinton's Rose Law Firm of an estimated half a million dollars. This was the man who was responsible for the Ethics in Government Act, which required

---

[43] *The Clinton Chronicles.*

Arkansas legislators to report conflicts of interest. Astonishingly, this act specifically *exempted* governor Bill Clinton, his appointees, and relatives. Go on, pinch yourself. You're not dreaming this. Before Hubbell left Washington he was responsible for finding a permanent attorney general for Bill Clinton. This was Janet Reno, who became head of the hilariously named US 'Justice' Department (which decides who, when, where, and whether, to prosecute). Webb Hubbell is not the only government-appointed crook that Janet Reno has come into contact with in her career. She had been District Attorney for Dade County, including downtown Miami, which was exposed as perhaps the most corrupt judicial system in the country. Reno's lack of action in the face of the evidence, led to an FBI undercover investigation which, in 1990, resulted in nearly half the judges in Miami being indicted on extortion charges. The decisions and judgements during Janet Reno's term at the Justice Department have served perfectly the aims of the New World Order, including the genocide at Waco (of which more later) and the suppression of information about drug running operations (including those out of Mexico, involving the leaders of the Mexican government). Researchers believe that Reno is a front for Webster Hubbell to be the *real* attorney general.

One of America's biggest drug trafficking operations, perhaps *the* biggest, was set up at the Mena airstrip in Arkansas in 1982 by Barry Seal, a pilot for the Drug Enforcement Administration![44] He moved his trade to Arkansas because of the hassle he was having from the authorities in his home state, Louisiana. He had no such hassle in Arkansas. Russell Welch, the policeman in charge of the Seal investigation, revealed: "He said 1983 was his most profitable cocaine smuggling period ever. He said that the airplanes that he had placed at the Mena Airport, there were four of them, a couple of Cessnas, a couple of Panthers, and one or two stragglers here and there, different airplanes. He said they were purchased solely for the purpose of cocaine smuggling." Welch added that the planes had special, and illegal, cargo doors which could be opened in flight to drop the drugs and money at other sites in Arkansas.

But where were the prosecutions? In the ten years during which the Mena drug operation was common knowledge, there was not one major prosecution. Yet when Clinton became president, he announced... guess what? Yes, a war on drugs. This was shortly before he revoked random drug testing for White House staff and dropped 121 posts at the Office of National Drug Control. Barry Seal is also part of the link between Bill Clinton, Oliver North, the Reagan-Bush administration, and Iran-Contra. According to court records, eye witness reports, and press accounts, Oliver North held a series of meetings at Little Rock in the early 1980s to set up

---

[44] "State Organised Crime", the Presidential Address by William J. Chambliss to The American Society of Criminology, 1988.

the illegal Contra weapons pipeline. One of the main operatives was Barry Seal and another was Terry Reed, a former combat pilot in Laos, who moved to Little Rock in 1983 and set up a training base for Contra terrorism at Nella Ark, eleven miles north of Mena. Reed said at his own trial in 1989 for fraud charges that at least one of the early meetings to plan the Nella Ark centre was attended by Bill Clinton's brother, Roger, and he said other meetings were attended by Clinton's close associate and drug runner, Dan Lasater. Yet again we see the One Party State in action. While the Republican Reagan-Bush presidency was involved in Iran-Contra, the 'opposition' in the form of Democrat governor, Bill Clinton, was covertly supporting it in Arkansas.

The power of the Elite to control the major newspapers and broadcast media was seen again in January 1995, when a 4,000 word article exposing the Barry Seal drug-running operation at Mena and its connections to Iran-Contra and the CIA was withdrawn from the *Washington Post*. It was immediately dubbed "The Greatest Story Never Told". The article was due to appear in the "Sunday Outlook" section, after eleven weeks of debate and argument among the staff. Lawyers had been through every line and approved it legally, the type had been set, and the illustrations completed. The contracts with the authors had been signed and Leonard Downie, the executive editor, had given his consent. Then suddenly, it was pulled and the Post's managing editor, Robert Kaiser (CFR), said it was a "non-existent story" and a "reprise of rumours and allegations". Sure it was. The owner of the *Washington Post* is the Bilderberger, Trilateralist, and member of the Council on Foreign Relations, Katherine Graham. The authors of the article were Doctor Roger Morris, formerly of the National Security Council under Johnson and Nixon, and Sally Denton, the former head of the Special Investigations Unit at the newsagency, UPI. Both have long records of this type of investigation. Their exposé was compiled from detailed research which included access to Barry Seal's bank and telephone records, invoices, appointment books, handwritten notes, personal diaries, and recorded conversations, plus police records and surveillance reports. The article said that Seal was flying planes out of Mena to export weapons to Bolivia, Argentina, Brazil, and the Contras in Nicaragua, and they returned full of cocaine for sale in New York, Chicago, Detroit, St Louis, and other cities. Morris and Denton say that Seal had such close ties with the CIA that he believed he could smuggle what he wanted, whenever he wanted, and they point out that nine separate attempts by state and federal authorities to stop him were blocked. All this took place, incidentally, during the Reagan-Bush "War on Drugs". The article withdrawn by the *Washington Post* had said: "Over the entire episode looms the unmistakable dark shape of US government complicity in vast drug trafficking and gun running". And it asked the questions that the mainstream media have failed to ask:

"For three presidents of both parties – Messrs Reagan, Bush, and Clinton – the old enduring questions of political scandal are once again apt: What did they know about Mena? When did they know it? Why didn't they do anything to stop it?" [45]

The involvement in drug trafficking of Bill Clinton, George Bush, and the CIA was also revealed by businessman Terry Reed and his co-author, John Cummings, in their 1994 book, *Compromised: Clinton, Bush, And The CIA.*[46] Reed was a former US Airforce Intelligence Officer who became a successful businessman. He was recruited by the CIA to set up a CIA front company in Mexico selling high technology and consultancy. When Reed realised it was being used to ship drugs, he tried to get out of the operation and to return to Arkansas, then governed by Clinton. As usual, Clinton and the CIA sought to silence and discredit Reed by accusing him of what *they* were doing. He was charged by Clinton and the Arkansas authorities with drug running! Reed also reveals in his book how *Time* magazine and other publications and newspapers were involved in disinformation and cover-ups to keep the truth about drugs from the public.

Barry Seal was not convicted for his drug crimes. Instead he was murdered. This happened as he was beginning to speak openly about what he knew. He told how he was ordered by the CIA and the Drug Enforcement Administration to photograph Sandinista officials in Nicaragua loading drugs onto a plane for shipment to the United States. This photograph was used by President Reagan in a televised speech in March 1986 as propaganda against the Nicaraguan regime. This led to Congress voting another $100 million in aid to the Contra terrorists in Nicaragua who were running drugs in league with the CIA. This drug running operation was done with the knowledge of the then Vice President Bush. Seal later admitted to reporters that the Sandinistas in his photograph were not loading drugs at all. He also spoke of the Contra drug smuggling network and its connection with the Colombian cartels. Soon after this, in February 1987, Seal was dead.

This period was littered with murders and suspicious deaths in Arkansas. On August 23rd 1987, two boys, Kevin Ives and his friend Don Henry, were out walking in the early hours in the area of the Mena airstrip. Later they were found dead on a railway line. The State Medical Examiner, Fahmy Malak, a man appointed by Bill Clinton, ruled that the deaths were an accident. The parents disagreed and asked for a second opinion, a request that was met with resistance from the authorities on all fronts. They won a court order requesting samples for the second opinion of everything the crime laboratory had, but Malak still refused to hand them over. Eventually

---

[45] Details of the article were reported in the London *Sunday Telegraph*, (January 29th 1995) p18.
[46] Terry Reed and John Cummings, *Compromised: Clinton, Bush, And The CIA*, (1994).

other opinion showed that Don Henry had been stabbed in the back and Kevin Ive's skull had been crushed before they were placed on the railway line. Malak still said it was an accident. The boys had both fallen asleep on the tracks, he said. It's just the place you would choose to go to sleep, isn't it?

Six people who talked to the police about the boys' murders were themselves killed. Keith McKaskie knew what was planned for him. He said goodbye to his family and friends in 1988 and days later he was murdered. The following year, Jeff Rhodes, a young guy from Benton, Arkansas, rang his father to say he had to get out of town because he knew too much about the deaths of the boys and McKaskie. Two weeks later Rhodes was found shot dead. Keith Coney was fleeing for his life on his motorcycle when he collided with a truck; Gregory Collins was shot; Richard Winters and Jordan Ketelson were both killed by shotgun blasts. The head of the Saline County Drug Task Force who had uncovered evidence of the Arkansas Police Department's involvement with drug smuggling and the cover-up of the boys' murder, was forced into hiding. This was all going on while President Clinton was governor for Arkansas.

Investigating Bill Clinton or making allegations against him would appear, from endless evidence, to be a very dangerous occupation. Danny Casolaro, a reporter investigating Clinton and an alleged bonds racket, was found dead in a West Virginia hotel. Paul Wilcher, a Washington lawyer, was investigating Clinton and was due to meet Danny Casolaro's former attorney. Wilcher was found dead sitting on the toilet in his apartment. Prosecuting attorney, Charles Black, asked Governor Clinton for funds to continue the Mena drugs investigation. The money never came, but Black's mother was brutally murdered. Police said there was no connection. Ed Willey, the manager of Clinton's campaign finance committee, was killed with gunshot wounds. Verdict: "Suicide". John Wilson, a city councillor in Washington who was reported to be planning to expose Clinton's dirty tricks, was found hanged in 1993. Verdict: "Suicide". Kathy Ferguson, the wife of Danny, an Arkansas police patrolman and Clinton bodyguard, talked about a number of sexual incidents involving Clinton, and she said her husband had taken Paula Jones to Clinton's hotel room where he, allegedly, dropped his trousers and propositioned her. Kathy Ferguson was found dead with a gun in her hand. Verdict: "Suicide". Husband Danny then denied Clinton's connection with Paula Jones. Danny is still alive. Paula Jones says Kathy was telling the truth. Jon Parnell Walker, a senior investigator for the Resolution Trust Corporation, was pressing for an investigation into the collapsed Madison Guaranty Savings and Loan company, linked to Clinton under the heading the "Whitewater Affair". He fell from the balcony of a new apartment in Arlington, Virginia. Verdict: "Suicide". C. Victor Raider II was co-chairman of Clinton's presidential campaign, but they fell out. Raider and his son, Montgomery, died when their small plane crashed. Herschel Friday was a member of Raider's committee and an expert pilot. He died when his plane exploded. Dentist Ronald Rogers was on his way to talk to a journalist about Clinton when his plane crashed in clear weather. Luther "Jerry" Parks from Little Rock had compiled a study of Clinton's sexual activities. Clinton owed him $81,000 for providing guards during the presidential campaign and his wife said he had threatened to reveal the information he had unless he was paid. Parks was shot dead on September 26th 1993. Park's son, Gary Parks, said his father had names, dates, places – everything about Clinton's liaisons. He said he also had details of Clinton's drug taking and that of his brother, Roger. Shortly before his father's murder, the phone lines at his home were cut, the security system turned off, and the files on Clinton were stolen. In Arkansas, no autopsy need be performed on anyone ruled to have committed suicide, even if the evidence points to murder. This law was introduced by Bill Clinton in one of his last acts as governor.

The death most publicised in connection with Bill Clinton is that of his lifelong friend, Vincent Foster, a lawyer at Hillary Clinton's company, the Rose Law Firm. His death by 'suicide' came during investigations into the financial scandal known as the Whitewater Affair. The Clintons said their investment in the Madison Savings and Loans company was a loss-maker. Others say it was a scam to skim off federal money. What is beyond question is that it cost the taxpayers $60 million. Robert Fiske was named as special prosecutor to lead the 'investigation' into Whitewater and that same week, the Rose Law Firm began to shred documents. One of the shredders, Jeremy Hedges, said: "They had his [Fosters] initials pretty much all over…everything from the box to the manila files to – I even saw his signature on one of the Rose Firm letterheads."[47] A demonstration was held outside the Rose offices when people heard what was going on. Again in that same week, there was a fire at the Worthen Bank Building owned by Jackson Stephens, one of the founders of BCCI, and Clinton's main financial backer. Stephen's bank advanced the Clinton presidential campaign $2.8 million. Less than two years earlier, the bank had earned a profit on a transaction involving student loans controlled by Bill Clinton. The size of the profit? $2.8 million.[48] Clinton channelled ADFA funds through the Worthen Bank after 1988. The fire there destroyed documents related to the Whitewater investigation.

On July 20th 1993, Vincent Foster, a senior partner with Hillary Clinton and Webb Hubbell in the Rose Law Firm before his appointment as White House deputy counsel, and the man handling the Clinton's personal legal affairs, was found shot dead at Fort Marcy Park, off the George Washington Parkway on the west bank of the Potomac River across from the capital. The verdict was our old friend: suicide. The gun was still in his hand, which is hardly what would have happened as he reacted to the consequences of the

[47] Interview on the video, *The Clinton Chronicles*.
[48] Quote from Jim Johnson, former Arkansas State Senator and State Supreme Court Judge, on the video *The Clinton Chronicles*.

shot. The suicide verdict was made before there had been either an autopsy or a ballistics test. Larry Nichols has a police memo proving that Foster was found in his car, not the park.

In March 1994, when the speculation would not go away, the White House issued a photograph of Foster's body at the scene which was said to prove that it was suicide. The gun was in his right hand. Foster was left-handed. The photo shows the body surrounded by brown leaves. But he had died in the summer and reporters at the scene soon after he died said there were no leaves on the ground. The White House also announced (five months after Foster's death) that four members of Bill Clinton's staff *had ransacked Foster's office the night he died*! They included Patsy Thomasson, Hillary Clinton's personal assistant. It was done, they said, for reasons of "national security". God help us. Patsy Thomasson was a leading assistant to Clinton's pal Dan Lasater, when he was, as shown in court, dealing drugs.[49] Thomasson was also named in law enforcement files for drug trafficking and it was she who stopped drug testing for White House employees.

This is the President of the United States we are talking about here. This is the White House, the supposed centre of power in the most powerful country in the world. And people go on allowing it to happen. Clinton was actually re-elected in 1996!

There is another intriguing aspect to the Foster story. Documents shown to the London *Sunday Telegraph* reveal that Foster was jetting around the world and making strange visits to Switzerland while still working in private practice at the Rose Law firm.[50] Records show that he was flying with Delta Airlines (at discount rates only available to senior government officials or those involved in work for the federal government), *before* he was publicly connected in any way to the government. Twice he made trips to Switzerland with American Airlines and Swiss Air, staying for little more than 24 hours before returning home. Switzerland is a major coordinating centre for the Global Elite. These visits took place on November 3rd 1991 and December 7th 1992. The latter was in the transition period between the Bush and Clinton administrations. On July 1st 1993, Foster used his American Express card to purchase another ticket to Geneva, but then cancelled. Later that month he was dead. His wife,

[49] Nicholas Guarino, the editor of *The Wall Street Underground*, wrote an article accusing Bill Clinton of being implicated in murder, drug running, extortion, rape, threats, beatings, break ins, bribery, thefts, arson, conflicts of interest, money laundering, insider trading, election fraud, obstruction of justice, campaign fraud, witness tampering, and destruction of subpoenaed documents. The content of the article was summarised in *The Spotlight*, (December 19th 1994) p1, 3.
[50] "Secret Swiss Link to White House Death", *Sunday Telegraph*, (May 21st 1995) p22.

Lisa, knew nothing of these trips to Switzerland, apparently. Many researchers link Foster to the Arkansas computer firm, Systematics, owned by...Jackson Stephens. They also link him to Mossad.

The suspicious deaths and the intimidation go on. In the midst of all of this, Larry Nichols was approached by attorney Gary Johnson, who wanted to help him expose the money laundering and general corruption at Clinton's ADFA scam. Coincidentally, Johnson lived next door to Gennifer Flowers, one of the women Clinton denied having a sexual relationship with. What anyone does in their private life is up to them, but it is what followed here that Americans might consider worth addressing. Gary Johnson had a security camera at his front door and this captured Clinton entering Gennifer Flower's apartment. He went in with his own key. Johnson had this recorded on tape and could prove that Clinton was lying. Attorney Gary Johnson was attacked at his home and suffered the most terrible injuries. The people who did this stole his tape of Bill Clinton. This is America in the 1990s. How could all these things be covered up, glossed over, and the Clintons not face a public investigation into all these matters I have highlighted? Larry Nichols has the answer:

> "A lot of people wonder how Bill Clinton could control a state the size of Arkansas with the absolute authority that he did. It's not hard. You see, after twelve years, after kissing the people that have the money, Bill Clinton controlled the legal system, he controlled the judges, he controlled the attorneys, he controlled the banks." [51]

Which is precisely what the Elite do on a global scale. And when Clinton went off to the White House, he played the same game. Democracy is no longer just phoney, it is virtually non-existent. A new kid on the block in the American media is House Speaker Newt Gingrich, the latest 'star' of the Republican Party, who lambasts Clinton and demands 'change'. This is what Clinton demanded before continuing business as usual. What happened to the proposed Clinton blitz on the medical system? He and Hillary were going to take on the drug companies, they said, and the shares in those companies went down. Then the Clintons changed their minds and the shares went up. What happened in between? It doesn't matter who is president of the United States or prime minister of the United Kingdom because the same force will be in power until we do something about it.

President Bush helped to engineer the Gulf War, pressed for the introduction of the GATT 'free trade' agreement, and the expansion of the North American Free Trade Area (NAFTA) throughout the Americas. His successors from the 'opposing' party, Bill Clinton and Al Gore, both

[51] Interview for *The Clinton Chronicles*.

supported the Gulf War, and they have supervised the passing of the GATT through Congress and proposed the expansion of NAFTA into South America.[52] Who led the Republican Party in its support for GATT and voted with the Clinton Democrats? Who also voted for NAFTA? Clinton's great 'critic', Newt Gingrich, and another Republican leader, Bob Dole. At the Trilateral Commission meeting in Copenhagen, Denmark, in May 1995, two US members, former Speaker of the House, Tom Foley, and Senator William Roth, were reportedly questioned about why Gingrich and Dole had made mild criticisms of the World Trade Organisation before supporting it. Foley and Roth assured the Trilateral Commission members that Gingrich and Dole were merely involved in "necessary political posturing" and their support was "never in doubt".[53] Sums up the political process, really. When 'Republican' Dole ran for president, his co-chairman for finance was... Jackson Stephens...the backer of 'Democrat', Bill Clinton!

It was the same Newt Gingrich, a vehement promoter of Israel, who made a speech at a gathering of military and intelligence officers in Washington in 1995 calling for the subversion of Iran. The scheme he articulated was first expressed by an Israeli government propagandist called Martin Indyk, who was appointed by Bill Clinton to serve as Middle East policy 'expert' on the National Security Council. The same anti-Iran and anti-Iraq policy appeared in the March/April 1994 issue of *Foreign Affairs*, the magazine of the Council on Foreign Relations, of which Gingrich is said to be a "proud member". Bill Clinton is also a member of the CFR and so is his national security advisor, Anthony Lake, who called for the "dual containment" of Iran and Iraq in the *Foreign Affairs* magazine. How nice to have such amazing agreement between 'opponents'. On September 2nd 1994, Avonoam Bar-Yosef, writing in the prominent Israeli daily, *Ma'Ariv*, said that seven of the leading members of Bill Clinton's National Security Council were Jewish. The article, headlined "The Jews who run Clinton's Court", quoted the rabbi of the Adath Yisrael synagogue, as saying: "...for the first time in American history...the US has no longer a government of Goyim [Gentiles], but an administration in which the Jews are full partners in decision making at all levels".

Newt Gingrich's wife, Marianne, is collecting $2,500 a month as vice-president for business development for the Israel Export Development Company, which aims to attract American businesses to a high tech business park in Israel. She first met her boss, David Yerushalmi, while on a tour of Israel sponsored by the Israel lobbying group, the American-Israel Public

[52] *The Spotlight*, (May 8th 1995) p6.

[53] David Rockefeller praised Clinton publicly for his support for GATT in the *Arkansas Democratic Gazette* of May 21st 1995, and Rockefeller was described as a "leading voice" advising Clinton on trade policies in Central and South America. Advising? Dictating.

Affairs Committee.[54] Arne Christianson, a former official of the same American-Israel Public Affairs Committee, is now a top policy advisor to her husband, Newt Gingrich. The Bush and Clinton administrations, as with Clinton and Gingrich, share many common threads and on anything that involves the New World Order agenda, they all vote the same way. They are also awash with members of the Council on Foreign Relations and the Trilateral Commission, the vehicles for the Rockefellers and the Elite to manipulate the US and the world.

THE BRITISH ONE PARTY STATE

In the United Kingdom, as elsewhere, there is a nexus of people and organisations which connect banking, business, and politics. We have government ministers linked to companies and organisations which their legislation has affected. We have members of parliament taking bribes to ask questions in the House of Commons on behalf of companies. We have them paid to 'lobby' for interest groups. We have former cabinet ministers walking out of government and into top posts. Lord Wakeham was the energy secretary who supervised the privatisation of the UK's state-owned electricity industry. The merchant bank, N.M. Rothschild, has made a fortune from its work on government privatisations – including that of the electricity industry and the coal industry, thanks to contracts agreed while Lord Wakeham was in charge at the energy department. When Lord Wakeham left the government, he became a director of...N.M. Rothschild. Norman Lamont, the Chancellor of the Exchequer, was sacked by Prime Minister John Major and became a director of...N.M. Rothschild. Lamont worked for the Rothschilds before going into government, as did the Treasury Secretary, Anthony Nelson, and John Major's former Welsh Secretary, John Redwood, who unsuccessfully challenged him for the leadership in July 1995.

The story of the Redwood challenge is very interesting. John Redwood, formerly of All Souls College, Oxford, was 'seconded' from N.M. Rothschild to head the Downing Street policy unit of Margaret Thatcher, a role Lord Victor Rothschild, the political manipulator and alleged spy, had enjoyed under the premiership of Edward Heath (Conservative, Bil) and unofficially under Harold Wilson (Labour, Bil). Redwood's policy unit was behind the orgy of privatisations of state utilities which has handed control of essential public services to the banking elite. This policy has made enormous sums of money for N.M. Rothschild. Redwood then returned to Rothschilds before becoming an MP via the safe Conservative seat of Wokingham in Berkshire. If a monkey stood for the Conservatives in Wokingham, it would be elected. Once in parliament, he (Redwood, not the monkey) was appointed to the Department of Trade and Industry at the

[54] *The Spotlight*, (February 27th 1995) p6.

time his original privatisation plans were being introduced.[55] Now there's a coincidence for you. Isn't life just amazing?

In early June 1995, the Bilderberg Group met at Burgenstock in Switzerland. According to *Spotlight* sources,[56] the Bilderberg elite decided that John Major would be given a choice: get back into line and support a Federal Europe with a central bank and a single currency or be removed from office. In that same month, Major was persuaded to resign as leader of the ruling Conservative Party and offer himself for re-election. He said he was fed-up with the rumours of a challenge to his leadership by MPs opposing further centralisation of power in Europe. "Put up or shut up", was the message. The man who "put up" was John Redwood who publicly opposed a federal Europe. His main supporter in the election was his N.M. Rothschild buddy, Norman Lamont, another man 'opposing' a centralised Europe. What was the outcome of this challenge, however? Redwood lost and Major used this as an opportunity to purge his cabinet of those arguing against a Federal Europe. More than that, a deal was probably done in which Major agreed to hand over power to Michael Heseltine who favours a federal Europe. Major and Heseltine had a three-hour meeting on the day of the vote and after his 'victory', Major appointed Heseltine as "Deputy" Prime Minister at the head of a network of power. It may be that Heseltine was given the reins of government (under the control of the Global Elite) and in return Major was assured of enough votes to survive as a figurehead, puppet prime minister. So who benefited by that challenge from John Redwood and Norman Lamont, the two "anti-federalists" from N.M. Rothschild? Those who want to see a United States of Europe – the very thing Redwood said he stood to oppose. What another amazing coincidence then, that a few days before the Redwood 'challenge', we find among the guests at the Bilderberg meeting in Switzerland the name...Norman Lamont. He went as a Rothschild representative together with Emma Rothschild, Lord Victor Rothschild's daughter. Well, I never. Norman "save our sovereignty" Lamont attending a meeting of the organisation that has been behind the manipulation to create a Federal Europe for more than 40 years. The same meeting which decided that John Major must come into line on Europe or be ousted. Norman, my old son, you have been rumbled. The Labour MP, Giles Radice, the chairman of the European Movement, would have seen Lamont at Burgenstock because Radice was also there. How strange he didn't mention that while Stormin' Norman was so publicly 'opposing' a federal Europe. Radice must have forgotten. Another British government 'name' at Burgenstock was Lamont's Conservative colleague William Waldegrave, the then secretary of state for agriculture and a man implicated in the arms to Iraq scandal. Waldegrave has close connections with the Rothschilds and served under Lord Victor Rothschild in Ted Heath's Downing Street Policy unit

---

[55] *Private Eye* magazine, No. 875, (Friday June 30th 1995) p5.
[56] *The Spotlight*, (July 3rd 1995) p1.

(1971–73). Interestingly, James Goldsmith, the billionaire financier who formed a political party to "oppose" a European superstate, is a frontman for the House of Rothschild and a second cousin of Baron Edmund de Rothschild. He's also a close friend of George bush. It is important to remember that the Elite seek to lead the organisations both for and "against" what they desire, to ensure complete control of the "debate" and its outcome.

Also on the board of N.M. Rothschild are Lord Armstrong (TC, Bil), the former head of the civil service and cabinet secretary during Margaret Thatcher's privatising mania. So are Sir Clive Whitmore, former permanent secretary at the Home Office; Sir Frank Cooper, former permanent secretary at the Ministry of Defence; and Sir John Fairclough, former chief scientific adviser. N.M. Rothschild has twenty-six non-executive directors on the board, several connected with government. The company was involved in the privatisations of British Gas, British Coal, the electricity industry, the water industry, the Forestry Commission, and the Royal Ordnance Factories. According to the *Daily Telegraph* of January 26th 1995, it has developed the image of "the government's favourite bank" in the light of its success in being selected so often by a process "independent" of government departments, which chose the banks to advise the companies being privatised. Sir Michael Richardson was vice chairman of N.M. Rothschild and chairman of the Rothschild company, Smith New Court, when this privatisation work was being won during the Margaret Thatcher years. Sir Michael, a senior Freemason, is a close associate of Margaret Thatcher.

We can always rely on the media to expose these matters, however. The *Sunday Telegraph* of January 29th 1995, ran an article justifying the Rothschild/Wakeham/government connections and saw nothing wrong with them. *The Sunday Telegraph*, like *The Daily Telegraph*, is owned by the Bilderberger, Conrad Black, and on the board of Telegraph Newspapers plc is Evelyn de Rothschild, the chairman of…N.M. Rothschild! The article failed to mention that. They must have forgotten, too. The House of Commons Register of Members' Interests revealed that 200 of the 243 Conservative backbenchers during the Major government elected in 1992 held a total of 276 paid directorships and 365 paid consultancies. The potential for corruption is quite, quite, extraordinary. And when do they find time to represent their voters? Maybe this is why virtually no MP or member of Congress actually read the detail of the GATT agreement before voting it into law! The same with representatives throughout Europe who didn't read the detail of the Maastrict Agreement on centralising power in a European Union before they voted in favour. And what of the Labour Party, that other wing of the One Party State? They supported both GATT and the Maastrict Agreement, as did the Liberal Democrats. Here we see modified Hegelianism again. Two 'opposite' forces, socialism and capitalism, were brought into opposition by the Elite in the early years of this century in Britain and they have fused into one force, which now differs only in words, not deeds. There are certainly scores of unanswered questions relating to leaders and high ranking members of the Labour Party through this century.

Doctor Kitty Little is a long time researcher into the corruption and infiltration within the British Intelligence agencies. Her scientific career has included research for the Ministry of Aircraft Production during the Second World War followed by nine years at the Atomic Energy Research Establishment at Harwell. In her submission to the 1995 Nolan Committee on Standards in Public Life, she tells the story of an attempt to recruit her to the Communist Party at Oxford University in 1940. Oxford University, you will recall, was a bastion of the Milner Circle and the Round Table, particularly All Souls, New Chapel, and Balliol. The communists, she said, had gone "underground" by joining the university Labour Party and she attended a meeting of a Labour Party "study group" in a room at University College. The main speaker at the meeting, who clearly believed he was among "friends", began to reveal the plot to "destabilise the United Kingdom and Commonwealth, ready for a Marxist takeover". She later realised that this was part of the plan to introduce the global centralised control called the New World Order. The plot was outlined by the speaker at that Oxford meeting to destroy United Kingdom defences, engineer a Marxist takeover of Rhodesia and South Africa, and to use what became known as the European Community as a smokescreen to hide the changeover to a centralised, Marxist, rule of Europe. The plan was also to destroy British manufacturing industry. He went on to describe how members of the political section of this subversive organisation were going to infiltrate the British parliament and civil service, some entering each of the political parties. Many would go into the right wing of the Labour Party, others to the left wing of the Conservatives. Eventually there would be a fusion into a new "Centre" party. He said that the British distrusted extremists and so posing as "moderates" occupying the centre ground would allow them to dismiss their opponents as "Right wing extremists". This subversive organisation did not have a name, he said, because that would make it harder for people to prove it existed. The speaker said that he had been chosen to be the head of the political section of this organisation and he expected himself one day to become the prime minister of the United Kingdom. All this was said in 1940 and that man did indeed become prime minister.

His name was Harold Wilson.

Wilson was the British prime minister throughout the period between 1964 and 1976, except for the four years between 1970-74 when the Conservative Party leader, Edward Heath, was in office. Harold Wilson and Ted Heath were both Bilderbergers and both close associates of Lord Victor Rothschild. Wilson took over the Labour Party leadership with the death of Bilderberger, Hugh Gaitskell, in 1963. Significantly, Gaitskell was not in favour of a federal Europe. His death was very convenient because Wilson became leader at an opportune time. Conservative Prime Minister, Harold Macmillan (Comm 300, RIIA), was driven from office by the Profumo spy scandal in the same year that Gaitskell died, opening the way for the Bilderberger Sir Alec Douglas Hume (Lord Home) to take over the Premiership. Hume would later be a chairman of the Bilderberg Group and also served on the Committee of 300. The following year Hume faced – and was defeated by – Harold Wilson, in the 1964 election. The political upheavals in Britain mirrored those in the United States where Lyndon Johnson became president in 1963 after the Kennedy assassination in which, in my view, Lord Victor Rothschild was involved.

Dr Little says that when she made her story public, the *Daily Express* journalist and writer of intelligence 'exposés', Chapman Pincher, showed a copy of her allegations to Harold Wilson. He was issuing libel writs like confetti at the time, but his only reaction to Dr Little was to say she had mistaken him for a Tom Wilson. She knew she had done nothing of the kind, but she checked the entire university records and there was not even one "T" Wilson enrolled there in this century! She knew Wilson as an Economics Fellow at Oxford because it was he who researched and compiled most of the Beveridge Report which created the welfare state and the social security system after the war. Beveridge, she says, was little more than a figurehead who put his name to it. On the surface, the report was admirable in many ways, but from the perspective of the 1990s it can perhaps be seen to have wider implications. It created dependency and control while destroying opportunities for self-reliance and independence outside the Elite-controlled system. Now that dependency has been created, the welfare state is being dismantled and what is left is being handed over to 'privatisation' – the elite bankers in other words. This is leaving people at the mercy of some very unpleasant people and organisations. Should the underclass react violently to this, the Elite have another opportunity to introduce harsher laws under problem-reaction-solution.

Dr Little said in her submission to the Nolan Inquiry, that the intentions set out by the young Harold Wilson in Oxford were transmitted to Moscow and by the end of 1941 a double agent in the Kremlin had given the details to Britain's MI5. This was circulated to senior MI5 officers, but no action was taken. During this period, Kitty Little said, the "senior subversive infiltrator" within British Intelligence was Lord Victor Rothschild, the man who controlled the use of Regulation 18b during the war. He was also named in a 1994 book as the unidentified "fifth man" in the Burgess-Maclean-Philby-Blunt communist spy scandal, although his involvement in covert activities was far, far greater than claimed in that book.

Dr Little has had access to sources at some very high levels over the last 50 years. She says that Lord Rothschild was not the "fifth man" in a KGB spy scandal. Instead, he was the spider at the centre of a web of infiltration and corruption. He controlled the activities of Philby, Burgess, Maclean, Blunt and Guy Liddell, the acting head of MI5. She names another man in this circle as Tommy Harris, about whom little is known, except that he was a good cook. Harris cooked meals for the group when they met regularly at his home. Maclean was not directly involved with them. His work at the Foreign Office was to feed geology reports to Guy Rothschild in France who used them to control essential resources, especially uranium. According to Dr Little, the Rothschilds now control 80% of the world's uranium. This spider's web of corruption within the British establishment was not about spying for the Soviet Union. This is more camouflage. The aim was to further the ambitions of the New World Order. Harold Wilson's nameless subversive organisation had (has) three sections, the political (led by him), the economic, and the 'biological'. The head of the biological section was the overall controller. Until his death, that was Lord Victor Rothschild. Who is it today?

Lord Rothschild helped to finance MI5 agent, Peter Wright, in the production, with Chapman Pincher, of the 'exposé' book called *Their Trade Is Treachery*, which names the late MI5 chief, Sir Roger Hollis, as the fifth man and 'clears' Lord Rothschild. Later Rothschild arranged for Wright to produce another book, the infamous *Spycatcher*, which also named Hollis. Margaret Thatcher's vehement opposition to the book's publication ensured it was a best seller around the world and added to its credibility as an 'exposé'. Leading this opposition to *Spycatcher* on behalf of the government was Lord Armstrong, the cabinet secretary to Margaret Thatcher and friend of Rothschild. It was in a court hearing over *Spycatcher* that Lord Armstrong (Bil, TC) made his famous distinction between lying and being "economical with the truth". When he retired from government office, Lord Armstrong became a director of...N.M. Rothschild. In a letter to the Speaker of the House of Commons on May 1st 1987, Dr Kitty Little says:

> *"Early in the war Wing Commander Arnold, then head of a section in MI5, had reason to think that Rothschild was not to be trusted. He took steps to have the most sensitive material kept from him, but found Rothschild's backers too powerful to do more than that. Later, when Sir Roger Hollis was Director-General, he asked Wing Commander Arnold for a detailed report of events from that era.*
>
> *"When Wilson became leader of the Labour Party a very serious problem arose, since it was the head of the political section of the subversive organisation who was in line to become the next Prime Minister. Shortly before his death, the late Sir Theobald Matthew, the then Director of Public Prosecutions, told me that he considered that he and the Director General of MI5 had almost sufficient legally admissible evidence to prosecute. Sir Theobald said that in his opinion when a Minister used his official position to take action to promote objectives of a criminal organisation...in a manner that would be criminal if he were acting as a private citizen, then those actions are still criminal. This is only logical, since Ministers are better placed than*

*private citizens to do irreparable harm to the nation. Sir Theobald died while
Wright organised a smear campaign against Sir Roger Hollis and the Deputy
Director-General, that was launched with the aid of Lord Rothschild and
Philby. And so Wilson escaped prosecution."* [57]

It is astonishing how many people die at the most convenient times. Dr
Little says that Lord Rothschild was actively seeking to discredit MI5 and
after 1979 ordered Peter Wright and Chapman Pincher to indulge in
character assassination and disinformation. It is notable that *Spycatcher*
claimed an MI5 plot to destabilise the Wilson Labour government in the
period we are talking about. Could this not be yet another smokescreen to
hide the truth that in fact MI5 was making legitimate investigations?
Rothschild covertly collaborated with 'socialist' Harold Wilson (Bil) and
worked openly with 'Conservative' Edward Heath (Bil, TC), who occupied
10 Downing Street between them for eleven years. Heath invited Rothschild
to head his government's policy unit, the Central Policy Review Staff, and to
select its personnel![58] One of Rothschild's roles was to supervise British
Intelligence and to reorganise the Foreign Office. I wonder if this included
Group 13, the Foreign Office assassination squad? Yes, the British Foreign
Office has its own assassination squad. From this time the run down of
Britain's aircraft, shipbuilding, car, steel and machine tool industries began to
quicken – exactly as Wilson had predicted in 1940. And the man behind the
plan under Wilson and Heath was Victor Rothschild who was working
towards a European superstate and the end of national sovereignty. During
their periods in office, both Heath and Wilson made organisational changes
to MI5. Wilson limited the techniques of investigation that were allowed,
and demanded to be told if any MPs were under investigation. Heath went
further and placed many other decision makers "out of bounds" for the
security services and the police. These two opponents had a number of
things in common, including their enthusiasm for the European Community.
Edward Heath took Britain into Europe and is to this day a vehement
campaigner for full integration into a centralised Europe with a European
central bank and currency. Wilson began the move to metrication in Britain,
which is ending British forms of measurement and replacing them with the
European version. Dr Little says she was told that Heath and Wilson were
friends when they first arrived at Oxford University in the 1930s. She says of
Harold Wilson's sudden resignation little more than a year after winning the
1974 General Election:

---

[57] Letter to Bernard Weatherill, Speaker of the House of Commons, May 1st 1987.
[58] "Subversive infiltrators into Westminster and Whitehall. Promotion of a Federal Europe."
Submission to the Committee on Standards in Public Life by Dr Kitty Little, January 1995.
The Nolan Committee decided not to accept her detailed information about the calculated
destruction of Britain. They said it was "outside their brief". Sure it was.

"I have every reason to think that before the end of 1975 they [MI5] were within sight of having sufficient legally admissible evidence for a prosecution. Wilson resigned. Callaghan succeeded him as Prime Minister, and had the members of MI5 who had been carrying out the investigation of Wilson's criminal activities removed, on the grounds that they were 'Right wing extremists'." [59]

Jim Callaghan (Bil) has since kept abreast of foreign policy as a joint president of the Royal Institute of International Affairs. His fellow presidents are Lord Carrington (TC, Bil, Comm 300) and Harold Wilson's former chancellor and home secretary, Lord (Roy) Jenkins (TC, Bil), who, with Lord (David) Owen (TC, Bil), Bill Rogers (Bil), and Shirley Williams, left the Labour Party in the early 1980s to form a centre party, the SDP, now the Liberal Democrats. All these people worked closely with another prominent Labour government minister under Harold Wilson and James Callaghan: the Bilderberger, Trilateralist, chairman of the IMF Interim Committee, Committe of 300 member, and council member of the Royal Institute of International Affairs, Denis Healey. I wonder if, when they were in the highest political offices in the land, Wilson, Heath, Jenkins, and Healey ever got together and pondered on the remarkable twist of destiny that led four people who were at Oxford University in the same period, to become the leading political names of the 1960s and 1970s, just as the United Kingdom was committing itself to the European Community. Indeed Jenkins would go on to be president of the European Commission and Heath would take the UK into the community. Wilson (Jesus College, University College), Healey (Balliol), Jenkins (Balliol), and Heath (Balliol) are such an inspiration to us all. Look what an Oxford education can do for you. In this same period, even the Liberal Party leaders did Oxford proud in the form of Jo Grimond (Balliol, Bil), and Jeremy Thorpe (Trinity College), the author of the book, *Europe: The Case For Going In.* Later leaders of the Liberal Party (now the Liberal Democrats), David Steel and Paddy Ashdown are also Bilderbergers and supporters of the European superstate. Once again, maybe all these connections are simply a coincidence, but you have every right to know they exist. It's called democracy. All those members of the Bilderberg Group involved in the creation of, and membership of, the European Community does challenge the idea of coincidence a little though, don't you think? But then, as George McGhee, a US ambassador to West Germany and Bilderberg attendee said: "the treaty of Rome, which brought the Common Market into being, was nurtured at Bilderberg meetings".[60] Precisely.

One other point about the findings of Kitty Little and similar researchers

[59] Letter to Bernard Weatherill, Speaker of the House of Commons, May 1st 1987.

[60] Robert Eringer, *The Global Manipulators*, (Pentacle Books, Bristol, 1980). Quoted in *Treason At Maastricht*, p17.

is that of Rhodesia, the country named after its creator, Cecil Rhodes. It is now Zimbabwe. The new Constitution for Rhodesia replaced dictatorship by white rule with dictatorship by Robert Mugabe for the benefit of the Elite. It was agreed upon in the autumn of 1979 at a conference at Lancaster House in London, chaired by Lord Carrington, who had taken over as foreign secretary from David Owen after Margaret Thatcher's election victory a few months earlier. The constitution was presented to the assembled Rhodesian political leaders, black and white, by Carrington, who insisted on an answer by the end of the week. One man in the Rhodesian delegation who would have seen the inherent flaws in this was John Giles, a constitutional expert. On Tuesday October 4th 1979, on the very day that the Rhodesians were due to discuss the Carrington proposals, John Giles went missing and was later found dead. Dr Kitty Little was at Lancaster House that day to meet Ian Smith, a friend of many years. She has been trying ever since to make the background to both the conference and the death of John Giles public. The previous day, Dr Little says, Giles had been to Hamley's (the famous London toy shop) to buy Christmas presents for his children. On the morning he disappeared he rang his wife, sounding very cheerful and upbeat, but later that morning he was observed looking suddenly very worried about something. In the afternoon, an official car, a Granada Ghia, came to pick him up. He was never seen alive again.

While Lord Carrington's proposals, in the absence of Giles, tied the Rhodesian delegation in mental knots and won the day, the police were advised that Giles was missing. The next morning, John Giles was found dead on a path close to the rear entrance of Lancaster House. Verdict: "Suicide". His death would not have been made public at all, unless an ambulance man had alerted the press. The coroner, who did not call policemen at the scene to give evidence, decided that Giles had jumped from a first floor window at Lancaster House, which those who have been to the spot say was an impossibility, given where the body was found. And that's another thing. The Lancaster House staff used the service door of the building and would have had to step over the body to get in and out. It was supposed to have laid there through a whole afternoon, evening, and night. Yet it wasn't found until the following morning.

The case was handled by the local police and the authorities refused to discuss it with the Rhodesian–Zimbabwe Special Branch. No police file exists on John Giles, I understand. Kitty Little insists that Ken Flower, the head of the Rhodesian Central Intelligence Organisation was, or had been, a member of Britain's intelligence section, MI6. She also says that it is now known that MI6 was working to destabilise Rhodesia in order to force the dictatorship swap that Lancaster House was really designed to produce. According to Dr Kitty Little's impeccable sources, Ken Flower might qualify for the *Guinness Book Of Records* as the doublest of double agents! While head of Rhodesian Intelligence he was also working for MI6, the KGB, East European Intelligence, the CIA, and a number of African Intelligence networks. He worked with the "D" group of MI6 operatives who, to quote Dr Little, "did nasty things and had them blamed on Ian Smith". Zimbabwe is obviously very important to the Elite and the multinational corporations, one of which, Rio Tinto Zinc, had enjoyed the experience of having Lord Carrington on its board.

There is considerable evidence to support Kitty Little's contention. Two months after the Lancaster House conference, it was revealed that Margaret Thatcher (Bil) and Lord Carrington (TC, Bil, RIIA, Comm 300) had ordered a massive surveillance operation on the delegates. Telephones were tapped, rooms bugged, diplomatic communications were monitored, and the British used Rhodesian security to interpret the African language. This was revealed by reporter Barrie Penrose in the London *Sunday Times* of February 3rd 1980, under the headline, "Minister's Phone was Tapped by Secret Services". This, said the article, was why "Lord Carrington could conduct the conference on the basis of brinkmanship. The intelligence services told him what the brinks were". Which leads to another question: if the rooms and phones were bugged, why did they not know what had happened to John Giles until he was found dead the next morning? Ummm. Kitty Little contends that Margaret Thatcher was kept in the dark by Carrington about a host of foreign policy subjects and only selected information was allowed to reach her. This clearly would have coloured her views of which policy to follow. It is emerging that for all her apparent power, the "Iron Lady" was another puppet, perhaps even more than most.

In the light of what Kitty Little says, it is interesting that (as I mentioned earlier) I was approached by the wife of a former official of the South African government, who said she had seen documents explaining how the Trilateral Commission had ordered Britain out of Rhodesia. Both foreign secretaries involved, Lord Carrington (Conservative) and David Owen (Labour) are connected to the Trilateral Commission. Carrington was a member and Owen would become one soon after Carrington replaced him as foreign secretary.

After the sudden death of John Smith (TC, Bil), the "new" Labour Party under Tony Blair (Bil) was immediately supported by the Elite and its frontmen like media mogul, Rupert Murdoch. They wanted Blair to be prime minister and they manipulated him to power. His chancellor, Gordon Brown (Bil), gave the Elite-created Bank of England control over setting interest rates within days of coming to office, so mirroring the Federal Reserve in the US. The leadership of the three main political parties in the UK are agreed on almost all that matters to the New World Order agenda, as they were in the days of Wilson, Heath and Jo Grimond/Jeremy Thorpe. When you look behind the words and camouflage, there is hardly a jot of difference between them on the way ahead – integration into the European

Union and a single currency and bank. They only differ, in public anyway, on the timescale. On the fundamentals of economic policy it is hard to prise them apart.

So what has been the effect of all this on a key ambition of the manipulators – the creation of a Federal Europe with centralised control? While we've been having this farce of a debate over whether the UK should agree to a single currency and a European Central Bank, the truth is that we are already committed to it. The politicians involved know it too. They are just kidding you, laughing at you probably. The UK Conservative Party claims (for public consumption only) to oppose the centralisation of power in Europe while Conservative members in the European Parliament are also members of the alliance grouping known as the European People's Party, which openly calls for a United States of Europe. This is actually written in its constitution![61] One way the confidence trick has been hidden is by increasing dramatically the numbers of laws being introduced at all levels of government, particularly in Europe. By the mid-1980s, the published laws emanating from Brussels together with parliamentary legislation, Ministerial Rules, and Orders in Council, exceeded in just six months, the sum total of all laws introduced in Britain before 1900.[62] This tidal wave of legislation is not an accident. It is there to ensure that millions of pages are voted into law without the lobby fodder politicians, or even the government ministers, having time to read them, let alone assess what they really mean amid the calculated gobbledygook and ambiguity. Another smokescreen is the belief that those who run the European Union are stupid and incompetent. Not at the highest levels they're not. Butter mountains and wine lakes may seem to be the result of incompetence, but who benefited from these policies? The multinational corporations who were able to absorb all the smaller farmers and producers put out of business by the surpluses. That was the idea. It all has to be done covertly because if the public knew what a federal Europe really means they would not agree to it. In 1947, a group of Conservatives and Liberals produced a document called *Design For Europe* and one paragraph revealed their approach very clearly:

> *"Moreover – and it is as well to state this bluntly at the outset – no government dependent upon a democratic vote could possibly agree in advance to the sacrifice which any adequate plan must involve. The people must be led slowly and unconsciously into the abandonment of their traditional economic defences..."* [63]

---

[61] *Treason At Maastricht*, p82, 89.

[62] Dr Kitty Little, "Subversive Infiltrators into Westminster and Whitehall. Promotion of a Federal Europe", (January 1995) p5, paragraph 19.

[63] Ibid p8, paragraph 29.

Edward Heath was agreeing to the political union of Britain in Europe as early as April 1962 when he was Lord Privy Seal. He told the Ministerial Council of the Western European Union that, "...you have decided that those who join the Economic Communities as full members must also join the Political Union. I am sure that this was the right decision." (Command Paper 1720.) Meanwhile the people were being told that the Common Market was only a free trade zone. Before Mr Heath (Bil) took Britain into Europe, he attended a meeting in Paris in October 1972 to negotiate the conditions with the French President, Georges Pompidou (Bil), a former employee of Guy Rothschild. John Davies, Heath's Secretary of State for Industry, was at the meeting and told the Conservative Party's Monday Club that the following had been agreed: UK technology would be merged with European industry. Britain had led research and development for more than 50 years and so it was 'only fair' that someone else should have a turn – France. As Britain ran down her manufacturing industry, London would become the money market of Europe. Heath further agreed to run down sterling and abolish the monarchy.[64] (The barrage of bad publicity that has destabilised the Royal family in recent years is designed to destroy the monarchy. Who has been tapping their 'phone calls? The manipulators. Prince Charles and Princess Diana are being played off against each other by 'advisors'. The target year for the end of the monarchy is 1999.) Edward Heath (Bil) and Sir Alec Douglas Hume (Bil) signed on behalf of the UK, a Treaty of Accession to the Treaty of Rome and we were in the European spiders web.

Also accepted by Mr Heath at the time of Britain's entry and by Harold Wilson and James Callaghan during the 'renegotiation' of British membership, was that Britain would renounce her national sovereignty and become part of a federal Europe. Local government was reorganised to reshape the country in preparation for this, and devolution of power to the regions of the UK is being promoted to prepare for the plan for a Europe of 'regions'. These regions would be given limited powers akin to the county councils of today and they would be administered by those who control the European superstate. The Maastricht Treaty on European Union even uses the word "municipal" elections when it talks of national elections within Europe.[65] Very appropriate, given the game plan. In 1980, the European Commission published their map of regions. Those which have been proposed in the former Yugoslavia as a result of the war are virtually the same as those on that map. When the absence of 'England' on the map was questioned, Dr Little and her colleagues were told that the national government would no longer be an "administrative unit". But while all this agreement was going on behind the scenes around the

[64] Dr Kitty Little, "Subversive Infiltrators into Westminster and Whitehall. Promotion of a Federal Europe", (January 1995) p10, paragraph 34.
[65] *Treason At Maastricht*, p54

time of British entry, Mr Heath was denying in public that there would be any loss of sovereignty. The lack of interest in the people's wishes reached a new low when a document published by the European Assembly in February 1984 said that anyone who even *voted* in the June 1984 European elections, would be deemed to have supported the idea of European Union! Equally outrageous was that the Maastricht Treaty on European Union had not even been published at the time of the UK general election which Prime Minister John Major claimed had approved the document! Isn't democracy just fantastic? We're having elections now in which only the clairvoyant can make an informed choice. When Douglas Hurd, the then foreign secretary, signed the Maastricht Treaty in February 1992, he committed Britain to a United States of Europe. He and the government will tell you differently. They will say there is a get-out clause which says:

> *"Unless the United Kingdom notifies the Council that it intends to move to the third stage* [political and monetary union], *it shall be under no obligation to do so."*

What they don't tell you is this Protocol was over-ruled by another on page P/UP–UEM/en61, which has these paragraphs:

> *"The high contracting parties…declare the irreversible character of the Community's movement to the third stage of Economic and Monetary Union by* **signing** [my emphasis] *the new Treaty provisions on Economic and Monetary Union.*
>
> *"Therefore all Member states shall, whether they fulfil the necessary conditions for the adoption of a single currency or not, respect the will for the community to enter swiftly into the third stage, and therefore no Member state shall prevent the entry into the third stage."*

Mr Hurd signed those provisions and therefore committed the UK to those terms. In other words, having lost the power of veto, the UK either accepts political and monetary union or pulls out of the show altogether. The public 'debate' is a fraud. Mr Hurd, Mr Major, and the pro-Europe Chancellor, Kenneth Clarke (Bil) knows that. So does Tony Blair (Bil), an Elite "chosen one" and Paddy Ashdown (Bil). Mr Hurd was one of those who stood in the Conservative leadership election after Margaret Thatcher was removed, on the orders of the Bilderberg Group, for her opposition to political and monetary union. Mr Hurd, who recommended Henry Kissinger for his knighthood, was well schooled in European affairs. He was private secretary to Ted Heath (1968–70) when Heath was leader of the opposition, and was then appointed his political secretary (1970–74) after Heath became Prime Minister. Hurd was also a minister of state at the Foreign Office under Lord Carrington in the run up to the Falklands War.

One of the people who helped to whip up the atmosphere which led to the demise of Mrs Thatcher, was Sir Geoffrey (now Lord) Howe (Comm 300), a former president of the European Council of Ministers. So what awaits us now, unless we get off our backsides very quickly? A Europe of regions controlled by the unelected European Commissioners and the six members of the Executive Board of the European Central Bank who will have control of the single currency and the reserves of each member 'State'. These six people, who will control the whole of the European Union, shall "be appointed from among persons of recognised standing and professional experience in monetary or banking matters". (Maastricht Treaty, Article 109a, page UP-UEM/eu41.) In their eight years of guaranteed security of tenure, these super six bankers of the Global Elite "may not seek or take instructions from Community Institutions...or any other body". The European dictatorship will be complete.

That is what the One Party Staters have been working towards behind their masks of opposition. Their ambitions are almost fulfilled. Only you – we – can stop them.

THE GLOBAL ONE PARTY STATE

Meanwhile the wars, which achieve so much for the Elite, continue. When the truth about the Iran-Iraq War, the Gulf War, and the Bosnian conflict comes out, as one day it will, the trails will lead to some very famous people and some front line companies – especially those involved in armaments – in the United Kingdom, the United States, and other countries. Who armed Saddam Hussein? Britain and America did. Who armed the Iranians? Britain and American did. Who armed the Serbs in Bosnia? Britain and America did. The time will come when the proof will be overwhelming that this is the case and some leading armament companies and politicians are going to face some serious questions. If you know more, please tell me.

In an article in *The Spotlight* on December 19th 1994, writer Warren Hough, claims that Henry Kissinger was accused by French President, François Mitterand, of being the "master manipulator" of the Yugoslav conflict. The allegation is said to have been made at a meeting of the European Security Conference in Budapest, Hungary. Warren Hough's article continued:

> "*As part of their war plans, the Serb leaders spent millions of dollars on contracts and payoffs in the US Wall Street sources say that most of these short-lived deals were apparently set up to make money for Kissinger's consulting firm, Kissinger Associates,* [founding director Lord Carrington, a 'peace' negotiator in the former Yugoslavia] *and for two of Kissinger's cronies, Lawrence Eagleburger and Brent Scowcroft. This populist newspaper, after reviewing confidential bank records in New York City, warned as early as 1992 that Eagleburger (a former secretary of state)*

and Scowcroft (White House national security director in the Bush administration) concealed a compromising 'cash nexus' to the Serbs while they were formulating supposedly impartial US positions toward the warring ethnic factions of the former Yugoslavia."

Interestingly, an 'advisor' to the Serb leader Radovan Karadzic, has been Sir Alfred Sherman who has operated from an apartment in Pale near Sarajevo, next door to Karadzic's office, according to published research. Sherman is known as the "inventor of Margaret Thatcher" and he was at the forefront of the manoeuvring that led to her election as leader of the British Conservative Party. She later awarded him a knighthood and together they founded the "think tank", the Centre for Policy Studies[66] from where the economic madness of the 1980s partly originated. The Serbs were funded by the Elite via Belgrade banks involved in massive drug money laundering. It is also amazing how many 'foundations' were set up in the former Yugoslavia by the financial speculator and Rothschild frontman, George Soros (Bil). He has them in Bosnia, Croatia, Slovenia and Belgrade. Soros is a close friend of Lawrence Eagleburger at Kissinger Associates, the former US ambassador to Belgrade and close ally of Slobodon Milosevic! Now what's that I can smell? Air freshener anyone? According to writer and researcher Ben C. Vidgen, writing in *Nexus* magazine in February 1996, America, Germany and Israel were running a secret airlift of arms to Croatia and Bosnia from the start of the conflict.

French journalists revealed in 1994 that CIA agents were luring Bosnian Muslims into reckless and hopeless counter-attacks against the Serbs on false promises of US support. The White House call these reports "malicious lies". But then George Kenney, an American official in charge of Yugoslav affairs at the US State Department until he quit in disgust on August 11th 1992, said that Muslims were indeed tricked into rejecting a number of partial truce offers on the assumption that American aid would ensure them victory. Warren Hough says that while the Muslims were set up, the Kissinger network was playing the "good guy, bad guy" game, which the manipulators use so often. It involved the two Serb leaders, Slobodan Milosevic and Radovan Karadzic. Hough wrote:

"Under this scenario, Milosevic — the client of Kissinger Associates — publicly repudiated and condemned the illegal onslaught of Karadzic's troops against Bosnian Muslims. But covertly the Milosevic government furnished the 'renegade' forces of Karadzic with all the armaments and other support they needed to wage an implacable 'war of extermination' against their Muslim neighbours. Muslim resupplies were, of course, blocked by the UN arms embargo."

---

[66] *Secret Societies*, p279.

The research claims also that Saudi Arabia, itself a fascist tyranny, was being set up by this plan. According to *Spotlight*, King Fahd was repeatedly reassured by his ambassador in Washington that the US planned to lift the arms embargo in time to allow decisive reinforcements to reach the embattled Muslims. As a result the King convinced other Islamic leaders to have faith in Washington. Now the Saudi monarchy is denounced as a gullible fellow-traveller of the CIA, or as a traitor to Islam. Which, of course, suits the manipulators wonderfully well. In the light of all this, there are some interesting connections between the 'peace' negotiators in Bosnia. Lord Carrington (RIIA, Bil, TC, Comm 300), Lord Owen (Bil, TC) and Sweden's Carl Bildt (Bil) followed each other as official peace negotiators for the European Union in the former Yugoslavia. The United Nations peace negotiator, who worked closely with his great friend, Lord Owen, was Jimmy Carter's Secretary of State, Cyrus Vance (CFR, TC, Bil, Comm 300), and a director of the Rothschild bank, Manufacturers Hanover Trust. When Vance resigned, the UN appointed another negotiator to work with Lord Owen – Thorvald Stoltenberg, of Norway. Yes, you guessed it again, a member of the Trilateral Commission and the Bilderberg Group. And when they each failed to achieve peace, who was it who suddenly flew to Bosnia, amid worldwide publicity, as an 'independent' peace negotiator? Why, it was Jimmy Carter (CFR), the Trilateral Commission's first President of the United States. Later came Richard Holbrooke (TC, CFR, Bil), the peace envoy of Bill Clinton (CFR, TC, Bil) and the US ambassador to Yugoslavia was Warren Zimmerman (also TC, CFR), who reported, like Holbrooke, to Clinton's Secretary of State, Warren Christopher, of the CFR and Trilateral Commission. And who was it who arrived in Rwanda on an undisclosed "diplomatic mission" days before the outbreak of that horrific conflict? Lord Carrington and Henry Kissinger!

Maybe this is all smoke without fire. Maybe the Trilateral Commission and the Bilderberg Group just happen to run peace negotiation courses. Maybe pigs can fly. Make up your own mind. My feeling about the former Yugoslavia when I wrote the first edition of this book was that the conflict was being used overwhelmingly to embarrass the UN Peacekeeping Forces and NATO. This was designed to create a situation of "something must be done" which would lead to greater powers for the UN/NATO alliance and, in effect, create a world army. As usual, the more atrocities and suffering that the public see, the greater the demand that "something must be done". What has happened since? The Bosnian conflict has led to the creation of a 60,000-strong NATO 'peacekeeping' force which includes some 30 countries. It is a world army under central control – exactly as the Elite plan demanded. It is the biggest multinational force to be assembled since the second World War and it has been made possible by untold human suffering. The main front man for this NATO world army was Bill Clinton (CFR, TC, Bil), the yes man for David Rockefeller and the Elite. One of those appointed to oversee the civilian operation in Bosnia after the 'peace' agreement was Carl Bildt (Bil), and the officer in charge of the multinational force (world army) was named as US Admiral Leighton Smith (CFR). If you want confirmation that the world army in Bosnia is part of the Elite plan look no further than a full page advertisement in the Washington Post on December 6th 1995. It was placed by an organisation calling itself the Committee for American Leadership in Bosnia and it supported Bill Clinton's plan for a world army in Bosnia. The ad was signed by, among others, Zbigniew Brzezinski (CFR, Bil and a founder of the Trilateral Commission); Congressman Stephen Solarz (CFR); Rothschild frontman and currency speculator, George Soros (Bil); Michael Armacost (CFR), the president of the Elite's Brookings Institute; and Leslie Gelb (TC), the president of the Council on Foreign Relations and a columnist on the *New York Times*. The policy on Bosnia is the Elite's policy from start to finish. We have one party states within a one party world under a one party army.

How many more have to suffer before the political stooges stop being duped? How many more tragedies do there have to be before the human race says "*Enough!*" and takes control of its own destiny? If that is to happen, we need to stop looking to politicians for the answers and start organising ourselves in our own communities to build local economies and organisations which can operate outside this manipulation. A good statement of intent, in my view, would be a mass boycott of all state, national, and European elections. To vote under the present circumstances is to give credence to a system that is an insult to freedom and democratic choice, a system that is designed to control us and not to set us free. By refusing to vote and have any part of it, we can show how we feel. We can say to the manipulators: We know what you are doing and the game is up. We will no longer be manipulated into supporting and maintaining the one party state and a one party world.

Chapter 14

Psychological fascism

"The sophisticated exercise of control utilises the ability to keep people oppressed yet contented. Much better to make them think it was their idea to go to the gallows."
Anon

The underlying theme of all you have read is the manipulation of the human mind. You cannot control billions of people with tanks in the streets and soldiers at the door. You can only do it by divide and rule – and by programming the mass consciousness (public opinion) into believing that what you want to do is a good idea or the only option.

This is crucial to both understanding how the manipulation works and to thinking on a more streetwise vibration which will make it far more difficult for us to be misled. For example, say that you want to introduce cameras in the streets, an armed and more authoritarian police force, and the erosion of personal freedoms. You don't want the public to oppose these policies, indeed you want them to *demand* that you introduce them. What do you need for this to happen? More high profile, violent crime, which creates enormous fear in the community. Achieve that and people will be knocking on your door demanding that you put cameras in their streets and give more guns and power to the police. Problem-reaction-solution. And what better way to induce more crime than to create a society of 'haves' and 'have nots' dependent on welfare payments and then start dismantling the welfare state? You give people a choice of going without basic needs or of taking someone else's money and property. And when they do the latter, the victims of the crime and the mass of people who see the reports of the crime demand that "something must be done".

All aspects of society are being used to promote this mental coup d'état. The 'education' system is not there to inform children and young people, it is there to indoctrinate them; the same with the media and advertising. The tax exempt foundations coordinate the Elite's 'education' policy in the United States schools and universities, and in the United Kingdom this is done, in part, by a secret clique known as the All Souls Group. This meets three times a year at (most appropriately) Rhodes House at Oxford University. Such education policies are designed to turn out clones of the system and world government supporters, although the overwhelming majority of people in the teaching profession will not realise this.

I included in *The Robots' Rebellion* an extract from a document found, apparently by accident, in 1986 called *Silent Weapons For A Quiet War*. Another version is reported to have been in the hands of US Naval Intelligence in 1969. It is a wonderful explanation of the technique of mass brainwashing. The version I have was found inside an IBM photocopier bought at a second hand sale in America and it describes a policy of mass mind control. This lengthy and detailed document was dated 1979, but it outlines a policy that has been implemented since the 1950s. The document says that: "The quiet war was... declared by the international elite at a meeting held in 1954". The Bilderberg Group first met in 1954. It is likely that the methods laid out in the document will be inspired by the Tavistock Institute of Human Relations in London and its interconnecting offshoots. Here is a flavour of the content:

> "Experience has proven that the simplest method of securing a silent weapon and gaining control of the public is to keep them undisciplined and ignorant of basic systems principles on the one hand, while keeping them confused, disorganised, and distracted with matters of no real importance on the other hand.

This is achieved by:
1. *disengaging their minds; sabotaging their mental activities; providing a low-quality programme of public education in mathematics, systems design and economics, and discouraging technical creativity.*
2. *engaging their emotions, increasing their self indulgence and their indulgence in emotional and physical activities by:*
a) *unrelenting emotional affrontations and attacks (mental and emotional rape) by way of a constant barrage of sex, violence, and wars in the media – especially the TV and the newspapers.*
b) *giving them what they desire – in excess – "junk food for thought" – and depriving them of what they really need.*
c) *rewriting history and law and subjecting the public to the deviant creation, thus being able to shift their thinking from personal needs to highly fabricated outside priorities.*

These preclude their interest in, and discovery of, the silent weapons of social automation technology. The general rule is that there is profit in confusion; the more confusion, the more profit. Therefore the best approach is to create problems and then offer solutions.

In summary:
Media: *Keep the adult public attention diverted away from the real social issues, and captivated by matters of no real importance.*

> ***Schools:*** *Keep the young public ignorant of real mathematics, real economics, real law, and real history.*
> ***Entertainment:*** *Keep the public entertainment below a sixth grade level.*
> ***Work:*** *Keep the public busy, busy, busy, with no time to think; back on the farm with the other animals."*

That doesn't describe today's world, does it? All the main aspects of the coup d'état are there and we can see this strategy at work every day. When a government is planning to introduce legislation against a target group as part of the plan to enforce conformity and remove freedoms, the process of softening up public opinion against that target group begins months, sometimes years, before there is even a hint of new laws. The idea is to turn public opinion against the target group through propaganda and engineered events. When the legislation is finally presented, the potential opposition is already either greatly reduced or destroyed altogether. Take the example of the Criminal Justice Bill introduced by the British government in 1994. It was a dreadful piece of work and a tremendous strike against basic freedoms, but it sailed through Parliament with virtually all-party support. One of its many targets were the 'travellers', the groups of people who live in mobile homes of many kinds and move between various places throughout the year. They have been dubbed 'New Age' travellers by the media. The travellers are not perfect – who is? – but it will be enlightening to look at how they were treated. In the year to eighteen months before the Criminal Justice Bill was announced, you could hardly open a newspaper or watch the TV news without seeing a story which suggested that travellers were a 'problem' in need of a 'solution'. Police were stopping and harassing the traveller convoys as they moved from site to site; councils were refusing to allow them to cross their borders; conflicts were breaking out between travellers and police as the anger and frustration mounted. All was captured and broadcast on the main television news bulletins. Agents provocateur connected to British Intelligence were in there stirring things up just as the cameras were on the spot, in the way such agencies operate all over the world.

Once negative events and propaganda have been projected at public opinion, out go the opinion-polling organisations with their clipboards. The people who ask the questions on the street don't know what they are involved in. They are just asking the questions they are told and paid to ask. But opinion polls are not there to *measure* public opinion so the people can be given what they desire. They are there to *direct* public opinion, often using loaded questions to attract the desired reply. Tell people that 80% of the population believe something and those of the sheep – baa, baa – mentality will quickly conform and believe the same. Eighty per cent of people cannot be wrong, can they? Oh yes they can, if they have given their minds away. The other role of opinion polls is to check if the propaganda against a target group is working. Once the opinion polls say that a sufficient majority now believe the target group is a problem and "something must be done", the legislation (the solution) is taken out of the file and put before Parliament. This approach has another advantage in that the potential political opposition, what little there is, fears the electoral consequences of opposing laws to 'solve' a 'problem' about which the public has now been programmed to believe that "something must be done". Therefore highly controversial legislation like the Criminal Justice Bill (which removes basic freedoms) goes through Parliament and into law virtually on the nod. Once this Bill was making its way into law, suddenly all the "travellers are a problem" stories disappeared and at the time of this writing, have never reappeared. They will only return when even more harsh legislation against them is being planned. Until then, public opinion will go on being softened up to accept legislation against other target groups on the Elite's hit list and the public will go on reacting like robots in exactly the way required. Unless we choose to take control of our own minds.

Organisations like the Tavistock Institute of Human Relations (and their brothers and sisters in the United States such as the Stanford Research Institute, and the Rand Corporation) research into how people will react, individually and collectively, to events, changes, and 'buzz words'. It was Tavistock, according to research that I've read,[1] which devised the policy of 'future shocks', the means by which the collective human mind is bombarded with so many changes, events, and contradicting information that it overloads, switches off, and becomes subservient. This is happening all over the world today, most obviously in the United States and Japan, where the population is being given one event after the other to fill them with fear and insecurity. The aim is to destabilise Japanese society and break its resistance to fundamental change.

Many of the so called 'spontaneous' trends that are taken on by the young are introduced by these and other organisations and then hyped into a frenzy by advertising and the controlled media. People talk about the "latest craze" and very few stop to ask, "Where did this start and who was behind it?" We hear about the "craze that's sweeping America" and that's all. The 'Flower Power' period of the 1960s was hijacked and directed by this same mind manipulating force. The CIA and British Intelligence were experimenting with the effects of the drug LSD in the 1950s, before it was unleashed on the market and destroyed any possibility of substantial positive change emerging from that time. In 1953, the CIA commandeered the entire supply of LSD from the Swiss manufacturers, Sandoz (which was owned by S.G. Warburg of London). Later they did the same with Eli Lilly when it began to produce LSD in the United States. People were so doped and duped that they thought LSD was a weapon of 'freedom'. Some still do. I'm not sure the CIA and British Intelligence had that in mind, somehow.

---

[1] See Dr John Coleman's *Conspirators' Hierarchy: The Story Of The Committee Of 300*.

The Diversion Technique

All that I am talking about here comes under the heading of 'diversion'. This is one of the most effective of the mind manipulation weapons used against the human psyche. It takes many forms. If you are being held captive, one way to escape is to start a diversion. It may be an argument or a fight among fellow prisoners. Once the trouble starts, everyone's attention, including that of the guards, focuses on the incident. This gives you the opportunity to slip away unseen. The bullfighter's technique is another obvious form of diversion as he focuses the attention of the bull on his cape, so allowing himself to avoid injury.

In the world of propaganda and public mind manipulation, we are constantly being subjected to this. Accusations of anti-Semitism against New World Order investigators is a classic example of diversion. You concentrate attention on the issue of the messenger's alleged racism and divert attention from what he or she is saying about their research. We have the strategy of infiltrating 'moderate' wings of political parties while covertly following an extreme game plan. This is a diversion which stops extremists being identified while they, themselves, denounce their legitimate opposition as extremists. We hear from time to time of 'revelations' about intelligence agencies, but how many are real revelations and how many are systematically leaked to divert people from what is really going on? An example: publish a book by a 'spy' who names certain people as foreign agents. Hype it up through your controlled media and get the government to vehemently oppose it, so adding to its credibility. Persuade people to accept that the names revealed by the 'whistle-blower' are correct and those who were really involved are in the clear. If you want to introduce controversial legislation or a government is being forced to reveal unpleasant information about itself, then under the rules of diversion, this should be done on a day you know another major story is going to break. This lessens the space and prominence given to what you say because of the massive media coverage of the other big story.

On the day the British Home Secretary, Michael Howard, announced the introduction of identity cards, the Loyalist Paramilitary groups in Northern Ireland announced a ceasefire in line with the one agreed by the Republican IRA. This reduced by a tremendous amount, the coverage and reaction in the media to Michael Howard's identity cards. I do not believe this was a coincidence, especially since the paramilitaries and the British government are in regular contact through the secret society network and other channels, no matter what they may say publicly. Indeed, the secret communication between the IRA and their 'enemy', the British government, has been publicly exposed.

The attempts to blame two Libyans for the bomb on Pan Am Flight 103 which killed 270 people at Lockerbie, Scotland, in December 1988 is another case of diversion. None of the evidence points to Libya. That is a

convenient scapegoat to move attention from what really happened and to
undermine the Gaddafi regime. The evidence of independent studies and
documentaries clearly points to other Middle East connections, the CIA,
and other intelligence agencies. The Lockerbie crash site was swarming with
American agents, as locals and journalists have pointed out. Police surgeon,
David Fieldhouse, said he issued death certificates after examining 59
bodies, but later he found that police records contained details of only 58
bodies.[2] What happened to the missing body, no-one seems to know. Could
it just have been the body that would have shed some light on what
happened and who did it? And if the authorities didn't know what was
going to occur, why were 'VIPs' warned not to take that flight after their
seats had been booked? Among them were Pik Botha, the South African
minister, and others accompanying him, including the head of BOSS, the
South African intelligence agency (which has close ties with the CIA and
Mossad). They cancelled their reservations on Flight 103 shortly before
departure after a tip-off from intelligence sources.[3] Pik Botha told the
British businessman, Tiny Rowlands, that these sources were the kind that
"couldn't be dismissed".[4]

Libya has been used as a diversion for years. Colonel Gaddafi was portrayed
as the monster of monsters, until it became more useful to give that title to
George Bush's old friend, Saddam Hussein. The bombing of Tripoli by US
planes flying from British bases in 1986 was part of this. Dozens of Libyan
civilians, including children, were murdered by the Americans (with British
support) in retaliation for "Libyan terrorism" at a disco in West Berlin, for
which, again, there was no evidence, as later conceded by German
investigators. I know nothing about Gaddafi for sure, but I have heard
suggestions that he's hated by the US. There is another view that this
"hatred" is a front for CIA terrorist training based in Libia, which, it is said,
has honed the skills of the IRA, the Red Brigades, and other terrorist
groups. It's hard to tell, but here I am looking only at the strange
connections surrounding the Lockerbie bomb. The man who wrote the
paper for Ronald Reagan which proposed a campaign to destroy the Gaddafi
regime with lies and disinformation was (by his own admission) the CIA
operative, Vincent Cannistraro. He worked for three years on the campaign
with Oliver North and this led to the bombing of Tripoli. Who was the man
appointed to head the CIA 'investigation' into Lockerbie which decided that
two Libyans were responsible? It couldn't be? Yes it could: Vincent
Cannistraro. Part of the CIA campaign against Libya included the murder by
the CIA of the British policewoman, Yvonne Fletcher, in St James Square,

[2] *The Sunday Telegraph*, (February 5th 1995).
[3] Oswald Le Winter, CIA operative 1968-85, speaking on the documentary, *The Maltese
Double Cross*, which was shown to British MPs in 1994.
[4] Ibid.

London, on April 17th 1984. This murder was blamed on the staff at the Libyan People's Bureau. Some researchers believe she was shot by a CIA marksman from 8 St James Square, close to the Bureau, say some researchers. This building had been occupied from only a few months before by a company with known CIA connections.

Despite this information and the fact that no evidence points to an involvement by Libya in the Lockerbie bombing, the United Nations (Global Elite) continue to impose sanctions on that country! And the British prime minister has refused to allow a trial of the two Libyans to take place in a neutral country. Either the British government at the highest levels is breathtakingly dumb or they know more about Lockerbie than they are prepared to reveal to the people who elected them. The United States and the Elite use the create-a-monster technique all the time to divert attention from the fact that they are installing and pulling the strings of far more extreme regimes throughout the world. There was no talk of monsters and terrorism in 1988 when the USS Vincennes fired a missile 'by accident' to shoot down an Iranian passenger jet with 290 on board.[5] The Vincennes was in the Persian Gulf to support Saddam Hussein, then America's friend and ally in the Iraqi war with Iran. The commander of the ship was 'severely punished': he was awarded the Legion of Merit Award by George Bush for "exceptionally meritorious conduct in the performance of outstanding service" and for the "calm and professional atmosphere" under his command during the period the jet was destroyed.[6]

The stepping-stones strategy is another diversion. The Elite know the goal they are aiming for and the stepping-stones required to manipulate public opinion towards that end. But if they are going to persuade people to accept those stepping stones, each one must be presented in isolation. If once they are seen by the general public as links in a chain leading towards a global centralised tyranny, obviously the game is up. If you want barcoded human beings linked to a central computer, you must first get them to accept credit and identity cards. You can be even more subtle by announcing first of all that the identity cards will not be compulsory, as Michael Howard did at the Conservative Party Conference in 1994. Shouts of dismay from the audience who want them to be compulsory make you look positively moderate in comparison, and initial opposition from the civil liberties groups is diluted because the government says, "But they are not compulsory; people have the choice". Of course, the plan is to make them compulsory and then go on to barcoding, but the stepping-stones diversionary approach demands that this be done in distinct stages, so that people in general don't realise what is

---

[5] There was another air disaster in the 1980s, which cost 329 lives. It was the bombing of the Air India flight off Ireland in 1985 which has since been traced to a paramilitary camp in Alabama where mercenaries are trained for terrorist activities.

[6] Noam Chomsky, *Letters From Lexington*, (AK Press, Edinburgh, Scotland) p119–120.

going on. These tactics are used at all levels of society. If you want to develop an area of unspoilt, isolated land, and you announce plans to build a housing estate or industrial complex, it would attract enormous opposition. Instead, the first stage is to propose a road to allow people greater 'access' to the area. Once this has been achieved a few buildings begin to appear, then more and more, until you have built, in stages, what you intended all along. This is one reason why the information in this book and others like it is so important. Once you know the ultimate aims, the stepping-stones towards them become so easy to see.

THE 'FREE' PRESS

None of this mind manipulation could happen without the media. Again, only a few people in the media know they are playing a key role in programming the human mind to walk the road to a global tyranny. The overwhelming majority of journalists have no idea how they are being used. I would go further. From my experience inside the media for many years and more recently on the other side of the microphone and notebook, I believe the two *least* knowledgeable and streetwise professions – in general – are journalism and politics. As I suggested earlier, they are two aspects of the same illusion. The politicians act as if they rule the world and the media report events as if politicians are the global decision makers. Thus, the *real* controllers can stay in the shadows, unreported and unidentified. There are exceptions when you meet a very bright journalist who can see behind the façades. They know they are imprisoned within a media structure which severely limits what they can say and do. But they take every opportunity to get across as much information as they can. I have met a few of those people and they are a joy to talk to. If only that were true of the rest. Most journalists on local and regional papers and local radio are either time-servers, who are programmed to turn out the same old establishment line without question while thinking their years in the profession make them streetwise, or they are youngsters fresh out of university who have no experience of the world and the manipulation that goes on. There are, I stress, exceptions, but I am speaking generally here. I don't say this out of condemnation, but as this mindset stands between the events in the world and the way the information about them is communicated to the public, it is important that we know the nature of the filters and the filtering that goes on.

I remember talking in Southern England one night in the terms I have outlined in this book. There was one person in the audience who seemed to have a permanent question mark above her head. This turned out to be the local journalist. When I saw her report, it was headlined "Icke's old theory about the New World Order". I was intrigued. "Old theory?" Had this newspaper talked about the global conspiracy before, then? No, as it happens. The headline referred to the reporter's contention that what I said that night about the nature of the New World Order was not new because George Bush had used the same words years before! If that was an isolated example of the thought processes which provide our news, it wouldn't be a problem. But it isn't. I could fill another book with stories of my experiences with people bravely claiming to be journalists who have asked questions and written articles that would make a two-year-old look like the peak of maturity.

At the national and international level, the number of journalists knowingly manipulating the human mind is far greater than the local and regional media, but it is still a relative few. The rest just conform to the traditional structure and approach and allow themselves to be manipulated to manipulate their audience. I worked in the BBC Television national newsroom for years and everyone around me appeared to be extremely genuine. Most of them were very nice people who loved their children and would not wish to leave them to face a centralised global dictatorship. But every day they turn out stories which feed their millions of viewers the line the Elite want them to see and hear.

To manipulate the world, you don't need to have people running around all the time, like one of those stage performers trying to keep a dozen plates spinning on the end of a stick. Once you have created the structure, anyone coming into that organisation, say a newspaper or television newsroom, has to conform to what is already there. If you can get your representatives into the positions which appoint others into that organisation, it is even better, because you can then fill the place with clones of your own attitudes. Also, journalists are there to report events. If you can engineer significant events, the journalists will report them. You don't have to control every journalist to do this; the event will be reported anyway. Most of the time, the background information and explanation of that event will come from official sources. Watch a television news bulletin today if you can, and see where the words the reporter is speaking are overwhelmingly coming from: official sources. So without even manipulating a single journalist, your engineered event, be it a "terrorist bomb" or "economic problem", is both reported and explained in the way you want.

The coverage of the horrific bombing in Oklahoma City in April 1995 was yet another example of puppet-strings journalism. Whatever official statements were issued, the media jumped on them immediately and accepted them as fact, without question. I listened to the BBC's Radio Five at that time and they introduced a lady from an organisation I had never heard of in America. There was not one question about what her organisation represented, who funded it, or what its background was. The interviewer just fed her questions and allowed her, unchallenged, to give her 'expert' opinion on the people she believed had carried out the attack. In BBC Television's review of 1995, the so called "heavyweight" news presenter, John Humphreys, parrotted the government line on Oklahoma and named McVeigh and the militias as the "enemy within" even before there had been a trial! And they call themselves 'journalists'. It's unbelievable.

When you are looking at the news, make a note of how short the individual items are. There is usually only enough time, even in major stories, to say this is what has happened and this is the (official) explanation. I was laughed at by millions when I questioned that the figure I was seeing on the television news was the real Saddam Hussein back in 1991. There was this man on the screen and the reporter or newsreader was saying it was Saddam. We were told whom he had met that day, and, on one occasion, how he had swum across a river to show his people he was alive and well after the Gulf War. *Now* we know from a defector from Iraq that it was not the real Saddam, but his stand-in lookalike. The media is being conned day by day and it then cons its audience. Ask 99% of journalists about the Bilderberg Group, the Council on Foreign Relations, the Trilateral Commission, and the Elite in general, and they will look at you in bewilderment. They won't even have heard of them, let alone know what their role is.

But there are some journalists in strategic positions who do know and support what those organisations are doing. The media is such a vehicle for the coup d'état that if it ever got into the hands of the Elite, the potential would be limitless. But we don't have to worry because, as we are told so often, we have an independent media. Ummm. Independent of what and whom? In the August/September 1993 edition of the Netherland's based magazine, *Exposure*, details were published of the controlling boards of the three television networks in the United States, NBC, CBS, and ABC. These networks are supposed to be in 'competition' and it is this very 'competition' that is part of the 'independence' which ensures we enjoy unbiased news. That's the theory, anyway. The *Exposure* research came from the work of the American New World Order investigator, Eustace Mullins. From what I read, Eustace and I would have very little in common on most things, but either the people he names were controlling the networks at the time of the article, or they were not. The following is provable fact: NBC is a subsidiary of RCA, a media conglomerate which appears regularly on the career details of a number of people named throughout this book. Among the NBC directors named in the Mullins article were: John Brademas (CFR, TC, Bil), a director of the Rockefeller Foundation; Peter G. Peterson (CFR), former head of Kuhn, Loeb, and Co (Rothschild), and a former Secretary of Commerce; Robert Cizik, chairman of RCA and of First City Bancorp, which was identified in Congressional testimony as a Rothschild bank; Thomas O. Paine, president of Northrup Co (the big defence contractor) and director of the (Elite-controlled) Institute of Strategic Studies in London; Donald Smiley, a director of two Morgan Companies, Metropolitan Life and US Steel; Thornton Bradshaw, chairman of RCA, director of the Rockefeller Brothers Fund, Atlantic Richfield Oil, and the Aspen Institute of Humanistic Studies (both of the latter headed by 'environmentalist' and elite Bilderberger, Robert O. Anderson). Clearly the NBC board has considerable Rockefeller-Rothschild-Morgan influence.

Another American TV network, ABC, had on its board of directors: Ray Adam, director of J.P. Morgan, Metropolitan Life (Morgan), and Morgan Guaranty Trust; Frank Cary, chairman of IBM, and director of J.P. Morgan and the Morgan Guaranty Trust; Donald C. Cook (CFR, Bil), general partner of Lazard Freres banking house; John T. Connor (CFR) of the Kuhn, Loeb (Rothschild) law firm, Gravath, Swaine and Moore, former Assistant Secretary of the Navy, US Secretary of Commerce, director of the Chase Manhattan Bank (Rockefeller/Rothschild), General Motors, and chairman of the J. Henry Schroder Bank and Schroders Inc, of London (see the funding of Hitler); Thomas M. Macioce, director of Manufacturers Hanover Trust (Rothschild); George Jenkins, chairman of Metropolitan Life (Morgan) and Citibank (which has many Rothschild connections); Martin J. Schwab, director of Manufacturers Hanover (Rothschild); Alan Greenspan (CFR, TC, Bil), chairman of the Federal Reserve, director of J.P. Morgan, Morgan Guaranty Trust, Hoover Institution, *Time* magazine, and General Foods; Ulric Haynes Jr, director of the Ford Foundation and Marine Midland Bank (owned by the Hong Kong and Shanghai Bank). Again, we see the same Rockefeller-Rothschild-Morgan line-up on the board of the ABC network which, we are told, is independent of NBC. The ABC company was taken over by Cities Communications, whose most prominent director is Robert Roosa (CFR, Bil), senior partner of Brown Brothers Harriman, which has close ties with the Bank of England. Roosa and David Rockefeller are credited with selecting Paul Volcker to chair the Federal Reserve Board.

Which brings us to CBS, the third of the 'independent' networks. Its financial expansion was supervised for a long time by Brown Brothers Harriman and its senior partner, Prescott Bush who was a CBS director. CBS banks through the Morgan Guaranty Trust and reports of CBS connections with the CIA and British Intelligence are legion among New World Order researchers. Some know it as the Conspiracy Brainwashing System. The CBS board included: William S. Paley (Comm 300), the chairman (for whom Prescott Bush personally organised the money to buy the company); Harold Brown (CFR), executive director of the Trilateral Commission, and former Secretary of the Air Force and Defence; Roswell Gilpatric (CFR, Bil), from the Kuhn, Loeb (Rothschild) law firm, Cravath, Swaine, and Moore, and former director of the Federal Reserve Bank of New York; Henry B. Schnacht, director of the Chase Manhattan Bank (Rockefeller/Rothschild), the Council on Foreign Relations, Brookings Institution, and Committee for Economic Development; Michel C. Bergerac, chairman of Revlon, and director of Manufacturers Hanover Bank (Rothschild); James D. Wolfensohn (CFR, TC, Bil), former head of J. Henry Schroder Bank, who has close links with the Rothschilds and the Rockefellers, (in 1995, Bill Clinton successfully nominated him to head the World Bank); Franklin A. Thomas (CFR), head of the Ford Foundation; Newton D. Minow (CFR), director of the Rand Corporation and, among

many others, the Ditchley Foundation, which is closely linked with the
Tavistock Institute in London and the Bilderberg Group. People connected
with research into how the public mind reacts to events and information are
on the board of a United States television network? What?

Again with CBS, we are looking at the same names at the helm, and all
three networks are closely interlocked with the Council on Foreign Relations
and the Trilateral Commission. How can it possibly be claimed that the three
television networks in America, through which the overwhelming majority of
Americans get their news, are independent? They are controlled or strongly
influenced by the *same* people! Look at the potential for recruiting only those
producers, journalists, and editors who support your views and aims, and for
sacking those who challenge your interference in what is and isn't shown.
Look at the potential for selling a common line on events and news stories to
ensure the American people have no other explanations than those you want
them to believe. In July 1995, ABC was merged with the Walt Disney empire
and the giant Westinghouse Electric made its move to buy CBS. Two months
later, Turner Broadcasting, the company behind CNN Television, announced
plans to merge with Time Warner. The deal was struck between the Time
Warner chairman, Gerald M. Levin (TC) and Ted Turner (Comm 300), a
leading supporter of the new global order. We have seen the history of Time
Warner in *Chapter 12*. The concentration of power gathers pace.

The same familiar Elite control the three television networks and
America's main newspapers, like the *New York Times*, the *Washington Post*,
and the *Los Angeles Times*. This is without even mentioning all the other
media outlets and international news agencies (like Reuters) which the Elite
control and the agencies run by the major newspapers which feed a common
line to the smaller papers via the wire machines and syndicated columnists.
The mind manipulation possibilities this offers are just incredible. Scores of
leading US journalists and editors are members of the Council on Foreign
Relations and the Trilateral Commission and they are covertly working to
that party line in their selection, dissection and presentation of news and
information. Typical was a 'report' by the famous CBS News anchorman,
Walter Cronkite, into the wealth and power of the Rockefellers. He closed
by saying that if any family had to have as much power and money as the
Rockefellers, it was a good thing it was the Rockefellers.[7] Violin, anyone? I
am grateful for the research into UK media ownership in the early 1990s by
Colonel Barry Turner, which he published in 1992 as a paper entitled
"Control of the Communications Media and Conditioning of the Public
Mind". Much of the following information about names and newspapers is
thanks to his painstaking work. The leading 'quality' newspaper in the UK is
The Daily Telegraph. This is owned through the Hollinger Group by the

---

[7] *The Rockefellers*, CBS, (Friday, December 28th 1973). Today the *ABC News* anchorman and
senior editor, Peter Jennings, is a Bilderberger.

Canadian, Conrad Black. The group owns more than 200 newspapers and magazines in the United Kingdom, the United States, Canada, and Israel, and the group started life as a front company set up by the British intelligence as I explained earlier. Conrad Black is a member of the elite Steering Committee of the Bilderberg Group, a Trilateralist, and a member of the Institute for Strategic Studies. The senior international advisors to the Hollinger Group are Henry Kissinger (CFR, TC, Bil, RIIA, Comm 300) and Lord Carrington (TC, RIIA, Bil, Comm 300). Some members of the Hollinger International Supervisory Board are Zbigniew Brzezinski (CFR, TC, Bil); Giovanni Agnelli (Bil, Black Nobility, Comm 300); David Brinkley (CFR), news commentator with ABC News; Paul Volker (CFR, TC, Bil), the chairman of the Federal Reserve Board responsible for Reaganomics and Thatcherism; Lord Rothschild, chairman of Rothschild Holdings; and Lord Hanson, chairman of Hanson plc. On the board of *The Daily Telegraph* is Evelyn de Rothschild, chairman of the N.M. Rothschild merchant bank. N.M. Rothschild are merchant bankers to the Hollinger Group to complete the cosy relationship.

A former editor-in-chief and board member at *The Daily Telegraph* is Andrew Knight, another member of the Bilderberg Group Steering Committee and the Ditchley Foundation, and formerly of *The Economist* magazine (director, Evelyn de Rothschild), a publication set up to press for an end to the Corn laws and promote the principle of 'free trade'. Knight moved on to become executive chairman of Rupert Murdoch's *News International* which owns *The Sun*, *The News Of The World*, and *The Times* and *Sunday Times*. Murdoch owns newspapers, magazines, and television networks that are estimated to have a potential audience of three billion people. That is without his interests in the film industry. He is now linking in with a global telephone and communications network, MCI, and has made a bid for parts of the vast Berlusconi media empire in Italy. According to *The European* newspaper, he is also planning to substantially increase his media interests across Europe.[8] In a feature in *The Spotlight* newspaper headed: "What is Murdoch Up To And Who Is Backing Him?" the writer Dan McMahan linked the rise of this media mogul to names like Harry Oppenheimer (South Africa, Anglo-American, De Beers), Armand Hammer (Occidental Petroleum), the Bronfman family (who are close to the Hollinger Group and the Anti-Defamation League), and the Rothschilds.[9] It is not the front men we need to look at so much as who is behind them pulling their strings. It is they who make the money available and manipulate the politicians to allow great media takeovers and cartels to emerge. With unbelievable hypocrisy, Conrad Black's *Daily Telegraph* said of Murdoch's

---

[8] "Is Rupert Murdoch preparing an assault on fortress Europe?", *The European*, (July 7th–13th 1995) p21.
[9] "Murdoch takes five days to win news group for £800m", *Daily Telegraph*, (February 4th 1986).

domain: "This is a huge and potentially dangerous concentration of media power..." [10] And the *Telegraph* owner's empire is not?

The controlled media can feed the same basic messages to the public and hypnotise the collective mind to accept them. And if the same messages are coming from apparently unconnected media outlets, it must be true because "they are all saying it". Just as we have a One Party political state, so we have a One Media State. In the UK, you would think that the Murdoch *Sun* and the *Independent* or *Guardian* were miles apart and offering different opinions. But if you analyse what they are all agreed on and the way they operate, none are vehicles for a radical alternative to what we have. They actually say the same. They just say it differently. The least radical newspaper in Britain is the one claimed to be most radical: *The Guardian*, the tome of the mindset I call the Robot Radicals. The founding editor of *The Guardian*'s 'rival', *The Independent*, was Andreas Whittam Smith. He was a member of the Trilateral Commission during his years at the top of that newspaper. The political 'choice' is an illusion and so is the media 'choice'. Indeed the two are indivisible.

When I started to have more and more success in making this suppressed information available to the public, the campaign to discredit me was stepped up. I was delighted in a way, because it proved I am twitching a few nerve ends among those who wish to control the human mind. *The Jewish Chronicle*, which parrots words like freedom and truth, began to write outrageous misrepresentations of what I am saying and doing. I was having conversations with the press officer of the Board of Deputies of British Jews – a lovely woman – who was speaking to one David Icke, while she was reading about a very different David Icke in the *Jewish Chronicle*. Understandably she was confused. I wasn't because what was happening was so predictable. The sight of a paper like the *Chronicle* posturing its morality while lying through its teeth is not a pretty one.

However, it was the *Guardian*, the daily house magazine of the Robot Radical mindset, that I found most interesting. One of its reporters, a Paul Brown, arrived at a meeting in Glastonbury and built an article around one man who had not read my books, yet was handing out leaflets opposing them! The anti-Icke piece came from a newspaper which claims to represent freedom. Excuse me while I fall down, laughing hysterically. In the article were the (barely) one-dimensional clichés about 'disciples' and other childish nonsense, but nowhere was there a mention of the Bilderberg Group and its RIIA, CFR, TC network which I had spent much of the evening talking about. But what is it the *Illuminati Protocols* say?

> "*All our newspapers will be of all possible complexions – aristocratic, republican, revolutionary, even anarchical – for so long, of course, as the constitution exists...Like the Indian idol, Vishnu, they will have a hundred*

[10] Three Part Series, January 30th, February 6th, February 13th 1984.

hands, and every one of them will have a finger on any one of the public opinions required. When a pulse quickens these hands will lead opinion in the direction of our aims, for an excited patient loses all power of judgement and easily yields to suggestion. Those fools who will think they are repeating the opinion of a newspaper of their own camp will be repeating our opinion or any opinion that seems desirable for us. In the vain belief that they are following the organ of their party, they will in fact follow the flag which we hang out for them."

Protocol 12

And most journalists, probably including Mr Brown, will not have a clue about how they are being used. Someone wrote to me who had read *The Robots' Rebellion* and was a daily reader of *The Guardian* because he thought it had the integrity that others lacked. He was stunned to read Brown's article, which he said was a gross misrepresentation of what I am saying and doing. "I thought I could trust *The Guardian*" he said. You can't. You can't trust any of them. It was the same with a 'journalist' called Rosemary Carpenter on the Daily Express. She was given access to the information revealed in this book and yet she dismissed it without any checking or research. Mind blowing. From where do the public get their information about political parties at election time? The controlled media. If the media will not support you, or are vehemently against you, it is virtually impossible to be elected. If you are a politician looking to win or stay in power, you have to listen to what the media is demanding. If you don't, they will turn against you and even reveal some unpleasant information which they have long known about, but have kept under wraps while you were playing their game. When Rupert Murdoch began to make positive statements about the British Labour leader Tony Blair (Bil) following the 'untimely' and sudden death of his predecessor, John Smith, this was considered highly significant for Blair's chances of becoming prime minister. The sad thing is that it *was* significant.

The media have to keep the banks and advertisers happy. That's where the power really lies. The Global Elite pyramid coordinates major advertisers into pressurising papers into following or not following, a particular line. "Print that and we withdraw our advertising" is a powerful weapon. But, of course, we have the media 'watchdogs' which are there to protect us from media abuse. The chairman of the newspaper 'watchdog', the Press Complaints Commission, is Lord Wakeham, the former cabinet minister, who controversially went from government to the board of N.M. Rothschild. And while Lord Rees Mogg (Bil), the former editor of *The Times*, was chairman of the television and radio 'watchdog', the Broadcasting Complaints Commission, he was also a Rothschilds' director. Sir Zelman Cowan, another former chairman of the old complaints body, the Press Council, was involved in 1991 with the takeover of the Australian Fairfax Group by Conrad Black's Hollinger Group. Lord Armstrong, the former head of the Civil Service and cabinet secretary (who went on to become a director of N.M. Rothschild) also joined the board of Carlton Television, which broadcasts to London and the 'Independent' television network in the UK. I could go on and on across the UK media, revealing the interconnections between certain names and companies. Rest assured, however, there is really nothing to worry about. As the then Home Secretary, Douglas Hurd, said in *The Financial Times* on January 19th 1989: "Broadcasting will not be run by tycoons." Phew, that's a relief! I rather prefer the opinion on the true state of affairs within the media of John Swinton, a journalist on the *New York Times*, who is reported to have told his staff at his retirement dinner:

> *"There is no such thing as a free press. You know it and I know it. There is not one of you who would dare to write his honest opinions. The business of the journalist is to destroy truth, to lie outright, to pervert, to vilify, to fawn at the feet of Mammon, and to sell himself, his country, and his race, for his daily bread. We are tools and vassals of rich men behind the scenes. We are jumping jacks; they pull the strings, we dance; our talents, our possibilities, and our lives are the property of these men. We are intellectual prostitutes."*

But here again, we come back to the same theme. The media is our creation. It reflects the collective mind of humanity and if it did not, it could not survive and prosper as it does. We can debate which came first, the collective mind's attitudes or the programming of those attitudes, but if you read the average tabloid newspaper and then spend an hour in the average bar, you will see that the thought patterns of the paper and the people are largely the same. Vast numbers of people think and act like a tabloid newspaper. They have allowed themselves to become tabloid thinkers with tabloid minds. We now have tabloid radio and tabloid television, too, which follows from the success of the tabloid newspapers. They all want it short, incredibly superficial, and with each item full of either mockery, condemnation, instant judgements, the official line, and/or defence of the status quo. Oh yes, and if you can get lots of tits and bums in there at every opportunity, so much the better, because women are only here to lust after. Have I just described the content of a tabloid newspaper or the content of a conversation you will hear in almost any bar when 'the lads' get together? Both. And that's the point. Those thought patterns in the collective mind created the reality we call the media. Tabloid newspapers reflect, and program, the thoughts of great tracts of humanity in an ever-downward spiral. The more our thoughts are programmed, the more open we become to even more severe programming. The media won't change until the collective mind changes and that will result only from changes in individual thinking. We create our own reality and the media is no different. Whatever dominates the thought patterns of the collective mind will be the physical reality. The members of the human race in general want someone else to do their thinking for them, and they have allowed their minds to close to the point where they do not want to discuss anything that isn't superficial or full of mockery and instant judgements of others. Hence the media we have today. We have thought that into existence, too. When we change, it will change.

MASS HYPNOSIS

The media's greatest effect on the human mind is not so much its detail, but the mass hypnosis created by the same basic themes occurring over and over. Most people don't pick up detail from newspapers, let alone the broadcast media where you get one chance to hear something and there is no way you can go back and hear it again, let alone extract more detail from it. These themes include the criteria for how we should judge ourselves and each other; for what is credible or incredible, sane or insane. This background bombardment of our subconscious with a common 'party line' of information plays a major part in the way the conscious and subconscious sees itself and the world. As a result, we are allowing the sum total of the media to program our thought patterns and create our reality. I learned so much about this process when I was the focus of unbelievable national ridicule in the early 1990s. Most of what the media said about me was 100% the opposite of what I was saying and writing, but the people overwhelmingly believed what the media told them and I was ridiculed by millions for things I wasn't saying and didn't believe. This is happening to other people every day. The mass hypnosis has also turned millions into spectators of the world, rather than participants. We allow others to *do*, while we observe and sit in the stand, watching the few play the game which decides the future of the human race...*our* human race. This is symbolised by sport and the endless television soaps in which we are spectators of the manufactured lives of overwhelmingly cardboard, one-dimensional characters. We often live their lives instead of our own. I love sport and there are soaps that I enjoy, too, but the danger comes when that is all we have in our lives. As one of the *Illuminati Protocols* said in the 1800s:

> "*In order that the masses themselves may not guess what they are about we further distract them with amusements, games, pastimes, passions, people's palaces...Soon we shall begin through the press to propose competitions in art, in sport of all kinds: these interests will finally distract their minds from questions in which we should find ourselves compelled to oppose them. Growing more and more unaccustomed to reflect and form any opinions of their own, people will begin to talk in the same tone as we, because we alone shall be offering them new directions of thought...of course through such persons as will not be suspected of solidarity with us.*"
> **Protocol 13**

We think of hypnotism only in terms of a single person lying down on a couch and listening to the words of a hypnotist speaking softly into the ear. Or we may think of the stage hypnotist who has a group of people doing silly things in front of a guffawing audience. Some even demand that this should be banned because it is dangerous. These are obvious forms of hypnosis. But we don't realise that we are subtly being hypnotised and encouraged to do and think silly things every day of our lives. Instead of lying on the couch listening to the soft words of the hypnotist, we sit in the chair listening to newsreaders, film stars, advertising voice overs, and sundry presenters. The messages pound our conscious and subconscious mind and we are programmed to think the way the controllers who own the media, the banks, the drug companies, the armament companies, the oil companies, ad infinitum, want us to think. Is there anyone left reading this book who still believes that the idea of a global conspiracy with the tiny few controlling the vast majority is a fantasy, and impossible? Surely not.

The esoteric knowledge about the nature of the human psyche is used to great effect. While those in the spiritual movement are laughed at for their explanations of the human mind-spirit, this same knowledge is being used by the manipulators to covertly hypnotise us and program our subconscious. Doctor Wilson Bryan Key, a professor of journalism, made a study of these techniques and wrote three books, *Media Sexploitation*, *The Clam Plate Orgy*, and *Subliminal Seduction*. He discovered that millions of dollars are being spent by advertisers for the subliminal[11] [programming of the subconscious] manipulation and indoctrination of audiences. Dr Key revealed the existence of the Tachistoscope, a film projector with a high speed shutter which flashes messages every five seconds for $1/3000$th of a second. These messages could not be seen by the naked eye, but were absorbed by the subconscious. The message would then filter down from the subconscious to the conscious level as a thought, desire, or opinion, which the person believes is their own. Years ago, a flash-frame picture of a Coca-Cola bottle used to be inserted into a cinema film just before the interval. The audience couldn't see it, but their subconscious could. Sales of Coca-Cola during cinema intervals went up significantly.

Through the 1950s and 60s the experimentation into this subliminal interaction with the subconscious expanded rapidly. In 1962 and 1966, Doctor Hal C. Becker patented subliminal devices which increased the potential of such technology. He operated a successful weight reduction clinic in New Orleans using subliminal messages directed at the subconscious and his anti-theft programme was operated in department stores in Canada and the United States. Messages which were inaudible to the ear were broadcast across the stores, saying "don't steal". Thefts from the

---

[11] 'Subliminal' refers to messages which bypass our conscious level of awareness and program our subconscious, the level which creates our reality.

stores were reduced. In 1986, a more advanced security system emerged which broadcast its messages under piped music. A computer ensured that the sound of the message went up and down with the loudness of the music. These subliminal messages have been shown to work. So what else are they being used for?

Some years ago there was a furore in France when the picture of François Mitterand was seen to flash into view on the opening titles to the news. This was when Mitterand was running for president. It was a mistake by the TV company, for sure. But what kind of mistake? An error in putting the flash picture in the titles at all, or a mistake in leaving it in for too long, so that the conscious and as well as the subconscious saw it? The potential for subliminal messages to affect the outcome of elections and to direct the thinking of the mass population is simply fantastic. If they can make more people buy bottles of Coca-Cola with these techniques, why can't they make more people vote for the party and the candidate they want? They can. Of course they can. And given what you have read up to now, do you think they would use that potential to manipulate the public mind or would they refuse to do that because it was undemocratic? Once the technology and the knowledge is available, there is nothing that can't be communicated to the subconscious through this technique of mass hypnosis.

Once more, we come back to the esoteric knowledge. The manipulators know how the psyche works and how it is possible to program responses without the conscious level of awareness knowing it is happening. The technology now exists which can be set up near a television or radio transmitter and will send out messages which lock into the wavelength of the television broadcast as a 'carrier wave', a carrier of the subliminal message. These subliminal messages are coming out of the television set without even the television station knowing it is happening. The messages can tell people how to vote, who they should love and who they should hate, what they should buy, and what they should think. Say you want to start a riot. Send out subliminal messages to the area for a while, and then produce one or two agents provocateur and an event to focus anger. In no time you will have the people, already primed subliminally, going absolutely crazy. Then you say you need more power for the police and the military to 'solve' this 'problem'.

The television has become the greatest tool of mind manipulation and it starts with children only a few years old. Some researchers believe children are especially susceptible to this form of programming. Most people watch the television as if mesmerised by the screen. Conversation is destroyed. Instead of talking *to* people, we are talked *at* by the television set. Our lives are conditioned by the themes and indoctrination pouring from the screen. We are told what is right and wrong, good and bad, success and failure, in and out. It is our resident hypnotist in the corner of the room. Many people fall asleep in front of the television because their minds are bombarded to the point of overload by the incessant flow of opinions and information. What does a hypnotist do before he or she begins to make those subconscious suggestions? They put their clients into a state of relaxation, a dozy half-sleep, because that is when the conscious mind is quiet and the subconscious can be most effectively accessed. What better way, therefore, to program television viewers with subliminal messages than to have them half asleep in the chair. In fact, people could even be put into that state by the subliminal messages coming from the set. And what is the real effect of the computer games and virtual reality technology that turns some children into zombies? Virtual reality is a good name because the whole system is designed to encourage the human race to accept a virtual reality and call it life. Dr Wilson Bryan Key, the investigator of these matters, said that subliminal technology can so affect many people that they can be programmed to start eating and drinking too much, change their sexual habits, and embark on an almost endless list of other manifestations of extreme behaviour. The subconscious is programmed with thought patterns and it creates that physical reality. These techniques are becoming more sophisticated and developed all the time. Susan Bryce highlighted one development in her article in *Exposure* magazine in the June/July 1993 issue:

> *"Data on the relationship between heartbeats and suggestibility reveals that music or voice timed to the rhythm of the human heart beat of 72 pulses per minute, can affect human behaviour...Experimental commercials prepared using 72 beats per minute as pacing for drumbeats, music, and voice have been tested in a special theatre with a random audience of housewives and husbands. The advertisement was for a new analgesic [headache potion]. Results showed that had the analgesic commercial been broadcast to the roughly 30 million people watching NBC Evening News, five million would have developed headaches within three hours of viewing it."* [12]

The technology has been developed to send out messages as microwaves and extremely low frequency waves (ELFs) which can speak to the mass subconscious and cause physical illness. It is important to appreciate that the knowledge held secretly about the human mind and body is far more advanced than anything we are allowed to see in the public arena. Again, it is part of the "need to know" policy. If someone has knowledge and technology which most people do not realise exists, the potential for manipulation is enormous. The esoteric knowledge passed through the secret society network across the years has been a major factor in the creation of this two-speed science. The public is told about a limited and intentionally flawed science which goes back to Darwin and others, while the far more advanced version remains hidden. The mind-spirit, the eternal part of us, is a series of interconnecting and interacting magnetic energy fields. These react with

[12] *Exposure* magazine, (June/July 1993) p12.

other magnetic energy fields and this is why people who live under electricity power lines are more prone to certain illnesses. The electromagnetic field thrown out by the power lines imbalances the magnetic mind-spirit of the people living nearby. This imbalance is passed through the multiple levels of our being to the physical body where it manifests as cancer or some other disease. It can also directly affect cellular functioning to create physical illness. Therefore, if the manipulators can broadcast waves at certain frequencies, they can imbalance our cellular and non-physical magnetic levels and cause physical, mental, and emotional illness. Former FBI agent, Ted Gunderson, has said that magnetic radioactive discs have long been used covertly as cancer-inducing "silent killers" to remove unwanted politicians and others. These can cause cancers which grow at astonishing speeds. Experiments on the effects of ELF waves and chemical warfare substances are routinely carried out on unsuspecting populations around the world. We hear about these things on the news with reports of a "strange and unexplained plague/disease" which has broken out over a small area of a country. I am told that an area of New Mexico is plagued by a "hum" that no-one can explain, which causes headaches and illness in susceptible individuals.

Some people find it hard to believe that messages can be broadcast to the subconscious. But what is television and radio? They are words and pictures which are broadcast in wave form and decoded back into words and pictures by technology. When you think of the advanced knowledge that is secretly known about the nature of the human brain/psyche, is it too much of a mental leap to see that it is possible to broadcast messages on wavelengths designed to communicate with the subconscious? In fact, as I explain at length in *The Robots' Rebellion*, the existence of such technology is provable. Experiments have shown that if people are subjected to these waves for little more than a minute, they begin to react as the messages tell them to. In their minds, these messages appear to be their own thoughts, when in reality they are tuning into wavelengths broadcast from outside of their psyche. In such a situation, these people are fully-paid-up robots. Two such techniques are called Radio Hypnotic Intracerebral Control and Electronic Dissolution of Memory. Researchers say that these can remotely induce an hypnotic trance, deliver suggestions, and erase all memory of both the instructions and whatever it is the person has done in response to those instructions. What a tool if you want to assassinate a 'troublemaker'; create some terrible event to discredit a group or person; abduct someone and blame it on 'aliens'; or produce a problem-reaction-solution situation. In 1975, the journalist James Moore claimed to have secured a 350-page manual on the subject from CIA sources. Part of that document said:

> "Medically, these radio signals are directed at certain parts of the brain. When a part of your brain receives a tiny electrical impulse from outside sources, such as vision, hearing, etc, an emotion is produced – anger at the sight of a

*gang of boys beating an old woman, for example. The same emotion of anger
can be created by artificial radio signals sent to your brain by a controller. You
could instantly feel the same white hot anger without any apparent reason."*

It makes you wonder about some of the messages being received by
mediums and channellers. Psychically sensitive people are consciously tuning
into other wavelengths of reality. It is possible, indeed probable, that some are
tuning into wavelengths broadcast from technology on this planet. In the
world of secret science, they know it is possible for channellers to
communicate with other wavelengths of reality. They know how it is done
and they use mediums/channellers in their experiments. According to the
books on the mind control and advanced science establishment at Montauk[13]
in the USA in the 1970s, the Elite scientists were able to produce the image
on a computer screen of what their psychic was thinking. They later
broadcast his thought waves from a transmitter at the base and found that
people in the area had been affected in their own minds by the thoughts
being broadcast. The manipulators know also that more and more people are
listening to what channellers say. What a great opportunity to use this process
to further manipulate. Once again, our protection is to think for ourselves
and accept no information on face value without thinking hard about it and
checking the facts as best you can. That includes what you read in this book.

Project MKUltra

Alongside the development of mass mind control techniques have come those
aimed at specific individuals. The most notorious is the MKUltra programme
run by the CIA. Other offshoots and variations on this have been programmes
known as Monarch, Bluebird, Artichoke, MKDelta, and MKNaomi. Their
even more advanced successors still go on today and the victims have often hit
the global headlines as 'lone assassins'. MKUltra began in the 1950s under the
Canada-based Scottish psychiatrist, Doctor Ewen Cameron, who became a
close friend of CIA chief Allen Dulles after Cameron served as the
Canadian/United States psychiatrist at the Nuremberg War Trials. Cameron
was one of the psychiatrists who examined the man who claimed to be Rudolf
Hess. That was an appropriate appointment because what Cameron did to his
'patients' under the CIA's MKUltra programme mirrored some of what the
Nazis did to their victims, too. Under the supervision of people like the Dulles
brothers and other members of the US Elite establishment, many of the Nazi
mind control experts and leading scientists were secretly removed from
Germany, as the Allies closed in. They were taken to the United States to
continue their work into mind control and what we would call flying
saucers, anti-gravity technology. Some estimate that as many as 10,000 active

---

[13] Preston B. Nichols and Peter Moon, *The Montauk Project* and *Montauk Revisited*, (Sky
Books, New York, 1992, 1994).

Nazis escaped, leaving the farce of the Nuremberg War Trials to deal out 'justice' to those who had often been guilty of far less terrible crimes than the ones the Americans had helped to escape. Yes, the Nazis carried out horrible experiments on people, including children. Of that I have no doubt. But does anyone really think that is not continuing in the underground establishments in America and elsewhere today? The Nazi mentality did not end in 1945. It just changed locations and, literally, went underground.

The CIA was formed out of the wartime OSS, the Office of Strategic Services. This formation of the new Central Intelligence Agency was done under the supervision of British Intelligence, which had centuries of accumulated experience in covert operations. Many of the key personnel in the CIA were Nazis who had served under Hitler. One, Reinhard Gehlen of the SS, was employed by Allen Dulles to set up the CIA network in Europe after the war. I say 'employed'. In fact Gehlen has said that it was more like a partnership between the CIA (headed by the Hitler-supporting Allen Dulles) and the worldwide Nazi network. Gehlen said that the collaboration with Dulles was a "gentlemen's agreement" which "for a number of reasons was never set out in black and white...such was the element of trust that has been built up between the two sides during...intensive personal contact, that neither had the slightest hesitation in founding the entire operation on verbal agreement and a handshake".[14] The 'verbal agreement' wouldn't have anything to do with the danger of written evidence seeping out and blowing the story, I suppose. Writer and researcher, Noam Chomsky, says that Gehlen set up a secret US-Nazi army, which extended its operations to Latin America (where it supported the Nazi-type regimes imposed on the people by the United States). The CIA was formed *by* Nazis, *for* Nazis, to promote the Nazi mentality. British Intelligence was a major instigator because it too is a Nazi organisation at its core, and so is the deeply corrupt international 'police' operation known as Interpol, which has been headed by known Nazis. The CIA, under Allen Dulles, funded psychiatrist Ewen Cameron from the early 1950s, as documents released in 1977 under the US Freedom of Information Act have confirmed. Most of the documents were destroyed or not released, but there were enough to offer just a glimpse of the nightmare that was MKUltra. The project included the use of drugs (like LSD) and grotesque mind manipulation techniques known as 'depatterning' and 'psychic driving'. The CIA admitted supporting research into human mind and behaviour control at 150 institutions and these included hospitals, prisons, drug companies, and 44 universities. At least 185 scientists were involved. Like the Nazis' experiments, the targets were largely those considered 'lesser human beings' such as prostitutes, foreigners, people with non-white skins, and drug addicts. Thousands of prisoners were also forced to take part, and hospital and mental patients were used without their consent as experiment-fodder for these crazy people. Let no-one tell me this is

---

[14] *Casebook On Alternative 3*, p32.

not still happening today all over the world, including the UK. Soldiers in the US forces were used, too. Thousands were given LSD in the 1970s while being told they were testing gas masks and other protective gear. This puts in a new light the severe damage to the health of soldiers given vaccinations during the Gulf War, who are now demanding compensation.

The CIA funded Ewen Cameron through an organisation called the Society for Human Ecology, yet another CIA front, which was connected to Cornell University in New York. Cameron and Dulles wanted to develop forms of drugs, electronic stimulation, and hypnosis which would remove a person's natural personality and replace it with an 'improved one'. Another major aim was to preprogram people to carry out assassinations which could then be written off as the work of some 'lone nutter'. This goal was quite quickly achieved. In 1969, the CIA psychologist, José Delgado, published his book, *Physical Control Of The Mind: Toward A Psychocivilised Society*. He wrote:

> *"Physical control of brain functions is a demonstrated fact...it is even possible to create and follow intentions, the development of thoughts and visual experiences. By electrical stimulation of specific cerebral structures, movements can be induced by radio command, hostility may appear and disappear, social hierarchy can be modified, sexual behaviour may be changed, and memory, emotions, and the thinking process may be influenced by remote control..."* [15]

Speaking in 1966, Delgado said that his experiments "...support the distasteful conclusion that motion, emotion, and behaviour can be directed by electrical forces and that humans can be controlled like robots by push buttons".[16] Which is precisely what happened to the killers of people like John Lennon,[17] the would-be assassin of President Reagan, and, almost certainly, the assassin of King Faisal of Saudi Arabia, who was shot dead in 1975. The King, who routinely had free copies of the *Protocols* distributed to foreign tourists, was murdered by a relative who travelled from America to do it. This technique is also used to program people who run into streets or restaurants shooting in all directions, and to carry out the most awful crimes which add to the fear and the "something must be done" mentality. This demands – and gets – harsher laws and sentences, a more armed police force, and cameras in the streets. By the way, Lennon's assassin, Mark Chapman, was "mentally assessed" by Bernard Diamond, the same psychiatrist who "assessed" Sirhan Sirhan, the patsy in the Bobby Kennedy murder. Just a coincidence!

---

[15] J.M. Delgado, *Physical Control Of The Mind: Toward A Psychocivilised Society*, (1969).

[16] Quoted in *When The State Rapes: The Mind Control Papers, Part II*, p2, 6. This study is distributed by Mediaecco and Contact Network International, PO Box 66, 8400 AB Gorredijk, The Netherlands.

[17] Files released inder the Freedom of Information Act reveal what a threat John Lennon's influence was considered to be by the US authorities.

LSD was widely used in the Cameron experiments. It creates confusion, a key aspect of mind control. One of the early victims was Frank Olsen, a chemist specialising in airborne disease. He was given LSD while suffering from "depression and paranoia" and two weeks later threw himself to his death from the window of a New York hotel. The CIA funded a series of 'safe houses' for experimentation in San Francisco and New York. Here MKUltra operatives observed through two-way mirrors how the clients of CIA-hired prostitutes responded after being secretly given LSD. At Ewen Cameron's headquarters, the Allan Memorial Institute in Montreal, Canada, he 'treated' unsuspecting people for a variety of mental problems and systematically dismantled their personalities in MKUltra experiments. In the *Observer* magazine of October 16th 1994, writer Elizabeth Nickson told the stories of many of Cameron's victims, including her own mother. One patient, a woman from Vancouver, was suffering from post-natal depression and fatigue. She was kept in a drug-induced sleep for 86 days by Cameron and when he was finished with her, she had lost all memory of her life, including the ability to read and write. She even needed toilet training. As a result of this pressure on her family, she lost her husband and six children. This was the same Ewen Cameron who was fêted by his fellow psychiatrists and made president of the string of leading psychiatric bodies, including the World Psychiatric Association. The president and directors of the MKUltra project included the president of the New York Hospital-Cornell Medical Centre and the head of the Smithsonian Institute. This was the establishment top brass, not some mad professor working alone.

One of Cameron's techniques links in with what I said earlier. He used a tape machine called the Cererophone which was placed under the pillow of the sleeping victim to repeat messages over and over. He would also record a key phrase used by the victim in conversations with him and play it back at 30 second intervals as the victim slept. This was "psychic driving". The result was that the victim became obsessed with the phrase and could not think about anything else. Such was the emotional result that drugs would be used to sedate the person. Psychic driving, the input of the 'new' personality, often followed electro-therapy, the destruction of the natural personality. This was called the "depatterning" process.

Cameron used a technique called the Page-Russell shock treatment, named after the two British doctors who developed it. The victims would be given an initial electric shock, followed by five to nine smaller ones, two or three times a day for up to thirty days. Hospital workers at the time have reported that the screaming echoed around the hospital. The 'patients' would try to escape from this horror. Once this depatterning was completed and the victim thoroughly confused, a helmet would be clamped on their heads and negative messages would be repeated into the victim's mind for maybe twenty hours a day. These messages would repeat phrases like "My mother hates me, my husband hates me, I am a failure", and so on, using recordings of the victim's own voice. Cameron would also wire their legs and give them an electric shock after the completion of each message.

With the old personality now destroyed, the process would be used to build a new one in Cameron's image. And this, lest we forget, was funded by the CIA with taxpayers' money at the behest of Allen Dulles, the man who, with others, controlled the Nuremberg War Trials that sentenced scores of lower-ranked Nazis to death for doing far less than he and Cameron were doing. All of this continues in a much more advanced way today. I have been told of mind control research of a similar kind in some UK universities and if you know more, please tell me.

Most people have no idea how easy the law makes it for you to be imprisoned in a mental institution. It really is so easy. A friend of mine who was going through a traumatic spiritual awakening (he was seeing the world for what it really is) was pressured by his family to agree to attend a private mental hospital. He chose to go for their sake. But when he decided to leave the hospital after chatting with the doctors, he was forcibly stopped. He was also forced to take drugs. What the staff of that hospital were doing was perfectly legal. Once you agree to have treatment at such a place, you lose all your rights to leave if the staff decide that you should not. As the doctors at that level of the profession largely have no idea about the nature of the psyche, despite being called 'psychiatrists', they can imprison you and force you to take drugs to 'treat' quite natural phenomena. If we are not vigilant, the excuse of 'mental illness' will be used to intern those who say they can communicate with other frequencies ['schizophrenia'] and those who claim there is a global conspiracy ['paranoia']. Someone like me who talks about both becomes a 'paranoid schizophrenic', which is exactly how they imprisoned dissenters in the psychiatric hospitals of the Soviet Union.

Eventually, at the start of the Bush presidency, the CIA settled out of court with nine of the victims of MKUltra for the largest sum of money possible without the approval of the Attorney General. Another 69 are still battling for compensation. This is not helped by the admission of Richard Helms, the CIA chief at the time of Watergate, that he destroyed most of the MKUltra documents in 1973. What we are looking at here is the sharp end of the policy to turn the human race from unique and free-thinking expressions of creation into a herd of sheep and robots. It is a combination of technology, engineered events, and control of both politics and (crucially) the media. Behind it is the familiar roll call. The document *Silent Weapons For A Quiet War* reveals the input of the Rockefeller Foundation in funding research through Harvard University into the potential for computers to control human thinking. The aim is to have physical money replaced entirely by credit card electronic money, and then to replace credit cards and identity cards with a microchip just under the skin. Intel Corporation was awarded a five-year contract in 1994, to develop just such a device at its Rio Rancho, New Mexico, facility. This chip would be linked to a global computer using the excuse that all financial transactions had to be registered at the new world central bank. The computer would know everything there is to know about us at all times and would be able to send messages the other way, from the computer to us, feeding us messages and programming our consciousnesses. Robots would be exactly the word.

This prospect is nothing new. CIA psychologist Dr José Delgado said in 1966 that the day would come when brain control could be turned over to non-human operators, by establishing two-way communication between the implanted brain and a computer. In the 1970s, Sweden was stunned to hear that microchips were being implanted into hospital patients without their knowledge, as part of a mind control experiment. This was sanctioned by Olof Palme, the Bilderberger Prime Minister of Sweden. The dangers are so potent and so obvious. As Senator Sam J. Ervin, the head of a Senate subcommittee on behaviour modification, said in 1973:

> "...behavioural technology...in the United States today touches upon the most basic sources of individuality, and the very core of personal freedom. To my mind the most serious threat...is the power this technology gives one man to impose his views and values on another...If our society is to remain free, one man must not be empowered to change another man's personality and dictate the values, thoughts, and feelings of others." [18]

Throughout the *Silent Weapons* document and the Elite philosophy in general, we see the desire to do exactly that. We see the theme of the chosen elite controlling the 'stupid herd' in all areas of our lives. It starts with the children in the schools and the young people in the universities. Get 'em young and you have got them for good. I never cease to wonder when I speak at universities how the majority of students are already programmed to think like clones of the system by the age of seventeen and eighteen. Their inability to think for themselves is quite stunning, with very honourable exceptions. *Silent Weapons For A Quiet War* emphasises to its own agents the importance of controlling what children and young people are told. The teachers are trained to think in a certain way and to believe that the information they are communicating is true. Even if they doubt it, the authorities insist that it is taught anyway. "If you don't like it Mr or Mrs Teacher, get out and we will replace you with someone who will do as they are told." As the rock group, Pink Floyd, say in their well-known song, children are programmed by the education system to be "Just another brick in the wall". But how much debate goes on about these matters? Teachers, parents, the teaching unions, and the politicians go on endlessly about the funding of schools and the shortage of school books. Where is the concern about what is actually taught in the schools

---

[18] Introduction to the 1974 report of the Senate sub committee on the role of the US Government in behaviour modification.

and what is written in those books? And yet there is no other subject on Earth that is more important than the programming of the human mind. From that all else comes. The *Silent Weapons* document describes the mind-controlling technique brilliantly. It says of the Quiet War:

> *"It shoots situations, instead of bullets; propelled by data processing, instead of grains of gunpowder; from a computer, instead of a gun; operated by a computer programmer, instead of a marksman; under the orders of a banking magnate, instead of a military general. It makes no obvious noises, causes no obvious physical or mental injuries, and does not obviously interfere with anyone's daily social life.*
>
> *"Yet it makes an unmistakable 'noise', causes unmistakable physical and mental damage, and unmistakably interferes with daily social life, i.e., unmistakable to a trained observer, one who knows what to look for. The public cannot comprehend the weapon, and therefore cannot believe they are being attacked and subdued by a weapon.*
>
> *"The public might instinctively feel that something is wrong, but because of the technical nature of the silent weapon, they cannot express their feeling in a rational way, or handle the problem with intelligence. Therefore, they do not know how to cry for help, and do not know how to associate with others to defend themselves against it.*
>
> *"When a silent weapon is applied gradually, the public adjusts/adapts to its presence and learns to tolerate its encroachment on their lives until the pressure (psychological via economic) becomes too great and they crack up. Therefore the silent weapon is a type of biological warfare. It attacks the vitality, options, and mobility of the individuals of a society by knowing, understanding, manipulating, and attacking their sources of natural and social energy, and their physical, mental, and emotional strengths and weaknesses."*

In others words, divide and rule, and introduce your global dictatorship via the stepping-stones approach and few will realise what is really going on until it is too late. In fact, many will even laugh at or condemn those who point out what is happening. Well the readers of this book, and many others like it, *do* know what is really going on. And if we are truly committed to a better world and to freedom of thought and expression, the information is impossible to ignore. The work we all have to do to break the hold the programmers have on so many human minds is considerable, but it is perfectly achievable – and will be achieved – if we are prepared to get involved. There is nothing more powerful than a human mind determined to think and act for itself. Such a phenomenon is a manipulator's nightmare and, like everyone on this planet, you have that power.

You only have to use it.

Chapter 15

Cult or con?

A prime example of the 'buzz word' approach to mind manipulation is the term 'cult'. The plan has been to engineer events and propaganda which devalue the word cult in the public mind and then, once that is achieved, to apply the label "cult" to any group or organisation which the Elite wish to discredit and destroy. That means anyone who is challenging the status quo or living in ways that undermine centralised control.

The Concise Oxford Dictionary definition of cult is "A system of religious worship as expressed in ceremonies; devotion or homage to person or thing". So every religion is a cult by that definition, and so is the banking and financial system, where they are devoted and pay homage to a 'thing': money. The All-Seeing Eye secret society network is a cult because it worships the Luciferic, Prison Warder Consciousness through ceremonies, devotion, and homage. The whole of the United Kingdom is a cult, or at least those many people who are devoted to and pay homage to the monarchy. Almost everything becomes a cult under that criterion. However, that is not what the manipulators want you to think. They have used events to turn the word cult into a much narrower meaning – dangerous religious 'nutters', brainwashed and programmed to worship a messiah figure. The plan is well advanced in feeding the public mind with such messages to the point where anything labelled a cult is subject to a reflex action response of: "Dangerous nutters – something must be done".

There are three ways you can manipulate events to suit that plan. You can set up the 'cult' from the start and control the whole thing; you can infiltrate a group or community with agents provocateur who then act in ways which discredit the innocent members, or you can simply blame a group of people or sect for something they did not do. Whichever way you choose, the outcome is the same – the word 'cult' is further devalued in the collective consciousness. Two events which have been enormously successful in poisoning the public to the word 'cult' have been the Jonestown Massacre of 1978 and Waco in 1993. The Jonestown encampment in Guyana was the headquarters of the People's Temple sect controlled by its 'messiah' figure, Jim Jones. Its members, overwhelmingly black, had followed Jones to Guyana from the original base in California, then under the governorship of Ronald Reagan. An estimated 900 people died at Jonestown on November

18th 1978, in what was said to have been a "mass suicide" achieved through cyanide poisoning and shooting. At Waco in Texas 15 years later, we were asked to believe the same official story of a "mass suicide" by the Branch Davidian sect run by its 'messiah' figure, David Koresh. Who benefits from people believing these official explanations? Those who want the word 'cult' to mean 'dangerous nutters'. Intriguingly, therefore, we can point out many connections with the intelligence agencies.

One of the main financial backers of Jonestown was Dr Lawrence Layton senior, who was formerly in charge of research and development at one of the US Army's top chemical and biological warfare research centres at the Dugway Proving Ground in Utah. This has been connected by researchers to cattle mutilations blamed on 'aliens', disease warfare, and genetic experimentation. Layton was also director of the Missile and Satellite Development at the Navy Propellant Division at Indian Head, Maryland. His wife's fortune came, in part, from the I.G. Farben cartel. Their son, Lawrence Layton Jr, was in the sect firing squad which executed Congressional Representative, Leo Ryan, who had travelled to Jonestown to investigate the People's Temple. Ryan was seriously unpopular with the CIA. He had co-authored the Hughes-Ryan Amendment which obliged the CIA to give Congress prior notice of covert operations. What a coincidence that Ryan, a man battling to make the CIA accountable to the people, should be in Jonestown, Guyana, at just the moment the shooting started.

The Laytons are a prominent Southern family who fought for the Confederates during the civil war. They have many connections with the intelligence agencies. Lawrence Layton Jr's sister, Debora Layton Blakey, was married to George Philip Blakey, the man who placed the downpayment on the property at Jonestown purchased by Jim Jones. Blakey was a former contract agent for the CIA in Angola and a number of researchers claim that Jonestown was used as a cover to train 'rebels' for the CIA covert operations in Angola. There are other CIA connections to the Jonestown massacre. Richard Dwyer, the deputy head of the US Embassy in Guyana and the local CIA chief, was known to be involved. On a tape recorded at Jonestown when the violence flared, the voice of Jim Jones can be heard shouting, "Get Dwyer out of here". By his own admission, Dwyer was seen stripping the dead of their wallets and other identification on the orders of Zbigniew Brzezinski, a founder of the Trilateral Commission and then Jimmy Carter's National Security Advisor.[1] The People's Temple members were active in their support of the Guyana President, Forbes Burnham, who openly admitted his links with the CIA. When Jim Jones went to Brazil in 1961 "to administer to the downtrodden", his transportation and food were paid for by the US Embassy, and he told local residents that he was working for Naval Intelligence. He was accompanied by his lifelong friend, Dan

[1] Kenneth Wooden, *The Children Of Jonestown*, (McGraw-Hill, New York, 1981) p196.

Mitrione, who worked for the CIA instructing Third World police forces on interrogation and torture techniques. The connections between Jones, Jonestown, and the intelligence agencies are many. James T. Richardson, professor of sociology at the University of Nevada, published a study of the People's Temple in the *Journal For The Scientific Study Of Religion*, in 1980. He wrote:

> *"Because of the negligence of US officials in not ordering immediate autopsies on those who died in Guyana, we will never know how many died of suicide and how many were murdered. Dr Leslie Mootoo, Chief Medical Examiner for the Guyana Government and the first medically-trained person to arrive at Jonestown after the event, told reporters: 'I do not believe there were ever more than 200 persons who died voluntarily.' He said this after inspecting a number of bodies and the scene of their deaths. This question has been most fully discussed in a series of articles by Deirdre Griswold in Worker's World…a series which also poses some questions about possible CIA involvement in the Jonestown tragedy. Griswold, who accuses the US Government of deliberately destroying evidence by not performing autopsies, points out a number of intriguing ties between the People's Temple and the CIA. She says some of the white leaders at Jonestown may have been CIA agents, and Jonestown may have been a pawn in political struggles involving the US, Cuba, and Guyana…"*

There is also evidence that Jonestown was a mind control experiment and a part of MKUltra. Large quantities of psychiatric drugs were found there, enough to drug 200,000 people a year, and the members were known to wear identification tags similar to those that people are given in hospital. Indeed, the Jonestown complex included a substantial and sophisticated hospital while conditions in the rest of the compound were poor. The mix of blacks, women, and prisoners, mirrored the victims chosen for MKUltra mind experimentation. The blacks were bound and gagged when they arrived in Guyana and taken to the compound to work 18 hours a day. The links between Jonestown, MKUltra, and Nazi-style ideology are explored by Michael Meiers in *Was Jonestown A CIA Medical Experiment? A Review Of The Evidence*. He argues that Jonestown was the final field experiment of MKUltra and that Jim Jones was a long-time CIA asset who had been secretly supported by Ronald Reagan's California administration in the years before the operation moved to Guyana. Meiers says the mind control story can be traced back at least to 1965 when Jones and the People's Temple first moved to Ukiah, California. He reports:

> *"…the group immediately infiltrated the Mendocino State Mental Hospital which would provide not only test persons [TPs as the Nazis called them] for his [Jones's] preliminary medical experiments, but also a training ground for*

medical technicians needed for the ultimate experiment. Within a very short period of time, every employee at the hospital was a member of the People's Temple. From nurses to therapists, from counsellors to cleaning women, every worker on the facility was replaced by a Temple member. California virtually gave the Mendocino State Mental Hospital to Jim Jones." [2]

The aftermath and official explanations for the massacre were a familiar tale of provable lies and contradictions. The number of people reported to have been living in Jonestown was around 1100. This was based, it would appear, on a passport count. But after the tragedy, the number of dead was given as only 400 and later 913. As many as 200 were 'missing'. This is a significant figure because the elite guard around Jim Jones numbered between 120 and 200. While the People's Temple membership was predominantly black, the elite guard was overwhelmingly white. Elite guard or CIA guard? Despite the official figure of 900 dead, only 400 were found and the speculation was rife over what happened to the other 500. It was at this point, according to testimony by the military commander investigating Jonestown, that he was told by US government official, Robert Pastor, to stop identifying the bodies. Pastor was the top aide to Zbigniew Brzezinski. Surely identification of the bodies was essential if you really wanted to know what happened! In the days following this order from Brzezinski's aide, the missing 500 bodies were miraculously found. Where had they been hiding, pray? I promise you I am not joking here. They were found, according to the official version, *underneath the other 400!* You only have to look at the pictures of the first bodies to be found to see that there is no way they were lying on top of another 500. But that is the official version to this day.

Ladies and gentlemen, they are just laughing at us. The charred body said to be that of Jim Jones was never properly identified and he almost certainly escaped with the white guards. The whole thing stinks, just like the assassinations of Martin Luther King and JFK which, 'coincidentally', were being reinvestigated at the time of Jonestown by a House Select Committee. One attorney, Mark Lane, had connections with both Jonestown and the assassination hearings. He was the attorney for the People's Temple and for the 'patsy' James Earl Ray, the alleged 'lone assassin' of Dr King. Mark Lane, who has also worked for the Liberty Lobby, the publishers of *The Spotlight* newspaper, called the People's Temple a "paradise on Earth". This so discredited him after Jonestown that his contention that James Earl Ray was innocent was subsequently met with disdain by many.

There were rumours that the People's Temple included a death squad which disposed of anyone who threatened or spoke badly about the sect. The government has always denied that, but Jim Jones was known to have a

---

[2] Michael Meiers, *Was Jonestown A CIA Medical Experiment? A Review Of The Evidence*, Studies in American Religion, Vol. 35, (The Edward/Merlin Press, 1988).

hit list and the leading names on it died violently in the months that followed the massacre. At the top of the list was George Moscone, the Mayor of San Francisco. He was shot dead nine days after the tragedy. Moscone's election campaign had been backed by substantial donations from the People's Temple and he had made Jim Jones the head of the San Francisco Housing Authority. Many of Jones's followers were also employed by the City Welfare Department and they used this privilege to recruit the poor and homeless to the sect. The second name on the Jones hit list was Jenny Mills, a former official of the People's Temple, who wrote a book with her husband, *My Six Years With God*, which was extremely critical of Jones and his group. In the summer of 1979, Jenny Mills, her husband, and her daughter were shot dead at their home in Berkeley. Their murder remains unsolved. A journalist, Kathy Hunter, who had reported the deaths of seven members who had been killed for trying to leave the original headquarters compound in California, also died in strange circumstances. It is the old, old, story we have seen repeated so many times in this book. But ask most people today and if they remember the Jonestown Massacre, they will speak of religious 'nutters' who committed suicide while under the influence of a 'mad messiah' and cult leader. That is what they are supposed to think.

Jonestown, the massacre, and its repercussions, served the manipulators well. It was a cover to train mercenaries for the CIA's covert activities in Angola; it provided on-the-spot political support for CIA asset, Forbes Burnham; it eliminated the CIA's tenacious political opponent, Leo Ryan; it undermined the House Select Committee on Assassinations by discrediting James Earl Ray's attorney, Mark Lane; it gave valuable information about mind control to the MKUltra Project; and it further poisoned the public mind to the word 'cult'.

You will find many of the elements of Jonestown in the story of Waco. On April 19th 1993, more than 80 men, women, and children were burnt alive when the US government, in the form of the FBI and the Bureau of Alcohol, Tobacco, and Firearms (BATF), attacked the Mount Carmel compound of the Branch Davidians, near Waco, Texas. We are asked to believe once again that this was a 'mass suicide' by a group of crazed and brainwashed followers of a weird and dangerous 'messiah' figure, David Koresh. I could not disagree more with the views that David Koresh was supposed to have had (if what is claimed is true). He appears to have been a very mixed up man. But the focus on Koresh has been used to obscure the issue of how and why all those people died at the hands of government agencies.

It is the same with all these mind-manipulating events. At the time they happen, the official version dominates the papers and the television screens. The public soak it up and overwhelmingly accept it. Then, as the weeks pass and more open-minded researchers begin to uncover the true background, a very different version of events emerges. However, the official version is communicated to a colossal audience all over the world at the height of the publicity and coverage of the event, while the true, or at least truer, version comes to light later when interest has died down. The mainstream media usually ignores such information and the challenge to the official whitewash is marginalised into books like this or in magazines selling to a relatively small audience. So while the alternative explanations, even proof, exists to demolish the propaganda as a pack of lies, the mass of the people never know that this is the case. They go on believing that what they were told in the beginning continues to be the truth of what happened. Because of this, the vast majority of people still believe that Waco was the mass suicide of a mad cult. But was it?

The BATF first used guns to attack the Branch Davidian compound on February 28th 1993. This attack was 'justified' by official claims that the sect members had broken gun laws. They bought and sold guns to earn money, as many do in Texas. I don't understand how a religious group can buy and sell guns, or even own them, but what they did was legal. Yet here were agents of the BATF trying to shoot their way into the compound. And, according to Ron Engleman, a presenter at KGBS Radio in Dallas, the BATF had rung the media to tell them about the raid. That's why the cameras were there. An investigative video called *Waco: The Big Lie*, was compiled by attorney Linda Thompson, of the American Justice Federation. Again, Linda Thompson's belief system and approach to life could not be further from my own, but if we are only going to accept the research of those we agree with on *everything*, we become a dupers dream. Her video uses footage from the February attack and the mass murder at the end of the 51-day siege that followed. I don't necessarily agree with everything the video claims and there are many questions about it I would like to ask, but it certainly reveals a very different version of what happened.

In the first attack in the February, we see four BATF men dressed in black on the Mount Carmel building. They are all armed, but no shots are coming from the building. Three of these men are seen to climb through a window while the fourth stays on the roof outside. When his colleagues have disappeared through the window, he throws in a grenade and begins to open fire in that direction. Bullets burst through the wall from the inside. But is this the Branch Davidians returning fire or the three BATF men retaliating in response to their 'buddy's' actions? All three of those men who entered that window were found dead, the video claimed. Why would their colleague kill them, if that was what happened? Only he knows and since he was dressed in black with only his eyes uncovered, no-one outside of the authorities knows who he is. However, according to Linda Thompson, the three men who were killed were all Bill Clinton bodyguards during his presidential campaign. Some mainstream journalists have denied this, but you have a right to know that these other explanations exist.

During the weeks of the siege which followed this initial raid, the official story of Waco went around the world. Not only were American minds conditioned to the negative meaning of 'cult', so was anyone who read a paper or watched the television anywhere on the planet. The propaganda against Koresh and the Branch Davidians was incessant. At night, the compound was floodlit to keep everyone awake and recordings of rabbits being slaughtered were broadcast at full volume. These are the sort of minds that control 'law enforcement' agencies like the BATF, the FBI and the CIA. Eventually, Bill Clinton and his Webb Hubbell-selected attorney general, Janet Reno, gave permission for the action which was to cost the lives of so many innocent people. Janet Reno said the action was taken "for the sake of the children". These were the same children who were burnt alive soon afterwards. This justification of saving the children came from the claims that the Davidians were guilty of child abuse. This may or may not have been true in the case of David Koresh, but Janet Reno has since admitted there was no evidence to prove this at the time of the massacre, and the 'evidence' put forward since is extremely questionable, often provably untrue.

The public were not told as events in Waco unfolded, that surveillance technology is now extremely advanced and by using tiny cameras, sensitive sound equipment, and infra red cameras, the BATF and FBI knew exactly what was happening inside the building and where all the people were gathered. The tanks attacked the compound early on April 19th. On the Linda Thompson video, we see a tank at 6am moving back and forth over a small area at the front of the building. This, Thompson claims, was directly over the underground bunker where the women and children would have been sheltering at night from the floodlights and the noise. The tank was almost certainly crushing the bunker and trapping the people. Why else would it have been going back and forth on the same spot? We then see other tanks knocking down the walls of the building and fires breaking out which quickly consume the complex, killing all inside. Who started the fire? It was said to be mass suicide, but why does it appear from the video footage that some tanks had flame throwers on the front? And why was the Parkland Hospital in Dallas called by the FBI at six o'clock that morning and asked how many beds they had in their burns unit?[3] Again, some journalists challenge this version of events, but the public has a right to hear all sides, not just the government's. Then they can make up their own minds.

The mind manipulators squeezed full value from this propaganda coup. David Koresh was compared with mass murderers of history and Waco was actually compared with Bosnia by Steven V. Roberts, a senior writer at *US News And World Report*.[4] Unbelievable. He also asked in the article: "How does a society deal with a messianic personality who resists all attempts at

---

[3] KGBS radio presenter, Ron Engleman, told Radio Free America that he confirmed through a contact at the hospital that this call was made.

[4] *US News And World Report*, (May 3rd 1993).

persuasion or pressure?" The answer, Mr Roberts, is that they usually elect him President of the United States. Talking of which, Bill Clinton, who had sanctioned the attack, sought to justify what followed by saying: "There is, unfortunately, a rise in this sort of fanaticism all across the world. We may have to confront it again". Well done, Bill. Exactly to script. I think that State Representative, John Padfield who certainly didn't support the views of the Branch Davidians, was much closer to the truth when he said:

> *"I think the BATF intentionally went way beyond their bounds to put on a huge media show just to demonise guns and self-sufficient people and to win favor with the new anti-gun President. I really believe the evidence will show BATF had no intention of serving a warrant or conducting themselves in a professional manner. After all, if Koresh was such a dangerous person, why didn't they simply pick him up when he went jogging or to town?"* [5]

It was not the first time the deadly duo of BATF and FBI had been responsible for killing innocent people in a siege. There is the infamous Randy Weaver case, when 400 agents were deployed against the Weaver family in their mountain-top home in Idaho in August 1992. Randy Weaver, a court later heard, had been set up as an agent provocateur by the BATF. The idea was to frame him on gun charges to force him to become an informer. But he refused and eventually the FBI-BATF terrorist squad killed Weaver's 14-year-old son as he was running away from them back to the house. They killed his wife while she was holding a baby in the doorway, killed the family dog, and wounded Weaver himself and a friend, Kevin Harris. From what I have heard, I would agree with little that Randy Weaver believed in, but so what? If we don't treat all people equally, whether we agree with them or not, we create a tyranny.

In 1994, we were told of another 'mass suicide' by a 'cult' in Switzerland. Given what I knew about Jonestown and Waco, I watched the coverage of the story with added interest. When the story broke, it was a 'mass suicide' by followers of two 'messianic' leaders. The next day, it was suddenly a mass murder by the two leaders and an international police hunt was launched. A day or so later, one of the two leaders was found to be among the dead. Now it was mass murder by the other leader. Another few days passed and he was also found to be among the dead. In December 1995, another 16 members, or *alleged* members, were found shot dead in France. So who killed them? No-one seems to know or care, but such is the attention span and the retention of detail by newspaper readers and television viewers that most will have absorbed only the theme that here was another mad, bad, and dangerous cult. This lack of attention to detail by most people, in the face of the tidal wave of information with which we are deluged every day, is a highly effective tool of the mind manipulators. According to Professor Massimo

Introvigne at the Centre for the Study of New Religion in Turin, Italy, there are at least circumstantial and historical connections between the Order of the Solar Temple involved in the Swiss tragedy and both the French secret service and the P2 Freemasonry cell.[6] We have since had the accusations against a Japanese sect over the poison gas released into the underground system and by the time you read this there may well have been other stories to devalue the word 'cult'. Either this Supreme Truth organisation is an Elite front (very possible) or it is the victim of anti-'cult' propaganda. The BATF agent, Dan Curtis, summed up the game when he defined a cult at the trial of eleven Branch Davidians as "a group of people who live together differently from the rest of society".[7] And that would never do, would it? Just as the Elite seek to destroy countries who are in danger of setting a good example of alternative lifestyles and economics, so they do the same with groups living in ways which show that the status quo is not the only option. 'Choice' becomes 'bad', 'different' becomes 'dangerous'.

The media yet again play their role to perfection as the messenger boys and girls of this propaganda. When the Waco story broke, I was questioned by the media about my 'cult'. I have no 'cult' of any kind because I don't worship or pay homage to anything, but I was described by the *Daily Record* newspaper in Scotland as a 'Cult Lord', and I found a picture of myself in the paper next to that of the murderer, Charles Manson! I was on the same page as David Koresh, too. Can you believe these people who run newspapers? On the day the 'mass suicide' was discovered in the Swiss community, I was asked by the supposedly 'thinking person's' BBC news programme, *Newsnight*, to be interviewed about such 'cults', presumably because I was considered by them to be a 'cult leader'. Maybe they read the *Daily Record*. Talk about barely one-dimensional! It is simply pathetic. But what a dream to have that media mindset available if you are a manipulator. I am a leader of nothing, except my own mind. The media ought to try it sometime. It's wonderful.

In the light of this background to the 'cult' tragedies, it is important that 'cult-buster' groups are questioned and investigated just as much as the 'cults' they attack. These groups have sprung up all over the world. I can understand the motivation behind some of them because there are mind controlling sects preying on the emotions of people, particularly the young, and many, if not most, of these can be linked with the intelligence agencies. They are part of problem-reaction-solution with the Elite creating or exploiting the 'cult' and controlling the opposition to them, the 'cult-busters'. One of the latter is the America-based Cult Awareness Network (CAN), a front for the Anti-Defamation League. Glenn Krawczyk, a freelance writer and former

---

[6] *New Dawn* magazine, (Melbourne, Australia, May/June, 1995) p7.
[7] Dick Reavis, "Witness for the Prosecution", *The San Antonio Current*, (February 10th 1994) p6.

researcher with the satellite TV science programme, *Beyond 2000*, has made a
study of CAN, and his findings were published in the October–November
1994 edition of *Nexus* magazine.[8] He found one of the prime movers behind
CAN is Doctor Louis Jolyn "Jolly" West, who is connected to a similar group
called the American Family Foundation. West was the psychiatrist the
authorities chose to 'analyse' Jack Ruby in Dallas, after Ruby had murdered
Lee Harvey Oswald, the 'patsy' in the Kennedy assassination. In 1973, West
was Director of the University of California Neuropsychiatric Institute and
chairman of the Department of Psychiatry at the University, from where
came Tom Grubbs, a psychologist linked to Jonestown.

West proposed a Center for the Study and Reduction of Violence, at which
he planned to treat 'undesirable behaviour' with the latest neuropsychiatric and
genetic manipulation techniques. Goodness knows what he would have got up
to, and yet he had enthusiastic support from California Governor, Ronald
Reagan. Fortunately the California legislature could see what was happening
and labelled the idea, "Nazi science". West knew all about that because he had
been, as confirmed by CIA records, a long-time operative on the agency's
mind control programmes, including MKUltra. Dr West's specialities include
interrogation using deprivation techniques, hypnosis and psychoactive drugs,
behaviour modification through electrical stimulation of the brain, and
electronic devices to track and monitor his victims. That is the mentality of
one of the main figures behind the Cult Awareness Network (CAN). So what
constitutes a 'cult' in this man's misguided mind? According to his own
published papers, they include the following:

> "(1) neo-Christian cults; (2) Hindu and Eastern religious cults; (3) occult,
> witchcraft and satanism cults; (4) spiritualist cults; (5) Zen and other Sino-
> Japanese philosophical cults; (6) race cults; (7) flying saucer and outer space
> cults; (8) psychological cults [like CAN, presumably]; (9) political cults;
> and (10) certain communal and self-help or self-improvement groups that
> become transformed into cults."

What about the "walking to the shops to buy tonight's dinner" cults? I
can't think why he missed that one. The list confirms what I was saying
earlier about the way the Elite want to discredit the word 'cult' and then
apply it to any group or lifestyle they wish to undermine and destroy. The
aim is to marginalise and wipe out all thinking that challenges the desired
norm. One of West's cronies, Dr Martin Orne, a former head of the Office
of Naval Research's Committee on Hypnosis, said: "Even in present day
America, when an individual hears God speak to him, it is a toss-up whether
he will become a successful leader of a new religious cult or will come to the

---

[8] *Nexus* magazine is an excellent publication which covers stories and information the
mainstream media will not print. See bibliography.

attention of a psychiatric unit". It was a 'deprogrammer' or, in truth, a reprogrammer with CAN, called Rick Ross who tipped off the BATF about guns at the Waco Compound. It was Ross who 'deprogrammed' 14-year-old Kiri Jewell, who claimed that Koresh sexually abused her, 'evidence' which has been seriously questioned. Ross was working at the time with Priscilla Coates, a national spokesperson for the Cult Awareness Network. The use of 'lethal force' against the Branch Davidians was recommended by Patricia Ryan, the President of CAN.[9]

Significantly, it was during Dr "Jolly" West's campaign for the 'behaviour modification' unit in California in 1974, that the Symbionese Liberation Army (SLA) came to public prominence when they kidnapped Patricia Hearst, the daughter of the newspaper tycoon, Randolf Hearst. This happened in the same state of California under Ronald Reagan, from where the Peoples' Temple of Jim Jones also emerged. The SLA was supposed to be a Marxist urban warfare group and the propaganda about them terrorised the state for months. In fact, only nine people were involved. Patricia Hearst became active in SLA actions after her abduction. This included an armed bank robbery and the stories began to flow about her being brainwashed by this 'cult'. The SLA was destroyed when 150 officers and agents expelled 5,000 rounds of ammunition in front of live television cameras during prime time. Later Patricia Hearst was given a mental examination by two 'experts' on brainwashing...Dr Louis Jolyn West and Dr Martin Orne, of the Cult Awareness Network.

The founder of CAN, Ted Patrick, has a long list of criminal convictions against him which result from his 'counselling' techniques on cult 'victims'. These include kidnapping, conspiracy, false imprisonment, abduction and assault, possession of cocaine, and violation of probation. A case brought against Patrick in 1976 revealed that he had held one of his abductees prisoner for 86 days at 12 locations and subjected her to "frightful experiences".[10] These are just some of the people who are protecting the innocent from cults! You now increasingly see the word cult used to discredit groups and alternative communities that are anything but 'brainwashed dangerous nutters'. Once the word 'cult' is applied, it is considered OK to treat the people involved as subhuman, with no rights as human beings. Yet, as US judge T.S. Ellis told 'deprogrammer' Galen Kelly: "One man's cult is another man's community, no matter how wacky you or I might think that is".

There are other groups dubbed as 'cults', however, which suit the Elite and they are allowed to become global empires. One is the Unification Church, started in Korea and now based in New York. It is led by Sun Myung Moon and is better known as the Moonies. This is an extremely sinister organisation, in my view, with New World Order overtones. On January 15th 1995, the London *Sunday Express* revealed that the former British

[9] *Houston Chronicle*, (April 8th 1993).

[10] Helander vs Patrick, Bridgeport, Conneticut, USA, 1976.

Prime Minister, Edward Heath (Bil), had been paid handsomely to make the keynote speech at the Moonies' Summit Council for World Peace in Korea. In March 1994, he also spoke at Sun Myung Moon's World Peace Conference, where the main speaker was the former Soviet Union leader, Mikhail Gorbachev, the friend of Henry Kissinger and David Rockefeller. The Knight of Malta and former US Secretary of State and Supreme Allied Commander of NATO, Alexander Haig, has spoken at Moonie events. So has the former US Defense Secretary, Frank Carlucci (CFR, TC). The Unification Church has a worldwide business empire which includes *The Washington Times*, *The New York City Tribune*, and *The Middle East Times*. Their list of front groups and businesses in the NameBase system runs to 28 pages and 667 names.[11] Moon's son and heir apparent, Justin, runs an arms company in Massachusetts called Saeilo Incorporated.[12] Once more the links with the intelligence agencies of the Elite have been identified. The Moonies paid $50,000,000 to buy the University of Bridgeport in Connecticut and one of the new trustees named was Jack E. Thomas, the assistant chief of staff at US airforce intelligence, and special assistant to the CIA director for nine years. The Unification Church has support from the South Korean Central Intelligence Agency (KCIA). Bo Hi Pak, the KCIA liaison officer to US intelligence stationed at the Korean Embassy in Washington, became one of Moon's top aides and president of *The Washington Times*. Moon's editor at the *Washington Times* is Arnaud de Borchgrave, a former leading correspondent of the CIA-connected *Newsweek*, owned by the *Washington Post* company of Katherine Graham (CFR, TC, Bil). De Borchgrave is closely connected by marriage to the Rothschild family, the longtime and leading financial and political backers of Israel, a state they were, in effect, responsible for creating.

The Church of Scientology (established by L. Ron Hubbard) was named by former CIA officer, Miles Copeland, as one of two religious-type groups with which the CIA made 'arrangements'. The other was called Moral Re-Armament. The Elite make sure they work through both sides whenever possible, in this case the 'cult' and the 'cult-busters'. In doing so they control the actions and events the public mind sees and absorbs. From the evidence that I have seen and my own intuition, I sense the time approaching when a coordinated global campaign will be activated which seeks to discredit all alternative thinking, movements, and lifestyles. It is a time to be strong and determined and allow the power of love to win through.

This same technique is being used against investigators into the global conspiracy. As more of the web and background is unravelled, there is a desperate need by the Elite to discredit this information by discrediting the messengers. It is a technique known as "Ad Hominem" – if a truth you

[11] Investigative Research Specialists, "List of Moonie Fronts", 1992.
[12] *The Spotlight*, (December 11th 1995) p2.

don't like is being communicated, attack the messenger, not the message. I am now seeing an expanding range of articles about 'conspiracy theorists' and how they are all 'Right wing extremists'. As with the word 'cult', the propagandists want to stimulate an immediate public reaction of 'Nazi' to anyone who reveals information about the global manipulation. This is where the 'Left', those I call the Robot Radicals, are so helpful to the Elite. They parrot this nonsense by reflex action. Another buzz term is "historical revisionist". This is also being used in a negative way. What such a person is doing is challenging the conventional version of history. Do those who speak of historical revisionists as Nazis really believe that everything we are told about history is true? Surely not. Then why can't we be adult enough to look at what the revisionists say and make up our own mind about what we think is right? Because the Elite would lose control of history, that's why.

My experience and observations lead me to believe that parts of the "New Age" scene are among the most easy to manipulate. It is the naïvety which makes it so. I have heard Bill Clinton described as a "lightworker" by some in the New Age movement who have done no research whatsover into the background to the man. I hear all the instant, off-the-shelf responses about 'cults' from people involved in the very groups, organisations, and lifestyles which the word 'cult' is being manipulated to target! Some of those who have done most to spread false stories and gossip about me have been those who speak of truth and light. I used to be amazed at that, but no more. One story doing the New Age rounds is that I have so much money I live as a tax exile in Jersey. As I've only been to Jersey for a total of four days in my life, I clearly don't get home much! I read in spiritual magazines of the need for a world government as the expression of Oneness and the coming together of all peoples in One World. It sounds great, unless you do the research and see how the New Age Movement is being manipulated too.

I attended a lovely spiritual event at Wembley, London, in the summer of 1994. It was to celebrate the Oneness of all things and the need to express love in the world, all of which I agree with. But manipulation of the human mind doesn't only come in one all-pervading blob. We have designer-manipulation which is targeted at a particular belief system. As people were leaving Wembley, there was a group outside handing out little glossy leaflets carrying the message of Babaji Francesco, "the man who has come to bring love and wisdom to all the Earth". Mr Francesco, it turns out, is the founder of an organisation called Associazione S.U.M. – Stati Uniti del Mondo (the United States of the World). On the first page of the leaflet is a message about love from Mr Francesco in which he tells us that our tears are his tears and for those who follow him all pain shall be removed. Excuse me, I feel quite ill suddenly. He says that he has come to teach us that everything is One. Thank you very much. But wait, what else has he come to teach us? That only by meeting the Earth's problems at a worldwide level can they be overcome. This

couldn't mean, could it, that we need a world government, currency and
army? Oh yes it could. His leaflet says:

> *"Babaji Francesco, in order to resolve all problems, proposes the unification
> of the Nations of the Earth and maintains the need of a one and only World
> Government composed of delegates of each nation. He deems important the
> realisation of a one and only world army composed of volunteers of each
> country, for the protection of all Peoples of the Earth, that they should be
> effective and timely to avoid useless genocide like that which took place in
> Rwanda, Yugoslavia, Somalia, etc...He also affirms that, in order to cancel
> the public debt of each country, all states should cancel all debts between each
> other and that it is necessary to eliminate all present currencies and replace
> them with a one and only world currency that should have equal value in each
> nation so that speculations, competitions, and wars would be replaced by unity,
> brotherhood and peace among all human beings."*

All of which is straight from the pages of the Global Elite game plan and
the *Illuminati Protocols*. Either the man who has come to teach us and lead us
into this utopia needs to do some urgent research into the New World Order
or he has other reasons for equating the need for love and Oneness with a
centralised global tyranny. The Raëlian Foundation I spoke of earlier is also
promoting all the Elite's ambitions because of what their 'messiah', Claude
Raël, claims he was told by the extraterrestrial "Elohim". When I attended a
New Age type exhibition in the north of England, it was fascinating to see
how many organisations I came across either supporting the United Nations
and the concepts of world government and/or offering people another
excuse to give their minds away to some "Supreme Master" or other. Don't
be thought-controlled by a religion – be thought controlled by a guru
instead! I picked up a magazine called *Share International*, the publication
edited by the Scottish-born painter and 'esotericist' Benjamin Creme who,
the publicity says, has been "trained and supervised over many years by his
own Master". The magazine, which claims to circulate within 70 countries,
is based in the Netherlands and the United Kingdom with branches and
connections in many other countries, including the United States. The
magazine promotes the "Maitreya", the "World Teacher", who, according to
Creme, has "miraculously" appeared to people all over the planet. This
"World Teacher" will only appear to everyone, he says, when the media
invites him to. We have so far waited since 1977 for this while the "World
Teacher" has, says Creme, continued to live in the Asian Community in
London between his materialisations all over the world. When invited by the
media, Maitreya will, says Creme, address an international press conference
which will lead to the "Day of Declaration", the time when the "World
Teacher" will appear on radio and television networks worldwide and will
mentally overshadow all people, simultaneously. All will hear his words

through telepathic communication, apparently. Ummm, again. What's going on here, I wonder? Costly advertisements appear constantly in the New Age magazines about "Maitreya". Every advertisement features the "Maitreya" appearing "miraculously" to thousands of people in Nairobi in 1988, although I can't say the picture looks anything like that to me. The exact locations of the Maitreya "manifestations" are never given. To do so would contravene the free will of the people involved, Creme tells us.

The April 1995 edition of *Share International* which I bought at the exhibition was dominated by an interview with Sir Shridath Ramphal, the former Secretary General of the Commonwealth, calling for world government and the need for a leader of the calibre of Franklin D. Roosevelt! The interview is followed by a report on the Commission on Global Governance headed by Ramphal which included calls for, in effect, a world (UN) army, centralised global economic control, and a world government. This, in turn, was followed by three pages called "Priorities for a New World Order". Benjamin Creme, in answers to letters, also informs us that the only way to counter events like Bosnia and Rwanda is "to have a United Nations with an army powerful enough, supported by all nations, who must give enough men and armaments". Coincidentally, that is just what Henry Kissinger says, and Babaji Francesco. Creme adds that if "Jimmy Carter lives long enough, I believe he will become a member of a 'group of wise men' which will function as the future ruling committee of the United States". The Trilateral Commission will be delighted, I'm sure, and what's this about a "ruling committee"? Whatever happened to democracy? Mind you, an article in the magazine tells us that:

> "...*a true disciple will apply himself to his 'indicated task' with all the energy at his disposal, forgetful of his own personality, with the one purpose of contributing all that lies within him towards serving and the realisation of the Plan. This must inevitably also lead to his own progress – not towards self-satisfaction, but by evoking dormant capacities that will mould him into an ever more efficient instrument of* **service in the hands of the masters***.*" [my emphasis]

Oh dear, oh dear, oh dear. Here we go again. People follow, masters rule. "Maitraya" is one of the Alice Bailey 'Masters' and it is on her 'teachings' that Creme's organisation is based. At the same New Age exhibition I found two other Alice Bailey-inspired organisations, the Lucis Trust, formerly the Lucifer[12] Trust, and its offshoot organisation, World Goodwill. The latter was

[12] The term Lucifer is believed by some to mean "Bringer of Light", as I outlined in *The Robots' Rebellion*. Rabbi Marvin S. Antelman claims in *To Eliminate The Opiate* that the change of name from Lucifer to Lucis in 1924 was to hide the fact that it was involved with Devil worshipping groups linked with the All-Seeing Eye cult. (p54).

founded by Alice Bailey in 1932 in the run up to the Second World War
which led to the creation of the United Nations. World Goodwill is now
little more than a New Age promoter of the United Nations from its centres
in Whitehall Court, London, Geneva, and New York. Its many publications
offer gushing praise for the UN as the answer to the ills of the planet. One
leaflet is called "The Great Invocation Cooperation with the United
Nations". It says:

> *"An inclusive attitude of mind and heart and active cooperative goodwill
> between peoples and nations are necessary prerequisites to the establishment of
> a new world order of peace and prosperity for all humanity...As a result of
> mental conflict, separateness, and lack of understanding, a point of tension has
> now been reached in world affairs; therefore a new opportunity of creative
> progress exists for which the United Nations stands. ...The United Nations
> is today an instrument of universality and an agency for unity, peace and
> prosperity in the world."*

Give me strength. The World Goodwill arm of the Lucis Trust distributes
articles by UN staff and links the spiritual view of wholeness and oneness
with centralised global institutions. It publishes a quarterly newsletter which
reads like a UN fan club. The one I picked up in the spring of 1995
included, like Benjamin Creme's *Share International*, an article about Sir
Shridath Ramphal and his Commission on Global Governance [a world
government and world army are the only way forward]. It also included a
message from Global Elite frontman, Dr Boutros Boutros-Ghali, the UN
Secretary General, who tells us that: "...a new array of problems of
undeniable global dimensions are beyond the ability of any single country or
group of states to solve". We'd better have a world government then, eh,
Boutros? Other publications distributed by World Goodwill call for all
people to be given identity cards, and one says that:

> *"The United Nations, through the General Assembly, specialised agencies,
> and its various councils, commissions and committees must be supported; there
> is, as yet, no other organisation to which man can hopefully look. Therefore,
> he must support the United Nations, but, at the same time, let this group of
> world leaders know what is needed."*

It is worth subscribing to the World Goodwill newsletter, if only to see the
extent of the infiltration of the Global Elite mentality into areas like
spirituality and education. One UN education project alone, I read, involves
a network of 3,200 schools in 122 countries. The UNESCO Associated
Schools Project is "dedicated to preparing children and young people to live
in a global society and to develop their attitudes of 'Earth patriotism' [See
global village, global neighbourhood, etc] that are vital in an increasingly

interdependent world". Children and young people are being indoctrinated to look to the United Nations for the answers and the Lucis Trust/World Goodwill organisation are supporting this. As with most people helping the Global Conspiracy, 99% of them will have no idea what they are really being used to promote. Most of the people who support these organisations will be doing so because they believe in what they say. They have children and grandchildren and the last thing they want is to leave them a global fascist tyranny. But that is what they are, unknowingly, helping to create.

I spoke to a guy at the *Share International* stall at the New Age exhibition and he was a lovely man. He had no idea what he was involved with and answered every question with "Well, as I understand it..." and "Well, it says in the magazine..." He'd given his mind away. At another stall I found another group of genuine people promoting The Brahma Kumaris, the World Spiritual University with more than 3,000 teaching centres in 62 countries. This is a non-governmental organisation affiliated with the United Nations Department of Public Information and winner of seven UN Peace Messenger Awards. It has consultative status with the UN Economic and Social Council and UNICEF and has endless links with the UN. In 1988, it launched the first Peace Messenger initiative dedicated to the UN. Part of this was the publication of a book called *Visions Of A Better World*, in which international leaders and famous people from all walks of life made their contributions. Again, at least 99% of those involved with the Brahma Kumaris will not realise what they are being used to promote by the One World Government brigade. I also never cease to be amazed at the numbers of apparently open-minded people who have, in truth, given their minds away to the man, sorry the "living god on Earth", called Sai Baba. These are people who dismiss religion as mind control and urge others to think for themselves!

Designer manipulation of belief systems is very subtle, but extremely effective and the same centralised tyranny can be presented in many ways to suit the mindset of different groups of people. We can expect a stream of guru-type figures and 'spiritual' organisations being manipulated to do this or knowingly doing so. If spiritual people and groups accept the one world government plan as part of the journey to wholeness and oneness they will be supported by the UN and the manipulators. If they do not, they will be labelled a 'cult'. That is the manipulators' dual approach to the re-emerging spirituality. We need to remember that nothing is ever what it seems at first glance. If we look at everything from that perspective, we become so much harder to disinform. This is vital because there is one 'cult' that dominates all others on this planet. It is the 'cult' which is devoted to, and pays homage to, a highly negative consciousness which is expressed as the worship of power and control. It is called The Global Elite and the All-Seeing Eye.

Chapter 16

The 'Global Village'

"Single acts of tyranny may be ascribed to the opinion of a day, but a series of oppressions, begun at a distinguished period, unalterable through every change of ministers, too plainly prove a deliberate, systematical plan of reducing us to slavery."

Thomas Jefferson

The New World Order has come a long way since the start of the present banking system, the creation of Freemasonry, the United States, and the French Revolution.

When you look at how far the Elite plan has been allowed to progress, it is a sobering thought. And one which I trust will activate the determination within each of us to regain control of our own destiny. This we can and will do, but the bottom line is knowing that the manipulation exists, how it works, and to what end. Without that knowledge, we are at the mercy of the manipulators, because a calculated long-term strategy will go on being presented as singular events unconnected with each other. For those who still believe that the plan for a world government, central bank, currency, and army, together with a microchipped population linked to a global computer, is a conspiracy 'theory', I will end this section with a summary of just how far along that road we have travelled without realising it.

WORLD GOVERNMENT

The United Nations is evolving rapidly into just such an institution. From its early days as a global talking-shop, it has created a massive network of interconnecting organisations which cover all areas of our lives, from health to aid to environment to a world police force to science to religion, and so it goes on. The time is approaching when it will be given its own source of funding, independent of the nation states. Perhaps some funding 'crisis' will be engineered, with some major nations failing to keep up contributions and a 'solution' will have to be found – a form of United Nations taxation of some kind or other. In 1993 Joseph Connor (CFR) was appointed undersecretary-general for administration and management at the UN. He was chairman of Price Waterhouse, the Elite accountants, who have a designate on the

Committee of 300. Mr Connor has been warning that the UN faces bankruptcy and something must be done.[1] Now there's a surprise. More conflict will demand more 'solutions', and in desperation people will look to the United Nations for answers. Centralised answers. Most of the people who work for the United Nations believe they are doing the right thing. They don't know what they are involved in. They are pawns in a game they don't understand. The real agenda is hidden behind terms like "global village", "global neighbourhood", the "global commons" and the need for "One World". The covert plan for the United Nations is exactly the same as that unfolding in Europe. The pressure is being applied with ever greater severity for centralisation of political power and decision making within the ever-expanding European Union which is now a maze of centralised power structures and legislation affecting every facet of daily life. The face of that organisation has changed beyond measure in the last forty years. It has been a metamorphosis from trading area to centralised tyranny and the same stepping-stones process is happening within the United Nations. The President of the European Parliament, Klaus Hänsch, made his ambitions clear in *The European* newspaper of May 1995, when he called for a European Union in which nations would 'pool' their sovereignty for the greater good [centralised control]; a Union which assumed its full responsibility for peace and security, acting in close collaboration with the United Nations [world army]; a Europe which "lives up to the dreams and the vision of its founding fathers" [world government, central bank, currency, and army]. Popular enthusiasm for this "new European project" had to be generated, he said. I'll give it a miss, if it's all the same with you, Klaus.

One of the most vehement advocates of political and monetary union in Europe is the German Chancellor Helmut Kohl. This is no surprise when, like his predecessors Willy Brandt and Helmut Schmidt, he is a loyal member of the Bilderberg Group. Kohl is alleged to be a Grand Orient Freemason and is connected to B'nai B'rith which bestowed its highest honour, the Order of Joseph, upon him.[2] Kohl knows the game plan, alright, and works passionately for its success. Jacques Santer, the president of the European Commission, is another Bilderberger running a tyrannical campaign for political and monetary union.

This evolution to centralised control has been done gradually, quietly, and secretly and only by looking back over the years can we see how much power the nation states, the regions, and communities, have given away. Decision making that affects our everyday existence has moved further and further away from the towns, cities, villages, and countries in which we live. First to the national parliaments and civil service cartel, then to Europe, and, unless we stop being puppets on a string, eventually it will continue to move away still further to the global government. The Trilateral Commission's influence can

---

[1] *The Guardian*, (December 12th 1995) p12.

[2] *Secret Societies*, p218.

be seen in the support by the European Commission for Japan to become a permanent member of the United Nations Security Council and to have a greater say in UN affairs.[3] The Trilateral Commission was created to coordinate the work of the manipulating elites in the US, Europe, and Japan, as part of the move to world government. The game plan is coming closer to the surface with every month, as the Global Elite begin to filter the prospect of a world government into the public domain. The former Secretary General of the Commonwealth, Sir Shridath Ramphal, voiced the plan at an International Development Conference in Washington in January 1995, when he said that the UN should be empowered to "raise global revenue for global purposes". The conference supported the policy with great enthusiasm. Ramphal, the co-chairman of the Commission on Global Governance in Geneva, Switzerland, added that national sovereignty was outmoded. "The time has come to establish arrangements of global governance," he said. "We need a new order in world affairs. Large numbers of people recognise this and understand by a 'new world order' nothing less than the birth of a new world."

The attempt to achieve this coup on the human race will be done by making the present world so awful and chaotic that anyone promising a new world will be followed like the Pied Piper, purely out of desperation (just like they did with Hitler – the 'saviour' for Germany's post-war misery). I believe the Elite have a global computer into which all the data of world events and public reaction is constantly fed. The computer is programmed to process this data and produce a list of events projecting years ahead, which need to happen if the human mind is to accept world government. This way the Elite plan can be prepared far in advance. Ramphal is a long-time standard-bearer for world government. He has also served on other global commissions like the Brandt Commission and the Brundtland Commission on Environment and Development. It was members of these Global Elite-created commissions, and another led by the murdered Bilderberger, Olof Palme, the Swedish Prime Minister, who formed the Commission on Global Governance in 1992, chaired by Ramphal and another prime minister of Sweden, Ingvar Carlsson. And who, pray, is this I see listed on the Commission on World Governance? Why it's...Maurice Strong (Comm 300), the 'Green' oil millionaire, the Maurice Strong who fronted the 1992 Earth Summit in Brazil, and sits on the board of the Aspen Institute owned by elite Bilderberger, Robert O. Anderson of Atlantic Richfield Oil. Also listed is Jacques Delors, that archcentraliser and former top man in the European Union. Commission on Global Governance = New World Order. Another world government lobby event, the Global Forum on the First 'Global Civilisation', was arranged by the Gorbachev Foundation USA, for the autumn of 1995. Gorbachev played his part magnificently in triggering the prearranged 'freedom' in the Soviet Union and its subordinate states to set the scene for the absorption of those

---

[3] Reported in the London *Financial Times*, (March 9th 1995) p4.

countries into the European Union and the United States of the World. The 'Cold War' was also a case of thesis v antithesis = synthesis. The 'freeing' of the Soviet Union was planned, not spontaneous. Among those invited to the event in San Francisco, the official birthplace of the UN, were George Shultz (TC, CFR, Bil, Comm 300, Kissinger Associates), George Bush (TC, CFR, Comm 300), Margaret Thatcher (Bil), Al Gore (CFR), Zbigniew Brzezinski (TC, CFR, Bil), Paul Volcker (TC, CFR, Bil), and Ted Turner (Comm 300), head of the CNN global news channel which has merged into the Time Warner empire. The pre-event literature published by the Gorbachev Foundation said the forum would challenge political leaders to provide a framework for stability and *regulated* human interactions [my emphasis]. The Foundation added that the forum was designed to:

> "...*focus on the fundamental challenges and opportunities confronting humanity as we enter the next century and a new millennium. It is being held in the belief that at this momentous juncture in history, we are giving birth to the first global civilisation.*"

In other words, world government and all the trimmings. Expect to see a series of 'commissions', 'conferences' and 'summits' to discuss the creation of world government in the months and years ahead. Expect, also, an attempt to rewrite the US Constitution to allow the New World Order to impose its policies on the USA. Another group to watch is the Bilderberg-related, New Atlantic Initiative (NAI), headed by the same crowd with Margaret Thatcher as a patron. It seeks to fuse the US with the European Union and make NATO a world army.

WORLD CENTRAL BANK AND CURRENCY

Ramphal also calls for the establishment of an "apex" economic body within the United Nations, an Economic Security Council. This fits in with the Global Elite's plan to fuse all economic power under one roof, or within one computer. The United Nations and its economic arms, the World Bank, the International Monetary Fund (IMF), the Organisation of Economic Cooperation and Development (OECD), and their stream of interconnected offshoots, control the world's economic development, along with other Elite groupings like the Bank of International Settlements and the International Banking Commission. They decide who has development funds, what they are spent on, and the economic changes that must happen within nation states before any money changes hands. It is a world economic dictatorship run at the behest of the few. Within this network, too, is the World Trade Organisation and the GATT 'free trade' agreement, which is gathering ever more power to prevent nation states from protecting their home industries and production from unwanted imports. Many of these imports come from areas of the world where the native population is exploited in the most inhuman way.

With countries increasingly unable to protect their own population from this economic warfare, the people of the world become ever more dependent on a world economic system over which they have no control. As cross-border tariffs on imported goods are removed by GATT, so that loss of revenue is being met by the people of those countries. They are subsidising the New World Order. A report by the US Treasury in June 1994 suggested that GATT will reduce tariffs by nearly $750 billion over the following decade. Along with the pressure for centralisation of political power in Europe has come the connected demand for a European Central Bank and a single European currency. For political power to be effective, it has to be backed up by economic power. If you control the currency and the central bank to which all other banks are subordinate, you control the whole of Europe. This will eventually encompass the states of the former Soviet Union, also. If we allow this to happen, the centralised European tyranny will have been achieved by a mental coup d'état, without a gun being fired. The American continent's version of this, the North American Free Trade Area (NAFTA), and the Asia-Australia version (APEC), are designed to evolve in precisely the same way, until all connect with the United Nations as a world government, central bank, and currency. The plan is for NAFTA to become the American Union, APEC to become the Pacific Union, and together with the already established European Union, they would come under the control of a global government. At a 1995 meeting of the Trilateral Commission in Denmark, inside sources suggest that the plan was revealed for a Transatlantic Free Trade Area (TAFTA) to combine the European Union with the North American Free Trade Area. Sir Leon "Mr GATT" Brittan, the European Trade Commissioner, has since called for something similar and the British Foreign Secretary, Malcolm Rifkind (Bil), did the same at the 1995 Conservative Party Conference. Ireland's Peter Sutherland (Bil, TC), the GATT negotiator and first Director-General of the World Trade Organisation, was at the Trilateral meeting to speak about the "changing world economy". At the same time the German Foreign Minister, Klaus Kinkel, was in Chicago addressing the Council on Foreign Relations about the Transatlantic Free Trade Area. Bill Clinton and the European Union have formerly agreed on "joint action" on many issues including trade. Anyone who challenges the Elite plan for Europe is immediately jumped upon. Bernard Connolly, the British economist working for the European Commission on the single currency plan, was suspended by Jacques Santer (Bil) for writing a book exposing the scam. Neil Kinnock, a European Commissioner and former UK Labour leader, was publicly censured by Santer for merely questioning that the timetable for a single currency might be too tight, at a private meeting. The European Union is already a centralised dictatorship. They are spending £40 million of our money on a publicity campaign to condition people to accept their policy of a single currency, the "Euro" as it is to be called.[4]

---

[4] *The Sunday Times*, (December 17th 1995) p2.

Remember the motivation and the methods. If you want to install a single currency and bank, you have to create a perceived need for them. Therefore you trigger a banking crisis and currency chaos. On the face of it, when such things happen and they are reported on the news, they appear to be bad for the bankers and financiers, and for many they are. But not for the Global Elite, because they need such crises to manipulate their plan into reality and, as they know what is coming, they not only can insulate their own resources from the effect of their actions, they can actually make an economic killing. George Soros (Bil), the Hungarian with a US passport, is one of the most famous currency speculators. He 'gambles' billions of dollars to destabilise currencies and markets, making unimaginable fortunes in the process. Soros, a former student at the London School of Economics, moved to the US to establish his vehicle for "speculation", the Quantum Group, which is dominated by Swiss and Italian financiers. Funnily enough Switzerland and Italy are also the base of the Black Nobility. Researcher, William Engahl, names Soros as a frontman for the Anglo-French Rothschild banking group.[5] One of the board members of the "Soros" Quantum Fund is Richard Katz, the head of Rothschild Italia S.p.A. in Milan and a board member of N.M. Rothschild.[6] Another Quantum director is Nils O. Taube, a partner with Lord Rothschild of St James' Place Capital.[7] An associate of Soros in several speculations was the late Sir James Goldsmith,[8] a Rothschild relative who now claims to "oppose" centralisation of power in Europe. It was Soros who fronted the attack on the pound that led to the British Chancellor, Norman Lamont (Bil), withdrawing the UK from the European monetary system, the ERM, so increasing calls for one European currency. Lamont is an employee of the Rothschilds, and Soros is a frontman for them. Currency 'speculations' are neither speculations nor accidental. They are carefully planned and executed to ensure a specific effect.

In late 1994 and early '95, the Elite plunged Mexico into economic chaos which seriously affected the value of the dollar, just as they did before when Mexico wanted to use its oil potential to gain economic independence from the USA. In doing so, those US banks who knew the peso's collapse was coming, made a fortune. While the Mexican people suffered from the consequences, Citibank reported an 81% increase in earnings for the last quarter of 1994 and the New York daily, *Newsday*, reported profit gains for Chemical Bank of 22% and the Rockefeller/Rothschild Chase Manhattan of 19% for the same period. All were heavy investors in the peso, but switched their investments at exactly the right time to take advantage of its imminent fall.

---

[5] *Secret Societies*, p285.
[6] Ibid.
[7] Ibid.
[8] Ibid.

Mexico is being pushed into an economic catastrophe through debt to the banks of the Global Elite because they want to forgive the debt, or some of it, in return for control of all of Mexico's oil and other natural resources. Who proposed the $40 billion bail out of Mexico which has substantially increased its debts to America, so accelerating the scam? The Democrat, Bill Clinton. Who supported him? The Republicans, Newt Gingrich and Bob Dole. In June 1995, the leaders of the 67 industrialised countries met in Halifax, Nova Scotia, a week after the Bilderberg meeting in Switzerland, and agreed to increase the role and powers of the IMF. Their excuse for this? The financial collapse of the Mexican peso! Bill Clinton also called for a national identity card in the United States to deal with the "wave of illegal immigration [from Mexico] that was sure to follow". Meantime small business people the world over are being ruined by a market rigged in favour of the multinational banks and corporations which control the politicians who pass the legislation.

WORLD ARMY

The progress to a world army has advanced quickly through the 1980s and '90s. The idea is to manipulate conflicts which will lead to demands for greater military powers for the United Nations Peacekeeping Forces. They will then be fused with NATO into a world army. What would a world army do? Invade any country or community that refuses to bow to the world government, central bank, and currency. The Gulf War in 1991 was created in part to hasten this process with NATO countries funding and fighting that conflict under the United Nations flag. The conflict in the former Yugoslavia has been manipulated to this same end. As a result of the horrors of Bosnia, we now have a 60,000-strong, 30 nation world army assembled in the former Yugoslavia working under centralised control, the biggest multinational force to be seen since the second World War. Exactly to the Elite plan. Any occasion which sees NATO forces operating outside their designated area is another precedent which takes us closer to the world army. We can expect to see moves, too, which extend NATO's area of operation, particularly into the Middle East and the former Soviet Union, and you will see moves to expand the number of nations in NATO in the same way that the European Union is expanding. The UN troops will continue to evolve from peacekeepers to peace enforcers and then, once that precedent is set, to enforcers of policies issued by the global political and economic elite. When the UN troops are seen to be ineffective in places like Rwanda, the former Yugoslavia, and Somalia, the public perceive this as a bad thing. But for the manipulators, this failure is essential. If the UN Peacekeeping operations were working effectively, there would be no demand to give them more powers. They have to be seen to be not working (problem) to attract the desired reaction (something must be done), and open the way to the greater powers (the solution). The immediate victims of this are the men, women and children, slaughtered by the Elite-engineered civil wars designed to show that the UN forces need more power. We can expect more Rwandas and Bosnias until public opinion either bows to the manipulation for a world army or acts to bring an end to the New World Order. The former UN Secretary-General, the Elite-stooge, Dr Boutros Ghali, was echoing the words of Henry Kissinger at the 1991 meeting of the Bilderberg Group when he called for the formation of a UN Army under its own command with the right to go into a nation state at will and without the need to consult other countries for permission. In his Washington speech, Sir Shridath Ramphal said that the UN should be "backed by the ability to rapidly deploy UN forces," and he said that protecting the security of states was clearly authorised under the UN charter. The following day, Jessica Mathews, a senior fellow of the Council on Foreign Relations, called for exactly the same, a UN Standing Army, when writing in the Elite-controlled, *Washington Post*.

Readers of *The Spotlight* newspaper have been sending in pictures of UN troops in the United States on manoeuvres all across the country and UN tanks and equipment being transported by rail trucks. The authorities have denied the existence of any such thing. As I detail at some length in *The Robots' Rebellion*, government organisations like the Federal Emergency Management Agency (FEMA) are fronts for the creation of holding areas (concentration camps) for those who oppose the New World Order conspiracy once it has launched its physical coup d'état across the world, particularly in America and Europe, against those who challenge the tyranny. Indeed in some areas this has already begun. FEMA was created under an Executive Order (which required no debate in Congress), and signed by President Jimmy Carter, the Trilateral Commission frontman. This allows FEMA to take control of the United States during any "national emergency" declared by a president. These powers include martial law and the right of the military to enforce whatever FEMA decides. All the laws are already in force which allow a military take-over of the United States. They have been passed by Presidential Executive Order and any time a president calls a state of emergency they can be invoked. At the forefront of this plan are the Delta Forces in their black uniforms and unmarked black helicopters. These have often been seen at the scene of cattle mutilations, which some researchers connect with extraterrestrial activity. People can ignore all this and walk away if they like, but their children will reap the consequences if we hand over our responsibility for much longer.

The Spotlight edition of December 5th 1994, revealed the creation of a joint UN-NATO force called the Allied Rapid Reaction Corps (ARRC) which will have four "multinational" divisions of some 80,000 troops when combat ready. According to the article, the designated commander-in-chief is Sir Jeremy MacKenzie, a Lieutenant General in the British Army. The justification of this force was the failure of the UN and NATO operations in the former Yugoslavia! A report quoted by *Spotlight* from the North Atlantic Assembly, an offshoot of NATO, says that the multinational interventions in the Balkans have been "characterised by massive failure and shortcomings" (problem). To cope with this new challenge, the report continued, NATO required a new organisation (solution). The joint NATO-UN Allied Rapid Reaction Corps had already completed its first exercises under UN auspices by the time of the *Spotlight* article, a NATO report obtained by the paper confirmed. Some 2,000 troops were involved in a rapid deployment of riot control forces from northwestern Germany to "...an imaginary crisis spot in the United Kingdom". The veteran military analyst Lieutenant Colonel Matthew Coulterm, said when told of this:

> *"Troops that practise multinational military intervention in the internal domestic quarrels of Great Britain today will be preparing to do the same thing in the US tomorrow. We must cut off the head of this one-world monster before it bites us."* [9]

Ironically when the Bosnian hostage crisis unfolded in May 1995, some politicians called for a UN-NATO rapid reaction force. It already existed! The process of centralising the world military is also happening with the police forces. A little debated or publicised clause in the Maastricht treaty for European Union established the K4 Committee to create a European police network operating outside democratic control. This must have been one of the clauses the voting fodder politicians missed when they failed to read the treaty before passing it into law. K4 is supposed to coordinate pan-European police action against drug trafficking, money laundering, and illegal immigration. It will also establish a European police network called Europol and a massive database of information about the population. Some have described it as a European FBI. Under the Maastricht Treaty, the 'democratically' elected European Parliament will have the right to be 'consulted' about the policies of K4, but has no right to change or veto them! The membership of K4 is also to be kept secret and inaccessible to journalists and human rights groups. Tony Bunyan, a director of the civil liberties group, Statewatch, said that K4 is "a major step forward in the creation of the European state infrastructure that will be largely unaccountable and undemocratic". The British government and establishment which talks from time to time of its concern about the centralisation of power in Europe is a keen supporter of K4. This is because the rhetoric of those in power is only for public consumption. The overwhelming majority of them support the centralisation of Europe, whatever they may claim.

---

[9] "NATO, UN Contract, Marriage Made In Hell", *The Spotlight*, (December 5th 1994) p1.

THE MICROCHIPPED POPULATION

This is the part of the Elite strategy which some people find hardest to accept. We believe that we would never allow it to happen. Well, let's take a look at how close it is. Already domestic animals are being microchipped in ever greater numbers and linked to a computer. It's been sold to pet owners on the basis of: "You'll never lose Rover or Fido again". The Queen of England has had some of her corgis microchipped. Who next, Prince Charles? Alongside this, the move to phase out the use of coins and notes is being quickened and all money transactions will be electronic via a credit card and/or smart card. This is planned to become a joint identity/money card with all personal details on a microchip. If things go to plan, all these transactions will be recorded by a global computer – the "beast", possibly, mentioned in the Biblical Revelations. The "mark of the beast," the microchip, is planned to be moved from the smart card to the human body when a story can be hatched to persuade people to accept it. Some researchers suggest that the human barcoding system will include three sets of six digits in the computer – hence 666, "the number of the Beast". Once we have agreed to the end of cash and there is no turning back, we will have to accept the microchip implant or we will have no means of purchasing anything when they decide to phase out smart cards. Also it will be sold to people as a convenience which will end credit card fraud and lost cards. It is the ultimate control. Everything about you, including your location, will be constantly observed by the computer. Some people believe that the Global Elite computer system is based underground in Brussels, Belgium. It is claimed to be called the Krypt or Crypt and located in 100,000 square feet of office space under the city. Similar computer centres are believed to be located at the Air Force Academy, Cheyenne Mountain, Colorado, USA, and the Alice Springs, Australia. These systems lock into government computers across the world to gather information on every man, woman and child on the planet who has a social security number or a personal identification of some type kept on a database. Your details will be on these computers now, waiting for the microchipping to start. The plans are well advanced and microchipping has already been widely promoted and in many areas of life, introduced.

Today if you go into a shop to buy food and your credit card is refused by the computer, you can pay with cash. What happens when there is no cash? You are at the mercy of the computer. If it refuses your card or microchip, you have no means to purchase anything. We will then be robots in every sense, an extension of a computer program. In the US, Food Stamps and some other benefits are being converted to the card based Electronic Benefit Transfer (EBT) and the whole social security system is planning to do the same. The plan to phase out cash moves apace. A United Kingdom company, AIM UK, which specialises in "automatic identification", produced a face with a bar coding on the forehead as part of its publicity material. One of this company's products is Radio Frequency Identification which reads electronic labels in manufacturing, warehousing, shops, and on people. The technology now being developed will allow every thought and action to be monitored and recorded. The London *Sunday Times* of April 16th 1995, also reported that:

> *"The next computer you buy may be the last one you will need. In future, scientists want to insert electronic chips into our heads so we can plug directly into the information superhighway. British researchers are among international teams working on an implant to translate human thought into computer language. In a generation, one group says, people with a peppercorn-sized chip in the back of the neck will be able to talk to machines."*

Or, rather, the machines will be able to talk to *them*. People with satellite television are amazed to find that their individual decoder cards can be programmed from the TV headquarters. When you ring to subscribe to a 'scrambled' channel, the operator activates a beam which programmes your card and the picture appears while you are still on the phone! If they can do that to a card, they can do it to a microchip inside a human being. The Elite plan includes the microchipping of all babies at birth. It would take only a fraction of a second to do. The technology already exists and the only thing that remains is to persuade public opinion to accept it, or even demand it. One way this will be done is to highlight missing children stories, including the abduction of babies from maternity wards. While I have been writing this book, there have been such incidents in the United Kingdom and immediately the 'solution' offered was electronic tagging. This is a tiny step from an implanted microchip. The electronic tagging of criminals is also a stepping-stone to the microchip. With the mind control techniques I discussed in the last chapter, it is no problem to program a woman to go into a hospital and steal a baby to create the something-must-be-done scenario. She would have no recollection of her programming and she would believe it was her decision. A highly acclaimed electronics engineer in the United States was developing a microchip implant to help spinal injury patients when, he said, the project was hijacked by the one-world brigade. The story of Dr Carl W. Sanders was reported in the investigative magazine, *Nexus*, in the summer of 1994. He said that he attended 17 meetings of the One-Worlders in places like Brussels and Luxemburg. The meetings, he claimed, were "tying together the finances of the world". Dr Sanders said:

> *"I was at one meeting where it was discussed: 'How can you control a people if you can't identify them?' People like Henry Kissinger and CIA folk attended these meetings. It was discussed: 'How do you make people aware of the need for something like this chip?' All of a sudden the idea came: 'Let's make them aware of lost children, etc.'*

"This was discussed in meetings almost like people were cattle. The CIA came up with the idea of putting pictures of lost children on milk cartons. Since the chip is now accepted, you don't see the pictures anymore, do you? It's served its purpose." [10]

Dr Sanders said the manipulators want the chip to contain a name and a picture of the person's face, an international Social Security number, fingerprint identification, physical description, family and medical history, address, occupation, income tax information, and criminal record. Another selling point of this, no doubt, would be the end of passports. The chip recharges itself by turning the changes in body temperature into a dynamo system and the most effective places they have found for this are the forehead and the back of the wrist. The BBC 'science' programme, *Tomorrow's World*, revealed in September 1995, how in the UK, people are already being microchipped with their medical records. This stuff is happening NOW! The implications of allowing ourselves to be microchipped are far wider than I've even outlined. It also involves the suppression of the spiritual transformation now underway. The Sanders chip, he said, can be used to modify behaviour. During the Vietnam War, he told *Nexus*, they had a "Rambo Chip" which stimulated a greater flow of adrenaline. Timothy McVeigh, the man charged with the Oklahoma bombing, says he was microchipped while serving in the US Army. How many mind-controlled service and ex-service personnel are out there with microchips within them that can be activated at will? Dr Sanders pointed out that if you stop the output of the pituitary gland, you can stop the flow of oestrogen, cause instant menopause, and stop conception. The chip can be a form of mass birth control, another theme of the New World Order. Messages from the computer to the implanted chip can change mass behaviour, act as an emotional upper and downer, a sexual stimulant and depressant, and trigger violence at will. And the major stepping-stones to the microchipped human being are the microchipped identity card and the end of cash. *Don't let it happen.*

Supermarkets are now experimenting with barcoded cards which customers will use to keep a tally of their purchases and then pay for them when they leave, without the need for a checkout assistant. The big supermarket chains already have the facility for customers to pay by credit card in ways very similar to this. The next step is to say how much more convenient it would be if customers had a little microchip under the skin without the need to use a card. Give your freedom away. You know it makes sense. Look at the supermarket queues you will avoid! In February 1995, the now defunct London *Today* newspaper included a centre page article predicting that cash would be phased out by the end of this decade and replaced with electronic money. 'Trials' are underway in England, as

---

[10] *Nexus* magazine, (June/July 1994) p15.

they are across the world. The new European currency will almost certainly be electronic.

As I write this, there has been a story on the news that the new European currency will be delayed until the next century because of the time it will take to print all the money and mint the coins. I can hear the punch line now: "Oh we have found a way of speeding up the process – we'll have an electronic currency!" The British government has made the UK the first country to introduce compulsory DNA profiles of everyone charged with a criminal offence. The DNA makeup of a human being is a potentially catastrophic tool in the wrong hands because the underground science knows far more about these things than the public are told or even mainstream science knows. In the light of all these provable developments, it focuses the mind to reflect on the predictions in the Biblical Revelation:

> "*And he* [the beast or antichrist] *causes all, both small and great, rich and poor, free and slave, to receive a mark on their right hand or on their foreheads, and that no-one may buy or sell except one who has the mark or the name of the beast or the number of his name. Here is wisdom. Let him who has understanding calculate the number of the beast for it is the number of a man: His number is 666.*"
> **Revelation 13:16–18**

The Hopi native American people also have an ancient prophecy that no-one will be able to buy or sell without the mark of the bear. When this mark becomes visible, the prophecy says, the third Great War will come. If you look at the mark a bear makes when it sharpens its claws on a tree, there is a remarkable resemblance to the bar code of today. The New World Order is pushing ahead at this time faster than ever before to secure food control, energy control, business and credit control and the sum total of all these things and more: people control. That's what the manipulators mean when they speak of One World and the Global Village. A global fascist tyranny. A global plantation. The plan now is to divide and destabilise societies with terrorism and economic upheaval to dupe their collective minds into allowing what is left of basic freedoms to be destroyed. Japan is one obvious target of destabilisation, but all are in their sights unless we get wise to it. The idea is to stimulate fear in every heart. Nothing is too unspeakable to the Global Elite in pursuit of this. We can stop all of it and we *will* stop it, but only when people choose to stop being pawns and victims. The Global Elite are *not* all powerful. They exist and control only because the human mind has opted out of responsibility and allowed them to run the world. With everyone who regains control of their own mind, the task of the Elite gets harder and harder.

If people are shocked by what they have read here, then I'm glad. I saw a badge, made in America, which said: "The Truth will set you free – but first it will piss you off!" Reality often does shock and it's time for human beings to look reality in the face – and change it to a better one. The reality which has been exposed here is the reality the collective human mind has created. It's time to grow up. Human apathy and naïvety are the greatest weapons of the Elite. Opening ourselves spiritually and realising the full glory of Creation is wonderful. But if people float around in some spiritual mist, their feet dangling from the ceiling, they are copping out, in my view, and the complacency I see in so many areas of the spiritual movement is staggering in the light of events in the world.

I hear people who think that addressing or talking about something that is 'negative' must be avoided at all costs. It is disempowering, I hear. Knowledge is never disempowering. But ignoring it is. What is more negative and disempowering than being manipulated every day towards a global fascist dictatorship while having no idea that it is even happening? What is more negative than having thoughts planted into our minds which we believe to be our own? And what does negative energy do, if it is not addressed? It stays negative, or gets more so. Is that what the spiritual movement wants? Is that empowering? Or is it much easier to live in some semi-dream world where words like love and peace are scattered around like confetti while the Elite go on unchallenged because to expose their manipulation is considered too 'negative'?

It is easy to speak words, much harder to live them. And if we are going to change this world for the better, then words like love, peace, respect, and freedom need to be lived and not just parroted like some New Age speaking clock. As its foundation, any guide to freedom needs a thorough knowledge of why and how that freedom has been removed in the first place. Without that, there can be no answers. But answers there are if we have the courage and the vision to stop playing around and get on with it.

People of Planet Earth. It is wakey, wakey, time.

Part Two

The Freedom

I believe in... me

Our deepest fear is not that we are inadequate. Our deepest fear is that we are powerful beyond measure. It is our light, not our darkness, that most frightens us. We ask ourselves "who am I to be brilliant, gorgeous, talented, fabulous?" Actually, who are you not to be? You are a child of God. Your playing small doesn't serve the world. There's nothing enlightened about shrinking so that other people won't feel insecure around you. We are all meant to shine, as children do... we were born to make manifest the Glory of God that is within us.

And as we let our light shine, we unconsciously give other people permission to do the same. As we're liberated from our own fear, our presence automatically liberates others.

Attributed to Nelson Mandela.

Chapter 17

We are the Prison Warders

Freedom may seem so far from our grasp when you read of the global manipulation. In reality, it is but a thought away. That thought is our freedom. If we are going to remove the global dictatorship – and we are *are* – it will be done by changing the way we think and feel about ourselves. Who are the real Prison Warders who have systematically delinked us from our true and infinite potential?

We are.

You, me, all of us. I outlined some ideas in *The Robots' Rebellion* for the way we can organise and evolve our societies to ensure the freedom of thought and expression we seek. But they were only ideas, not rigid structures. Society, and how it is organised, reflects, like everything, human thought. If we feel fear, guilt, resentment, and hatred, and we desire for others to take over our responsibility, those thought patterns will create the dictatorship institutions of today. However, if we feel love, respect and forgiveness, for self and others, and we desire to retake control of our minds and responsibility, then society will express those thoughts. The answer to the ills I have described in this book is within us and how we think and feel about ourselves. Everything that happens in this physical world is the result of a thought or thoughts. If we change thought, we change the physical world. In this closing section of the book, I am going to address this process because it is the means through which we can, and will, create a better world. The inner revolution becomes the outer revolution. The Earth is a mirror of the human mind.

It is appropriate at this stage to recap on a major theme of the book: creating our own reality. Look at your world and your life and you are looking at what you think of yourself at the very core of your being. It is easier to look outside ourselves for someone else to blame for what is happening to us. But we attracted those experiences and so the answer lies within, not without. We are absorbing magnetic energy from the cosmos and higher levels of ourselves and broadcasting that energy out through the chakra/vortex system into the world, all the time. As that energy passes through us, it picks up our energy pattern. This precisely reflects our physical, emotional, mental, and spiritual state of being. Through this means, the subconscious creates a physical replica of itself before our eyes, in people, places and experiences which reflect its sense of self. At any moment in any day, we are casting around us a magnetic image of what we think of ourselves. It is this which creates our reality by magnetically attracting to us experiences which correspond with that pattern. If you think you will always be poor, that is the magnetic energy pattern you will cast around you. This will attract poverty to you on the basis of like attracts like. Look at yourself and most of the people you know. Observe for a while how many negative statements you and they make about the world and themselves. "I can't do this", "I could never do that." The common theme is: "I'm not good enough". As a result, we achieve little because that is what we expect to achieve.

This is understandable to an extent, because thanks to religion and the education/media system, we are deluged with messages telling us we are 'sinners' or 'unworthy' in some way. If you are a woman without a 'perfect' body, you are unworthy; if you are a little man with a bald head, you are unworthy; if you work in a factory, you are unworthy compared with the guy in the suit; if you were born out of wedlock, you are unworthy compared with those with 'official' parents. There is a never-ending list of images which, if we do not conform to some or all of them, we are considered, and consider ourselves, a failure or less worthy than someone else. All this is crap, but it is persuasive crap if people are told it often enough from childhood. This is, in fact, the most powerful and effective of the mind manipulations I have been exposing. If we can be made to feel unworthy, of little consequence, and only here to do as we are told by our 'betters', then that is the magnetic energy field we broadcast and that is the physical reality we create. In doing so, we are handing our minds and our world to those who broadcast a reality in which they have the right to control everything and everyone.

Years ago, as a journalist, I visited a hostel for women who had been attacked by their husbands or partners. I was amazed to find that a number of these women were on their second, third or even fourth partner who had been physically violent towards them. I am not amazed anymore, because I can see why this was so. The women were attracting that punishment to them by what they thought of themselves. I did not meet one woman in that hostel who had any self-esteem and when I chatted with them, that lack of self-esteem clearly went back long before the first man attacked them. This is not to dismiss what they suffered, nor to excuse what the men did to them. The men were also reflecting what they thought of themselves, because anyone who exhibits hatred and violence towards others is projecting outwardly a hatred of self. The victims are only mirrors for what the men think of themselves. The reason these two inner imbalances are attracted to each other is because the woman (who has such low self-esteem that she has an inner belief that she deserves to be punished), attracts the man (who wishes to punish others to avoid looking within). This is done through the attraction of two magnetic 'capes'. When one violent relationship breaks down, the woman simply attracts another until the cause (the lack of self-love) is removed. It's the same with the man. Love at first sight, dislike at first sight...all such reactions are the result of this process.

The family connection is important to emphasise here. Apart from the relative few who eventually break away from the mental and emotional domination of their parents, most people are massively influenced by the messages of childhood. Everyone is, to some extent, and these messages can be positive or, far too often, negative. Our overwhelming source of information in the first few crucial years of our physical lives is our parents. And what they tell us about the world is a reflection of what they think of themselves. They were the products of their own upbringing and what their parents thought of themselves. If our parents and grandparents were given negative images of themselves and their potential, they are likely to have passed this onto us. This is not done out of malice, merely misunderstanding. Our parents are the products of their upbringing, just as we are of ours. Each generation of victims creates, largely unknowingly, the next generation of victims. But we don't have to. The cycle can be broken and that is what we are here to do. We are here to take the baton of conditioning and limitation from our parents, break those patterns, and hand a baton of freedom onto our children.

As the mind control and the human divisions of class, job, sex, colour and creed, have grown, the childhood messages for the majority have been extremely negative. If you are a woman, you are led to believe that you are here to serve men and conform to your place in a man's world. A career of your own? What about your husband? In these circumstances, standing in a man's shadow becomes the woman's reality and that is the life she attracts and therefore creates. If we are born into a vast council housing estate amid poverty and unemployment, it is easy to see how through childhood and into adulthood we can be persuaded that life will always be like that. We can believe that there is no way out of this cycle. It becomes our reality. We don't expect to escape from our lot in life and so we don't, because we are attracting to us what we expect. We don't expect to have a say in what happens in the world and, again, that is what we create. It is the same with those who suffer from inhuman deprivation in parts of Africa, Asia, and Central and South America. Children born into those conditions naturally believe that this is what life must be like because they have known nothing else. They inherit, and then pass on, the mindset that the West is rich and they are poor and it will always be so. As a result they remain poor and exploited because that is the magnetic reality they attract. If you can create the mindset, you create the physical reality, and this is what the manipulators seek to do.

Now look at this from the Global Elite point of view. The children of the key families at the peak of the pyramid are brought up through childhood to believe that not only will they always be rich materially, they are also programmed to believe that they have a birthright and a genetic inheritance which ensures they will control the world and deserve to do so. That is what they believe and that becomes their magnetic reality. This energy pattern which they broadcast around them attracts the experiences and opportunities to manifest in their lives what is going on inside. They do indeed control a world made up largely of people broadcasting, and creating, the reality that they are unworthy and have no control over their lives. One reality dominates the other and it is not difficult to see why. Of course, the attitude of the Global Elite which says they are superior and have a right to control others is a reflection of deep imbalances within them, a lack of love and respect for self, manifesting outwards as a lack of love and respect for others. This will make them unfulfilled and unhappy people, always seeking happiness and a sense of fulfilment by yet more control and domination of others. But at the level of controlling the world, their day by day reality is very much that they are the controllers. Therefore they are. And each generation within the families of the Global Elite will program that into their offspring, so maintaining the reality through the decades. Whatever else is going on inside, someone who believes they are born to control will always dominate those who believe they are unworthy and need to look to others to tell them what to think and do. The 'master' and the 'slave' create each other.

There will be those who claim that all this cannot be true because while they are always saying they are confident of achieving this or winning that, they never do. That's because they don't really believe it. Far from describing what we feel inside, words are often used to hide what is happening within us. They are fronts, smokescreens, to our true self. Words only have real power when we believe what we say. This is why two people can make the same speech and one will get a standing ovation and the other polite applause. If we truly feel the words we speak, they project an energy of enormous power, for it is the combination of the words and our inner self in unison. If another person just reads the words competently and professionally without feeling them with all their being, that potential power will not be there. I can say I am a black woman. I find it easy to say that. But I don't believe it because I am not a black woman, I am a white man. Words are just words unless we believe them. It is not words that create our reality, it is what is going on inside of our multidimensional, magnetic, self.

When people verbally attack politicians or those in power of any kind, they believe they are proving that they won't be pushed around by authority. Often the opposite is the case. People may attack politicians as "useless" or bankers as "greedy parasites", but what happens when anything goes wrong? To whom do those same people look for answers and responsibility? Themselves? No. Politicians and bankers. What are "they" going to do about it, they ask. The words are just a façade, an illusion that people are taking control of their lives. The inner being is still giving its mind and life away to others and that continues to be the physical reality, no matter what the words may say.

The New World Order is the natural outcome of each generation handing over its responsibility and potential. The collective mind of the human race is the sum total of all human thought. Whatever dominates human thought will dominate the collective mind and this also creates a global magnetic reality. If the dominating thought patterns in the collective mind include a desire for someone else to take responsibility for our lives and do all the things we can't be bothered to do, then the magnetic pattern thus produced will create a collective, global, version of that – the network called the New World Order. It will attract together the imbalanced energy fields of the Global Elite to fulfil that reality. The Global Elite are the collective equivalent of a dominating husband who tells his wife everything she must do and think. That woman will have attracted that man and vice versa because of what is going on within both of them. So it is with the collective mind and the New World Order. It is our creation.

We are the Global manipulators because the people identified in this book are the global reflection, the mirror, of the way we manipulate each other. Look at how we all manipulate people by using fear and guilt to get our own way. We often do it without realising it because it has become so much a part of the human psyche. The Global Elite are simply doing the same on a global scale. Look at how people play two sides off against each other to bring about a desired result in a family or business. The Elite are only doing the same on a bigger stage. It is only the scale that is different. They represent the sum total of human behaviour on that vibration of control and domination which billions of people are using in their own lives day by day. So when we look at the Rothschilds, the Henry Kissingers, and the David Rockefellers who are provably manipulating the human race along a dark and deeply unpleasant road, in my view, they are only the reflection of what is happening in the collective human mind. When we love, respect, and forgive ourselves and each other, and when we desire to take responsibility for our own lives, that will be the reality we will create around us and, together, we will create globally. The New World Order of centralised dictatorship will not be able to exist in such circumstances because it will not be the collective desire and, therefore, the collective reality. We will have thought it out of existence. There is no such thing as a "natural order". What we call the "natural order" is merely the physical expression of the dominating thought patterns in any society or on a particular frequency. When the thought patterns change, so does the "natural order".

There are many thought patterns that form together to create our inner sense of self and our outer physical reality. It's not only the way we think now. It includes all the thought patterns, the inner resentments, hurts, fears, and guilts, we have held on to from earlier in our lives and in previous physical lives, sometimes going back aeons. If your life today does not reflect the way you are consciously thinking, it can be that way for a number of reasons. One is that you are holding on to patterns from the past which you may not even be aware of. How can you tell what they are? Look at your life. It reflects what is going on inside. What is it about your attitude to yourself that is attracting your present experience? It is only by our subconscious creating an outer, physical, reflection of itself that we can identify what we are carrying deep within our psyche. Many people, at this time of the Great Transformation of the Earth and the human race, are going through highly negative experiences, mostly affecting the emotional level where so much of this psychological baggage from the past is accumulated. Although it may not seem so at the time (as I know from my own experiences), this process is actually very positive. It is giving us the opportunity to face our inner self and let go of the pain and weight of the past. We don't live in and enjoy the *now* because our 'now' is dominated by the baggage of the past and the worry of the future.

Two other forces that help to create our present experience by affecting our inner pattern are our desire to serve the Earth and the human race, and, connected with that, the astrological vibrations we are feeling day by day. When we come with a specific task to make a contribution to improving life on Earth, and there are countless millions, potentially billions, of such people on the planet at this time, we carry preprogrammed patterns which will help us to do the job. Sometimes such people will not be doing what they consciously want to do, but they will be following a pattern from their higher consciousness which will attract to them the experiences necessary to carry out their chosen task in this incarnation. Astrological factors will be part of this, as they are for all people. The planets are like transmitters broadcasting a distinct vibration. Depending where they are on their orbits in relation to the Earth, different planetary vibrations, or combinations of them, are more powerful at different times in their effect on this planet. A good astrologer identifies these combinations and outlines their likely effect. Things don't *have* to happen in response to these astrological changes because we have freewill, but they are more *likely* to happen.

At birth we absorb the energy pattern in the atmosphere of our birthplace. This will reflect the positions of the planets at that moment. So, as the planets continue to travel the heavens during our physical lifetime, we will be affected by them in a rather different way from someone born at another time and place because our inner 'birth pattern' will be different. Again a good astrologer – and the ability varies enormously as with every other profession – will be able to predict likely effects on people if they know their exact time of birth and where they were born. They will also be able to make a reasonable assessment of what we have chosen to achieve in this life by assessing the energies we absorbed at birth. When and where we are born is rarely random. The movement of the planets and changing Earth vibrations they trigger are affecting us every second, and I believe it will be shown as the transformation proceeds that our DNA is synchronised with the planets.

There are many factors which go into the make-up of our inner energy pattern and therefore the physical reality it creates. But one thing above all will lead us to a positive, joyous, freedom more effectively than anything else. That is to love, forgive, and respect ourselves. The first step to that is to deprogramme our minds from the manipulated messages of the Global Elite and allow ourselves to be, think, and feel, what we really are. The real us, not the robot version.

DEPROGRAMMING THE MIND

An ever-increasing number of people are deprogramming themselves from a lifetime of subtle and less than subtle mental dictatorship. The minute-by-minute messages from the media, religion, and the 'education' system, together with the inherited 'values' we absorb without question, have been designed to create a concrete prison of dogma in our consciousness. I refer to religion and the other empires of manipulation as psychological fascism. It turns our mind into a rigid enemy, when it should be our flexible friend.

Letting go of dogma is the key. It doesn't matter what form your dogma may take; there will be an opposing dogma to challenge yours. As these are brought into conflict, a divide-and-rule scenario follows. This is why religions and political parties were created. To the Global Elite, and therefore the Prison Warder consciousness, the so called 'far Left' is just as important as the 'far Right'. The dogmatic Christians are just as important as the dogmatic Muslims or Hindus. The unions are just as vital as the 'bosses'. You need two to tango and two to fight. Creating extremes and playing them off against each other has been one of the most effective weapons in the Prison Warder control of this physical world. Tyranny takes many forms, most of them not obvious. More than that, most people who behave in dictatorial, authoritarian ways, don't even realise they are doing so. They are so sure that they are right, they don't stop to observe that they are imposing their beliefs on someone else and using the banner of 'freedom' to do it. Mental dictators don't all look like Adolf Hitler or Josef Stalin. They can also stand in picket lines, go on freedom marches, or sit around a candle in Glastonbury.

We desperately need the re-emergence of female energy on the planet, but not to the extent that we replace one dogma with another. When it was suggested that I be interviewed on the BBC radio programme, *Woman's Hour*, the programme researcher asked what a man could possibly tell women about female energy. This lady opposed, quite rightly, male chauvinism, but then expressed female chauvinism, another dogma which operates on exactly the same thought pattern as the one she was opposing! Some homosexuals who, again rightly, demand an end to their oppression and victimisation, campaign for their beliefs in ways that oppress and victimise others, often other homosexuals. They will, collectively, stop attracting discrimination when they stop giving it out. A British MP demanded that violent criminals be thrashed on live television after the National Lottery draw. What effect would this have, did she say? Less violence in society! And in the United States, perhaps the sickest and most violent society in the world, the death penalty is being extended to more states. Why? To deter violence and murder. They are killing people with electric chairs and firing squads because, presumably, they say life is sacred and anyone who takes life should be murdered. The mental gymnastics required for this beggars belief. All these examples are the same thought patterns promoted as opposites. They are dogmas, prisons of the mind. What we believe is right for us we surely need to believe is also right for everyone. If we don't, we are not serious about freedom for all, only freedom for ourselves and our own dogma.

The difference between dictatorship and freedom is allowing all information into the public arena and respecting another's right to make of it what feels good to them. Disagreement and harmony are not contradictions if respect for another view is there. When I challenge people and organisations in this book, it is not because of what they believe. They can believe what they like, that is their choice. I challenge them because from my perspective they seek to impose those views and to suppress others. They can believe to their hearts' content that a world government and a microchipped population is a great idea. It is when they impose those things on others that a challenge becomes legitimate and necessary. We need to keep in focus what we mean when we talk of freedom. If we don't do that, we might, unknowingly, be acting in ways that stop ourselves and others being truly free. I will highlight here three groups who campaign for freedom in various ways and it's interesting to see how the old thinking and dogmas can be promoted as the new. If we don't see the difference, then we remain programmed, manipulated, and freedom will be beyond our grasp.

THE ROBOT RADICALS

This is the name I give to those locked into the thought pattern considered to be on the 'Left' or 'radical' wings of the Elite-created Left/Right spectrum of alleged political 'opposites'. This thought pattern has its whole view of life controlled by where it considers itself and others to be on that mythical Left/Right scale. You are either Left or Right. There is no 'in-between' to a Robot Radical, precisely as the manipulators intended. It all appears so simple. Left is good and Right is bad and you must be one or the other. It is a thought pattern which speaks of freedom, but actually believes in anything but. It is another form of inflexible, mental dictatorship decked out as freedom – the freedom to pursue and impose its own dogma. The Robot Radicals are a manipulator's dream. Smash the Tories and all will be well. Summon the revolution of the people against the fascist state. That's what they said in France during their revolution. That's what they said in Russia during theirs. Millions were slaughtered in the name of 'people power' and one tyranny was replaced by another. Those on the Robot Radical vibration do not appreciate that the same force that controls their 'opposition' also controls them. They are the foot soldiers and propagandists for the Elite and the overwhelming majority have no idea that this is so. Any suggestion of a global clique manipulating Left and Right is such an attack on their simple good-guys-bad-guys/freedom-fascist view that they find it easier to ignore or condemn the messenger than to open their minds to the evidence.

The nature of this mindset was brought home to me when *The Robots' Rebellion* was published in the UK in 1994. It contains a wealth of information about the background to the ills that the Robot Radicals say they oppose. I do not claim that every last word and detail is accurate, because we are dealing with the history of a secret strategy, after all, but it makes (I and many, many, others believe) a significant contribution to the debate. Was it accepted as such by the Robot Radicals? Not quite. My use of extracts from the *Protocols Of The Elders Of Zion* was too much for political purity to take. It didn't matter that I had emphasised, as I do in this book, that this is not a plot by Jewish people; it didn't matter that I renamed them the *Illuminati Protocols* for the specific reason of getting away from their association with Jewish people; it didn't matter that these *Protocols*, which came to light in the late 1800s, contain details of the very plan of manipulation which has provably unfolded through the twentieth century. It doesn't matter because the Nazis used the *Protocols* against Jews after Hitler was given a copy by a man of Jewish extraction, Alfred Rosenberg, and so anyone else who mentions them must be condemned. How the Elite must laugh with glee. A Robot Radical refuses to be selective or discerning and divide the two issues of who was *blamed* for the *Protocols* from what they actually *say*. What they are missing is a flexibility of mind and yet it could be theirs now, this second, if they summoned the courage to make that choice.

For some years in the 1980s, I was a national speaker for the British Green Party. I was attracted by their desire to protect the planet and their alleged support for freedom of information. When a Green Party group in Salford, Manchester, asked me to speak about my book at the Green Party national conference in the Autumn of 1994, I was banned by the party hierarchy for, in effect, inciting racial hatred. The campaign was whipped up by two Robot Radicals called Derek Wall and David Black, the author of a charming little article about me headed "Son of God or Son of the Devil?" They were supported by others in the Green Party's Robot Radical clique, like Penny Kemp. I have a letter from the conference organiser which says that of the members of the committee who issued the ban only *two* had read the book and both went into the meeting determined to say it was not racist. They ended up being persuaded to vote for a ban by those who had not read it! And the membership which is so 'anti-hierarchy' allowed its own hierarchy to deny their right to hear me speak.

There are many genuinely open-minded people in the Green Party groups around the UK, but at the collective level, it is just another strand in the Elite web of mind control and self-deception. The sad thing is, they don't realise it. I had intended to use the opportunity at the conference to talk about the underlying manipulation which is creating the problems the Green Party was set up to address, and the way that pollution-free energy sources are being suppressed which supercede anything the Green Movement has been promoting. The membership did not get the opportunity to hear this, however. The hierarchy in this 'anti-hierarchy' party had decided what they should and should not hear. Much better to do that than to have a black-and-white belief system challenged. It has become another Robot Radical party, at the hierarchy level, which talks of freedom, but refuses to live it.

You see this attitude constantly expressed in the various forms of Robot Radicalism, represented in the UK by newspapers like *The Guardian*, *The New Statesman*, and *The Socialist Worker*. So it is with other 'radical' parties and organisations who see freedom as having the right for their beliefs to take over the centres of control from those they disagree with. One form of imposition replacing another. And each new generation is enticed into the web and locked into this Robot Radical thought wave which not only makes life easy for the manipulating elite, it also imprisons the new recruits in a barely-one-dimensional view which shuts out their higher consciousness. It is just another mental prison.

It is a reflection of the thought patterns of the Global Elite. The Elite manipulate minds by emphasising some information and suppressing or ignoring the rest. So do the Robot Radicals. They claim to be anti-racist, but, in reality, they are only against non-politically-correct racism. If you claim to be against racism, it must mean all racism, surely. To see any race as inferior is not only deeply unpleasant, it is downright silly from the view of life that I hold. Our minds, our consciousness, incarnates into endless physical bodies and life situations, white, black, yellow, Jewish, Arab, all of them. To judge someone by their genetic spacesuit − body − is the ultimate misunderstanding, I feel. But the Robot Radicals posture their political purity (or knowingly work for the manipulators) by attacking as racists those who are legitimately investigating the global conspiracy, while they ignore completely the blatant examples of Jewish racism.

The child-like mind of the Robot Radical cannot challenge Jewish racism because the Nazis they so despise are anti-Jewish, and so they must not say a word against Jewish racism because they might be seen to be supporting the Nazis. Showing themselves to be against *all* racism is far less important to a Robot Radical than playing their silly political games on a black and white chessboard. So while New World Order researchers are condemned as racists because they name some people who happen to be Jewish (and far more who are not), nothing is said by the Robot Radicals about the *Talmud*, the Jewish Book of Law, which is among the most appallingly racist documents on the planet. There is silence, too, about rabbis who say they would never drink wine that had not been bottled by a Jew. Yet there would be vehement condemnation of someone who said they would never drink wine that *had* been bottled by a Jew. The stench of hypocrisy fills the air.

In the same way, there is silence from the Robot Radicals when people like the Frenchman, Jean Briere, are fined or jailed for expressing an opinion. Briere, a former spokesman for the French Green Party, was given a three-month suspended prison sentence and fined £1,800 for "anti-Semitic and anti-Israeli remarks". He had said the Jewish lobby had influenced the US to start the Gulf War and he described Israel as "racist, militaristic, theocratic, and expansionist". The Robot Radicals would have been united in their condemnation of Briere and yet had he spoken those words about America and Americans, those same Robot Radicals would have burst into spontaneous applause.

What is the difference between the anti-Jewish laws in Nazi Germany and laws under which you can be fined and imprisoned for saying what Briere said? What is the difference between the controlled anti-Jewish media under Hitler and the way the Japanese magazine, *Marco Polo*, was closed down by its parent company in 1995 because of a campaign by the global Jewish hierarchy to stop its advertising revenue after it published an article questioning some of the official stories of the Nazi concentration camps? Both come under the heading of authoritarianism, but don't ask a Robot Radical to see that. Their dogma could not cope with it. These apparent 'opposites' like Right and Left, fascists and Robot Radicals, are actually operating on the same thought patterns. They just use different words to describe the same thing: imposing their dogma on everyone else while seeking to deny a platform to views and information they disagree with.

When I spoke in Glastonbury, Somerset, in 1995, a Robot Radical from the local Green Party handed out leaflets and went to the media condemning me and *The Robots' Rebellion* for spreading racial hatred. This campaigner for freedom, a David Taylor, wanted to ensure that I would not have the opportunity to speak in Glastonbury again, so denying the people the right to make up their own minds. He listed a series of staggering misrepresentations and untruths on his leaflet in support of his case. This did not surprise me when I realised that Mr Taylor, despite his campaign and condemnation, had not actually read the book! I kid you not. When asked about the manipulation of the Freemasons, he replied that they were an organisation that did a lot for charity, and when faced with the information about the way Roosevelt had provably manipulated America into an already manipulated Second World War, he said that unless the Americans had come into the war, Hitler would have won. Mr Taylor was speaking and acting for a collective mindset that grips the consciousness of hundreds of millions of Robot Radicals all over the world. No wonder the Global Elite have had such a free ride thus far.

The Robot Radical mindset is a telling mixture of naïvety and arrogance and that is one heck of a combination! How ironic that the people who have done most to attack me for trying to make suppressed information available are those who claim in their angelic, politically-correct, lily-white sense of their own purity, that they stand for freedom from tyranny. The Robot

Radicals *are* a tyranny and they are just too full of their own political perfection to realise it. And on the other 'extreme' you have the Robot Right, the same tyrannical thought pattern as the Robot Radicals, but wearing a different uniform. The Robot Radicals are convinced of their moral purity and the Robot Right are convinced of their genetic purity. But they are the same thought pattern disguised as opposites.

Nothing has illustrated the arrogance and naïvety of the Robot Radical mindset in my recent experience, more than two people called Matthew Kalman and John Murray. They publish a magazine in Britain called *Open Eye*. This is some irony because I have rarely come across eyes and minds that were more obviously slammed shut. They claim to be interested in exposing manipulation and corruption and yet appear to take every opportunity to attack and undermine those who are successful in raising these issues in the main public arena. It was they who have led people to believe that I am a Nazi or Nazi sympathiser and anti-Jewish. They wrote two grubby articles, one of which was published in the Robot Radical weekly, *The New Statesman*, under the heading "New Age Nazism". The fact that I am neither 'New Age' or a 'Nazi' is brilliantly symbolic of the standard of their research. Apparently, anyone who has an open mind about history and the official line is, by definition, a potential Nazi to Kalman and Murray. They also admit contributing 'information' about me to *The Guardian* and for an outrageous article by 'journalist', Mark Honigsbaum, in the London *Evening Standard*, entitled "The Dark Side of David Icke". At no time before these articles were written did either Kalman or Murray even take the trouble to talk to me. Kalman is also editor of a Jewish 'alternative' magazine called *New Moon*, the November 1995 front cover of which portrayed me as Adolf Hitler. Inside was a Kalman and Murray 'review' of this book in which they claimed I was saying it is all a plot by Jewish people to take over the world. You've read the book and you can see the opposite is true. So why are they saying this? Virtually every article attacking me in this way was written by Kalman and Murray or had the 'information' supplied by them. Either this duo are just being incredibly immature and silly (a strong probability) or they have another agenda. In my view, whatever their motivation, they have revealed magnificently how the best defence the Elite have against exposure is the Robot Radical mentality.

If people were in control of their own minds, the nonsense communicated by Kalman and Murray would be of no consequence. Unfortunately the Robot Radical mind can't wait to give itself away. Most depressing was the number of people who believed the laughable 'research' behind these articles. Some began to hand out protest leaflets at my meetings. Many were from the Anti-Nazi League. The leaflets were equally, often staggeringly, inaccurate. Most of the people doing it had not read my books or heard me speak. They were reacting to what they read in the media, almost all of which was inspired by our friends Kalman and Murray! Some invitations for

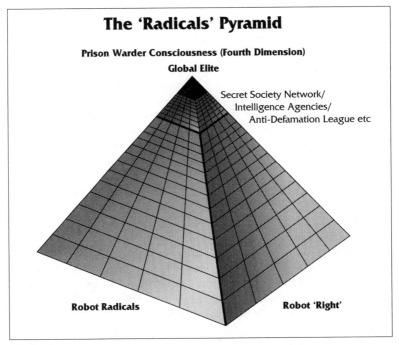

The 'Radicals' Pyramid

Prison Warder Consciousness (Fourth Dimension)
Global Elite

Secret Society Network/
Intelligence Agencies/
Anti-Defamation League etc

Robot Radicals   **Robot 'Right'**

Figure 16

me to speak were also withdrawn on the strength of the same information. The manipulators must be laughing themselves to death. Others behind the efforts to dub me a Nazi are, I am told by a good source, connected to the Raëlian Foundation of which I wrote earlier.

What the Robot Radicals can't see, and don't want to see, is that the Global Elite fund Jewish groups and anti-Jewish groups; communist groups and anti-communist groups; the far Left and the far Right. The Elite have no need to bring these 'opponents' into conflict because they are so imbalanced within their being that they find each other like heat-seeking missiles and attempt to destroy each other without any help from anyone. Whenever a person stands up to make suppressed information public, the Elite network uses both wings in the discrediting campaign. It uses its Robot Right organisations to come out in support of the writer or speaker and then activates its Robot Radical organisations to attack the person for being a tool of the far Right. That is precisely what has been tried with me, and most of the people involved will not realise how they are being manipulated.

If you really want to discredit someone, you arrange for anti-Jewish or anti-whatever events such as the smashing of graves, assaults on people, even a terrorist bomb in the extreme. You then point the finger at your target person or group. You say they are either directly responsible or 'incited' the actions by what they are writing and saying. Adolf Hitler used this very technique when the Nazis burned down the German Parliament building, the Reichstag, in 1933 and blamed it on the communists. This method has an added bonus for a manipulator – it creates fear in their own community or group, thus making them easier to control. I am not saying that there are no genuine attacks on Jewish and other groups by desperately unbalanced and misguided people, but to say that *all* of them are genuine is equally naïve. The combination of naïvety and arrogance will ensure that most of the members of both 'Left' and 'Right' don't realise that they are being used by the same force (*Figure 16, on previous page*). I would recommend that both the Robot Radicals and the Robot Right repeat over and over those words of John F. Kennedy. Whether he really meant them or not is by the by. The words themselves are brilliant:

> *"We seek a free flow of information...a nation that is afraid to let the people judge the truth and falsehood in an open market is a nation afraid of its people."*

That is what we have in this world today. Self-interest groups afraid of the people, and the Robot Radicals and the Robot Right are the same as all the rest.

NEW AGE – OR THE OLD AGE REVISITED?

The inflexibility of thought I am addressing here can be found in all areas of 'alternative' thinking and lifestyles, including that which is known as the New Age. Significant parts of the New Age are, I believe, becoming little more than another religion which believes in reincarnation and it is seeking to impose its gathering dogma on others. I have been fascinated to experience how those who speak of freedom of thought and expression really mean freedom of thought and expression which agrees with their own. This is what the old thinking does, as revealed by the Robot Radicals, and yet here the old thinking is packaged as new thinking for a New Age. I feel we have to be careful about this because much of this 'new thinking' appears to me to be like an old car resprayed. On the outside it looks new and fresh, but it is the same old vehicle underneath and the rust is starting to show.

One of the foundations of the New Age thinking is to urge people to ignore what the world may tell them they should think and to follow what their heart and intuition tells them. I could not agree more. But what do I see happening? I see people being told by elements within the New Age what they should think and do. This is not done as a suggestion, it is almost an order. Failing to accept this 'advice' is seen as confirmation that you have gone "off your path". For "off your path" read "the path that someone else thinks you should be on". Are such people not seeking to impose their intuition and their belief system on others instead of respecting another's right to follow their heart and instincts in the way they demand to be allowed to follow their own? I thought this was something the New Age was supposed to be challenging, not perpetuating. I see censorship in the New Age to keep out what would question the gathering and solidifying dogma at its core, and if people now awakening to a new reality are sucked into this, they could be swapping one form of thought control for another. What is right for one is not right for everyone and once you begin to impose dogmas, it's the Old Age revisited.

If you look at any organisation or movement, it invariably follows the same pattern. First it emerges to question the status quo of the time with another set of beliefs. Then, instead of evolving in the light of new information and experience, it solidifies and turns those original beliefs into a dogma which becomes the status quo of the next generations. This dogma is defended with the same unyielding vehemence as the old dogma displayed in the past. Anyone who continues to seek and move on in their thinking and perceptions, is condemned as "extreme", "loony" and not to be taken seriously – the same response of the old dogma when it was defending itself. At this point, such a movement or organisation ceases to be a vehicle for positive change and becomes a block on that change. The Green Movement has been through this process. It is now a block on further understanding because it refuses to encompass areas of spiritual and scientific thought which question its original thinking. The New Age Movement moved beyond the Green hierarchy by encompassing the multidimensional view of people and planet. But it, too, is now solidifying. It is fast becoming, in significant areas, what the Green Movement has become: a form of suppression, dogma, and diversion, not freedom. The New Age says we are all equal and yet creates the same hierarchical divisions of us and them, teachers and pupils, gurus and followers, that the Old Age has done.

One mindset which has swept the New Age is the idea that some "Ashtar Command"[1] is going to send down spaceships to take off the chosen few. Maybe it's just me, but that sounds remarkably like a cop-out and another version of the theme of ages – the messiah coming to save the good guys and good gals. All this can do – and does – is to create another form of dependency, another rigid belief system, when surely the transformation of humanity is about triggering everyone's potential to be whatever they wish to be. I have learned of an Elite project called Operation Bluebeam which is sending out thought waves on the wavelengths that channellers use. These messages are designed to mislead and divert people by purporting to come from extraterrestrials and other dimensions. Two of the inventions of Operation Bluebeam, according to an excellent source, are the "Ashtar Command" and the "Ascension" information. But make up your own mind.

Workshops, meetings, and such like are great if they are designed to set free, to allow people to remember who they are and what they can do. But if

---

[1] The "Ashtar Command" information sounds really doubtful to me. I get seriously negative "vibes" whenever I hear the name. Still, as with Sai Baba, each to their own.

they are structured as the 'Enlightened One' teaching the less enlightened, it is another means of giving the mind away. I see people promoted as "Britain's leading healer" or "Britain's leading psychic" or even "Maitreya, the Christ and World Teacher, a hero, a titan in men's midst". What is going on here? We are all healers and all psychic. Who on Earth can say that one is better than the rest and why do we feel the need to claim that anyway? We are all each other, all part of the same whole, all with the potential of tapping into the healing force and passing it on to others. I believe we should be working together, not claiming superiority. But parts of the New Age are showing every sign of being the Old Age under another flag.

The New Age has made a positive contribution and in many areas it is positive in its intent and achievements today. The world is a more enlightened place with the New Age movement than without it. The same with the Green movement to an extent. But if we allow ourselves to be sucked into their dogma, we will be held back from further discovery. No-one knows it all, or even nearly so. Therefore there is always more to know. Getting caught up in rigid perceptions will keep us from that never-ending flow of knowledge that is ours for the taking if, and only if, we keep our minds and hearts free from dogma.

CHRISTIAN PATRIOTISM

The phenomena of the same thought patterns dressed up in different ways is true of many areas of global conspiracy investigation. This consists of a vast array of different people and backgrounds, and I am not generalising about everyone. But I find here, too, the dogma and the illusion of freedom. The question I always ask when someone is proposing "freedom" is "Freedom to do what?" If you look at many of the conspiracy investigators and organisations, particularly in the United States, you often find that they are not talking about freedom, at all. In the USA, the loudest voice challenging the New World Order is that of Christian Patriotism. This thought pattern believes that the problems in America and the world result from the decline of Christianity and the answer is to restore the United States as a patriotic Christian nation. That'll fix it. Is this the same patriotic Christian nation that destroyed without mercy the Native American civilisations which had lived on that continent for thousands of years? Is this the same nation that forced children generation after generation to be taught someone else's beliefs and to be condemned if they didn't accept them? It surely is. Those two dogmas of Christianity and Patriotism are, irony of ironies, two of the rigid mindsets which have been used continually over the centuries to bring about the very New World Order the Christian Patriot now so opposes. They have been used because they are views of life with no shades of grey and whenever such thinking appears, manipulation is never far away. A child could do it.

I hear and read the views of some of those who are seeking to expose the New World Order and I am glad that they are speaking out. But when I see where they are coming from with their alternative society, I sometimes cringe in horror. I wrote to one guy in America congratulating him on his efforts to expose the conspiracy, but when he sent me material about his organisation and its views, I was appalled. I was looking at tyranny spelled out as freedom. If all we are doing is seeking to replace the control and imposition of the Global Elite with the control and imposition of Christian Patriotism, or some other dogma, we are wasting our time. There is a difference between having smaller units of government with control in the hands of people and communities and the chest-out-chin-up-fight-for-your-country-flag-in-hand-god-on-our-side patriotism that has been used by the Elite to play country against country century after century. So again, if we fall into the dogma trap, we can jump out of the pan and into the fire. We need to be selective in what we accept because no-one has all the answers.

This process of personal selection is not something that is encouraged, nor often even understood. The Robot Radical thought pattern, for instance, believes that if you take a piece of information from a person or group you must, by definition, agree with *everything* that person or group stands for or says. Because I take information from sources like *The Spotlight* newspaper in the USA, I must therefore agree, according to the Robot Radicals, with *everything* that newspaper believes. I don't. There is an enormous amount about its outlook on life that is not only different, but opposite to mine. It is a bastion of Christian Patriotism, for a start. But it does some excellent research and has a long and proven record of accuracy. I am not going to ignore that research because I don't agree with everything the paper stands for. I am searching for truth, not someone else's version of political correctness.

Because I quote from research by the Lyndon LaRouche organisation, the *Executive Intelligence Review*, I must, by definition in the Robot Radical mind, agree with *everything* they say and do. I don't. Nothing like. But the Robot Radical looks on in bewilderment at that. If you only look at information that comes from people who share your own view of life, you deny yourself unimaginable amounts of information from other sources. This is what the Robot Radicals do, which is why they are so naïve and limited in their appreciation of what is happening in the world. They are not interested in whether information is true, only the source from which it came. If the source is not politically correct in their childish minds, the information is condemned and dismissed without a second thought.

One of the most compelling aspects of conspiracy research is the way that thousands of people who would agree on almost nothing else, agree on the basic foundations of the manipulation, names, organisations, events. There are people investigating the conspiracy with whom I have virtually nothing in common in terms of our views on life. But if they come up with information which cross checks with what others are coming up with, then I will use it.

In Britain, Colonel Barry Turner has provided some excellent background for me from time to time. I don't share his views on some things, nor he mine, but we do share a passionate desire to expose the global tyranny. Therefore there is mutual exchange of information and support towards that end. It's called being adults. I have spent years challenging the policies of British Conservative MPs like Teddy Taylor and Theresa Gorman, but that doesn't mean that I am not going to support them in their contention that the United Kingdom has gone too far in handing sovereignty to a centralised European cartel. The very idea of supporting a Conservative MP on anything would give a coronary to a red or green Robot Radical. Yet it is this very selectivity and lack of dogma that frees us from the programming quicker than anything else and sets us on the road to mental, emotional, and physical freedom. Being selective and following our own intuition is the only way to avoid that. Opening our minds doesn't require us to accept everything we hear. It requires us to look at all views and information and to take from them what feels right to us and not just to someone else.

One final point about the conspiracy research scene which relates very much to the theme of the same thought patterns manifesting in different guises. There is an I-know-it-all arrogance in some areas of conspiracy 'research'. Apparently, a conspiracy researcher has been telling people that I stopped going to his shop because I realised he knew more than I did. I know nothing of the man or his shop, but his invented story reveals much about the mentality of some involved in this area. Why aren't we sharing information and supporting each other instead of claiming superiority? Conspiracy research is becoming another 'club' with its hierarchy and 'gurus'. Such rigidity makes it child's play to manipulate and infiltrate. Once we think we know it all, we are revealing how little we know. This book runs to 500 pages and yet it only scratches the surface of what is happening.

So What is Freedom?

Those three versions of 'freedom', the Robot Radicals, elements of the New Age and Christian Patriotism, are not to my eyes, freedom at all. They are different ways of saying: "I know best". Freedom, for me, is the right of everyone to follow the path they feel is correct for them and to respect another's right to choose a different path. The only time their behaviour deserves to be challenged is when they seek to impose their views on others. This requires a switch in our attitudes. It means allowing people to believe things that we don't agree with and to support their right to speak of those views openly without suppression. We need to start trusting ourselves. If a person says something we find distasteful, and we are correct in that response, the people in general will reject what is being put to them. Better it is out in the open, anyway. When all information and views are allowed access to the public stage, people can make a genuine choice of what they wish to believe. We have a fusion of knowledge and not an exclusion of knowledge.

Centuries of the latter have led to the imbalanced understandings of the human race because we have been subjected to imbalanced, one-sided, information. Truth does not come in neatly packaged parcels with names like socialism, fascism, Christianity, or New Age. We need to search for it by looking at all information and following our hearts. Yet one-way freedom is what I so often see. It is one-way freedom when Christian or Muslim fundamentalists try to stop meetings of those who disagree with their view of life and when prison and death sentences are issued on people for believing something different. I don't agree, as you may have noticed, with the Robot Radicals, but they have every right to speak their views. If freedom means anything, it means freedom for all.

This is crucial to the process of personal deprogramming. We cannot be free until in our minds and our hearts we allow others to be free. The idea that we are mentally and spiritually free because we are following what we believe to be right is an illusion. We are only truly free when we are as determined that others should be able to do the same. The suppression of one human being or animal is the suppression of all of us. When we have no desire to impose our views on others and when we celebrate diversity of thought and lifestyle that have been freely chosen, then we can begin to say that the programming of this world and the Elite machine is breaking up and falling away within us. But not until.

GETTING STREETWISE

When people begin to soften their inflexible thoughts and responses, the influence the daily programming has upon them is diffused also. They begin to see the subtleties of mind manipulation in a way a rigid mind cannot. This mental switch is open to everyone, no matter how unyielding their minds might be now. It can happen in an instant, once you decide you want it to happen. Scanning the information and the views available to us and picking out those aspects which we each feel good about involves taking pieces from everywhere and fitting them together to form our own evolving truth. When we are asked to put a label on what we think and believe in these circumstances, we cannot answer. We are not 'Left', nor 'Right', nor 'Centre'. We are not a 'religion'. We just are. There are no instant labels for that. There are no labels at all. We refuse to be pigeon-holed because we are constantly seeking and evolving. If people can name an "ism" of any kind to describe what they believe, they are in some form of mental prison. The difference it makes when you let go of the labels and the off-the-peg opinions and views promoted by the "isms" is beyond words. You see the world so much more clearly. The smokescreens begin to disperse. An open mind is not a naïve one. Quite the opposite. Deprogramming demands that we are constantly selective in what we accept minute by minute through the media and other sources. For example, if people are opposing something it would seem obvious that they are against it. But is this always the case?

If you want to do something controversial, it is much easier if you also control the 'opposition' to what you are doing. You can ensure that while people have the illusion of democratic opposition and the right to protest, those leading the main opposition group or groups will lead their followers to ultimate, if 'glorious', failure. Everyone goes away thinking they all did their best and could do no more, when the whole thing was being controlled as an exercise in 'democracy' which was designed to fail in its goal of stopping whatever policy is involved. The sheep mentality is so ingrained in the human race that it takes very few to infiltrate, direct, and control. Look at how one of the key officials of the Nation of Islam was working for the FBI in the period of Malcolm X and the black civil rights movement in the 1960s. That story could be repeated a million times and more in 'radical' organisations all over the world. Some of the protest groups use violence. The Animal Liberation Front and Class War in Britain are two of them. When Class War, which claims to be 'anti-state', trigger violent clashes with the police during peaceful protest marches, who benefits? Those in authority who want to dismiss the peaceful opponents to their policies as "violent extremists" and those who wish to introduce more authoritarian laws to meet the challenge from the growth in (manufactured) "violent extremists". Put it this way. If Class War was an arm of British Intelligence, they could not do a better job of undermining the vast majority of people who wish to protest peacefully. When thousands of people gather to protest peacefully against the treatment of animals and a few idiots become violent or plant bombs, who benefits? Those in authority who wish to continue to treat animals with great cruelty while dismissing the protesters as "violent extremists". An open mind can see this, a rigid mind cannot.

FEELING AND HEALING

Even more important than thinking for ourselves is to *feel* for ourselves. In the centre of the chest we have a feeling centre called the heart chakra or heart vortex. It is from here that we express love in the fullest sense. It is from here also, and the solar plexus chakra, that we instinctively feel if something is right for us. It doesn't need words or explanations, it just feels right. This is our intuition speaking to us and our intuition is our connection to our higher consciousness. When I am faced with a choice between what my mind or my intuition is telling me, I go with the intuition every time these days. I often can't explain why I go to a certain place or embark on an area of exploration and research. It simply feels right to do so. The mind, even an open one, can be influenced by the daily programming to some extent and it can go through lists of reasons why what our intuition is suggesting is not a good idea. "What will my friends think? What about this or that consequence? Don't do it, you fool!" The feeling centre is not subject to those pressures because it is connected to a level of consciousness and knowledge that is beyond the manipulations of this physical world. As the spiritual renaissance proceeds, the feeling centre is being powerfully reactivated among those who are awakening, and intuition is going to be the guide of the future. It will not always lead us to where our rational mind wants to be, but it will always lead us to where we *need* to be for our own and the planet's evolution. If I had followed my rational mind since 1990, I would still be sitting in television studios presenting sports programmes. I find the thought of still doing that quite awful!

It is the intuition more than anything that can help us to weave a path through the maze of misleading messages and manipulation our eyes and minds face every day. When this feeling centre becomes more sensitive to us, we will know that something feels instinctively right or wrong. When the mind opens and becomes less influenced by dogma and trivia, the more powerfully we feel our intuition. The mind steps aside, gets out of the way. It has a part to play, of course, as part of a balance, but it is not there to dominate. A rigid mind, full of programmed perceptions, overpowers the intuition and delinks us from that flow of inspiration and guidance from our higher levels of understanding – mission control. In these circumstances, the feeling centres shut down like dormant volcanos. Therefore I do not accept that everyone on the planet is doing precisely what they came to do, as some New Age thinking believes. We are all born into the circumstances we choose, but as we travel through life we can be diverted by other influences if we allow ourselves to accept the programming and close down the potential of the feeling centres, particularly the heart vortex, to guide us. If we do that we can become like a ship without a rudder and complete very few of the tasks we came to achieve. I am sure there must be many people who incarnated this time to play a big role in the transformation who have become so shut down by their programmed minds that they are laughing at, or condemning, those who are doing what they came to do! This situation, however, can be put right very quickly. Once we allow that flow of inspiration from higher levels to gather its power and guide us, the magnetic interaction with other energy fields – people, places, situations – will draw to us all the support, experiences, and opportunities we need to evolve both individually and collectively. This flow of inspiration and guidance is not to give our responsibility away. The guidance is not coming from some outside force. It is coming from a higher level of us. It is still the "I", the multidimensional self. When we reconnect powerfully with that, we are instantly deprogrammed.

I am asked by many people for advice on what they should do and I always reply in the same way. I don't know what is best for anyone else. I only know what I feel is best for me. The only person who knows what you should do, where you should go, or what you should think and say, is…*you*.

What does your heart tell you? Right. Go for it!

Chapter 18

The freedom called love

We can only be truly free when we respect ourselves and love ourselves, but humanity, collectively and individually, finds this so hard to do. As a result, we project into the world this self-dislike, even self-hatred, the spiritual cancer within us. The inner turmoil becomes the outer turmoil reported on the news bulletins. Some of the most aggressive people I have met have been those who hate themselves and have no love or respect for themselves. If our thoughts and attitudes change, so must life on this planet. If we heal ourselves, we heal the world. The Prison Warder Consciousness knows all this. To maintain the outer chaos and conflict, they know that we humans have to be manipulated into inner chaos and conflict. We will then be broadcasting the thought waves, energies, that reflect our inner state of dis-ease and dis-harmony into the energy fields of the Earth, thus creating the outer, planetary, dis-ease and dis-harmony, which is so essential to the maintenance of the vibratory prison. Dogmatic religion has been used to fantastic effect over thousands of years to fuel and exploit emotions like fear and guilt, and the feeling of being 'unworthy'. This has encouraged people to hand over their right to think and feel to a Bible and a priest because they have not had the confidence or self-belief to realise that they have a right, and an infinite gift, to make their own decisions. As the power of religion has waned in the face of 'science', politics, and economics, these have become the new religions with new books and priests – scientists, politicians, economists – to whom we can concede our right to think and feel. We are encouraged to deny our own infinite potential. We are "born sinners", apparently, and I cringe when I hear the mass of humanity described as the "common people" or "the ordinary man and woman in the street", or when politicians describe the population as "our people", as if we are children who must be looked after by their higher intelligence.

There are no 'ordinary people'. There are no 'common people'. There are only glorious expressions of the one consciousness that is creation. Each aspect is unique, equally special, and loved by the source of all that is. Each one is on an eternal journey of evolution through experience and all have the potential to do anything and be anything we want to be.

The process of awakening and deprogramming will be stifled and, at worst, suffocated unless we let go of these programmed responses like fear, guilt, and the sense of worthlessness. Every second, we are taking in energies from the cosmos around us and from other levels of our own consciousness. These are the 'feeling', 'intuitive', energies I have spoken about. This flow and connection comes in through the base chakra (vortex) in the genitals area and up through the central channel to the other major chakras. It also flows the other way, too. From here it affects all areas of our physical, emotional, mental, and spiritual being. When this flow is powerful and harmonious we are operating at our full intuitive potential, but this can only be achieved when we are at peace with ourselves. Like everything, emotions such as fear, guilt, and resentment, are an energy. These deep-seated and often long-held emotions act like dark knots of energy which eat us away and are, if not dealt with and released, a major cause of dis-eases such as cancer and heart problems. They block or diminish the natural, powerful, flow of intuitive energies, as they pass through our levels of being.

You might see these knots of energy symbolically like dams or big rocks in a fast flowing river, slowing down the flow and causing disharmony as eddies and whirlpools are created. In a way, the vibratory prison is like a vast knot of negative energy which is holding back the flow of energies in this part of the cosmos; hence other levels and civilisations are as keen as we are to remove it. When we lack self-worth and have feelings of fear and guilt, it holds us back from reconnecting with our true, whole, selves. Yet, when you look from the spiritual perspective at what makes us feel fearful and guilty, it all seems so ridiculous. Fear, guilt, and resentment are not emotions we have to feel. They are emotions we create for ourselves by locking into the programming which is passed on and intensified across the generations.

FEAR

Look at the bottom line of human existence, something that cannot be taken away from us: today is the first day of the rest of our eternity, and the Source of all that is has a love for all of us that is equal, beyond words, and eternal. As we reconnect with levels of ourselves which are outside the jamming vibration, we can begin to feel this incredible love and broadcast it into this physical world. When you connect with that love, a love without judgement or condition, there simply is no fear or guilt. You know there is nothing to fear. It is of our own creation and it is within the power of our hearts and minds to un-create it. To be without fear is not to be without awareness. I have heard it said that fear is essential for survival because it is that which stops us walking across the street in front of a car or jumping into a lion's cage. But fear and awareness are not the same. You don't have to be fearful to know the consequences of something and avoid them. In fact fear is often the cause of unpleasant events, not the protection from them.

It is the use and manipulation of fear that has allowed people like Averell

Harriman and Henry Kissinger to tell two countries the (often invented) aggressive intentions of the other and so bring about conflict. Each country strikes out of the fear of what the other is planning, or alleged to be planning, to do. Each one thinks: "We must destroy them before they destroy us". "Get your retaliation in first," as a soccer manager I knew used to say. War is overwhelmingly the physical manifestation of fear. It is the opposite polarity to love, trust, and respect – the protectors from war and disharmony. If we remove fear from ourselves, we remove our contribution to fear in the world. Removing fear from the world, removes war and disharmony. Once again it starts with us.

Fear is indivisibly connected with a lack of self-worth and self-respect. All three are the result of looking outside ourselves for confirmation that we are OK. The reason most people say they can't speak in public is fear. And the fear comes from being concerned about what the audience thinks of them. They are looking to the audience to confirm that what they are saying and doing is right and they fear those people will either reject what they say or think them to be an idiot. Put the would-be public speaker in an empty room or among their trusted family and friends and they would be fine expressing their views. Put them in front of an audience and they can hardly speak for nerves and lack of confidence. When you begin to reconnect and understand the true nature of the human being, you begin to look within for confirmation that you're an OK person. It doesn't matter what people think of you and what you say. They have a right to think what they like – and so have you.

The only person you have to convince that what you are doing is right, is *you*. Of course we need to listen to all views and information, but if you are in tune with that flow of intuition from higher levels of yourself, you, and no-one else, will know what is right for you to do and say. Once you realise that, and live it, you no longer stand up in front of an audience worrying about what they will think of you because you accept that they have every right to disagree. You know that what really matters is what *you* think of you. Perhaps the most effective form of information suppression is the fear of those who think differently to the status quo, but are frightened of speaking out and passing on what they know and feel. It is time for that to end.

Many people tell me they fear for my safety because of the 'powers' I am challenging and exposing in this book and *The Robots' Rebellion*, and for what I say in the media and on the speaking tours. I can honestly say, hand on heart, that I feel no such fear. I try to avoid unnecessary hassle that will affect my ability to communicate information to a wide audience, but when I believe something to be right and in need of communication, I do not fear the consequences. First of all, I feel enormously protected in a way I could not express in words, and secondly, what's the worst that can happen? My eternal self leaves this physical shell and moves on to another parallel world, another wavelength of reality. That doesn't sound too bad to me. I have had the benefit of experiencing years of severe and, for a while, constant ridicule in the United Kingdom. It was impossible to walk down a street, literally anywhere, without being pointed at, shouted at, and laughed at. This has diminished, but it still goes on today among those who have accepted without a thought or question what the media say I stand for. Such experiences have shown me how completely the vast majority give their minds away and, most important on a personal level, that no matter what people say about you or do about you, no-one can stop you if you refuse to be intimidated and you look to yourself for self-assurance and not to others. What does it matter what others think of you? People change what they think all the time and if we constantly seek to conform to the prevailing beliefs we just become clones of another's opinion – often programmed opinion – instead of masters of our own hearts, minds, and destiny. There is nothing to fear.

GUILT

When I host weekend workshops and we talk about guilt, I never cease to be amazed at the wonderful people before me who speak, movingly, of the guilt they feel. Beautiful spirits who ooze warmth and love reveal sometimes a lifetime of inner turmoil and emotional pain caused by guilt. It blights their lives and, in terms of self-worth and the flow of intuitive energies from the higher realms, it is terribly destructive. Guilt, like fear, is a creation designed to control. But, again, when you analyse what makes us feel guilty, it is programmed 'values', mostly from generations long passed. There are Roman Catholic priests all over the world with sexual feelings they battle to suppress and with a sense of guilt at those natural feelings which fills their days with emotional distress. Do you know why they are forced to go through this nonsense? Because one Pope decided in 1074 that clergy should be celibate. Sex and relationships are perhaps the most awesome of the countless vehicles for the creation of guilt. If people have had a sexual experience with someone who is not their official partner, they feel guilty and if news of it gets out, they are made to feel even more guilty by a society which has been programmed to inherit 'values' without question.

How would the tabloid newspapers fill their pages every day without passing judgement on the morals of the rich and famous? And how many people with much to offer the world have been destroyed by such 'exposés', in papers who would not know a moral if it bit them on the bum? But hold on a minute, here. Who said that expressing love for another human being (another aspect of ourselves) is wrong unless it is the official partner? Did you decide that? The guy down the street? Who? Religion decided it thousands of years ago, as I explain in *The Robots' Rebellion*. And who or what was controlling religion? These same people were also vehemently insistent at the time they decided on this form of "morality" that the Earth was flat and Jerusalem was the centre of the universe. And yet we go on judging ourselves and others and either feeling guilty or making others feel guilty on the basis of what people thousands of years ago decided was right. It's just crazy.

Who owns your body? You or someone else? Who owns your emotions and your spiritual self? You or someone else? If you accept the above imposition the answer is someone else. You are allowing them to impose thought and behaviour patterns upon you which, if you go against them, create an enormous sense of guilt. This area of love, sex, and relationships is a minefield of guilt which is holding back so many people from reconnecting with their true and whole self. When you look behind the words and the cliches surrounding relationships, we are not looking at love. We are looking at a form of possession. I love you, therefore I own you. Yet what is *real* love? It is a love so endless and without judgement or condition, that we love a person for what they are, not what we say they must be if we are to love them. We love them so much that we want them to experience whatever they need to experience to ensure that they can learn, evolve, and achieve what they have come here to do. We have no wish to possess another human being, only to love them. How many can truly say on that basis that they love someone? I am not saying here that we shouldn't respect the feelings of a partner. Of course we should, but we have feelings, too, and a lifeplan for our experience, service to Creation, and evolution. When you look at what makes people feel emotional pain over sex and relationships, it is largely the result of programming. It has little to do with what is right or wrong and everything to do with what that society has been programmed to *perceive* as right or wrong over hundreds of years.

If a person was born into a rigid, sexually suppressive society, their emotions would be blitzed by their partner expressing physical love for another, even though the love that partner had for them remained undiminished or was even strengthened. But if that same person was born in a loving and sexually open society in which expressing physical love for each other was as natural as the sea and sky, there would not be the same emotional pain in exactly the same circumstances. Sex has been turned, by design I most strongly feel, into a form of suppression, control, and limitation. Guilt is the major factor in achieving all three. And if the power of the base (sexuality) chakra can be diminished, we don't absorb energy to our full potential. This affects our life span and creativity. On the one hand, sex has been presented as something sinful and dirty, thanks to the influence of religion, and on the other it has become for many a merely physical experience, a means of releasing physical desires and frustrations. Both, I believe, are a travesty of what sex really is. Indeed I would say there was a chasm of difference between sex (physical) and spiritual love (physical/ spiritual).

The act of spiritual love is an explosion of spiritual energy. It is the multidimensional expression of spiritual, emotional, and physical love and all those energies are created and merged to affect positively both the individuals and the Earth. Spiritual love between two people is a positive contribution to the world because of the love and thought patterns it creates. So why are we supposed to feel guilty about it? Some Eastern philosophies acknowledge this truth and their view of sex and relationships is consequently different from the Western version which, as I saw in a quite awful publication by the British government's Health Education Authority,[1] has turned sex into the spiritual equivalent of artificial insemination.

At the moment of orgasm our physical, emotional, mental, and spiritual levels are as One and we are as One with our highest potential. All our energy centres are wide open. This is a moment when we can reconnect and feel the bliss of that experience if the intent is loving and spiritual. As with everything, however, there is a downside to this if the intent is negative. Orgasm under those circumstances opens up the energy centres to connection with the lower vibrational, malevolent consciousness and this, I believe, is why so many of the dark esoteric ceremonies involve sex and orgasmic experience. Whenever I look at something which helps us to reconnect with our highest potential, be it sexual love, self-love, or the free flow of information, I find that it has been, by calculated design at the Prison Warders level, distorted and manipulated. Our view of sex and relationships is one very important example of this and it creates a tidal wave of guilt in the collective human mind. I will return to this theme in a future book devoted to this subject. Again, we need to follow our intuition. Does it feel right to express physical love for someone, whoever they may be? Your mind may be shouting "guilt" at you in a gathering panic. But what does your feeling centre, your heart, say? If it says yes and it feels like the most natural thing in the world, then what could possibly be wrong with that? It is possible to love more than one person at the same time. It is possible to love all people and all lifeforms at the same time, in many different ways. It is possible to love those who love us and love those who hate us. So why do we say that everyone needs to love everyone to build a better world and yet feel guilty on the occasions when our bodies are involved? What a contradiction it all is. The body is only a vehicle for the eternal self, after all. A magnificent vehicle, yes, and an extension of us while in incarnation, but still a vehicle and not the eternal self. I am not calling for a sort of open-house-all-in-together-free-love society. It is up to the individuals involved to decide what their heart and intuition tells them. If people want to live together and not have sexual experience with anyone else, great, wonderful, fantastic. But while they have a right to make the decision of what they believe is right for them, others have an equal right to make a different choice. It is not a better or worse choice, it is merely different. So there is no justification for guilt to be felt by those involved, nor for guilt to be imposed by others who seek to make everyone else conform to their version of morality.

---

[1] "The 69 [sic] Bravest Sex Questions" (bold, spicy, frank... they're the ones you've always wanted to ask!). Yawn. Published by *Company Magazine* in association with the Health Education Authority.

There is so much that society demands we should feel guilty about. We look back at the way we treated our parents. We feel guilty if we did not fulfil in our lives what our parents wanted us to achieve. We think we have let them down. We feel guilty at the way, perhaps, we treated our own children or other loved ones. We feel guilty if we work so much that we don't see enough of our families. We feel guilty if we don't work enough and can't give our children the material things they are programmed to want. You name it and someone, somewhere, will feel guilty about it.

Enough!

Fear and guilt are there to control us, divide us, diminish us, and limit us. Let them go. These things have to be seen from a much bigger, spiritual, perspective. First of all we choose where and with whom we incarnate. We choose our parents and they choose us. Instead of holding onto the guilt and resentment of what we see as an unpleasant childhood or the feeling of letting down our parents, we need to ask ourselves why we chose those experiences and why our parents did. What was that interaction of people designed to achieve for all parties? My father gave me a hard time mentally and emotionally, but that experience turned out to be essential to tap the mental and emotional toughness I needed to cope with what has happened to me since 1990. The experiences my wife and children have had as a result of what I have said and done has had the same effect on them. Experiences that seem terrible in the moment can be seen, with the hindsight and knowledge of passing years, to be gifts which allow us to deprogramme from the shallow, manipulated, superficial world we have allowed to solidify around us. We are not here to fulfil our parents' ambitions for us. We are here to serve the planet in the most effective way, fling open the prison door, and speed our own, and the collective, evolution. In the same way, we are not here to impose our beliefs and ambitions on our children. We have not come to serve a system created by the manipulators which insists we must work day after day under someone else's control or feel guilty or unworthy if we don't. Nor are we here to play the material game by allowing guilt about our children to make us feel terrible when we can't give them what their friends may have. We can give them something that is beyond price. We can give them unconditional love and we can help them to reconnect with their highest potential. You can't buy that at the computer game store.

Another form of guilt is that felt by awakening people at not thinking 'perfect', loving thoughts about everyone all the time. We need to be kind to ourselves here. In this imbalanced world, some terrible events happen and we are not going to be immune to the emotions they attract. When I saw Bill and Hillary Clinton sitting with assembled children and television cameras in the White House taking political advantage of the Oklahoma bombing, I did not have loving thoughts, I can tell you. Nor am I immune from the frustation of being attacked by those who talk of "freedom". It is the way we deal with those emotions that matters. That is very different from not feeling them. We really would be robots if that were the case. The more we open up to our higher consciousness, the easier it is to keep thinking positively, but it's a process we evolve through and if we feel bad about feeling bad, it will only hold us back by accumulating more guilt.

PATTERN BREAKING

Another form of guilt is this word, karma. It is expressed in many religions and cultures and can be summed up by "what you do to others will be done to you". I accept that karma exists and I believe it can be expressed as creating our own reality. It is not a punishment, it is a gift. I also feel, as I have said in other books, that karma is created by the intent behind an action, not the action itself. If we do something with good intent and it doesn't work out, we learn from the experience, but there is no 'karma'. If, however, we do something that appears to be positive, but it has an ulterior, negative intent behind it, there will be a karmic reaction which will lead us into a situation in which we face what we have done to another. The reason for this is that positive intent and negative intent create different thought patterns and so attract a different reality. But there are two points to make about karma. One is that it is too often presented as punishment and people feel guilty when negative things happen to them because it must be the result of something terrible they have done. And the second is that to explain everything that happens to us as our 'karma' (how we have behaved in the past) is, in my view, misleading and simplistic.

In this amazing period of spiritual and, therefore, physical transformation, large numbers of people are going through sometimes extreme experiences, negative and positive. These are not all 'karmic' experiences, from where I am sitting. They are the prearranged means by which we are being given the opportunity to deprogramme ourselves. These experiences may be the breakup of a long-term relationship, the loss of a job, an illness, or our whole life being turned upside down in some other way. The common denominator of all of them is to make our status quo disappear. Whatever choices we make in the light of these events, one thing is certain: the status quo, life as it has been, is not an available option. They ensure some kind of change, often a massive one.

The colossal spiritual awakening that I experienced in 1990-91 happened so publicly that my television career was destroyed. My status quo was demolished and a great change in my life had to take place. That was not my 'karma', in the sense of punishment for past deeds; it was the opportunity to break out of the prison of thought control. If life gets too comfortable and cosy in the same thought pattern – rut – it can be very difficult to step out of it and move on. Sometimes an upheaval in our lives is necessary to present us with such an opportunity. It seems terrible at the time, but from my own experience and the countless people I have met who have been through this process, you always look back at such events as gifts and not punishment. Energy codings in our consciousness are triggered, often by astrological influences, to create change within our magnetic aura and, therefore, our physical lives. This is especially true today with the Great Transformation upon us.

The process I have described is pattern breaking, in this case, our personal thought patterns. But we are also affecting other, collective, thought patterns as we open up to the higher frequencies. A lot of people ask why life can be so tough sometimes, even when we have given our commitment to do whatever is necessary to support the transformation. I have asked that question myself, many times! As I said earlier, some of it will be caused by the facing and cleansing of inner thought patterns from the past we didn't know we had, but I believe that people who have come specifically to support the transformation also operate like spiritual kidney machines. They absorb negative emotions and thought patterns into their energy fields and transform them into another, higher, state. At the time these are being processed by the person, however, they will be living that emotion and experience. They might feel depressed, angry, or in despair, when there is nothing apparently happening in their life that should make them feel like that. Then those feelings will go quite suddenly without any obvious reason. This, for me, is the process of collective pattern breaking and negative energy dispersal. It is a very positive contribution. But people who are doing this without knowing it often feel guilty at some of the emotions they are feeling. So much is happening that we don't understand and only when we stop judging ourselves from the viewpoint of the programmed status quo will we be able to release our feelings of guilt and fear.

RESENTMENT

This is another emotional cancer which manifests in so much individual and global self-destruction. If we create our own reality, whatever we experience is of our creation. We attract to us an energy field – person and experience – which can reflect our inner self as a physical reality before our eyes. Or, as in the case of the Robot Radicals, they unknowingly help to highlight information by attacking it, so helping us to fulfil our task. Those other people we resent for what they have done to us have their own imbalances to face and maybe we can help them to do that by our reaction to their behaviour. How we react is an opportunity to look at our inner self. And there is certainly no justification for the resentment we still hold against another person because they were an outer expression, a mirror, of the inner us. Responsibility for what happens to us begins and ends with *us*. People resent the success of others when the only difference between them is the different realities they have created. And who suffers from the resentment we hold onto about others? We do. We punish ourselves by clinging to such patterns and it negatively affects our sense of self and reality. We're the losers in this, not those we resent. One good way I find of letting go of guilt and resentment is to visualise the person or experience involved with a thread connecting them to me. I then project love at the person and experience, thank them for the gift of knowledge, and visualise the thread being cut and the person/experience drifting away, no longer part of my inner pattern. The Global Elite use resentment to great effect to start conflicts and to keep them going as each side becomes more resentful at the acts of the other. One expression of this is the so called "tit for tat" killings in the world's trouble spots. If we release our resentment, we help the planet and humanity as a whole to release theirs. But the biggest winner when we do this is ourselves.

If you have done something in your life that you regret or you feel guilty for the effect it has had on others, remember this: you have all eternity to put right what you have done and the experience you put someone through was precisely what that person needed for his or her evolution. You are sitting there feeling guilty when, viewed from a higher level of understanding, you have made a positive contribution to their eternal journey. Turn this around from the other perspective of what others have done to you and you see resentment in the same light. And if you have made 'mistakes', how do you know they have not been an essential, and preplanned, part of your own learning which can help you and others? Who is the best person to help an alcoholic or drug addict? Someone who has read about it in a book or passed an exam? Or someone who has been there and knows exactly what it is like? There are no such thing as mistakes, only learning from experience. Accept 'mistakes' as a gift, absorb the knowledge, and move on. Fear, resentment and guilt are yet more by-products of dogma. They result from rigid responses to rigid 'values'. Step out of the dogma and you step out of the by-products.

I AM WHAT I AM

There is a great song by Shirley Bassey called *I Am What I Am* and there is one particularly telling line which says: "I am what I am and what I am needs no excuses". Says it all. When you follow the guidance of that feeling centre, your heart, you are doing whatever you need to do with whomever you need to do it. You are not your brother, or the guy across the street, or the famous person on the television screen. You are you and you are a wonderful you. Every bit as special and unique as anyone else. And your path is not my path or anyone else's. It is yours and yours alone. So while we are all part of the same whole, all part of each other, we are the sum total of all our experiences since we first became conscious and that means we are at different points in the journey, with different things to offer and different things to learn. If we allow fear, resentment, and guilt to make us conform to another's thought pattern and value system, we give away the uniqueness of our contribution to the world and we lose the opportunity for experiences designed specifically for us. It doesn't matter what you have done in the past. That has gone. It is what you are *now*, this moment, that is important. I don't care if you have served a prison sentence for an unpleasant crime. I don't care if you have been Jesus Christ or Adolf Hitler. What are you *now*, this second?

Hold on to the uniqueness that is you. Why should you conform to someone else's pattern? Why should you be what someone else insists that you be? You have spent forever developing that uniqueness. Why be a clone now? The pressure to conform is simply the pressure to control. The Global Elite and its Illuminati-Brotherhood cannot control and manipulate billions of people who are expressing their full potential and their uniqueness of view. It can only be done by mass mind control that directs the overwhelming majority to think the same. Only then do you have the herd mentality, the unthinking, unquestioning sheep, following the guy at the front. How would you control a herd of sheep if they all went their different ways, refusing to follow the one at the front and instead following their own hearts and what felt right for them? You simply cannot control them. So being the unique you and resisting the pressure to be a clone is not only to follow your own path and express your true self. It is also, by definition, to dismantle the means of global control.

Nothing has succeeded in denying our uniqueness more than religion. God save us from religion. It has been a tool and a creation of the Prison Warders and it has done more than anything over the centuries to enforce the uniformity essential to mass control. It is, as I have said before, psychological fascism. The divisions of race and colour are used in the same way. If you are born into a certain religion or culture, you must follow their rules. If you do not, you are a traitor. Such an approach is not an expression of love and freedom. It is the suppression of both. If you are a victim of such a religion or culture by birth, you do have a choice. You can conform and take, in the short term, but only the short term, the road of least resistance. Or, like gathering numbers, you can acknowledge your own uniqueness, your own mind, and your power to control your own destiny. Remember, too, that you chose to incarnate in the situation that you have. So why did you make that choice? Just to be another clone? It is rather more likely that it was to give yourself the opportunity to serve Creation, your own evolution, and your fellow men and women by striking out from the mental prison and shouting to everyone who can hear: "I will not be imprisoned by the mind of another. I am what I am and what I am needs no excuses!"

I read an article by a Jewish-born writer called Jon Ronson who wrote of the way his religion and culture have reacted to him. He could quite easily have been speaking of the extreme versions of Christianity, Islam, Hinduism, or so many you-will-believe-this-because-I-say-so cultures and belief systems. Jon Ronson wrote an article in the London *Time Out* magazine about his attendance at the Jewish funeral of his grandmother, in which he recalled:

"I'm the only person in the room who doesn't understand what the hell's going on. I'm jealous of the warmth of their identity, embarrassed and guilty of my ignorance. Everybody is singing the Hebrew verse, and I am reading the England translations…2,000 years of 100 per cent, pure-bred Orthodox Ronsons without a hint of goyism [Gentile] in the genes, and the bloodline ends here."

Ronson wrote another article three weeks later in another magazine or paper detailing the reaction of fellow Jews to his remarks. Someone sent me a photocopy of this anonymously through the post and so I can't tell you the date or the publication. He highlighted one letter which "spat out", as he put it, the fact that he was no better than David Irving, a man who has been vilified for challenging the official stories of the Nazi gas chambers. The letter went on: "I speak for *all* [my emphasis] Jews when I say how you have betrayed and shamed us. We are pleased that your bloodline ends here." There we have yet another individual claiming to speak for all and telling everyone what they should think and do. A clone leading clones. The people who have bodies which are Jewish or Roman Catholic or Islamic or whatever, cannot be legitimately referred to as one entity. They are, like all races and peoples, an example of Creation's infinite beauty and uniqueness. The Jewish hierarchy in their desperation to control are denying the full expression of thought and potential that Jewish people can offer the world. It is the same with other extreme religions, too. And this is causing so much pain for those who wish to be themselves and not what the self-appointed thought-police demand that they be. In his article, Ronson said of the letter from the man claiming to speak for all Jews:

"The letter shocked the hell out of me at first, and then it made me smile. I photocopied it, and sent it – as reply – to the scores of Jews who had written to me in empathy with the column: Jews who have discovered heathenism to be a pleasanter, and more viable, experience than the cut-throat, school-bully, world of official Judaism…On top of the photocopy, I wrote: 'This is what we're leaving behind. Makes you proud doesn't it?'

"And does it make me proud? It's hard being part of the new, disenfranchised generation of young Jews: Jews who feel, deep down, that our culture is a destructive, arcane, racist, and sectarian one. (I hate hearing Jews bad-mouthing Blacks and Asians. Why do they do this? To deny our past? To help us forget we were the oppressed minority, the 'dirty immigrant?' To make us feel more British?)

"And still we refuse to allow our children to mix with non-Jews. We still clutch, unquestioningly, onto Zionism, even its distasteful aspects. We are self destructing…One aunt, after reading my column, phoned the rest of the family to accuse me of anti-Semitism. My family were split down the middle…The idiot that compared me to David Irving will undoubtedly read

this and become even more incensed. But don't you realise — you're the one
who's driving us away. And, judging by the volume of mail I received, you're
driving us away in droves."

However, freedom for one must mean freedom for all and Jon Ronson
would later reveal his one dimensional view of freedom. While he wishes to
be free to be himself, he is less inclined that others should enjoy the same
priviledge. As a journalist on the London *Guardian*, he rang a BBC TV
programme called *Good Morning With Anne And Nick* which had invited me
to discuss the first edition of this book. After Ronson's call the invitation was
withdrawn by the programme, a decision "justified" by an excuse which
insulted the intelligence. Ronson later wrote an article about me which, as
witnesses will confirm, gave an outrageously inaccurate account of our short
meeting. When you respect another's freedom, Mr Ronson, you will enjoy
freedom yourself. But not until. You create your own reality, as we all do.

If you are being imprisoned by Judaism, Roman Catholicism, Islam,
Hinduism, or one of the others, you have the opportunity to make a great
contribution to the freedom of yourself and those in your position. The
awakening of the human consciousness will turn the droves into a tidal wave
of people walking away from this intergenerational thought and behaviour
control. Many volunteers have incarnated into these cultures and religions at
this time to do just that. As these structures crumble and fall, the hierarchies
will be seen as they really are: able to lead and cling on to power only by
fear, guilt, and mental and emotional suppression.

Don't deny what you believe, what you think and feel, just because they
are different to the prevailing culture in which you find yourself. Those
beliefs and feelings are you. If you deny them, you are denying the real you.
What good is that to anyone? Fear, guilt, dogma: these are the vehicles of
human control. Without them there can be no control, no Global Elite. You
can let them go now if you so choose. In doing this, you will be
contributing to creating the world we wish to see for ourselves and those
who follow. The means to build that world lies within you and within me.
So what are we waiting for?

Chapter 19

Free at last

The river is flowing, flowing, and growing,
The river is flowing, back to the sea.
Mother Earth carry me, a child I will always be;
Mother Earth carry me, back to the sea.

I don't know the person behind the eyes that are reading these words. I
don't know where you come from or your race, colour, creed, or income.
I frankly don't care because these temporary states are only vehicles for
experience, anyway.

But I do know a great deal about you in other ways. I know that you are
part of me and I am part of you because we are all aspects of the same
infinite consciousness that we call God and Creation. I know that you are a
unique expression of that consciousness as the sum total of all your
experiences. I know your potential to love and create is without limit and
without end. I know these things because every lifeform on this planet and
anywhere else you would care to name, has those same abilities, that same
limitless potential. You can do anything you want to do and be anything you
wish to be. You just have to believe it and make it happen. It is the
awakening understanding of our true selves and the end of limitation which
will bring an end to the manipulation I have detailed in this book. This is
already happening.

The speed with which life will change on Earth in our generation will defy
the imagination. I know that many people who have opened up to another
understanding find it hard to accept just how fast the new world and the new
Earth will emerge over the next 35 years, even the next ten. But think of it in
these terms. We are trapped in a vibratory prison. Imagine it is a physical
prison cell. While inside that cell, our potential to act and achieve is
enormously limited. But the moment the door is opened, that potential soars.
Suddenly, it is not only the door that is opened to us. It is the world, also. Yet
the time span between those two states of severe limitation and freedom is the
fraction of a second it takes to step through the door. In the time it took to
make that one step, our lives would be transformed. The principle is the same

with the vibratory prison. The moment that blocking, jamming frequency is dispersed and humanity returns to 'wholeness' and multidimensional reconnection with its higher consciousness, this world will change for the better in an incredibly short time. We are now in the transitional period between those two states of being...the prison and the freedom.

I believe that the period we call Atlantis was the last full scale attempt to break the blocking frequency. Consciousness of high evolution entered the three-dimensional prison and became incarnate on Earth to challenge the Prison Warder vibration. I feel that many of these spiritual volunteers (who arrived with the best of intent) became intoxicated by this rare vibratory environment and were negatively affected by it under a thought-bombardment from the Fourth Dimension. Those Atlantean volunteers who allowed their vibratory state to fall below that of the jamming frequency, found themselves trapped and unable to leave until they had, through experience, raised their frequency again to a level that allowed them to escape. They, like the rest of the prisoners, embarked on a cycle of incarnation and reincarnation trying to create experiences and learning that would restore them to a state of love and enlightenment that would open the vibratory door. Those who managed it were said, in symbolic language, to have 'ascended' to the 'Father'.

Such an achievement was extremely difficult because the consciousness within the prison was delinked from its powerful connection with the higher consciousness outside. This has created the reincarnation cycle, which, for some, I believe, involves incarnating with little pattern or plan. The dense physical world has become like a drug with minds – souls – attracted to certain lifestyles and experiences like a cocaine addict is consumed by his or her addiction. I am sure that many of the people I call the Elite have had scores of physical lifetimes in which they pursued the same pattern of control and manipulation. Thought patterns of many kinds can become like a rut, a needle stuck in a record, repeating over and over. They might be attracted to certain family lines because they know those lines will allow them to continue with their addiction.

Other Atlanteans managed to stay in greater contact with their higher consciousness while still in the prison and continued to select their incarnations with a view to gaining experience of this strange and suppressing vibration in preparation for a future mass incarnation to break the jamming frequency. This is the period we are living through today. Since Atlantis, other highly evolved consciousnesses have entered the prison to experience and prepare for this time.

My own view is that the 'volunteer' consciousness has come back from the future and that the star system known as the Pleiades is very much involved. This relates to the idea of simultaneous 'time' in which the past, present, and future are all happening at once. Mind blowing, I know. I get a headache just thinking about it. But I do feel that the consciousness of those who are here specifically to free the Earth and the human race from suppression and oppression, came from a time-space reality far in the 'future' of this universe. Time travel is very much a reality, as perhaps even the elite human scientists have now understood. It is possible that from the volunteers' and the extraterrestrials' perspective, they have come to change the course of their 'past' to avoid some sort of catastrophe unfolding in their 'present'. Maybe even Atlantis happened in another time-space dimension of the Earth and not this one. Just a thought. Now please excuse me while I disappear up my own backside!

There have been memorable group incarnations of volunteers to bring higher frequencies to the planet and to diffuse the negative vibrations. One of these group incarnations came 2,000 years ago when the man, probably called Y'shua, was involved (as I explore at length in *The Robots' Rebellion*). I believe that consciousness came from the future too, and that it is back on Earth today. If you look at the prophecies of many people and texts like those of Nostradamus, parts of the Bible, the Mayans of Central America, the Native Americans, and so many others throughout history, they all have a common theme: a period of fantastic change when a new world and a new Earth will emerge. Some believe this will happen in this decade and across the millennium into the next century. Another common theme between such predictions, I believe, are that they were channelled to this reality from frequencies outside the prison where the knowledge of what will occur is available to us.

There are two main reasons, I feel, why all the predictions have pointed to the last years of the 1990s and beyond. These relate to astrology and something called the Photon Belt or Beam. There are, according to astrologers, a number of rare planetary alignments and sequences in the latter period of the 1990s which are likely to trigger enormous change on all levels of people and planet – a transformation indeed of the old evolutionary cycle. The vibrations of the planets affect us very powerfully. As the pull of the moon moves the tides of whole oceans, so our bodies are affected by the same spiritual magnetism. Our bodies consist overwhelmingly of water because they are like batteries, storing and processing energy. Blood is the physical version of our energy meridians and blood is subject to influence by the planets, as is our body in general. Some highly significant astrological events have already occurred like the Uranus-Neptune alignments in 1993 and the effects of Pluto in 1995 which are speeding the awakening of those who are ready. The year 2000 coincides with the highest point of the upwards cycle of the Orion constellation to which the pyramid builders apparently aligned their geometry, and it was in the 11th millennium BC, within the window period suggested for great geological upheavals on the Earth, that Orion reached the lowest point of its cycle. Astrological events affect earthquakes and weather systems because of the vibrational change they create on Earth, as does collective human thought. Also on May 5th

2000, the sun and the planets, Neptune, Uranus, Venus, Mercury, and Mars all align with each other. The vibrational effects of this are likely to be fantastic. Another important date may well be December 21st 2012, when the calender system left by the Mayans in Central America more than 1600 years ago, predicted that a great cycle for the Earth would end. It appears to me that May 5th 2000 is the moment when the freedom vibration begins to take over from the fear vibration as the dominant force in the human psyche as Uranus, the planet of breakthroughs, discovery, rebellion, freedom, and experimentation, enters into a colossal vibratory tussle in the heavens with Saturn, the planet of tradition, old values, limitation, discipline, rules, regulations, and control. The gifted British astrologer, Gloria Treloar,[1] says of this event:

> *"When these two planets challenge each other it signals a change in mass consciousness. Events and circumstances during this transit will start to shatter false 'security' which has been fixed in old social values and belief systems promoted through fear. Experimenting with new concepts which give a greater sense of liberty and independence has been the bottom line since the sixties felt the first vibration of the Age of Aquarius. Rebels with a cause emerged to fight injustice, narrow vision, and controlling influences. It was a rehearsal for the final decade of the century when breakthroughs (Uranus) would begin to happen on an aggregate level, rather than a generational one. The effect will manifest in disruption and it is meant to — only through chaos can creative and harmonic change emerge!"*

Underpinning these astrological events in this period is the Photon Belt. Many psychics and esoteric scientists are now agreed on the existence of a belt of highly charged energy centred on the Pleiades star system, an estimated 500 light years from the Earth. It is from here that much channelled information which feels right to me is purported to come. I believe that the Pleiades (maybe in our 'future') is a base for the positive extraterrestrial support we are being given at this time, and quite possibly the home of extraterrestrials who have abused the Earth and humanity, too. As with the Earth, the Pleiades will have those of positive and negative intent. It is no coincidence, either, that the Pleiades was the focus of much mythology in the ancient civilisations of Greece, China, and others. The astronomer, José Comas Sola, made a special study of the Pleiades – the "Seven Sisters" as they are called – and he suggested that they form a system which includes our Sun and a number of others. Each Sun, he said, had its own planetary system. In his study of the star system, Paul Otto Hesse claimed to have discovered a belt of immensely powerful energy which he termed the Photon Belt. According to estimates, it takes this solar system 24,000 (some

---

[1] See bibliography.

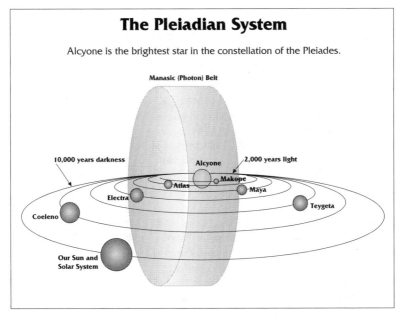

The Pleiadian System

Alcyone is the brightest star in the constellation of the Pleiades.

Manasic (Photon) Belt

10,000 years darkness   Alcyone   2,000 years light

Makope

Atlas

Electra   Maya

Coeleno   Teygeta

Our Sun and
Solar System

Figure 17

say 26,000) years to orbit the Pleiades and the star reckoned to be at the centre of the belt (*Figure 17*) known as Alcyone (Al-see-ah-nee). Again, there is much ancient legend across many cultures about this star. It would appear that we have reached the point where this solar system is entering the Photon Belt and its highly, highly, charged energy. The influence of the belt on the Earth began in the early 1960s and affected the thinking of many people, but it was as nothing compared with what will happen over the next 35 years. While it takes 2,000 years to pass fully through the belt, the biggest impact is when we first enter, and the vibrations and molecular structure of everything has to cope with dramatically changing conditions. This will affect the thinking, behaviour, and physical bodies of all lifeforms.

We are now beginning to see the mainstream scientific community confirming phenomena long predicted by psychics and felt instinctively by sensitive people. Cosmic rays of (in modern times) unprecedented power are being detected. Normally the rays are measured in millions of electron volts, but scientists at the Dugway Proving Grounds in Utah, have measured cosmic rays with an energy of 320 billion, billion electron volts. This had previously been considered "impossible". Something similar has also been measured by scientists in Japan. Roger Highfield, the Science Editor of the London *Daily Telegraph* wrote:

> *"Something out there — no-one knows what — is hurling high energy particles around the universe, in this case the most energetic ever observed by*

scientists…Not even the power released by the most violent exploding stars could account for them. Indeed conventional theory says such particles should not exist…" [2]

These are the energies that are changing life on this planet by the minute, never mind the day, and these same energies are rebalancing the Fourth Dimension, so dispersing the negativity and manipulation from there. The Global Elite are losing their power source. I was also fascinated to see how the cycles of sunspots synchronise so remarkably with the cycles of the Earth's evolution left by the ancient Maya of central America. Sunspots are produced when the sun is emitting an immensely powerful magnetism which comes to the Earth on the so called solar wind.[3] These cycles are fundamental, I believe, to the spiritual transformation and the multidimensional shifts which the planet, and humanity, are experiencing. We are going through enormous magnetic change and this has great consequences for the electronics and computer systems which, of course, are the basis of the world financial system.

On Earth today in this period of incredible opportunity are millions of volunteers from many universal civilisations and time-space realities who have come here to be at the front of the snowplough. Some are former Lemurian and Atlantean consciousnesses, and others who have come into the prison since then. But what has happened in the past is of no relevance now, except in the experiences and the knowledge that has been gleaned to make the task easier. It doesn't matter if your consciousness has been an Atlantean or a cabin boy in a previous life, you are the sum total of all your experiences and it is what you do *now* that matters. The volunteers on Earth today have been living what we would call 'normal' lives, mostly with no idea what they are really here for or where they have come from. This has been essential to become knowledgeable and grounded in the world as it is, and to lock into the rigid thought patterns they have come to challenge. Experiences, many extreme and sometimes very negative on the surface, have been attracted to them to help their minds break out of the programming of this world and to access their higher consciousness. Often it is when you are as low as you can go that you shed the old, programmed skin and reveal the new one, the real you, underneath. As a channelled message said: "Opportunity is often disguised as a loss".[4] This happened to me in 1991, when the fantastic ridicule I attracted from virtually the entire United Kingdom allowed me to

---

[2] "Hunt for the Most Powerful Particle of All", *Daily Telegraph*, (July 5th 1995).

[3] See the work of Maurice Cotterell, particularly *The Mayan Prophecies*, (Element, Shaftesbury, Dorset; Rockport, Massachusetts, and Brisbane, Australia, 1995). This is written with Adrian Gilbert.

[4] *Earth – Pleiadian Keys To The Living Library* channelled by Barbara Marciniak, (Bear & Company, Sante Fe, 1995) p135.

let go of the old perceptions and the concern of what others thought of me. I entered another reality in which being true to myself and my heart became far more important than worrying what anyone would think of me. I can't recommend it highly enough.

Within the subtle levels of the volunteers were preprogrammed spiritual 'alarm clocks' which have been activated increasingly since the late 1980s. They have suddenly opened their eyes to another understanding and they are now creating another reality. Some have been in the financial world, or business, religion, education, and medicine. Others have been mothers at home, unemployed people, or those who have retired. Their background and role in life up to this point matters only as experience. The real reason for this incarnation is just beginning for most of them and their numbers gather by the day as more wake up and realise who they are. They are reconnecting across the jamming vibration to wholeness and their lives and perceptions are changing dramatically. They are remembering. The same opportunity is available to everyone on the planet. In the years to come, the masks will be removed. We are going to see how many spiritual volunteers there are within the system of control. As they awaken, they will bring down these Elite bastions from within. At the same time, we will see that many of those who have spoken the words of the New Age, the environmental, and the 'radical', are in fact tuned to a rather less pleasant consciousness. By their deeds we shall recognise them, not by their words.

The process of diffusing and removing the jamming frequency is very simple in one way, but, in this misguided world, it can involve some vast emotional and spiritual upheavals in our lives to deprogramme us to the point where we can achieve it. As people awaken and let go of the programming, their consciousness also lets go of that programming's vibratory suppression which is holding down their own frequency. When the mind and feeling centres are opened and allowed to expand, their frequency rises and if this is allowed to continue, it will reach the point where it can synchronise with frequencies of reality outside the vibratory prison. This allows these higher frequencies to be filtered down our levels of being to this conscious level, and then broadcast out into this physical world. When this state of being is achieved, those people become walking, talking, transmitters of a higher frequency. The more people who awaken to do this, the more the cumulative effect is raising the frequency of the planet as a whole. This is allowing non-physical frequencies within the prison to rise, because in some way, this dense physical level will hold back the others if it doesn't shift and raise itself. It acts like a drag or an anchor on the other frequencies within the prison and until this dense physical level moves, they can't.

We are looking here at a multidimensional shift across many parallel universes in this period of transformation and not just on this single planet. When this multidimensional shift happens, largely as a result of what we do on Earth now in conjunction with the effect of the planets and the Photon

Belt, the jamming frequency will be overwhelmed and the prison door will fly open. We will be free and whole again. The nightmare will be over. The jamming frequency is already diffusing and breaking up, and light is pouring into our world. As the process gathers pace, the portals or gateways to other time-space realities (dimensions) are beginning to open. The period of quarantine is also coming to a close. These gateways, in places like Stonehenge, Machu Picchu in Peru, Tibet, Knossos in Crete, Ayers Rock, Lake Titicaca in the Andes, Mount Fuji, Mount Shasta, and the lands of ancient Sumer and Babylon (now Iraq) are opening as circumstances allow. This is like opening a valve which allows energies and vibrations from other dimensions to flood into this one.

A merging of dimensions and realities is beginning to happen which is offering the opportunity for those who are ready, emotionally and mentally (vibrationally in other words), to advance to a far higher state of consciousness, love, wisdom, and understanding. These energies and the effect of the Photon Belt are activating data stored in our consciousness and our physical bodies. Knowledge is being unlocked from the cells, bones, and our DNA which will, eventually, be restored to its twelve-stranded potential. This will return us to full brain capacity, instead of the 8 to 20% the human race works with currently. Each cell has a consciousness and its coding is controlled by our thoughts. This is why we can think ourselves ill and think ourselves healthy. Our emotions stimulate and release chemicals into our bodies which have positive and negative physical effects. Laughter is a great healer because of the chemicals it releases, and hatred, anger, fear, and guilt cause dis-ease for the same reason. Health is actually free and we will be able to regenerate our cells by our own thoughts. Our bodies age and become infirm because that is the reality programmed into the human mind and that is the reality we create. We don't have to age in the way that we do. Our thoughts ensure that we age, not our bodies. The power of thought to heal the body is something the drug companies (Global Elite) don't want us to know. Our bodies are going through incredible changes and this will increase with each year.

As the time-space portals reopen, more extraterrestrials will be visiting this dimension and we will be seeing more UFO activity. An average of 150 UFO sightings a day are reported world wide and it is reckoned that only about one in ten sightings are actually reported. I would emphasise the caution, however, that the scientists and military of the Global Elite have flying saucer, anti-gravity technology and we need to be very careful not to be conned by its use in the guise of an "alien" threat to justify centralised control. I believe this to be a distinct possibility, the ground for which is being prepared. This whole area of UFOs and extraterrestrials is a minefield which demands great caution and a very flexible mind. ETs, like everyone, can be positive and negative in their intent, and it is vital that we don't treat them as 'gods'. They are not to be feared, because we will attract that reality, nor to be worshiped as saviours. We are our own saviours.

There is a great deal of disinformation circulating about ETs and UFOs and picking the wheat from the chaff requires a constantly open, but filtering, mind, and constant vigilance. The opening portals and merging of dimensions is breaking the linear time locks which distinguish past, present, and future. That version of time is collapsing and we will realise, amazing as it may seem, that the past, the present, and the future, are happening at the *same* time. The effect of collapsing linear time is that the hours and days will seem to pass incredibly quickly until the point is reached when another version of time emerges. These are difficult concepts to grasp because so much knowledge has been kept from us and so much limited thinking has been imposed.

Many people, more than ever before in modern times, are being attracted to ancient sacred sites and most are unsure of exactly what is happening when they go there and feel often powerful energies pass through them into the Earth. They know something has happened because they can feel it and they know as more people awaken that the same experiences can be retold by millions around the world. I was asking the same questions when it began to happen to me in 1990. I believe that the energies we feel passing through us at such moments are the higher frequencies filtering down our levels of being and we are grounding them on this frequency, so quickening its vibration. In 1987, hundreds of thousands of people gathered at sacred sites all over the world for the event known as Harmonic Convergence when there was a mass grounding of higher frequencies onto this level. This was the trigger that activated my own spiritual alarm clock and the pace of awakening has increased in great leaps since then. This work is helping the frequency of this physical level to raise itself out of the misunderstandings that have plagued this world.

A frequency carries information, knowledge, and the higher the frequency, the more developed and evolved the knowledge. It is this frequency change that will transform the world we live in because information is freedom. We talk of freedom of information, but it is the information itself which is the freedom. What we think is what we create and what we think is based on what we feel and know – information, knowledge. As the frequency continues to rise, there is an explosion of knowledge re-entering our world. Nothing and no-one will be the same again. The true origin of the great sacred sites will be known, and since all spiritual change is reflected on the physical level, this is a period when a constant stream of scientific, historical, and geological discoveries will be made to overturn our whole view of history and who we are. There is world-shattering information waiting to be found in Egypt, I am convinced. In the same way that the rising frequencies are triggering data and codes stored in our bodies, so it is happening with thought codings stored in the stones of ancient sites. The energies of these sites are filling with knowledge, which is available to anyone operating on a vibration high enough to access it.

The higher frequencies can be filtered down and grounded anywhere and once you are connected with those higher levels, you are doing it all the time, often without even realising it. But there are points on the Earth's surface – many of which are marked by the standing stones and circles, mounds, hills, and other places held sacred by the ancients – where this can be done most powerfully and effectively. As acupuncture has long understood, the physical body is kept alive by a web of energy lines known as meridians and these also connect into vortex points, the spirals of energy called chakras, where these lines cross. They are like spinning spiral power stations on a grid of electricity lines. When these energies are flowing with balance and harmony, the person is physically, emotionally and mentally well. When they are imbalanced or blocked, they will be suffering from some form of physical, emotional, or mental dis-ease, dis-harmony.

It is the same with the Earth. This energy grid of the Earth has been much affected by negative events and limitation of thought. The energy passing through these lines is a form of consciousness, because everything is consciousness in different states of being. So these lines are affected by other consciousness – like the thoughts of human minds. When those thoughts are full of fear, anxiety, guilt, pain, and other negative emotions, the negative thought patterns are absorbed by the energy grid and its power and balance diminished. They are also carried around the globe on the grid network, and so the negative energy created by a war on one side of the world affects everyone because it is passed around the planet. These lines are designed to enjoy positive-negative and male-female harmony, but they have become dominated by the negative and male energies resulting from the inner turmoil and imbalances of humanity. In this transition period, it is necessary to repair the grid by removing the negative blockages, and channel high frequency energies into its system to raise the frequency. Millions are now involved in this. Other levels of their consciousness are guiding them to the right place at the right time, via the feeling centre and the magnetism. They are using their physical bodies as transformers and transmitters to broadcast the new frequency to this planet.

The point of maximum impact on the jamming frequency is the collective mind of humanity. With every individual mind which opens itself and deprogrammes its thinking, we are another step closer to that critical mass point of the Hundredth Monkey Syndrome, when a big collective switch will occur. Those who are working now to open their own consciousness and to heal and deprogramme themselves, are at the front of the snowplough, the pioneers, who are adding to that critical mass and making the big switch possible. If you are one of them, you have every right to be proud of yourself. Anyone can do it, anyone at all. You just make the choice, follow your heart at all times, and you are on your way. If we now look at the Elite's manipulation from the perspective I have outlined here, we can see that the themes of spiritual transformation, freedom, and global conspiracy are indivisible. We can also appreciate the wider picture within which the manipulation in this world needs to be seen if we are to fully understand its nature:

1. When we close our minds and hearts, our frequency falls (we become less informed and sometimes incredibly stupid). When we open our minds and hearts our frequency is raised (we become more knowledgeable, wise, and understanding). We can also raise our frequency to the point where we can cross the jamming vibration and escape from the prison.

   If you are the Prison Warder consciousness on the Fourth Dimension which wants to retain this vibratory prison and the negative energy production unit it has become, you can only do that if human minds, as a whole, remain closed. Therefore you develop a network of manipulation on this physical level designed to keep people from the higher knowledge and their infinite potential. You create religions which tell people what to think – or not to think. You encourage the population to focus their thinking on absurdities and trivia, and give their minds away to religious books which most people, even 'believers', do not bother to read, let alone understand.

   This gives the power to churchmen to tell the population what the religious book says and means. When this religious imposition begins to wane as even the closed-minded humans realise it is a vehicle of oppression, you introduce a new 'science' which claims there is no after-life of any kind and when this physical life is over, the lights go out forever. You ensure that the scientist is seen as the cutting edge of human knowledge and so if he or she says there's no after-life, that's the way it must be. You also develop other vehicles for this drivel and call it Humanism. This encourages humans not to relink with their higher levels because they become convinced they have no higher levels. The mind is the brain and the brain is the mind, and that's it, so there.

2. When people who are connected with the higher levels become incarnate on Earth, you make sure they are condemned and ridiculed, lied about, and undermined in any way possible, to stop their information being accepted and taken seriously. When they have gone you even take the opportunity to turn their words on their head and create a religion in their name which is the epitome of everything they came to challenge.

3. You develop a media, business, and political network controlled by people operating on your vibration to manipulate the human mind and keep it closed, uninformed and confused. You create a money system which keeps people under a lifetime of pressure just trying to survive. This gives them no time to think and feel and ask questions about life and the world. They are too busy getting through to tomorrow to worry

about anything like that. Thinking about the wider world is a luxury they don't have the time to do, or so they believe. We work too much and think and feel too little.

You divide and rule via manufactured divisions such as race, colour, creed, religion, income bracket, and an endless list of other 'us and them' devices. This creates the same division and confusion in the collective mind, thus ensuring that it is never united enough or on a high enough vibration, which would breach the jamming vibration in an instant. Those involved with the Elite are just vehicles for the Prison Warder consciousness to work through them and follow an agenda which is serving a much wider plan that even the Elite do not understand. They think they are in control, but they are not. They are stooges, a means to an end.

4. When you realise that an attempt is coming to remove your control of the Earth by raising the frequencies within the prison, you step up your attempts to dominate the human consciousness. You press ahead even faster towards the global control of government, banking, the currency, information, and the military, and you increase the pace at which you introduce the microchipped population because you know that if you can electronically tag every human being and link them to a centralised computer, you can artificially suppress their minds and frequency, so preventing them from being vehicles for grounding the vibrations that will break open the prison or access levels of understanding that can tell them they are in a prison. You also activate your dirty tricks agencies to undermine alternative thinking and concepts by branding them as mad and dangerous 'cults'.

    A global attempt to destroy the 'grounded' alternative movements is underway while, at the same time, another team of dirty tricksters is continuing to manipulate the New Age movement into floating around in some spiritual mist following the instructions of 'Masters' and 'Ashtar Commands'. The manipulators want to stimulate imbalance because that means control and a limited perspective and potential. They don't care *why* people give their minds away, so long as they do. Sending out broadcasts on what you might call "psychic frequencies" to mislead the New Age field is, in my view, undoubtedly happening. If they can get the spiritually-minded to hand over their thinking to some master or extraterrestrial 'command' they can neutralise their effect in the physical world. It is those people who have a spiritual-physical balance, those who wish to manifest spiritual values in physical change, that the manipulators fear, not New Age dogma.

5. You know that if the frequency of the energy grid is raised, so is that of the planet. You work through compatible human minds to build roads, factories, power stations, and transmission towers, at key points on the grid. The black magicians of the Global Elite know that if you can

control the energy passing through the grid, you can control the collective mind of the human race. The village and road built through the centre of the stone circles at Avebury in Wiltshire, England, is a prime example. This strategy pours negative energy into the network at these points, weakening the flow within the lines, and suppressing the frequency.

I have spoken to many people recently who have begun to identify a pattern in the United Kingdom of roads and broadcasting transmitters of various kinds which are sited very near or on well known Earth acupuncture points and chakra vortices. It goes beyond the bounds of random coincidence. The people who make these decisions often have no idea of the energy grid significance, but who is feeding thoughts into their consciousness or who is passing down the instructions from the upper reaches of the global pyramid of manipulation? The Fourth Dimensional manipulators. You can also create wars and suffering in particularly important areas of the grid, like Iraq and the former lands of Mesopotamia, between the River Euphrates and the River Tigris, the site of ancient Sumer and Babylon when they knew far more about the energy grid than mainstream science does today. Everything I talked about earlier in the book about the physical level manipulation and the engineering of wars is the reflection of a much higher understanding of energies, vibrations, and consciousness, and their relationship to the Earth and the human mind. George Bush would not have said: "We'll attack Iraq and pour negative energy into the energy grid because this will affect the world". But whatever and whoever was pulling the strings to make war with Iraq sure as heck knew the implications for the energy grid of doing so.

The effects of the Photon Belt and the vibratory tussle now at large on Planet Earth between the jamming vibration and the freedom vibration can be seen more obviously by the week. I passed on channelled information in earlier books going back to 1990 which talked of dramatically changing weather patterns in this decade and beyond, with colossal rainfall and floods, and of many other extreme weather and geological phenomena. The changing weather patterns worldwide are now obvious with enormous tracts of ice the size of countries breaking away from the polar ice shelves which were once considered permanent. Nothing is permanent except life itself. Rainfall records continue to be broken year after year; the seas rise, and rivers cover the land in ways that defy the eye. In other areas there are great droughts. Look back at the ancient prophecies and you will find all of these things.

We are told, often with little conviction, that this is the result of global warming, the Greenhouse Effect. I beg to differ. This is a diversion from what is really happening, I believe. We are witnessing the result of the Photon Belt and the higher frequencies being grounded, the portals opening, and the move from a three-dimensional reality into the fourth and fifth dimensions.[4] At the same time, the old vibration seeks to hold on to its domain and this is reflected physically as those awakening and changing their thinking and the Elite who wish to impose still further the old patterns of control and domination. This is the tussle symbolised by Uranus and Saturn. This and the Photon energies are stirring up the subtle levels of the planet consciousness – Mother Nature, Gaia, the Earth Spirit – and this is having magnetic consequences in the Earth's energy field. The planet is the physical body of a consciousness with a mind and emotions. The Earth is not just a physical sphere spinning in space. She thinks and feels, just like we do. She is part of us, and we of her. The weather and geological changes are leading, I believe, to a switch of the magnetic poles and, possibly, a physical shift of the axis. How traumatic all this has to be on the road to a better world is up to us, the human race. It is no coincidence that, looking at the records of insurance companies alone, geological and weather events have increased in both scale and number very significantly since the time of the Harmonic Convergence in 1987.

This immense transformation we are living through is likely to be one of extremes and opposites before all comes into harmony. It is the chaos period as one vibration breaks up and another moves in. Those with an open mind and heart will absorb the new space-time realities. Others who follow the propaganda of the Global Elite and the Prison Warder consciousness will cling on to the old vibration in their desperation to find security. They will become even more vehement in their religious, political, and economic dogma. They will resist the rising vibrations if they choose that path, and this will have mental, emotional, and physical effects. The two states of being, the programmed mind and the open mind, will be more obvious with every month to those who know what is happening. The Prison Warders, via the Global Elite, will increase their efforts to speed the New World Order, but they will not ultimately succeed. This transition period may well stimulate many negative events, but if we raise our own consciousness and hold onto our positive sense of self, we will not attract such events to us, unless, of course, it is part of our chosen path to experience them. Our state of mind is our protection from harm. Astrologer, Gloria Treloar, told me:

> *"Uranus in square to Jupiter (May 5th 2000) signals a time of social and economic change and a restructuring of values. Belief systems will be transformed. Those already open to a different study of truth from the one that has been indoctrinated down the years, will now take a further leap in consciousness; those who have been on the sidelines, a little apprehensive about*

---

[4] Nothing is black and white, however. The Elite have at their disposal technology that can affect the weather and create great storms, particularly in a small area, by manipulating the magnetic energy fields. Extraterrestrials certainly have this knowledge.

even a small step, will suddenly cast aside their fears, take a look outside
themselves and move into that higher state – breakthrough! It won't be easy,
but a happening so stunningly and refreshingly transformative can never be
described as a breeze. It's a hurricane which roars through the psyche uprooting
old trees of knowledge and shaking foundations to make way for the new.
Although the transit of these planets will be uncomfortable, whatever the
individual and collective process experiences, it will eventually prove a small
price to pay for liberation."

If we follow our intuition, we will magnetically attract to ourselves everything we need to guide us through this period. Many people have said that my books, and others, have fallen at their feet from the shelf of a bookshop. This appears to be a 'mystery', but it is not. The magnetic energy field of the book and the person's subconscious interact because the subconscious knows that its conscious level would benefit from reading the book. At its most powerful, this magnetic attraction pulls the book from the shelf. It is like two magnets attracting each other. If we are open minded, this process will ensure that we will be in the right place at the right time, with the right people, no matter what chaos may be happening around us.

In an ideal situation, the transition from one frequency to another is a very straightforward process. But given the vibratory prison and the vast number of closed minds on the planet at this time, this is no ideal situation. The human and Earth consciousness are not yet rising together as one. There are very different minds linked to very different frequencies pulling in all directions. As I understand it, the dense physical level is one place where consciousnesses linked to an infinite number of wavelengths can live together side by side in the same world. The manufactured divisions which our generations have inherited and perpetuated are the result of divided thought patterns. These patterns fighting for supremacy would cause some chaos anyway, but this is now happening in a period in which much higher frequencies are becoming part of this reality also, and raising the whole vibration of the Earth. The subtle energy levels of the planet have become subject to astonishing vibratory pressures and it is these which are changing the weather so fundamentally. They will, if they continue to build, bring geological upheavals of a kind not experienced or even dreamed about in the modern world. There is so much evidence now emerging that indicates massive changes in our environment. In the UK, the water tables in London, Birmingham and other cities are rising rapidly, some by two metres and more per year. This has fundamental consequences for daily life.[5]

Hard as it may be to accept at first, the geological and weather catastrophes are created largely by the human mind and the wavelengths it broadcasts. The way the collective mind thinks affects the planetary mind, Gaia, and if

---

[5] "Water levels undermine safety of city buildings", *The Times*, (October 6th 1995) p12.

she becomes imbalanced emotionally and mentally, this has physical effects, just as it does in the human body. But such a scale of physical change does not have to be. It is within our minds and hearts to make this transition far smoother than that. As more people deprogramme and allow their minds and hearts to open, they will cease to be part of the old vibration as they are able to connect with, and ground, the higher, freedom vibrations of love and harmony. The greater the number who step out of the old vibration and into the new, the smoother and more harmonious the transition will be. But whatever happens, the years of the vibratory prison are almost over. The only question left is how bumpy will be its last days, and if we are to lessen that impact, the time for action is urgent.

So, as always, the answers lie with us. If we can heal ourselves and stop being manipulated by the Prison Warder consciousness, via the Global Elite, the whole process will be easier and the end of the jamming frequency will be hastened. If we heal ourselves, open ourselves, and trust ourselves, we will heal each other and we will heal the world. It is happening now.

Chapter 20

I love you, Dr Kissinger

This book has been written with honesty, without fear, and in the desire to uncover the cause of the ills of this planet and the means through which we can heal them.

Not every last fact will be 100% accurate, nor every assumption, because we are dealing with people and organisations who wish that such information remains hidden. Dispersing the smokescreens is a life's work. I come from the direction of no religious, racial, or political dogma. I only wish to challenge the imposition of belief systems by those who use violence, fear, guilt, and the suppression of information. I also desire for love to flood this planet and for all humanity to access its full and infinite potential. If anyone decides to take parts of this book out of context and pronounce it 'racist', they will be making a statement about their own state of being, not mine. I wouldn't know how to be racist if my life depended upon it.

I seek freedom for myself, for humanity, and for this planet and all her lifeforms. If there are those who believe, or claim to believe, otherwise, that is their right. But I know what is in my heart and that is good enough for me. Such people will benefit, too, from remembering that their children and grandchildren, of whatever colour, culture, or background, will have to live in the world we leave them. Would they prefer us to leave them freedom or the New World Order? To be accused of racism when you have love and freedom in your heart can be frustrating, but no scale of criticism will stop me. It is time for humanity to stop running away. Time to let go of fear.

You will have noted, I'm sure, how the first section of the book is far longer than the second. This is not an imbalance. It is symbolic of how simple the answers are to all that I have outlined in this book. The principles within these last few chapters contain all that we need to change the reality of this world. We need to love, respect, and forgive ourselves and, through that, love, respect and forgive everyone else. One will come with the other. It begins with self. I don't have to set out new economic and political structures and tell people how they must live to create a better society. Who the hell am I to tell someone else what they should do, anyway? I know what is right for me, not you. From the transformation of mind which love, respect, and forgiveness of self will trigger, all these other answers will naturally evolve. We have the tyrannical structures of today because that is the reality the collective mind has created by its attitude to itself. When we change that attitude, we change the world. The pyramid becomes a circle. The human race, in general, doesn't like itself, let alone love itself. That is reflected in the physical reality. When love abounds within us, love will wrap its arms around the planet and it is on that foundation that all else will follow.

LOVE

By love, I mean a much greater love than the emotional attachment and possession that so much 'love' on Earth has become. I don't mean "I love you if I fancy you, darling". Nor "I love you if what you do is acceptable to me, or if you conform to my idea of someone who deserves to be loved". I mean "I love you, whatever you do". It means to read this book and then say: I love you, Dr Kissinger. I love you David Rockefeller, George Bush and Bill Clinton. That kind of love. Without condition or possession. It is the love we have for our children. We don't always agree with what they do and say, but we love them just the same.

If we can see each other in that light, the ills of this planet will fade away. With this unconditional love for self and each other, we would not produce economic arguments for why homeless people must sleep in the streets. The economic system would become subordinate to love and reflect that love. The idea that we would allow one person to be without adequate shelter would be unthinkable. We would stop charging interest on money, remove the debt so far accumulated, and spend what was necessary, interest free, to build enough good quality homes for people to live in. The love in our hearts would accept nothing less. We would dismantle the economic tyranny and encourage communities to take back the power over their lives, providing what is necessary for the benefit of people, not some Global Elite. Love would eliminate the pain and suffering we impose on the animal kingdom. We would recognise that the privileged minority on this planet cannot, with love, go on living off the backs of the Third World and then ease their conscience by putting a few pounds in a charity tin here and there. Love would insist that we withdraw from such economic dictatorship and allow those oppressed billions to live their lives for the benefit of themselves and not the multinational corporations. There would be no more CIA fascist coups to thwart elected governments determined to serve the needs of the people when love abounds in the collective human heart.

Love would cease to cooperate with the present structures of global power and in doing so, it would show just how little power they really have. They only exist because we created them and because we continue to cooperate and bow to their will. The real power in a pyramid lies at the base, not the top. Nothing survives if it is not founded on love and the present structures of control will not survive. The governments we select in a world of love would reflect that desire to serve, to set free, and not impose. How many people today vote with love in their hearts? People vote, overwhelmingly, for what they believe is best, materially, for them in the short-term. That is the reality they create – governments which serve themselves, short-term self-interest, and not the interests of others. We get what we vote for, because we get what we are feeling in our hearts when we, collectively, decide how to vote.

If the human race voted out of love, it would attract and elect such people into government. It is no good hurling all the blame at politicians for what is happening in the world. Politicians can only get elected by telling people what they have been programmed to want to hear. What people want to hear is what is in it, materially, for them. The kind of politicians we elect are an exact reflection of the collective attitudes which voted for them. When the collective human mind changes, so will the kind of politician we elect. Try getting elected on a policy of ending the Western dictatorship of the Third World which would affect the incomes and imports of the industrialised countries. No chance. Only with love in the collective heart will that be possible. Power to the people with the power of love.

Love for self will transform our lives, not least in the way we heal ourselves and others. Today, the medical services are controlled by the multinational drug companies. Sixty per cent of the US drug industry is owned by the Rockefellers alone. As a result, what claims to be state-of-the-art 'medicine' offers the scalpel or the drug in response to almost every ill. Both are motivated, at their controlling levels, by profit, not people. Wealth and not health. The infinite knowledge of healing in the world which understands how imbalances in our eternal selves create physical disease is kept out of 'official' medicine. The body-as-machine approach of Darwin and others is still the one taught in medical schools and hospitals. It has become so farcical, that a hospital doctor I once met treats the nurses with homeopathy, but cannot treat his patients in that way, except secretly, because the wrath of the official drug-company-controlled medical establishment would be brought down upon him. Millions die of cancer while many cures are suppressed. If you can't sell it at a vast profit under contract to a drug company, every effort is made to destroy methods of healing that would remove the so called "incurable" diseases of today. There are no incurable diseases. Every one is caused by an energy imbalance – an imbalance that can be returned to harmony and, in doing so, the body returned to health. This is happening every day outside the medical establishment.

Love for self will insist on taking back power over our own bodies. The drug companies dominate because the human race has, largely, handed over control of the body to doctors and pharmacists. It is an expression, yet again, of the way humans look outside themselves for answers. We look outside for confirmation that we are OK; for someone else to blame when something goes wrong; and for the answers to our discomfort when our body is ill. The answers for all three are inside us, in our view of ourselves. Self-hatred and frustration leads to cancer and heart disease, and every other ill can be linked to a mental, emotional, or spiritual imbalance, all of which can be corrected. I can thoroughly recommend a book called *You Can Heal Your Life* by Louise Hay[1] for more detail about this. As we begin to love ourselves and let go of the fears, guilts, and resentments accumulated over the years and the aeons of time, disease in the world will plummet. The cause of it will have diminished. We will see the illness that does occur as a sign of something amiss inside us. We will then address that, and think ourselves well again. Our physical dis-ease is also the result of our inner dis-ease, the magnetic pattern our thoughts create.

Love is not just a word. It is the power that holds creation together. It is the power that holds *us* together and, as we can see, whenever love is missing, a life, or a world, simply falls apart.

RESPECT

This, together with love, is the self-balancing mechanism of any balanced society. An imbalanced society creates endless rules and regulations to say "you will" and "you won't" to overcome the lack of respect. When you have respect for the Earth, you don't need laws and government agencies to tell you not to damage or pollute the environment. You would not dream of doing so. When you respect life as sacred, you don't need laws against cruelty to animals because you would not dream of harming a fellow expression of creation. When you respect another's right to live their life as he or she sees fit, you don't seek to impose your view on them. You respect and celebrate their right to be different. Not wrong. Different. When such respect is awash in the collective human mind, people will be living their lives in a way they believe to be right, while allowing others to do the same. All will shape their behaviour so they do not impose their thinking upon another. There will be no need for laws as we know them today because love and respect will be the balance that allows different beliefs to live in harmony.

This respect for others comes, as always, from respect for self. A lack of respect for others is the outward expression of a diminished respect for self. When we respect ourselves, we stop looking to others to tell us what to do and think. We have respect for our own infinite capacity to decide what we can do in any situation. We might seek another's advice and view, but in the end self-respect decides for itself. Self-respect also has the confidence to go against the majority view when appropriate and to decide its own morals and values. It refuses to bow to all the "shoulds" and "musts" that we are subjected to, and subject ourselves to, from the earliest years of childhood, most of them inherited from previous generations, sometimes thousands of

---

[1] Louise Hay, *You Can Heal Your Life*, (Eden Grove, London, 1988). First published by Hay House Inc., USA, 1984.

years before. You must do this, you should do that, I must do this, I must do that. Who says? The American therapist, Albert Ellis, called this phenomenon "mustabation". The musts certainly abate in the face of self respect. Love and respect for self are the most powerful combination in Creation. With them as our guiding light, there can be no fear, or guilt, or psychological fascism. And without those, there is no New World Order.

FORGIVENESS

The burden of guilt carried by the human race, much of it going back to previous lives, is caused by a refusal to forgive ourselves. If we do not forgive ourselves, we find it so much harder to forgive others. If we don't forgive others, we eat ourselves away with resentment, and seek revenge against those we consider to have acted badly towards us. Hence we have the conflicts and feuds that span the generations and the inherited prejudice and divisions which the Global Elite so exploit. If we vent our anger and resentment on the people I have named in this book, some of whom will not know what they are really involved in, what good will that do? It is right that we know what is going on and those who are seeking to control us. Without that knowledge, we will go on being manipulated. But the people connected with the New World Order do not need or deserve our hatred. No-one does. They are victims, too, the physical result of the emotional and spiritual imbalances within them which desire to control and dominate others. The last thing they need is more hatred. They need our love. By that, I don't mean a love that walks away and allows all this to continue unchallenged. I mean a love that does challenge the imposition, but without hatred or a desire for revenge. I love you, I love you, I love you, Dr Kissinger. I am you and you are me. We are each other. But I will challenge the New World Order mentality until the moment it is time for me to leave this planet and move on. The two approaches, the love and the challenge, are not incompatible. Nor is forgiveness of the personnel while working to expose their game plan.

Forgiveness of self and each other will bring an end to the story I have told. Let the divisions between us fall away, for they have been manufactured on the classic principle of divide and rule. That is the reason behind the engineered wars and the divisions of race, colour, country, class and income bracket. While there is an us and a them, we are a manipulator's party trick. When the us and them becomes *we*, which is what we really are, all part of each other, the manipulation will end. Let us put our arms around each other, the Arab and the Jew, the Christian and the Muslim, the manipulator and the manipulated. It's been a nightmare, but the nightmare is almost over. It's time to dream.

You are a beautiful spirit. You can be whatever you want to be. You are unique and you are loved in a way that we find so hard to comprehend on this planet. There are times when I feel that love from all, and for all, of

Creation. It is a love without fear, guilt, resentment, judgement or division. It is an experience beyond words and it is ours, yours, for the taking, the thinking, the feeling. We've been away too long, my friends. It is time to go home and reconnect with all that is. In the words of a lovely song recorded for the Comic Relief Appeal:

> *When we stand together,*
> *It's our finest hour.*
> *We can do anything, anything, anything, anything,*
> *Keep believing in love's power.*
>
> *Love can build a bridge,*
> *Between your heart and mine,*
> *Love can build a bridge,*
> *Don't you think it's time?* [2]

There are gathering millions who are screaming "YES!" to that question. As love, respect, and forgiveness sweep across the human mind and we love out of existence the misunderstandings of the past, we are destined to be the first generations for thousands of years who will leave our children a better world than the one we found. That is our gift to, and from, this glorious planet.

My fellow expressions of God, what a great time to be alive.

---

[2] *Love Can Build A Bridge*, (N. Judge, J. Jaruis, P. Overstreet, © London Records 90 Ltd.).

Postscript

Good evening, Mr President

A s this book went to press, I attended a performance of a stage show and obtained the tickets from the box office in the normal way. As I walked up the stairs into the arena, I met a friend who was looking worried and bemused. What was the problem? Seconds earlier she had heard a security guard say to someone that the security seats were in row S, numbers 25, 26, 27 and 28. I could understand why she was confused. She knew from an earlier conversation that the tickets I had for myself and another friend, Ayem, were row S, numbers 25 and 26! What goes on?

We went to the seats to see what would happen and as we sat down all the heads were turning to the back of the arena. Someone was arriving, surrounded by 'heavies', amid an explosion of flashing cameras. My friend then came over and solved the mystery. "It's Jimmy Carter" she said. "What?" At that moment, Jimmy Carter, the first Trilateral Commission President of the United States, walked along my row and sat down with his wife...*next to me!* I shook his hand as he arrived. "Good evening, Mr President." I just about resisted the temptation to enquire about the health of David Rockefeller. Here was I, a man who had exposed Carter in *The Robots' Rebellion* and even more so in this book, now sitting next to him surrounded by CIA guards. I laughed till I cried. What really struck me was that the energy working through those genuinely committed to the spiritual transformation is so strong that the New World Order has no chance of success. Mr Rockefeller, Dr Kissinger, Mr Carter et al, it's over my friends. I could have been allocated any seat among the three and a half thousand in the arena. I could have gone to any performance of the show over more than a year. But Ayem and I were there on that night sitting next to that man. Incredible.

During the performance I said to Ayem that I felt I was taking energy from Carter's aura. I didn't know exactly what it was, but there was definitely a flow from him to me. By the end of the show I was feeling a little agitated and later I was seriously agitated. In the end I was writhing around on the bed screaming and growling like some crazed animal. Two friends, including Ayem, kneeled beside me projecting love towards me. One level of my consciousness was in total control because I knew what was happening. For maybe 15 to 20 minutes, I was experiencing the consciousness that controls

501

the world and has done so for thousands of years. Its malevolence, hatred, arrogance, anger and lack of positive emotion was utterly stunning. When I felt I had experienced enough, I opened my heart energy (love) and in seconds the Prison Warder Consciousness was gone. I learned two things from that experience. Firstly, the Prison Warder Consciousness has no control over love, and secondly, the personalities behind the New World Order over thousands of years have been possessed by this malevolence. So were the Nazis. I could clearly understand why they have acted in the ways they have throughout history.

Lying there, feeling the grotesque emotions of the Prison Warder Consciousness, the following words came so powerfully into my mind...

Forgive them, they know not what they do.

Bibliography

This is a list of the books you may wish to consult for more detailed information of specific subject areas. They contain some excellent research. I don't agree with all that they say, indeed I strongly disagree with views expressed in several of them, but I am interested in their names-places-dates research, not their belief system.

Allen, Gary; *The Rockefeller File*, ('76 Press, Seal Beach, California, 1976).

Andrews, George C.; *Extra-Terrestrials Among Us*, (Llewellyn Publications, St Paul, Minnesota, 1993).

Andrews, George C.; *Extra-Terrestrial Friends And Foes*, (IllumiNet Press, Lilburn, GA, USA, 1993).

Antelman, Rabbi Marvin S.; *To Eliminate The Opiate*, (Zahavia Ltd, New York-Tel Aviv, 1974).

Armstrong, George; *The Rothschild Money Trust*, (1940).

Atkinson, Rodney, and Norris McWhirter; *Treason At Maastricht, The Destruction Of The Nation State*, (Compuprint Publishing, Newcastle-Upon-Tyne, 1995).

Baigent, Michael, Richard Leigh, and Henry Lincoln; *Holy Blood, Holy Grail*, (Jonathon Cape, London, 1982).

Bhutto, Benazir; *Tochter Der Macht: Autobiograhie*, (Droemer Knaur, 1989).

Bowen, Russel S.; *The Immaculate Deception*, (American West Publishers, Carson City, 1991).

Bromberger, Merry and Serge; *Jean Monnet And The United States Of Europe*, (Coward-McCann Publishers, New York, 1969).

Brzezinski, Zbigniew; *Between Two Ages: America's Role In The Technetronic Era*, (Viking Press, New York, 1970).

Bullock, Alan; *Hitler, A Study In Tyranny*, (Pelican Books, London, 1960).

Burdick, Thomas, and Charlene Mitchell; *Blue Thunder*, (Simon and Schuster, New York, 1990).

Chomsky, Noam; *Letters From Lexington, Reflections On Propaganda*, (Common Courage Press, Monroe, Maine, USA, and AK Press, Edinburgh, Scotland, 1993).

503

Chomsky, Noam; *What Uncle Sam Really Wants*, (Odonian Press, Berkeley, California, Fifth printing, 1993).

Chomsky, Noam; *World Orders, Old And New*, (Pluto Press, 345 Archway Road, London, N6 5AA).

Coleman, Dr. John; *Conspirators' Hierachy: The Story Of The Committee Of 300*, (American West Publishers, Bozeman, MT, USA, 1992).

Collins, Tony; *Open Verdict, An Account Of 25 Mysterious Deaths In The Defense Industry*, (Sphere Books, London, 1990).

Cooper, William; *Behold A Pale Horse*, (Light Technology Publishing, Sedona, Arizona, 1991).

Cowles, Virginia; *The Rothschilds, A Family Of Fortune*, (Weidenfeld and Nicolson, London, 1973).

Deacon, Richard; *The Truth Twisters*, (Macdonald, London, 1987).

Delair, J.B., and D.S. Allan; *When The Earth Nearly Died*, (Gateway Books, Bath, 1995).

Demaris, Ovid; *The Last Mafioso*, (Bantam Books, New York, 1981).

Deyo, Stan; *The Cosmic Conspiracy*, (West Australian Texas Trading, revised edition, 1992).

Drummey, James J.; *The Establishment's Man*, (Western Islands, Appleton, Wisconsin, 1991).

Dubois, Josiah E. Jr.; *Generals In Grey Suits*, (The Bodley Head, London, 1953).

Dulles, John Foster; *American Red Cross*, (Harper, New York, 1950).

Dziurski, Major Alojzy; *Freedom Fighter*, (J.A. Dewar, Victoria, Australia, 1983).

Editors of the *Executive Intelligence Review*; "Dope Inc.", (*Executive Intelligence Review*, Washington D.C., 1992).

Ehrlich, Dr. Paul R.; *The Population Bomb*, (Ballantine Books, New York, 1968).

Engdahl, F. William; *A Century Of War: Anglo-American Oil Politics And The New World Order*, (Dr Bottiger Verlags-GmbH, Distributed in the USA by Paul and Co., Massachusetts, 1992).

Essene, Virginia, and Sheldon Nidle; *You Are Becoming A Galactic Human*, (S.E.E. Publishing, California, 1994).

Eveland, Wilbur Crane; *Ropes Of Sand: America's Failure In The Middle East*, (W.W. Norton and Co, 1980).

George, David Lloyd; *Is It Peace?*, (Hodder and Stoughton, London, 1923).

George, John, and Laird Wilcox; *Nazis, Communists, Klansmen And Others On The Fringe*, (Prometheus Books, New York, 1992).

Giancana, Sam and Chuck; *Double Cross: The Explosive Inside Story Of The Mobster Who Controlled America*, (Warner Books, New York, 1992).

Goodman, Linda; *Star Signs: The Secret Codes Of The Universe*, (Pan, London, 1987).

Green, Stephen; *Taking Sides: America's Secret Relations With A Militant Israel*, (William Morrow and Co, New York, 1984).

Hall, Manly P.; *America's Assignment With Destiny, The Adepts In The Western Esoteric Tradition, Part Five*, (The Philosophical Research Society, Los Angeles, California, 1979).

Hancock, Graham; *Fingerprints Of The Gods*, (Heinemann, London, 1995).

Hanfstaengl, Ernst; *Hitler – The Missing Years*, (London, 1957).

Hay, Louise L.; *You Can Heal Your Life*, (Hay House Inc and Eden Grove Editions, London, 1988).

Helsing, Jan van; *Secret Societies And Their Power In The 20th Century*, (Ewertverlag, Gran Canana, Spain, 1995).

Hersh, Seymour M.; *The Samson Option: Israel's Nuclear Arsenal And American Foreign Policy*, (Random House, New York, 1991).

Heymann, David C.; *A Women Named Jackie*, (New American Library, New York, 1989).

Heymann, Hans; *Plans For Permanent Peace*, (Harper and Brothers, New York, 1941).

House, Colonel Edward Mandell; *Philip Dru: Administrator*, (B.W. Huebsch, 1912).

Hurt, Henry; *Reasonable Doubt: An Investigation Into The Assassination Of John F. Kennedy*, (Holt, Rinehart and Winston, New York, 1985).

Issacson, Walter, and Thomas Evan; *The Wise Men: Six Friends And The World They Made*, (Simon and Schuster, New York, 1986).

Jasper, William F.; *Global Tyranny...Step by Step: The United Nations And The Emerging New World Order*, (Western Islands, Appleton, Wisconsin, 1992).

Kasun, Jacqueline; *The War Against Population*, (Ignatius Press, San Francisco, 1988).

Keith, Jim; *Casebook On Alternative 3: UFOs, Secret Societies, And World Control*, (IllumiNet Press, Lilburn, GA, USA, 1994).

Knight, Stephen; *The Brotherhood*, (Panthar Books, London, 1983).

Koestler, Arthur; *The Thirteenth Tribe – The Khazar Empire And Its Heritage*, (Hutchinson, London, 1976).

Kurzman, Dan; *Ben-Gurion: Prophet Of Fire*, (Simon and Schuster, New York, 1983).

Lane, Mark; *Plausible Denial*, (Thunders' Mouth Press, New York, 1992).

Lilienthal, Alfred M.; *What Price Israel?* (Henry Regnery, Chicago, 1953).

MacNeil, Jim, Pieter Winsemius, and Taizo Yakushiji; *Beyond Interdependence: The Meshing Of The World's Economy And The Earth's Ecology*, (Oxford University Press, New York, 1991).

Marciniak, Barbara; *Bringers Of The Dawn*, (Bear and Co., Sante Fe, 1992).

Marciniak, Barbara; *Earth: Pleiadian Keys To The Living Library*, (Bear and Co., Sante Fe, 1995).

Marrs, Jim; *Crossfire: The Plot That Killed Kennedy*, (Carrol and Graf Publishers, New York, 1989).

McIllany, William H. II; *The Tax Exempt Foundations*, (Arlington House, Westport CT, USA, 1980).

Mead, Professor G.R.S.; *Fragments Of A Faith Forgotten*, (The Theosophical Publishing Society, London, 1906).

Meiers, Michael; *Was Jonestown A CIA Experiment? A Review Of The Evidence*. Studies in American Religion, Vol 35, (The Edward Merlin Press, 1985).

Milan, Michael; *The Squad: The US Government's Secret Alliance With Organised Crime*, (Shapolsky Publishers, New York, 1989).

Morgenstern, George; *Pearl Harbor: The Story Of The Secret War*, (Institute for Historical Review, Costa Mesa, California, 1991).

Morrow, Robert D.; *The Senator Must Die: The Murder Of Robert F. Kennedy*, (Roundtable Publishing, Santa Monica, 1988).

Mullins, Eustace; *The World Order, Our Secret Rulers*, (Self Published, USA, Second Edition, 1992).

Nichols, Preston B., with Peter Moon; *The Montauk Project*, (Sky Books, New York, 1992).

Nichols, Preston B., with Peter Moon; *Montauk Revisited*, (Sky Books, New York, 1992).

O'Brien, Christian; *The Genius Of The Few*, (Turnstone Press, Wellingborough, Northamptonshire, 1985).

Perloff, James; *The Shadows Of Power: The Council On Foreign Relations And The American Decline*, (Western Islands, Appleton, Wisconsin, USA, 1988).

Piper, Michael Collins; *Final Judgement, The Missing Link In The JFK Assassination Conspiracy*, (The Wolfe Press, Washington DC, 1995).

Quigley, Carroll; *The Anglo-American Establishment*, (Books in Focus, New York, 1981).

Quigley, Carroll; *Tragedy And Hope*, (Macmillan, New York, 1966).

Raël, Claude Vorilhon; *The Message Given To Me By Extra-Terrestrials, They Took Me To Their Planet*, (AOM Corporation, Tokyo, Japan, 1986).

Ramsey, Captain A.H.M.; *The Nameless War*, (Omni Publications, London, 1952).

Reed, Douglas; *Controversy Of Zion*, (Dolphin Pres, London, 1978).

Schafly, Phyllis, and Rear Admiral USN (ret) Chester Ward; *Kissinger On The Couch*, (Arlington House, New York, 1975).

Sedir, P.; *Histoire Et Doctrine Des Rose-Croix*, (Paris, 1910).

Shasti, Hari Prasad; *The Ramayana Of Valmiki*, (Shanti Sadan, London, 1976, three volumes).

Short, Martin; *Inside The Brotherhood*, (Grafton Books, London, 1990).

Sitchin, Zecharia; *The 12th Planet*, (Avon, New York, 1976).

Sklar, Holly, (editor); *Trilateralism: The Trilateral Commission And The Elite Planning For World Management*, (South End Press, Boston, USA, 1980).

Skousen, W. Cleon; *The Naked Capitalist*, (self published, Salt Lake City, Utah, 1970).

Snow, John Howland; *The Case Of Tyler Kent*, (The Long House, New Canaan, Connecticut, 1946, 1962).

Stich, Rodney; *Defrauding America*, (Diablo Western Press, Alamo, California, 1994).

Suster, Gerald; *Hitler And The Age Of Horus*, (Sphere Books, London, 1981).

Sutton, Anthony C.; *Wall Street And The Bolshevik Revolution*, (Veritas Publishing Company, Morley, Western Australia, 1981).

Sutton, Anthony C.; *Wall Street And The Rise Of Hitler*, (Heritage Publications, Melbourne, Australia, and Bloomfield Books, Sudbury, Suffolk, England, 1976).

Sutton, Anthony C.; *An Introduction To The Order, How The Order Controls Education*, and *How The Order Creates War And Revolution*, (Veritas Publishing Co., Bullsbrook, Western Australia, 1985).

Tarpley, Webster Griffin, and Anton Chaitkin; *George Bush, The Unauthorised Biography*, (Executive Intelligence Review, Washington D.C., 1992).

Taylor, Ian T.; *In The Minds Of Men, Darwin And The New World Order*, (TFE Publishing, Toronto, Canada, 1984).

Thompson, Richard L.; *Alien Identities*, (Govardhan Hill Publishing, San Diego, 1993).

Valenan, Valdamar; *The Matrix*, (Arcturus Books, 1988).

Van der Beugel, Ernst H.; *From Marshall Aid To Atlantic Partnership*, (Elsevier Publishing Co., Amsterdam, New York, 1966).

Viereck, George Sylvester; *The Strangest Friendship In History: Woodrow Wilson And Colonel House*, (Liveright, New York, 1932).

Walker, Martin J.; *Dirty Medicine*, (Sling Shot Publications, London, 1993).

Wean, Gary L.; *There's A Fish In The Courthouse*, (Casitas Books, Oak View, California, 1987).

Wise, Jennings C.; *Woodrow Wilson: Disciple Of Revolution*, (Paisley Press, New York, 1938).

Wooden, Kenneth; *The Children Of Jonestown*, (McGraw-Hill, New York, 1981).

Nexus Magazine is a very good source of information about the New World Order and it stocks many books and videos, including *Waco: The Big Lie*.
The international addresses are:
Head Office: PO Box 30, Mapleton, Qld 4560, Australia.
USA Office: PO Box 177, Kempton, IL 60946-0177, USA.
UK Office: 55 Queens Road, East Grinstead, West Sussex, RH19 1BG.
Europe Office: PO Box 372, 8250 AJ Dronten, The Netherlands.

Perceptions magazine can be contacted via:
Quality of Life, 27 Old Gloucester Street, London WC1N 3XX or
c/o 10736 Jefferson Blvd, Suite 502, Culver City, California, Postal Zone 90230.
Tel: (310) 313 5185 or fax: (310) 313 5198

Contact Network International, *Exposure* magazine, can be contacted via:
PO Box 118, Noosa Heads, Queensland 4567, Australia. Tel/fax: (61) 074 852 966 or
PO Box 75, 9663 RC, Nieuwe Pekela, The Netherlands. Tel/fax: (31) 0597 645291.

The Spotlight newspaper is published weekly out of Washington DC by the Liberty Lobby. I don't share its Christian Patriotism, but it is a really excellent source of up-to-date information about the New World Order. The address is: *The Spotlight*, 300 Independence Avenue, SE, Washington DC 20003.
It is possible to have it posted anywhere in the world.

On Target magazine which investigates the global conspiracy is published in the UK and written by Colonel (ret) Barry Turner. He can be contacted c/o 22 Hampton Road, Oswestry, Shropshire, SY11 1SJ.

All these books, newspapers, and magazines, need to be read as sources of information and views, but not as unquestionable fact. They won't always interpret the situation accurately because they are dealing with covert manipulation, and they will often have their own belief system to defend. But you will find out far more about what is really going on in the world from the list above than you will from the mainstream media.

For personal astrological readings with Gloria Treloar, please contact her with a SAE c/o Berachah Colour Healing Centre, Wellhouse Lane, Glastonbury, Somerset BA6 8BJ.

If you would like to contact this book's illustrator and cover artist Neil Hague, please do so via the Bridge of Love address.

If you would like help with the design or production of a publishing project, please contact Samantha Masters at the Bridge of Love address.

Index

509

Index of illustrations

Other books and videos by David Icke

THE BIGGEST SECRET: The follow up to *...And The Truth Shall Set You Free* and devastating for the British Royal Family and the elite who control the world. Quite simply the most astonishing book ever published.

REVELATIONS OF A MOTHER GODDESS: A new video in which for nearly three hours David Icke talks with Arizona Wilder who conducted human sacrifice rituals for the British Royal Family and many other world famous people in the UK and USA. Absolutely stunning, riveting and will put you on the edge of your seat.

THE FREEDOM ROAD: A new triple video. In this 6-hour, profusely illustrated presentation, David Icke tells the astonishing human story from the ancient world to the present day and ends with the countdown to 2012. What has happened? What is happening? What will happen? All are revealed in this eye-opening, heart-opening, mind-opening, video package.

SPEAKING OUT: A new two hour interview with David Icke as he reveals the nature of the global manipulation and the spiritual solutions available to everyone. Great for introducing people who are new to the subject.
This title is only available from Truth Seeker Company @ 800-321-9054

I AM ME, I AM FREE: With humour and powerful insight, David Icke exposes the mental and emotional prisons which billions build around themselves and offers the key to personal and collective liberation.

LIFTING THE VEIL: Another new book by David Icke, compiled from interviews with an American journalist. An excellent summary of Icke's work and a perfect introduction for those new to these subjects.
This title is only available from Truth Seeker Company @ 800-321-9054

TURNING OF THE TIDE: On video and audio cassette. A 2-hour presentation, funny and informative, and a great way to introduce your friends to Icke's work.

Books, videos, and cassettes by David Icke are available from the following:

Bookworld Services, Inc.	**Bridge of Love Publications**
1933 Whitfield Park Loop	**PO Box 43**
Sarasota	**Ryde**
Florida 34243	**Isle of Wight**
USA	**PO33 2YL**
	England
Order No 1-800-444-2524	**Tel/fax 01983-566002**

Earlier books by David Icke, *The Robots' Rebellion, Heal The World, Days Of Decision* and *The Truth Vibrations* are available from the UK address.

Where to contact us...

If you want to bring David to your city, book him for a conference, media interviews or you have information you think may help him, please contact us at the following addresses:

Bridge of Love Publications
8912 E. Pinnacle Peak Road
Suite 8-493
Scottsdale
Arizona 85255
USA

Tel: **602-657-6992**
Fax: **602-657-6994**
Email: **bridgelove@aol.com**

Bridge of Love Publications
PO Box 43
Ryde
Isle of Wight
PO33 2YL
ENGLAND

Tel/Fax: **01983 566002**
Email: **dicke75150@aol.com**

Visit the David Icke website for more information: **www.davidicke.com**

To contact David Icke's media coordinator:

Royal Adams
1825 Shiloh Valley Drive
Wildwood, MO 63005
Tel: 314-458-7824
Fax: 314-458-7823
Email: radams1825@aol.com